Data Engineering with

Second Edition

Acquire the skills to design and build AWS-based data transformation pipelines like a pro

Gareth Eagar

BIRMINGHAM—MUMBAI

Data Engineering with AWS
Second Edition

Senior Publishing Product Manager: Gebin George

Acquisition Editor – Peer Reviews: Tejas Mhasvekar

Project Editor: Namrata Katare

Content Development Editor: Elliot Dallow

Copy Editor: Safis Editing

Technical Editor: Srishty Bhardwaj

Proofreader: Safis Editing

Indexer: Rekha Nair

Presentation Designer: Pranit Padwal

Developer Relations Marketing Executive: Vignesh Raju

First published: December 2021

Second edition: October 2023

Production reference: 2061123

Published by Packt Publishing Ltd.
Grosvenor House
11 St Paul's Square
Birmingham
B3 1RB, UK.

ISBN 978-1-80461-442-6

www.packt.com

Contributors

About the author

Gareth Eagar has over 25 years of experience in the IT industry, starting in South Africa, working in the United Kingdom for a while, and now based in the USA.

Having worked at AWS since 2017, Gareth has broad experience with a variety of AWS services, and deep expertise around building data platforms on AWS. While Gareth currently works as a Solutions Architect, he has also worked in AWS Professional Services, helping architect and implement data platforms for global customers.

Gareth also frequently speaks on data-related topics.

To my amazing wife and children, thank you for your patience and understanding as I spent countless hours writing the revised edition of this book. Your support for me taking on this project, and making the space and time for me to write, means so much to me.

A special thanks to Disha Umarwani, Praful Kava, and Natalie Rabinovich, who each contributed content for the first edition of this book. And many thanks to Amit Kalawat, Leonardo Gomez, and many others for helping to review content for this revised edition.

About the reviewers

Vaibhav Tyagi is a skilled and experienced cloud data engineer and architect with 10 years of experience. He has a deep understanding of AWS cloud services and is proficient in a variety of data engineering tools, including Spark, Hive, and Hadoop.

Throughout his career, he has worked for Teradata, Citigroup, NatWest, and Amazon, and has worked on, among other things, designing and implementing cloud-based pipelines, complex cloud environments, and the creation of data warehouses.

I would like to thank my wife and children who have been my biggest cheerleaders and put up with my long working hours. I am truly grateful for their love and support. And thank you to my friends who have also been a great source of support.

Gaurav Verma has 9 years of experience in the field, having worked at AWS, Skyscanner, Discovery Communications, and Tata Consultancy Services.

He excels in designing and delivering big data and analytics solutions on AWS. His expertise spans AWS services, Python, Scala, Spark, and more. He currently leads a team at Amazon, overseeing global analytics and the ML data platform. His career highlights include optimizing data pipelines, managing analytics projects, and extensive training in big data and data engineering technologies.

Learn more on Discord

To join the Discord community for this book – where you can share feedback, ask questions to the author, and learn about new releases – follow the QR code below:

https://discord.gg/9s5mHNyECd

Table of Contents

Section 2: Architecting and Implementing Data Engineering Pipelines and Transformations   143

Chapter 5: Architecting Data Engineering Pipelines   145

Chapter 6: Ingesting Batch and Streaming Data   169

Section 3: The Bigger Picture: Data Analytics, Data Visualization, and Machine Learning   335

Chapter 11: Ad Hoc Queries with Amazon Athena   337

Section 4: Modern Strategies: Open Table Formats, Data Mesh, DataOps, and Preparing for the Real World   439

Chapter 14: Building Transactional Data Lakes   441

Chapter 16: Building a Modern Data Platform on AWS 515

Preface

We live in a world where the amount of data being generated is constantly increasing. While a few decades ago, an organization may have had a single database that could store everything they needed to track, today most organizations have tens, hundreds, or even thousands of databases, along with data warehouses, and perhaps a data lake. And these data stores are being fed from an increasing number of data sources (transaction data, web server log files, IoT and other sensors, and social media, to name just a few).

It is no surprise that we hear more and more companies talk about being data-driven in their decision making. But in order for an organization to be truly data-driven, they need to be masters of managing and drawing insights from these ever-increasing quantities and types of data. And to enable this, organizations need to employ people with specialized data skills.

Doing a search on LinkedIn for jobs related to data returns nearly 800,000 results (and that is just for the United States!). The job titles include roles such as data engineer, data scientist, and data architect.

This revised edition of the book includes updates to all chapters, covering new features and services from AWS, as well as three brand-new chapters. In these new chapters, we cover topics such as building transactional data lakes (using open table formats such as Apache Iceberg), implementing a data mesh approach on AWS, and using a DataOps approach to building a modern data platform.

While this book will not magically turn you into a data engineer, it has been designed to accelerate your journey toward data engineering on AWS. By the end of this book, you will not only have learned some of the core concepts around data engineering, but you will also have a good understanding of the wide variety of tools available in AWS for working with data. You will also have been through numerous hands-on exercises, and thus gained practical experience with things such as ingesting streaming data, transforming and optimizing data, building visualizations, and even drawing insights from data using AI.

Who this book is for

This book has been designed for two groups of people; firstly, those looking to get started with a career in data engineering, and who want to learn core data engineering concepts. This book introduces many different aspects of data engineering, providing a comprehensive high-level understanding of, and practical hands-on experience with, different focus areas of data engineering.

Secondly, this book is for those people who may already have an established career focused on data, but who are new to the cloud, and to AWS in particular. For these people, this book provides a clear understanding of many of the different AWS services for working with data, and gives them hands-on experience with a variety of these AWS services.

What this book covers

Each of the chapters in this book takes the approach of introducing important concepts or key AWS services, and then providing a hands-on exercise related to the topic of the chapter:

Chapter 1, An Introduction to Data Engineering, reviews the challenges of ever-increasing dataset volumes, and the role of the data engineer in working with data in the cloud.

Chapter 2, Data Management Architectures for Analytics, introduces foundational concepts and technologies related to big data processing.

Chapter 3, The AWS Data Engineer's Toolkit, provides an introduction to a wide range of AWS services that are used for ingesting, processing, and consuming data, and orchestrating pipelines.

Chapter 4, Data Governance, Security, and Cataloging, covers the all-important topics of keeping data secure, ensuring good data governance, and the importance of cataloging your data.

Chapter 5, Architecting Data Engineering Pipelines, provides an approach for whiteboarding the high-level design of a data engineering pipeline.

Chapter 6, Ingesting Batch and Streaming Data, looks at the variety of data sources that we may need to ingest from, and examines AWS services for ingesting both batch and streaming data.

Chapter 7, Transforming Data to Optimize for Analytics, covers common transformations for optimizing datasets and for applying business logic.

Chapter 8, Identifying and Enabling Data Consumers, is about better understanding the different types of data consumers that a data engineer may work to prepare data for.

Chapter 9, A Deeper Dive into Data Marts and Amazon Redshift, focuses on the use of data warehouses as a data mart and looks at moving data between a data lake and data warehouse. This chapter also does a deep dive into Amazon Redshift, a cloud-based data warehouse.

Chapter 10, Orchestrating the Data Pipeline, looks at how various data engineering tasks and transformations can be put together in a data pipeline, and how these can be run and managed with pipeline orchestration tools such as AWS Step Functions.

Chapter 11, Ad Hoc Queries with Amazon Athena, does a deeper dive into the Amazon Athena service, which can be used to run SQL queries directly on data in the data lake, and beyond.

Chapter 12, Visualizing Data with Amazon QuickSight, discusses the importance of being able to craft visualizations of data, and how the Amazon QuickSight service enables this.

Chapter 13, Enabling Artificial Intelligence and Machine Learning, reviews how AI and ML are increasingly important for gaining new value from data, and introduces some of the AWS services for both ML and AI.

Chapter 14, Building Transactional Data Lakes, looks at new table formats (including Apache Iceberg, Apache Hudi, and Delta Lake) that bring traditional data warehousing type features to data lakes.

Chapter 15, Implementing a Data Mesh Strategy, discusses a recent trend, referred to as a data mesh, that provides a new way to approach analytical data management and data sharing within an organization.

Chapter 16, Building a Modern Data Platform on AWS, introduces important concepts, such as DataOps, which provides automation and observability when building a modern data platform.

Chapter 17, Wrapping Up the First Part of Your Learning Journey, concludes the book by looking at the bigger picture of data analytics, including real-world examples of data pipelines, and a review of emerging trends in the industry.

To get the most out of this book

Basic knowledge of computer systems and concepts, and how these are used within large organizations, is helpful prerequisite knowledge for this book. However, no data engineering-specific skills or knowledge are required. Also, a familiarity with cloud computing fundamentals and core AWS systems will make it easier to follow along, especially with the hands-on exercises, but detailed step-by-step instructions are included for each task.

> **Note:**
> If you are using the digital version of this book, we advise you to access the code from the book's GitHub repository (a link is available in the next section), rather than copying and pasting from the PDF or electronic version. Doing so will help you avoid any potential formatting errors when copying and pasting code.

Download the example code files

The code bundle for the book is hosted on GitHub at `https://github.com/PacktPublishing/Data-Engineering-with-AWS-2nd-edition`. We also have other code bundles from our rich catalog of books and videos available at `https://github.com/PacktPublishing/`. Check them out!

Download the color images

We also provide a PDF file that has color images of the screenshots/diagrams used in this book. You can download it here: `https://packt.link/gbp/9781804614426`.

Conventions used

There are a number of text conventions used throughout this book.

`CodeInText`: Indicates code words in text, database table names, folder names, filenames, file extensions, pathnames, dummy URLs, user input, and Twitter handles. For example: "Include a `WHERE Year = 2020` clause."

A block of code is set as follows:

```
datalake_bucket/year=2023/file1.parquet
datalake_bucket/year=2022/file1.parquet
datalake_bucket/year=2021/file1.parquet
datalake_bucket/year=2020/file1.parquet
```

When we wish to draw your attention to a particular part of a code block, the relevant lines or items are set in bold:

```
datalake_bucket/year=2023/file1.parquet
datalake_bucket/year=2022/file1.parquet
datalake_bucket/year=2021/file1.parquet
datalake_bucket/year=2020/file1.parquet
```

Bold: Indicates a new term, an important word, or words that you see on the screen. For instance, words in menus or dialog boxes appear in the text like this. For example: "In addition, you can use **Spark SQL** to process data using standard SQL."

Warnings or important notes appear like this.

Tips and tricks appear like this.

Get in touch

Feedback from our readers is always welcome.

General feedback: Email feedback@packtpub.com and mention the book's title in the subject of your message. If you have questions about any aspect of this book, please email us at questions@packtpub.com.

Errata: Although we have taken every care to ensure the accuracy of our content, mistakes do happen. If you have found a mistake in this book, we would be grateful if you reported this to us. Please visit http://www.packtpub.com/submit-errata, click **Submit Errata**, and fill in the form.

Piracy: If you come across any illegal copies of our works in any form on the internet, we would be grateful if you would provide us with the location address or website name. Please contact us at copyright@packtpub.com with a link to the material.

If you are interested in becoming an author: If there is a topic that you have expertise in and you are interested in either writing or contributing to a book, please visit http://authors.packtpub.com.

Share your thoughts

Once you've read *Data Engineering with AWS, Second Edition*, we'd love to hear your thoughts! Scan the QR code below to go straight to the Amazon review page for this book and share your feedback.

https://packt.link/r/1804614424

Your review is important to us and the tech community and will help us make sure we're delivering excellent quality content.

Download a free PDF copy of this book

Thanks for purchasing this book!

Do you like to read on the go but are unable to carry your print books everywhere? Is your eBook purchase not compatible with the device of your choice?

Don't worry, now with every Packt book you get a DRM-free PDF version of that book at no cost.

Read anywhere, any place, on any device. Search, copy, and paste code from your favorite technical books directly into your application.

The perks don't stop there, you can get exclusive access to discounts, newsletters, and great free content in your inbox daily

Follow these simple steps to get the benefits:

1. Scan the QR code or visit the link below

https://packt.link/free-ebook/9781804614426

2. Submit your proof of purchase
3. That's it! We'll send your free PDF and other benefits to your email directly

Section 1

AWS Data Engineering Concepts and Trends

In section one, we examine why data is so important to organizations today, and introduce foundational concepts of data engineering, including coverage of governance and security topics. We also learn about the AWS services that form part of the data engineer's toolkit, and get hands-on with creating an AWS account and using services such as Amazon S3, AWS Lambda, and AWS Identity and Access Management (IAM).

This section comprises the following chapters:

- *Chapter 1, An Introduction to Data Engineering*
- *Chapter 2, Data Management Architectures for Analytics*
- *Chapter 3, The AWS Data Engineer's Toolkit*
- *Chapter 4, Data Governance, Security, and Cataloging*

1

An Introduction to Data Engineering

Data engineering continues to be a fast-growing career path and a role in high demand, as data becomes ever more critical to organizations of all sizes. For those that enjoy the challenge of putting together the "puzzle pieces" that build out complex data pipelines to ingest raw data, and then transform and optimize that data for varied data consumers, it can be a really rewarding career.

In this chapter, we look at the many ways that data has become an important, and increasingly valuable, corporate asset. We also review some of the challenges that organizations face as they deal with increasing volumes of data, and how data engineers can use cloud-based services to help overcome these challenges. We then set the foundations for the hands-on activities in this book by providing step-by-step details on creating a new **Amazon Web Services (AWS)** account.

Throughout this book, we are going to cover a number of topics that teach the fundamentals of developing data engineering pipelines on AWS, but we'll get started in this chapter with these topics:

- The rise of big data as a corporate asset
- The challenges of ever-growing datasets
- The role of the data engineer as a big data enabler
- The benefits of the cloud when building big data analytic solutions
- Hands-on – create or access an AWS account for following along with the hands-on activities in this book

Technical requirements

You can find the code files of this chapter in the GitHub repository using the following link: `https://github.com/PacktPublishing/Data-Engineering-with-AWS-2nd-edition/tree/main/Chapter01`.

The rise of big data as a corporate asset

You don't need to look too far or too hard to hear about the many ways that big data and data analytics are transforming organizations and having an impact on society as a whole. We hear about how companies such as *TikTok* analyze large quantities of data to make personalized recommendations about which video clip to show a user next. We also read countless articles about how the new generation of chatbots (like *ChatGPT* from *OpenAI* or *Bard* from *Google*) have been trained on massive datasets, and as a result, are able to have human-like conversations on a wide range of topics. We experience how companies like *Amazon* and *Netflix* are able to recommend products or videos we may be interested in, based on our purchase and viewing history. All of these companies have innovated and added customer value by performing complex analyses on very large datasets.

We also see the importance of data in large companies, as demonstrated by those companies creating a new executive C-level position – the **Chief Data Officer (CDO)**. According to an article (`https://hbr.org/2021/08/why-do-chief-data-officers-have-such-short-tenures`) in the Harvard Business Review, the role of CDO was first established by Capital One (a technology-driven U.S. bank) in 2002. By 2012, it was estimated that 12% of firms had a CDO according to a NewVantage Partners survey, and by 2021, this had grown to 65% of firms having a CDO.

There is no doubt that data, when harnessed correctly and optimized for maximum analytic value, can be a game-changer for an organization. At the same time, those companies that are unable to effectively utilize their data assets risk losing a competitive advantage to others that do have a comprehensive data strategy and effective analytic and machine learning programs.

Organizations today tend to be in one of the following three states:

- They have an effective and modernized data analytics and machine learning program that differentiates them from their competitors.
- They are conducting proof of concept projects to evaluate how modernizing their analytic and machine learning programs can help them achieve a competitive advantage.

- Their leaders are having sleepless nights worrying about how their competitors are using new analytics and machine learning programs to achieve a competitive advantage over them.

No matter where an organization is in its data journey, if it has been in existence for a while, it has likely faced a number of common data-related challenges. Let's look at how organizations have typically handled the challenge of ever-growing datasets.

The challenges of ever-growing datasets

Organizations have many assets, such as physical assets, intellectual property, the knowledge of their employees, and trade secrets. But for too long, organizations did not fully recognize that they had another extremely valuable asset, and they failed to maximize the use of it – the vast quantities of data that they had gathered over time.

That is not to say that organizations ignored these data assets, but rather, due to the expense and complex nature of storing and managing this data, organizations tended to only analyze and keep a subset of their data.

Initially, data may have been stored in a single database, but as organizations and their data requirements grew, the number of databases exponentially increased. Today, with the modern application development approach of microservices, companies commonly have hundreds, or even thousands, of databases. Faced with many data silos, organizations invested in data warehousing systems that would enable them to ingest data from multiple siloed databases into a central location for analytics. But due to the expense of these systems, there were limitations on how much data could be stored, and some datasets would either be excluded or only aggregate data would be loaded into the data warehouse. Data would also only be kept for a limited period of time, as data storage for these systems was expensive, and therefore, it was not economical to keep historical data for long periods. There was also a lack of widely available tools and compute power to enable the analysis of extremely large, comprehensive datasets.

As organizations continued to grow, multiple data warehouses and data marts would be implemented for different business units or groups, and organizations still lacked a centralized, single-source-of-truth repository for their data. Organizations were also faced with new types of data, such as semi-structured or even unstructured data, and analyzing these datasets using traditional tools was a challenge.

As a result, new technologies were invented that were better able to work with very large datasets and different data types. **Hadoop** was a technology created in the early 2000s at Yahoo as part of a search engine project that wanted to index 1 billion web pages. Over the next few years, Hadoop, and the underlying **MapReduce** technology, became a popular way for all types of companies to store and process very large datasets. However, running a Hadoop cluster was a complex and expensive operation requiring specialized skills.

The next evolution for big data processing was the development of **Spark** (later taken on as an Apache project and now known as **Apache Spark**), a new processing framework for working with big data. Spark showed significant increases in performance when working with large datasets due to the fact that it did most processing in memory, significantly reducing the amount of reading and writing to and from disks. Today, Apache Spark is often regarded as the gold standard for processing large datasets and is used by a wide array of companies.

In parallel with the rise of Apache Spark as a popular big data processing tool was the rise of the concept of data lakes – an approach that uses low-cost object storage as a physical storage layer for a variety of data types, Apache Hive as a central catalog of all the datasets, and makes that data available for processing with a wide variety of tools, including Apache Spark. AWS's own website uses the following definition of data lakes:

> *A data lake is a centralized repository that allows you to store all your structured and unstructured data at any scale. You can store your data as-is, without having to first structure the data, and run different types of analytics—from dashboards and visualizations to big data processing, real-time analytics, and machine learning to guide better decisions.*

Data lakes were great for centralizing data but were often run by a centralized team that would look to ingest data from all the data silos in an organization, transform and aggregate the data, and make it available centrally for use by other teams. While this was a definite improvement on having databases and data warehouses spread out with no central repository or governance, there was still room for improvement.

By centralizing all the data and having a single team manage this repository of data, the teams working to transform and extract additional value out of the data were often not the people most familiar with the business context behind the data.

To address this, Zhamak Dehghani (a data consultant working for Thoughtworks at the time) developed a new approach, which eventually became known as a **data mesh**. While we will cover a brief introduction to data mesh architecture here, we will cover this topic in more detail in *Chapter 15, Implementing a Data Mesh Architecture*.

With a data mesh architecture, the idea is to make the teams that generate the data responsible for creating an analytics version of the data, and then make that data easily accessible to the rest of the organization without needing to make multiple copies of the data.

By 2022, this concept had gained widespread appeal, and many companies were working to implement a data mesh approach for their data. Some took a limited view of what a data mesh was and considered it primarily a means of sharing data between teams without needing to physically move or copy the data. However, a full data mesh implementation went well beyond the technology of how to share data. A data mesh implementation meant a change to the processes of how operational data was converted into analytical data, and along with it, the personas that were responsible for the data. A data mesh implementation was not just a technical implementation but rather a change to the culture and operation of teams within an organization.

Whereas in many organizations, large-scale analytics had been done by a centralized team, with a data mesh approach, the team that owns an application that generates data must *productize* that data to make it available to the rest of the business. Much like DevOps had changed how development teams worked to create and support software, the data mesh approach meant that product teams needed to work differently in how they generated and shared analytical data. They would appoint a data product manager who would be responsible for the task of taking operational data and creating an analytics data product from that. For the product they created, they would take ownership of ensuring data quality, the freshness of data, communication around changes to the product (such as schema changes), and so on. They would effectively be product managers, outlining a roadmap for the data analytics product they would create, and they would be responsive to customer feedback on the data product.

With a data mesh, there would still be a central data team, but this team would be responsible for creating a centralized data platform, which all the different data product teams could then use. So rather than being data engineers that transformed data, the centralized team would focus on being data platform engineers, creating a standardized platform that met best practices. They would then make this platform available to individual development teams to use in order to create and share their own data analytic products.

Having looked at how data analytics became an essential tool in organizations, let's now look at the roles that enable maximizing the value of data for a modern organization.

The role of the data engineer as a big data enabler

Amid the increasing recognition of data as a valuable corporate asset and the introduction of new technologies to store and process vast amounts of data, there has been an increase in the opportunities and roles available for data-related careers.

Let's look at a sample use case where a sales manager for a consumer goods organization wants to better understand which alternate products a customer considers before purchasing their product. In addition, they also want to have a better way of predicting product demand by category based on external factors, such as the expected weather.

Achieving the desired outcomes as specified by the sales manager will require bringing in data from multiple internal and external sources. Datasets that could be relevant to this scenario may include the following:

- Customer, product, and order relational databases
- Web server logs from the consumer-facing storefront
- Third-party sales data from online marketplaces where relevant products are sold (such as Amazon.com)
- Other relevant third-party datasets that may influence sales (for example, weather-related data)

Multiple teams would need to be involved in the project, with the following 3 roles playing a primary part in implementing the required solution:

- Data engineer
- Data scientist
- Data analyst

Let's take a look at how these three roles would contribute to this new project.

Understanding the role of the data engineer

The role of a **data engineer** is to do the following:

- Design, implement, and maintain the pipelines that enable the ingestion of raw data into a storage platform

- Transform that data to be optimized for analytics, based on data consumer requirements
- Make that data available for various data consumers using their tool of choice

A data engineer must also ensure that they comply with all required security and governance requirements while performing the above tasks.

In our scenario, the data engineer will first need to design the pipelines that ingest raw data from various internal and external sources. To achieve this, they will use a variety of tools, depending on the source system and whether it will be scheduled batch ingestion or near real-time streaming ingestion (as discussed in *Chapter 6, Ingesting Batch and Streaming Data*).

The data engineer is also responsible for transforming the raw input datasets to optimize them for analytics, using various techniques (as discussed in *Chapter 7, Transforming Data to Optimize for Analytics*). The data engineer must also create processes to verify the quality of data, add metadata about the data to a data catalog, and manage the lifecycle of code related to data transformation.

Finally, the data engineer may need to assist in integrating various data consumption tools with the transformed data, enabling data analysts and data scientists to use their preferred tools to draw insights from the data.

The data engineer uses tools such as **Apache Kafka**, **Apache Spark**, and **Presto,** as well as other commercially available products, to build the data pipeline and optimize data for analytics.

The data engineer is much like a civil engineer for a new residential development. The civil engineer is responsible for designing and building the roads, bridges, train stations, and so on to enable commuters to easily commute in and out of the development. In a similar way, the data engineer is responsible for designing and building the infrastructure required to bring data into a central source and for optimizing the data for use by various data consumers.

Understanding the role of the data scientist

The role of a **data scientist** is to draw complex insights and make predictions based on various datasets, using machine learning and artificial intelligence. The data scientist will combine a number of skills, including computer science, statistics, analytics, and math, in order to help an organization answer complex questions and make informed decisions using data.

Data scientists need to understand the raw data and know how to use that data to develop and train complex machine learning models that will help recognize patterns in the data and predict future trends. In our scenario, the data scientist may build a machine learning model that uses past sales data, correlated with weather information for each day in the reporting period.

They can then design and train this model to help business users get predictions on the likely top-selling categories for future dates based on the expected weather forecast (ice creams sell better on hot days, and umbrellas sell better on rainy days).

Where the data engineer is like a civil engineer building infrastructure for a new development, the data scientist is developing new and advanced products for the residents of the development, such as advanced types of transport in and out of the development. Data scientists create the machine learning models that enable data consumers and business analysts to draw new insights and predictions from data. However, much like the designer of a new airplane is dependent on having an airport where the plane can land and take off, the data scientist is dependent on data engineers creating data pipelines to bring in the data required to train new machine learning models.

Understanding the role of the data analyst

The role of a **data analyst** is to examine and combine multiple datasets in order to help a business understand trends in the data and to make more informed business decisions. While a data scientist develops models that make future predictions or identifies non-obvious patterns in data, the data analyst works with well-structured and modeled data to understand current conditions and to highlight recent patterns from the data.

A data analyst may answer questions such as which menu item sold best in different geographic regions over the past month, or which medical procedure had the best outcome for patients of different ages. These insights help an organization make better decisions for the future.

In our scenario, the data analyst may run complex queries against the different datasets that are available (such as an orders database or web server logs), joining together subsets of data from each source to gain new insights. For example, the data analyst may create a report highlighting which alternate products are most often browsed by a customer before a specific product is purchased. The data analyst may also make use of advanced machine learning models developed by the data scientists to gain further valuable insights.

Where the data engineer is like a civil engineer building infrastructure, and the data scientist is developing new, advanced forms of transportation, the data analyst is like a skilled pilot, using their expertise to get users to their end destination.

Understanding other common data-related roles

Organizations may have other role titles and job descriptions for data-related positions, but generally, these will be a subset of the roles described in the preceding sections.

For example, a **big data architect** or **data platform architect** could be a subset of the **data engineer** role, focused on designing the architecture for big data pipelines, but not building the data-specific pipelines. Or, a **data visualization developer** may be focused on building out visualizations using business intelligence tools, but this is effectively a subset of the **data analyst** role.

Larger organizations tend to have more focused job roles, while in a smaller organization, a single person may take on the role of data engineer, data scientist, and data analyst.

In this book, we will focus on the role of the data engineer, and dive deep into how a data engineer is able to build complex data pipelines using the power of cloud computing services. Let's now look at how cloud computing has simplified how organizations are able to build and scale out big data processing solutions.

The benefits of the cloud when building big data analytic solutions

For a long time, organizations relied on complex systems that they would run in their own data centers to help them capture, store, and process large amounts of data. But over the last decade or so, there has been a trend of an increasing amount of data that organizations want to store and analyze, and on-premises systems have struggled to scale to keep up with demand. Scaling up these traditional tools for managing ever-increasing dataset sizes has been expensive, complex, and time-consuming, and organizations have been seeking alternative solutions to cope with the increasing data volumes.

Ever since Amazon launched **AWS** in 2006, organizations have been realizing the benefits of running their workloads in the cloud. Cloud computing enables scalability, cost efficiency, security, and automation that most companies find impossible to achieve within their own data centers, and this applies to the area of data analytics as well. One of the first AWS services was **Amazon Simple Storage Service (Amazon S3)**, a cloud-based object store that offers essentially unlimited scalability at low cost, and yet provides durability and availability that most data center managers could only dream of achieving. Today, Amazon S3 has become the physical storage layer for many thousands of data lake projects, and a wide ecosystem of analytic tools has been created to work with the service.

Successful data engineers need to understand the tools available in the cloud for building out complex data analytic projects and understand which set of tools is best to achieve the outcome needed for their project. In this book, you will learn more about AWS services for working with big data, and you will gain hands-on experience in developing a data engineering pipeline in AWS.

To get started, you will need either an existing AWS account, or you will need to create a new AWS account so that you can follow along with the practical examples. In the next section, we provide step-by-step instructions for creating a new AWS account.

Hands-on – creating and accessing your AWS account

The projects in this book require you to access an AWS account with administrator privileges. If you already have administrator privileges for an AWS account and know how to access the AWS Management Console, you can skip this section and move on to *Chapter 2, Data Management Architectures for Analytics*.

If you are making use of a corporate AWS account, you will want to check with your AWS cloud operations team to ensure that your account has administrative privileges. Even if your daily-use account does not allow full administrative privileges, your cloud operations team may be able to create a **sandbox** account for you.

What is a sandbox account?

A sandbox account is an account isolated from your corporate production systems with relevant guardrails and governance in place and is used by many organizations to provide a safe space for teams or individual developers to experiment with cloud services.

If you cannot get administrative access to a corporate account, you will need to create a personal AWS account or work with your cloud operations team to request specific permissions needed to complete each section. The exercises in this book assume you have administrative access and the full details of required granular permissions will not be covered, but you can review the AWS documentation for information on granular permission requirements for each service.

An important note about costs associated with hands-on tasks in this book

If you are creating a new personal account or using an existing personal account, you will incur and be responsible for AWS costs as you follow along in this book. While some services may fall under AWS Free Tier usage, some of the services covered in this book will not. **We strongly encourage you to set up budget alerts within your account and to regularly check your billing console.**

See the AWS documentation on setting up billing alarms to monitor your costs at `https://docs.aws.amazon.com/AmazonCloudWatch/latest/monitoring/ monitor_estimated_charges_with_cloudwatch.html`.

Creating a new AWS account

To create a new AWS account, you will need the following things:

- An email address (or alias) that has not been used before to register an AWS account
- A phone number that can be used for important account verification purposes
- Your credit or debit card, which will be charged for AWS usage outside of the Free Tier

A tip regarding the phone number you use when registering

It is important that you keep your contact details up to date for your AWS account as, if you lose access to your account, you will need access to the email address and phone number registered for the account to restore access. If you expect that your contact number may change in the future, consider registering a virtual number that you will always be able to access and that you can forward to your primary number. One such service that enables this is Google Voice (`http://voice.google.com`).

The following steps will guide you through creating a new AWS account:

1. Navigate to the AWS landing page at `http://aws.amazon.com`.
2. Click on the **Create an AWS Account** link in the top right-hand corner.
3. Provide an **email address**, provide a **name** for your account, and then click on **Verify email address**. You will be emailed a verification code to verify your email, which you need to enter on the form to continue.

A tip about reusing an existing email address

Some email systems support adding a "+" sign followed by a few characters to the end of the username portion of your email address in order to create a unique email address that still goes to your same mailbox. For example, `atest.emailaddress@gmail.com` and `atest.emailaddress+dataengineering@gmail.com` will both go to the primary email address inbox. If you have used your primary email address previously to register an AWS account, you can use this tip to provide a unique email address during registration but still have emails delivered to your primary account.

4. Once you verify using the code emailed to you, specify a new secure **password** for your account (one that you have not used elsewhere). Then click on **Continue**.

5. Select **Business** or **Personal** for the account type (note that the functionality and tools available are the same no matter which one you pick).

6. Provide the requested personal information and then, after reviewing the terms of the **AWS Customer Agreement**, click the checkbox if you agree to the terms, and then click **Continue**.

7. Provide a credit or debit card for payment information and select **Verify and Continue**.

8. Provide a **phone number** for a verification text or call, enter the characters shown for the **security check**, and complete the verification.

9. Select a **support plan** (basic support is free, but only provides self-service access to support resources) and complete the signup.

10. You will receive a notification that your account is being activated. This usually completes in a few minutes, but it can take up to 24 hours. Check your email to confirm account activation.

What to do if you don't receive a confirmation email within 24 hours

If you do not receive an email confirmation within 24 hours confirming that your account has been activated, follow the troubleshooting steps provided by AWS Premium Support at `https://aws.amazon.com/premiumsupport/knowledge-center/create-and-activate-aws-account/`.

Accessing your AWS account

Once you have received the confirmation email confirming that your account has been activated, follow these steps to access your account and create a new admin user:

1. Access the AWS console login page at http://console.aws.amazon.com.

2. Make sure **Root user** is selected, and then enter the email address that you used when creating the account.

3. Enter the password that you set when creating the account.

> **Best practices for securing your account**
>
> When you log in using the email address you specified when registering the account, you are logging in as the account's *root user*. It is a recommended best practice that you do not use this login for your day-to-day activities but rather, only use this when performing activities that require the root account, such as creating your first **Identity and Access Management (IAM)** user, deleting the account, or changing your account settings. For more information, see https://docs.aws.amazon.com/ IAM/latest/UserGuide/id_root-user.html.
>
> It is also strongly recommended that you enable **Multi-Factor Authentication (MFA)** on this and other administrative accounts. To enable this, see https://docs.aws. amazon.com/IAM/latest/UserGuide/id_credentials_mfa_enable_virtual. html.

In the following steps, we are going to create a new IAM administrative user account:

1. In the AWS Management Console, confirm which **Region** you are currently in. You can select any region, such as the region closest to you geographically.

Selecting a region

The region you select in the AWS console is the geographical area of the world where the AWS resources you create will be deployed. It generally makes sense to deploy to the region closest to where you are located; however, this is not always the case. For example, not all AWS services are available in all regions (for a list of services available per region, see `https://aws.amazon.com/about-aws/global-infrastructure/regional-product-services/`).

Another factor to consider is that the pricing for AWS services differs from region to region, so also take this into account when selecting a region to use for the exercises in this book. Finally, make sure that you are always in the same region when working through the exercises in each chapter.

For more information on selecting a region, refer to the AWS blog post *What to Consider when Selecting a Region for your Workloads* at `https://aws.amazon.com/blogs/architecture/what-to-consider-when-selecting-a-region-for-your-workloads/`.

In the following screenshot, the user is in the **Ohio** region (also known as **us-east-2**).

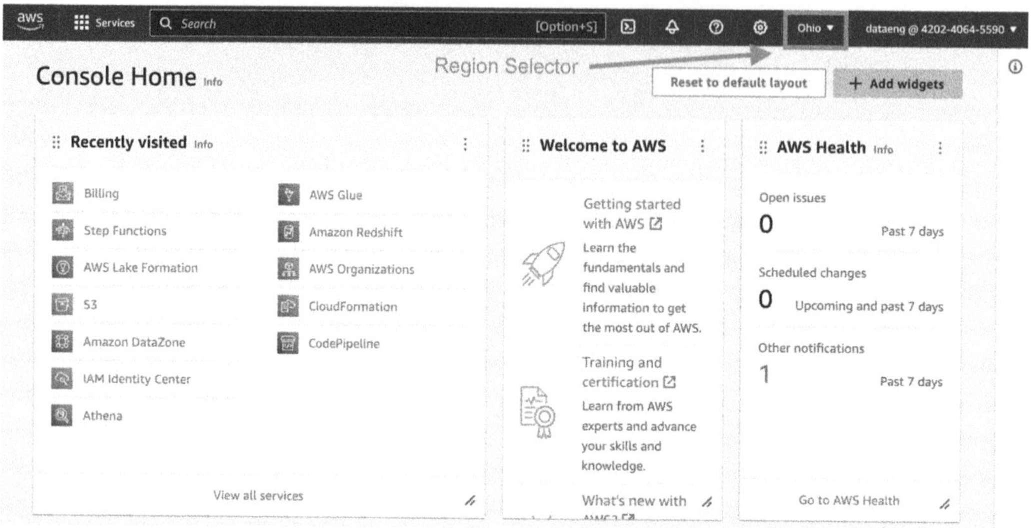

Figure 1.1: AWS Management Console

2. In the **Search** bar at the top of the screen, type in IAM and press *Enter*. This brings up the console for **Identity and Access Management (IAM)**.

3. On the left-hand side menu, click **Users** and then **Add users**.

4. Provide a username, and then select the checkbox for **Enable console access - *optional***.

5. Select **Custom password**, provide a password for console access, select whether to force a password change on the next login, then click **Next**.

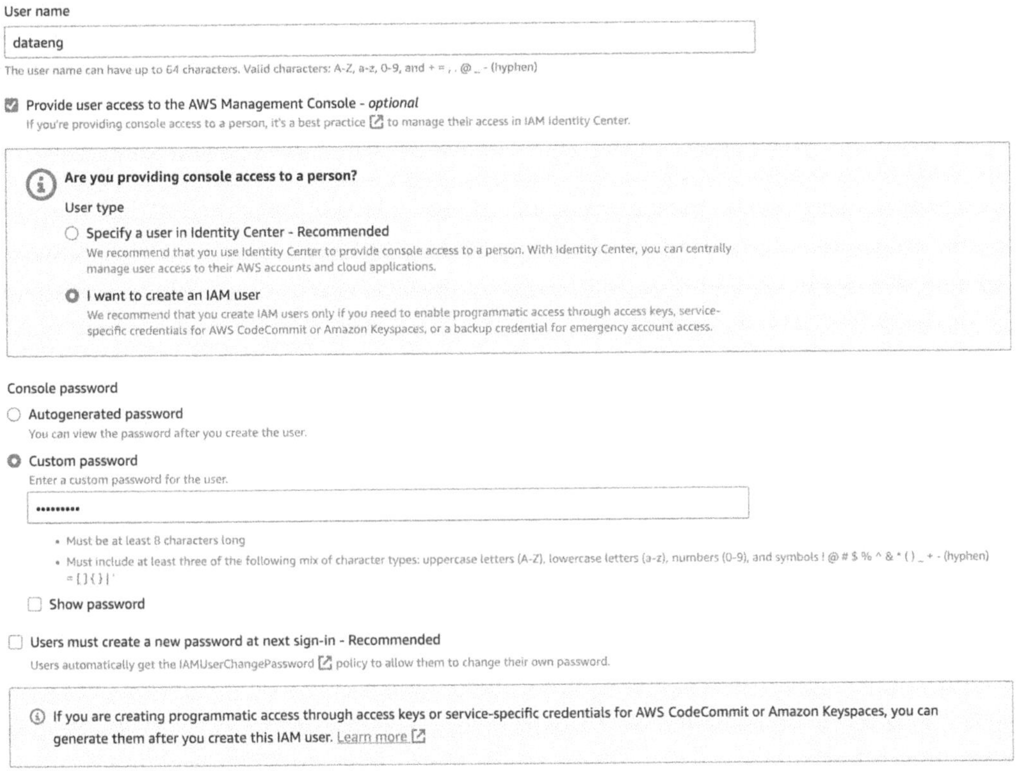

User name

dataeng

The user name can have up to 64 characters. Valid characters: A-Z, a-z, 0-9, and + = , . @ _ - (hyphen)

☑ Provide user access to the AWS Management Console - *optional*
If you're providing console access to a person, it's a best practice ☑ to manage their access in IAM Identity Center.

ⓘ **Are you providing console access to a person?**

User type

○ **Specify a user in Identity Center - Recommended**
We recommend that you use Identity Center to provide console access to a person. With Identity Center, you can centrally manage user access to their AWS accounts and cloud applications.

◉ **I want to create an IAM user**
We recommend that you create IAM users only if you need to enable programmatic access through access keys, service-specific credentials for AWS CodeCommit or Amazon Keyspaces, or a backup credential for emergency account access.

Console password

○ **Autogenerated password**
You can view the password after you create the user.

◉ **Custom password**
Enter a custom password for the user.

●●●●●●●●●

• Must be at least 8 characters long
• Must include at least three of the following mix of character types: uppercase letters (A-Z), lowercase letters (a-z), numbers (0-9), and symbols ! @ # $ % ^ & * ( ) _ + - (hyphen) = [ ] { } | '

☐ Show password

☐ Users must create a new password at next sign-in - Recommended
Users automatically get the IAMUserChangePassword ☑ policy to allow them to change their own password.

ⓘ If you are creating programmatic access through access keys or service-specific credentials for AWS CodeCommit or Amazon Keyspaces, you can generate them after you create this IAM user. Learn more ☑

Figure 1.2: Creating a new user in the AWS Management Console

6. For production accounts, it is best practice to grant permissions with a policy of least privilege, giving each user only the permissions they specifically require to perform their role. However, AWS managed policies can be used to cover common use cases in test accounts, and so to simplify the setup of our test account, we will use the **Administrator-Access** managed policy. This policy gives full access to all AWS resources in the account.

    On the **Set permissions** screen, select **Attach policies directly** from the list of policies, select **AdministratorAccess**, then click **Next: Tags**.

7. Optionally, specify tags (key-value pairs), then click **Next**.

8. Review the settings, and then click **Create user**.

9. Take note of the **Console sign-in URL** link that you will use to sign into your account.

For the remainder of the tutorials in this book, you should log in using the URL link provided and the username and password you set for your IAM user. You should also strongly consider enabling MFA for this account, a recommended best practice for all accounts with administrator permissions.

Summary

In this chapter, we reviewed how data is becoming ever more important for organizations looking to gain new insights and competitive advantage, and introduced some core big data processing technologies and approaches. We also looked at the key roles related to managing, processing, and analyzing large datasets, and highlighted how cloud technologies enable organizations to better deal with the increasing volume and variety of data.

In our first hands-on exercise, we provided step-by-step instructions for creating a new AWS account, which can be used through the remainder of this book as we develop our own data engineering pipeline.

In the next chapter, we dig deeper into current approaches, tools, and frameworks that are commonly used to manage and analyze large datasets, including data warehouses, data marts, data lakes, and data mesh. We also get hands-on with AWS again, but this time we will use the AWS **Command Line Interface** (CLI) to create new Amazon S3 buckets.

Learn more on Discord

To join the Discord community for this book – where you can share feedback, ask questions to the author, and learn about new releases – follow the QR code below:

`https://discord.gg/9s5mHNyECd`

2

Data Management Architectures for Analytics

In *Chapter 1, An Introduction to Data Engineering*, we looked at the challenges introduced by ever-growing datasets, and how the cloud can help solve these analytic challenges. However, there are many different cloud services, open-source frameworks, file formats, and architectures that can be used in analytic projects, depending on the business requirements and objectives.

In this chapter, we will discuss how analytical technologies have evolved and introduce the key technologies and concepts that are foundational for building modern analytical architectures, irrespective of whether you build them on **Amazon Web Services (AWS)** or elsewhere.

The content in this chapter lays an important foundation, as it will provide an introduction to the concepts that we will build on in the rest of the book.

In this chapter, we will cover the following topics:

- The evolution of data management for analytics
- A deeper dive into data warehouse concepts and architecture
- An overview of data lake architecture and concepts
- Bringing together the best of data warehouses and data lakes
- Hands-on – using the AWS **Command Line Interface (CLI)** to create **Simple Storage Service (S3)** buckets

Technical requirements

To complete the hands-on exercises included in this chapter, you will need access to an AWS account in which you have administrator privileges (as covered in *Chapter 1, An Introduction to Data Engineering*).

You can find the code and other content related to this chapter in the GitHub repository at the following link: `https://github.com/PacktPublishing/Data-Engineering-with-AWS-2nd-edition/tree/main/Chapter02`.

The evolution of data management for analytics

Innovations in data management and processing over the last several decades have laid the foundations for modern-day analytic systems. When you look at the analytics landscape of a typical mature organization, you will find the footprints of many of these innovations in its data analytics platforms. As a data engineer, you may come across analytic pipelines that were built using technologies from different generations, and you may be expected to understand them. Therefore, it is important to be familiar with some of the key developments in analytics over time, as well as to understand the foundational concepts of analytical data storage, data management, and data pipelines.

Databases and data warehouses

There are two broad types of database systems, and both of these have been around for many years:

- **Online Transaction Processing (OLTP)** systems are primarily used to store and update transactional data in high volumes. For example, OLTP-type databases are often used to store customer records, including transaction details (such as purchases, returns, and refunds).

- **Online Analytical Processing (OLAP)** systems are primarily used for reporting on large volumes of data. It is common for OLAP systems to take data from multiple OLTP databases, and provide a centralized repository of data that can be used for reporting purposes.

In this book, we are focused primarily on data analytics, and therefore most of our discussions will be around OLAP systems.

Both OLTP and OLAP data processing and analytic systems have evolved over several decades. In the 1980s, the focus was on batch processing, where data would be processed in nightly runs on large mainframe computers.

In the 1990s, the use of databases exploded, and organizations found themselves with tens, or even hundreds, of databases supporting different business processes. Generally, these databases were for transactional processing (OLTP), and the ability to perform analytics across systems was limited.

As a result, in the 1990s, data warehouses (OLAP systems) became a popular tool with which data could be ingested from multiple database systems into a central repository, and the data warehouse could focus on running analytic reports.

The data warehouse was designed to store **integrated**, **highly curated**, and **trusted** data, that was also very structured (formatted with a well-defined schema). Data would be ingested on a regular basis from other highly structured sources, but before entering the data warehouse, the data would go through a significant amount of pre-processing, validation, and transformations. Any changes to the data warehouse schema (how the data was organized, or structured), or the need to ingest new data sources, would require a significant effort to plan the schema and related processes.

Over the last few decades, businesses and consumers have rapidly adopted web and mobile technologies, and this has resulted in rapid growth in data sources, data volumes, and the options for analyzing an increasing amount of data. In parallel, organizations have realized the business value of the insights they can gain by combining data from their internal systems with external data from their partners, the web, social media, and third-party data providers. To process consistently larger data volumes and increased demands to support new consumers, data warehouses have evolved through multiple generations of technology and architectural innovations.

Early data warehouses were custom-built using common relational databases on powerful servers, but they required IT teams to manage host servers, storage, software, and integrations with data sources. These were difficult to manage, and so in the mid-2000s, there was an emergence of purpose-built hardware appliances designed as **modular data warehouse appliances, built for terabyte- and petabyte-scale big data processing**. These appliances contained new hardware and software innovations and were delivered as easy-to-install and easy-to-manage units from popular vendors such as **Oracle, Teradata, IBM Netezza, Pivotal Greenplum**, and others.

Dealing with big, unstructured data

While data warehouses have steadily evolved over the last 25+ years to support increasing volumes of highly structured data, there has been exponential growth in the amount of semi-structured and unstructured data produced by modern digital platforms (such as mobile and web applications, sensors, IoT devices, social media, and audio and video media platforms).

These platforms produce data at a high velocity, and in much larger volumes than data produced by traditional structured sources. To gain a competitive advantage by transforming customer experience and business operations, it has become essential for organizations to gain deeper insights from these new data sources. Traditional data warehouses are good at storing and managing flat, structured data from sources such as a set of tables, organized as a relational schema. However, they are not well suited to handling the huge volumes of high-velocity semi-structured and unstructured data that are becoming increasingly popular.

As a result, in the early 2010s, new technologies for big data processing became popular. **Hadoop**, an open-source framework for processing large datasets on clusters of computers, became the leading way to work with big data. These clusters contained tens of hundreds of machines with attached disk volumes that could hold tens of thousands of terabytes of data managed under a single distributed filesystem known as the **Hadoop Distributed File System (HDFS)**.

Many organizations deployed **Hadoop distributions** from providers such as **Cloudera, Hortonworks, MapR**, and **IBM** to large clusters of computers in their data centers. These Hadoop packages included cluster management utilities, as well as pre-configured and pre-integrated open-source distributed data processing frameworks such as **MapReduce, Hive, Spark**, and **Presto**.

However, building and scaling on-premises Hadoop clusters typically required a large upfront capital investment in machines and storage. And, the ongoing management of the cluster and big data processing pipelines required a team of specialists that included the following:

- Hadoop administrators specialized in cluster hardware and software
- Data engineers specialized in processing frameworks such as Spark, Hive, and Presto

As the volume of data grew, new machines and storage continually needed to be added to the cluster.

Big data teams managing on-premises clusters typically spent a significant percentage of their time managing and upgrading the cluster's hardware and software, as well as optimizing workloads.

Cloud-based solutions for big data analytics

Over the last decade or so, organizations have increasingly adopted public cloud solutions to handle the challenge of increasing data volumes and diversity. Making use of cloud solutions for big data processing has a number of benefits, including:

- On-demand capacity
- Limitless and elastic scaling

- Global footprint
- Usage-based cost models
- Freedom from managing hardware

After AWS launched Amazon EMR in 2009 (a managed platform for running Hadoop frameworks), and Amazon Redshift in 2013 (a cloud-native data warehouse), the number of other companies developing cloud-based solutions for big data analytics rapidly increased.

Today, companies like **Google Cloud Platform (GCP)**, **Microsoft Azure**, **Snowflake**, and **Databricks** provide a number of solutions for ingesting, storing, and analyzing large datasets in the cloud.

Over time, these cloud data warehouses and other cloud-based big data systems have rapidly expanded their feature sets to exceed those of high-performance, on-premise data warehousing appliances, and Hadoop clusters. Besides no upfront investment, a petabyte scale, and high performance, these cloud-based services provide elastic capacity scaling, a usage-based cost model, and freedom from infrastructure management.

Over the last decade, the number of organizations building their big data processing applications in the cloud has accelerated. In the last 5 years alone, thousands of organizations have migrated their existing data warehouses and Hadoop applications from on-premise vendor products and appliances to cloud-based services.

Another trend brought on by the move to the cloud has been the adoption of highly durable, inexpensive, and virtually limitless cloud object stores. Cloud object stores, such as Amazon S3, can store hundreds of petabytes of data at a fraction of the cost of on-prem storage, and support storing data regardless of its source, format, or structure. They also provide native integrations with hundreds of cloud-native and third-party data processing and analytics tools.

These new cloud object stores have enabled organizations to build a new, more integrated analytics data management approach with decoupled compute and storage, called a **data lake** architecture. A data lake architecture makes it possible to create a single source of truth by bringing together a variety of data of all sizes and types (structured, semi-structured, or unstructured) in one place: a central, highly scalable repository built using inexpensive cloud storage. A wide variety of analytic tools have been created or modified to integrate with these cloud object stores, providing organizations with many options for building data lake-based big data platforms.

Instead of lifting and shifting existing data warehouses and Hadoop clusters to the cloud as they are, many organizations are instead refactoring their previously on-premises workloads to build an integrated cloud data lake. In this approach, all data is first ingested, processed, and stored in the data lake to build a single source of truth, and then a subset of the "hot" data is loaded into the dimensional schemas of a cloud data warehouse to support lower-latency access.

In recent years, another term has been coined to refer to a variety of new technologies that enable integrating the best of data lakes and data warehousing capabilities, called the data lake house approach. There have been solutions from commercial companies (such as AWS, GCP, Snowflake, and Databricks), as well as open-source community-led initiatives (such as Apache Hudi, and Apache Iceberg) that have referred to a data lake house (also sometimes called a *Lakehouse*).

While we will cover these new approaches in more detail in this chapter in the *Bringing together the best of data warehouses and data lakes* section, some of the new capabilities include:

- The ability to quickly ingest any type of data
- Storing and processing petabytes of unstructured, semi-structured, and structured data
- Support for **ACID** transactions (which references 4 key properties of a transaction - namely its atomicity, consistency, isolation, and durability – enabling multiple concurrent users to read, insert, update, and delete records in a dataset managed by the data lakehouse)
- Low-latency data access
- The ability to consume data with a variety of tools, including SQL, Spark, machine learning frameworks, and business intelligence tools

Before we dive deeper into the *data lake house* architecture, let's first review some of the fundamentals of data warehouses.

A deeper dive into data warehouse concepts and architecture

An **Enterprise Data Warehouse** (**EDW**) is the central data repository that contains structured, curated, consistent, and trusted **data assets** that are organized into a well-modeled schema. The **data assets** in an EDW are made up of all the relevant information about key business domains and are built by integrating data sourced from the following places:

- Run-the-business transactional applications (ERPs, CRMs, and line-of-business applications) that support all the key business domains across an enterprise.
- External data sources such as data from partners and third parties.

An EDW provides business users and decision-makers with an easy-to-use, central platform that helps them find and analyze a well-modeled, well-integrated, single version of truth for various business subject areas such as customers, products, sales, marketing, the supply chain, and more. Business users analyze data in the warehouse to measure business performance, find current and historical business trends, find business opportunities, and understand customer behavior.

In the remainder of this section, we will review the foundational concepts of a data warehouse by discussing a typical data management architecture with an EDW at the center, as depicted in *Figure 2.1*. Typically, a data-warehouse-centric architecture includes the following:

- Data sources from across the business that provide raw data to the data warehouse via **Extract, Transform, Load (ETL)** or **Extract, Load, Transform (ELT)** processes (more on this later in this chapter)
- One or more data warehouses (and, optionally, multiple subject-focused data marts)
- End user analytic tools for consuming data from the warehouse (such as SQL-based analytic tools, and business intelligence visualization systems)

The following diagram shows how an enterprise data warehouse fits into an analytics architecture:

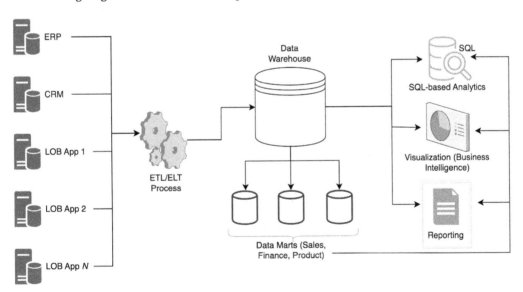

Figure 2.1: Enterprise data warehousing architecture

At the center of our architecture is the EDW, which hosts a set of *data assets* that contain current and historical data about key business subject areas. We also have optional data marts that contain a subset of the data from the warehouse, focused on and optimized for queries in a specific business domain (sales, finance, product, etc.).

On the left-hand side, we have our source systems and an ETL pipeline to load the data into the warehouse and transform the data. On the right-hand side, we can see several systems/applications that consume data from the data warehouse and data marts.

Before we dive deeper into the technical architecture and optimization techniques used in modern data warehouses, let's review some of the foundational concepts around data modeling in data warehouses.

Dimensional modeling in data warehouses

Data assets in the warehouse are typically stored as relational tables that are organized into widely used dimensional models, such as a **star schema** or **snowflake schema**. Storing data in a warehouse using a dimensional model makes it easier to retrieve and filter relevant data, and it also makes analytic query processing flexible, simple, and performant.

Let's dive deeper into two widely used data warehouse modeling techniques, and see how we can organize sales domain entities as an example. Note that this example is just a subsection of a much larger data warehouse schema.

Figure 2.2 illustrates how data in a sales subject area can be organized using a star schema:

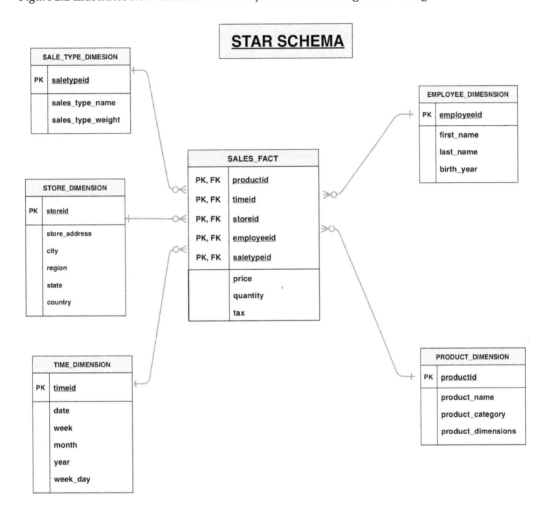

Figure 2.2: Sales data entities organized into a star schema

In data warehouses, tables are generally separated into **fact tables** and **dimension tables**. In *Figure 2.2*, the data entities are organized like a star, with the sales fact table forming the middle of the star, and the dimension tables forming the corners.

A fact table stores granular numeric measurements/metrics for a specific domain (such as sales). In *Figure 2.2*, we have a SALES_FACT table that stores facts about an individual sales transaction, such as the sales **price** and **quantity** sold. The fact table also has a large number of **foreign key** columns that reference the primary keys of associated dimension tables.

The dimension tables store the context under which fact measurements were captured. In *Figure 2.2*, for example, we have dimension tables with information on **stores**, **products**, and other dimensions related to each sale transaction. Each individual dimension table essentially provides granular attributes related to one of the dimensions of the fact (such as the store where the sale took place).

For example, for a specific sale, we record the price, quantity, and tax for the sale in the fact table, and then we reference dimensions such as the store_id for the store in which the sale took place and the product_id for the product that was sold. Instead of storing all the details for the store in the fact table (such as street address, region, country, and phone number), we just store the store_id related to the specific sale as a foreign key. When we want to query sales data, we can do a **join** between the SALES_FACT table and the STORE_DIMENSION table to report on the sale details (price and quantity) along with the region and country of the store (or any other details captured in the dimension table). We can also do a join between other dimension tables to retrieve details about the product sold, the employee that did the sale, the day of the week of the sale, etc.

Dimensional attributes are key to finding and aggregating measurements stored in the fact tables in a data warehouse. Business analysts typically slice, dice, and aggregate facts from different dimensional perspectives to generate business insights about the subject area represented by the star schema. They can find answers to questions such as:

- What is the total volume of a given product sold over a given period?
- What is the total revenue in a given product category?
- Which store sells the greatest number of products in a given category?

In a **star schema**, while data for a subject area is normalized by splitting measurements and context information into separate **fact** and **dimension** tables, individual dimension tables are typically kept denormalized so that all related attributes of a dimensional topic can be found in a single table.

This makes it easier to find all related attributes of a dimensional topic in a single table (fewer joins, and a simpler-to-understand model), but for larger dimension tables, a denormalized approach can lead to data duplication and inconsistencies within the dimension table. Large denormalized dimension tables can also be slow to update.

One approach to work around these issues is a slightly modified type of schema, the **snowflake schema**, which is shown in *Figure 2.3*:

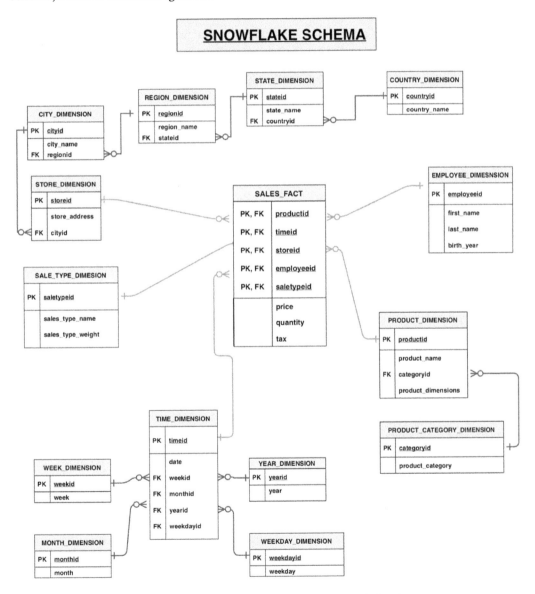

Figure 2.3: Sales data entities organized into a snowflake schema

The challenges of inconsistencies and duplication in a star schema can be addressed by **snow-flaking** (basically normalizing) each dimension table into multiple related dimension tables (normalizing the original *product* dimension into *product* and *product category* dimensions, for example). This normalization of tables continues until each individual dimension table contains only attributes with a direct correlation with the table's primary key. The highly normalized model resulting from this snowflaking is called a **snowflake schema**.

The snowflake schema can be designed by extending the star schema or can be built from the ground up by ensuring that each dimension is highly normalized and connected to related dimension tables forming a hierarchy. A snowflake schema can reduce redundancy and minimize disk space, compared to a star schema, which often contains duplicate records. However, on the other hand, the snowflake schema may necessitate complex joins to answer business queries and may slow down query performance.

To decide on whether to use a snowflake or star schema, you need to consider the types of queries that are likely to be run against the dataset and balance the pros and cons of potentially slower and more complex queries with a snowflake schema versus less performant updates and more complexity in managing changes to dimension tables with a star schema.

Let's now take a closer look at the role of data marts, which can be used to provide a data repository that is easier to work with, with a schema focused on a specific aspect of a business.

Understanding the role of data marts

Data warehouses contain data from all relevant business domains and have a comprehensive yet complex schema. Data warehouses are designed for the cross-domain analysis that's required to inform strategic business decisions. However, organizations often also have a narrower set of users who want to focus on a particular line of business, department, or business subject area. These users prefer to work with a repository that has a simple-to-learn schema, and only the subset of data that focuses on the area they are interested in. Organizations typically build **data marts** to serve these users.

A data mart is focused on a single business subject repository (for example, marketing, sales, or finance) and is typically created to serve a narrower group of business users, such as a single department. A data mart often has a set of denormalized fact tables organized into a much simpler schema compared to that of an EDW. Simpler schemas and a reduced data volume make data marts faster to build, simpler to understand, and easier to use for end users. A data mart can be created either as:

- **Top-down**: Data is taken from an existing data warehouse, focused on a slice of business subject data
- **Bottom-up**: Data is sourced directly from the transactional databases that are used to run a specific business domain of interest

Both data warehouses and data marts provide an integrated view of data from multiple sources, but they differ in the scope of data they store. Data warehouses provide a central store of data for the entire business, or division, and cover all business domains. Data marts serve a specific business function by providing an integrated view of a subject area relevant to that business function.

So far, we have discussed various aspects of data warehouses and data marts, the central data repositories of our *EDW architecture* from *Figure 2.1*. Now, let's do a deeper dive into the technical architecture and optimizations that make modern data warehouses effective at querying large volumes of data.

Distributed storage and massively parallel processing

In *Figure 2.4*, we see the underlying architecture of an **Amazon Redshift** cluster. There are various different types of Redshift nodes, and *Figure 2.4* shows a Redshift cluster based on **RA3 nodes** (which we will take a closer look at in *Chapter 9, A Deeper Dive into Data Marts and Amazon Redshift*):

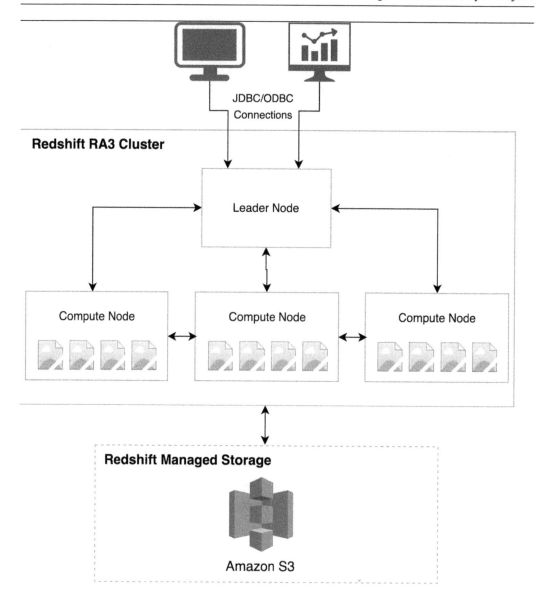

Figure 2.4: MPP architecture of an Amazon Redshift RA3 cluster

As seen in *Figure 2.4*, an Amazon Redshift cluster contains a leader node and one or more compute nodes:

- The **leader node** interfaces with client applications, receives and parses queries, and coordinates query execution on compute nodes.

- Multiple **compute nodes** have high-performance storage for storing a subset of the warehouse data and run query execution steps in parallel on the data that they store.

- For RA3 node types (as illustrated in this diagram), Amazon S3 is used as **Redshift Managed Storage (RMS)** for warehouse data, and the compute node high-performance local storage is used as a cache for hot data.

Each compute node has its own independent processors, memory, and high-performance storage volumes that are isolated from other compute nodes in the cluster (this is called a shared-nothing architecture).

Cloud data warehouses implement a distributed query processing architecture called **Massively Parallel Processing (MPP)** to accelerate queries on massive volumes of data. In this approach, the cluster leader node first compiles the incoming client query into a distributed execution plan. It then coordinates the execution of segments of compiled query code on multiple compute nodes of the data warehouse cluster, in parallel. Each compute node executes assigned query segments on a portion of the distributed dataset.

Columnar data storage and efficient data compression

In addition to providing massive storage and cluster computing, modern data warehouses also boost query performance through **column-oriented** storage and **data compression**. In this section, we'll examine how this works, but first, let's understand how OLTP databases store their data.

OLTP applications typically work with entire rows that include all the columns of the table (for example, reading/writing a sales record, or looking up a catalog record). To serve OLTP applications, backend databases need to efficiently read and write full rows to the disk. To speed up full-row lookups and updates, OLTP databases use a row-oriented layout to store table rows on the disk. In a **row-oriented** physical data layout, all the column values of a given row are co-located, as depicted in *Figure 2.5*:

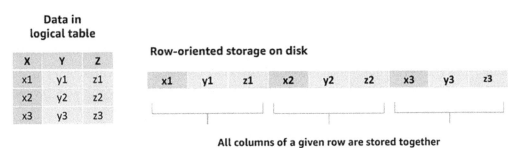

Figure 2.5: Row-oriented storage layout

Most analytics queries that business users run against a data warehouse are written to answer a specific question and typically include grouping and aggregations (such as sum, average, or mean) on a large number of rows, but of a narrow set of columns from the fact and dimension tables (these typically contain many more columns than the narrow set of columns included in the query). Analytics queries typically need to scan through a large number of rows but need data from only a narrow set of columns that relate to the specific query. A **row-oriented** physical data layout forces analytics queries to scan a large number of full rows (all columns), even though they need only a subset of the columns from these rows. Analytics queries on a row-oriented database can thus require a much higher number of disk I/O operations than necessary.

Modern data warehouses store data on disks using a **column-oriented** physical layout. This is more suitable for analytical query processing, which only requires a subset of columns per query. While storing a table's data in a column-oriented physical layout, a data warehouse breaks a table into groups of rows, called row chunks/groups. It then takes a row chunk at a time and lays out data from that row chunk, one column at a time, so that all the values for a column (that is, for that row chunk) are physically co-located on the disk, as depicted in *Figure 2.6*:

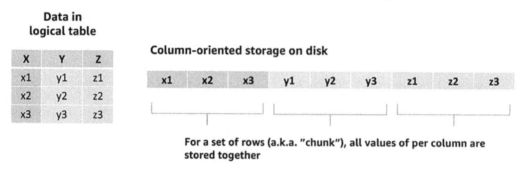

Figure 2.6: Column-oriented storage layout

Data warehouses repeat this for all the row chunks of the table. In addition to storing tables as row chunks and using a column-oriented physical layout on disks, data warehouses also maintain in-memory maps of the locations of these chunks. Modern data warehouses use these in-memory maps to pinpoint column locations on the disk and read the physically co-located values of the column. This enables the query engine to retrieve data for only the narrow set of columns needed for a given analytics query. By doing this, the disk I/O is significantly reduced compared to what would be required to run the same query on a row-oriented database.

In addition to using a column-orientated storage layout, modern data warehouses also employ multiple **compression algorithms** for a table. The warehouse is able to match individual columns with the compression algorithm that is most optimal for the given column's type and profile of its data content.

In addition to saving storage space, compressed data requires much lower disk I/O to read and write data to the disk. Compression algorithms provide much better compression ratios when all values being compressed have the same data type and have a larger percentage of duplicates. Since column-oriented databases lay out values of the same column (hence, the same data type, such as strings or integers) together, data warehouses achieve good compression ratios, resulting in faster read/writes, and smaller on-disk footprints.

Now that we have a better understanding of the architecture of modern data warehouses, let's look at the processes (often referred to as pipelines), that are used to move data into a data warehouse, and to transform the data to optimize it for analytics.

Feeding data into the warehouse — ETL and ELT pipelines

To bring data into the warehouse (and optionally, data marts), organizations typically build data pipelines that do the following:

- Extract data from source systems.
- Transform source data by validating, cleaning, standardizing, and curating it.
- Load the transformed source data into the enterprise data warehouse schema, and optionally a data mart as well.

In these pipelines, the first step is to **extract** data from source systems, but the next two steps can either take on a **Transform-Load** or **Load-Transform** sequence (so either ETL or ELT).

The data warehouses of a modern organization typically ingest data from a diverse set of sources, such as **ERP** and **CRM** application databases, files stored on **Network-Attached Storage (NAS)** arrays, **SaaS** applications, and external partner applications. The components that are used to implement the **Extract** step of both ETL and ELT pipelines typically need to connect to these sources and handle diverse data formats (including relational tables, flat files, and continuous streams of records).

The decision as to whether to build an ETL or ELT data pipeline is based on the following:

- The complexity of the required data transformations
- The skills and tools the organization has available to build data transformation steps
- The speed at which source data needs to be made available for analysis in the data ware-house after it's produced in the source system.

Figure 2.7 shows a typical ETL pipeline for loading data into a data warehouse:

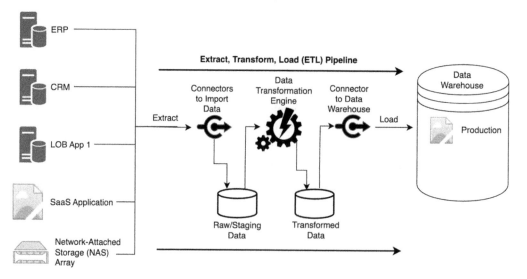

Figure 2.7: ETL pipeline

With an **ETL** pipeline, transformations are performed outside of the data warehouse using custom scripts, a cloud-native ETL service such as AWS Glue, or a specialized ETL tool from a commercial vendor such as Informatica, Talend, DataStage, Microsoft, or Pentaho.

An ETL pipeline may be a single system that has connectors to extract and load the data in addition to doing the transformations, or there may be multiple systems in the pipeline. For example, an ETL pipeline could consist of the following:

- One or more systems that extract data from various sources (databases, SaaS solutions, file storage, etc.) and write the data to a raw/staging storage area
- One or more transformation jobs that read data from the raw/staging storage area, transform the data, and then write it to a transformed storage area
- Another system that reads data from the transformed storage area and loads the data into the data warehouse

A transformation engine may run multiple transformation jobs to perform tasks such as validating data, cleaning data, and transforming data for the target data warehouse dimensional schema.

An ETL approach to building a data pipeline is typically used when the following are true:

- Source database technologies and formats are different from those of the data warehouse
- The engineering team wants to perform transformations using a programming language (such as PySpark) rather than pure SQL
- Data transformations are complex and compute-intensive

On the other hand, an ELT pipeline extracts data (typically highly structured data) from various sources and loads it as is into the staging area of the data warehouse. The database engine powering the data warehouse is then used to perform transformation operations on the staged data and writes the transformed data to a production table (ready for consumption).

Figure 2.8 shows a typical ELT pipeline:

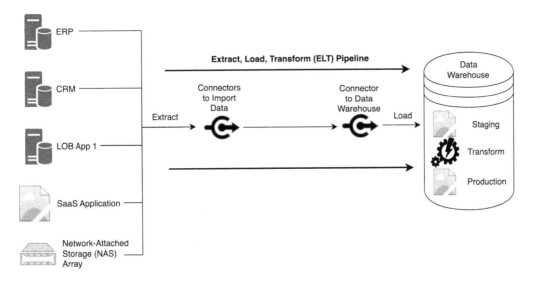

Figure 2.8: ELT pipeline

The ELT approach allows for rapidly loading large amounts of source data into the warehouse. Furthermore, the MPP architecture of modern data warehouses can significantly accelerate the transformation steps in ELT pipelines. The ELT approach is typically leveraged when the following are true:

- Data sources and the warehouse have similar database technologies, making it easier to directly load source data into the staging tables in the warehouse.

- A large volume of data needs to be quickly loaded into the warehouse.
- All the required transformation steps can be executed using the native SQL capabilities of the warehouse's database engine.

With an ELT approach, the data transformation tasks are generally performed using SQL code. While there is a large amount of SQL knowledge and skills available on the market, there are other options for performing transformations (such as by using Apache Spark with PySpark or Scala code). Using an ELT approach limits your transformations to using SQL, which may or may not be best based on the skill sets and requirements of your organization.

The primary difference between ETL and ELT is about where the data transformation takes place. With ELT, the data is loaded directly into the data warehouse, and the data warehouse engine is used for the transformation (typically using SQL to create a new, transformed version of the data). With ETL, an engine outside of the data warehouse first transforms the data before writing it to the data warehouse.

In this section, we learned how data warehouses can store and process petabytes of structured data. Modern data warehouses provide high-performance processing using a dimensional data model (such as star or snowflake), compute parallelism, and a columnar physical data layout with compression. Data management architectures at modern organizations, however, also need to store and analyze exploding volumes of semi-structured and unstructured data. In the next section, we'll learn about a newer architecture, called data lakes, that today's leading organizations typically implement to store, process, and analyze structured, semi-structured, and unstructured data.

An overview of data lake architecture and concepts

As we saw in the previous section, EDWs have been the go-to repositories for storing highly structured tabular data sourced from the transactional databases used by business applications. However, the lack of a well-defined tabular structure makes typical data warehouses less suitable for storing unstructured and semi-structured data. Also, while they are good for use cases that need SQL-based processing, data warehouses are limited to processing data primarily using only SQL, and SQL is not the right tool for all data processing requirements. For example, extracting metadata from unstructured data, such as audio files or images, is best suited for specialized machine learning tools.

A cloud data lake is a central, highly scalable repository in the cloud where an organization can manage exabytes of various types of data, including:

- Structured data (row-column based tables)

- Semi-structured data (such as JSON and XML files, log records, and sensor data streams)
- Unstructured data (such as audio, video streams, Word/PDF documents, and emails)

Data from any of these sources can be quickly loaded into the data lake as is (keeping the original source format and structure). Unlike with data warehouses, data does not need to first be converted into a standard structure before it is consumed.

A cloud data lake also natively integrates with cloud analytic services that are decoupled from data lake storage and enables diverse analytic tools, including **SQL**, code-based tools (such as **Apache Spark**), specialized **machine learning tools**, and **business intelligence** visualization tools.

In the next section, we dive deeper into the architecture of a typical data lake.

Data lake logical architecture

Let's take a closer look at the architecture of a cloud-native data lake by looking at its logical architecture, as shown in *Figure 2.9*:

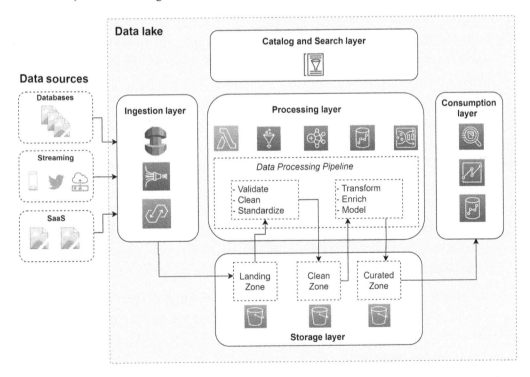

Figure 2.9: Logical layers of a data lake architecture

We can visualize a data lake architecture as a set of independent components organized into five logical layers. A layered, component-oriented data lake architecture can evolve over time to incorporate new innovations in data management and analytics methods, as well as to make use of new tools. This keeps the data lake responsive to new data sources and changing requirements. In the next section, we will dive deeper into these layers.

The storage layer and storage zones

At the bottom of the data lake architecture illustrated in *Figure 2.9* is the storage layer, built on a cloud object store such as Amazon S3. This provides virtually unlimited, low-cost storage that can store a variety of data, irrespective of the structure or format.

The storage layer is organized into different **zones**, with each zone having a specific purpose. Data moves through the various zones of the data lake, with new, modified copies of the data in each zone as the data goes through various transformations. There are no hard rules about how many zones there should be, or the names of zones, but the following zones are commonly found in a typical data lake:

- **Landing/raw zone**. This is the zone where the ingestion layer writes data, as is, from the source systems. The landing/raw zone permanently stores the raw data from the source.
- **Clean/transform zone**. The initial data processing of data in the landing/raw zone, such as validating, cleaning, and optimizing datasets, writes data into the clean/transform zone. The data here is often stored in optimized formats such as **Parquet** and is often partitioned to accelerate query execution and downstream processing. Data in this zone may also have had PII information removed, masked, or replaced with tokens.
- **Curated/enriched zone**. The data in the clean/transformed zone may be further refined and enriched with business-specific logic and transformations, and this data is written to the curated/enriched zone. This data is in its most consumable state and meets all organizational standards (in terms of cleanliness, file formats, and schema). Data here is typically partitioned, cataloged, and optimized for the consumption layer.

Depending on the business requirements, some data lakes may include more or fewer zones than the 3 zones highlighted above. For example, a very simple data lake may just have two zones (the raw and curated zones), while some data lakes may have 5 or more zones to handle intermediate stages or specific requirements.

Catalog and search layers

A data lake typically hosts a large number of datasets (potentially thousands), from a variety of internal and external sources. These datasets are often useful to multiple teams across the organization, and these teams need the ability to search for available datasets and review the schema and other metadata of those datasets.

A **technical catalog** is used to map the many files stored in the storage layer into a logical representation of databases and tables, with each table having columns of a specific data type (the table schema). A technical catalog, such as the AWS Glue Data Catalog, stores the metadata that defines the relationship between physical files on storage and a table definition in the catalog. Consumption tools (such as Amazon Athena) can use the technical catalog to understand which files to read from the storage layer when a user queries a specific database and table.

A **business catalog** focuses on the metadata that is important to the business. This may include attributes such as the data owner, the date the dataset was last updated, a description of the table purpose, column definitions, and more. The business catalog may also integrate with the technical catalog in order to provide information on the table schema in the business catalog interface. The business catalog should also support the ability to do advanced searches, enabling teams to find data that is relevant to their use cases. We do a deep dive into data cataloging in *Chapter 4, Data Governance, Security, and Cataloging*.

Ingestion layer

The **ingestion layer** is responsible for connecting to diverse types of data sources and bringing their data into the landing/raw zone of the storage layer. This layer may contain a variety of independent tools, each purpose-built to connect to a data source with a distinct profile in terms of:

- Data structure (structured, semi-structured, or unstructured)
- Data delivery type (table rows, data stream, data file)
- Data production cadence (batch or streaming)

This approach provides the flexibility to easily add new tools to match a new data source's distinct profile.

A typical ingestion layer may include tools such as **AWS Database Migration Service (DMS)** for ingesting from various databases, **Amazon Kinesis Firehose** for ingesting streaming data, and **Amazon AppFlow** for ingesting data from SaaS applications. We do a deep dive into the ingestion layer in *Chapter 6, Ingesting Batch and Streaming Data*.

The processing layer

Once the ingestion layer brings data from a source system into the landing zone, it is the **processing layer** that makes it ready for consumption by data consumers. The processing layer transforms the data in the lake through various stages of data cleanup, standardization, and enrichment. Along the way, the processing layer stores transformed data in the different zones – writing it into the clean zone and then the curated zone, and then ensuring that the technical data catalog gets updated. Tools commonly used in this layer include **AWS Glue** and **Amazon EMR**.

Components in the ingestion and processing layers are used to create ELT pipelines. In these pipelines, the ingestion layer components extract data from the source systems and load the data into the data lake, and then the processing layer components transform it to make it suitable for consumption by components in the consumption layer. We will do a deep dive into the processing layer in *Chapter 7, Transforming Data to Optimize It for Analytics*.

The consumption layer

Once data is ingested and processed to make it consumption-ready, it can be analyzed using several techniques, such as interactive query processing, business intelligence dashboarding, and machine learning. To perform analytics on data in the lake, the consumption layer provides purpose-built tools that are able to access data from the storage layer, and the schema from the catalog layer (to apply schema-on-read to the lake-hosted data). We will do a deeper dive into data consumption in *Chapter 8, Identifying and Enabling Data Consumers*.

Data lake architecture summary

In this section, we learned about data lake architectures and how they can enable organizations to manage and analyze vast amounts of structured, unstructured, and semi-structured data.

Analytics platforms at a typical organization need to serve warehousing-style structured data analytics use cases (such as for complex queries and BI dashboarding), as well as use cases that require managing and analyzing vast amounts of unstructured and semi-structured data. As a result, organizations typically end up building both a data warehouse and a data lake, often with little interaction between the warehouse and the lake.

In the next section, we will look at modern data management and analytic architectures that integrate the best of both data warehouses and data lakes.

Bringing together the best of data warehouses and data lakes

In today's highly digitized world, data about customers, products, operations, and the supply chain can come from many sources and can have a diverse set of structures. To gain deeper and more complete data-driven insights into a business topic (such as a customer journey, customer retention, product performance, etc.), organizations need to analyze all topic-relevant data, of all structures, from all sources, together.

A data lake is well suited to storing all these different types of data inexpensively and provides a wide variety of tools to work with and consume the data. This includes the ability to transform data with frameworks such as **Apache Spark**, to train machine learning models on the data using tools such as **Amazon SageMaker**, and to query the data using **SQL** with tools such as **Amazon Athena**, **Presto**, or **Trino**.

However, there are some limitations to traditional data lakes. For example, traditional implementations of data lakes do not support the **ACID** (atomicity, consistency, isolation, and durability) properties common in most databases. Also, due to the use of inexpensive object storage as the storage layer, the query performance does not match what is possible with data warehouses that use high-performance, SSD-based local storage.

These limitations cause complexity when you have multiple teams working on the same dataset, as one team updating data in the data lake while another team attempts to query the data lake can lead to inconsistencies in the queries. Also, when you have heavily used dashboards and reporting as is common with **Business Intelligence** applications, the performance of queries on data lake data may not meet requirements.

These challenges are often worked around by loading a subset of the data from the data lake into a data warehouse, such as **Amazon Redshift** or **Snowflake**. This offers the performance needed for demanding business intelligence applications and also provides consistency when multiple teams are working with the same dataset. However, data warehouse storage is expensive, and some use cases require joining data across a diverse set of data and it is not economical to load all this data into the data warehouse.

To work around these challenges, new table formats have been created that simplify the process of updating data lake tables in a transactionally safe way, and new functionality is available to enable federated queries (joins of data across different storage engines) in an approach often referred to as a **data lake house**.

The data lake house approach

During the year 2020, a number of vendors started using a new term to talk about an approach that brought together the best of data warehouses and data lakes. Some vendors referred to this as a **Lakehouse**, while others called it a **data lake house**, or **data lakehouse**. In addition to these differences in the name of the approach, the different vendors had slightly different definitions of what a lake house was.

Even today you can read blogs and articles about different lake house approaches from companies such as AWS, Azure, Google, Snowflake, Databricks, Dremio, and Starburst. Because of this, I would consider the lake house terminology more of a marketing term than a technical term. Ultimately, there is no standard definition of a lake house, beyond the intention of different vendors to provide the best of both data warehouses and data lakes with their own technology stacks.

However, there are a number of widely adopted technologies and approaches that enable these companies to blur the lines between a data warehouse and a data lake.

New data lake table formats

Over the past few years, a number of new table formats have been proposed that are effectively a new generation of the original Hive table format, a format developed at Facebook more than a decade ago. While Hive has been fundamental in enabling the creation and growth of data lakes, there are a number of challenges with the Hive format that put significant limits on Hive-based data lakes. As a result, today there are three primary competing new table formats that can be used to develop modern data lakes.

While each of these table formats has its own strengths and weaknesses, they are all intended to enable simplified and more consistent updates and reads of data lake data (especially when you have multiple teams working with the same dataset), as well as to offer performance improvements, and the ability to query a table as it was at a certain point in time (often referred to as time travel). Many big data solution providers are adding support for one or more of these table formats, as they build out their "data lake house" offerings. These new table formats provide functionality for working with data in a data lake that is similar to what traditionally was only available in databases and data warehouses.

The three main new-generation table formats are:

- **Delta Lake.** This is a table format created by the Databricks company and is offered both as a commercial paid version with enhanced functionality and as an open-source version, which is a Linux Foundation project. A number of commercial and open-source tools are able to work with Delta Lake files, including Apache Spark, Presto, Snowflake, Redshift, and others.

- **Apache Hudi.** This is a table format that was created by Uber, and later donated to the Apache Software Foundation, and is now available as an open-source solution. Hudi has been fairly widely adopted, and blog posts/case studies that mention the use of Apache Hudi include those from companies such as Amazon Transportation Service, Walmart, Robinhood, and GE Aviation.

- **Apache Iceberg.** This table format was created by two engineers at Netflix and later donated to the Apache Software Foundation, making it available as an open-source solution. Companies that have publicly referenced making use of Apache Iceberg, or who have contributed to the open-source project, include Airbnb, Expedia, Adobe, Apple, and Lyft.

It is impossible to predict with certainty which one of these table formats (or potentially others yet to be popularized) will become dominant over the next few years, but recently it has seemed like Apache Iceberg is generating increasing interest and gaining more and more support from big data product vendors. We will cover these new table formats in more detail in *Chapter 14, Transactional Data Lakes*. For now, though, let's look at how federated queries enable querying across different database engines.

Federated queries across database engines

Another approach that has become common in the quest to combine the best of data lakes and data warehouses is functionality that enables queries across different database engines or storage platforms. For example, cloud data warehouses such as Amazon Redshift and Snowflake are able to query data loaded into the data warehouse, as well as data in an Amazon S3-based data lake.

With this approach, the most recent 12 months of data could be loaded into a data warehouse, while the previous 4 years of data could be stored in the data lake. Most queries would only query the most recent 12 months of data, and that would be stored within the highly performant storage of the data warehouse. However, for those queries that needed to access the historical information, the data warehouse could join tables in the S3 data lake with the recent data in the data warehouse.

This query federation can extend beyond just joining tables in the data warehouse and tables in the S3-based data lake to querying data in other storage engines as well. For example, with Amazon Redshift, you can define external tables that point to data in a PostgreSQL or MySQL database.

With federated queries, the requirement to copy data between different data systems through ETL pipelines is reduced. However, querying across different systems does not perform as well as querying on local-only data, so there are use cases where you would still want to copy data between systems. Nevertheless, having the ability to query data across systems is useful in many situations, and helps create a more integrated big data ecosystem. AWS messaging around the lake house concept has often included highlighting this ability to have access to data in different systems, with a shared data catalog, and without needing to always create a copy of the source data in each system.

In later chapters, the hands-on exercises will cover various tasks related to ingesting, transforming, and querying data in the data lake, but in this chapter, we are still setting up some of the foundational tasks. In the next section, we will use the AWS **Command Line Interface** (**CLI**) to create a number of Amazon S3 buckets.

Hands-on – using the AWS Command Line Interface (CLI) to create Simple Storage Service (S3) buckets

In *Chapter 1, An Introduction to Data Engineering*, you created an AWS account and an AWS administrative user and then ensured you could access your account. Console access allows you to access AWS services and perform most functions; however, it can also be useful to interact with AWS services via the **CLI** at times.

In this hands-on section, you will learn how to access the AWS CLI, and then use the CLI to create Amazon S3 buckets (a storage container in the Amazon S3 service).

Accessing the AWS CLI

The AWS CLI can be installed on your personal computer/laptop or can be accessed from the AWS Console. To access the CLI on your personal computer, you need to generate a set of access keys.

Your access keys consist of an **access key ID** (which is comparable to a username), and a **secret access key** (which is comparable to a password). With these two pieces of information, you can authenticate as your user and perform all actions that your user is authorized to perform.

However, if anyone else were able to get your access key ID and secret access key, then they would have access to the same permissions. In the past, there have been instances where users have accidentally exposed their access key ID and secret access key, enabling malicious third parties to fraudulently use their account.

As a result, the easiest and most secure way to access the CLI is via the AWS CloudShell service, which is accessible via the console.

Using AWS CloudShell to access the CLI

CloudShell provides a terminal interface in your web browser, as part of the AWS Console, that can be used to explore and manage AWS resources, using the permissions of the user with which you log in to the console. With this approach, there is no need to generate access keys for your user.

Use the following steps to access the CLI via AWS CloudShell:

1. Log in to the AWS Console (`https://console.aws.amazon.com`) using the credentials you created in *Chapter 1*.

2. Click on the CloudShell icon, or use the search bar to search for the **CloudShell** service.

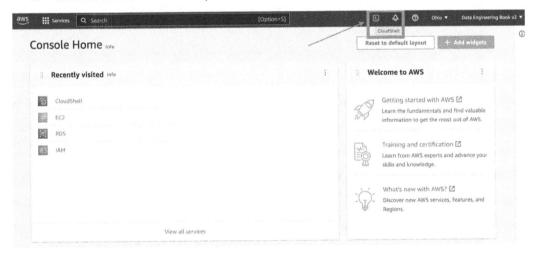

Figure 2.10: Accessing the AWS CloudShell service in the console

3. To interact with AWS services, you run the command aws. To learn how to interact with a specific service, you can run the aws command, followed by the name of the AWS service you want to interact with (such as S3), followed by help. For example, to learn how to use the Amazon S3 service, run the following command, which will display the help page for the S3 service:

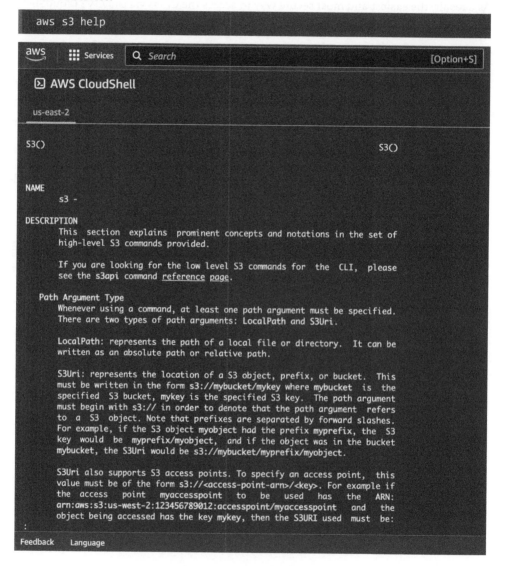

Figure 2.11: Displaying the AWS CLI help page for Amazon S3

4. Press the *SPACE* bar to display subsequent pages of the help, or press the letter *q* to quit the help pages.

Creating new Amazon S3 buckets

Amazon S3 is an object storage service that offers near-unlimited capacity with high levels of durability and availability. To store data in S3, you need to create a bucket. Once created, the bucket can store any number of objects.

Each S3 bucket needs to have a globally unique name, and it is recommended that the name be DNS-compliant. For more information on rules for bucket names, see https://docs.aws.amazon.com/AmazonS3/latest/userguide/bucketnamingrules.html:

1. To create an S3 bucket using the AWS CLI, run the following command at the Command Prompt in CloudShell. In the following command, replace <bucket-name> with a unique name for your bucket:

   ```
   $ aws s3 mb s3://<bucket-name>
   ```

   Remember that the bucket name you specify here must be globally unique. If you attempt to create a bucket using a name that another AWS account has used, you will see an error similar to the following:

   ```
   $ aws s3 mb s3://test-bucket
   make_bucket failed: s3://test-bucket An error occurred
   (BucketAlreadyExists) when calling the CreateBucket operation: The
   requested bucket name is not available. The bucket namespace is
   shared by all users of the system. Please select a different name
   and try again.
   ```

   If your aws s3 mb command returned a message similar to the following, then congratulations! You have created your first bucket.

   ```
   make_bucket: <bucket-name>
   ```

2. We can now create additional buckets that we are going to use in some of the hands-on exercises in later chapters. As discussed earlier in this chapter, data lakes generally have multiple zones for data at different stages. To set up our data lake, we want to create S3 buckets for the **landing zone, clean zone**, and **curated zone**. Refer back to the section titled *The storage layer and storage zones* earlier in this chapter for a description of each of the zones.

In order to ensure that each bucket name created is globally unique, you can append some unique characters to each name, such as your initials, and if necessary, some numbers. In the examples below, I am going to append gse23 to each bucket name to ensure it is unique.

Run the following three commands in the CloudShell terminal to create your buckets (replacing gse23 with your own identifier).

```
$ aws s3 mb s3://dataeng-landing-zone-gse23
$ aws s3 mb s3://dataeng-clean-zone-gse23
$ aws s3 mb s3://dataeng-curated-zone-gse23
```

We have now created the storage buckets that will form the foundation of the three zones of our data lake (landing zone, clean zone, and curated zone). In later chapters, we will ingest data into the landing zone, and then create transformed copies of that data in the other zones.

Summary

In this chapter, we learned about the foundational architectural concepts that are typically applied when designing real-life analytics data management and processing solutions. We also discussed three analytics data management architectures that you would commonly find in organizations today: data warehouse, data lake, and data lakehouse.

In the next chapter, we will provide an overview of several AWS services that are used in the creation of these architectures, including services for ingesting data, services that help perform data transformation, and services that are designed for querying and analyzing data.

Learn more on Discord

To join the Discord community for this book – where you can share feedback, ask questions to the author, and learn about new releases – follow the QR code below:

https://discord.gg/9s5mHNyECd

3

The AWS Data Engineer's Toolkit

Back in 2006, Amazon launched **Amazon Web Services (AWS)** to offer on-demand delivery of IT resources over the internet, essentially creating the cloud computing industry. Ever since then, AWS has innovated at an incredible pace, continually launching new services and features to offer broad and deep functionality across a wide range of IT services.

Traditionally, organizations built their own big data processing systems in their data centers, implementing commercial or open-source solutions designed to help them make sense of ever-increasing quantities of data. However, these systems were often complex to install, requiring a team of people to maintain, optimize, and update, and scaling these systems was a challenge, requiring significant expenditure on infrastructure and delays while waiting for hardware vendors to install new compute and storage systems.

Cloud computing has enabled the removal of many of these challenges, including the ability to launch fully configured software solutions at the push of a button and have these systems automatically updated and maintained by the cloud vendor. Organizations also benefit from the ability to scale out by adding resources in minutes, all the while only paying for what was used, rather than having to make large upfront capital investments.

Today, AWS offers over 200 different services, including a number of analytics services that can be used by data engineers to build complex data analytic pipelines. There are often multiple AWS services that can be used to achieve a specific outcome, and the challenge for data architects and engineers is balancing the pros and cons of a specific service and evaluating it from multiple perspectives, before determining the best fit for the specific requirements.

In this chapter, we introduce a number of these AWS-managed services commonly used for building big data solutions on AWS, and in later chapters, we will look at how you can architect complex data engineering pipelines using these services. As you go through this chapter, you will learn about the following topics:

- AWS services for ingesting data
- AWS services for transforming data
- AWS services for orchestrating big data pipelines
- AWS services for consuming data
- Hands-on – triggering an AWS Lambda function when a new file arrives in an S3 bucket

Technical requirements

You can find the code files of this chapter in the GitHub repository at the following link: `https://github.com/PacktPublishing/Data-Engineering-with-AWS-2nd-edition/tree/main/Chapter03`.

An overview of AWS services for ingesting data

The first step in building big data analytic solutions is to **ingest data** from a variety of sources into AWS. In this section, we will introduce some of the core AWS services designed to help with this; however, this should not be considered a comprehensive review of every possible way to ingest data into AWS.

Don't feel overwhelmed by the number of services we cover in this section! We will explore approaches to deciding on the right service for your specific use case in later chapters, but it is important to have a good understanding of the available tools upfront.

Amazon Database Migration Service (DMS)

One of the most common ingestion use cases is to sync data from a database system into an analytic pipeline, either landing the data in an Amazon S3-based data lake or in a data warehousing system such as **Amazon Redshift**.

AWS DMS is a versatile tool that can be used to migrate an existing database system into a new database engine, such as migrating an existing **Oracle** database into an **Amazon Aurora PostgreSQL** database. In addition, Amazon DMS can be used to replicate between the same database engine (such as from an on-prem PostgreSQL server to an Amazon Aurora PostgreSQL-compatible server).

When migrating to the same engine, DMS uses the database engine native tools in order to make the migration easy and performant. From an analytics perspective, AWS DMS can also be used to run continuous replication from a number of common database engines into an **Amazon S3 data lake**.

As discussed previously, data lakes are often used as a means of bringing data from multiple different data sources into a centralized location to enable an organization to get the big picture across different business units and functions. As a result, there is often a requirement to perform continuous replication of a number of production databases into Amazon S3.

For our use case, we want to *sync* our production *customer*, *products*, and *order* databases into the data lake. Using DMS, we can do an initial load of data from the databases into S3, specifying the format that we want the file written out in (such as CSV or Parquet), and the specific ingestion location in S3. At the same time, we can also set up a DMS task to do ongoing replication from the source databases into S3 once the full load is completed.

With transactional databases, the rows in a table are regularly updated, such as if a customer changes their address or telephone number. When querying the database using **Structured Query Language (SQL)**, we can see the updated information, but in most cases, there is no practical method to track changes to the database using only SQL. Because of this, DMS uses the database transaction log files from the database to track updates to rows in the database and writes out the target file in S3 with an extra column added (**Op**) that indicates which operation is reflected in the row – an insert, update, or deletion. The process of tracking and recording these changes is commonly referred to as **Change Data Capture (CDC)**.

Picture a situation where you have a source table with a schema of **custid, lastname, firstname, address**, and **phone**, and the following sequence of events happens:

- A new customer is added with all fields completed
- The phone number was entered incorrectly, so the record has the phone number updated
- The customer record is then deleted from the database

We would see the following in the CDC file that was written out by DMS:

```
I, 9335, Smith, John, "1 Skyline Drive, NY, NY", 201-555-9012
U, 9335, Smith, John, "1 Skyline Drive, NY, NY", 201-555-9034
D, 9335, Smith, John, "1 Skyline Drive, NY, NY", 201-555-9034
```

The first row in the file shows us that a new record was *inserted* into the table (represented by the I in the first column). The second row shows us that a record was *updated* (represented by the U in the first column). Finally, the third entry in the file indicates that this record was *deleted* from the table (represented by the D in the first column).

We would then have a separate update process that would run to read the updates and apply those updates to the full load, creating a new point-in-time snapshot of our source database. The update process would be scheduled to run regularly, and every time it runs, it would apply the latest updates as recorded by DMS to the previous snapshot, creating a new point-in-time snapshot. We will review this kind of update job and approach in more detail in *Chapter 7, Transforming Data to Optimize It for Analytics*.

Amazon DMS is available either in a provisioned mode (where you select the size of the replication instance used to connect to the source database, do any transformation, and then write to the target) or in a serverless mode (where DMS automatically configures, scales, and manages the resources needed for the migration based on requirements).

When to use: Amazon DMS simplifies migrating from one database engine to a different database engine or syncing data from an existing database to Amazon S3 on an ongoing basis.

When not to use: Amazon DMS does put some load on the production database during migrations, so you need to take this into account.

AWS web page: https://aws.amazon.com/dms/

Amazon Kinesis for streaming data ingestion

Amazon Kinesis is a managed service that simplifies the process of ingesting and processing streaming data in real time, or near real time. There are a number of different use cases that Kinesis can be used for, including ingestion of streaming data (such as log files, website clickstreams, or IoT data), as well as video and audio streams.

Depending on the specific use case, there are a number of different services that you can select from that form part of the overall Kinesis service. Before we go into more detail about these services, here is a high-level overview of the various Amazon Kinesis services:

1. **Kinesis Data Firehose:** Ingests streaming data, buffers for a configurable period, then writes out to a limited set of targets (**S3**, **Redshift**, **OpenSearch Service**, **Splunk**, and others)

2. **Kinesis Data Streams**: Ingests real-time data streams, processing the incoming data with a custom application and low latency

3. **Kinesis Data Analytics**: Reads data from a streaming source and uses SQL statements or **Apache Flink** code to perform analytics on the stream

4. **Kinesis Video Streams**: Processes streaming video or audio streams, as well as other time-serialized data such as thermal imagery and RADAR data

In addition to the four core services listed above that make up the Kinesis service, there is also Kinesis Agent, which can be used to package and send data to Kinesis services.

Amazon Kinesis Agent

AWS provides Kinesis Agent to easily consume data from a system and write that data out in a stream to either Kinesis Data Streams or Kinesis Data Firehose.

Amazon Kinesis Agent is available on GitHub as a Java application under the Amazon Software License (`https://github.com/awslabs/amazon-kinesis-agent`), as well as in a version for Windows (`https://github.com/awslabs/kinesis-agent-windows`).

The agent can be configured to monitor a set of files, and as new data is written to the file, the agent buffers the data (configurable for a duration of between 1 second and 15 minutes) and then writes the data to either Kinesis Data Streams or Kinesis Data Firehose. The agent handles retry on failure, as well as file rotation and checkpointing.

An example of a typical use case is a scenario where you want to analyze events happening on your website in near real time. Kinesis Agent can be configured to monitor the Apache web server log files on your web server, convert each record from the Apache access log format into JSON format, and then write records out reflecting all website activity every 30 seconds to Kinesis, where Kinesis Data Analytics can be used to analyze events and generate custom metrics based on a tumbling 5-minute window.

When to use: Amazon Kinesis Agent is ideal for when you want to stream data to Kinesis that is being written to a file in a separate process (such as log files).

When not to use: If you have a custom application where you want to emit streaming events (such as a mobile application or IoT device), you may want to consider using the **Amazon Kinesis Producer Library** (**KPL**), or the **AWS SDK**, to integrate sending streaming data directly from your application.

Amazon Kinesis Firehose

Amazon Kinesis Firehose is designed to enable you to easily ingest data in near real time from streaming sources and write out that data to common targets, including Amazon S3, Amazon Redshift, Amazon OpenSearch Service, as well as many third-party services (such as **Splunk**, **Datadog**, and **New Relic**).

With Kinesis Firehose, you can easily ingest data from streaming sources, process or transform the incoming data, and deliver that data to a target such as Amazon S3 (among others). A common use case for data engineering purposes is to ingest website clickstream data from the Apache web logs on a web server and write that data out to an S3 data lake (or a Redshift data warehouse).

In this example, you could install Kinesis Agent on the web server and configure it to monitor the Apache web server log files. Based on the configuration of the agent, at a regular schedule, the agent will write records from the log files to the Kinesis Firehose endpoint.

The Kinesis Firehose endpoint would buffer the incoming records, and either after a certain time (1-15 minutes) or based on the size of incoming records (1 MB-128 MB), it would write out data to the specified target. Kinesis Firehose requires you to specify both a size and a time limit, and whichever is reached first will trigger the writing out of the file.

When writing files to Amazon S3, you also have the option to transform incoming data into **Parquet** or **ORC** format or perform custom transformations of the incoming data stream using an Amazon Lambda function. Kinesis Data Firehose also supports **dynamic partitioning**, enabling you to specify a custom partitioning configuration. With dynamic partitioning, as your data is written to your S3-based data lake it can be partitioned based on custom partition keys contained in the data payload.

When to use: Amazon Kinesis Firehose is the ideal choice for when you want to receive streaming data, buffer that data for a period, and then write the data to one of the targets supported by Kinesis Firehose (such as Amazon S3, Amazon Redshift, Amazon OpenSearch Service, an HTTP endpoint, or a supported third-party service).

When not to use: If your use case requires very low-latency processing of incoming streaming data (that is, immediate reading of received records) or you want to use a custom application to process your incoming records or deliver records to a service not supported by Amazon Kinesis Firehose, then you should consider using **Amazon Kinesis Data Streams** or Amazon **Managed Streaming for Apache Kafka** (**MSK**) instead.

AWS web page: https://aws.amazon.com/kinesis/data-firehose/

Amazon Kinesis Data Streams

While Kinesis Firehose buffers incoming data before writing it to one of its supported targets, Kinesis Data Streams provides increased flexibility for how data is consumed and makes the incoming data available to your streaming applications with very low latency (AWS indicates data is available to consuming applications within as little as 70 milliseconds of the data being written to Kinesis).

Companies such as Netflix use Kinesis Data Streams to ingest terabytes of log data every day, enriching their networking flow logs by adding in additional metadata, and then writing the data to an open-source application for performing near real-time analytics on the health of their network.

You can write to Kinesis Data Streams using Kinesis Agent, or you can develop your own custom applications using the AWS SDK or the **Amazon KPL**, a library that simplifies writing data records with high throughput to a Kinesis data stream.

Kinesis Agent is the simplest way to send data to Kinesis Data Streams if your data can be supported by the agent (such as when writing out log files), while the AWS SDK provides the lowest latency, and the Amazon KPL provides the best performance and simplifies tasks such as monitoring and integration with the **Kinesis Client Library** (**KCL**).

There are also multiple options available for creating applications to read from your Kinesis data stream, including the following:

- Using other Kinesis services (such as Kinesis Firehose or Kinesis Data Analytics).
- Running custom code using the AWS Lambda service (a serverless environment for running code without provisioning or managing servers).
- Setting up a cluster of Amazon EC2 servers to process your streams. With this approach, you can use the KCL to handle many of the complex tasks associated with using multiple servers to process a stream, such as load balancing, responding to instance failures, checkpointing records that have been processed, and reacting to resharding (increasing or decreasing the number of shards used to process streaming data).

Kinesis Data Streams supports two capacity modes. With **Provisioned** mode, you need to specify the number of shards for the data stream upfront, and can then resize the number of shards based on changing requirements. With **On-Demand** mode, you do not need to do any capacity planning or sizing of the Kinesis cluster, as the cluster automatically scales to meet throughput requirements.

When to use: Amazon Kinesis Data Streams is ideal for use cases where you want to process incoming data as it is received, or you want to create a high-availability cluster of servers to process incoming data with a custom application.

When not to use: If you have a simple use case that requires you to write data to specific services in near real time, you should consider Kinesis Data Firehose if it supports your target destination. If you are looking to migrate an existing Apache Kafka cluster to AWS, then you may want to consider migrating to Amazon MSK. If Apache Kafka supports third-party integration that would be useful to you, you may want to consider Amazon MSK.

AWS web page: `https://aws.amazon.com/kinesis/data-streams/`

Amazon Kinesis Data Analytics

Amazon Kinesis Data Analytics simplifies the process of processing streaming data using an Apache Flink application.

An example of a use case for Kinesis Data Analytics is to analyze incoming clickstream data from an e-commerce website to get near-real-time insight into the sales of a product. In this use case, an organization may want to know how the promotion of a specific product is impacting sales to see whether the promotion is effective, and Kinesis Data Analytics can enable this using a Flink application to process records being sent from their web server clickstream logs. This enables the business to quickly get answers to questions such as *"how many sales of product x have there been in each 5-minute period since our promotion went live?"*

When to use: If you want to use Apache Flink to analyze data or extract key metrics over a rolling time period, Kinesis Data Analytics significantly simplifies this task. If you have an existing Apache Flink application that you want to migrate to the cloud, consider running the application using Kinesis Data Analytics.

AWS web page: `https://aws.amazon.com/kinesis/data-analytics/`

Amazon Kinesis Video Streams

Amazon Kinesis Video Streams can be used to process time-bound streams of unstructured data such as video, audio, and RADAR data.

Kinesis Video Streams takes care of provisioning and scaling the compute infrastructure that is required to ingest streaming video (or other types of media files) from potentially millions of sources. Kinesis Video Streams enables playback of video for live and on-demand viewing and can be integrated with other Amazon API services to enable applications such as computer vision and video analytics.

Appliances such as video doorbell systems, home security cameras, and baby monitors can stream video through Kinesis Video Analytics, simplifying the task of creating full-featured applications to support these appliances.

When to use: When creating applications that use a supported source, Kinesis Video Streams significantly simplifies the process of ingesting streaming media data and enabling live or on-demand playback.

AWS web page: https://aws.amazon.com/kinesis/video-streams

A note about AWS service reliability

AWS services are known to be extremely reliable, and generally significantly exceed the uptime and reliability of what most organizations can achieve in their own data centers. However, as Werner Vogels (Amazon's CTO) has been known to say, *"Everything fails all the time."*

In November 2020, the Amazon Kinesis service running out of data centers in the Northern Virginia Region (us-east-1) experienced a period of a number of hours where there were *increased error rates* for users of the service. During this time, many companies reported having their services affected, including Roomba vacuum cleaners, Ring doorbells, The Washington Post newspaper, Roku, and others.

This is a clear reminder that while AWS services generally offer extremely high levels of availability, if you require absolutely minimal downtime, you need to design the ability to fail-over to a different AWS Region in your architecture.

Amazon MSK for streaming data ingestion

Apache Kafka is a popular open-source distributed event streaming platform that enables an organization to create high-performance streaming data pipelines and applications, and **Amazon MSK** is a managed version of Apache Kafka available from AWS.

While Apache Kafka is a popular choice for organizations, it can be a challenge to install, scale, update, and manage in an on-premises environment, often requiring specialized skills. To simplify these tasks, AWS offers Amazon MSK, which enables an organization to deploy an Apache Kafka cluster with a few clicks in the console and reduces the management overhead by automatically monitoring cluster health and replacing failed components, handling OS and application upgrades, deploying in multiple availability zones, and providing integration with other AWS services.

With Amazon MSK, you need to specify compute and storage capacity for the cluster; however, Amazon MSK is also offered as a serverless cluster type. With this option, you do not need to specify and manage cluster capacity, as **Amazon MSK Serverless** automatically deploys and scales the required compute and storage. To decide between provisioned and serverless, you need to compare the pricing for your use case, but generally, MSK Serverless is best suited for unpredictable workloads where there are spikes and troughs in streaming throughput.

When to use: Amazon MSK is an ideal choice if your use case is a replacement for an existing Apache Kafka cluster, or if you want to take advantage of the many third-party integrations from the open-source Apache Kafka ecosystem. As Amazon MSK is a managed version of the open-source Apache Kafka solution, if having an open-source solution that enables easy migration to non-AWS environments is important to you, then Amazon MSK may be a good choice.

When not to use: Amazon Kinesis may be a preferred streaming solution if you are creating a new solution from scratch and you are looking for the best integration with other AWS services.

AWS web page: https://aws.amazon.com/msk/

Amazon AppFlow for ingesting data from SaaS services

Amazon AppFlow can be used to ingest data from popular SaaS services (such as Salesforce, Google Analytics, Microsoft SharePoint Online, and many more), and to transform and write the data out to common analytic targets (such as Amazon S3, Amazon EventBridge, and Amazon Redshift, as well as being able to write to some SaaS services).

For example, AppFlow can be used to ingest lead data from **Marketo**, a developer of marketing automation solutions, where your organization may capture details about a new lead. Using AppFlow, you can create a flow that will automatically create a new **Salesforce** contact record whenever a new Marketo lead is created.

From a data engineering perspective, you can create flows that will automatically write out new opportunity records created in Salesforce into your S3 data lake or Redshift data warehouse, enabling you to join those opportunity records with other datasets to perform advanced analytics.

AppFlow can be configured to run on a schedule or in response to specific events (for certain sources), and can filter, mask, and validate data, and perform calculations from data fields in the source. AWS also regularly adds additional integrations to the AppFlow service, and, in November 2022, it announced 22 new data connectors, bringing the total number of connectors to over 50.

In addition to connectors for a number of AWS services, there are connectors for third-party services such as Datadog, Facebook, Google Analytics, GitHub, LinkedIn, Salesforce, SAP OData, ServiceNow, Slack, Snowflake, Stripe, QuickBooks, Zoom, and many others.

For details on all AppFlow connectors, review the AppFlow documentation at `https://docs.aws.amazon.com/appflow/latest/userguide/app-specific.html`.

When to use: Amazon AppFlow is an ideal choice for ingesting data into AWS if one of your data sources is a supported source.

When not to use: Amazon AppFlow has limited functionality for transforming data that is ingested. If you require more complex transformations as part of ingestion, or if the data sources you require are not supported, consider similar third-party toolsets (such as Hevo Data), or consider building a custom ingest pipeline using AWS Glue.

AWS web page: `https://aws.amazon.com/appflow/`

AWS Transfer Family for ingestion using FTP/SFTP protocols

AWS Transfer Family provides a fully managed service that enables file transfers directly into and out of Amazon S3 using common file transfer protocols, including **FTP**, **SFTP**, FTPS, and AS2.

Many organizations today still make use of these protocols to exchange data with other organizations. For example, a real-estate company may receive the latest **Multi-Listing Service (MLS)** files from an MLS provider via SFTP. In this case, the real-estate company will have configured a server running SFTP and created an SFTP user account that the MLS provider can use to connect to the server and transfer the files.

With AWS Transfer for SFTP, the real-estate company could easily migrate to the managed AWS service, replicating the account setup that exists for their MLS provider on its on-premises server with an account in its AWS Transfer service. With little to no change on the side of the provider, when future transfers are made via the managed AWS service, these would be written directly into Amazon S3, making the data immediately accessible to data transformation pipelines created for the Amazon S3-based data lake.

When to use: If an organization currently receives data via FTP, SFTP, FTPS, or AS2, it should consider migrating to the managed version of this service offered by Amazon Transfer.

When not to use: There are other AWS Marketplace options for running a managed file transfer service, so you should compare options based on both features and pricing in order to determine the best match for your requirements.

Some of these other services, such as SFTP Gateway (see `https://help.thorntech.com/`), offer options across multiple clouds, so if multi-cloud is important to you, you may prefer a third-party service.

AWS web page: `https://aws.amazon.com/aws-transfer-family/`

AWS DataSync for ingesting from on premises and multicloud storage services

There is often a requirement to ingest data from existing on-premises storage systems, and **AWS DataSync** simplifies this process while offering high performance and stability for data transfers.

Network File System (NFS) and **Server Message Block (SMB)** are two common protocols that are used to allow computer systems to access files stored on a different system. With DataSync, you can easily ingest and replicate data from file servers that use either of these protocols. DataSync also supports ingesting data from on-premises object-based storage systems that are compatible with core **AWS S3 API** calls, as well as from **Hadoop Distributed File System (HDFS)**, commonly used for on-premises data lakes, and from other cloud object stores (such as Azure Blob Storage and Google Cloud Storage).

DataSync can write to multiple targets within AWS, including Amazon S3 and Amazon EFS, making it an ideal way to sync data from on-premises storage, on-premisis data lakes, as well as other cloud services, into your AWS S3-based data lake. For example, if you have a solution running in your data center that writes out end-of-day transactions to a file share, DataSync can ensure that the data is synced to your S3 data lake. Another common use case is to transfer large amounts of historical data from an on-premises system or HDFS data lake into your S3 data lake.

When to use: AWS DataSync is a good choice when you're looking to ingest current or historical data from compatible on premises storage systems, or other cloud storage services, to AWS over a network connection.

When not to use: For very large historical datasets where sending the data over a network connection is not practical, you should consider using the Amazon Snow family of devices.

AWS web page: `https://aws.amazon.com/datasync/`

The AWS Snow family of devices for large data transfers

For use cases where there are very large datasets that need to be ingested into AWS, and either a good network connection is lacking or just the sheer size of the dataset makes it impractical to transfer them via a network connection, the **AWS Snow family of devices** can be used.

The AWS Snow family of devices are ruggedized devices that can be shipped to a location and attached to a network connection in the local data center. Data can be transferred over the local network and the device is then shipped back to AWS, where the data will be transferred to Amazon S3. All the devices offer encryption of data at rest, as well as high-security features such as tamper-resistant enclosures and **Trusted Platform Modules** (**TPMs**) that can detect unauthorized modifications to the hardware, software, or firmware of the devices.

The Snow devices also offer compute ability, enabling edge computing use cases (edge computing is where you run applications closer to a user, so outside of the core AWS cloud environment). An example edge computing use case is for a factory in a remote area without good internet connectivity, where they can use a Snow device in the factory to collect and process factory IoT data (such as using machine learning models running on the Snow device to predict maintenance issues based on the IoT data).

There are multiple devices available for different use cases, as summarized here:

1. **AWS Snowcone**: Lightweight (4.5 lb/2.1 kg) device with 8-14 TB of usable storage, 2 vCPUs, and 4 GB of RAM for the compute
2. **AWS Snowball Edge**: Medium-weight (49.7 lb/22.5 kg) device with up to 104 vCPUs, 416 GB of RAM, and 210 TB of usable SSD storage

The Snowball Edge devices are available either as **compute-optimized** or **storage-optimized**. The compute-optimized device can have up to 28 TB of SSD storage and includes the option of having an NVIDIA Tesla V100 GPU for compute-intensive applications (such as machine learning or video analysis). The storage-optimized device can have up to 210 TB SSD of storage but does not provide an option for GPU compute.

When to use: The AWS Snow family of devices is ideal for migrating very large volumes of data from on-premises or remote locations to Amazon S3 and can also be used for edge computing use cases and for data migration from locations that have poor internet connectivity.

When not to use: You need to evaluate the available bandwidth from the source environment where you need to migrate data from in order to determine whether a solution such as DataSync may be able to transfer your data quicker than using a Snow device. See the *Best practices for moving your data to AWS* video from *re:Invent 2021*, available at https://youtu.be/9r9PmMpJGKg?t=219, for a comparison of DataSync and Snow devices for large transfers.

AWS web page: https://aws.amazon.com/snow/

AWS Glue for data ingestion

AWS Glue provides a serverless Apache Spark environment where you can create code-based solutions for both data ingestion and transformation.

AWS Glue includes a number of built-in connectors for connecting to certain AWS and third-party services, including Amazon RDS, Amazon Redshift, Amazon DocumentDB, MongoDB, MongoDB Atlas, and various JDBC-accessible sources.

In addition, AWS Glue makes it possible to subscribe to a number of connectors from the AWS Marketplace. These include connectors created by AWS and available at no charge, such as the **Google BigQuery connector** (`https://aws.amazon.com/marketplace/pp/prodview-sqnd4gn5f ykx6?ref_=beagle&applicationId=GlueStudio`). It also includes connectors from third parties that may have associated licensing costs, such as the **CData Connector for Salesforce** (`https://aws.amazon.com/marketplace/pp/prodview-sonh33r7xavhw?sr=0-11&ref_=beagle&applicat ionId=GlueStudio`).

You can use these connectors when creating AWS Glue jobs in order to connect to a diverse set of sources and to import data as part of your AWS Glue job.

When to use: AWS Glue enables you to import data into AWS as part of a Glue job, using pre-built connectors. This is useful when there is no AWS-managed service for importing data from the required source, or when you want to import data as part of a Glue-based ETL job. The AWS Marketplace includes a number of these pre-built connectors, some at no charge, and others that have a subscription-based cost.

When not to use: AWS Glue uses a Spark-based ETL job to ingest data from a variety of sources, but if you are looking to just ingest data without needing to do Spark-based transformations, then consider the AWS ingestion-focused managed services for your use case (such as Amazon AppFlow or AWS DMS).

Learn more about Glue connectors: `https://docs.aws.amazon.com/glue/latest/ug/ connectors-chapter.html`

Having examined a number of options for ingesting data into your AWS environment, we will now move on to an overview of services for transforming your data.

An overview of AWS services for transforming data

Once your data is ingested into an appropriate AWS service, such as Amazon S3, the next stage of the pipeline needs to **transform** the data to optimize it for analytics and to make it available to your data consumers.

Some of the tools we discussed in the previous section for ingesting data into AWS can perform light transformations as part of the ingestion process. For example, Amazon DMS can write out data in Parquet format (a format optimized for analytics), as can Kinesis Firehose. However, heavier transformations are often required to fully optimize your data for a differing set of analytic tasks and diverse data consumers, and in this section, we will examine some of the core AWS services that can be used for this.

AWS Lambda for light transformations

AWS Lambda provides a serverless environment for executing code and is one of AWS's most popular services. You can trigger your Lambda function to execute your code in multiple ways, including through integration with other AWS services, and you only pay for the duration that your code executes, billed in 1-millisecond increments, and based on the amount of memory that you allocate to your function. Lambda can scale from a few executions per day to thousands of executions per second.

In the data engineering world, a common use case for Lambda is for performing validation or light processing and transformation of incoming data. For example, if you have incoming CSV files being sent by one of your partners throughout the day, you can trigger a Lambda function to run every time a new file is received, have your code validate that the file is a valid CSV file, perform some computation on one of the columns and update a database with the result, and then move the file into a different bucket where a batch process will later process all files received for the day.

Another use case is to process an incoming stream of data. For example, you can use Lambda along with Amazon Kinesis Data Streams or Kinesis Data Firehose to process real-time streaming data from a mobile application.

With the ability to run for up to 15 minutes, and with a maximum memory configuration of 10 GB, it is possible to do more advanced processing as well. For example, you may receive a ZIP file containing hundreds of small XML files, and you can process that with a Lambda function that unzips the file, validates each XML file to ensure that it is valid XML, performs calculations on fields in the file to update various other systems, concatenates the contents of all the files, and then writes that out in Parquet format in a different zone of your data lake.

Lambda is also massively parallelized, meaning that it can easily scale for highly concurrent workloads. In the preceding example of processing ZIP files as they arrive in an S3 bucket, if hundreds of ZIP files were all delivered within a period of just a few seconds, a separate Lambda instance would be spun up for each file, and AWS would automatically handle the scaling of the Lambda functions to enable this. By default, you can have 1,000 concurrent Lambda executions within an AWS Region for your account, but you can work with AWS support to increase this limit to the tens of thousands.

AWS Lambda supports many different languages, including **Python**, which has become one of the most popular languages for data engineering-related tasks. In the hands-on activity part of this chapter, we will create a Lambda function that is automatically triggered when a new file is uploaded to a specific S3 location.

AWS Glue for serverless data processing

AWS Glue has multiple components that could have been split into multiple separate services, but these components can all work together, so AWS has grouped them together into the AWS Glue family. In this section, we will look at the core Glue components related to data processing.

Serverless ETL processing

There are a number of common code-based engines that are popular for performing data-engineering-related tasks. These include:

1. **Apache Spark** is an open-source engine for the distributed processing of large datasets across a cluster of compute nodes, which makes it ideal for taking a large dataset, splitting the processing work between the nodes in the cluster, and then returning a result. As Spark does all processing in memory, it is highly efficient and performant and has become the tool of choice for many organizations looking for a solution for processing large datasets.

2. **Python**, which traditionally runs on a single node, has become an extremely popular language for performing data-science-/data-engineering-related tasks on small to medium-sized datasets.

3. **Ray.io** is an open-source framework that enables running Python code over multiple compute nodes, enabling Python code to be used to process much larger datasets.

The following diagram depicts two of the Glue engines – a single-node Glue Python shell on the left, and a multi-node Glue Apache Spark cluster on the right:

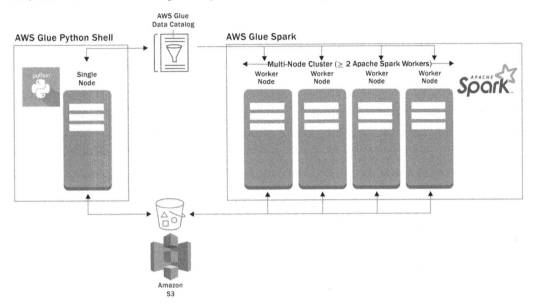

Figure 3.1: Glue Python shell and Glue Spark engines

Both engines can work with data that resides in Amazon S3 and with the **AWS Glue Data Catalog**. Both engines are serverless from the perspective of a user, meaning a user does not need to deploy or manage servers; a user just needs to specify the number of **Data Processing Units (DPUs)** that they want to power their job. Glue ETL jobs are charged based on the number of DPUs configured, as well as the amount of time for which the underlying code executes in the environment.

While AWS Glue does provide additional Spark libraries and functionality to simplify some common ETL tasks, their use is optional, and existing open-source Spark code can be easily run in AWS Glue. AWS Glue also supports **Spark Streaming**, an extension of the core Spark API designed to process live data streams.

You can write new Spark code directly (or use existing Spark code) with the AWS Glue ETL service or you can generate Spark code through a GUI-based tool with the **Glue Studio Visual Editor**. In *Chapter 7, Transforming Data to Optimize for Analytics*, we will get hands-on with Glue Studio to join two datasets.

AWS Glue DataBrew

AWS Glue DataBrew is another serverless visual data preparation tool that lets you easily apply transformations to your data, without needing to write or manage any code. DataBrew includes over 250 built-in data transformations, which can be easily assembled via the DataBrew UI to create a *DataBrew recipe*, enabling you to apply multiple transformations to a dataset.

DataBrew includes functionality for both profiling data (gathering statistics on the different columns in the dataset) and for monitoring data quality. It also includes many different types of transformations, such as formatting data, obfuscating PII data, splitting or joining columns, converting timezones, detecting and removing outliers, and many more. For example, you can run a DataBrew profile job that can detect PII data, and then create a DataBrew job that can mask, encrypt, or hash sensitive data.

DataBrew is commonly used by data analysts and data scientists to clean and prepare data for additional processing. In *Chapter 8*, *Identifying and Enabling Data Consumers*, we will do a hands-on exercise on using Glue DataBrew to transform some data.

AWS Glue Data Catalog

To complement the ETL processing functionality described previously, AWS Glue also includes a *data catalog* that can be used to provide a logical view of data stored physically in the storage layer. Objects (such as databases and tables) in the catalog can then be directly referenced from your ETL code.

Glue Data Catalog is a **Hive metastore**-compatible catalog, meaning that it can be used with any system that is able to work with a Hive metastore. As discussed in *Chapter 2*, under the heading *Catalog and search layer*, you get two types of catalogs – business and technical. The Hive metastore, and therefore Glue Data Catalog, is a *technical* catalog.

As an example, if you used **AWS DMS** to replicate your **Human Resources** (**HR**) database in S3, you would end up with a prefix (directory) in S3 for each table from the source database. In this directory, we would generally find multiple files containing the data from the source table – for example, 20 CSV files containing the rows from the source employee table.

Glue Data Catalog can provide a logical view of this dataset and capture additional metadata about the dataset. For example, the data catalog consists of a number of databases at the top level (such as the **HR** database), and each database contains one or more tables (such as the employee table).

In addition, each table in the catalog contains metadata, such as the column headings and data types for each column (such as employee_id, lastname, firstname, address, and dept), a reference to the S3 location for the data that makes up that table, and details on the file format (such as CSV).

In the following screenshot, we see a bucket that contains objects under the prefix hr/employees and a number of CSV files that contain data imported from the employee database:

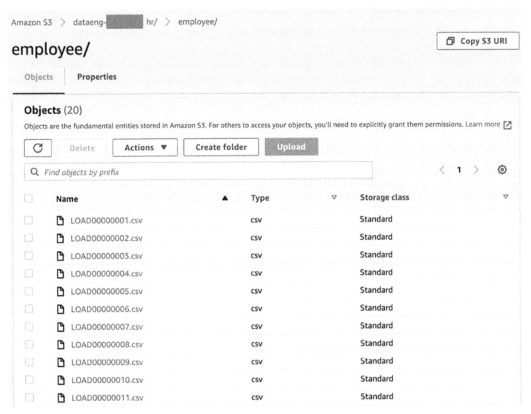

Figure 3.2: Amazon S3 bucket with CSV files making up the employee table

The screenshot of the following AWS Glue Data Catalog shows us the logical view of this data. We can see that this is the employee table and it references the S3 location shown in the preceding screenshot. In this logical view, we can see that the employee table is in the HR database, and we can see the columns and data types that are contained in the CSV files.

	Name	employee
	Description	
	Database	hr
	Classification	csv
	Location	s3://dataeng-temp/hr/employee/
	Connection	
	Deprecated	No
	Last updated	Wed Dec 09 21:46:50 GMT-500 2020
	Input format	org.apache.hadoop.mapred.TextInputFormat
	Output format	org.apache.hadoop.hive.ql.io.HiveIgnoreKeyTextOutputFormat
	Serde serialization lib	org.apache.hadoop.hive.serde2.lazy.LazySimpleSerDe
	Serde parameters	field.delim ,

Table properties											
skip.header.line.count	**1**	sizeKey	**6300**	objectCount	**20**	UPDATED_BY_CRAWLER	**hr-employee-crawler**				
CrawlerSchemaSerializerVersion	**1.0**	recordCount	**40**	averageRecordSize	**156**	CrawlerSchemaDeserializerVersion	**1.0**				
compressionType	**none**	columnsOrdered	**true**	areColumnsQuoted	**false**	delimiter	**,**	typeOfData	**file**		

Schema

Showing: 1 -

	Column name	Data type	Partition key	Comment
1	emp_id	bigint		
2	last_name	string		
3	first_name	string		
4	hire_date	bigint		
5	street_address	string		

Figure 3.3: AWS Glue Data Catalog showing a logical view of the employee table

Within the AWS ecosystem, a number of services can use AWS Glue Data Catalog. For example, Amazon Athena uses AWS Glue Data Catalog to enable users to run SQL queries directly on data in Amazon S3, and Amazon EMR and the AWS Glue ETL engine use it to enable users to reference catalog objects (such as databases and tables) directly in their ETL code.

AWS Glue crawlers

AWS Glue crawlers are processes that can examine a data source (such as a path in an S3 bucket) and automatically infer the schema and other information about that data source so that AWS Glue Data Catalog can be automatically populated with relevant information.

For example, we could point an AWS Glue Crawler at the S3 location where DMS replicated the *employee* table of our *HR* database. When the Glue Crawler runs, it examines a portion of each of the files in that location, identifies the file type (CSV or Parquet), uses a classifier to infer the schema of the file (column headings and types), and then adds that information into a database in Glue Data Catalog.

Note that you can also add databases and tables to Glue Data Catalog using the Glue API or via SQL statements in Athena, so using Glue crawlers to automatically populate the catalog is optional. In *Chapter 6, Ingesting Batch and Streaming Data*, we will do a hands-on exercise to configure the Glue Crawler to add newly ingested data to Glue Data Catalog.

Amazon EMR for Hadoop ecosystem processing

Amazon EMR provides a managed platform for running popular open-source big data processing tools, such as **Apache Spark, Apache Hive, Apache Hudi, Apache HBase, Presto, Pig**, and others. **Amazon EMR** takes care of the complexities of deploying these tools and managing the underlying clustered compute resources.

Like many other AWS services, Amazon EMR can run in a provisioned mode (where you specify specific compute resources to use), or it can be run in a serverless mode.

With EMR provisioned mode, you can create an EMR cluster on EC2 nodes, specifying the specific instance types you want to use, and many other detailed configuration parameters (big data applications you want to deploy, automatic scaling options, networking, and more). This option provides you the most control and flexibility for cluster and application configuration, enabling you to fine-tune the performance of your applications. However, this does require you to build up expertise to understand the configuration options and their impact on application performance, such as the optimal EC2 instance type to use for different applications.

Alternatively, you can select to run Spark workloads using **Amazon EMR** on an **Elastic Kubernetes Service (EKS)** cluster. If your organization already makes use of EKS to run applications, you can have EMR automatically deploy containers to run Spark workloads using the EKS compute. EMR does not provision the EKS cluster (it only provisions the Spark-based container to run on the cluster), so you are required to have an existing cluster and the skills to maintain and configure EKS.

EMR Serverless provides you with an option to run certain workloads without needing to decide on and select EC2 instance types. With EMR Serverless, you can create an application that runs either Spark or Hive as the processing engine, and then select a maximum for CPU, memory, and storage for that application. You can optionally select to pre-initialize Spark drivers and workers for your application, which then creates a warm pool of workers for an application. While there is a cost to have the warm pool running, it does enable submitted jobs to start processing immediately, and you can optionally specify a timeout, after which the application will stop if idle. If you do not pre-initialize capacity, it may take a few minutes for a submitted job to run, but it is the most cost-effective way to run your jobs as you do not pay for application idle time. Once an application is running, you can submit multiple Spark jobs to the application.

As discussed above, Amazon EMR can be used to run Apache Spark, and you might be wondering why AWS has multiple services (Glue and EMR) that effectively offer the same big data processing engine. While either service can be used to perform big data processing using the Apache Spark engine, there are differences from a management, integration, and cost perspective.

AWS Glue requires the least amount of configuration, as you just need to specify a worker type and a maximum number of DPUs for each job and can then submit a Spark job to run. Using EMR Serverless requires a bit more configuration as you need to configure an application, and can then submit jobs to that application. However, you have more control over both the number of CPUs and the memory for each worker, and the cost for equivalent processing power is slightly lower than Glue.

Amazon EMR provisioned clusters (on EC2 or EKS) require more expertise to manage but provide the most control for fine-tuning your Spark jobs. They also support a wide range of big data processing applications beyond Spark (such as Hive, Presto, and Trino) and are the lowest-cost method for running Spark jobs using a managed AWS service.

One of the other differences is that AWS Glue has a number of built-in connectors, as well as a marketplace with additional connectors, that can make it easier to integrate your Spark code with external systems.

The following diagram shows an EMR cluster provisioned on EC2, including some of the open-source projects that can be run on the cluster:

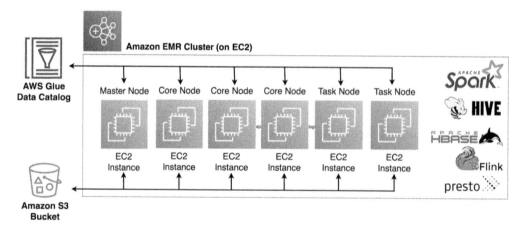

Figure 3.4: High-level overview of an EMR cluster running on EC2

Each EMR provisioned cluster requires a master node, at least one **core node** (a worker node that includes local storage), and then optionally a number of **task nodes** (worker nodes that do not have any local storage).

Having looked at how we can transform data in our data lake, let's now look at the AWS services that enable us to orchestrate the different components of our data pipeline.

An overview of AWS services for orchestrating big data pipelines

As discussed in *Chapter 2, Data Management Architectures for Analytics*, a data pipeline can be built to bring in data from source systems, and then transform that data, often moving the data through multiple stages, further transforming or enriching the data as it moves through each stage.

An organization will often have tens or hundreds of pipelines that work independently or in conjunction with each other on different datasets and perform different types of transformations. Each pipeline may use multiple services to achieve the goals of the pipeline, and orchestrating all the varying services and pipelines can be complex. In this section, we will look at a number of AWS services that help with this **orchestration** task.

AWS Glue workflows for orchestrating Glue components

In the *An overview of AWS services for transforming data* section, we covered AWS Glue, a service that includes a number of components. As a reminder, they are as follows:

- A serverless Apache Spark or Python shell environment for performing ETL transformations

- Glue Data Catalog, which provides a centralized logical representation (database and tables) of the physical data stored in Amazon S3

- Glue crawlers, which can be configured to examine files in a specific location, automatically infer the schema of the file, and add the file to the AWS Glue Data Catalog

AWS Glue workflows are a functionality within the AWS Glue service that has been designed to help orchestrate the various AWS Glue components. A workflow consists of an ordered sequence of steps that can run Glue crawlers and Glue ETL jobs (Spark or Python shell).

The following diagram shows a visual representation of a simple Glue workflow that can be built in the AWS Glue console:

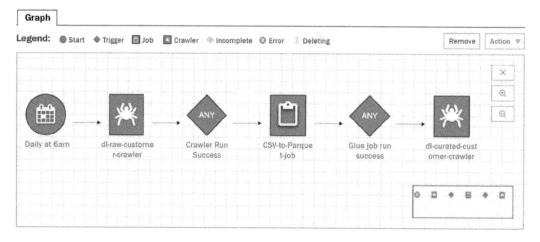

Figure 3.5: AWS Glue workflow

This workflow orchestrates the following tasks:

1. It runs a *Glue Crawler* to add newly ingested data from the raw zone of the data lake into Glue Data Catalog.

2. Once the Glue Crawler completes, it triggers a *Glue ETL job* to convert the raw CSV data into Parquet format and writes it to the curated zone of the data lake.

3. When the Glue job is complete, it triggers a Glue Crawler to add the newly transformed data to the curated zone in Glue Data Catalog.

Each step of the workflow can retrieve and update the state information about the workflow. This enables one step of a workflow to provide state information that can be used by a subsequent step in the workflow. For example, a workflow may run multiple ETL jobs, and each ETL job can update state information, such as the location of files that it outputted, which will be available to be used by subsequent workflow steps.

The preceding diagram is an example of a relatively simple workflow, but AWS Glue workflows are capable of orchestrating much more complex workflows. However, it is important to note that Glue workflows can only be used to orchestrate Glue components, which are ETL jobs and Glue crawlers.

If you only use AWS Glue components in your pipeline, then AWS Glue workflows are well suited to orchestrate your data transformation pipelines. But if you have a use case that needs to incorporate other AWS services in your pipeline (such as AWS Lambda), then keep reading to learn about other available options.

AWS Step Functions for complex workflows

Another option for orchestrating your data transformation pipelines is **AWS Step Functions**, a service that enables you to create complex workflows that can be integrated with over 220 AWS services, without needing to maintain code.

Step Functions is serverless, meaning that you do not need to deploy or manage any infrastructure, and you pay for the service based on your usage, not on fixed infrastructure costs.

With Step Functions, you use JSON to define a state machine using a structured language known as the **Amazon States Language** (**ASL**). Alternatively, you can use **Step Functions Workflow Studio** to create a workflow using a visual interface that supports dragging and dropping, and this creates the JSON ASL for you. The resulting workflow can run multiple tasks, run different branches based on a choice, enter a wait state where you specify a delay before the next step is run, and loop back to previous steps, as well as various other things that can be done to control the workflow.

When you start a state machine, you include JSON data as input text that will be passed to the first state in the workflow. The first state in the workflow uses the input data, performs the function it is configured to do (such as running a Lambda function using the input passed into the state machine), modifies the JSON data, and then passes the modified JSON data to the next state in the workflow.

You can trigger a step function using **Amazon EventBridge** (such as on a schedule or in response to something else triggering an EventBridge event), as well as various other AWS services (such as Amazon API Gateway, AWS CodePipeline, or AWS IoT Rules Engine). You can also trigger a step function on-demand, by calling the Step Functions API.

The following is an example of a Step Functions state machine:

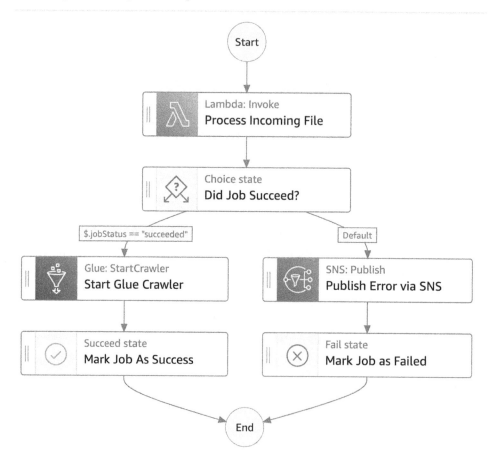

Figure 3.6: AWS Step Functions state machine

This state machine performs the following steps:

1. An EventBridge rule is triggered whenever a file is uploaded to a particular Amazon S3 bucket, and the EventBridge rule starts our state machine, passing in a JSON object that includes the location of the newly uploaded file.

2. The first step, **Process Incoming File**, runs a Lambda function that takes the location of the uploaded file as input and processes the incoming file (for example, converting from CSV into Parquet format). The output of the Lambda function indicates whether the file processing succeeded or failed. This information is included in the JSON passed to the next step.

3. The **Did Job Succeed?** step is of type `Choice`. It examines the JSON data passed to the step, and if the `jobStatus` field is set to `succeeded`, it branches to **Start Glue Crawler**. Otherwise, it branches to **Publish Error via SNS**.

4. In the **Start Glue Crawler** step, an AWS Glue Crawler is triggered. When this completes, a Step Functions flow runs that marks this step function execution as being successful.

5. In the **Publish Error via SNS** step, a message is published to an SNS topic, which sends an email or text message to an operator to inform them that the job failed. When this completes, a Step Functions flow runs that marks this step function execution as having failed.

In *Chapter 10, Orchestrating the Data Pipeline*, we have a hands-on exercise for orchestrating a pipeline using AWS Step Functions.

Amazon Managed Workflows for Apache Airflow (MWAA)

Apache Airflow is a popular open-source solution for orchestrating complex data engineering workflows. It was created by **Airbnb** in 2014 to help its internal teams manage its increasingly complex workflows and became a top-level Apache project in 2019.

Airflow enables users to create processing pipelines programmatically (using the Python programming language) and provides a user interface to monitor the execution of the workflows. Complex workflows can be created and Airflow includes support for a wide variety of integrations, including integrations with services from AWS, Microsoft Azure, Google Cloud Platform, and others.

However, installing and configuring Apache Airflow in a way that can support the resilience and scaling required for large production environments is complex, and maintaining and updating the environment can be challenging. As a result, AWS created **Managed Workflows for Apache Airflow (MWAA)**, which enables users to easily deploy a managed version of Apache Airflow that can automatically scale out additional workers as demand on the environment increases and scale in the number of workers as demand decreases.

An MWAA environment consists of the following components:

1. **Scheduler**: The scheduler runs a multithreaded Python process that controls what tasks need to be run, and where and when to run those tasks.

2. **Worker/executor**: The worker(s) execute(s) tasks. Each MWAA environment contains at least one worker, but when configuring the environment, you can specify the maximum number of additional workers that should be made available. MWAA automatically scales out the number of workers up to that maximum, but will also automatically reduce the number of workers as tasks are completed and if no new tasks need to run. The workers are linked to your VPC (the private network in your AWS account).

3. **Meta-database:** This runs in the MWAA service account and is used to track the status of tasks.

4. **Web server:** The web server also runs in the MWAA service account and provides a web-based interface that users can use to monitor and execute tasks.

Note that even though the meta-database and web server run in the MWAA service account, there are separate instances of these for every MWAA environment, and there are no components of the architecture that are shared between different MWAA environments.

When migrating from an on-premises environment where you already run Apache Airflow, or if your team already has Apache Airflow skills, then the MWAA service should be considered for managing your data processing pipelines and workflows in AWS. However, it is important to note that while this is a managed service (meaning that AWS deploys the environment for you and upgrades the Apache Airflow software), it is not a serverless environment.

With MWAA, you select a core environment size (small, medium, or large), and are charged based on the environment size, plus a charge for the amount of storage used by the meta-database and for any additional workers you make use of. Whether you run one 5-minute job per day or run multiple simultaneous jobs 24 hours a day 7 days a week, the charge for your core environment will remain the same. With serverless environments such as Amazon Step Functions, billing is based on a consumption model, so there is no underlying fixed charge.

Having looked at the services that can be used to orchestrate our data pipelines, let's now move on to an overview of the AWS services that can be used to query and analyze our data.

An overview of AWS services for consuming data

Once the data has been transformed and optimized for analytics, the various data consumers in an organization need easy access to the data via a number of different types of interfaces. Data scientists may want to use standard SQL queries to query the data, while data analysts may want to both query the data in place using SQL and also load subsets of the data into a high-performance data warehouse for low-latency, high-concurrency queries, and scheduled reporting. Business users may prefer to access data via a visualization tool that enables them to view data represented as graphs, charts, and other types of visuals.

In this section, we will introduce a number of AWS services that enable different types of data consumers to work with our optimized datasets. We won't cover all the services that can be used to consume data in this section, but instead will highlight the primary services relevant to a data engineering role.

Amazon Athena for SQL queries in the data lake

Amazon Athena is a serverless solution for using standard SQL queries to query data that exists in a data lake or in other data sources. As soon as a dataset has been written to Amazon S3 and cataloged in AWS Glue Data Catalog, users can run complex SQL queries against the data without needing to set up or manage any infrastructure.

What is SQL?

SQL is a standard language used to query relational datasets. A person proficient in SQL can draw information out of very large relational datasets easily and quickly, combining different tables, filtering results, and performing aggregations.

Data scientists and data analysts frequently use SQL to explore and better understand datasets that may be useful to them. Enabling these data consumers to query the data in an Amazon S3 data lake, without needing to first load the data into a traditional database system, increases productivity and flexibility for these data consumers.

Many tools are designed to interface with data via SQL and these tools often connect to the SQL data source using either a **JDBC** or **ODBC** database connection. Amazon Athena enables a data consumer to query datasets in the data lake (or other connected data sources) through the AWS Management Console interface or through a JDBC or ODBC driver.

Graphical SQL query tools, such as **SQL Workbench**, can connect to Amazon Athena via the JDBC driver, and you can programmatically connect to Amazon Athena and run SQL queries in your code through the ODBC driver.

Athena Federated Query, a feature of Athena, enables you to build connectors so that Athena can query other data sources, beyond just the data in an S3 data lake. Amazon provides a number of pre-built open-source connectors for Athena, enabling you to connect Athena to sources such as **Amazon DynamoDB** (a NoSQL database), as well as other Amazon-managed relational database engines, and even Amazon CloudWatch Logs, a centralized logging service. Using this functionality, a data consumer can run a query using Athena that gets active orders from Amazon DynamoDB, references that data against the customer database running on PostgreSQL, and then brings in historical order data for that customer from the S3 data lake – all in a single SQL statement.

At re:Invent 2022, AWS announced **Amazon Athena for Apache Spark,** a new functionality that enables running Apache Spark jobs with Athena. With this new feature, you can launch a Jupyter notebook from within the Athena console, and query data in the data lake using Apache Spark code.

Amazon Redshift and Redshift Spectrum for data warehousing and data lakehouse architectures

Data warehousing is not a new concept or technology (as we discussed in *Chapter 2, Data Management Architectures for Analytics*), but **Amazon Redshift** was the first cloud-based data warehouse to be created. Launched in 2012, it was AWS's fastest-growing service by 2015, and today there are tens of thousands of customers that use it.

A Redshift data warehouse is designed for reporting and analytic workloads, commonly referred to as **Online Analytical Processing (OLAP)** workloads. Redshift provides a clustered environment that enables all the compute nodes in a cluster to work with portions of the data involved in a SQL query, helping to provide the best performance for scenarios where you are working with data that has been stored in a highly structured manner, and you need to do complex joins across multiple large tables on a regular basis. As a result, Redshift is an ideal query engine for reporting and visualization services that need to work with large datasets.

A typical SQL query that runs against a Redshift cluster would be likely to retrieve data from hundreds of thousands, or even millions, of rows in the database, often performing complex joins between different tables, and likely doing calculations such as aggregating, or averaging, certain columns of data. The queries run against the data warehouse will often be used to answer questions such as *"What was the average sale amount for sales in our stores last month, broken down by each ZIP code of the USA?"* or *"Which products, across all of our stores, have seen a 20% increase in sales between Q4 of last year and Q1 of this year?"*

In a modern analytic environment, a common use case for a data warehouse would be to load a subset of data from the data lake into the warehouse, based on which data needs to be queried most frequently and which data needs to be used for queries requiring the best possible performance.

In this scenario, a data engineer may create a pipeline to load customer, product, sales, and inventory data into the data warehouse on a daily basis. Knowing that 80% of the reporting and queries will be on the last 12 months of sales data, the data engineer may also design a process to remove all data that's more than 12 months old from the data warehouse.

But what about the 20% of queries that need to include historical data that's more than 12 months old? That's where Redshift Spectrum comes in, a feature of Amazon Redshift that enables a user to write a single query that queries data that has been loaded into the data warehouse, as well as data that exists outside the data warehouse, in the data lake. To enable this, the data engineer can configure the Redshift cluster to connect with AWS Glue Data Catalog, where all the databases and tables for our data lake are defined. Once that has been configured, a user can reference both internal Redshift tables and tables registered in Glue Data Catalog.

The following diagram shows the Redshift and Redshift Spectrum architecture:

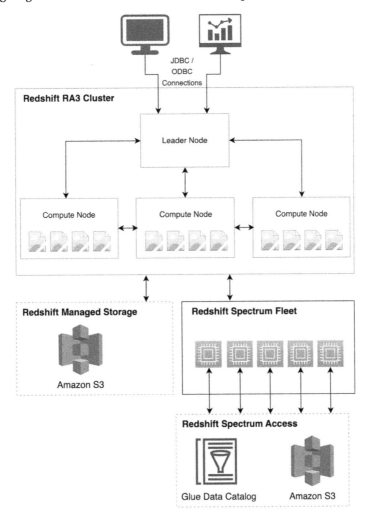

Figure 3.7: Redshift architecture

In the preceding diagram, we can see that a user connects to the Redshift leader node (via JDBC or ODBC). This node does not query data directly but is effectively the *central* brain behind all the queries that run on the cluster. In a scenario where a user is running a query that needs to query both current (last 12 months of) sales data and historical sales data in Amazon S3, the process works as follows:

1. Using a SQL client, the user makes a connection, authenticates with the Redshift leader node, and sends through a SQL statement that queries both the `current_sales` table (a table in which the data exists either in the local SSD cache of the cluster, or within **Redshift Managed Storage (RMS)**, and contains the past 12 months of sales data) and the `historical_sales` table (a table that is registered in Glue Data Catalog, and where the data files are located in the Amazon S3 data lake, which contains historical sales data going back 10 years).

2. The leader node analyzes and optimizes the query, compiles a query plan, and pushes individual query execution plans to the compute nodes in the cluster.

3. The compute nodes query data they have locally (for the `current_sales` table) and query AWS Glue Data Catalog to gather information on the external `historical_sales` table. Using the information they gather, they can optimize queries for the external data and push those queries out to the Redshift Spectrum layer.

4. Redshift Spectrum is outside of a customer's Redshift cluster and is made up of thousands of worker nodes (Amazon EC2 compute instances) in each AWS Region. These worker nodes are able to scan, filter, and aggregate data from the files in Amazon S3 and then stream the results back to the Amazon Redshift cluster.

5. The Redshift cluster performs final operations to join and merge data and then returns the results to the user's SQL client.

6. Note the difference between **RMS** and data in S3 that Redshift Spectrum is able to query. Files that Redshift stores in RMS are managed by Redshift and are not accessible outside of Redshift. A Redshift cluster will automatically move data between the S3-based RMS and local SSD storage in each node of the cluster and is designed to ensure that frequently queried data is available from the local SSD drives for best performance. With Redshift Spectrum, any data in Amazon S3 that has been cataloged in Glue Data Catalog can be queried by a fleet of compute instances that are available to all Redshift clusters. This could be data in a variety of formats (such as JSON, CSV, Parquet, or others) and can be queried by other tools, such as Amazon Athena, since this data is not managed by Redshift.

7. Redshift also includes a number of advanced features, such as data sharing between Redshift clusters, automatic optimization of tables, integration with machine learning through Redshift ML, and the ability to mask data through data masking policies. We will do a deeper dive into Amazon Redshift in *Chapter 9, Loading Data into a Data Mart*, and this includes a hands-on exercise for loading data into Redshift and then querying that data.

Overview of Amazon QuickSight for visualizing data

"*A picture is worth a thousand words*" is a common saying, and it is a sentiment that most business users would strongly agree with. Imagine for a moment that you are a busy sales manager, it's Monday morning, and you need to quickly determine how your various sales territories performed last quarter before your 9 a.m. call.

Your one option is to receive a detailed spreadsheet showing the specific sales figures broken down by territory and segment, as per *Figure 3.8*:

Sales Data by Territory and Segment			
Territory	SMB	Midmarket	Enterprise
East Q3	$ 168,778	$ 210,696	$ 423,875
East Q4	$ 196,254	$ 244,995	$ 492,878
South Q3	$ 99,361	$ 168,572	$ 263,119
South Q4	$ 116,895	$ 198,320	$ 309,552
Central Q3	$ 132,882	$ 203,082	$ 296,332
Central Q4	$ 156,332	$ 238,920	$ 245,000
Mountain Q3	$ 127,699	$ 213,247	$ 271,440
Mountain Q4	$ 146,780	$ 245,112	$ 312,000
West Q3	$ 156,147	$ 210,558	$ 396,885
West Q4	$ 185,889	$ 250,664	$ 526,995

Figure 3.8: Sales table showing sales data by territory and segment

The other option you have is to receive a graphical representation of the data in the form of a bar graph, as shown in *Figure 3.9*. Within the interface, you can filter data by territory and market segment, and also drill down to get more detailed information:

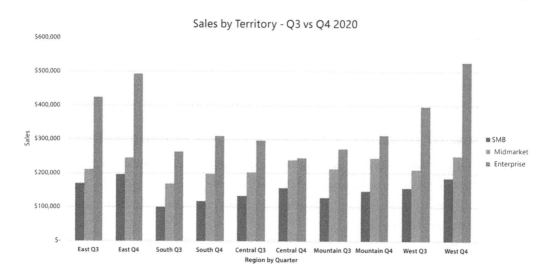

Figure 3.9: Sample graph showing sales data by territory and segment

Most people would prefer the graphical representation of the data, as they can easily visually compare sales between quarters, segments, and territories, or identify the top sales territory and segment with just a glance. As a result, the use of business intelligence tools, which provide visual representations of complex data, is extremely popular in the business world.

Amazon QuickSight is a service from AWS that enables the creation of these types of complex visualizations, but beyond just providing static visuals, the charts created by QuickSight enable users to filter data and drill down to get further details. For example, our sales manager could filter the visual to just see the numbers from Q4 or to just see the enterprise segment. The user could also drill down into the Q4 data for the enterprise segment in the West territory to see sales by month, for example.

Amazon QuickSight is serverless, which means there are no servers for the organization to set up or manage, and there is a simple monthly fee based on the user type (either an author, who can create new visuals, or a reader, who can view visuals created by authors).

A data engineer can configure QuickSight to access data from a multitude of sources, including accessing data in an Amazon S3-based data lake via integration with Amazon Athena. In *Chapter 12, Visualizing Data with Amazon QuickSight,* we will do a hands-on exercise to create a simple visualization with QuickSight.

In the next section, we will wrap up the chapter by getting hands-on with building a simple transformation that converts a CSV file into Parquet format, using Lambda to perform the transformation.

Hands-on — triggering an AWS Lambda function when a new file arrives in an S3 bucket

In the hands-on portion of this chapter, we're going to configure an S3 bucket to automatically trigger a Lambda function whenever a new file is written to the bucket. In the Lambda function, we're going to make use of an open-source Python library called **AWS SDK for pandas**, created by AWS Professional Services to simplify common ETL tasks when working in an AWS environment. We'll use the AWS SDK for pandas library to convert a CSV file into Parquet format and then update AWS Glue Data Catalog.

Converting a file into Parquet format is a common transformation in order to improve analytic query performance against our data. This can either be done in bulk (such as by using an AWS Glue job that runs every hour to convert files received in the past hour), or it can be done as each file arrives, as we are doing in this hands-on exercise. A similar approach can be used for other use cases, such as updating a total_sales value in a database as files are received with daily sales figures from a company's retail stores across the world.

Let's get started with the hands-on section of this chapter.

Creating a Lambda layer containing the AWS SDK for pandas library

Lambda layers allow your Lambda function to bring in additional code, packaged as a **.zip** file. In our use case, the Lambda layer is going to contain the AWS SDK for pandas Python library, which we can then attach to any Lambda function where we want to use the library.

To create a Lambda layer, do the following:

1. Access the 2.19.0 version of the AWS SDK for pandas library in GitHub at https://github. com/aws/aws-sdk-pandas/releases. Under **Assets**, download the awswrangler-layer-2.19.0-py3.9.zip file to your local drive. Note that there is a direct link to this file on the GitHub site for this book at https://github.com/PacktPublishing/Data-Engineering-with-AWS-2nd-edition/tree/main/Chapter03.

2. Log in to the **AWS Management Console** as the administrative user you created in *Chapter 1, An Introduction to Data Engineering* (https://console.aws.amazon.com).

3. Make sure that you are in the Region that you have chosen for performing the hands-on sections in this book. The examples in this book use the us-east-2 (**Ohio**) Region.

4. In the top search bar of the AWS console, search for and select the **Lambda** service.

5. In the left-hand menu, under **Additional Resources**, select **Layers,** and then click on **Create layer**.

6. Provide a **name** for the layer (for example, awsSDKpandas219_python39) and an optional description, and then upload the .zip file you downloaded from GitHub. For **Compatible runtimes-optional**, select **Python 3.9**, and then click **Create**. The following screenshot shows the configuration for this step:

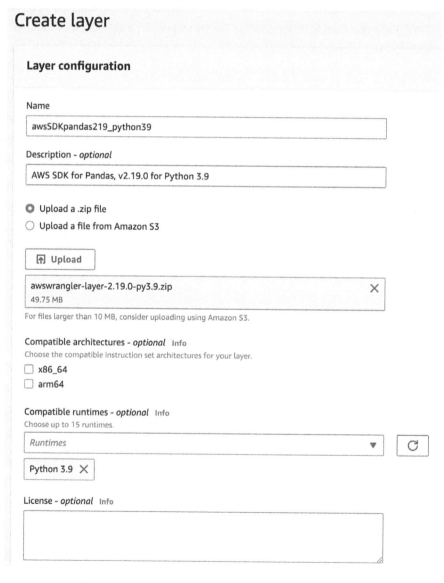

Figure 3.10: Creating and configuring an AWS Lambda layer

By creating a Lambda layer for the AWS SDK for pandas library, we can use AWS SDK for pandas in any of our Lambda functions just by ensuring this Lambda layer is attached to the function.

Creating an IAM policy and role for your Lambda function

In the previous chapter, we created three Amazon S3 buckets – one for a landing zone (for ingestion of raw files), one for a clean zone (for files that have undergone initial processing and optimization), and one for the curated zone (to contain our finalized datasets, ready for consumption).

In this section, we will create a Lambda function to be triggered every time a new file is uploaded to our landing zone S3 bucket. The Lambda function will process the file and write out a new version of the file to a target bucket (our clean zone S3 bucket).

For this to work, we need to ensure that our Lambda function has the following permissions:

1. Read our source S3 bucket (for example, `dataeng-landing-zone-<initials>`).

2. Write to our target S3 bucket (for example, `dataeng-clean-zone-<initials>`).

3. Write logs to Amazon CloudWatch.

4. Access to all Glue API actions (to enable the creation of new databases and tables).

To create a new AWS IAM role with these permissions, follow these steps:

1. In the search bar at the top of the AWS console, search for and select the **IAM** service, and in the left-hand menu, select **Policies** and then click on **Create policy**.

2. By default, the **Visual editor** tab is selected, so click on **JSON** to change to the **JSON** tab.

3. Provide the JSON code from the following code blocks, replacing the boilerplate code. Note that you can also copy and paste this policy by accessing the policy on this book's GitHub page (`https://github.com/PacktPublishing/Data-Engineering-with-AWS-2nd-edition/blob/main/Chapter03/DataEngLambdaS3CWGluePolicy.json`). Note that if doing a copy and paste from the GitHub copy of this policy, you must replace `dataeng-landing-zone-<initials>` with the name of the landing zone bucket you created in *Chapter 2*, and replace `dataeng-clean-zone-<initials>` with the name of the clean zone bucket you created in *Chapter 2*.

This first block of the policy configures the policy document and provides permissions for using CloudWatch log groups, log streams, and log events:

```
{
    "Version": "2012-10-17",
    "Statement": [
```

```
            {
                "Effect": "Allow",
                "Action": [
                    "logs:PutLogEvents",
                    "logs:CreateLogGroup",
                    "logs:CreateLogStream"
                ],
                "Resource": "arn:aws:logs:*:*:*"
            },
```

This next block of the policy provides permissions for all Amazon S3 actions (get and put) that are in the Amazon S3 bucket specified in the resource section (in this case, our clean zone and landing zone buckets). Make sure you replace dataeng-clean-zone-<initials> and dataeng-landing-zone-<initials> with the names of the S3 buckets you created in *Chapter 2*:

```
            {
                "Effect": "Allow",
                "Action": [
                    "s3:*"
                ],
        "Resource": [
                    "arn:aws:s3:::dataeng-landing-zone-INITIALS/*",
                    "arn:aws:s3:::dataeng-landing-zone-INITIALS",
                    "arn:aws:s3:::dataeng-clean-zone-INITIALS/*",
                    "arn:aws:s3:::dataeng-clean-zone-INITIALS"
                ]
            },
```

In the final statement of the policy, we provide permissions to use all AWS Glue actions (create job, start job, and delete job). Note that in a production environment, you should limit the scope specified in the resource section:

```
        {
            "Effect": "Allow",
            "Action": [
                "glue:*"
            ],
            "Resource": "*"
        }
    ]
}
```

4. Click on **Next Tags** and then **Next: Review**.

5. Provide a name for the policy, such as `DataEngLambdaS3CWGluePolicy`, and then click **Create policy**.

6. In the left-hand menu, click on **Roles** and then **Create role**.

7. For the trusted entity, ensure **AWS service** is selected, and for the service, select **Lambda** and then click **Next: Permissions**. In *step 4* of the next section (*Creating a Lambda function*), we will assign this role to our Lambda function.

8. Under **Attach permissions**, select the policy we just created (for example, `DataEngLambdaS3CWGluePolicy`) by searching and then clicking the tick box. Then, click **Next**.

9. Provide a role name, such as `DataEngLambdaS3CWGlueRole`, and click **Create role**.

Creating a Lambda function

We are now ready to create our Lambda function that will be triggered whenever a CSV file is uploaded to our source S3 bucket. The uploaded CSV file will be converted into Parquet, written out to the target bucket, and added to the Glue catalog using the AWS SDK for pandas library:

1. In the AWS console, search for and select the **Lambda** service, and in the left-hand menu, select **Functions** and then click **Create function**. *Make sure you are in the same Region as where you created your AWS buckets* in *Chapter 2*.

2. Select **Author from scratch** and provide a **function name** (such as `CSVtoParquetLambda`).

3. For **Runtime**, select **Python 3.9** from the drop-down list.

4. Expand **Change default execution role** and select **Use an existing role**. From the drop-down list, select the role you created in the previous section (such as `DataEngLambdaS3CWGlueRole`):

Function name

Enter a name that describes the purpose of your function.

```
CSVtoParquetLambda
```

Use only letters, numbers, hyphens, or underscores with no spaces.

Runtime Info

Choose the language to use to write your function. Note that the console code editor supports only Node.js, Python, and Ruby.

```
Python 3.9
```

Architecture Info

Choose the instruction set architecture you want for your function code.

○ x86_64

○ arm64

Permissions Info

By default, Lambda will create an execution role with permissions to upload logs to Amazon CloudWatch Logs. You can customize this default role later when adding triggers.

▼ **Change default execution role**

Execution role

Choose a role that defines the permissions of your function. To create a custom role, go to the IAM console ⤴.

○ Create a new role with basic Lambda permissions

● Use an existing role

○ Create a new role from AWS policy templates

Existing role

Choose an existing role that you've created to be used with this Lambda function. The role must have permission to upload logs to Amazon CloudWatch Logs.

```
DataEngLambdaS3CWGlueRole
```

View the DataEngLambdaS3CWGlueRole role ⤴ on the IAM console.

Figure 3.11: Creating and configuring a Lambda function

5. Do not change any of the **Advanced settings** and click **Create function**.

6. Click on **Layers** in the first box (*Function overview*), and then click **Add a layer** in the **Layers** box.

7. Select **Custom layers**, and from the dropdown, select the AWS SDK for pandas layer you created in a previous step (such as `awsSDKpandas219_python39`). Select the latest version and then click **Add**.

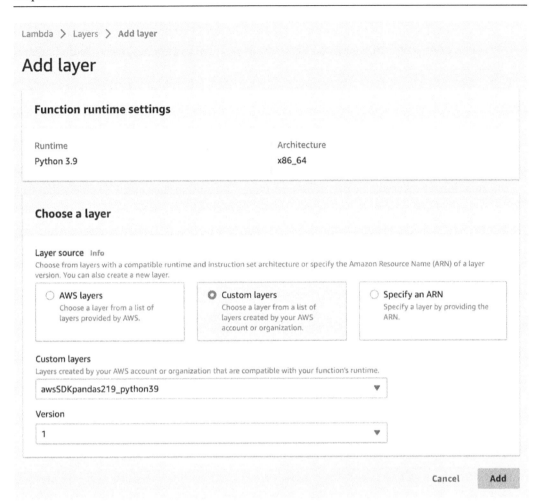

Figure 3.12: Adding an AWS Lambda layer to an AWS Lambda function

8. Scroll down to the **Code Source** section in the Lambda console. The following code can be downloaded from this book's GitHub repository. Make sure to replace any existing code in `lambda_function` with this code.

In the first few lines of code, we import boto3 (the AWS Python SDK), awswrangler (which is part of the AWS SDK for pandas library that we added as a Lambda layer), and a function from the urllib library called unquote_plus:

```
import boto3
import awswrangler as wr
from urllib.parse import unquote_plus
```

We then define our main function, lambda_handler, which is called when the Lambda function is executed. The event data contains information such as the S3 object that was uploaded and was the cause of the trigger that ran this function. From this event data, we get the S3 bucket name and the object key. We also set the Glue catalog db_name and table_name based on the path of the object that was uploaded (review the comments in the code below for an explanation of how this works).

```
def lambda_handler(event, context):
    # Get the source bucket and object name as passed to the Lambda
function
    for record in event['Records']:
        bucket = record['s3']['bucket']['name']
        key = unquote_plus(record['s3']['object']['key'])

    # We will set the DB and table name based on the last two
elements of
    # the path prior to the filename. If key = 'dms/sakila/film/
LOAD01.csv',
    # then the following lines will set db to 'sakila' and table_
name to 'film'
    key_list = key.split("/")
    print(f'key_list: {key_list}')
    db_name = key_list[len(key_list)-3]
    table_name = key_list[len(key_list)-2]
```

We now print out some debugging information that will be captured in our Lambda function logs. This includes information such as the Amazon S3 bucket and key that we are processing. We then set the output_path value here, which is where we are going to write the Parquet file that this function creates. **Make sure to change the** output_path **value of this code to match the name of the target S3 bucket you created earlier:**

```
      print(f'Bucket: {bucket}')
      print(f'Key: {key}')
      print(f'DB Name: {db_name}')
      print(f'Table Name: {table_name}')

      input_path = f"s3://{bucket}/{key}"
      print(f'Input_Path: {input_path}')
      output_path = f"s3://dataeng-clean-zone-INITIALS/{db_name}/
  {table_name}"
      print(f'Output_Path: {output_path}')
```

We can then use the AWS SDK for pandas library (defined as wr in our function) to read the CSV file that we received. We read the contents of the CSV file into a pandas DataFrame we are calling input_df. We also get a list of current Glue databases, and if the database we want to use does not exist, we create it:

```
      input_df = wr.s3.read_csv([input_path])

      current_databases = wr.catalog.databases()
      wr.catalog.databases()
      if db_name not in current_databases.values:
          print(f'- Database {db_name} does not exist ... creating')
          wr.catalog.create_database(db_name)
      else:
          print(f'- Database {db_name} already exists')
```

Finally, we can use the AWS SDK for pandas library to create a Parquet file containing the data we read from the CSV file. For the S3 to Parquet function, we specify the name of the DataFrame (input_df) that contains the data we want to write out in Parquet format. We also specify the S3 output path, the Glue database, and the table name:

```
      result = wr.s3.to_parquet(
          df=input_df,
          path=output_path,
          dataset=True,
          database=db_name,
          table=table_name,
          mode="append")
      print("RESULT: ")
```

```
        print(f'{result}')
        return result
```

9. Click on **Deploy** at the top of the **Code Source** window

10. Click on the **Configuration** tab (above the **Code Source** window), and on the left-hand side, click on **General configuration**. Click the **Edit** button and modify the **Timeout** to be 1 minute (the default timeout of 3 seconds is likely to be too low to convert some files from CSV into Parquet format). Then, click on **Save**. *If you skip this step, you are likely to get an error when your function runs.*

Configuring our Lambda function to be triggered by an S3 upload

Our final task is to configure the Lambda function so that whenever a CSV file is uploaded to our landing zone bucket, the Lambda function runs and converts the file into Parquet format:

1. In the **Function Overview** box of our Lambda function, click on **Add trigger**.

2. For **Trigger configuration**, select the **S3** service from the drop-down list.

3. For **Bucket**, select your landing zone bucket (for example, `dataeng-landing-zone-<initials>`).

4. We want our rule to trigger whenever a new file is created in this bucket, no matter what method is used to create it (**Put**, **Post**, or **Copy**), so select **All object create events** from the list.

5. For **suffix**, enter `.csv`. This will configure the trigger to only run the Lambda function when a file with a `.csv` extension is uploaded to our landing zone bucket.

6. Acknowledge the warning about **Recursive invocation**, which can crop up if you set up a trigger on a specific bucket to run a Lambda function and then you get your Lambda function to create a new file in that same bucket and path. This is a good time to double-check and make sure that you are configuring this trigger in the `LANDING ZONE` bucket (for example, `dataeng-landing-zone-<initials>`) and not the target `CLEAN ZONE` bucket that our Lambda function will write to:

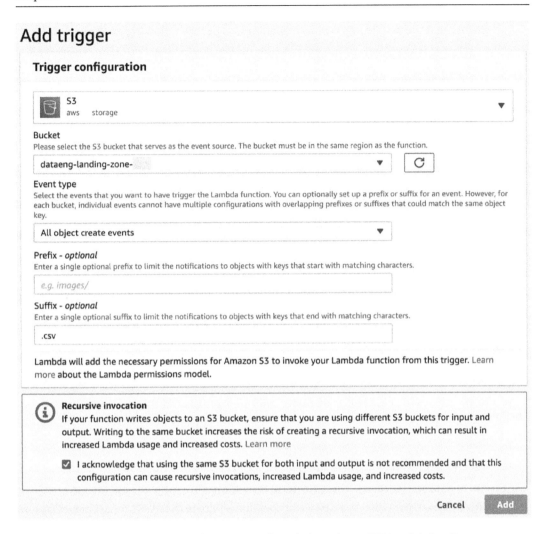

Figure 3.13: Configuring an S3-based trigger for an AWS Lambda function

7. Click **Add** to create the trigger.

8. Create a simple CSV file called test.csv that you can use to test the trigger or download test.csv from the GitHub site for this chapter (https://github.com/PacktPublishing/ Data-Engineering-with-AWS-2nd-edition/blob/main/Chapter03/test.csv).

Ensure that the first line has column headings, as per the following example:

```
name,favorite_num
Gareth,23
Tracy,28
Chris,16
Emma,14
```

Ensure you create the file with a standard text editor, and not Word processing software (such as Microsoft Word) or any other software that will add additional formatting to the file.

9. Navigate to the Amazon S3 console (`https://s3.console.aws.amazon.com/s3`) and click on the `dataeng-landing-zone-initials` bucket that you previously created. Then click on **Create folder** and provide a folder name of `cleanzonedb`. The top-level folder we create here is going to be used as the name of the database that will be created in Glue Data Catalog to store our new table.

10. Navigate into the `cleanzonedb` folder, and create a second-level folder (this will be used as the name of the table that gets created in Glue Data Catalog). Name the second-level folder `csvtoparquet`.

11. Navigate into the `csvtoparquet` folder, click on **Upload**, and then upload the `test.csv` file you previously created. The file should be uploaded into `dataeng-landing-zone-initials/cleanzonedb/csvtoparquet`.

12. If everything has been configured correctly, your Lambda function will have been triggered and will have written out a Parquet-formatted file to your target S3 bucket and created a Glue database and table. You can access the Glue service in the AWS Management Console to ensure that a new database and table have been created in the data catalog and can run the following command in CloudShell to ensure that a Parquet file has been written to your target bucket. Make sure to replace `dataeng-clean-zone-initials` with the name of your target S3 bucket:

```
aws s3 ls s3://dataeng-clean-zone-initials/cleanzonedb/csvtoparquet/
```

The result of this command should display the Parquet file that was created by the Lambda function.

Summary

In this chapter, we covered a lot! We reviewed a range of AWS services at a high level, including services for ingesting data from a variety of sources, services for transforming data, and services for consuming and working with data.

We then got hands-on, building a solution in our AWS account that converted a file from CSV format into Parquet format and registered the data in AWS Glue Data Catalog.

In the next chapter, we will cover a really important topic that all data engineers need to have a good understanding of and that needs to be central to every project that a data engineer works on, and that is the topic of data governance.

Learn more on Discord

To join the Discord community for this book – where you can share feedback, ask questions to the author, and learn about new releases – follow the QR code below:

https://discord.gg/9s5mHNyECd

4

Data Governance, Security, and Cataloging

Data governance and security are some of the most important topics to cover in a book that is all about data. Having the most efficient data pipelines, the fastest data transformations, and the best data consumption tools is not worth much if the data is not kept secure and governed correctly. Data must also be stored and accessed in a way that complies with local laws, and the data needs to be cataloged so that it is discoverable and useful to the organization.

Sadly, it is not uncommon to read about data breaches and poor data handling by organizations, and the consequences of this can include reputational damage to the organization, as well as potentially massive penalties imposed by the government. And once an organization causes damage to their customers (such as exposing them to potential identity theft through a data breach), it is difficult for the organization to regain that trust.

It is also not uncommon for organizations to find that they have massive quantities of data, but that they are not able to maximize the value of that data since it is siloed (contained across many different systems that are not connected) or of poor quality, or users just have no trust in the data they have access to.

In this chapter, we will do a deeper dive into best practices for handling data responsibly, and for making sure that the value of data can be maximized for an organization. We will cover the following topics:

- The many different aspects of data governance
- Data security, access, and privacy

- Data quality, data profiling, and data lineage
- Business and technical data catalogs
- AWS services that help with data governance
- Hands-on – configuring Lake Formation permissions

Technical requirements

To complete the hands-on exercises included in this chapter, you will need an AWS account where you have access to a user with administrator privileges (as covered in *Chapter 1, An Introduction to Data Engineering*).

You can find the code files of this chapter in the GitHub repository using the following link: `https://github.com/PacktPublishing/Data-Engineering-with-AWS-2nd-edition/tree/main/Chapter04`

The many different aspects of data governance

Data governance is a wide-ranging topic, covering many different aspects. If you do a Google search for the definition of data governance, you are likely to see many different definitions. At its core though, data governance is the various things an organization needs to do to ensure the secure, compliant, and effective use of data, from the time the data is created through to when it is archived or deleted.

This includes processes that make the data **discoverable**, **understandable**, and **usable**, while ensuring that the data is of **high quality** and is **protected and secured**. This covers all data within an organization; however, for the purposes of this book, we will only be focusing on data governance for analytic data.

Most organizations consist of many different business units or teams, and each of these generates their own data, and also has their own specific requirements for accessing data from other parts of the organization. But if a team has no way to centrally publish their datasets, or to discover datasets published by other parts of the organization, this significantly impacts the value of the data. Data is most valuable to an organization when all data generated can be used across all parts of the organization (in a well-governed manner).

But just being able to discover data generated across the organization is not helpful if the data is not of good quality, cannot be easily understood, or cannot be trusted. Also, if it is not easy to get access to discovered data in a secure way, without significant delays and complicated processes, then the value of that data is impacted.

But governance also extends to ensuring that the data that is generated is secured and handled in a responsible way.

Data security dictates how an organization should protect data to ensure that it is stored securely (such as in an encrypted state), and that access by unauthorized entities is prevented. For example, all the things an organization does to prevent falling victim to a ransomware attack, or having their data stolen and sold on the dark web, fall under data security.

The **responsible handling of data** involves making sure that only people who need access to specific datasets have that access (such as ensuring that data is not just generally open to all users of a system without considering whether they need access to that data to perform their jobs). Responsible handling also means ensuring that an organization only uses and processes data on individuals in approved ways, and that organizations provide data disclosures as required by law.

As the security of data needs to be the top priority for an organization, let's start with a deeper dive into the topics of security, privacy, and data handling.

Data security, access, and privacy

Not providing adequate protection and security for an organization's data, or not complying with relevant governance laws, can end up being a very expensive mistake for an organization.

According to an article on CSO Online titled *The biggest data breach fines, penalties, and settlements so far* (`https://www.csoonline.com/article/3410278/the-biggest-data-breach-fines-penalties-and-settlements-so-far.html`), penalties and expenses related to data breaches have cost companies over $4.4 billion (and counting).

For example, Equifax, the credit agency firm, had a data breach in 2017 that exposed the personal and financial information of nearly 150 million people. As a result, they agreed to pay at least $575 million in a settlement with several United States government agencies, and U.S. states.

But beyond financial penalties, a data breach can also do incalculable damage to an organization's reputation and brand. Once you lose the trust of your customers, it can be very difficult to earn that trust back.

Beyond data breaches where personal data is stolen from an organization's system, failure to comply with local regulations relating to how data is handled can also be costly. There are an increasing number of laws that define under what conditions a company may collect, store, and process personal information. Not complying with these laws can result in significant penalties for an organization, even in the absence of a data breach.

For example, Google was hit with a fine of more than $50 million for failing to adequately comply with aspects of a European regulation known as the **General Data Protection Regulation** (**GDPR**). Google appealed the decision, but in 2020, the decision was upheld by the courts, leaving the penalty on Google in place.

Common data regulatory requirements

No matter where you operate in the world, there are very likely several regulations concerning data privacy and protection that you need to be aware of, and plan for, as a data engineer. A small selection of these include the following:

- The **General Data Protection Regulation** (**GDPR**) in the European Union
- The **California Consumer Privacy Act** (**CCPA**) and the **California Privacy Rights Act** (**CPRA**) in California, USA
- The **Personal Data Protection** (**PDP**) **Bill** in India
- The **Protection of Personal Information Act** (**POPIA**) in South Africa

These laws can be complex and cover many different areas, which is far beyond the scope of this book. However, generally, they involve individuals having the right to know what data a company holds about them; ensuring adequate protection of personal information that the organization holds; enforcing strict controls around data being processed; and in some cases, the right of an individual to request their data being deleted from an organization's system.

In the case of GDPR, an organization is subject to the regulations if they hold data on any resident of the European Union, even if the organization does not have a legal presence in the EU.

In addition to these broad data protection and privacy regulations, many regulations apply additional requirements to specific industries or functions. Let's take a look at some examples:

- The **Health Insurance Portability and Accountability Act** (**HIPAA**), which applies to organizations that store an individual's healthcare and medical data
- The **Payment Card Industry Data Security Standard** (**PCI DSS**), which applies to organizations that store and process credit card data

Understanding what these regulations require and how best to comply with them is often complex and time-consuming. In this chapter, we will look at general principles that can be applied to protect data used in analytic pipelines; however, this chapter is not intended as a guide on how to comply with any specific regulation.

GDPR specifies that in certain cases, an organization must appoint a **Data Protection Officer (DPO)**. The DPO is responsible for training staff involved in data processing and conducting regular audits, among other responsibilities.

If your organization has a DPO, ensure you set up a time to meet with the DPO to fully understand the regulations that may apply to your organization and how this may affect analytic data. Alternatively, work with your **Chief Information Security Officer (CISO)** to ensure your organization seeks legal advice on which data regulations may apply.

If you must participate in a compliance audit for an analytic workload running in AWS, review the *AWS Artifact* service (`https://aws.amazon.com/artifact/`), a self-service portal for on-demand access to AWS's compliance reports.

Core data protection concepts

There are several concepts and terminology related to protecting data that are important for a data engineer to understand. In this section, we will briefly define some of these.

Personally identifiable information (PII)

Personally identifiable information (PII) is a term commonly used in North America to reference any information that can be used to identify an individual. This can refer to either the information on its own being able to identify an individual or where the information can be combined with other linkable information to identify an individual. It includes information such as full name, social security number, IP address, and photos or videos.

PII also covers data that provides information about a specific aspect of an individual (such as a medical condition, location, or political affiliation).

Personal data

Personal data is a term that is defined in GDPR and is considered to be similar to, but broader than, the definition of PII. Specifically, GDPR defines personal data as follows:

> *Any information relating to an identified or identifiable natural person ("data subject"); an identifiable natural person is one who can be identified, directly or indirectly, in particular by reference to an identifier such as a name, an identification number, location data, an online identifier or to one or more factors specific to the physical, physiological, genetic, mental, economic, cultural or social identity of that natural person.*

GDPR, Article 4, Definitions (`https://eur-lex.europa.eu/legal-content/EN/`
`TXT/HTML/?uri=CELEX:32016R0679#d1e1374-1-1`)

Encryption

Encryption is a mathematical technique of encoding data using a key in such a way that the data becomes unrecognizable and unusable. An authorized user who has the key used to encrypt the data can use the key to decrypt the data and return it to its original plaintext form.

Encrypted data may be able to be decrypted by a hacker without the key through the use of advanced computational resources, skills, and time. However, a well-designed and secure encryption algorithm increases the difficulty of decrypting the data without the key, increasing the security of the encrypted data.

There are two important types of encryption and both should be used for all data and systems:

1. **Encryption in transit**: This is the process of encrypting data as it moves between systems. For example, a system that migrates data from a database to a data lake should ensure that the data is encrypted before being transmitted, that the source and target endpoints are authenticated, and the data can then be decrypted at the target for processing. This helps ensure that if someone can intercept the data stream during transmission, the data is encrypted and therefore unable to be read and used by the person who intercepted the data. A common way to achieve this is to use the **Transport Layer Security (TLS)** protocol for all communications between systems.

2. **Encryption at rest**: This is the encryption of data that is written to a storage medium, such as a disk. After each phase of data processing, all the data that is persisted to disk should be encrypted.

Encryption (in transit and at rest) is a key tool for improving the security of your data, but other important tools should also be considered, as covered in the subsequent sections.

Anonymized data

Anonymized data is data that has been altered in such a way that personal data is irreversibly de-identified, rendering it impossible for any PII data to be identified. For example, this could involve replacing PII data with randomly generated data in such a way that the randomization cannot be reversed to recreate the original data.

Another way anonymization can be applied is to remove most of the PII data so that only a few attributes that may be considered PII remain, but with enough PII data removed to make it difficult to identify an individual. However, this contains risk, as it is often still possible to identify an individual even with only minimal data. A well-known study (`https://dataprivacylab. org/projects/identifiability/paper1.pdf`) found that with just the ZIP code, gender, and date of birth information, 87% of the population in the United States can be uniquely identified.

Pseudonymized data/tokenization

Pseudonymized data is data that has been altered in such a way that personal data is de-identified. While this is similar to the concept of anonymized data, the big difference is that with pseudonymized data, the original PII data can still be accessed (if a user has a legitimate need to access the PII data and has the necessary system authorization).

Pseudonymized data is defined by GDPR as data that cannot be attributed to a specific data subject without the use of separately kept *"additional information."*

There are multiple techniques for creating pseudonymized data. For example, you can replace a full name with a randomly generated token, a different name (so that it looks real but is not), a hash representing the name, and more. However, whichever technique is used, it must be possible to still access the original data.

One of the most popular ways to do this is to have a tokenization system generate a unique, random token that replaces the PII data.

For example, when a raw dataset is ingested into the data lake, the first step may be to pass the data through the **tokenization** system. This system will replace all PII data in the dataset with an anonymous token and record each **real_data token substitution** in a secure database. Once the data has been transformed, if a data consumer requires access and is authorized to access the PII data, they can pass the dataset to the tokenization system to be detokenized (that is, have the tokens replaced with the original, real values).

The benefit of a tokenization system is that the generated token is random and does not contain any reference to the original value, and there is no way to determine the original value just from the token. If there is a data breach that can steal a dataset with tokenized data, there is no way to perform reverse engineering on the token to find the original value.

However, the tokenization system itself contains all the PII data, along with the associated tokens. If an entity can access the tokenized data and is also able to comprise the tokenization system, they will have access to all PII data.

Therefore, it is important that the tokenization system is completely separate from the analytic systems containing the tokenized data, and that the tokenization system is protected properly.

On the other hand, **hashing** is generally considered the least secure method of de-identifying PII data, especially when it comes to data types with a limited set of values, such as social security numbers and names.

Hashing uses several popular hashing algorithms to create a hash of an original value. An original value, such as the name *"John Smith,"* will always return the same hash value for a specific algorithm.

However, all possible social security numbers and most names have been passed through popular hashing algorithms and lookup tables have been created, known as **rainbow tables**. Using these rainbow tables, anyone can take a hashed name or social security number and quickly identify the original value.

For example, if you use the SHA-256 hashing algorithm, the original value of *"John Smith"* will always return *"ef61a579c907bbed674c0dbcbcf7f7af8f851538eef7b8e58c5bee0b8cfdac4a."*

If you used the SHA-256 hashing algorithm to de-identify your PII data, it would be very easy for a malicious actor to determine that the preceding value referenced *"John Smith"* (just try Googling the preceding hash and see how quickly the name John Smith is revealed). While there are approaches to improving the security of a hash (such as salting the hash by adding a fixed string to the start of the value), it is still generally not recommended to use hashing for any data that has a well-known, limited set of values, or values that could be guessed.

Authentication

Authentication is the process of validating that a claimed identity is that identity. A simple example is when you log in to a **Google Mail** (**Gmail**) account. You provide your identity (your Gmail email address) and then validate that it is you by providing something only you should know (your password), and possibly also a second factor of authentication (by entering the code that is texted to your cell phone, for example).

Authentication does not specify what you can access but does attempt to validate that you are who you say you are. Of course, authentication systems are not foolproof. Your password may have been compromised on another website, and if you had the same password for your Gmail account, someone could use that to impersonate you. If you have **multi-factor authentication** (**MFA**) enabled, you receive a code on your phone or a physical MFA device that you need to enter when logging in, and that helps to further secure and validate your identity.

Federated identity is a concept related to authentication and means that responsibility for authenticating a user is done by another system. For example, when logging in to the AWS Management Console, your administrator could set up a federated identity so that you use your Active Directory credentials to log in via your organization's access portal, and the organization's Active Directory server authenticates you. Once authenticated, the Active Directory server confirms to the AWS Management Console that you have been successfully authenticated as a specific user. This means you do not need a separate username and password to log in to the AWS system, but you can use your existing Active Directory credentials to be authenticated to an identity in AWS.

Authorization

Authorization is the process of authorizing access to a resource based on a validated identity. For example, when you log in to your Google account (where you are authenticated by your password, and perhaps a second factor such as a code that is texted to your phone), you may be authorized to access that identity's email, and perhaps also the Google Calendar and Google Search history for that identity.

For a data analytics system, once you validate your identity with authentication, you need to be authorized to access specific datasets. A data lake administrator can, for example, authorize you to access data that is in the Conformed Zone of the data lake, but not grant you access to data in the Raw Zone.

Putting these concepts together

Getting data protection right, and ensuring that you comply with local compliance regulations, does not happen by itself. It is important that you plan for and thoughtfully execute the process of protecting your data and ensuring data compliance. This will involve using some of the concepts introduced previously, such as the following:

- Making sure PII data is replaced with a token as the first processing step after ingestion (and ensuring that the tokenization system is secure).
- Encrypting all data at rest with a well-known and reliable encryption algorithm and ensuring that all connections use secure encrypted tunnels (such as by using the TLS protocol for all communications between systems).
- Implementing federated identities where user authorization for analytic systems is performed via a central corporate identity provider, such as Active Directory. This ensures that, for example, when a user leaves the company and their Active Directory account is terminated, their access to analytic systems in AWS is terminated as a result.

- Implementing least privilege access, where users are authorized for the minimum level of permissions that they need to perform their job.

This is also not something that a data engineer should do in isolation. You should work with your organization's security and governance teams to ensure you understand any legal requirements for how to process and secure your analytical data. You should also regularly review, or audit, the security policies in place for your analytic systems and data.

Ensuring the security of your data, protecting PII, and making sure that data is used appropriately need to be a top priority for every organization. However, if the data that is being generated is not of high quality, and not trusted and understood by people across your organization, then the value of that data is limited. In the next section, we look at important ways to manage the quality of your data, and ways to build trust in your data across the organization.

Data quality, data profiling, and data lineage

In this section, we look at three different, but related, concepts: data quality, data profiling, and data lineage. Each of these aspects of data governance are important tools for ensuring that data that is shared within your organization is of high quality, and that teams across your organization can have confidence when accessing and using the data.

Data quality

Having high-quality data is essential for ensuring that an organization is equipped to make the best data-driven decisions, and to be effective in all activities that are data-driven (such as marketing campaigns).

There are many different aspects to measuring **data quality**, and data quality is important in all phases of the data lifecycle. If data in the source production database is not captured correctly, then when that data is copied over to analytical systems, the analytical systems will have incorrect or missing data. For example, if the source system does not enforce that the date of birth is captured when creating a new customer record, then an analytical system using that data cannot rely on using a date of birth field, as it may be null for some records. Invalid records can also be created when users do manual data entry, as they may make a typo or capture a number incorrectly.

However, data quality issues can be introduced at any part of the data pipeline. As data is bought in from multiple different systems, datasets are joined, and calculations are made, data can be corrupted. Also, at times, ETL jobs in a pipeline may fail or be interrupted at some point, and the resulting data that is generated may be incomplete. This can lead to further issues down the line with subsequent jobs.

Data quality can be measured in many different ways, depending on the perspective of the person reviewing the data. Some of the common ways that data quality is measured include:

- **Accuracy** – does the data reflect the real facts?
- **Completeness** – does the data have all the required fields completed, such as date of birth or email?
- **Consistency** – does data from different data sources match and do the formats, such as the date format, match?
- **Timeliness** – is the data up to date?

For a data engineer, though, the primary concern is whether the content of the data is as expected. For example, if a column in a dataset is expected to be an integer, but some rows have strings in that field, then that could potentially cause the ETL pipeline to fail. Or, if a data processing job depends on each row having a valid email address, but some rows are missing an email address (or have an invalid email address), this again could cause a job to fail. Another example is where a column is meant to have a percentage between 0 and 100, and some rows have values that are outside of that range.

As a result, it is common for data engineers to create a data quality check job as part of the data pipeline. In these data quality jobs, the data engineer will specify a number of rules that are used to evaluate the quality of data, and a data quality report can be generated that provides details on the results. For example, a data quality rule could be created that checks to make sure that the email address field has a valid value for at least 90% of rows in the dataset. Or, the data quality check could ensure that every phone number value in a dataset consists of exactly 10 characters. The data engineer can then decide on what action to take for rows that do not pass the data quality rule check.

There are various commercial and open-source tools that can be used to help create these jobs to evaluate data quality, and the AWS Glue service also includes functionality for evaluating data against a set of rules. Later in this chapter, we will do a deeper dive into AWS Glue Data Quality functionality.

Data profiling

Data profiling is the process of analyzing a dataset, and then reporting on various aspects of the data content. This is useful to give both data engineers and other potential users of the data better insight into the underlying data. Data profiling can also be very useful to quickly identify potential data quality issues in a dataset, as we explain below.

A data profiling job analyzes all the data in a dataset, and then provides metrics for each column in the dataset. For example, if one of the columns in the dataset is a string, the data profiling job may report on the following attributes of that column:

Missing values. This reports on how many rows have a null, or no data, for this column. If we are planning to use a dataset for an email-based marketing campaign, but the data profiling job indicates that 54% of rows have a null for the email address, then we can very quickly determine that this dataset would not be good for our planned use case.

Distinct values. This reports on how many distinct values are contained in this column. For example, if the column was to report on which US state a customer was in, we would expect there to be no more than 50 distinct values, since there are 50 states in the USA. If a higher number was reported for this column, then we would have to assume that data was not captured consistently, such as some rows having **NY** recorded for state, while other rows have captured the full name of **New York**.

Unique values. This reports on how many rows have a unique value for this column (i.e., it is the only row that contains a specific value for this column).

Minimum/maximum string length. This reports on the number of characters for the shortest string in the column, as well as the longest string in the column.

A dataset that includes number-based columns (such as integers or doubles) may report on similar values, but instead of reporting on minimum/maximum string length, for numbers, the report may include the minimum/maximum value. For a column that records a percentage that is expected to be between 0 and 100, if the minimum reported was a negative number, or the maximum recorded was over 100, then this would indicate likely data quality issues.

In this way, data profiling is closely related to data quality, as it helps to identify potential data quality issues very quickly. But data quality requirements may be different for different users of a dataset.

For example, a team that uses the master customer data table for reporting on the number of users in each country or state may not care whether every customer record has an email address and phone number, but does require the name of the *Country* or *State* that is part of the user's address to be captured consistently. On the other hand, a marketing team that wants to send email-based promotions to all users may not care whether the customers' *Country* or *State* has been captured consistently, but does require that they have a valid *email address* for every customer.

In this way, data profiling does not make any assessment about the quality of data, but rather just reports on the profile, or shape, of the data. The end user who wants to use a specific dataset for a specific purpose can then review the data profile information to get a quick assessment as to whether the dataset seems to be appropriate for their use or not. If the data profile does not highlight any obvious problems with the data based on the specific use case, the data engineer can request access to the dataset and then establish a data quality job to further analyze the data.

For example, even if the data profile report indicates that 100% of rows have an email address captured, the data engineer can create a data quality rule to validate whether every email address appears to be valid by ensuring each email address contains an "at" sign and a string with a dot separator in the domain portion of the email address. In this way, if one of the data records has an email value of "anna@gmail," this would not be a null value, so the data profiling report may still indicate that 100% of records have an email address specified. But it is the data quality rule that would evaluate the specific value and be able to determine that the domain portion has not been correctly captured.

Data lineage

Another concept in data management that helps to build trust in a dataset is the understanding of how a dataset has been created, which can be captured with data lineage. **Data lineage** allows a user to view information about the original sources of a dataset, as well as the transformations that have been applied to those sources.

For example, let's say you work for a company that has a streaming movie business and you need to identify the top 10 movies for each country that you operate in. To do this, you create a table called `country_top_movies` by joining your `customer`, `movies`, and `streaming_stats` tables. In your ETL job, you group by country and limit the results to the top 10 movies for each country.

When you look at the data lineage for this job, you will see the three source tables, as well as details about the transformations that were applied to these tables after the join.

When a data analyst is searching for a dataset, being able to view the data lineage that shows how that table was created helps to build trust that the table is appropriate for their use case. They gain insight into what the source tables were and the types of transformations that were applied, and using that information can decide whether the resulting dataset meets their requirements.

The results of data quality checks, information on the data profile, and a visualization of data lineage can all be recorded in a data catalog, enabling users to search for datasets and dig deeper into information about that dataset. Let's look at the role of data catalogs in more detail.

Business and technical data catalogs

You have probably heard about swamps, even if you have never actually been to one. Generally, swamps are known to be wet areas that smell pretty bad, and where some trees and other vegetation may grow, but the area is generally not fit to be used for most purposes (unless, of course, you're an ogre similar to Shrek, and you make your home in the swamp!).

In contrast to a swamp, when most people think about a lake, they picture beautiful scenery with clean water, a beautiful sunset, and perhaps a few ducks gently floating on the water. Most people would hate to find themselves in a swamp if they thought they were going to visit a beautiful lake.

In the world of data lakes, as a data engineer, you want to provide an experience that is much like the pure and peaceful lake described previously, and you want to avoid your users finding that the lake looks more like a swamp. However, if you're not careful, your data lake can become a data swamp, where there are lots of different pieces of data around, but no one is sure what data is there. Then, when they do happen to find some data, they don't know where the data came from or whether it can be trusted. Ultimately, a data swamp can be a dumping ground for data that is not of much use to anyone. Or, more dangerously, it can allow people to use datasets that may not be the right dataset for the purpose and the data quality may be low or out of date. Making business decisions on the wrong dataset can lead to the wrong decision being made, which can negatively impact a company financially, or reputationally.

To avoid creating a data swamp, you need a well-organized data catalog.

Implementing a data catalog to avoid creating a data swamp

With some careful upfront planning and the right tools and policies, it is possible to avoid a data swamp and instead offer your users a well-structured, easy-to-navigate data lake.

Avoiding a data swamp is easy in theory – you just need two important things:

- A central data catalog that can be used to keep a searchable record of all the datasets in the data lake
- Policies that ensure useful metadata is added to all the entries in the data catalog, and policies for ensuring that only high-quality data is allowed to be added to the data catalog

While that may sound pretty straightforward, the implementation details matter and things are not always as simple in real life. You need to have a data platform that has rules in place to only allow data to be added to the central catalog that meets your specific requirements (such as certain metadata that must be associated with the dataset, and ensuring that the dataset meets certain data quality rules).

If you allow anyone to publish any dataset in your central catalog, you are very likely to end up with a data swamp. There may be many datasets published in the catalog, but users will not be able to identify which are trustworthy and useful datasets, or which are updated regularly, and will not have the context to help them understand where the dataset came from (its lineage) and what business purpose it serves.

When we talk about a central catalog, we are generally referring to a business data catalog, and the business catalog is usually associated with one or more technical catalogs. Let's take a closer look at the different types of catalogs.

Business data catalogs

The business data catalog (often referred to just as the data catalog) is a central repository that stores metadata about the different datasets in your environment. The purpose of the catalog is to enable users across your organization to discover available datasets and learn more about those datasets through the associated metadata.

For example, you may have a dataset called *Top Movies by Country* that lists the top 10 most streamed movies over the past 8 hours for each country your movie steaming company operates in. This dataset is created by an ETL job that runs every 8 hours, joining data from multiple different database tables. The ETL job and dataset are created by the **Playback Operations** team, as they need this data so that their streaming video player can display the current most popular movies based on the country a user is in. The table that is created has the following fields:

- Country
- Movie_Rank
- Movie_ID
- Title
- Genre
- Runtime
- Release_Year

When the Playback Operations team added the *Top Movies by Country* dataset to the business data catalog, they included the following metadata:

- **Description of the dataset**: Top 10 movies over last 8 hours grouped by country
- **Tags**: top10; ranking; countries; movies
- **Owning team**: Playback Operations
- **Data Owner**: Anchal Priya
- **Update Frequency**: 8 hours

As part of the process of creating the new dataset entry in the business data catalog, the dataset entry is linked with the technical catalog, meaning that the details about each of the fields in the dataset are also included in the business data catalog.

The data catalog also captures certain metadata automatically, such as the date/time when the dataset was last updated, a data quality score that can be automatically imported from the data quality tool, and the popularity of the dataset based on how many other users have requested access to the dataset. It is also possible to have the lineage and profile of the dataset stored in the data catalog, giving other users a better understanding of how this data was generated.

Recently, the marketing team started a new project that depends on having data about which genre of movies are most popular in each country (such as Action in Brazil, and Comedy in Argentina). They initially thought that they would need to create their own new ETL job to join many different datasets to get this information, but wisely decided that they should first search the corporate data catalog to see if there is an existing dataset that may have this information.

One of the data analysts on the marketing team logs in to the data catalog, and searches for *top movie genres by country*. In the search results, the *Top Movies by Country* dataset is listed, and the data analyst is able to explore more information about the dataset, view the list of fields, and even see feedback that other users of the dataset have left. In this way, the data catalog is much like the catalog of products on eCommerce sites like Amazon.com. Users can search for products, explore more information about the products, and look at reviews left by others who provide feedback on the products.

The data analyst realizes that this dataset has the data they need in order to be able to easily identify the top movie genre by country. Within the data catalog, they are able to click a button to request access to the data, and provide a short note indicating why they need access. This automatically gets routed to the dataset owner (Anchal Priya, as recorded in the catalog) who can then approve or deny the request. If approved, an automatic process grants the data analyst on the marketing team access to the dataset.

Popular data catalog solutions outside of AWS include the **Collibra Data Catalog**, the **Informatica Enterprise Data Catalog**, **Atlan**, and **Amundsen** (an open-source data catalog). At the AWS re:Invent conference in December 2022, AWS announced **Amazon DataZone**, a new service that includes business data-catalog-type functionality.

Amazon DataZone is a service from AWS that provides built-in data governance features, helping to unlock the power of data across an organization. This includes functionality for a business data catalog, as we cover in more detail in *Chapter 15, Implementing a Data Mesh Strategy*.

As shown in this section, the purpose of the business data catalog is to enable users to discover and browse datasets that are available within the organization. Let's now take a look at technical catalogs, which are primarily used by analytic applications to work with data in a data lake.

Technical data catalogs

Technical catalogs are those that map data files in a data lake (such as files stored in Amazon S3 storage) to a logical representation of those files in the form of databases and tables. The Hive metastore is a well-known technical catalog that stores metadata for Hive tables (such as the table schema, location, and partition information). These are primarily technical attributes of the table, and the AWS Glue Data Catalog is an example of a Hive-compatible Metastore (meaning analytic services designed to work with a Hive metastore catalog can use the Glue catalog).

Services such as Amazon Athena, AWS Glue ETL, and Amazon EMR enable you to run queries on data in an Amazon S3 data lake, just by referencing a database and table name and without needing to know the actual location in S3. When you run a query on a specific database/table, the analytic service references the technical catalog to determine where the underlying files that make up this table are located in Amazon S3. In addition, the analytic service can also access information on the schema of the table (column names and column types), as well as the format of those files (such as CSV or Parquet format), so that it uses the correct reader to access the data.

A business data catalog (discussed in the previous section) can often integrate with the technical catalog. For example, with Amazon DataZone it is possible to import databases that have been registered in the Glue technical data catalog. Once imported, a user can add additional business metadata that users of the DataZone catalog can use to discover datasets. When users search the DataZone catalog, they can search and view the business metadata that was manually added, but can also access technical metadata imported from Glue, such as the schema (a list of columns and data types). In a similar way, third-party tools such as the Collibra data catalog can also integrate with the Glue catalog in order to import technical attributes.

In the next section, we do a deeper dive into AWS services that relate to data governance, and this includes a closer look at the technical data catalog provided by AWS.

AWS services that help with data governance

As already discussed in this chapter, data governance is a wide-ranging subject covering many different aspects of working with data. And within AWS, there are a number of different tools and services that assist with data governance, which we will explore in this section.

The AWS Glue/Lake Formation technical data catalog

The AWS Glue Data Catalog is a technical catalog that provides a logical mapping (databases, tables, and columns) to data that is stored in files in Amazon S3. However, in addition to cataloging data files in Amazon S3, the AWS Glue Data Catalog can also store schema and metadata information about tables in other databases, such as Amazon Redshift, Amazon RDS, Amazon DynamoDB, and more.

Within AWS, there are actually two services for interacting with the data catalog. So far, we have only discussed the **AWS Glue Data Catalog**, but the **AWS Lake Formation** service also provides an interface for the same catalog.

It is important to understand that there is only a single data catalog, but both Glue and Lake Formation provide an interface to the catalog. For example, if we edit the schema of the csvtoparquent table that we created in the hands-on exercise in *Chapter 3*, and use the Glue console to change the data type of the favorite_num column from bigint to int, we will see that reflected in the Lake Formation console as well.

In the following screenshot, we see the csvtoparquent table, showing the schema, in the AWS Glue console.

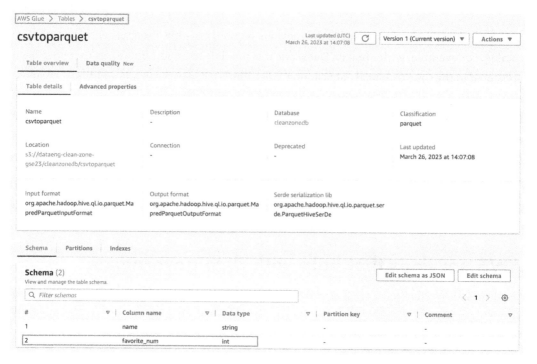

Figure 4.1: AWS Glue console showing table schema

If we look at the same table in the **Lake Formation** console, we can see similar information, including that the current version of this table is Version 1 (this was created when we updated Version 0 by changing the data type for the favorite_num column).

Figure 4.2: AWS Lake Formation console showing table schema

The Lake Formation and Glue consoles are similar in both design and functionality, and so whether you use the Glue or Lake Formation console comes down to personal preference.

The data catalog can be referenced by various analytical tools to work with data in the data lake. For example, Amazon Athena can reference the data catalog to enable users to run queries against databases and tables in the catalog. Athena uses the catalog to get the following information, which is required to query data in the data lake:

- The Amazon S3 location where the underlying data files are stored
- Metadata that indicates the file format type for the underlying files (such as CSV or Parquet)
- Details of the serialization library, which should be used to serialize the underlying data
- Metadata that provides information about the data type for each column in the dataset
- Information about any partitions that are used for the dataset

A data engineer must help put automation in place to ensure that all the datasets that are added to a data lake are cataloged and that the appropriate metadata is added.

In *Chapter 3, The AWS Data Engineers Toolkit,* we discussed AWS Glue Crawlers, a process that can be run to examine a data source, infer the schema of the data source, and then automatically populate the technical data catalog with information on the dataset.

A data engineer should consider building workflows that make use of Glue Crawlers to run after new data is ingested, to have the new data automatically added to the data catalog. Or, when a new data engineering job is being bought into production, a check can be put in place to make sure that the Glue API is used to update the data catalog with details of the new data.

Note that adding data to the technical catalog is a separate process from adding data to a business data catalog. While having data in the Glue/Lake Formation catalog enables many different AWS services to work with the data (such as Amazon Athena, Amazon EMR, etc.), the Glue/Lake Formation interfaces were not designed as business catalogs. As such, they do not provide the best interface for searching for different datasets, or for capturing business-related metadata (such as data owner, confidentiality level, data quality score, etc.). Therefore, to make data discoverable, you need a separate process to ensure that datasets are added to a business catalog.

AWS Glue DataBrew for profiling datasets

As discussed earlier in this chapter, data profiling examines a dataset in order to report on the profile, or shape, of the data. This includes information on each of the columns, such as the number of rows, distinct and unique values, min and max values for number data types, and min and max string length for string data types. It can also report on null or missing values within a column.

In order to generate profile information on a dataset, you can configure and run a **Glue DataBrew** profile job. When the job finishes examining a dataset, you can view information about the data profile within the Glue DataBrew console, and you can generate a JSON file that contains profile information for the dataset.

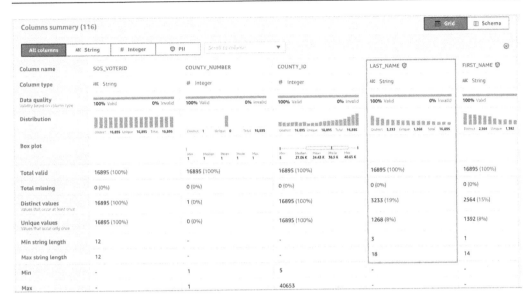

Figure 4.3: AWS Glue DataBrew profiling job results

In the above screenshot, we can see a sample data profile as shown in the AWS Glue DataBrew console. Note that this is just a subset of the data profile information that DataBrew generated, but in this screenshot, we can see, for example, that there is a LAST_NAME column with 16,895 rows. We can further see that there are 3,233 distinct values (last names that occur at least once), as well as 1,268 unique values (last names that occur only once in this dataset). We also see that the shortest last name is 3 characters long, and the longest last name has 18 characters.

AWS Glue Data Quality

The AWS Glue service includes functionality for monitoring and measuring the quality of your datasets. With **AWS Glue Data Quality**, you can either evaluate data that is in S3 and has been cataloged in the Glue Data Catalog, or you can evaluate data as part of a data processing job using **AWS Glue Studio**.

Glue Data Quality is based on the open-source **Deequ data quality framework** and uses the **Data Quality Definition Language (DQDL)** in order to define data quality rules. The following are some of the expressions that you can use in DQDL rules to test the quality of a dataset:

- **ColumnExists** – checks whether a column exists. For example, `ColumnExists "date_of_birth"`.

- **ColumnLength** – checks the length of each row in the column. For example, if your dataset has a postal code/ZIP code column and you know that the ZIP code should always be 5 characters in length, you can write a rule such as `ColumnLength "Postal_Code" = 5`.

- **Completeness** – checks the percentage of non-null rows for the specific column. For example, if you wanted to make sure that at least 95% of the rows in the dataset had a value for email, you could write a rule such as `Completeness "email" > 0.95`.

- **RowCount** – checks that the dataset contains a specified number of rows. This can be within a range, for example, we can check if the dataset has between 10,000 and 15,000 rows with the following rule: `RowCount between 10000 and 15000`.

There are many other rule types that can be used to evaluate data quality, either for data already cataloged in the data catalog or for data being processed with a Glue Studio job. Both Glue Studio and the Glue Data Catalog provide a visual tool for building a set of data quality rules.

In addition, the **AWS Glue DataBrew** service also includes a visual editor for implementing data quality rules to evaluate the quality of your data.

AWS Key Management Service (KMS) for data encryption

AWS KMS simplifies the process of creating and managing security keys for encrypting and decrypting data in AWS. The AWS KMS service is a core service in the AWS ecosystem, enabling users to easily manage data encryption across several AWS services.

There are a large number of AWS services that can work with AWS KMS to enable data encryption, including the following AWS analytical services:

- **Amazon AppFlow**
- **Amazon Athena**
- **Amazon EMR**
- **Amazon Kinesis Data Streams/Kinesis Firehose/Kinesis Video Streams**
- **Amazon Managed Streaming for Kafka (MSK)**
- **Amazon Managed Workflows for Apache Airflow (MWAA)**

- **Amazon Redshift**
- **Amazon S3**
- **AWS Data Migration Service (DMS)**
- **AWS Glue/Glue DataBrew**
- **AWS Lambda**

The full list of compatible services can be found at https://aws.amazon.com/kms/features/#AWS_ Service_Integration.

Permissions can be granted to users to make use of the keys for encrypting and decrypting data, and all use of AWS KMS keys is logged in the AWS CloudTrail service. This enables an organization to easily audit the use of keys to encrypt and decrypt data.

For example, with Amazon S3, you can enable Amazon S3 Bucket Keys, which configures an S3 bucket key to encrypt all new objects in the bucket with an AWS KMS key. This is significantly less expensive than using **Server Side Encryption – KMS (SSE-KMS)** to encrypt each object in a bucket with a unique key.

To learn more about configuring Amazon S3 Bucket Keys, see https://docs.aws.amazon.com/ AmazonS3/latest/userguide/bucket-key.html.

It is important that you carefully protect your KMS keys and that you put safeguards in place to prevent a KMS key from being accidentally (or maliciously) deleted. If a KMS key is deleted, any data that has been encrypted with that key is effectively lost and cannot be decrypted.

Because of this, you must schedule the deletion of your KMS keys and specify a waiting period of between 7 and 30 days before the key is deleted. During this waiting period, the key cannot be used, and you can configure a CloudWatch alarm to notify you if anyone attempts to use the key.

If you use AWS Organizations to manage multiple AWS accounts as part of an organization, you can create a **Service Control Policy (SCP)** to prevent any user (even an administrative user) from deleting KMS keys in child accounts.

Amazon Macie for detecting PII data in Amazon S3 objects

Amazon Macie is a managed service that uses machine learning, along with pattern matching, to discover and protect sensitive data. Amazon Macie identifies sensitive data, such as PII data, in an Amazon S3 bucket and provides alerts to warn administrators about the presence of such sensitive data. Macie can also be configured to launch an automated response to the discovery of sensitive data, such as a step function that runs to automatically remediate the potential security risk.

Macie can identify items such as names, addresses, and credit card numbers that exist in files on S3. These items are generally considered to be PII data, and as discussed previously, these should ideally be tokenized before data processing. Macie can also be configured to recognize custom sensitive data types to alert the user to sensitive data that may be unique to a specific use case.

The AWS Glue Studio Detect PII transform for detecting PII data in datasets

While Amazon Macie detects PII data directly in S3 files, an alternate option is to use the **AWS Glue Studio Detect PII transform** to detect PII data during a data processing job. When creating a job in AWS Glue Studio, you can add the **Detect Sensitive Data** transform and configure it based on your requirements. This includes selecting whether to examine every cell in the dataset for PII data or whether to just sample a limited number of rows for each column to detect PII data. You can also select what to do when PII data is detected, including options for redacting the text (replacing it with a preset string), applying a SHA-256 hash to the value, or just reporting on the PII data that is detected.

Amazon GuardDuty for detecting threats in an AWS account

While **Amazon GuardDuty** is not directly related to analytics on AWS, it is a powerful service that helps protect an AWS account. GuardDuty is an intelligent threat detection service that uses machine learning to monitor your AWS account and provide proactive alerts about malicious activity and unauthorized behavior.

GuardDuty analyzes several AWS-generated logs, including the following:

- CloudTrail S3 data events (a record of all actions taken on S3 objects)
- CloudTrail management events (a record of all usage of AWS APIs within an account)
- VPC flow logs (a record of all network traffic within an AWS VPC)
- DNS logs (a record of all DNS requests within your account)

By continually analyzing these logs to identify unusual access patterns or data access, Amazon GuardDuty can proactively alert you to potential issues, and also helps you automate your response to threats.

AWS Identity and Access Management (IAM) service

AWS IAM is a service that provides both authentication and authorization for the AWS Console, **command-line interface** (**CLI**), and **application programming interface** (**API**) calls.

AWS IAM also supports the federation of identities, meaning that you can configure IAM to use another identity provider for authentication, such as Active Directory or Okta.

Note that this section is not intended as a comprehensive guide to Identity and Access Management on AWS, but it does provide information on foundational concepts that are important for anyone working within the AWS cloud to understand. For a deeper understanding of the AWS IAM service, refer to the *AWS Identity and Access Management user guide* (`https://docs.aws.amazon.com/IAM/latest/UserGuide/introduction.html`).

Several IAM identities are important to understand:

- **AWS account root user**: When you create an AWS account, you provide an email address to be associated with that account, and that email address becomes the root user of the account. You can log in to the AWS Management Console using the root user, and this user has full access to all the resources in the account. However, it is strongly recommended that you do not use this identity to log in and perform everyday tasks, but rather create an IAM user for everyday use.

- **IAM user**: This is an identity that you create and can be used to log in to the AWS Console, run CLI commands, or make API calls. An IAM user can have a login name and password that's used for Console access, and can have up to two associated access keys that can be used to authenticate this identity when using the AWS CLI or API. While you can associate IAM policies directly with an IAM user, the recommended method to provide access to AWS resources is to make the user part of a user group that has relevant IAM policies attached.

- **IAM user groups**: An IAM user group is used to provide permissions that can be associated with multiple IAM users. You provide permissions (via IAM policies) to an IAM user group, and all the members of that group then inherit those permissions.

- **IAM roles**: An IAM role can be confusing at first as it is similar to an IAM user. However, an IAM role does not have a username or password and you cannot directly log in or identify as an IAM role. However, an IAM user can assume the identity of an IAM role, taking on the permissions assigned to that role. An IAM role is also used in identity federation, where a user is authenticated by an external system, and that user identity is then associated with an IAM role. Finally, an IAM role can also be used to provide permissions to AWS resources (for example, to provide permissions to an AWS Lambda function so that the Lambda function can access specific AWS resources).

To grant authorization to access AWS resources, you can attach an **IAM policy** to an IAM user, IAM user group, or IAM role. These policies grant, or deny, access to specific AWS resources, and can also make use of conditional statements to further control access.

These identity-based policies are JSON documents that specify the details of access to an AWS resource. These policies can either be configured within the AWS Management Console, or the JSON documents can be created by hand.

There are three types of identity-based policies that can be utilized:

1. **AWS-managed policies**: These are policies that are created and managed by AWS and provide permissions for common use cases. For example, the `AdministratorAccess` managed policy provides full access to every service and resource in AWS, while the `DatabaseAdministrator` policy provides permissions for setting up, configuring, and maintaining databases in AWS.

2. **Customer-managed policies**: These are policies that you create and manage to provide more precise control over your AWS resources. For example, you can create a policy and attach it to specific IAM users/groups/roles that provide access to a list of specific S3 buckets and limit that access to only be valid during specific hours of the day or for specific IP addresses.

3. **Inline policies**: These are policies that are written directly for a specific user, group, or role. These policies are tied directly to the user, group, or role, and therefore apply to one specific entity only.

The following policy is an example of a customer-managed policy that grants read access to a specific S3 bucket:

```
{
    "Version": "2012-10-17",
    "Statement": [
        {
            "Effect": "Allow",
            "Action": [
                "s3:ListBucket"
            ],
            "Resource": "arn:aws:s3::: de-landing-zone"
        },
    {
            "Effect": "Allow",
            "Action": [
                "s3:GetObject"
            ],
    ],
```

```
                    "Resource": ["arn:aws:s3::: de-landing-zone/*"]
          }
          ]
    }
```

The policy takes the form of a JSON document. In this instance, the policy does the following:

1. Allow access (you can also create policies that Deny access).

2. Allows access for Action of s3:GetObject and s3:ListBucket, meaning authorization is given to run the Amazon S3 GetBucket and ListBucket actions (via the Console, CLI, or API).

3. For ListBucket, the resource is set as the de-landing-zone bucket. For GetObject, the resource is set as de-landing-zone/*. This results in the principal being granted access to list the de-landing-zone bucket, and read access to all the objects inside the de-landing-zone bucket.

You could further limit this policy to only be allowed if the user was connecting from a specific IP address, at a certain time of day, or various other limitations. For example, to limit this permission to users from a specific IP address, you could add the following to the policy:

```
"Condition": {
                "IpAddress": {
                    "aws:SourceIp": [
                        "12.13.15.16/32",
                        "45.44.43.42/32"
                    ]
                }
            }
```

Once you have created a customer-managed policy, you can attach the policy to specific IAM user groups, IAM roles, or IAM users.

Traditional data lakes on AWS used IAM policies to control access to data in an Amazon S3-based data lake. For example, a policy would be created to grant access to different zones of the data lake storage in S3, and then that policy would be attached to different IAM users, user groups, or roles.

However, when creating a large data lake that may contain multiple buckets or S3 prefixes that relate to specific business units, it can be challenging to manage S3 permissions through these JSON policies. Each time a new data lake location is created, the data engineer would need to make sure that the JSON policy document were updated to configure permissions for the new location.

To make managing large S3-based data lakes easier, AWS introduced a service called **AWS Lake Formation**, which enables permissions for the data lake to be controlled by the data lake administrator from within the AWS Management Console (or via the AWS CLI or AWS API).

Using AWS Lake Formation to manage data lake access

AWS Lake Formation is a service that simplifies setting up and managing a data lake. A big part of the Lake Formation service is the ability to manage access (authorization) to data lake databases and tables without having to manage fine-grained access through JSON-based policy documents in the IAM service.

Lake Formation enables a data lake administrator to grant fine-grained permissions on data lake databases, tables, and columns using the familiar database concepts of grant and revoke for permissions management. A data lake administrator, for example, can grant SELECT permissions (effectively READ permission) for a specific data lake table to a specific IAM user or role.

Lake Formation permissions management is another layer of permissions that is useful for managing fine-grained access to data lake resources, but it works with IAM permissions and does not replace IAM permissions. A recommended way to do this is to apply broad permissions to a user or user group in an IAM policy, but then apply fine-grained permissions with Lake Formation.

Permissions management before Lake Formation

Before the release of the Lake Formation service, all data lake permissions were managed at the Amazon S3 level using IAM policy documents written in JSON. These policies would control access to resources such as the following:

- The data catalog objects in the Glue Data Catalog (such as permissions to access Glue databases and tables)
- The underlying physical storage in Amazon S3 (such as the Parquet or CSV files in an Amazon S3 bucket)
- Access to analytical services (such as Amazon Athena or AWS Glue)

For example, the IAM policy would provide several Glue permissions, including the ability to read catalog objects (such as Glue tables and table partitions) and the ability to search tables. However, the resources section of the policy would restrict these permissions to the specific databases and tables that the user should have access to.

The policy would also have a section that provided permissions to the underlying S3 data. For each table that a user needed to access in the Glue Data Catalog, they would need both Glue Data Catalog permissions for the catalog objects, as well as Amazon S3 permissions for the underlying files.

The last part of the IAM policy would also require the user to have access to relevant analytical tools, such as permissions to access the Amazon Athena service.

Permissions management using AWS Lake Formation

With **AWS Lake Formation**, permissions management is changed so that broad access can be provided to Glue catalog objects in the IAM policy, and fine-grained access is controlled via AWS Lake Formation permissions.

With Lake Formation, data lake users do not need to be granted direct permissions on underlying S3 objects as the Lake Formation service can provide temporary credentials to compatible analytic services to access the S3 data.

It is important to note that Lake Formation permissions access only works with compatible analytic services, which, at the time of writing, include the following AWS services:

- Amazon Athena
- Amazon QuickSight
- Amazon EMR
- Amazon Redshift Spectrum
- AWS Glue
- Amazon SageMaker Studio

If using these compatible services, AWS Lake Formation is a simpler way to manage permissions for your data lake. The data lake user still needs an associated IAM policy that grants them access to the AWS Glue service, the Lake Formation service, and any required analytic engines (such as Amazon Athena). However, at the IAM level, the user can be granted access to all AWS Glue objects. Then, the Lake Formation permissions layer can be used to control which specific Glue catalog objects (databases and tables) can be accessed by the user.

As the Lake Formation service passes temporary credentials to compatible analytic services to read data from Amazon S3, data lake users no longer need any direct Amazon S3 permissions to be provided in their IAM policies.

Hands-on — configuring Lake Formation permissions

In this hands-on section, we will use the AWS Management Console to configure **Lake Formation permissions**.

However, before we implement Lake Formation permissions, we're going to create a new data lake user and configure their permissions using just IAM permissions. We'll then go through the process of updating a Glue database and table to use Lake Formation permissions, and then grant Lake Formation permissions to our data lake user.

Configuring the Glue Crawler

While not covered in this chapter, we will provide a hands-on section with details on how to configure the Glue Crawler in *Chapter 6, Ingesting Batch and Streaming Data*.

Creating a new user with IAM permissions

To start, let's create a new IAM user that will become our data lake user. We will initially use IAM to grant our data lake user the following permissions:

- Permission to access a specific database and table in the Glue Data Catalog
- Permission to access specific S3 locations that contain the underlying files associated with our Glue table objects
- Permission to use the Amazon Athena service to run SQL queries against the data lake

First, let's create a new IAM policy that grants the required permissions for using Athena and Glue, but limits those permissions to only the CleanZoneDB in the Glue catalog. To do this, we're going to copy the Amazon-managed policy for Athena Full Access, but we will modify the policy to limit access to just a specific Glue database, and we will add S3 permissions to the policy. Let's get started:

1. Log in to the AWS Management Console and access the IAM service using this link: https://console.aws.amazon.com/iam/home.
2. On the left-hand side, click on **Policies**, and then for **Filter Policies**, type in Athena.
3. From the filtered list of policies, expand the AmazonAthenaFullAccess policy.
4. Click on the **Copy** button to copy the policy to your computer clipboard.

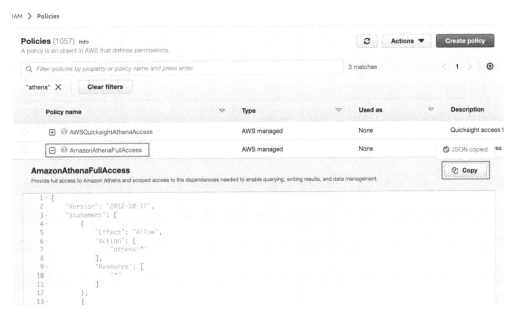

Figure 4.4: Copying the text of the AmazonAthenaFullAccess policy

5. At the top of the page, click on **Create policy**.

6. The visual editor is selected by default, but since we want to create a JSON policy directly, click on the **JSON** tab.

7. Paste the Athena Full Access policy that you copied to the clipboard in *step 4* into the policy, overwriting and replacing any text currently in the policy.

8. Look through the policy to identify the section that grants permissions for several Glue actions (glue:CreateDatabase, glue:DeleteDatabase, glue:getDatabase, and so on). This section currently lists the resource that it applies to as *, meaning that the user would have access to all databases and tables in the Glue catalog. In our use case, we want to limit permissions to just the Glue CleanZoneDB database (which was created in the hands-on section of *Chapter 3, The AWS Data Engineers Toolkit*). Replace the resource section of the section that provides Glue access with the following, which will limit access to the required DB only, although it also includes all tables in that database:

```
"Resource": [
    "arn:aws:glue:*:*:catalog",
    "arn:aws:glue:*:*:database/cleanzonedb",
    "arn:aws:glue:*:*:database/cleanzonedb*",
    "arn:aws:glue:*:*:table/cleanzonedb/*"
]
```

The following screenshot shows how this looks when applied to the policy:

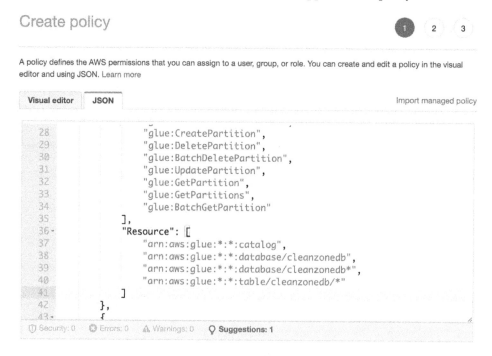

Figure 4.5: Updated policy with limited permissions for Glue resources

9. Immediately after the section that provides Glue permissions, we can add new permissions for accessing the S3 location where our CleanZoneDB data resides. Add the following section to provide these permissions, **making sure to replace <initials> with the unique identifier you used when creating the bucket** in *Chapter 2, Data Management Architectures for Analytics*:

```
{
    "Effect": "Allow",
    "Action": [
        "s3:GetBucketLocation",
        "s3:GetObject",
        "s3:ListBucket",
        "s3:ListBucketMultipartUploads",
        "s3:ListMultipartUploadParts",
        "s3:AbortMultipartUpload",
        "s3:PutObject"
    ],
```

```
        "Resource": [
            "arn:aws:s3:::dataeng-clean-zone-<initials>/*"
        ]
    },
```

The following screenshot shows the S3 permissions added to the policy:

| Visual editor | JSON | Import managed policy |

```
39              arn:aws:glue:*:*:database/cleanzonedb*,
40              "arn:aws:glue:*:*:table/cleanzonedb/*"
41          ]
42      },
43 ▾    {
44          "Effect": "Allow",
45 ▾        "Action": [
46              "s3:GetBucketLocation",
47              "s3:GetObject",
48              "s3:ListBucket",
49              "s3:ListBucketMultipartUploads",
50              "s3:ListMultipartUploadParts",
51              "s3:AbortMultipartUpload",
52              "s3:PutObject"
53          ],
54 ▾        "Resource": [
55              "arn:aws:s3:::dataeng-clean-zone-gse23/*"
56          ]
57      },
58 ▾    {
59          "Effect": "Allow",
60 ▾        "Action": [
61              "s3:GetBucketLocation",
```

ⓘ Security: 0   ⊗ Errors: 0   ⚠ Warnings: 0   ♡ Suggestions: 1

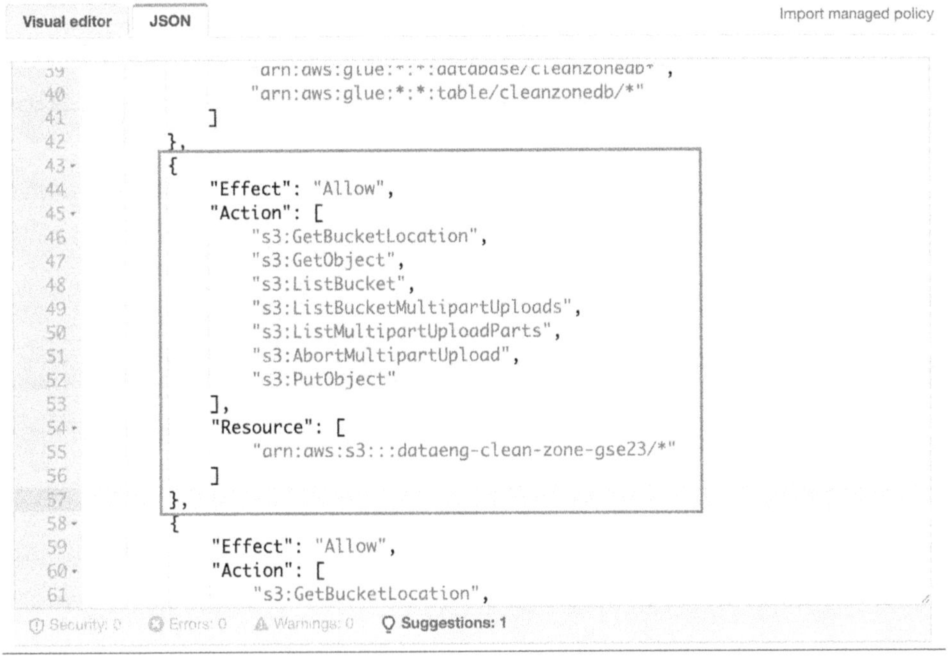

Figure 4.6: S3 permissions added to the policy

10. Once you have pasted in the new S3 permissions, click on **Next:Tags** at the bottom right of the screen.

11. Optionally, add any tags for this policy, and then click on **Next: Review**.

12. For Name, provide a policy name of AthenaAccessCleanZoneDB and click **Create policy**.

Now that we have created an IAM policy for providing the required permissions to the Glue catalog and S3 buckets, we can create a new data lake user and attach our new policy to the user.

Note that AWS recommends the use of **IAM Identity Center** to manage users in your AWS account, and this should be strongly considered when creating users in production, and even development, accounts. However, for our purposes, where we are using a single-purpose sandbox-type account for performing the hands-on exercises in this book, we will create an IAM user as this is a simpler setup.

Follow these steps to create the new IAM user:

1. In the IAM console, on the left-hand side, click on **Users**, and then click **Add users**.

2. For **User name**, enter datalake-user.

3. Click the checkbox for **Provide user access to the AWS Management Console - optional**.

4. Select the **I want to create an IAM user** option.

5. Select your preferred options for creating a password, and then click **Next**.

6. On the **Set permissions** page, select **Attach policies directly**.

7. In the **Permission policies** search bar, search for **Athena** and select the **AthenaAccess-CleanZoneDB** policy, which we created in the previous set of steps.

8. Click **Next**.

9. Review the new user details, and then click **Create user**.

10. Take note of the **Console sign-in URL**, which can be used to access the login screen for your account.

Now, let's create a new Amazon S3 bucket that we can use to capture the results of any Amazon Athena queries that we run:

1. In the AWS Management Console, use the top search bar to search for and select the **S3** service.

2. Click on **Create bucket**.

3. For **Bucket name**, enter aws-athena-query-results-dataengbook-<initials>. Replace <initials> with your initials or some other unique identifier.

4. Ensure **AWS Region** is set to the region you have been using for the other exercises in this book.

5. Leave all other options with their defaults, and click on **Create bucket**.

We can now verify that our new datalake-user has access to CleanZoneDB and that the user can run Athena queries on the table in this database:

1. Sign out of the AWS Management Console, and then sign in again using the new user you just created, datalake-user. Use the **Console sign-in URL** you previously noted down to access the login page.

2. From the top search bar, search for and select the **Athena** service.

3. Before you can run an Athena query, you need to set up a query result location in Amazon S3. This is the S3 bucket and prefix where all the query results will be written to. From the top right of the Athena console, click on **Edit Settings**.

4. For **Query result location**, enter the S3 path you created in *the previous Step 3* (for example, s3://aws-athena-query-results-dataengbook-<initials>/).

5. Click on **Save**.

6. Change to the **Editor** tab, and in the query window, run the following SQL query: select * from cleanzonedb.csvtoparquet.

7. If all permissions have been configured correctly, the results of the query should be displayed in the lower window. The file we created shows names and ages.

8. Log out of the AWS Management Console since we need to be logged in as our regular user, not datalake-user, for the next steps.

We have now set up permissions for our data lake using IAM policies to manage fine-grained access control, as was always done before the launch of the AWS Lake Formation service. In the next section, we will transition to using Lake Formation to manage fine-grained permissions on data lake objects.

Transitioning to managing fine-grained permissions with AWS Lake Formation

In the initial setup, we configured permissions for our data lake user to be able to run SQL queries using Amazon Athena, and we restricted their access to just cleanzonedb using an IAM permissions policy.

In this section, we are going to modify cleanzonedb and the tables in that database to make use of the Lake Formation permissions model.

Activating Lake Formation permissions for a database and table

As a reminder, **Lake Formation** adds a layer of permissions that work in addition to the IAM policy permissions. By default, every database and table in the catalog has a special permission enabled that effectively tells Lake Formation to just use IAM permissions and to ignore any permissions that may have been granted in Lake Formation. This is sometimes called the **Pass-Through** permission, as it allows security checks to be validated at the IAM level, but then passes through Lake Formation without doing any additional permission checks.

With our initial setup, we granted Glue Data Catalog permissions to datalake-user in an IAM policy. This policy allowed the user to access the cleanzonedb database, as well as all the tables in that database. Let's have a look at how permissions are set up on the cleanzonedb database and tables in Lake Formation:

1. Log in to the **AWS Management Console** and search for the Lake Formation service in the top search bar. Make sure you are logged in as your regular user, and not as datalake-user, which you created earlier in this chapter.

2. The first time you access the Lake Formation service, a **pop-up box** will prompt you to choose initial users and roles to be Lake Formation data lake administrators. By default, **Add myself** should be selected. Click **Get started** to add your current user as a data lake admin.

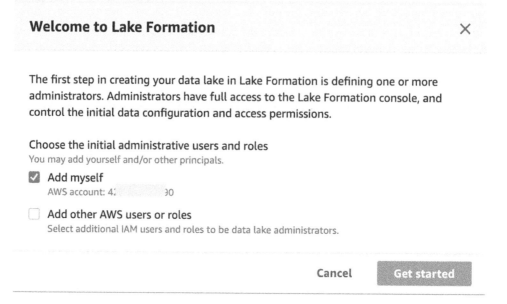

Figure 4.7: Adding your user as a Lake Formation administrator

3. Once selected, you should be taken to the Lake Formation **Data lake administrators** screen, where you can confirm that your user has been added as a data lake administrator.

4. On the left-hand side of the Lake Formation console, click on **Databases**. In the list of databases, click on the cleanzonedb database.

5. This screen displays details of cleanzonedb. Click on **Actions**, and then **View permissions**.

6. On the **View permissions** screen, we can see that two permissions have been assigned for this database. The first one is DataEngLambdaS3CWGlueRole, and this IAM role has been granted full permissions on the database. The reason for this is that DataEngLambdaS3CWGlueRole was the role that was assigned to the Lambda function that we used to create the database back in *Chapter 3, The AWS Data Engineers Toolkit*, so it is automatically granted these permissions.

Figure 4.8: Lake Formation permissions for the cleanzonedb database

The other permission that we can see is for the IAMAllowedPrincipals group. This is the pass-through permission we mentioned previously, which effectively means that permissions at the Lake Formation layer are ignored. If this special permission was not assigned, only DataEngLambdaS3CWGlueRole would be able to access the database. However, because the permission has been assigned, any user who has been granted permissions to this database through an IAM policy, such as datalake-user, will be able to successfully access the database.

7. To enable Lake Formation permissions on this database, we can remove the `IAMAllowedPrincipals` permission from the database. To do this, click the selector box for the `IAMAllowedPrincipals` permission and click **Revoke**. On the pop-up box, click on **Revoke**.

8. We now want to do the same thing for our `csvtoparquet` table in the database. To do this, click on **Databases** in the left-hand menu, then click on `cleanzonedb`. From the top right, click on **View tables**. Click the selector for the `csvtoparquet` table and click on **Actions/ View Permissions**. Click the selector for `IAMAllowedPrincipals` and click on **Revoke**. On the pop-up window, click on **Revoke**. This removes the special **Pass-Through** permission from the table.

Optional - checking permissions

If you want to see what effect this has, you can log out of the AWS Console and log in again as `datalake-user`. Now, when you try to run a query on the `csvtoparquet` table using Athena, you will receive an error message as Lake Formation permissions are in effect, and your `datalake-user` has not been granted permissions to access the table yet via Lake Formation.

Granting Lake Formation permissions

By removing the `IAMAllowedPrincipals` permission from the `cleanzonedb` database and the `csvtoparquet` table, we have effectively enabled Lake Formation permissions on those resources. Now, if any principal needs to access that database or table, they need both IAM permissions, as well as Lake Formation permissions.

If we had enabled Lake Formation permissions on all databases and tables, then we could modify our user's IAM policy permissions to give them access to all data catalog objects. We can do this because we would know that they would only be able to access those databases and tables where they had been granted specific Lake Formation permissions.

We previously created an edited copy of the `AmazonAthenaFullAccess` managed IAM policy to limit user access to specific data catalog databases and tables in the IAM policy. However, if all databases and tables had the `IAMAllowedPrincipals` permission removed and specific permissions granted to users instead, then we could apply the generic `AmazonAthenaFullAccess` policy.

We also previously provided access to the underlying S3 files using an IAM policy. However, when using Lake Formation permissions, compatible analytic tools are granted access to the underlying S3 data using temporary credentials provided by Lake Formation. Therefore, once Lake Formation permissions have been activated, we can remove permissions to the underlying S3 data from our user's IAM policy. Then, when using a compatible tool such as Amazon Athena, we know that Lake Formation will grant Athena temporary credentials to access the underlying S3 data.

Here, we will add specific Lake Formation permissions for our datalake-user to access the CleanZoneDB database and the csvtoparquet table:

1. Ensure you are logged in as your regular user (the one you made a data lake admin earlier) and access the Lake Formation console.
2. Click on **CleanZoneDB**, and then click **View tables**.
3. Click on the **csvtoparquet** table, and then click **Actions/Grant**.
4. From the **IAM users and roles** dropdown, click on the **datalake-user** principal.
5. For **Table permissions**, mark the permission for **Select**.
6. Under **Data permissions**, select **Column-based access**.
7. Select **Exclude columns**, and then under **Select columns**, select the favorite_num column.
8. Click on **Grant** at the bottom of the screen.

In the preceding steps, we granted our datalake-user **Select** permissions on the csvtoparquet table. However, we put in a column limitation, which means that datalake-user will not be able to access the favorite_num column. Enabling column-level permissions is not something that would be possible if we were just using IAM-level permissions, as column-level permissions is a Lake Formation-specific feature.

Now, if you log in to the AWS Management Console as datalake-user and run the same Athena query we ran previously (select * from cleanzonedb.csvtoparquet), your permissions will enable the required access.

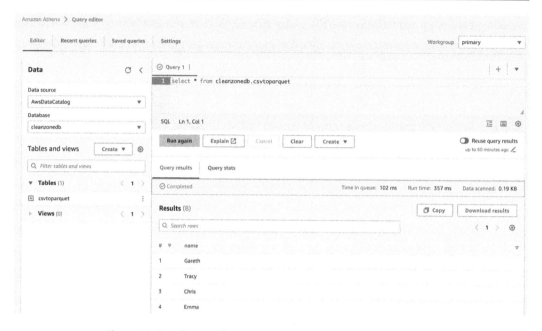

Figure 4.9: Running an Athena query with Lake Formation permissions

Note that in the results of the query, the `favorite_num` column is not included as we specifically excluded this column when granting permissions on this table to our `datalake-user`.

In this section, we transitioned to using Lake Formation for managing data lake permissions for the `cleanzonedb` database. We added fine-grained permissions in Lake Formation to limit `cleanzonedb` access to just our `datalake-user`, and excluded the `favorite_num` column from the list of columns that our user could query.

Summary

In this chapter, we reviewed important concepts around the many different aspects of data governance, including how a data catalog can be used to help prevent your data lake from becoming a data swamp.

We reviewed data profiling, data quality, and data lineage as important aspects of data governance, as well as an introduction to how to ensure that your data is secured correctly and used in accordance with relevant regulations (such as GDPR). Ensuring that your data is used correctly and that it offers the most value to your organization does not just happen, but rather requires a strong data governance program and focus.

In the next chapter, we will take a step back and look at the bigger picture of how a data engineer can architect a data pipeline. We will begin exploring how to understand the needs of our data consumers, learn more about our data sources, and review the transformations that are required to transform raw data into useful data for analytics.

Learn more on Discord

To join the Discord community for this book – where you can share feedback, ask questions to the author, and learn about new releases – follow the QR code below:

`https://discord.gg/9s5mHNyECd`

Section 2

Architecting and Implementing Data Engineering Pipelines and Transformations

In this section of the book, we examine an approach for architecting a high-level data pipeline and then dive into the specifics of data ingestion and transformation. We will examine different types of data consumers, learn about the important role of data marts and data warehouses, and finally put it all together by orchestrating our own data pipelines. We get hands-on with various AWS services for data ingestion (Amazon Kinesis and DMS), transformation (AWS Glue Studio), consumption (AWS Glue DataBrew), and pipeline orchestration (Step Functions).

This section comprises the following chapters:

- *Chapter 5, Architecting Data Engineering Pipelines*
- *Chapter 6, Ingesting Batch and Streaming Data*
- *Chapter 7, Transforming Data to Optimize for Analytics*
- *Chapter 8, Identifying and Enabling Data Consumers*
- *Chapter 9, A Deeper Dive into Data Marts and Amazon Redshift*
- *Chapter 10, Orchestrating the Data Pipeline*

5

Architecting Data Engineering Pipelines

Having gained an understanding of data engineering principles, the core concepts, and the available AWS tools, we can now put these together in the form of a data pipeline. A data pipeline is the process that ingests data from multiple sources, optimizes and transforms it, and makes it available to data consumers. An important function of the data engineering role is the ability to design, or architect, these pipelines.

In this chapter, we will cover the following topics:

- Approaching the task of architecting a data pipeline
- Identifying data consumers and understanding their requirements
- Identifying data sources and ingesting data
- Identifying data transformations and optimizations
- Loading data into data marts
- Wrapping up the whiteboarding session
- Hands-on – architecting a sample pipeline

Technical requirements

For the hands-on portion of this lab, we will design a high-level pipeline architecture. You can perform this activity on an actual whiteboard, a piece of paper, or using a free online tool called *diagrams.net*. If you want to make use of this online tool, make sure you can access the tool at `http://diagrams.net`.

You can find the code files of this chapter in the GitHub repository using the following link: `https://github.com/PacktPublishing/Data-Engineering-with-AWS-2nd-edition/tree/main/Chapter05`.

Approaching the data pipeline architecture

Before we get into the details of the individual components that will go into the architecture, it is helpful to get a 10,000 ft view of what we're trying to do.

A common mistake when starting a new data engineering project is to try and do everything at once, creating a solution that covers all use cases. A better approach is to identify an initial, specific use case and start the project while focusing on that one outcome, but keeping the bigger picture in mind.

This can be a significant challenge, and yet it is really important to get this balance right. While you need to focus on an achievable outcome that can be completed within a reasonable time frame, you also need to ensure that you build within a framework that can be used for future projects. If each business unit tackles the challenge of data analytics independently, with no corporation-wide analytics initiative, it will be difficult to unlock the value of corporation-wide data.

An ideal project will include sponsorship from the highest levels of an organization but will identify a limited-scope project to build an initial framework. This project, when completed, can be used as an internal case study to drive forward additional analytic projects.

In the 1989 film *Field of Dreams*, a farmer (played by Kevin Costner) hears a voice saying

> *"If you build it, he will come."*

Everyone in the town thinks he is crazy when he ends up sacrificing his crops to build a baseball field, but when he does, several long-dead baseball players come to the field to play. In business, a common mantra is the following:

> *"If you build it, they will come."*

This implies that if you build something really good, you will find customers for it. However, this is not a recommended approach for building data analytic solutions.

Some organizations may have hundreds, or even thousands, of data sources, and many of those data sources may be useful for centralized analytics. But that doesn't mean we should attempt to immediately ingest them all into our analytics platform so that we can see how a business may use them. When organizations have taken this approach, embarking on multi-year-long projects to build out large analytic solutions covering many different initiatives, they have often failed.

Rather, once executive sponsorship has been gained and an initial project with limited scope has been identified, the data engineer can begin the process of designing a data pipeline for the project.

Architecting houses and pipelines

If you were to build a new house, you would identify an appropriate piece of land and then contract an architect to work with you to create the plans for the building. The architect would do several things:

- Discuss your requirements with you (how you want to use the home, what materials you would like, how many bedrooms and bathrooms, and so on).
- Gather information on the land where you will be building (the size of the land, slope, and so on).
- Determine the type of materials that are best suited to build in that environment.

As part of this, the architect may create a rough sketch showing the high-level plan. Once that high-level plan is agreed upon, the architect can gather more detailed information and then create a detailed architectural plan. This plan would include the layout of the rooms, and then where the shower, toilet, lights, and so on would go and, based on that, where the plumbing and electrical lines would run.

For a data engineer creating the architecture for a data pipeline, a similar approach can be used:

- Gather information from project sponsors and data consumers on their requirements. Learn what their objectives are, what types of tools they want to use to consume the data, the required data transformations, and so on.
- Gather information on the available data sources. This may include what systems store the raw data, what format that data is in, who the system and data owner are, and so on.
- Determine what types of tools are available and which may be best suited for these requirements.

A useful way to gather this information is to conduct a whiteboarding session with the relevant stakeholders.

Whiteboarding as an information-gathering tool

Running a whiteboarding session with relevant stakeholders enables a data engineer to develop a high-level plan for the data pipeline, helping to gather the information required to start working on the detailed design. The purpose of the whiteboarding exercise is not to work out all the technical details and finalize the specific services and tools that will be used. Rather, the purpose is to agree with stakeholders on the overall approach for the pipeline and to gather the information that's required for the detailed design.

In this book, we will use an architectural approach, where we ingest data into an Amazon S3-based data lake. Data is initially ingested into a raw zone, and then we transform and optimize the data using several tools to move the data through different data lake zones. As we covered in *Chapter 2, Data Management Architectures for Analytics*, a data lake has multiple zones that the data moves through. Typically, this includes zones such as *raw*, *transformed*, *conformed*, and *enriched*, but a data lake can also include zones such as *staging* and *inference* (for data science purposes). There is no specific number of zones that a data lake requires, as zones should be based on business requirements, but for our whiteboarding session, we will show three zones.

Depending on data consumption requirements, we can then load subsets of the data into various data marts (such as Amazon Redshift, a cloud data warehouse service), making the data available to data consumers via various services.

The following diagram illustrates a high-level overview of the primary components of a typical data pipeline and the approach to developing the high-level pipeline architecture. Note that the diagram below shows data coming in on the left, and data consumers accessing the data on the right, which is a logical layout to understand the pipeline (data must be ingested before it can be consumed). However, when we approach designing the pipeline, we work backward, starting with the requirements of our data consumers, before then looking at data sources, and finally, meeting in the middle by looking at the required data transformations.

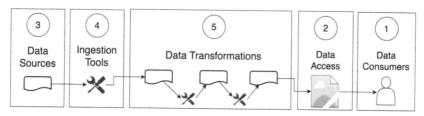

Figure 5.1: High-level overview of a data pipeline architecture

When approaching the design of the pipeline, we can use the following sequence (which is also reflected by the numbers in the preceding diagram):

- Understanding the business objectives, who the data consumers are, and their requirements
- Determining the types of tools that data consumers will use to access the data
- Understanding which potential data sources may be available
- Determining the types of toolsets that will be used to ingest data
- Understanding the required data transformations at a high level to take the raw data and prepare it for data consumers

As you can see, we should always work backward when designing a pipeline – that is, we should start with the data consumers and their requirements, and then work from there to design our pipeline.

Conducting a whiteboarding session

Once an initial project has been identified, the data engineer should bring together relevant stakeholders for a workshop to whiteboard the high-level approach. Ideally, all stakeholders should meet in person, have a whiteboard available, and should plan for a half-day workshop. Stakeholders should include a group of people that can answer the following questions:

- Who is the executive sponsor, and what is the business value and objective of the project?
- Who is going to be working directly with the data (the data consumers)? What types of tools are the data consumers likely to use to access the data?
- What are the relevant raw data sources?
- At a high level, what types of transformations are required to transform and optimize the raw data?

The data engineer needs to understand the business objectives, and not just gather technical information during this workshop. A good place to start is to ask for a business sponsor to provide an overview of current challenges, and to review the expected business outcomes, or objectives, for the project. Also, ask about any existing solutions or related projects, as well as any gaps or issues with those current solutions.

Once the team has a good understanding of the business value, the data engineer can begin white-boarding to put together the high-level design. We will work backward from our understanding of the business value of the project, which involves learning how the end-state data will be used to provide business value, and who the consumers of the data will be. From there, we can start understanding the raw data sources that will be needed to create the end-state data, and then develop a high-level plan for the types of transformations that may be required.

Let's start by identifying who our data consumers are and understanding their requirements.

Identifying data consumers and understanding their requirements

A typical organization is likely to have multiple different categories, or types, of data consumers. We discussed some of these roles in *Chapter 1, An Introduction to Data Engineering*, but let's review them again:

- **Business users**: A business user generally wants to access data via interactive dashboards and other visualization types. For example, a sales manager may want to see a chart showing last week's sales by sales rep, geographic area, or top product categories.

- **Business applications**: In some use cases, the data pipeline that the data engineer builds will be used to power other business applications. For example, Spotify, the streaming music application, provides users with an in-app summary of their listening habits at the end of each year (top songs, top genres, total hours of music streamed, and so on). Read the following Spotify blog post to learn more about how the Spotify data team enabled this: https://engineering.atspotify.com/2020/02/18/spotify-unwrapped-how-we-brought-you-a-decade-of-data/.

- **Data analyst**: A data analyst is often tasked with doing more complex data analysis, digging deeper into large datasets to answer specific questions. For example, across all customers, you may be wondering which products are most popular by different age or socio-economic demographics. Alternatively, you may be wondering what percentage of customers have browsed the company's e-commerce store more than 5 times, for more than 10 minutes at a time, and in the last 2 weeks but have not purchased anything. These users generally use structured query languages such as SQL.

- **Data scientist**: A data scientist is tasked with creating machine learning models that can identify non-obvious patterns in large datasets, or make predictions about future behavior based on historical data. To do this, data scientists need access to large quantities of raw data that they can use to train their machine learning models.

During the whiteboarding workshop, the data engineer should ask questions to understand who the data consumers are for the identified project. As part of this, it is important to also understand the types of tools each data consumer is likely to want to use to access data.

As information is discovered, it can be added to the whiteboard, as illustrated in the following diagram:

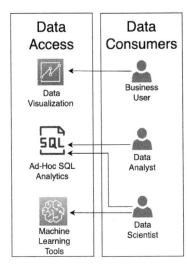

- **BUSINESS USERS:** This project will enable sales operations teams across the country. Total users appeox 25 - 30. They want easy access to summarized data via a data visualization tool that lets them filter, drill-down, work with different graphs, etc. Some of this have experience with Tableau for visualization, but we do not currently have enough licenses for all business users. Open to exploring alternate tools.

- **DATA ANALYSTS:** A team of 4 - 6 data analysts will be responsible for creating reports and drawing insights from the data that iwll be delivered to senior Sales Management. This team has in using SQL.

- **DATA SCIENTISTS:** A team of 2 - 3 data scientists will be tasked with creating Machine Learning models base don historical data that is part of this project. This team wants SQL access for exploring the data, as well as access to specialized machine learning tools.

Figure 5.2: Whiteboarding data consumers and data access

In this example, we can see that we have identified three different data consumers – a data analyst team, a data science team, and various business users. We have also identified the following:

- That the data analysts want to use ad hoc SQL queries to access data
- That the data science team wants to use both ad hoc SQL queries and specialized machine learning tools to access data
- That the business users want to use a **Business Intelligence** (BI) data visualization tool to access data

It is useful to ask whether there are any existing corporate standard tools that the data consumer must use, but it is not important to finalize the toolsets at this point. For example, we should take note if a team already has experience with Tableau (a common BI application) and whether they want to use it for data visualization reporting. However, if they have not identified a specific toolset to use, that can be finalized at a later stage.

Once we have a good understanding of who the data consumers are for the project, and the types of tools they want to use to work with data, we can move on to the next stage of whiteboarding, which is to examine the available data sources and means to ingest the data.

Identifying data sources and ingesting data

With an understanding of the overall business goals for the project, and having identified our data consumers, we can start exploring the available data sources.

While most data sources will be internal to an organization, some projects may require enriching organization-owned data with other third-party data sources. Today, there are many data marketplaces where diverse datasets can be subscribed to or, in some cases, accessed for free. When discussing data sources, both internal and external datasets should be considered.

The team that has been included in the workshop should include people who understand the data sources required for the project. Some of the information that the data engineer needs to gather about these data sources includes the following:

- Details about the source system containing data (is the data in a database, in files on a server, existing files on Amazon S3, coming from a streaming source, and so on)?

- If this data is internal data, who is the owner of the source system within the business? Who is the owner of the data?

- What frequency does the data need to be ingested on (continuous streaming/replication, loading data every few hours, or loading data once a day)?

- Optionally, discuss some potential tools that could be used for data ingestion.

- What is the raw/ingested format of the data (CSV, JSON, a native database format, and so on)?

- Does the data source contain PII or other data types that are subject to governance controls? If so, what controls need to be put in place to protect the data?

As information is discovered, it can be captured on the whiteboard, as illustrated in the following diagram:

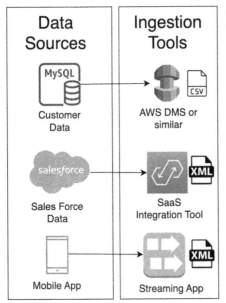

- **CUSTOMER DATA:** Stored in MySQL database. **System owner:** Database Team. **Data owner:** Marketing Team. **Data Load Frequency:** Daily. **Ingestion:** Investigate DMS for replication with Glue job to consolidate changes.

- **SALESFORCE DATA:** Company has Salesforce SaaS subscription. Project needs opportunity data loaded from Sales Force. **System owner:** Salesforce Admin team. **Data owner:** Enterprise Sales Team. **Data Load Frequency:** Hourly. **Ingestion:** SaaS Integration Tool (AWS AppFlow or Salesforce dataloader.io are possibilities)

- **MOBILE APP:** Need to ingest metrics in real-time from companies mobile app used by sales team. **System owner:** AppDev team. **Data owner:** Enterprise Sales Team. **Data Load Frequency:** Near real-time. **Ingestion:** Streaming service (Kinesis or MSK are possibilities).

Figure 5.3: Whiteboarding data sources and data ingestion

During the whiteboarding process, additional notes should be captured to provide more context or detail about the requirements. These can be captured directly on the whiteboard or captured separately.

In this example, we have identified three different data sources – customer data from a MySQL database, opportunity information from Salesforce, and near-real-time sales metrics from the organization's mobile application. We have also identified the following:

- The IT team that owns each source system and the business team that owns the data
- The velocity of ingesting the data (how often each data source needs to be ingested)
- Potential services that can be used to ingest the data

When discussing ingestion tools, it may be worthwhile to capture potential tools if you have a good idea of which tool may be suitable. However, the objective of this session is not to come up with a final architecture and decision on all technical components.

Additional sessions (as discussed later in this book) will be used to thoroughly evaluate potential toolsets against requirements and should be done in close consultation with source system owners.

During this whiteboarding session, we have worked backward, first identifying the data consumers, and then the data sources we plan to use. At this point, we can move on to the next phase of whiteboarding, which is to examine some of the data transformations that we plan to use to optimize the data for analytics.

Identifying data transformations and optimizations

In a typical data analytics project, we ingest data from multiple data sources and then perform transforms on those datasets to optimize them for the required analytics.

In *Chapter 7, Transforming Data to Optimize for Analytics,* we will do a deeper dive into typical transformations and optimizations, but we will provide a high-level overview of the most common transformations here.

File format optimizations

CSV, XML, JSON, and other types of plaintext files are commonly used to store structured and semi-structured data. These file formats are useful when manually exploring data, but there are much better, binary-based file formats to use for computer-based analytics. A common binary format that is optimized for read-heavy analytics (such as by compressing data and adding in useful metadata to optimize data reads) is the *Apache Parquet* format. A common transformation is to convert plaintext files into an optimized format, such as Apache Parquet.

Data standardization

When building out a pipeline, we often load data from multiple different data sources, and each of those data sources may have different naming conventions that refer to the same item. For example, a field containing someone's birth date may be called *DOB, dateOfBirth, birth_date,* and so on. The format of the birth date may also be stored as *mm/dd/yy, dd/mm/yyyy,* or in a multitude of other formats.

One of the tasks we may want to do when optimizing data for analytics is to standardize column names, types, and formats. By having a corporate-wide analytic program, standard definitions can be created and adopted across all analytic projects in an organization.

Data quality checks

Another aspect of data transformation may be the process of verifying data quality and alerting on any ingested data that does not meet the expected quality standards.

Data partitioning

A common optimization strategy for analytics is to partition data, grouping it at the physical storage layer by a field that is often used in queries. For example, if data is often queried by a date range, then it can be partitioned by a date field. If storing sales data, for example, all the sales transactions for a specific month would be stored in the same Amazon S3 prefix (which is very much like a directory). When a query is run that selects all the data for a specific day, the analytic engine only needs to read the data in the directory that stores data for the relevant month.

Data denormalization

In traditional relational database systems, data is normalized, meaning that each table contains information on a specific focused topic, and associated, or related, information is contained in a separate table. The tables can then be linked through the use of foreign keys.

In data lakes, combining data from multiple tables into a single table can often improve query performance. Data denormalization takes two (or more) tables and creates a new table, with data from both tables.

Data cataloging

Another important component that we should include in the transformation section of our pipeline architecture is the process of cataloging the dataset. During this process, we ensure that all the datasets in the data lake are added to the technical data catalog, and additional business metadata can be added to the business data catalog.

Now that we have an understanding of the common types of transformations, let's look at how this is applied to our whiteboarding session.

Whiteboarding data transformation

For the whiteboarding session, we do not need to determine all the details of the required transformations, but it is useful to agree on the main transformations for the high-level pipeline design.

Some of the information that the data engineer needs to gather about expected data transformations during the whiteboarding session includes the following:

- Is there an existing set of standardized column name definitions and formats that can be referenced? If not, who will be responsible for creating these standard definitions?

- What additional business metadata should be captured for datasets? For example, data owner, column descriptions, cost allocation tags, data sensitivity, and so on.

- What format should optimized files be stored in? Apache Parquet is a common format, but you need to validate that the tools used by the data consumers can work with files in Apache Parquet format.

- Is there an obvious field that data should be partitioned by?

- Are other required data transformations obvious at this point? For example, if you ingest data from a relational database, should the data be denormalized?

- What data transformation engines/skills does the team have? For example, does the team have experience creating Spark jobs using PySpark?

As information is discovered, it can be captured on the whiteboard, as illustrated in the following diagram:

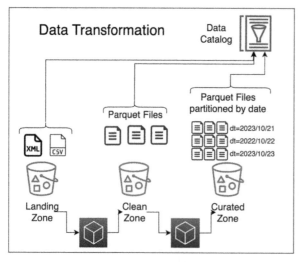

Data is ingested into the landing zone in raw format (CSV and XML)

- Quality checks are performed and data standardized. Data files are also converted to Parquet format. Resulting files are written to the clean zone.

- Data from relational database tables are denormalized based on use case requirements. New tables are enriched with additional data. Data is partitioned by year and month and written to the curated zone.

- As files are written into each zone, teh data is catalogged and meta-data is written to the data catalog.

- The team does have previous experience with creating Spark ETL jobs written in PySpark.

Figure 5.4: Whiteboarding data transformation

In this example, we create a data lake with three zones – the landing zone, the clean zone, and the curated zone (as previously discussed in *Chapter 2, Data Management Architectures for Analytics*):

- Raw files are ingested into the landing zone and will be in plaintext formats such as CSV and XML. When the files are ingested, information about the files is captured in the data catalog, along with additional business metadata (data owner, data sensitivity, and so on).

- We haven't identified a specific data transformation engine at this point, but we did capture a note indicating that the team has previous experience in creating Spark ETL jobs using PySpark. This means that AWS Glue may be a good solution for data transformation, but we will do further validation of this at a later stage.

- As part of our pipeline, we will have a process to run data quality checks on the data in the landing zone. If the quality checks pass, we will standardize the data (uniform column names and data types) and convert the files into Apache Parquet format, writing out the new files in the clean zone. Again, we will add the newly written-out files to our data catalog, including relevant business metadata.

- Another piece of our pipeline will now perform additional transformations on the data, as per the specific use case requirements. For example, data from a relational database will be denormalized, and tables can be enriched with additional data. We will write out the transformed data to the curated zone, partitioning the files by date as they are written out. Again, we will add the newly written-out files to our data catalog, including the relevant business metadata.

It's important to remember that the goal of this session is not to work out all the technical details but, rather, to create a high-level overview of the pipeline. In the preceding diagram, we did not specify that AWS Glue will be the transformation engine. We know that AWS Glue may be a good fit, but it's not important to make that decision now.

We have indicated a potential partitioning strategy based on date, but this is also something that will need further validation. To determine the best partitioning strategy, you need a good understanding of the queries that will be run against the dataset. In this whiteboarding session, it is unlikely that there will be time to get into those details, but after the initial discussion, this appeared to be a good way to partition data, so we have included it.

Having determined transformations for our data, we will move on to the last step of the whiteboarding process, which is determining whether we will require any data marts.

Loading data into data marts

Many tools can work directly with data in the data lake, as we covered in *Chapter 3, The AWS Data Engineer's Toolkit*. These include tools for ad hoc SQL queries (Amazon Athena), data processing tools (such as Amazon EMR and AWS Glue), and even specialized machine learning tools (such as Amazon SageMaker).

These tools read data directly from Amazon S3, but there are times when a use case may require much lower latency and higher performance reads of the data. Alternatively, there may be times when the use of highly structured schemas may best meet the analytic requirements of the use case. In these cases, loading data from the data lake into a data mart makes sense.

In analytic environments, a data mart is most often a data warehouse system (such as Amazon Redshift or Snowflake), but it could also be a relational database system (such as Amazon RDS for MySQL), depending on the use case's requirements. In either case, the system will have local storage (often high-speed flash drives) and local compute power, offering the best performance when you need to query across large datasets and specifically, when queries require joining across many tables.

As part of the whiteboarding session, you should spend some time discussing whether a data mart may be best suited to load a subset of data. For example, if you expect a large number of users to use your BI tool (for data visualizations), you may spend some time discussing which data will be used the most by these teams. You could then include a note in your whiteboarding session, about loading a subset of the data into a data warehouse system and connecting the data visualization tool to the data warehouse.

Wrapping up the whiteboarding session

After completing the whiteboarding session, you should have a high-level overview architecture that illustrates the main components of the pipeline that you plan to build. At this point, there will still be a lot of questions that have been left unanswered, and there will not be a lot of specific details. However, the high-level architecture should be enough to get broad agreement from stakeholders on the proposed plans for the project. It should have also provided you with enough information that you can start on a detailed design and set up follow-up sessions as required.

Some of the information that you should have after the session includes the following:

- A good understanding of who the data consumers for this project will be
- For each category of data consumer, a good idea of what type of tools they would use to access the data (SQL, visualization tools, and so on)
- An understanding of the internal and external data sources that will be used
- For each data source, an understanding of the requirements for data ingestion frequency (daily, hourly, or near-real-time streaming, for example)
- For each data source, a list of who owns the data and the source system containing the data
- A high-level understanding of likely data transformations
- An understanding of whether loading a subset of data into a data warehouse or other data marts may be required

After the session, you should create a final high-level architecture diagram and include notes from the meeting. These notes should be distributed to all participants to request their approval and agreement on moving forward with the project, based on the draft architecture.

Once an agreement has been reached on the high-level approach, additional sessions will be needed with the different teams to capture additional details and fully examine the requirements.

The final high-level architecture diagram, based on the scenario we have looked at in this chapter, may look as follows:

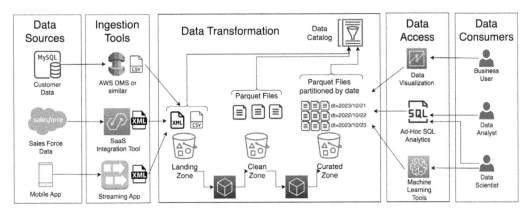

Figure 5.5: High-level architecture whiteboard

In addition to our high-level architecture diagram on the whiteboard, we will also capture associated notes about the various architectural components during the discussion. The notes that were captured for the scenario we discussed in this chapter may look like this:

Data Sources	Data Transformation	Data Consumers
- **CUSTOMER DATA:** Stored in MySQL database. **System owner:** Database Team. **Data owner:** Marketing Team. **Data Load Frequency:** Daily. **Ingestion:** Investigate DMS for replication with Glue job to consolidate changes. - **SALESFORCE DATA:** Company has Salesforce SaaS subscription. Project needs opportunity data loaded from Sales Force. **System owner:** Salesforce Admin team. **Data owner:** Enterprise Sales Team. **Data Load Frequency:** Hourly. **Ingestion:** SaaS Integration Tool (AWS AppFlow or Salesforce dataloader.io are possibilities) - **MOBILE APP:** Need to ingest metrics in real-time from companies mobile app used by sales team. **System owner:** AppDev team. **Data owner:** Enterprise Sales Team. **Data Load Frequency:** Near real-time. **Ingestion:** Streaming service (Kinesis or MSK are possibilities).	- Data is ingested into the landing zone in raw format (CSV and XML) - Quality checks are performed and data standardized. Data files are also converted to Parquet format. Resulting files are written to the clean zone. - Data from relational database tables are denormalized based on use case requirements. New tables are enriched with additional data. Data is partitioned by year and month and written to the curated zone. - As files are written into each zone, teh data is catalogged and meta-data is written to the data catalog. - The team does have previous experience with creating Spark ETL jobs written in PySpark.	- **DATA ANALYSTS:** A team of 4 - 6 data analysts will be responsible for creating reports and drawing insights from the data that iwll be delivered to senior Sales Management. This team has in using SQL. - **DATA SCIENTISTS:** A team of 2 - 3 data scientists will be tasked with creating Machine Learning models base don historical data that is part of this project. This team wants SQL access for exploring the data, as well as access to specialized machine learning tools. - **BUSINESS USERS:** This project will enable sales operations teams across the country. Total users appeox 25 - 30. They want easy access to summarized data via a data visualization tool that lets them filter, drill-down, work with different graphs, etc. Some of this have experience with Tableau for visualization, but we do not currently have enough licenses for all business users. Open to exploring alternate tools.

Figure 5.6: Notes associated with our whiteboarding

Now that you understand the theory of how to conduct a whiteboarding session, it's time to get some practical hands-on experience. This next section provides details about a fictional whiteboarding session and allows you to practice your whiteboarding skills.

Hands-on — architecting a sample pipeline

For the hands-on portion of this chapter, you will review the detailed notes from a whiteboarding session held for the fictional company GP Widgets Inc. As you go through the notes, you should create a whiteboard architecture, either on an actual whiteboard or on a piece of poster board. Alternatively, you can create the whiteboard using a free online design tool, such as the one available at `http://diagrams.net`.

As a starting point for your whiteboarding session, you can use the following template. You can recreate this on your whiteboard or poster board, or you can access the diagrams.net/Draw.IO template for this via the GitHub site of this book at `https://github.com/PacktPublishing/Data-Engineering-with-AWS-2nd-edition/blob/main/Chapter05/Data-Engineering-Whiteboard-Template.drawio`.

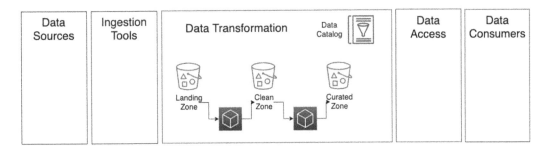

Figure 5.7: Generic whiteboarding template

Note that the three zones included in the template (landing zone, clean zone, and curated zone) are commonly used for data lakes. However, some data lakes may only have two zones, while others may have four or more zones. The number of zones is not a hard-and-fast rule but, rather, is based on the requirements of the use case you are designing for.

As you go through the meeting notes, fill out the relevant sections of the template. In addition to drawing the components and flow for the pipeline, you should also capture notes relating to the whiteboard components, as per the example in *Figure 5.6*. At the end of this chapter, you can compare the whiteboard you have created with the one that the data engineer lead for GP Widgets has created.

By completing this exercise, you will gain hands-on experience in whiteboarding a data pipeline and learn how to identify the key points about data consumers, data sources, and required transformations.

Detailed notes from the project "Bright Light" whiteboarding meeting of GP Widgets, Inc

Here is a list of attendees participating in the meeting:

- Ronna Parish, VP of marketing
- Chris Taylor, VP of enterprise sales
- Terry Winship, data analytics team manager
- James Dadd, data science team manager
- Owen McClave, database team manager
- Natalie Rabinovich, web server team manager
- Shilpa Mehta, data engineer lead

Meeting notes

Shilpa started the meeting by asking everyone to introduce themselves and then provided a summary of the meeting objectives:

- Plan out a high-level architecture for a new project to bring improved analytics to the marketing teams. During the discussion, Shilpa will whiteboard a high-level architecture.

- They reinforced that not all the technical details would be worked out in this meeting, but looking for agreement from all the stakeholders with a high-level approach and design is critical.

- It's already agreed that the project will be built in the AWS cloud.

Shilpa asked Ronna (marketing manager) to provide an overview of the marketing team requirements for project *Bright Light*:

- Project Bright Light is intended *to improve the visibility that the marketing team has into real-time customer behavior,* as well as **longer-term** *customer trends*, through the use of data analytics.

- The marketing team wants to give **marketing specialists** real-time insights into interactions on the company's e-commerce website. Some examples of these **visualizations** include a heatmap to show website activity in different geographic locations, redemptions of coupons by product category, top ad campaign referrals, and spend by zip code in the previous period versus the current period.

- All visualizations should enable a user to select a custom period, filter on custom fields, and drill down from summary information to detailed information. Data should be *refreshed on at least an hourly basis, but more often would be better.*

The **data analyst team** supporting the marketing department will run more complex investigations of current and historical trends:

- Identify the top 10% of customers over the past x days by spend, and identify their top product categories for use in marketing promotions.

- Determine the average time a customer spends on the website, as well as the number of products they browse versus the number of products they purchase.

- Identify the top returned products over the past day/month/week.

- Compare the sales by zip code this month versus sales by zip code in the same month 1 year ago, grouped by product category.

- For each customer, keep a running total of the number of widgets purchased (grouped by category), the average spend per sale, the average spend per month, the number of coupons applied, and the total coupon value.

We have tasked our **data science team** with building a machine learning model that can predict a widget's popularity based on the weather in a specific location:

- Research highlights how weather can impact e-commerce sales and the sales of specific products – for example, the types of widgets that customers are likely to buy on a sunny day compared to a cold and rainy day.

- The marketing team wants to target our advertising campaigns and optimize our ad spend and real-time marketing campaigns, based on the current and forecasted weather in a certain zip code.

- We regularly add new widgets to our catalog, so the model must be updated at least once a day, based on the latest weather and sales information.

- In addition to helping with marketing, the manufacturing and logistics teams have expressed interest in this model to help optimize logistics and inventory for different warehouses around the country, based on 7-day weather forecasts.

James Dadd (data science team manager) spoke about some of the requirements for his team:

- They would need **ad hoc SQL access** to **weather**, **website clickstream logs**, and **sales** data for at least the last year.

- They have determined that a provider on *AWS Data Exchange* offers historical and forecast weather information for all US zip codes. There is a subscription charge for this data, and the marketing team is working on allocating a budget for this. Data would be delivered **daily via AWS Data Exchange in the CSV format.**

- James indicated he had not had a chance to speak with the database and website admin teams about getting access to their data yet.

- The team currently uses **SparkML** for a lot of their machine learning projects, but they are **interested in cloud-based tools** that may help them speed up delivery and collaboration for their machine learning products. They also **use SQL queries to explore datasets.**

Terry Winship (data analytics team manager) indicated that her team specializes in **using SQL to gain complex insights from data**:

- Based on her initial analysis, her team would need access to the **customer, product, returns, and sales databases**, as well as **clickstream data from the web server logs**.

- Her team has experience in working with on-premises data warehouses and databases. She has been reading up about data lakes, and as long as the team can use SQL to query the data, they are open to using different technologies.

- She also has specialists on her team that **can create visualizations** for the marketing team to use. This team primarily has experience with using **Tableau** for visualizations, but the marketing team **does not have licenses to use Tableau**. There would be a learning curve if a different visualization tool were used, but they are **open to exploring other options**.

- Terry indicated that a **daily update of data from the databases** should be sufficient for what they need, but that they would need **near-real-time streaming for the clickstream web server log files** so that they could provide the most up-to-date reports and visualizations.

Shilpa asked Owen McClave (database team manager) to provide an overview of the database sources that the data science and data analytics teams would need:

- Owen indicated that all their **databases run on-premises** and run **Microsoft SQL Server 2016, Enterprise Edition**.

- Owen said he doesn't know much about AWS and has some concerns about providing administrative access for his databases to the cloud, since he does not believe the cloud is secure. However, he said that, ultimately, it is up to the data owners to approve whether the data can be copied to the cloud. If approved, he will work with the cloud team to enable data syncing in the cloud, so long as there is no negative impact on his databases.

- Chris Taylor (VP of sales) is the data owner of the databases that have been discussed today (customer, product, returns, and sales data).

Shilpa asked Chris Taylor (VP of sales) to provide input on the use of sales data for the project:

- Chris indicated that this analytics project has executive sponsorship from senior management and visibility by the board of directors.

- He indicated that sales data can be stored in the cloud, so long as the security team reviews and approves it.

Shilpa indicated that AWS has a tool called **Database Migration Service**, which can be used to replicate data from a relational database, such as SQL Server 2016, to Amazon S3 cloud storage. She said she would set up a meeting with Owen to discuss the requirements for this tool in more detail at a later point, as there are also various other options.

Shilpa requested that Natalie Rabinovich (web server team manager) provide more information on the web server log files that will be important for this project:

- Natalie indicated that they currently run the e-commerce website on-premises on **Linux servers running Apache HTTP Server**.
- A load balancer is used to distribute traffic between **four different web servers**. Each server stores its clickstream web server logs locally.
- The log files are **plaintext files in the Apache web log format**.
- Shilpa indicated that AWS has an agent called the **Kinesis Agent**, which can be used to read the log files and stream their contents to the AWS cloud. She queried whether it would be possible to install this agent on the Apache web servers.
- Natalie indicated that it should be fine, but they would need more details and to test it in a development environment before installing it on the production servers.
- Shilpa asked who the data owner was. Natalie indicated that the marketing team owns the web server clickstream logs from a business perspective.

Shilpa led a discussion on the potential data transformations that may be required on the data that is ingested for this project:

- Based on the description from James, it appears that data should be made available daily in the CSV format and can be loaded directly into the raw zone of the data lake.
- Using a tool such as Amazon DMS, we can load data from the databases into the raw zone of the data lake in the Parquet format.
- The Kinesis Agent can convert the Apache HTTP Server log files into the JSON format, streaming them to Kinesis Firehose. Firehose can then perform basic validation of the log (using Lambda), convert it into the Parquet format, and write directly to the clean zone.
- Shilpa indicated that an **initial transformation** could perform basic data **quality checks on incoming database data**, add contextual information as new columns (such as ingestion time), and then write the file **to the clean zone** of the data lake.

- Shilpa explained that partitioning datasets helps optimize both the performance and cost of queries. She indicated that partitions should be based on how data is queried and led a discussion on the topic. After some discussion, it was agreed that partitioning the database and weather by day (yyyyy/mm/dd) and web server logs by hour (yyyy/mm/dd/hh) may be a good partitioning strategy, but this would be investigated further and confirmed in future discussions.

- A **second transformation** could then be run against the data in the clean zone, performing tasks such as **denormalizing the relational datasets, joining tables to optimized tables, enriching data with weather data,** or performing any other required business logic. This optimized data would be **written to the curated zone** of the data lake. AWS Glue or Amazon EMR could potentially be used to perform these transformations.

- As each dataset is loaded, and then the transformed data is written out to the next zone, the **data will be added to the Glue Data Catalog.** Once data has been added to the data catalog, authorized users will be able to query the data using SQL queries, enabled by a tool such as Amazon Athena. **Additional metadata could be added** at this point, including items such as data owner, source system, data sensitivity level, and so on.

- Shilpa indicated that she will arrange future meetings with the various teams to discuss the business metadata that must be added.

- Shilpa wrapped up the meeting with a brief overview of the whiteboard, and she committed to providing a copy of the whiteboard architecture and notes to all attendees for further review and comment. She also indicated that she would schedule additional meetings with smaller groups of people to dive deep into specific aspects of the proposed architecture, providing additional validation.

Shilpa used a whiteboard in the meeting room to sketch out a rough architecture, and then after the meeting, she created the following diagram to show the architecture:

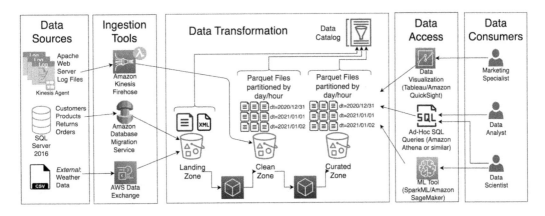

Figure 5.8: Completed whiteboard architecture for project Bright Light

Shilpa also added some notes to go with the whiteboard, sending out both the whiteboard architecture and the notes to the meeting attendees:

Data Sources

- **Apache Web Server Log Files:** From 4 Apache web servers. **System Owner:** Natalie Rabinovich. **Data Owner:** Marketing. **Ingestion:** Could use Kinesis Agent to transform to JSON and send to Kinesis Firehose. Firehose does validation (using Lambda function) and transforms to Parquet format. Could write direct to clean zone, partitioned by day (yyyy/mm/dd).

- **Databases:** Customers, Products, Returns, Orders on SQL Server 2016 Enterprise Edition. **System Owner:** Owen McClave. **Data Owner:** Sales Team. Potentially use Amazon DMS to replicate to Amazon S3 raw zone in Parquet format.

- **Weather Data:** External data source available via subscription. **Data Owner:** Marketing. **Ingestion:** Available from AWS Data Exchange marketplace. Lambda function can load data into Amazon S3 raw zone when available.

Data Transformation

- **Raw Zone:** Database and weather data replicated into raw zone. When files ingested triggers Lambda function to perform data quality checks and then loads into Clean Zone partitioned by yyyy/mm/dd.

- **Clean Zone:** Web server log files loaded directly into clean zone after Kinesis Firehose uses a Lambda function to perform data quality checks. Firehose configured to write to clean zone partitioned by yyyy/mm/dd. Database and weather files loaded from raw zone after data quality checks, and partition by yyyy/mm/dd.

- **Curated Zone:** Database files denormalized, enriched (with weather data potentially), other business logic added. Partitioned by either day (databases, weather) or hour (web server log files)

Data Consumers

- **Marketing Specialists:** Want to use business intelligence (visualization) tool to view up-to-date website analytics (ad-campaign referrals, coupon redemption, heatmap showing activity by geographic location). Refresh on at least hourly basis. Analytics team generally uses Tableau, but marketing team does not have licenses. Open to other BI tools.

- **Data Analysts:** Responsible for creating reports and insights using SQL queries. Database and weather data could be refreshed daily, but they would need web server clickstream log files refreshed at least hourly.

- **Data Scientists:** Need ad-hoc SQL access to databases, weather and web server log files. They currently use SparkML on-premises, but open to new cloud based tools that may make speed up delivery and collaboration for their machine learning products.

Figure 5.9: Completed whiteboard notes for project Bright Light

Compare the whiteboard you created to the whiteboard created by Shilpa, and note the differences. Are there things that Shilpa missed on her whiteboard or notes? Are there things that you missed on your whiteboard or notes?

The exercises in this chapter allowed you to get hands-on with data architecting and whiteboarding. We will wrap up this chapter by providing a summary, and then do a deeper dive into the topics of data ingestion, transformation, and data consumption in the next few chapters.

Summary

In this chapter, we reviewed an approach to developing data engineering pipelines by identifying a limited-scope project, and then whiteboarding a high-level architecture diagram. We looked at how we could have a workshop, in conjunction with relevant stakeholders in an organization, to discuss requirements and plan the initial architecture.

We approached this task by working backward. We started by identifying who the data consumers of the project would be and learning about their requirements. Then, we looked at which data sources could be used to provide the required data and how those data sources could be ingested. We then reviewed, at a high level, some of the data transformations that would be required for the project to optimize the data for analytics.

In the next chapter, we will take a deeper dive into AWS services to ingest batch and streaming data, learning more about how to select the best tool for our data engineering pipeline.

Learn more on Discord

To join the Discord community for this book – where you can share feedback, ask questions to the author, and learn about new releases – follow the QR code below:

https://discord.gg/9s5mHNyECd

6

Ingesting Batch and Streaming Data

Having developed a high-level architecture for our data pipeline, we can now dive deep into the varied components of the architecture. We will start with data ingestion so that in the hands-on section of this chapter, we can ingest data and use that data for the hands-on activities in future chapters.

Data engineers are often faced with the challenge of *the five Vs of data*. These are the **variety** of data (the diverse types and formats of data); the **volume** of data (the size of the dataset); the **velocity** of the data (how quickly the data is generated and needs to be ingested); the **veracity** or **validity** of the data (the quality, completeness, and credibility of the data); and finally, the **value** of data (the value that the data can provide the business with).

In this chapter, we will look at several different types of data sources and examine the various tools available within AWS for ingesting data from these sources. We will also look at how to decide between multiple different ingestion tools to ensure you are using the right tool for the job. In the hands-on portion of this chapter, we will ingest data from both streaming and batch sources.

In this chapter, we will cover the following topics:

- Understanding data sources
- Ingesting data from database sources
- Ingesting data from streaming sources
- Hands-on – ingesting data from a database source
- Hands-on – ingesting data from a streaming source

Technical requirements

In the hands-on sections of this chapter, we will use the AWS **Database Migration Service (DMS)** service to ingest data from a database source, and then we will ingest streaming data using Amazon Kinesis. To ingest data from a database, you need IAM permissions that allow your user to create an RDS database, an EC2 instance, a DMS instance, and a new IAM role and policy.

For the hands-on section on ingesting streaming data, you will need IAM permissions to create a Kinesis Data Firehose instance, as well as permissions to deploy a CloudFormation template. The CloudFormation template that is deployed will create IAM roles, a Lambda function, as well as Amazon Cognito users and other Cognito resources.

To query the newly ingested data, you will need permission to create an AWS Glue Crawler and permission to use Amazon Athena to query data.

You can find the code files of this chapter in the GitHub repository at the following link: `https://github.com/PacktPublishing/Data-Engineering-with-AWS-2nd-edition/tree/main/Chapter06`.

Understanding data sources

Over the past decade, the amount and the variety of data that gets generated each year has significantly increased. Today, industry analysts talk about the volume of global data generated in a year in terms of **zettabytes (ZB)**, a unit of measurement equal to a billion **terabytes (TB)**. By some estimates, a little over 1 ZB of data existed in the world in 2012, and yet by the end of 2025, there will be an estimated 181 ZB of data created, captured, copied, and consumed worldwide.

In our pipeline whiteboarding session (covered in *Chapter 5, Architecting Data Engineering Pipelines*), we identified several data sources that we wanted to ingest and transform to best enable our data consumers. For each data source that is identified in a whiteboarding session, you need to develop an understanding of the variety, volume, velocity, veracity, and value of data; we'll move on to cover those now.

Data variety

In the past decade, the variety of data used in data analytics projects has greatly increased. If all data was simply relational data in a database (and there was a time when nearly all data was like this), it would be relatively easy to transfer into data analytic solutions. But today, organizations find value, and often a competitive advantage, in being able to analyze many other types of data (web server log files, photos, videos, and other media, geolocation data, sensor data, other IoT data, and so on).

For each data source in a pipeline, data engineers need to determine what type of data will be ingested. Data is typically categorized as being of one of three types, as we examine in the following subsections.

Structured data

Structured data is data that has been organized according to a data model, and is represented as a series of rows and columns. Each row represents a record, with the columns making up the fields of each record.

Each column in a structured data file contains data of a specific type (such as strings or numbers), and every row has the same number and type of columns. The definition of which columns are contained in each record, and the data type for each column, is known as the data schema.

Common data sources that contain structured data include the following:

- **Relational Database Management Systems (RDBMSes)** such as MySQL, PostgreSQL, SQL Server, and Oracle
- Delimited files such as **Comma-Separated Value (CSV)** files or **Tab-Separated Value (TSV)** files
- Spreadsheets such as Microsoft Excel files in **xls** format

The data shown in the following table is an example of structured data. In this case, it is data on the calorie content of several foods from the USA MyPyramid Food Raw Data, available at `https://catalog.data.gov/dataset/mypyramid-food-raw-data`. This data extract has been sorted to show some of the foods with the highest calorie content in the dataset:

Food_Code	Display_Name	Portion_Display_Name	Total Calo
71411000	Potato skin with cheese & bacon	order (10 halves)	1667.4
24301010	Roasted duck	duck half	1283.52
21103120	Breaded fried steak (eat lean & fat)	large steak	1069.2
28141010	Fried chicken frozen meal	large meal (16 oz)	1024.92
27347100	Chicken or turkey pot pie	16-ounce pie (Hungry Man)	976.1
58200100	Wrap sandwich (meat, vegetables, rice)	wrap	818.37
21103120	Breaded fried steak (eat lean & fat)	medium steak	801.9
58106730	Meat & veggie pizza, thick crust	small pizza (8" across)	798.64
24401010	Roasted Cornish game hen	hen	792.54
58106530	Meat pizza, thick crust	small pizza (8" across)	785.4

Figure 6.1: An example of structured data

Structured data can be easily ingested into analytic systems, including Amazon S3-based data lakes, and data marts such as an Amazon Redshift data warehouse.

Semi-structured data

Semi-structured data shares many of the same attributes as structured data, but the structure, or schema, does not need to be strictly defined. Generally, semi-structured data contains internal tags that identify data elements, but each record may contain different elements or fields.

Some of the data types in the unstructured data may be of a strong type, such as an integer value, while other elements may contain items such as free-form text. Common semi-structured formats include JSON and XML file formats.

The data that follows is part of a semi-structured JSON formatted file for product inventory. In this example, we can see that we have two items – a set of batteries and a pair of jeans:

```
[{
        "sku": 10001,
        "name": "Duracell - Copper Top AA Alkaline Batteries - long
lasting, all-purpose 16 Count",
        "price": 12.78,
        "category": [{
        "id": "5443",
            "name": "Home Goods"
        }
        ],
        "manufacturer": "Duracell",
        "model": "MN2400B4Z"
    },
    {
        "sku": 10002,
        "name": "Levi's Men's 505 Jeans Fit Pants",
        "type": "Clothing",
        "price": 39.99,
        "fit_type": [{
                "id": 855,
                "description": "Regular"
            },
            {
                "id": 902,
```

```
                        "description": "Big and Tall"
                }
        ],
        "size": [{
                "id": 101,
                "waist": 32,
                "length": 32
        },
        {
                "id": 102,
                "waist": 30,
                "length": 32
        }
        ],
        "category": [{
                "id": 3821,
                "name": "Jeans"
        }, {
                "id": 6298,
                "name": "Men's Fashion"
        }],
        "manufacturer": "Levi",
        "model": "00505-4891"
    }
]
```

While most of the fields are common between the two items, we can see that the pair of jeans includes attributes for fit_type and size, which are not relevant to batteries. You will also notice that the first item (the batteries) only belongs to a single category, while the jeans are listed in two categories (Jeans and Men's Fashion).

Capturing the same information in a structured data type, such as CSV, would be much more complex. CSV is not well suited to a scenario where different records have a different number of categories, for example, or where some records have additional attributes (such as fit_type or size). JSON is structured in a hierarchical format (where data can be nested, such as for category, fit_type, and size) and this provides significant flexibility.

Storing data in a semi-structured format, such as JSON, is commonly used for a variety of different use cases, such as working with IoT data, as well as for web and mobile applications.

Unstructured data

As a category, unstructured data covers many different types of data where the data does not have a predefined structure or schema. This can range from free-form data (such as text data in a PDF or word processing file or emails) to media files (such as photos, videos, satellite images, or audio files).

Some unstructured data can be analyzed directly, although generally not very efficiently unless using specialized tools. For example, it is generally not efficient to search large quantities of free-form text in a traditional database, although there are specialized tools that can be used for this purpose (such as **Amazon OpenSearch Service**).

However, some types of unstructured data cannot be directly analyzed with data analytic tools at all. For example, data analytic tools are unable to directly analyze image or video files. This does not mean that we cannot use these types of files in our analytic projects, but to make them useful for analytics, we need to process them further to extract useful metadata from the files.

A large percentage of the data that's generated today is considered unstructured data, and in the past few years, a lot of effort has been put into being able to make better use of this type of data. For example, we can use image recognition tools to extract metadata from an image or video file that can then be used in analytics. Or, we can use natural language processing tools to analyze free-form text reviews on a website to determine customer sentiment for different products.

Refer to *Chapter 13, Enabling Artificial Intelligence and Machine Learning*, for an example of how Amazon Comprehend can be used to extract sentiment analysis from product reviews.

Data volume

The next attribute of data that we need to understand for each of our data sources relates to the volume of data. For this, we need to understand both the total size of the existing data that needs to be ingested, as well as the daily/monthly/yearly growth of data.

For example, we may want to ingest data from a database that includes a one-time ingestion of 10 years of historical data totaling 2.2 TB in size. We may also find that data from this source generates around 30 GB of new data per month (or an average of 1 GB per day of new data). Depending on the network connection between the source system and the AWS target system, it may be possible to transfer the historical data over the network, but if we have limited bandwidth, we may want to consider using one of the devices in the *Amazon Snow* family of devices.

For example, we could load data onto an Amazon Snowball device that is shipped to our data center, and then send the device back to AWS, where AWS will load the data into S3 for us.

Understanding the volume of historical and future data also assists us in doing the initial sizing of AWS services for our use case, and helps us budget better for the associated costs.

Data velocity

Data velocity describes the speed at which we expect to ingest and process new data from the source system into our target system.

For ingestion, some data may be loaded according to a batch schedule once a day, or a few times a day (such as receiving data from a partner on a scheduled basis). Meanwhile, other data may be streamed from the source to the target continually (such as when ingesting IoT data from thousands of sensors).

As an example, according to a case study on the AWS website, the BMW Group uses AWS services to ingest data from millions of BMW and MINI vehicles, processing TB of anonymous telemetry data every day. To read more about this, refer to the AWS case study titled *BMW Group Uses AWS-Based Data Lake to Unlock the Power of Data* (https://aws.amazon.com/solutions/case-studies/bmw-group-case-study/).

We need to have a good understanding of both how quickly our source data is generated (on a schedule or via real-time streaming data), as well as how quickly we need to process the incoming data (does the business only need insights from the data 24 hours after it is ingested, or is the business looking to gather insights in near real time?).

The velocity of data affects both how we ingest the data (such as through a streaming service such as Amazon Kinesis), as well as how we process the data (such as whether we run scheduled daily Glue jobs, or use Glue Streaming to continually process incoming data).

Data veracity

Data veracity considers various aspects of the data we're ingesting, such as the quality, completeness, and accuracy of the data.

As we discussed previously, the data we ingest may have come from a variety of sources, and depending on how the data was generated, the data may be incomplete or inconsistent. For example, data from IoT sensors where the sensor went offline for a while may be missing a period of data, or data captured from user forms or spreadsheets may contain errors or missing values.

We need to be aware of the veracity of the data we ingest so that we can ensure we take these items into account when processing the data. For example, some tools can help backfill missing data with averages, while others can help detect and remediate fields that contain invalid data.

Data value

Ultimately, all the data ingested and processed has been for a single purpose – finding ways to provide new insights and value to the business. While this is the last of the five Vs that we will discuss, it is the most important one to keep in mind when thinking of the bigger picture of what we are doing with data ingestion and processing.

We could ingest TB of data and clean and process the data in multiple ways, but if the end data product hasn't brought value to the business, then we have wasted both time and money.

When considering the data we are ingesting, we need to ensure we keep the big picture in mind. We need to make sure that it is worth ingesting this data and also understand how this data may add value to the business, either now or in the future.

Questions to ask

In *Chapter 5, Architecting Data Engineering Pipelines*, we held a workshop during which we identified some likely data sources needed for our data analytics project, but now, we need to dive deeper to gather additional information.

We need to identify who owns each data source that we plan to ingest, and then do a deep dive with the data source owner and ask questions such as the following:

- What is the format of the data (relational database, NoSQL database, semi-structured data such as JSON or XML, unstructured data, and so on)?
- How much historical data is available?
- What is the total size of the historical data?
- How much new data is generated on a daily/weekly/monthly basis?
- Does the data currently get streamed somewhere, and if so, can we tap into the stream of data?
- How frequently is the data updated (constantly, such as with a database or streaming source, or on a scheduled basis, such as at the end of the day or when receiving a daily update from a partner)?
- How will this data source be used to add value to the business, either now or in the future?

Learning more about the data will help you determine the best service to use to ingest the data, and help with the initial sizing of services and estimating a budget.

Now that we have reviewed how to take an inventory of the data sources you want to use, let's move on to examining specific ingestion types, starting with ingestion from relational databases.

Ingesting data from a relational database

A common source of data for analytical projects is data that comes from a relational database system such as MySQL, PostgreSQL, SQL Server, or an Oracle database. Organizations often have multiple siloed databases, and they want to bring the data from these varied databases into a central location for analytics.

It is common for these projects to include ingesting historical data that already exists in the database, as well as syncing ongoing new and changed data from the database. There are a variety of tools that can be used to ingest from database sources, as we will discuss in this section.

AWS DMS

The primary AWS service for ingesting data from a database is **AWS DMS**, though there are other ways to ingest data from a database source. As a data engineer, you need to evaluate both the source and the target to determine which ingestion tool will be best suited.

AWS DMS is intended for doing either one-off ingestion of historical data from a database or replicating change data (often referred to as **Change Data Capture** (**CDC**)) from a relational database on an ongoing basis. When using AWS DMS, the target is either a different database engine (such as an Oracle-to-PostgreSQL migration), or an Amazon S3-based data lake. In this section, we will focus on ingesting data from a relational database to an Amazon S3-based data lake.

We introduced the AWS DMS service in *Chapter 3*, *The AWS Data Engineer's Toolkit*, so make sure you have read the *Overview of Amazon Database Migration Service (DMS)* section in that chapter to get a good understanding of how the service works.

While AWS DMS was originally a managed service only (meaning that DMS provisioned one or more EC2 servers as replication instances), AWS announced an AWS DMS serverless option in June 2023. When using the AWS DMS serverless option, DMS automatically sets up, scales, and manages the underlying compute resources, helping to simplify the database migration process.

AWS Glue

AWS Glue, a Spark processing engine that we introduced in *Chapter 3, The AWS Data Engineer's Toolkit*, can make connections to several data sources. This includes connections to JDBC sources, and custom connectors available on the AWS Glue Marketplace, enabling Glue to connect to many different database engines, and through those connections transfer data for further processing.

AWS Glue is well suited to certain use cases related to ingesting data from databases. Let's take a look at some of them.

Full one-off loads from one or more tables

AWS Glue can be configured to make a connection to a database and download data from tables. Glue effectively does a `select *` from the table, reading the table contents into the memory of the Spark cluster. At that point, you can use Spark to write out the data to Amazon S3, optionally in an optimized format such as Apache Parquet.

Initial full loads from a table, and subsequent loads of new records

AWS Glue has a concept called *job bookmarks*, which enables Glue to keep track of which data was previously processed, and then on subsequent runs only process new data. Glue does this by having you identify a column (or multiple columns) in the table that will serve as a bookmark key. The values in this bookmark key must always increase in value, although gaps are allowed.

For example, if you have an audit table that has a `transaction_ID` column that sequentially increases for each new transaction, then this would be a good fit for ingesting data with AWS Glue while using the bookmark functionality.

The first time the job runs, it will load all records from the table and store the highest value for the `transaction_ID` column in the bookmark. For illustration purposes, let's assume the highest value on the initial load was 944,872. The next time the job runs, it effectively does a `select * from audit_table where transaction_id > 944872`.

Note that this process is unable to detect updated or deleted rows in the table, so it is not well suited to all use cases. An audit table, or similar types of tables where data is always added to the table but existing rows are never updated or deleted, is the optimal use case for this functionality.

Creating AWS Glue jobs with AWS Lake Formation

AWS Lake Formation includes several blueprints to assist in automating some common ingestion tasks. One of these ingestion blueprints allows you to use AWS Glue to ingest data from a database source. With a few clicks in the Lake Formation console, you can configure your ingest requirements (one-off versus scheduled, full table load or incremental load with bookmarks, and so on). Once configured, Lake Formation creates the Glue job for ingesting from the database source, the Glue Crawlers for adding newly ingested data into the Glue Data Catalog, and Glue workflows for orchestrating the different components.

Other ways to ingest data from a database

There are several other approaches to ingesting data from a database to an Amazon S3-based data lake, which we will cover briefly in this section.

Amazon EMR provides a simple way to deploy several common Hadoop framework tools, and some of these tools are useful for ingesting data from a database. For example, you can run Apache Spark on Amazon EMR and use a JDBC driver to connect to a relational database to load data into the data lake (in a similar way to our discussion about using AWS Glue to connect to a database).

If you are running MariaDB, MySQL, or PostgreSQL on Amazon **Relational Database Service (RDS)**, you can use RDS functionality to export a database snapshot to Amazon S3. This is a fully managed process that writes out all tables from the snapshot to Amazon S3 in Apache Parquet format. This is the simplest way to move data into Amazon S3 if you are using one of the supported database engines on RDS, and you want all tables exported to S3 on a scheduled basis. For more information, see the documentation at `https://docs.aws.amazon.com/AmazonRDS/latest/UserGuide/USER_ExportSnapshot.html`.

There are also several third-party commercial tools, many containing advanced features that can be used to move data from a relational database to Amazon S3 (although these often come at a premium price). This includes tools such as Qlik Replicate (previously known as Attunity), a well-known tool for moving data between a wide variety of sources and targets (including relational databases, data warehouses, streaming sources, enterprise applications, cloud providers, and legacy platforms such as DB2).

You may also find that your database engine contains tools for directly exporting data in a flat format that can then be transferred to Amazon S3. Some database engines also have more advanced tools, such as Oracle GoldenGate, a solution that can generate CDC data as a Kafka stream.

Note, however, that these tools are often licensed separately and can add significant additional expense. For an example of using Oracle GoldenGate to generate CDC data that has been loaded into an S3 data lake, search for the AWS blog post titled *Extract Oracle OLTP data in real time with GoldenGate and query from Amazon Athena,* or find it here: https://aws.amazon.com/blogs/big-data/extract-oracle-oltp-data-in-real-time-with-goldengate-and-query-from-amazon-athena/.

A reminder about CDC

We introduced the concept of CDC in *Chapter 3, The AWS Data Engineer's Toolkit,* but it is an important concept, so here is a reminder. When rows in a relational database are deleted or updated, there is no practical way to capture those changes using standard database query tools (such as SQL). But when replicating data from a database to a new source, it is important to be able to identify those changes so that they can be applied to the target. This process of identifying and capturing these changes (new inserts, updates, and deletes) from the database log files is referred to as CDC.

Deciding on the best approach to ingesting from a database

While all these tools can be used in one way or another to ingest data from a database, there are several points to consider when deciding on the best approach for your specific use case.

The size of the database

If the total size of the database tables you want to load is large (many tens of GB or larger), then doing a full nightly load would not be a good approach. The full load could take a significant amount of time to run and puts a heavy load on the source system while running. In this scenario, a better approach is to do an initial load from the database and then constantly sync updates from the source using CDC, such as by using *AWS DMS*.

For very large databases, you can use AWS DMS with an Amazon Snowball device to load data to the Snowball device in your data center. Once the data has been loaded, you return the device to AWS, and it will load it to Amazon S3. AWS DMS will capture all CDC changes while the Snowball device is being transferred back to AWS so that once the data is loaded, you can create an ETL job to apply changes to the full data load. This initial load via Snowball may take a week or longer due to the physical transport of the device back to AWS, plus the application of a week or more of CDC data. However, once the initial load and application of CDC data are complete, CDC changes can continue to be applied in near real time.

For smaller databases, you can consider using RDS' snapshot export functionality, AWS Glue, or native database tools to load the entire database to Amazon S3 on a scheduled basis. This will often be the simplest and most cost-effective method, but it is not right for every use case, being best suited to smaller databases (low tens of GB or smaller) and where having a daily update, rather than near-real-time updates, meets requirements.

Database load

If you have a database with a consistent production load at all times, you will want to minimize the additional load you place on the server to sync to the data lake. In this scenario, you can use DMS to do an initial full load, ideally from a read replica of your database if it's supported as a source by DMS. For ongoing replication, DMS can use database log files to identify CDC changes, and this places a lower load on database resources.

Whenever you do a full load from a database (whether you're using AWS DMS, AWS Glue, or another solution), there will be a heavier load on the database as a full read of all tables is required. You need to consider this load and, where possible, use a read replica of your database for the full load. If using Amazon RDS, see the following documentation for details on how to configure a read replica: `https://docs.aws.amazon.com/AmazonRDS/latest/UserGuide/USER_ReadRepl.html`.

If a smaller database is running on Amazon RDS, the best solution would be to use the export-to-S3-from-snapshot functionality of RDS if it's supported for your database engine. This solution places no load on your source database; however, as it loads from a snapshot of the database, it cannot be used for real-time data replication, but rather only for scheduled exports.

Data ingestion frequency

Some analytic use cases are well suited to analyzing data that is ingested on a fixed schedule (such as every night). However, some use cases will want to have access to new data as fast as possible.

If your use case requires access to data coming from a database source as soon as possible, then using a service such as AWS DMS to ingest CDC data is the best approach. However, remember that CDC data just indicates what data has changed (new rows having been inserted and existing rows updated or deleted), so you still require a process to apply those changes to the existing data to enable querying for the most up-to-date state.

If your use case allows for regularly scheduled updates, such as nightly, you can do a scheduled full load (if the database's size and performance impacts allow), or you can have a nightly process to apply the CDC data that was collected during the day to the previous snapshot of data.

In *Chapter 7, Transforming Data to Optimize for Analytics*, we will review several approaches for applying CDC data to an existing dataset.

Technical requirements and compatibility

When evaluating different approaches to and tools for ingesting data from a database source, it is very important to involve the database owner and admin team upfront to technically evaluate the proposed solution.

A data engineering team may decide on a specific toolset upfront, based on its requirements and its broad understanding of compatibility with the source systems. However, at the time of implementation, it may discover that the source database team objects to certain security or technical requirements of the solution, and this can lead to significant project delays.

For example, AWS DMS supports CDC for several MySQL versions. However, DMS does require that binary logging is enabled on the source system with specific configuration settings for CDC to work.

Another example is that AWS DMS does not support server-level audits when SQL Server 2008/2008 R2 is used as a source. Certain commands related to enabling this functionality will cause DMS to fail.

It is critical to get the buy-in of the database owner and admin team before finalizing a solution. All of these requirements and limitations are covered in the AWS DMS documentation (and other solutions or products should have similar documentation covering their requirements). Reviewing these requirements, in detail, with the database admin team upfront is critical to the success of the project.

In the next section, we will take a similar look at tools for and approaches to ingesting data from streaming sources.

Ingesting streaming data

An increasingly common source of data for analytic projects is data that is continually generated and needs to be ingested in near real time. Some common sources of this type of data are as follows:

- Data from IoT devices (such as smartwatches, smart appliances, and so on)
- Telemetry data from various types of vehicles (cars, airplanes, and so on)
- Sensor data (from manufacturing machines, weather stations, and so on)
- Live gameplay data from mobile games
- Mentions of the company brand on various social media platforms

For example, Boeing, the aircraft manufacturer, has a system called **Airplane Health Management (AHM)** that collects in-flight airplane data and relays it in real time to Boeing systems. Boeing processes the information and makes it immediately available to airline maintenance staff via a web portal.

In this section, we will look at several tools and services for ingesting streaming data, as well as things to consider when planning for streaming ingestion.

Amazon Kinesis versus Amazon Managed Streaming for Kafka (MSK)

The two primary services for ingesting streaming data within AWS are *Amazon Kinesis* and *Amazon MSK*. Both of these services were described in *Chapter 3, The AWS Engineer's Toolkit*, so ensure you have read those sections before proceeding.

In summary, both Amazon Kinesis and Amazon MSK are services from AWS that offer the ability to write streaming data to storage, and then have data consumers connect to that storage to read the messages. This is commonly used as a way to decouple applications producing streaming data from applications that are consuming data. Both services can scale up to handle millions of messages per second.

In this section, we will examine some of the primary differences between the two services and look at some of the factors that contribute to deciding which service is right for your use case.

Serverless services versus managed services

Amazon Kinesis Data Streams is available in two capacity modes – either *provisioned* or *on-demand*. With provisioned mode, you need to configure the number of shards (the base throughput unit of a Kinesis data stream) that is provisioned for the stream, while in on-demand mode, the number of shards is automatically allocated and managed by Kinesis.

In both modes, AWS manages the underlying compute resources for you. Therefore, with Kinesis, you never have to select EC2 instance sizes or EBS storage or deal with any of the underlying resources. You either select to provision and manage the number of shards for the Kinesis stream on your own (with provisioned mode) or you select to have AWS manage that for you with on-demand mode.

With *Amazon Kinesis Data Firehose*, much like Amazon Kinesis Data Streams in on-demand mode, the compute automatically scales up and down in response to message throughput changes without requiring any configuration.

In a similar way, *Amazon MSK* is also available in both a provisioned and a serverless mode. With provisioned mode, AWS manages the infrastructure for you, but you still need to be aware of and make decisions about the underlying compute infrastructure and software. For example, you need to select from a list of EC2 instance types to power your MSK cluster, configure VPC network settings, configure storage size and options, select the version of Apache Kafka to deploy, and fine-tune a range of Kafka configuration settings.

With Amazon MSK Serverless, the deployment is simpler as you do not need to make decisions about the EC2 instance size, storage, and version, but you also have less control over the Kafka cluster options.

If you have a team with existing skills in using Apache Kafka, and you need to fine-tune the performance of the stream, then you may want to consider MSK provisioned mode. If you're just getting started with streaming and your use case does not have a requirement to fine-tune performance, then Amazon Kinesis or Amazon MSK serverless mode may be a better option.

Open-source flexibility versus proprietary software with strong AWS integration

Amazon MSK is a managed version of Apache Kafka, a popular open-source solution. Amazon Kinesis is proprietary software created by AWS, although there are some limited open-source elements, such as Kinesis Agent.

With Apache Kafka, there is a large community of contributors to the software, and a large ecosystem providing a diverse range of connectors and integrations. Kafka provides out-of-the-box integration with hundreds of event sources and event sinks (including AWS services such as Amazon S3, but also many other popular products, such as PostgreSQL, Elasticsearch, and others).

With Amazon Kinesis, AWS provides strong integration with several AWS services, such as Amazon S3, Amazon Redshift, and Amazon OpenSearch Service. Kinesis also provides integration with a number of external services such as Splunk, DataDog, MongoDB, Sumo Logic, New Relic, and others through Amazon Kinesis Data Firehose.

When deciding between the two services, ensure that you consider the types of integrations your use case requires and how that matches with the out-of-the-box functionality of either Kinesis or MSK.

At-least-once messaging versus exactly once messaging

When working with streaming technologies, some use cases have specific requirements around how many times messages may be processed by data consumers. Amazon Kinesis and Apache Kafka (and therefore Amazon MSK) provide different guarantees around message processing.

Amazon Kinesis provides an *at-least-once* message processing guarantee. This effectively guarantees that every message generated by a producer will be delivered to a consumer for processing. However, in certain scenarios, a message may be delivered more than once to a consuming application, introducing the possibility of data duplication.

With **Apache Kafka** (and therefore Amazon MSK), as of version 0.11, the ability to configure your streams for *exactly-once* message processing was introduced. When you configure your Apache Kafka stream, you can configure the processing.guarantee=exactly_once setting to enable this.

With Amazon Kinesis, you need to build the logic for anticipating and appropriately handling how individual records are processed multiple times in your application. AWS provides guidance on this in the Kinesis documentation, in the *Handling Duplicate Records* section.

If your use case calls for a guarantee that all messages will be delivered to the processing application exactly once, then you should consider Amazon MSK. Amazon Kinesis is still an option, but you will need to ensure your application handles the possibility of receiving duplicate records.

A single processing engine versus niche tools

Apache Kafka is most closely compared to Amazon Kinesis Data Streams as both provide a powerful way to consume streaming messages. While both can be used to process a variety of data types, Amazon Kinesis does include several distinct sub-services for specialized use cases.

For example, if your use case involves ingesting streaming audio or video data, then Amazon Kinesis Video Streams is custom-designed to simplify this type of processing. Or, if you have a simple use case of wanting to write out ingested streaming data to targets such as Amazon S3, Amazon OpenSearch Service, or Amazon Redshift (as well as some third-party services), then Amazon Kinesis Data Firehose makes this task simple.

Deciding on a streaming ingestion tool

There are several factors to consider when deciding on which AWS service to use for processing your streaming data, as we covered in this section. Both Amazon Kinesis and Amazon MSK Serverless require minimal upfront configuration and ongoing maintenance, while Amazon MSK in provisioned mode provides the ability to fine-tune your cluster performance and options.

Amazon Kinesis has a subset of services for special use cases, so you should evaluate your use case against the various Kinesis services and see if one of these will meet your current and expected future requirements. If your use case has specific requirements, such as exactly once message delivery, the ability to fine-tune the performance of the stream, or needs integration with third-party products not directly available in Kinesis, then consider Amazon MSK. Finally, you should also compare the pricing for each service based on your requirements.

In the next few sections, you will get hands-on with ingesting data from a database using AWS DMS and then ingesting streaming data using Amazon Kinesis.

Hands-on — ingesting data with AWS DMS

As we discussed earlier in this chapter, AWS DMS can be used to replicate a database into an Amazon S3-based data lake (among other uses). Follow the steps in this section to do the following:

1. Deploy a CloudFormation template that configures a MySQL RDS instance and then deploys an EC2 instance to load a demo database into MySQL.
2. Set up a DMS replication instance and configure endpoints and tasks.
3. Run the DMS instance in full-load mode.
4. Run a Glue Crawler to add the tables that were newly loaded into S3 into the AWS Glue Data Catalog.
5. Query the data with Amazon Athena.
6. Delete the CloudFormation template in order to remove the resources that have been deployed.

NOTE

The following steps assume the use of your AWS account's default VPC and security group. You will need to modify the steps as needed if you're not using the default.

Deploying MySQL and an EC2 data loader via CloudFormation

AWS CloudFormation is a service that enables you to deploy infrastructure as code. Using CloudFormation templates provides the ability to deploy AWS services using either JSON- or YAML-formatted templates. This enables you to treat your infrastructure as code, meaning you can store the templates in a version control system (to manage changes to templates and integrate code reviews), and easily deploy infrastructure reliably and repeatably via CI/CD pipelines.

To get started, download the CloudFormation template from this book's GitHub site at https://
github.com/PacktPublishing/Data-Engineering-with-AWS-2nd-edition/blob/main/
Chapter06/mysql-ec2loader.cfn.

Save the file locally to your computer by right-clicking on **Raw** and then selecting **Save Link As**
in your browser window.

```
53 lines (45 sloc)   1.67 KB                                  Raw   Blame   

 1   ---
 2   AWSTemplateFormatVersion: 2010-09-09
 3   Description: Chapter 6 - Data Engineering with AWS
 4   Parameters:
 5     DBPassword:
 6       Type: String
 7       NoEcho: true
 8       Description: The database admin account password
 9       MinLength: 8
10       AllowedPattern: ^[a-zA-Z0-9]*$
11       ConstraintDescription: Password must contain only alphanumeric characters.
12     LatestAmiId:
13       Type: 'AWS::SSM::Parameter::Value<AWS::EC2::Image::Id>'
14       Default: '/aws/service/ami-amazon-linux-latest/al2023-ami-kernel-6.1-x86_64'
15   Resources:
16     MySQLInstance:
```

Figure 6.2: Download the CloudFormation template from GitHub

In the following steps, we are going to deploy a CloudFormation template that will do the following:

1. Request that the user provides a password (DBPassword) that will be set as the admin
   password for the MySQL instance.

2. Set a parameter (LatestAmiId) that provides a path to an *AWS Secrets Manager* entry that
   contains the **Amazon Machine Image** (**AMI**) ID for deploying an instance with Amazon
   Linux 2023 within which the region the user is working.

3. Create an Amazon RDS MySQL instance (MySQLInstance) with 20 GB of allocated storage,
   using the db.t3.micro instance type. Set the admin password for the instance to the value
   entered by the user as captured in the DBPassword parameter.

4. Create an Amazon EC2 instance (EC2Instance) of type t3.micro, provide user data that
   will run commands when the instance is launched to download a MySQL demo database,
   and write the database schema and data to the MySQL instance. Include the DependsOn
   option to indicate that the MySQLInstance resource must be created prior to this resource
   being created (this is to ensure that the MySQL instance is ready to receive the data that
   will be written via the EC2 instance we launch here).

Use the following steps to deploy the CloudFormation template:

1. Log in to the **AWS Management Console** (https://console.aws.amazon.com) and ensure that you are in the region that you have used for all the hands-on activities in this book.

2. In the top search bar, search for and select CloudFormation to access the CloudFormation console.

3. Click on **Create stack, With new resources (standard)**.

4. Under the **Specify template** section, select **Upload a template file**, click on **Choose file**, and select the mysql-ec2loader.cfn file you downloaded from GitHub.

5. Click on **Next**.

6. For **Stack name**, provide a name (such as dataeng-aws-chapter6-mysql-ec2).

7. In the **Parameters** section, provide a DBPassword that will be used as the password for your MySQL admin user.

8. Leave the **LatestAmiId** field with the default string, and then click **Next**.

9. Leave all other defaults and click **Next**.

10. Leave all defaults, and click on **Submit**.

CloudFormation will now take a few minutes to deploy your MySQL RDS instance and the EC2 instance that will download the demo database (called SakilaDB), and then load the demo database to the MySQL instance that was just created.

Once the deployment is finished, the stack status will change to **CREATE_COMPLETE**, as shown in the following screenshot.

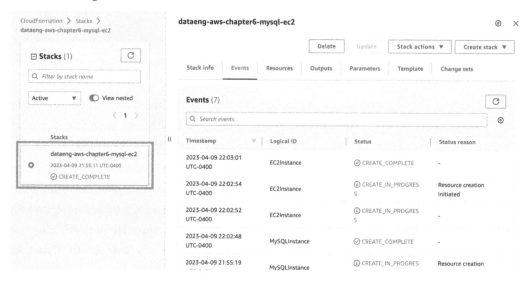

Figure 6.3: CloudFormation stack successfully created

You can continue with the next step to create an IAM policy and role for DMS to use while the deployment is still running. But you must ensure the deployment completes successfully before configuring DMS.

Creating an IAM policy and role for DMS

In this section, we will create an IAM policy and role that will allow DMS to write to our target S3 bucket:

1. In the AWS Management Console, search for and select **IAM** using the top search bar.
2. In the left-hand menu, click on **Policies** and then click **Create policy**.
3. By default, the **Visual editor** is selected, so change to text entry by clicking on the **JSON** tab.
4. Replace the boilerplate code in the text box with the following policy definition (which can also be copied from this book's GitHub site). Make sure you replace <initials> in the bucket name with the correct landing zone bucket name you created in *Chapter 2, Data Management Architectures for Analytics*:

```
{
    "Version": "2012-10-17",
    "Statement": [
        {
            "Effect": "Allow",
            "Action": [
                "s3:*"
            ],
            "Resource": [
                "arn:aws:s3:::dataeng-landing-zone-<initials>",
                "arn:aws:s3:::dataeng-landing-zone-<initials>/*"
            ]
        }
    ]
}
```

This policy grants permissions for all S3 operations (get, put, and so on) for the dataeng-landing-zone-<initials> bucket. This will give DMS the permissions needed to write out CSV files in the landing zone bucket with the data from our MySQL database.

5. Click **Next**.

6. Provide a descriptive policy name, such as DataEngDMSLandingS3BucketPolicy, and click **Create policy**:

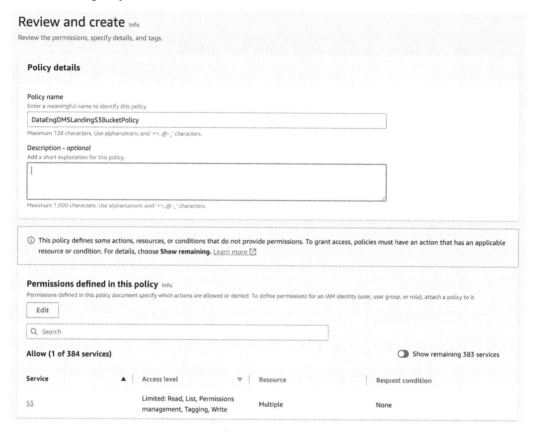

Figure 6.4: Creating an IAM policy to grant S3 permissions

7. In the left-hand menu, click on **Roles** and then click **Create role**.

8. For **Trusted entity type**, make sure **AWS service** is selected.

9. For **Use case**, search for and select **DMS**, make sure to click the selector for the DMS service, and then click **Next**.

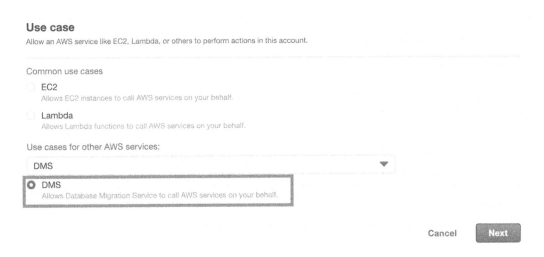

Figure 6.5: Creating a new role for the DMS service to use

10. Search for and select the policy you created in *step 6* (such as `DataEngDMSLandingS3Buck etPolicy`), and then click **Next**.

11. Provide a descriptive **Role name**, such as `DataEngDMSLandingS3BucketRole`, and click **Create role**.

12. Click on the newly created role and copy and paste the role **Amazon Resource Name (ARN)** property somewhere where you can easily access it; it will be required in the next section.

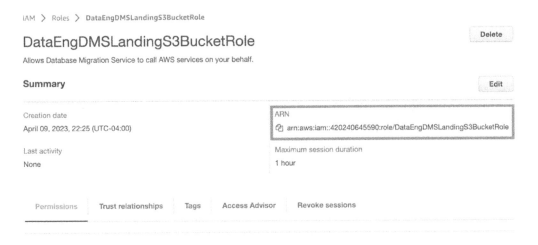

Figure 6.6: Capturing the ARN of the newly created role

Now that we have created the required IAM permissions, we will create a DMS replication instance, as well as other required DMS resources (such as source and target endpoints, as well as a database migration task).

Configuring DMS settings and performing a full load from MySQL to S3

In this section, we will create a DMS replication instance (a managed EC2 instance that connects to the source endpoint, retrieves data, and writes to the target endpoint), and also configure the source and target endpoints. We will then create a database migration task that provides the configuration settings for the migration. **Make sure that your CloudFormation template has been deployed completely before continuing with this section.**

In the following steps, you will configure DMS and start the full-load job:

1. In the AWS Management Console, search for **DMS** using the top search bar and click on **Database Migration Service**.
2. In the left-hand menu, click on **Replication Instances**.
3. At the top of the page, click on **Creation replication instance**.
4. Provide a **Name** for the replication instance; for example, `mysql-s3-replication`.
5. For **Instance class**, select `dms.t3.micro`.
6. For **High Availability**, select **Dev or test workload (Single-AZ)**.
7. For **Allocated storage**, enter `10` (the database we are replicating is very small, so 10 GB is enough space).
8. In the **VPC** dropdown, select the **default VPC**.
9. Leave everything else as the defaults and click **Create replication instance**. Note that it may take a few minutes for the replication instance to be created and ready.
10. In the left-hand menu, click on **Endpoints**.
11. At the top right, click on **Create endpoint**.

12. For **Endpoint type**, select **Source endpoint** and then click the box for **Select RDS DB Instance.**

13. For **RDS Instance**, use the drop-down list to select the MySQL database that was created by the CloudFormation template deployment.

14. Under **Endpoint configuration**, for **Access to endpoint database**, select **Provide access information manually.**

15. For **Password**, provide the password that you set for the database when deploying the CloudFormation template (*step 7* in the **Deploying the CloudFormation template** step)

16. Leave all other defaults and then click **Create endpoint** at the bottom right.

17. Now that we have created the source endpoint, we can create the target endpoint by clicking on **Create endpoint** at the top right.

18. For **Endpoint type**, select **Target endpoint.**

19. For **Endpoint identifier**, type in a name for the endpoint, such as s3-landing-zone-sakila-csv.

20. For **Target engine**, select **Amazon S3** from the drop-down list.

21. For **Amazon Resource Name (ARN) for service access role**, enter the ARN for the IAM role you recorded in *step 12* of the previous section.

22. For **Bucket name**, provide the name of the landing zone bucket you created in *Chapter 2, Data Management Architectures for Analytics* (for example, dataeng-landing-zone-<initials>).

23. For **Bucket folder**, enter sakila-db.

24. Expand the endpoint settings and click on **Add new setting**. Select AddColumnName from the settings list, and for the value, type True.

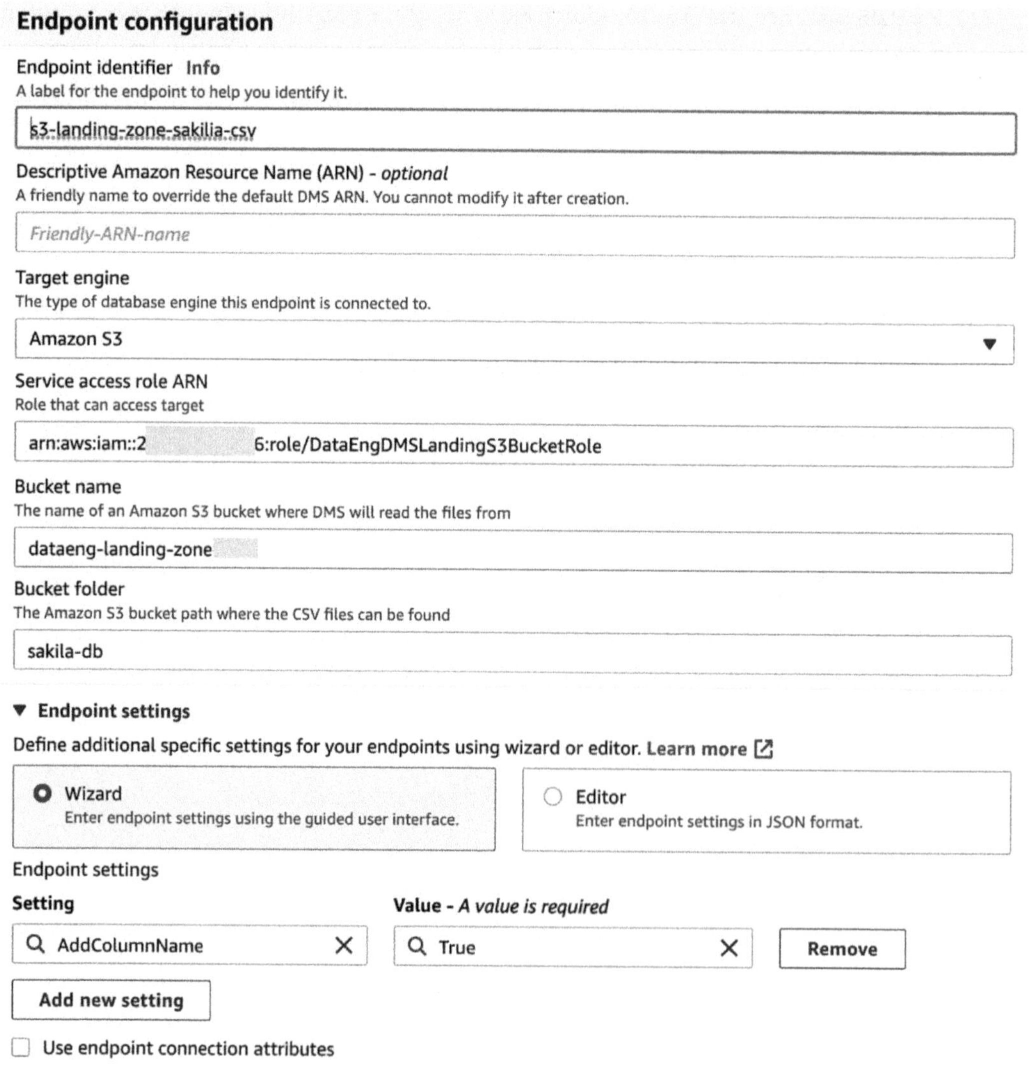

Endpoint configuration

Endpoint identifier Info
A label for the endpoint to help you identify it.

s3-landing-zone-sakilia-csv

Descriptive Amazon Resource Name (ARN) - *optional*
A friendly name to override the default DMS ARN. You cannot modify it after creation.

Friendly-ARN-name

Target engine
The type of database engine this endpoint is connected to.

Amazon S3   ▼

Service access role ARN
Role that can access target

arn:aws:iam::2   6:role/DataEngDMSLandingS3BucketRole

Bucket name
The name of an Amazon S3 bucket where DMS will read the files from

dataeng-landing-zone

Bucket folder
The Amazon S3 bucket path where the CSV files can be found

sakila-db

▼ **Endpoint settings**

Define additional specific settings for your endpoints using wizard or editor. **Learn more** ↗

⦿ Wizard	○ Editor
Enter endpoint settings using the guided user interface.	Enter endpoint settings in JSON format.

Endpoint settings

Setting	**Value -** *A value is required*	
Q AddColumnName ✕	Q True ✕	Remove

Add new setting

☐ Use endpoint connection attributes

Figure 6.7: AWS DMS S3 target endpoint

25. Click **Create Endpoint**.

26. On the left-hand side, click **Database migration tasks**, and then click **Create task**.

27. For **Task identifier**, provide a descriptive name for the task, such as dataeng-mysql-s3-sakila-task.

28. For **Replication instance**, select the instance you created in *step 4* of the previous section, such as `mysql-s3-replication`.

29. For **Source database endpoint**, select the source endpoint that links to your MySQL instance.

30. For **Target database endpoint**, select the S3 target endpoint you created previously.

31. For **Migration type**, select **Migrate existing data** from the dropdown. This does a one-time migration from the source to the target.

32. Leave the defaults for **Task settings** as they are.

33. For **Table mappings**, under **Selection rules**, click on **Add new selection rule**.

34. For **Schema**, select **Enter a schema**. For **Source name**, enter `%sakila%`, and for **Source Table name**, leave it set as `%`.

35. Leave the defaults for **Selection rules** and all other sections as they are and click **Create task**.

36. Once the task has been created, the full load will be automatically initiated and the data will be loaded from your MySQL instance to Amazon S3. Click on the task identifier and review the **Table statistics** tab to monitor your progress.

Our previously configured S3 event for all CSV files written to the landing zone bucket will be triggered for each file that DMS loads. This will run the Lambda function we created in *Chapter 3*, which will create a new Parquet version of each file in the **CLEAN ZONE** bucket. This will also register each table in the AWS Glue Data Catalog.

Querying data with Amazon Athena

The Lambda function that was run for each CSV file created by DMS also registers each new Parquet file as part of a table in the AWS Glue database.

We can now query the newly ingested data using the Amazon Athena service.

1. First, we need to create a new Amazon S3 folder to store the results of our Athena queries. In the **AWS Management Console**, search for and select **S3** using the top search bar.

2. Click on **Create bucket**, and for **Bucket name**, enter `athena-query-results-<INITIALS>`. Replace `<INITIALS>` in the bucket name with a unique identifier, such as the one you have used with other buckets in previous chapters.

3. Make sure the **AWS Region** is set to the Region you have used for the previous hands-on exercises. Leave all other defaults and click on **Create bucket**.

4. In the **AWS Management Console**, search for and select **Athena** using the top search bar.

5. Within the Athena console, click on the **Settings** tab.

6. Click on **Manage** in the **Settings** tab, and for **Location of query result**, provide the path of the bucket we just created (such as `s3://athena-query-results-gse23`), and then click **Save**.

7. Return to the **Editor** tab, and then in the **Database** dropdown on the left-hand side, select `sakila` from the drop-down list.

8. In the **New query** window, run the following query: `select * from film limit 20;`.

9. This query returns the results of the first 20 fictional films in the Sakila database.

10. If your query runs successfully and returns 20 results, that confirms that your DMS task was completed successfully. Since the infrastructure we deployed does have a low cost per hour while it is running, we can save costs by deleting the DMS replication instance and the resources deployed by the CloudFormation template. Open up the **DMS** service console, and on the left-hand side, click on **Database migration tasks**. We need to delete the task before we can delete the associated replication instance, so select the task, and from the **Actions** menu, click **Delete**, and then confirm the deletion in the pop-up box.

11. Once the replication task has been deleted, on the left-hand side, click on **Replication instances**. Select the replication instance you created earlier, and then from the **Actions** menu, select **Delete**. Confirm that you want to delete the replication instance by clicking on **Delete** in the pop-up box.

12. Open up the **CloudFormation service console**, and click on **Stacks** in the left-hand menu.

13. **Select the stack** that you deployed earlier, and then click on **Delete**. Confirm the deletion by clicking on **Delete stack** in the popup.

Congratulations! You have successfully replicated a MySQL database into your S3-based data lake. To learn more about ingesting data from MySQL to Amazon S3, see the following AWS documentation:

*   Using Amazon S3 as a target for AWS Database Migration Service (`https://docs.aws.amazon.com/dms/latest/userguide/CHAP_Target.S3.html`)

*   Using a MySQL-compatible database as a source for AWS DMS (`https://docs.aws.amazon.com/dms/latest/userguide/CHAP_Source.MySQL.html`)

Now that we have got hands-on with ingesting batch data from a database into our Amazon S3 data lake, let's look at one of the ways to ingest streaming data into our data lake.

Hands-on — ingesting streaming data

Earlier in this chapter, we looked at two options for ingesting streaming data into AWS, namely Amazon Kinesis and Amazon MSK. AWS provides an open-source solution for streaming sample data to Amazon Kinesis; therefore, in this section, we will use the Amazon Kinesis service to ingest streaming data. To generate streaming data, we will use the AWS open-source *Amazon Kinesis Data Generator* (*KDG*).

In this section, we will perform the following tasks:

1. Configure **Amazon Kinesis Data Firehose** to ingest streaming data, and write the data out to Amazon S3.

2. Configure **Amazon KDG** to create mock streaming data.

To get started, let's configure a new Kinesis Data Firehose instance to ingest streaming data and write it out to our Amazon S3 data lake.

Configuring Kinesis Data Firehose for streaming delivery to Amazon S3

Kinesis Data Firehose is designed to enable you to easily ingest data from streaming sources, and then write that data out to a supported target (such as Amazon S3, which we will do in this exercise). Let's get started:

1. In the AWS Management Console, search for and select **Kinesis** using the top search bar.

2. The Kinesis landing page provides links to create new streams using the Kinesis features of Kinesis Data Streams, Kinesis Data Firehose, or Kinesis Data Analytics. Select the Kinesis Data Firehose service, and then click on **Create delivery stream**.

3. In this exercise, we are going to use KDG to send data directly to Firehose, so for **Source**, select **Direct PUT** from the drop-down list. For **Destination**, select **Amazon S3** from the drop-down list.

4. For **Delivery stream name**, enter a descriptive name, such as `dataeng-firehose-streaming-s3`.

5. For the optional section of **Transform and convert records**, leave both options **unchecked.** **Transform source records with AWS Lambda** functionality can be used to run data validation tasks or perform light processing on incoming data with AWS Lambda, but we want to ingest the data without any processing, so we will leave this disabled. **Convert record format** can be used to convert incoming data into Apache Parquet or Apache ORC format. However, to do this, we would need to specify the schema of the incoming data upfront. We are going to ingest our data without changing the file format, so we will leave this disabled.

6. For **S3 bucket**, select the landing zone bucket you created previously; for example, `s3://dataeng-landing-zone-<initials>`.

7. For **Dynamic Partitioning**, leave this option set to **Not enabled**.

8. By default, Kinesis Data Firehose writes the data to S3 with a prefix to split incoming data by `YYYY/MM/dd/HH`. For our dataset, we want to load streaming data into a **streaming** prefix, and we only want to split data by the year and month that it was ingested. Therefore, we must set **S3 bucket prefix** to `streaming/!{timestamp:yyyy/MM/}`. For more information on custom prefixes, see `https://docs.aws.amazon.com/firehose/latest/dev/s3-prefixes.html`.

9. If we set a custom prefix for incoming data, we must also set a custom error prefix. Set **S3 bucket error output prefix** to `!{firehose:error-output-type}/!{timestamp:yyyy/MM/}`.

10. Expand the **Buffer hints, compression and encryption** section.

11. The S3 buffer conditions allow us to control the parameters for how long Kinesis buffers incoming data before writing it out to our target. We specify both a buffer size (in MB) and a buffer interval (in seconds), and whichever is reached first will trigger Kinesis to write to the target. If we used the maximum buffer size of 128 MB and a maximum buffer interval of 900 seconds (15 minutes), we would see the following behavior. If we receive 1 MB of data per second, Kinesis Data Firehose will trigger after approximately 128 seconds (when 128 MB of data has been buffered). On the other hand, if we receive 0.1 MB of data per second, Kinesis Data Firehose will trigger after the 900-second maximum buffer interval. For our use case, we will set **Buffer size** to `1 MB` and **Buffer interval** to `60` seconds.

12. For all the other settings, leave the default settings as they are and click on **Create delivery stream**.

Our Kinesis Data Firehose stream is now ready to receive data. So, in the next section, we will generate some data to send to the stream using the **KDG** tool.

Configuring Amazon Kinesis Data Generator (KDG)

Amazon **KDG** is an open-source tool from AWS that can be used to generate customized data streams and can send that data to Kinesis Data Streams or Kinesis Data Firehose.

The Sakila database we previously loaded was for a company that produced classic movies and rented those out of its DVD stores. The DVD rental stores went out of business years ago, but the owners have now made their classic movies available for purchase and rental through various streaming platforms.

The company receives information about its classic movies being streamed from its distribution partners in real time, in a standard format. Using KDG, we will simulate the streaming data that's received from partners, including the following:

- The streaming timestamp
- Whether the customer rented, purchased, or watched the trailer
- film_id that matches the Sakila film database
- The distribution partner's name
- The streaming platform
- The state that the movie was streamed in

KDG is a collection of HTML and JavaScript files that run directly in your browser and can be accessed as a static site in GitHub. To use KDG, you need to create an Amazon Cognito user in your AWS account, and then use that user to log in to KDG on the GitHub account.

AWS has created an Amazon **CloudFormation** template that you can deploy in your AWS account to create the required Amazon Cognito user. This CloudFormation template creates an AWS Lambda function in your account to perform the required setup.

Follow these steps to deploy the CloudFormation template, create the required Cognito user, and configure KDG:

1. Open the KDG help page in your browser by going to https://awslabs.github.io/amazon-kinesis-data-generator/web/help.html.

2. Read the information about how the CloudFormation template works to create Cognito credentials in your account. When you're ready, click on the **Create a Cognito User with CloudFormation** button.

3. The AWS Management Console will open to the CloudFormation **Create Stack** page.

   IMPORTANT: When opening the link, the Region may default to Oregon (us-west-2-), therefore, change **Region** in the console to the Region you are using for the exercises in this book, then accept the CloudFormation defaults, and click **Next**.

4. On the **Specify stack details** page, provide a **Username** and **Password** for your Cognito user and click **Next**.

5. For **Configure stack options**, leave all the default settings as they are and click **Next**.

6. Review the details of the stack to be created, and then click the box to acknowledge that **AWS CloudFormation may create IAM resources**. Then, click **Submit**.

   Refresh the web page and monitor it until the stack's status is CREATE_COMPLETE.

7. Once the stack has been successfully deployed, go to the **Outputs** tab and take note of the KinesisDataGeneratorUrl value. Click on the link and open a new tab.

8. Use the **username** and **password** you set as parameters for the CloudFormation template to log in to the Amazon KDG portal.

9. Set **Region** to the same Region in which you created the Kinesis Data Firehose delivery stream. If you need a mapping of Region IDs to region names, refer to the following documentation: https://docs.aws.amazon.com/AmazonRDS/latest/UserGuide/Concepts. RegionsAndAvailabilityZones.html.

10. For **Stream/delivery stream**, from the dropdown, select the Kinesis Data Firehose stream you created in the previous section.

11. For **Records per second**, set this as a **constant** of 10 records per second. Leave **Compress records unchecked**.

12. For the record template, we want to generate records that simulate what we receive from our distribution partners. Paste the following into the Template 1 section of KDG (this can also be copied and pasted from the GitHub site for this chapter at https://github.com/ PacktPublishing/Data-Engineering-with-AWS-2nd-edition/tree/main/Chapter06):

```
{
    "timestamp":"{{date.now}}",
    "eventType":"{{random.weightedArrayElement(
      {
        "weights": [0.3,0.1,0.6],
        "data": ["rent","buy","trailer"]
      }
```

```
        )}}",
    "film_id":{{random.number(
        {
            "min":1,
            "max":1000
        }
    )}},
    "distributor":"{{random.arrayElement(
        ["amazon prime", "google play", "apple itunes", "vudo",
"fandango now", "microsoft", "youtube"]
    )}}",
    "platform":"{{random.arrayElement(
        ["ios", "android", "xbox", "playstation", "smart tv",
"other"]
    )}}",
    "state":"{{address.state}}"
}
```

13. Click **Send data** to start sending streaming data to your **Kinesis Data Firehose** delivery stream. Because of the configuration that we specified for our Firehose stream, the data we are sending is going to be buffered for 60 seconds, and then a batch of data is written to our landing zone S3 bucket. This will continue for as long as we leave KDG running.

14. Allow KDG to send data for at least 5-10 minutes (3,000-6,000 records), and then click on **Stop Sending Data to Kinesis**. The longer this process runs, the more data you will have when querying this dataset in later chapters. If you want a larger dataset, consider leaving this process to run for 30-60 minutes before stopping sending data to Kinesis.

 By leaving KDG running for at least 5-10 minutes, it will have created enough data for us to use in later chapters, where we will join this data with data we migrated from our MySQL database. This is enough data to run the subsequent exercises, but you can leave KDG running for longer if you want a larger dataset to work with. However, this will cause your ETL jobs to run for longer, queries will take longer, etc.

We can now use a **Glue crawler** to create a table in our AWS Glue Data Catalog for the newly ingested streaming data.

Adding newly ingested data to the Glue Data Catalog

In this section, we will run a **Glue crawler** to examine the newly ingested data, infer the schema, and automatically add the data to the Glue Data Catalog. Once we do this, we can query the newly ingested data using services such as **Amazon Athena**. Let's get started:

1. In the AWS Management Console, search for and select **Glue** using the top search bar.

2. In the left-hand menu, click on **Crawlers** (under **Data Catalog**).

3. Click on **Create crawler**.

4. Enter a descriptive name for **Name**, such as dataeng-streaming-crawler, and click **Next**.

5. For **Data source configuration**, under **Data sources**, click on **Add a data source.**

6. Make sure **Data source** is set to **S3**, and for **Location of S3 data**, set the S3 path to your dataeng-landing-zone-<initials> bucket, and add a suffix of streaming. For example, s3://dataeng-landing-zone-<initials>/streaming/, but make sure to replace <initials> with the unique identifier you used, and make sure to include the ending slash after the suffix.

7. Leave all other settings as default, and then click on **Add an S3 data source.**

8. Click on **Next**.

9. For **Configure security settings**, click on **Create new IAM role**. Provide a suffix for the IAM role name, such as AWSGlueServiceRole-streaming-crawler, and then click **Create**.

10. Click **Next**.

11. For **Output configuration**, click on **Add database**. In the new tab that opens, provide a descriptive database name, such as streaming_db, and then click **Create database**.

12. Go back to your browser tab with the **Glue console**, and click the **refresh icon** to the right of **Target database**. From the dropdown, you should then be able to select the newly created streaming_db database. Leave the other settings as default (such as keeping the schedule as **On demand**), and then click **Next**.

13. Review the settings on the **Review and create** page, and then click **Create crawler**.

14. Select your new crawler from the list and click **Run**.

When the crawler finishes running, it should have created a new table for the newly ingested streaming data.

Querying the data with Amazon Athena

Now that we have ingested our new streaming data, and added the data to the AWS Glue Data Catalog using the AWS Glue crawler, we can query the data using Amazon Athena:

1. In the AWS Management Console, search for and select **Athena** using the top search bar.
2. On the left-hand side, from the **Database** drop-down list, select the database you created in the previous step (such as `streaming_db`).
3. In the query window, type in `select * from streaming limit 20`.

The result of the query should show 20 records from the newly ingested streaming data, matching the pattern that we specified for KDG. Note how the Glue Crawler automatically added the two fields that we configured as our partitions (year and month).

Summary

In this chapter, we reviewed several ways to ingest common data types into AWS. We reviewed how AWS DMS and AWS Glue can be used to ingest data from a relational database to S3, and how Amazon Kinesis and Amazon MSK can be used to ingest streaming data.

In the hands-on section of this chapter, we used both the AWS DMS and Amazon Kinesis services to ingest data and then used AWS Glue to add the newly ingested data to the AWS Glue Data Catalog and query the data with Amazon Athena.

In the next chapter, *Chapter 7, Transforming Data to Optimize for Analytics*, we will review how we can transform the ingested data to optimize it for analytics, a core task for data engineers.

Learn more on Discord

To join the Discord community for this book – where you can share feedback, ask questions to the author, and learn about new releases – follow the QR code below:

`https://discord.gg/9s5mHNyECd`

7

Transforming Data to Optimize for Analytics

In previous chapters, we covered how to architect a data pipeline and common ways of ingesting data into a data lake. We now turn to the process of transforming raw data in order to optimize the data for analytics, enabling an organization to efficiently gain new insights into their data.

Transforming data to optimize for analytics and create value for an organization is one of the key tasks for a data engineer, and there are many different types of transformations. Some transformations are common and can be generically applied to a dataset, such as converting raw files to Parquet format and partitioning the dataset. Other transformations use business logic in the transformations and vary based on the contents of the data and the specific business requirements.

In this chapter, we review some of the engines that are available in **AWS** for performing data transformations and also discuss some of the more common data transformations. However, this book focuses on the broad range of tasks that a data engineer is likely to work on, so it is not intended as a deep dive into **Apache Spark**, nor is it intended as a guide to writing **PySpark** or **Scala** code. Even so, there are many other great books and online resources focused purely on teaching Apache Spark, and you are encouraged to investigate these, as knowing how to code and optimize Apache Spark is a common requirement for data engineers.

The topics we cover in this chapter include the following:

- Overview of how transformations can create value
- Types of data transformation tools
- Common data preparation transformations

- Common business use case transformations
- Working with **change data capture (CDC)** data
- Hands-on: Building transformations with **AWS Glue Studio** and **Apache Spark**

Technical requirements

For the hands-on tasks in this chapter, you need access to the AWS Glue service, including AWS Glue Studio. You also need to be able to create a new S3 bucket and new IAM policies.

You can find the code files of this chapter in the GitHub repository using the following link: `https://github.com/PacktPublishing/Data-Engineering-with-AWS-2nd-edition/tree/main/Chapter07`

Overview of how transformations can create value

As we have discussed in various places throughout this book, data can be one of the most valuable assets that an organization owns. However, raw, siloed data has limited value on its own, and we unlock the real value of an organization's data when we combine various raw datasets and transform that data through an analytics pipeline.

Cooking, baking, and data transformations

Look at the following list of food items and consider whether you enjoy eating them:

- Sugar
- Butter
- Eggs
- Milk

For many people, these are pretty standard food items, and some (like the eggs and milk) may be consumed on their own, while others (like the sugar and the butter) are generally consumed with something else, such as adding sugar to your coffee or tea or spreading butter on bread.

But, if you take those items and add a few more (like flour and baking powder) and combine all the items in just the right way, you could bake yourself a delicious cake, which would not resemble the raw ingredients at all. In the same way, our individual datasets have value on their own to the part of the organization that they come from, but if we combine these datasets in just the right way, we can create something totally new and different.

Now, if you happen to be having a party to celebrate something, your guests will appreciate the cake far more than they would appreciate just having the raw ingredients laid out! But if your goal was to provide breakfast for your friends, you may instead choose to fry the eggs, make some toast and spread the butter on the toast, and offer the milk and sugar to your guests for them to add to their coffee.

In both cases, you're using some common raw ingredients, then adding some additional items, and finally using different utilities to prepare the food (an oven for the cake and a stovetop for the fried eggs). How you combine the raw ingredients, and what you combine them with, depends on whether you're inviting friends over for breakfast, or whether you're throwing a party and want to celebrate with a cake.

In the same way, data engineers can use the same raw datasets, combine them with additional datasets, process them with different analytics engines, and create totally new and different datasets. How they combine the datasets, and which analytics engine they use, depends on what they're trying to create, which, of course, ultimately depends on what the business purpose is.

For example, your marketing team may want to combine a dataset that lists sales of each product, for each day over the past year, with weather data for the past year (min and max temperature, and whether it rained or not). This would enable them to analyze which products sell best on hot days, cold days, and rainy days, so that they can tailor their marketing campaigns around this.

Another example is having the marketing team aggregate their campaign data by region, and combine this with sales data aggregated by region and by product category, to measure the effectiveness of their marketing campaigns in different regions and across different product lines. This enables the team to optimize their marketing campaigns based on past performance.

Transformations as part of a pipeline

In *Chapter 5, Architecting Data Engineering Pipelines*, we developed a high-level design for our data pipeline. We first looked at how we could work with various business users to understand what their requirements were (to keep our analogy going, whether they wanted a cake or breakfast). After that, we looked at three broad areas on which we gathered initial information, namely the following:

1. **Data consumers**: Who was going to be consuming the data we created and what tools would they use for data gathering (our guests)?

2. **Data sources**: Which data sources did we have access to that we could use to create our new dataset (our raw ingredients)?

3. **Data transformations**: We reviewed, at a high level, the types of transformations that may be required in our pipeline in order to prepare and join our datasets (the recipe for making a cake or for fried eggs).

We now need to develop a low-level design for our pipeline transformations, which will include determining the types of transformations we need to perform, as well as which data transformation tools we will use. In the next section, we begin by looking at the types of transformation engines that are available.

Types of data transformation tools

As we covered in *Chapter 3, The AWS Data Engineer's Toolkit*, there are a number of AWS services that can be used for data transformation. We reviewed a number of these services in that chapter, so make sure to review it again, but in this section, we will look more broadly at the different types of data transformation engines.

Apache Spark

Apache Spark is an in-memory engine for working with large datasets, providing a mechanism to split a dataset among multiple nodes in a cluster for efficient processing. Spark is an extremely popular engine to use for processing and transforming big datasets, and there are multiple ways to run Spark jobs within AWS.

With Apache Spark, you can either process data in batches (such as on a daily basis or every few hours) or process near real-time streaming data using **Spark Streaming**. In addition, you can use **Spark SQL** to process data using standard SQL, and **Spark ML** for applying machine learning techniques to your data. With **Spark GraphX**, you can work with highly interconnected points of data to analyze complex relationships, such as for social networking applications.

Within AWS, you can run Spark jobs using multiple AWS services. **AWS Glue** provides a serverless way to run Spark, and **Amazon EMR** provides both a managed service for deploying a cluster for running Spark as well as a serverless option. In addition, you can use AWS container services (**ECS** or **EKS**) to run a Spark engine in a containerized environment or use a managed service from an AWS partner, such as **Databricks**.

Hadoop and MapReduce

Apache Hadoop is a framework consisting of multiple open-source software packages for working with large datasets and can scale from running on a single server to running on thousands of nodes.

Before Apache Spark, tools within the Hadoop framework – such as **Hive** and **MapReduce** – were the most popular way to transform and process large datasets.

Apache Hive provides a SQL-type interface for working with large datasets, while MapReduce provides a code-based approach to processing large datasets. Hadoop MapReduce is used in a similar way to Apache Spark, with the biggest difference being that Apache Spark does all processing in memory. Hadoop MapReduce on the other hand, makes extensive use of traditional disk-based reads and writes to interim storage during processing.

For use cases with massive datasets that cannot be economically processed in memory, Hadoop MapReduce may be better suited. However, for most use cases, Apache Spark provides significant performance benefits, as well as the ability to handle streaming data, access to machine learning libraries, and an API for graph computation with GraphX. While Apache Spark has become the leading big data processing solution in recent years, there are many legacy Hadoop systems still being used to process data on a daily basis.

There are also components of Hadoop that are still commonly used for Spark processing. The Apache Hive metadata store (Data Catalog) is used by Spark to map databases and tables to physical files in storage. For example, the AWS Glue catalog (which we have discussed previously) is an Apache Hive-compatible metastore.

Within AWS, you can run a number of Hadoop tools using the managed Amazon EMR service. Amazon EMR simplifies the process of deploying Hadoop-based infrastructure and supports multiple Hadoop tools, including **Hive**, **HBase**, **Yarn**, **Tez**, **Pig**, and many others.

SQL

Structured Query Language (**SQL**) is another common method used for data transformation. The advantage of SQL is that SQL knowledge and experience are widely available, making it an accessible form of performing transformations for many organizations. However, a code-based approach to transformations (such as using Apache Spark) can be a more powerful and versatile way of performing transformations.

When deciding on a transformation engine, a data engineer needs to understand the skill sets available in the organization, as well as the toolsets and ultimate target for the data. If you are operating in an environment that has a heavy focus on SQL, with SQL skill sets being widely available and Spark and other skill sets being limited, then using SQL for transformation may make sense (although GUI-based tools can also be considered).

However, if you are operating in an environment that has complex data processing requirements, and where latency and throughput requirements are high, it may be worthwhile to invest in skilling up to use modern data processing approaches, such as Spark.

While we mostly focus on data lakes as the target for our data in this book, there are times where the target for our data transformations may be a data warehousing system, such as **Amazon Redshift** or **Snowflake**. In these cases, an **Extract, Load, Transform** (ELT) approach may be used, where raw data is loaded into the data warehouse (the *extract and load* portion of ELT), and then the transformation of data is performed within the data warehouse using SQL.

Alternatively, toolsets such as Apache Spark may be used with SQL, through **Spark SQL**. This provides a way to use SQL for transformations while using a modern data processing engine to perform the transformations, rather than using a data warehouse. This allows the data warehouse to be focused on responding to end-user queries, while data transformation jobs are offloaded to an Apache Spark cluster. In this scenario, we use an ETL approach, where data is **extracted** to intermediatory storage, Apache Spark is used to **transform** the data, and data is then **loaded** into a different zone of the data lake, or into a data warehouse.

Tools such as **AWS Glue Studio** provide a visual interface that can be used to design ETL jobs, including jobs that use SQL statements to perform complex transformations. This helps users who do not have Spark coding skills to run SQL-based transforms using the power of the Apache Spark engine.

GUI-based tools

Another popular method of performing data transformation is through the use of GUI-based tools that significantly simplify the process of creating transformation jobs. There are a number of cloud and commercial products that are designed to provide a drag-and-drop-type approach to creating complex transformation pipelines, and these are widely used.

These tools may not provide the versatility and performance that you can get from designing transformations with code, but they do make the design of ETL-type transformations accessible to those without advanced coding skills. Some of these tools can also be used to automatically generate transformation code (such as Apache Spark code), providing a good starting point for a user to further develop the code, reducing ETL job development time.

Within AWS, the **Glue DataBrew** service is designed as a visual data preparation tool, enabling you to easily apply transformations to a set of files. With Glue DataBrew, a user can select from a library of over 250 common transformations and apply relevant transformations to incoming raw files.

With this service, a user can clean and normalize data to prepare it for analytics or machine learning model development through an easy-to-use visual designer, without needing to write any code.

Another AWS service that provides a visual approach to ETL design is **AWS Glue Studio**, a service that provides a visual interface for developing Apache Spark transformations. This can be used by people who do not have any current experience with Spark and can also be used by those who do know Spark, as a starting point for developing their own custom transforms. With AWS Glue Studio, you can create complex ETL jobs that join and transform multiple datasets, and then review the generated code and further refine it if you have the appropriate coding skills.

Outside of AWS, there are also many commercial products that provide a visual approach to ETL design. Popular products include tools from **Informatica**, **Matillion**, **Stitch**, **Talend**, **Panoply**, **Fivetran**, and many others.

As we have covered in this section, there are multiple approaches and engines that can be used for performing data transformation. However, whichever engine or interface is used, there are certain data transformations that are commonly used to prepare and optimize raw datasets, and we'll look at some of these in the next section.

Common data preparation transformations

The first set of transformations that we look at are those that help prepare the data for further transformations later in the pipeline. These transformations are designed to apply relatively generic optimizations to individual datasets that we are ingesting into the data lake. For these optimizations, you may need some understanding of the source data system and context, but, generally, you do not need to understand the ultimate business use case for the dataset.

Protecting PII data

Often, datasets that we ingest may contain **personally identifiable information (PII)** data, and there may be governance restrictions on which PII data can be stored in the data lake. As a result, we need to have a process that protects the PII data as soon as possible after it is ingested.

There are a number of common approaches that can be used here (such as tokenization or hashing), each with its own advantages and disadvantages, as we discussed in more detail in *Chapter 4, Data Governance, Security, and Cataloging*. But whichever strategy is used, the purpose is to remove the PII data from the raw data and replace it with a value, or token, in a way that enables us to still use the data for analytics.

This type of transformation is generally the first transformation performed for data containing PII, and in many cases, it is done in a different zone of the data lake, designed specifically for handling PII data. This zone will have strict controls to restrict access for general data lake users, and the best practice would be to have the anonymizing process run in a totally separate AWS account. Once the transformation has anonymized the PII data, the anonymized files will be copied into the general data lake raw zone in the main processing account.

Depending on the method you want to use to transform PII data for anonymization, there may be multiple different toolsets that can be used. For example, in AWS both **AWS Glue Studio** and **AWS Glue DataBrew** can be used to detect and obfuscate PII data.

AWS Glue DataBrew provides more options for obfuscating the data. For example, with Glue DataBrew, you can redact data (replace PII data with a string of ######), replace/swap data (jumble the values in a column so that every value is moved to a different, random row), encrypt, or hash a PII value. With AWS Glue Studio, you can either redact or hash PII data.

Alternatively, for more complex use cases, you can use purpose-built managed services from commercial vendors that run in AWS, such as **PK Privacy from the company PKWARE**.

Optimizing the file format

Within modern data lake environments, there are a number of file formats that can be used that are optimized for data analytics. From an analytics perspective, the most popular file format currently is **Apache Parquet**.

Parquet files are column-based, meaning that the contents of the file are physically stored to have data grouped by columns, rather than grouped by rows as with most file formats (CSV files, for example, are physically stored to be grouped by rows). As a result, queries that select a set of specific columns (rather than the entire row) do not need to read through all the data in the Parquet file to return a result, leading to performance improvements.

Parquet files also contain metadata about the data they store. This includes schema information (the data type for each column), as well as statistics such as the minimum and maximum value for a column contained in the file, the number of rows in the file, and so on.

A further benefit of Parquet files is that they are optimized for compression. A 1 TB dataset in CSV format could potentially be stored as 130 GB in Parquet format once compressed. Parquet supports multiple compression algorithms, although **Snappy** is the most widely used compression algorithm.

These optimizations result in significant savings in terms of storage space used, and increased performance when running queries.

For example, the cost of an Amazon Athena query is based on the amount of compressed data scanned (at the time of writing, this cost was $5 per TB of scanned data). If only certain columns are queried of a Parquet file, then between the compression and only needing to read the data chunks for the specific columns, significantly less data needs to be scanned to resolve the query.

In a scenario where your data table is stored across perhaps hundreds of Parquet files in a data lake, the analytics engine is able to get further performance advantages by reading the metadata of the files. For example, if your query is just to count all the rows in a table, this information is stored in the Parquet file metadata, so the query doesn't need to actually scan any of the data. For this type of query, you will see that Athena indicates that 0 KB of data was scanned, therefore there is no cost for the query.

Or, if your query is for where the sales amount is above a specific value, the analytics engine can read the metadata for a column to determine the minimum and maximum values stored in the specific data chunk. If the value you are searching for is higher than the maximum value recorded in the metadata, then the analytics engine knows that it does not need to scan that specific column's data chunk. This results in both cost savings and increased performance for queries.

Because of these performance improvements and cost savings, a very common transformation is to convert incoming files from their original format (such as CSV, JSON, XML, and so on) into the analytics-optimized Parquet format.

Optimizing with data partitioning

Another common approach for optimizing datasets for analytics is to **partition** the data, which relates to how the data files are organized in the storage system for a data lake.

Hive partitioning splits the data from a table to be grouped together in different folders, based on one or more of the columns in the dataset. While you can partition the data based on any column, a common partitioning strategy that works for many datasets is to partition based on date.

For example, suppose you had sales data for the past four years from around the country, and you had columns in the dataset for **Day**, **Month**, and **Year**. In this scenario, you could select to partition the data based on the **Year** column.

When the data was written to storage, all the data for each of the past few years would be grouped together with the following structure:

```
datalake_bucket/year=2023/file1.parquet
datalake_bucket/year=2022/file1.parquet
datalake_bucket/year=2021/file1.parquet
datalake_bucket/year=2020/file1.parquet
```

If you then run a SQL query and include a `WHERE Year = 2020` clause, for example, the analytics engine only needs to open up the single file in the `datalake_bucket/year=2020` folder. Because less data needs to be scanned by the query, it costs less and completes quicker. Note that for most datasets there will be multiple Parquet files per partition, but each file would only contain data related to the partitioned year.

Deciding on which column to partition by requires that you have a good understanding of how the dataset will be used. If you partition your dataset by year but a majority of your queries are by the **business unit (BU)** column across all years, then the partitioning strategy would not be effective.

Queries you run that do not use the partitioned columns may also end up causing those queries to run slower if you have a large number of partitions. The reason for this is that the analytics engine needs to read data in all partitions, and there is some overhead in working between all the different folders. If there is no clear common query pattern, it may be better to not even partition your data. But if a majority of your queries use a common pattern, then partitioning can provide significant performance and cost benefits.

You can also partition across multiple columns. For example, if you regularly process data at the day level, then you could implement the following partition strategy:

```
datalake_bucket/year=2021/month=6/day=1/file1.parquet
```

This significantly reduces the amount of data to be scanned when queries are run at the daily level and also works for queries at the month or year level. However, another warning regarding partitioning is that you want to ensure that you don't end up with a large number of small files. The optimal size of each Parquet file in a data lake is between 128 MB and 1 GB. The Parquet file format can be split, which means that multiple nodes in a cluster can process data from a file in parallel. However, having lots of small files requires a lot of overhead for opening files, reading metadata, scanning data, and closing each file, and can significantly impact performance. Therefore, it is better to have fewer partitions with larger files than to have hundreds, or thousands, of partitions but each partition only has a single file that is a few MB in size.

Partitioning is an important data optimization strategy and is based on how the data is expected to be used, either for the next transformation stage or for the final analytics stage. Determining the best partitioning strategy requires that you understand how the data will be used next.

Data cleansing

Optimizing the data format and partitioning data are transformation tasks that work on the format and structure of the data but do not directly transform the data. Data cleansing, however, is a transformation that alters parts of the data.

Data cleansing is often one of the first tasks to be performed after ingesting data and helps ensure that the data is valid, accurate, consistent, complete, and uniform. Source datasets may be missing values in some rows, have duplicate records, have inconsistent column names, use different formats, and so on. The data cleansing process works to resolve these issues on newly ingested raw data to better prepare the data for analytics. While some data sources may be nearly completely clean on ingestion (such as data from a relational database), other datasets are more likely to contain data needing cleansing, such as data from web forms, surveys, manually entered data, or **Internet of Things (IoT)** data from sensors.

Some common data transformation tasks for data cleansing include the following:

1. **Ensuring consistent column names**: When ingesting data from multiple datasets, you may find that the same data in different datasets has different column names. For example, one dataset may have a column called date_of_birth, while another dataset has a column called birthdate. In this case, a cleansing task may be to rename the date_of_birth column heading to birthdate.

2. **Changing column data types**: It is important to ensure that a column has a consistent data type for analytics. For example, a certain column may be intended to contain integers, but due to a data entry error, one record in the column may contain a string. When running data analytics on this dataset, having a string in the column may cause the query to fail. In this case, your data cleansing task needs to replace all string values in a column that should contain integers with a null value, which will enable the query to complete successfully.

3. **Ensuring a standard column format**: Different data sources may contain data in a different format. A common example of this is for dates, where one system may format the date as MM-DD-YYYY, while another system contains the data as DD-MM-YYYY. In this case, the data cleansing task will convert all columns in MM-DD-YYYY into the format DD-MM-YYYY, or whatever your corporate standard is for analytics.

4. **Removing duplicate records:** With some data sources, you may receive duplicate records (such as when ingesting streaming data, where only-once delivery is not always guaranteed). A data cleansing task may be required to identify and either remove or flag duplicate records.

5. **Providing missing values:** Some data sources may contain missing values in some records, and there are a number of strategies to clean this data. The transformation may replace missing values with a valid value, which could be the average, or median, or the values for that column, or potentially just an empty string or a null. Alternatively, the task may remove any rows that have missing values for a specific column. How to handle missing values depends on the specific dataset and the ultimate analytics use case.

There are many other common tasks that may be performed as part of data cleansing. Within AWS, the *Glue DataBrew* service has been designed to provide an easy way to cleanse and normalize data using a visual design tool and includes over 250 common data cleansing transformations.

Once we have our raw datasets optimized for analytics, we can move on to looking at transforming our datasets to meet business objectives.

Common business use case transformations

In a data lake environment, you generally ingest data from many different source systems into a landing, or raw, zone. You then optimize the file format and partition the dataset, as well as applying cleansing rules to the data, potentially now storing the data in a different zone, often referred to as the clean zone. At this point, you may also apply updates to the dataset with CDC-type data and create the latest view of the data, which we examine in the next section.

The initial transforms we covered in the previous section could be completed without needing to understand too much about how the data is going to ultimately be used by the business. At that point, we were still working on individual datasets that will be used by downstream transformation pipelines to ultimately prepare the data for business analytics.

But at some point, you, or another data engineer working for a line of business, are going to need to use a variety of these ingested data sources to deliver value to the business for a specific use case. After all, the whole point of the data lake is to bring varied data sources from across the business into a central location, to enable new insights to be drawn from across these datasets.

The transformations that we discuss in this section work across multiple datasets to enrich, de-normalize, and aggregate the data based on the specific business use case requirements.

Data denormalization

Source data systems, especially those from relational database systems, are mostly going to be highly normalized. This means that the source tables have been designed to contain information about a specific individual entity or topic. Each table will then link to other topics with related information through the use of foreign keys.

For example, you would have one table for customers and a separate table for salespeople. A record for a customer will include an identifier for the salesperson that works with that customer (such as sales_person_id). If you want to get the name of the salesperson that supports a specific customer, you could run a SQL query that joins the two tables. During the join, the system queries the customer table for the specific customer record and determines the sales_person_id value that is part of the record for that customer. The system then queries the sales_person table, finding the record with that sales_person_id, and can then access the name of the salesperson from there.

Our normalized customer table may look as follows:

Customer_ID	Last_Name	First_Name	Address_Street	Address_City	Address_State	Phone_Number	Sales_Person_ID
1	Smith	Jonathan	123 Main Street	Springville	MA	555-943-1987	2
2	Mendez	Bruno	5449 South West Street	Jersey	PA	555-615-1609	3
3	Sachdeva	Viyoma	94 Midland Avenue	Oxford	NJ	555-664-0464	1

Figure 7.1: Normalized customer table

And our normalized sales_person table may look as follows:

Sales_Person_ID	Last_Name	First_Name	Territory_Code
1	Taylor	Chris	95
2	Williams	Carmen	42
3	Kelly	Michael	23

Figure 7.2: Normalized sales_person table

Structuring tables this way has write-performance advantages for **Online Transaction Processing (OLTP)** systems and also helps to ensure the referential integrity of the database. Normalized tables also consume less disk space, since data is not repeated across multiple tables. This was a bigger benefit in the early days of databases when storage was limited and expensive, but it is not a significant benefit today with low-cost object storage systems such as Amazon S3.

When it comes to running **Online Analytical Processing (OLAP)** queries, having to join data across multiple tables does incur a performance hit. Therefore, data is often denormalized for analytics purposes.

If we had a use case that required us to regularly query customers with their salesperson details, we may want to create a new table that is a denormalized version of our `customer` and `sales_person` tables.

The denormalized customer table may look as follows:

Customer_ID	Last_Name	First_Name	Address_Street	Address_City	Address_State	Phone_Number	Sales_Person_Last	Sales_Person_First
1	Smith	Jonathan	123 Main Street	Springville	MA	555-943-1987	Williams	Carmen
2	Mendez	Bruno	5449 South West Street	Jersey	PA	555-615-1609	Kelly	Michael
3	Sachdeva	Viyoma	94 Midland Avenue	Oxford	NJ	555-664-0464	Taylor	Chris

Figure 7.3: Denormalized customer_sales_person table

With this table, we can now make a single query that does not require any joins in order to determine the details for a salesperson for a specific customer.

While this was a simple example of a **denormalization** use case, an analytics project may have tens, or even hundreds, of similar denormalization transforms. A denormalization transform may also join data from multiple source tables and may end up creating very wide tables.

It is important to spend time understanding the use case requirements and how the data will be used, and then determine the right table structure and required joins.

Performing these kinds of denormalization transforms can be done with Apache Spark, GUI-based tools, or SQL. AWS Glue Studio can also be used to design these kinds of table joins using a visual interface.

Enriching data

Similar to the way we joined two tables in the previous example for denormalization purposes, another common transformation is to **join tables** for the purpose of enriching the original dataset.

Data that is owned by an organization is already valuable but can often be made even more valuable by combining data the organization owns with data from third parties, or with data from other parts of the business. For example, a company that wants to market credit cards to consumers may purchase a database of consumer credit scores to match against their customer database, or a company that knows that its sales are impacted by weather conditions may purchase historical and future weather forecast data to help them analyze and forecast sales information.

AWS provides a data marketplace with the **AWS Data Exchange** service, a catalog of datasets available via paid subscription, as well as a number of free datasets. AWS Data Exchange currently contains over 1,000 datasets that can be easily subscribed to. Once you subscribe to a dataset, the Data Exchange API can be used to load data directly into your Amazon S3 landing zone.

In these scenarios, you would ingest the third-party dataset to the landing zone of your data lake, and then run a transformation to join the third-party dataset with company-owned data.

Pre-aggregating data

One of the benefits of data lakes is that they provide a low-cost environment for storing large datasets, without needing to pre-process the data or determine the data schema up front. You can ingest data from a wide variety of data sources and store the detailed granular raw data for a long period inexpensively. Then, over time, as you find you have new questions you want to ask of the data, you have all the raw data available to work with and can run ad-hoc queries against the data.

However, as the business develops specific questions they want to regularly ask of the data, the answers to these questions may not be easy to obtain through ad-hoc SQL queries. As a result, you may create transform jobs that run on a scheduled basis to perform the heavy computation that may be required to gain the required information from the data, making it easier for business users to gain the insights they need.

For example, you may create a transform job that creates a denormalized version of your sales data that includes, among others, columns for the store number, city, and state for each transaction. You may then have a **pre-aggregation transform** that runs daily to read this denormalized sales data (which may contain tens of millions of rows per day and tens or hundreds of columns) and compute sales, by category, at the store, city, and state level, and write these out to new tables. You may have hundreds of store managers who need access to store-level data at the category level via a BI visualization tool, but because we have pre-aggregated the data into new tables, the computation does not need to be run every time a report is run.

Pre-aggregating data reduces time to insights for business users and provides significant performance improvements, and therefore you should look to understand the frequent queries that are run by your data consumers, to determine where pre-aggregating data could bring business benefits.

Extracting metadata from unstructured data

As we have discussed previously, a data lake may also contain **unstructured data**, such as audio or image files. While these files cannot be queried directly with traditional analytical tools, we can create a pipeline that uses **Machine Learning (ML)** and **Artificial Intelligence (AI)** services to extract metadata from these unstructured files.

For example, a company that employs real-estate agents (realtors) may capture images of all houses for sale. One of their data engineers could create a pipeline that uses an AI service such as **Amazon Rekognition** to automatically identify objects in the image and to identify the type of room (kitchen, bedroom, and so on). This captured metadata could then be used in traditional analytics reporting.

Another example is a company that stores audio recordings of customer service phone calls. A pipeline could be built that uses an AI tool such as **Amazon Transcribe** to create transcripts of the calls, and then a tool such as **Amazon Comprehend** could perform sentiment analysis on the transcript. This would create an output that indicates whether the customer sentiment was positive, negative, or neutral for each call. This data could be joined with other data sources to develop a target list of customers to send specific marketing communication.

While unstructured data such as audio and image files may at first appear to have no benefit in an analytics environment, with modern AI tools, valuable metadata can be extracted from many of these sources. This metadata in turn becomes a valuable dataset that can be combined with other organizational data, in order to gather new insights through innovative analytics projects.

While we have only highlighted a few common transforms, there are literally hundreds of different transforms that may be used in an analytics project. Each business is unique and has unique requirements, and it is up to an organization's data teams to understand which data sources are available, and how these can be cleaned, optimized, combined, enriched, and otherwise transformed to help answer complex business questions.

Another aspect of data transformation is the process of applying updates to an existing dataset in a data lake, and we examine strategies for doing this in the next section.

Working with Change Data Capture (CDC) data

One of the most challenging aspects of working within a data lake environment is the processing of updates to existing data, such as with **Change Data Capture** (**CDC**) data. We have discussed CDC data previously, but as a reminder, this is data that contains updates to an existing dataset.

A good example of this is data that comes from a relational database system. After the initial loading of data to the data lake is complete, a system (such as **Amazon DMS**) can read the database transaction logs and write all future database updates to Amazon S3. For each row written to Amazon S3, the first column of the CDC file would contain one of the following characters (see the section on Amazon DMS in *Chapter 3, The AWS Data Engineer's Toolkit*, for an example of a CDC file generated by Amazon DMS):

1. **I – Insert:** This indicates that this row contains data that was newly inserted into the table
2. **U – Update:** This indicates that this row contains data that updates an existing record in the table
3. **D – Delete:** This indicates that this row contains data for a record that was deleted from the table

Traditionally, though, it has not been possible to execute updates or deletes of individual records within a data lake. Remember that Amazon S3 is an object storage service, so you can delete and replace a file but you cannot edit or just replace a portion of a file.

If you just append the new records to the existing data, you will end up with multiple copies of the same record, with each record reflecting the state of that record at a specific point in time. This can be useful to keep the history of how a record has changed over time, and so sometimes a transform job will be created to append the newly received data to the relevant table in the data lake for this purpose (potentially adding in a timestamp column that reflects the CDC data-ingestion time for each row). At the same time, we want our end users to be able to work with a dataset that only contains the current state of each data record.

There are two common approaches to handling updates to data in a data lake, as we explore next.

Traditional approaches – data upserts and SQL views

One of the traditional approaches to dealing with CDC data is to run a transform job, on a schedule, that effectively merges the new CDC data with the existing dataset, keeping only the latest records. This is commonly referred to as performing an **upsert** (a combination of update and insert).

One way to do this is to create a transform in Spark that reads existing data into one DataFrame, reads the new data into a different DataFrame, and then merges the DataFrames using custom logic, based on the specific dataset. The transform can then overwrite the existing data or write data to a new date-based partition, creating a new snapshot of the source system. A certain number of snapshots can be kept, enabling data consumers to query data from different points in time.

These transforms can end up being complex, and it is challenging to create a transform that is generic across all source datasets. Also, when overwriting the existing dataset with the updated dataset, there can be disruptions for data consumers who are trying to read from the dataset while the update is running. And as the dataset grows, the length of time and compute resources required to read in the full dataset in order to update it can become a major challenge. There are various strategies for dealing with these challenges, but they are complex, and for a long time, each organization facing these challenges had to implement its own complex solutions.

In order to create a solution that could be used across multiple different datasets, one common approach is to create a configuration table that captures details about source tables. This config table contains information such as a column that should be considered the primary key and a list of columns on which to partition the output. When the transform job runs, it reads the configuration table in order to integrate that table's specific settings with the logic in the transform job.

AWS has a blog post that provides a solution for using **AWS DMS** to capture CDC data from source databases and then run an **AWS Glue** job to apply the latest updates to the existing dataset. This blog post also creates a **DynamoDB** table to store configuration data on the source tables, and the solution can be deployed into an existing account using the provided **AWS CloudFormation** template. For more information, see the AWS blog post titled *Load ongoing data lake changes with AWS DMS and AWS Glue*.

An alternative approach is to use **Athena views** to create a virtualized table that shows the latest state of the data. An Athena view is a query that runs whenever the virtual table is queried, using a SELECT query that is defined in the view. The view definition will join the source (the current table) and the table with the new **CDC data**, and return a result that reflects the latest state of the data.

Creating a view that combines the existing data and the new CDC data enables consumers to query the latest state of the data, without needing to wait for a daily transform job to run to consolidate the datasets. However, performance will degrade over time as the CDC data table grows, so it is advisable to also have a daily job that will run to consolidate the new CDC data into the existing dataset. Creating and maintaining these views can be fairly complex, especially when combined with a need to also have a daily transform to consolidate the datasets.

For many years, organizations have faced the challenge of building and maintaining custom solutions like these to deal with CDC data and other data lake updates. However, in recent years, a number of new offerings have been created to address these requirements more generically, as we see in the next section.

Modern approaches — Open Table Formats (OTFs)

Over the past few years, a number of new **Open Table Formats (OTFs)** have been developed to support the idea of a more *transactional data lake*. When we refer to a transactional data lake, we are referencing the ability of a data lake to contain properties that were previously only available in a traditional database, such as the ability to update and delete individual records. In addition, many of these new solutions also provide support for **schema evolution** and **time travel** (the ability to query data as it was at a previous point in time).

Technically, these new OTFs bring **ACID** semantics to the data lake:

1. **Atomicity**: An expectation that data written will either be written as a full transaction or will not be written at all, and the dataset will be returned to its state prior to the transaction on failure

2. **Consistency**: The expectation that even if a failure occurs, the dataset will stay consistent

3. **Isolation**: The expectation that one transaction on the dataset will not be affected by another transaction that is requested at the same time

4. **Durability**: The expectation that once a successful transaction has been completed, this transaction will be durable (it will be permanent, even if there is a later system failure)

Now, this does not mean that these modern data lake solutions can replace existing OLTP-based databases. You are not going to suddenly see retailers dump their PostgreSQL, MySQL, or SQL Server databases that run their **Customer Relationship Management (CRM)** systems and instead use a data lake for everything.

Rather, data lakes are still intended as an analytical platform, but these new solutions significantly simplify the ability to apply changes to existing records, as well as the ability to delete records from a large dataset. These solutions also help to ensure data consistency as multiple teams work on the same datasets. There is still latency involved with these types of transactions, but much of the complexity involved with consolidating new and updated rows in a dataset, and providing a consistent, up-to-date view of data with lower latency, is handled by these solutions.

In *Chapter 14, Building Transactional Data Lakes*, we will do a deeper dive into OTFs, but let's have a quick look at some of the most common offerings for these new transactional data lakes.

Apache Iceberg

Apache Iceberg was created by engineers at **Netflix** and is designed as an OTF for very large datasets. The code was donated to the Apache Software Foundation and became a top-level project in May 2020. Since then, it has become a very popular choice for creating a transactional data lake.

Iceberg supports schema evolution, time travel for querying at a point in time, atomic table changes (to ensure that data consumers do not see partial or uncommitted changes), and support for multiple simultaneous writers.

In August 2021, a new start-up, **Tabular**, was formed by the creators of Iceberg to build a cloud-native data platform powered by Apache Iceberg. Also, most of the large cloud providers (as well as other vendors) have added support for Apache Iceberg into many of their products (for example, AWS Glue provides native support for the Apache Iceberg table format).

Apache Hudi

Apache Hudi started out as a project within **Uber** (the ride-sharing company) to provide a framework for developing low-latency and high-efficiency data pipelines for their large data lake environment. They subsequently donated the project to the Apache Software Foundation, which in turn made it a top-level project in 2020. Today, Apache Hudi is a popular option for building out transactional data lakes that support the ability to efficiently upsert new/changed data into a data lake, as well as to easily query tables and get the latest updates returned. AWS supports running Apache Hudi within the Amazon EMR managed service, as well as with AWS Glue.

Databricks Delta Lake

Databricks, a company formed by the original creators of Apache Spark, have developed their own approach to providing a transactional data lake, which has become popular over the past few years. This solution, called **Delta Lake**, is an open table format for streaming and batch operations that provides ACID transactions for inserts, updates, and deletes. In addition, Delta Lake supports time travel, which enables a query to retrieve data as it was at any point in time. Databricks have open-sourced this solution and made it available on GitHub at `https://github.com/delta-io/delta`.

In addition to the open-source version of Delta Lake, Databricks also offers a fully supported commercial version of Delta Lake that is popular with large enterprises. For more information on the commercial version of Delta Lake, see `https://databricks.com/product/delta-lake-on-databricks`.

Handling updates to existing data in a data lake has been a challenge for as long as data lakes have been in existence. Over the years, some common approaches have emerged to handle these challenges, but each organization has had to effectively *reinvent the wheel* to implement their own solution.

Now, with a number of companies recently creating solutions to provide a more transactional-type data lake that simplifies the process of inserting, updating, and deleting data, it makes sense to explore these open table formats, as outlined in this section, and covered more fully in *Chapter 14, Building Transactional Data Lakes*.

So far in this chapter, we have covered data preparation transformations, business use case transforms, and how to handle CDC-type updates for a data lake. Now we get hands-on with data transformation using AWS Glue Studio.

Hands-on – joining datasets with AWS Glue Studio

For our hands-on exercise in this chapter, we are going to use *AWS Glue Studio* to create an Apache Spark job that joins streaming data with data we migrated from our MySQL database in the previous chapter.

Creating a new data lake zone – the curated zone

As discussed in *Chapter 2, Data Management Architecture for Analytics*, it is common to have multiple zones in a data lake, containing different copies of our data as it gets transformed. So far, we have ingested raw data into the landing zone and then converted some of those datasets into Parquet format, and written the files out in the clean zone. In this chapter, we will be joining multiple datasets together and will write out the new dataset to the curated zone of our data lake. The curated zone is intended to store data that has been transformed and is ready for consumption by data consumers. We created an Amazon S3 bucket for the curated zone in a previous chapter, so now we can create a new AWS Glue database for this zone of our data lake:

1. Log in to the **AWS Management Console** (https://console.aws.amazon.com).

2. In the **top search bar**, search for and select **Glue** to access the Glue console.

3. On the left-hand side, select **Databases**, and then click **Add database**.

4. For **Database name**, type curatedzonedb, and then click **Create database**.

We have now created a new curated zone database for our data lake, and in the next step, we will create a new IAM role to provide the permissions needed for our Glue transformation job to run.

Creating a new IAM role for the Glue job

When we configure the Glue job using Glue Studio, we will need to specify an IAM role that has the following permissions:

1. Read our source S3 bucket (for example, dataeng-landing-zone-gse23 and dataeng-clean-zone-gse23)

2. Write to our target S3 bucket (for example, dataeng-curated-zone-gse23)

3. Access to Glue temporary directories

4. Write logs to **Amazon CloudWatch**

5. Access to all Glue API actions (to enable the creation of new databases and tables)

To create a new AWS IAM role with these permissions, follow these steps:

1. In the top search bar of the **AWS Management Console**, search for and select the **IAM** service, and in the left-hand menu, select **Policies**, and then click on **Create policy**.

2. By default, the **Visual editor** tab is selected, so click on **JSON** to change to the **JSON** tab.

3. Provide the JSON code from the following code blocks, replacing the boilerplate code. This policy provides the required S3 permissions, and we will provide Glue and CloudWatch permissions via a managed policy in a later step.

    Note that you can also copy and paste this policy by accessing the policy on this book's GitHub page. If doing a copy and paste from the GitHub copy of this policy, you must replace <initials> in bucket names with the unique identifier you used when creating the buckets.

    The first block of the policy configures the policy document and provides permissions to get objects from Amazon S3 that are in the Amazon S3 buckets specified in the resource section. Make sure you replace <initials> with the unique identifier you have used in your bucket names:

    ```json
    {
        "Version": "2012-10-17",
        "Statement": [
            {
                "Effect": "Allow",
                "Action": [
                    "s3:GetObject"
                ],
                "Resource": [
                    "arn:aws:s3:::dataeng-landing-zone-<initials>/*",
                    "arn:aws:s3:::dataeng-clean-zone-<initials>/*"
                ]
            },
    ```

4. This next block of the policy provides permissions for all Amazon S3 actions (get, put, and so on) that are in the Amazon S3 bucket specified in the resource section (in this case, our curated zone bucket). Make sure you replace <initials> with the unique identifier you have used in your bucket names:

```
        {
            "Effect": "Allow",
            "Action": [
                "s3:*"
            ],
            "Resource": "arn:aws:s3:::dataeng-curated-zone-
    <initials>/*"
        }
    ]
}
```

5. Click on **Next: tags** and then click on **Next: Review**.

6. Provide a name for the policy, such as `DataEngGlueCWS3CuratedZoneWrite`, and then click **Create policy**.

7. In the left-hand menu, click on **Roles** and then **Create role**.

8. For **Trusted entity**, ensure **AWS service** is selected, and for **Use case** search for and select **Glue**, and then click **Next**. Listing Glue as a trusted entity for this role enables the AWS Glue service to assume this role to run transformations.

9. Under the **Attach permissions** policies, select the policy we just created (for example, `DataEngGlueCWS3CuratedZoneWrite`) by searching and then clicking in the checkbox.

10. Also, search for `AWSGlueServiceRole` and click on the checkbox to select this role (make sure that it is the managed `AWSGlueServiceRole` policy, and not a policy previously created, such as `AWSGlueServiceRole-streaming-crawler-Fefdx-s3Policy`). This managed policy provides access to temporary directories used by Glue, as well as **CloudWatch** logs and Glue resources.

11. Then, click **Next**.

12. Provide a role name, such as `DataEngGlueCWS3CuratedZoneRole`, and click **Create role**.

We have now configured the permissions required for our Glue job to be able to access the required resources, so we can now move on to building our transformation using Glue Studio.

Configuring a denormalization transform using AWS Glue Studio

We are now ready to create an **Apache Spark** job to denormalize the film data that we migrated from our MySQL database. The dataset we migrated is normalized currently (as expected for data coming from a relational database), so we want to denormalize some of the data to use in future transforms.

Ultimately, we want to be able to analyze various data points of our new streaming library of classic movies. One of the data points we want to understand is which categories of movies are the most popular, but to find the name of a category associated with a specific movie, we need to query three different tables in our source dataset. The tables are as follows:

1. `film`: This table contains details of each film in our classic movie library, including `film_id`, `title`, `description`, `release_year`, and `rating`. However, this table does not contain any information about the category that the film is in.

2. `category`: This table contains the name of each category of film (such as action, comedy, drama, and so on), as well as `category_id`. However, this table does not contain any information that links a category with a film.

3. `film_category`: This table is designed to provide a link between a specific film and a specific category. Each row contains a `film_id` value and associated `category_id`.

When analyzing the incoming streaming data about viewers streaming our movies, we don't want to have to do joins on each of the above tables to determine the category of movie that was streamed. So, in this first transform job that we are going to create, we denormalize this group of tables so that we end up with a single table that includes the category for each film in our film library.

To build the denormalization job using AWS Glue Studio, follow these steps:

1. In the AWS Management Console, use the top search bar to search for and select the **Glue** service.

2. In the left-hand menu, click on **ETL Jobs**.

3. Click on the **Visual ETL** option

4. On the left-hand side, under the **Visual** tab, click on **Amazon S3 (source)** as a new node.

5. On the right-hand side, under **Data source properties – S3**, ensure **Data Catalog table** is selected for **S3 source type**, and from the dropdown, select the `sakila` database.

6. For the **Table** dropdown, select `film_category`.

7. Set **Name** for this node to be `S3 - Film-Category`.

At this point, the Glue Studio screen should look as follows:

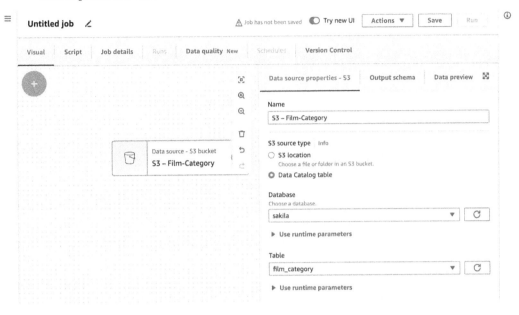

Figure 7.4: Glue Studio with first S3 data source

8. Click the **plus sign (+)** in the top left of the visual editor, and repeat *steps 4-7*, adding another S3 source for the `film` table, but set **Name** to S3 - Film. Once done, your Glue studio screen should look as follows:

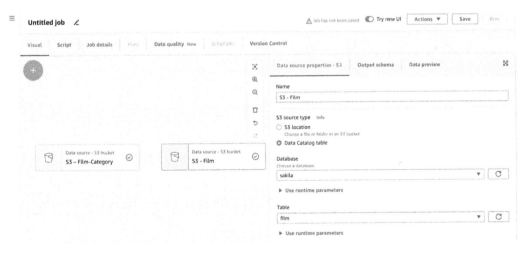

Figure 7.5: Glue Studio with two S3 data sources

9. In the **Designer** window, click on the **plus sign (+)** again, and from the **Transform** tab, select the **Join** transform.

10. The **Join** transform requires two "parent" nodes – the two tables that we want to join. To set the parent nodes, use the **Node parents** dropdown to select the **S3 – Film** and **S3 – Film-Category** tables.

11. You will see a red checkmark on the **Transform** tab, indicating an issue that needs to be resolved. Click on the **Transform** tab, and you will see a warning about both tables having a column with the same name. Glue Studio offers to automatically resolve the issue by adding a custom prefix to the columns in the right-hand table. Click on **Resolve it** to have Glue Studio automatically add a new transform that renames the columns in the right-hand table.

12. There are a number of different join types that Glue Studio supports. Review the **Join type** drop-down list to understand the differences. For our use case, we want to join all the rows from our left-hand table (film) with matching rows from the right-hand table (film_category). The resulting table will have rows for every film, and each row will also include information from the film_category table – in this case, the category_id value for each film. For **Join type**, select **Left join**, and then click **Add condition**. We want to match the film_id field from the film table with the film_id field from the film_category table. Remember, though, that we had Glue Studio automatically rename the fields in the film_category table, so for the film_category table, select the **(right)** film_id field.

Once done, your Glue Studio screen should look as follows:

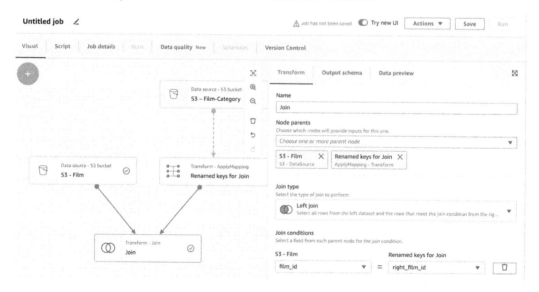

Figure 7.6: Glue Studio after first table join

13. Let's provide a name for the temporary table created as a result of the join. On the **Node properties** tab, change **Name** to `Join - Film-Category_ID`.

14. We don't need all the data that is in our temporary `Join - Film-Category_ID` table, so we can now use the **Glue Change Schema** transform to drop the columns we don't need, rename fields, and so on. Click on the **plus sign (+)** , and from the **Transforms** tab, select **Change Schema.**

15. Some of the fields that are related to our original data from when these movies were rented out from our DVD stores are not relevant to our new streaming business, so we can drop those now. At the same time, we can drop some of the fields from our `film_category` table, as the only column we need from that table is `category_id`. Select the **Drop** checkbox for the following columns:

    - `rental_duration`
    - `rental_rate`
    - `replacement_cost`
    - `last_update`
    - `(right) film_id`
    - `(right) last_update`

16. We can now add a transform, which will join the results of the **Change Schema** transform with our category table, adding the name of the category for each film. To add the **Category** table to our transform, click the **plus sign (+),** and from the **Data** tab, select **Amazon S3**. Ensure **Data Catalog Table** is selected, and for **Database**, select **sakila**; and for **Table**, select **Category**. To provide a descriptive name, change **Name** to `S3 - Category`.

17. We can now add our final transformation. Click the **plus sign (+)**, and from the **Transforms** tab, select **Join.**

18. We always need two tables for a join, so from the **Node properties** tab, use the **Node parents** dropdown to add the **Change Schema** transform as a parent of the join, and change **Name** to `Join - Film-Category`.

19. On the **Transform** tab, select **Left join** for **Join type**, and then click **Add condition**. From the **S3 – Category** table, select the `category_id` field, and from the **Change Schema** table, select the `(right) category_id` field.

20. Now we will add one last **Change Schema** transform to again remove unneeded fields, and rename fields where appropriate. Click the **plus sign (+)**, and from the **Transforms** tab, select **Change Schema**. Click the checkbox next to the following columns in order to drop them:

    - `last_update`
    - `(right) category_id`

21. Then, for the **Source key** value of **name**, change **Target key** to be `category_name`, as this is a more descriptive name for this field.

In this section, we configured our Glue job for the transform steps required to denormalize our film and category data. In the next section, we will complete the configuration of our Glue job by specifying where we want our new denormalized table to be written.

Finalizing the denormalization transform job to write to S3

To finalize the configuration of our transform job using Glue Studio, we now need to specify the target that we want to write our data to:

1. Add a target by clicking on the **plus sign (+)**, and from the **Targets** tab, select Amazon S3.

2. On the **Data target properties – S3** tab, ensure **Parquet** is selected for **Format** and **Snappy** for **Compression type**. Click on **Browse S3** for **S3 Target Location**, select the checkbox for the `dataeng-curated-zone-<initials>` bucket, and click **Choose**. In the **S3 Target Location** field, add a prefix after the bucket name of `/filmdb/film_category/`.

3. For **Data Catalog update options**, select **Create a table in the Data Catalog, and on subsequent runs, update the schema and add new partitions**.

4. For **Database**, select `curatedzonedb` from the drop-down list.

5. For **Table name**, type in `film_category`. Note that Spark requires lowercase table and column names, and that the only special character supported by Athena is the underscore character, which is why we use this rather than a hyphen.

Our **Data target properties – S3** configuration should look as follows:

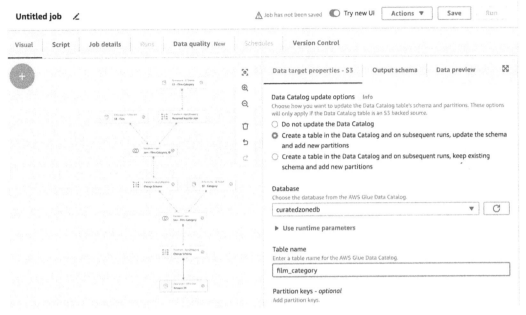

Figure 7.7: Data target properties – S3 configuration

A note about partition keys

Our sample dataset is very small (just 1,000 film records), but imagine for a moment that we were trying to create a similar table, including category information, for all the books ever published. According to an estimate from Google in 2010, there were nearly 130 million books that they planned to scan into a digital format. If our intention was to query all this book data to gather information on the books by category, then we would add a partition key, and specify `category_name` as a partition. When the data was written to S3, it would be grouped into different prefixes based on the category name, and this would significantly increase performance when we queried books by category.

6. We can now provide a name and permissions configuration for our job. In the top left, change from the **Visual** tab to the **Job details** tab.

7. Set the name of the job to be `Film Category Denormalization`.

8. For **IAM Role**, from the dropdown, select the role we created previously (`DataEngGlueC WS3CuratedZoneRole`).

9. For **Requested number of workers**, change this to 2. This configuration item specifies the number of nodes configured to run our Glue job, and since our dataset is small, we can use the minimum number of nodes. Since we are using the minimum number of nodes, auto-scaling will not make a difference, but it is **strongly encouraged** to use the option for **Automatically scale the number of workers** when configuring your jobs. This feature ensures that Glue dynamically changes the number of workers to match what is needed by your job, saving you money by minimizing idle workers.

10. For **Job bookmark**, ensure this setting is set to **Disable**. A job bookmark is a feature of Glue that tracks which files have been previously processed so that a subsequent run of the job does not process the same files again. For our testing purposes, we may want to process our test data multiple times, so we disable the bookmark.

11. For **Number of retries**, ensure this is set to **0**. If our job fails to run, we don't want it to automatically repeat.

12. Leave all other defaults, and at the top right, click on **Save**. Then, click on **Run** to run the transform job.

13. Click on the **Runs** tab in order to monitor the job run. You can also change to the **Script** tab if you want to view the Spark code that AWS Glue Studio generated.

14. When the job completes, navigate to the **Amazon S3** console and review the output location (such as `dataeng-curated-zone-gse23/filmdb/film_category`) to validate that the new Parquet files were created. Also, navigate to the **AWS Glue** console to confirm that the new table (`film_category`) was created in `curatedzonedb`.

In the preceding steps, we denormalized data related to our catalog of films and their categories, and we can now join data from this new table with our streaming data.

Create a transform job to join streaming and film data using AWS Glue Studio

In this section, we're going to use **AWS Glue Studio** to create another transform, this time to join the table containing all streams of our movies, with the denormalized data about our film catalog:

1. In the **AWS Management Console**, use the top search bar to search for and select the **Glue** service.

2. In the left-hand menu, click on **ETL jobs**.

3. Click on the **Visual ETL** option for **Create job**.

4. In the **Visual** tab, under **Add nodes**, select **Amazon S3 (source)**.

5. On the right-hand side, under the **Data source properties – S3 tab**, under **S3 source type**, ensure **Data Catalog table** is selected, and from the dropdown, select the curatedzonedb database.

6. For the **Table** dropdown, select film_category.

7. Set **Name** to S3 - Film_Category.

8. On the left-hand side, under the **Visual** tab, click on the PLUS (+) sign. Repeat *steps 4–7*, adding another S3 source for the **streaming** table from the streamingdb database, and setting the name to S3 - Streaming.

9. Click on the **plus sign (+)**, and from the **Transforms** tab, add a **Change Schema** transform for the **S3 – Streaming** data source (confirm that the **S3 – Streaming** source is selected by looking at **Node parents** on the **Node properties** tab).

10. Under the **Node properties** tab, change the **Name** of this transform element to Change Schema - Streaming.

11. On the **Transform** tab, under **Change Schema**, change the name of the film_id key to film_id_streaming (by changing the **Target key** value for film_id). Both of our S3 source tables have a film_id field, which is why we need to change the field name for one of the tables.

12. Click the **plus sign (+)** again, and under the **Transform** tab, add a **Join** transform and set **Join type** to **Left join**.

13. Under the **Transform** tab, ensure that the **Change Schema – Streaming** element and the S3 - Film_Category are listed as **Node parents.**

14. Under the **Transform** tab, for **Join conditions**, click on **Add condition**. Select film_id_streaming for the **Change Schema – Streaming** element, and film_id for the S3 - Film_Category element.

Your Glue Studio visual designer should look as follows:

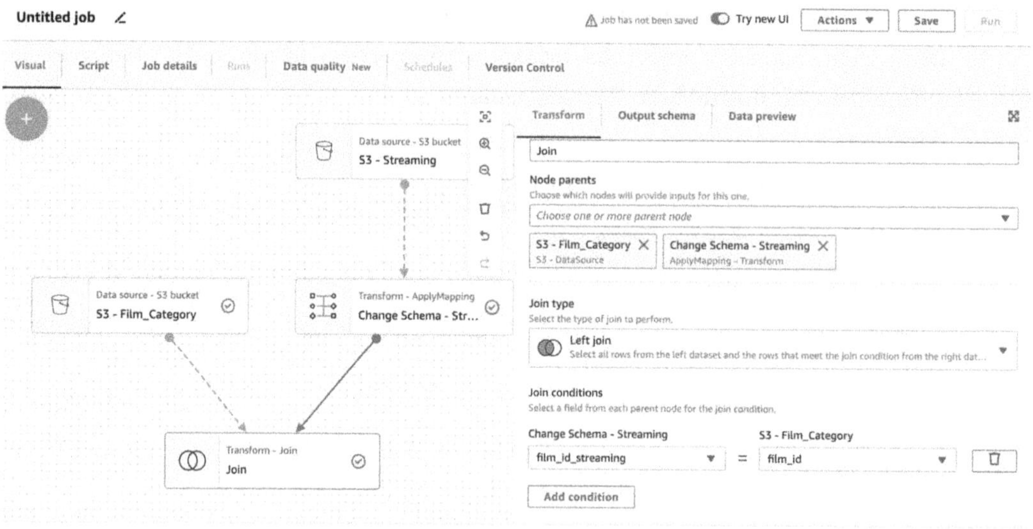

Figure 7.8: Glue Studio interface showing the first join

15. Add a target by clicking on the **plus sign (+)**, and under the **Targets** tab, click on Amazon S3.

16. For **Format**, select **Parquet** from the dropdown, and for **Compression type**, select **Snappy**.

17. For **S3 Target Location**, click **Browse S3**, click the selector for the dataeng-curatedzone-<initials> bucket, and click **Choose**. Add a prefix after the bucket of /streaming/streaming-films/.

18. For **Data Catalog update options**, select **Create a table in the Data Catalog, and on subsequent runs, update the schema and add new partitions**.

19. For **Database**, select curatedzonedb from the drop-down list.

20. For **Table name**, type in streaming_films.

Our **Data Target Properties** – **S3** configuration should look as follows:

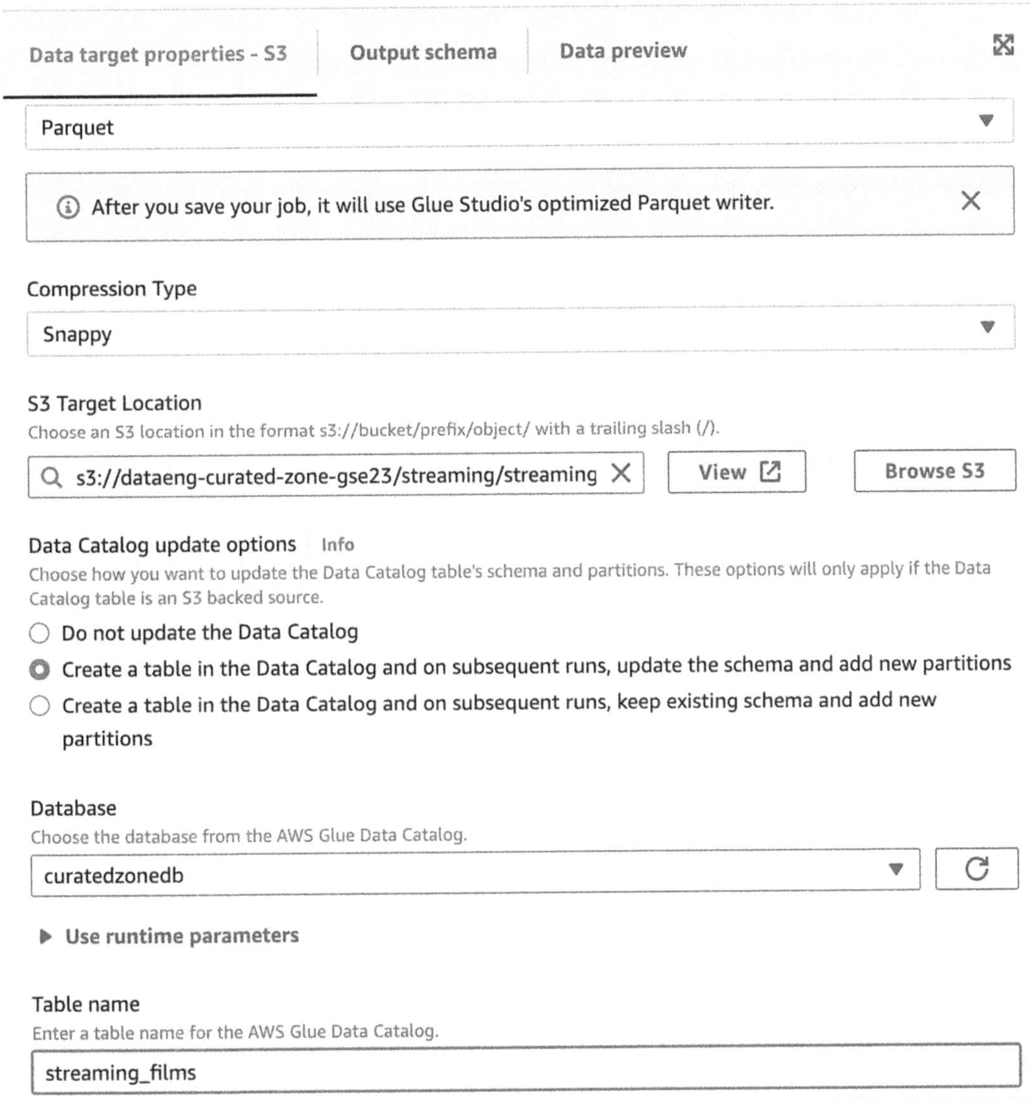

| Data target properties - S3 | Output schema | Data preview | ⤢ |

Parquet ▼

ⓘ After you save your job, it will use Glue Studio's optimized Parquet writer. ✕

Compression Type

Snappy ▼

S3 Target Location
Choose an S3 location in the format s3://bucket/prefix/object/ with a trailing slash (/).

🔍 s3://dataeng-curated-zone-gse23/streaming/streaming ✕   View ☐   Browse S3

Data Catalog update options   Info
Choose how you want to update the Data Catalog table's schema and partitions. These options will only apply if the Data Catalog table is an S3 backed source.

○ Do not update the Data Catalog
◉ Create a table in the Data Catalog and on subsequent runs, update the schema and add new partitions
○ Create a table in the Data Catalog and on subsequent runs, keep existing schema and add new partitions

Database
Choose the database from the AWS Glue Data Catalog.

curatedzonedb ▼   ↻

▶ **Use runtime parameters**

Table name
Enter a table name for the AWS Glue Data Catalog.

streaming_films

Figure 7.9: Glue Studio interface showing target configuration

21. We can now provide a name and permissions configuration for our job. Along the top list of tabs, change from the **Visual** tab to the **Job details** tab.

22. Set the name of the job to be `Streaming Data Film Enrichment`.

23. For **IAM Role**, from the dropdown, select the role we created previously (`DataEngGlueC WS3CuratedZoneRole`).

24. For **Number of workers**, change this to **2**.

25. For **Job bookmark**, make sure this is set to **Disable**.

26. For **Number of retries**, make sure this is set to **0**.

27. Leave all other defaults, and at the top right, click on **Save**. Then click on **Run** to run the transform job.

28. Click on the **Runs** tab in order to monitor the job run.

29. When the job status changes to **Succeeded**, click on **Databases** (under **Data Catalog)** to confirm that the new table (`streaming_films`) was created in the `curatedzonedb` database.

30. Navigate to the **Amazon S3** console and review the output location (`dataeng-curatedzone-<initials>/streaming/streaming-films/`) to validate that the files were created.

We have now created a single table that contains a record of all streams of our classic movies, along with details about each movie, including the category of the movie. This table can be efficiently queried to analyze streams of our classic movies to determine the most popular movie and movie category, and we can break this down by state and other dimensions.

Summary

In this chapter, we've reviewed a number of common transformations that can be applied to raw datasets, covering both generic transformations used to optimize data for analytics and business transforms to enrich and denormalize datasets.

This chapter built on previous chapters in this book. We started by looking at how to architect a data pipeline, then reviewed ways to ingest different data types into a data lake, and in this chapter, we reviewed common data transformations.

In the next chapter, we will look at common types of data consumers and learn more about how different data consumers want to access data in different ways, and with different tools.

Learn more on Discord

To join the Discord community for this book – where you can share feedback, ask questions to the author, and learn about new releases – follow the QR code below:

```
https://discord.gg/9s5mHNyECd
```

8

Identifying and Enabling Data Consumers

A data consumer can be defined as a person, or application, within an organization that needs access to data. Data consumers can vary from staff that pack shelves and need to know stock levels to the CEO of an organization that needs data to make a decision on which projects to invest in. A data consumer can also be a system that needs data from a different system.

Everything a data engineer does is to make datasets useful and accessible to data consumers, which, in turn, enables the business to gain useful insights from their data. This means delivering the right data, via the right tools, to the right people or applications, at the right time, to enable the business to make informed decisions.

Therefore, when designing a data engineering pipeline (as covered in *Chapter 5, Architecting Data Engineering Pipelines*), data engineers should start by understanding business objectives, including who the data consumers are and what their requirements are.

We can then work backward from these requirements to ensure that we use the appropriate tools to ingest data at the required frequency (streaming or batch, for example). We can also ensure that we create transformation pipelines that transform raw data sources into data that meets the consumer's specific requirements. And, finally, understanding our data consumers will guide us in selecting a target location and format for our transformed data that is compatible with the tools that best enable our data consumers.

Maintaining an understanding of how the data is consumed, as well as knowledge of any downstream dependencies, will also help data engineers support different types of data consumers as they work with a variety of datasets.

In this chapter, we will do a deep dive into data consumers by covering the following topics:

- Understanding the impact of data democratization
- Meeting the needs of business users with data visualization
- Meeting the needs of data analysts with structured reporting
- Meeting the needs of data scientists and ML models
- Hands-on – transforming data using AWS Glue DataBrew

Technical requirements

For the hands-on exercise in this chapter, you will need permission to use the AWS Glue DataBrew service. You will also need to have access to the AWS Glue Data Catalog and any underlying Amazon S3 locations for the databases and tables that were created in the previous chapters. If you are using the administrative user created in *Chapter 1*, then you will have the necessary permissions.

You can find the code files of this chapter in the GitHub repository using the following link: https://github.com/PacktPublishing/Data-Engineering-with-AWS-2nd-edition/tree/main/Chapter08

Understanding the impact of data democratization

At a high level, business drivers have not changed significantly over the past few decades. Organizations are still interested in understanding market trends and customer behavior, increasing customer retention, improving product quality, and improving speed to market. However, the analytics landscape, the teams and individual roles that deliver business insights, and the tools that are used to deliver business value have evolved.

Data democratization – the enhanced accessibility of data for a growing audience of users, in a timely and cost-efficient manner – has become a standard expectation for most businesses. Today's varied data consumers expect to be able to get access to the right data promptly, using their tool of choice to consume the data.

In fact, as datasets increase in volume and velocity, their gravity will attract more applications and consumers. This is based on the concept of *data gravity*, a term coined by Dave McCrory, which suggests that data has mass. That is, as datasets increase in size, they attract more users and become more difficult to move.

The takeaway here is that as data volumes grow, and the velocity at which data is ingested increases, the more business users demand easy access to high-quality data. Delivering on this becomes critical for enabling a business to stay competitive.

A growing variety of data consumers

Over the past few years, we have seen an increase in the number and type of data consumers within an organization, and these data consumers are constantly looking for new data sources and tools. As a result, in today's modern organizations, we can expect to find a wide variety of data consumers – from traditional business users and data analysts to data scientists, machine-to-machine applications, as well as new types of business users (as organizations become more data-driven, it's not only senior managers that need access to data, but employees at all levels of the organization need access to relevant, high-quality data).

Beyond just the ability to run SQL queries and generate scheduled reports based on a pre-existing dataset, we see data analysts who also want the ability to do ad hoc data cleansing and exploration, as well as the ability to join structured data with semi-structured data or metadata extracted from unstructured data. For example, they may want to examine how social media drives sales trends.

And business users now expect dashboards to be refreshed with real, or near-real-time, data. They also want these dashboards to be accessible from anywhere, on many different types of mobile devices. Furthermore, they are interested in more than just sales or ERP data. Analysts and business users are interested in social media data to identify consumer trends, and insurance and real estate companies are looking for data to be extracted from documents (such as medical reports or property appraisals). In the manufacturing industry, a variety of data consumers want access to data that's been collected from machines, devices, and vehicles for use cases such as proactively anticipating maintenance requirements.

Data consumers are also no longer limited to individual humans or teams. We are seeing a growing need for business applications to access data, be fed data, or be triggered based on an event or trend in the data. Call centers are interested in real-time transcripts of audio calls for sentiment analysis and tagging calls for manager review. They are also looking for applications and integrations that would use real-time call transcriptions, or full-text analysis of corporate documents, to reduce the time agents spend searching for answers. Engagement platforms map the customer journey and use every event (for example, email opened or email ignored) to tailor the customer experience.

Finally, organizations have a growing need for data science, and as such, the number of data scientist roles within those organizations is increasing. Data scientists develop **machine learning (ML)** models that can identify non-obvious patterns in large datasets or make predictions about future behaviors based on historical data. Data scientists usually require access to raw, non-aggregated data, and require large volumes of data to train a machine learning model and test the model for accuracy.

How a data mesh helps data consumers

With the increase in the number of datasets within an organization, and with a growing set of users wanting access to data across an organization, it can be very difficult for data consumers to find the data they need. Once a data consumer does find an available dataset, they need to be able to easily understand whether the dataset they found will meet their needs, and also need to get access to the data without complicated processes and the need to create multiple copies of the dataset.

A data mesh strategy (which we cover in more detail in *Chapter 15, Implementing a Data Mesh Strategy*), includes some core principles that help make datasets more easily discoverable, understandable, and accessible by data consumers. One of the data mesh principles is that of a self-serve data platform, and this platform is intended to streamline the experience of data consumers discovering, accessing, and using datasets.

The self-serve data platform often includes a business data catalog as the mechanism to make data discoverable. Data consumers can go to the catalog to search and discover all the datasets available in an organization. Each dataset published to the catalog should include additional metadata that helps the data consumer better understand the data (such as where the data comes from, who owns it, and business metadata providing more context around the dataset). The catalog should also provide a mechanism for a consumer to request access to a dataset, and then, if needed, the ability to automatically route that request to the appropriate person to approve the access. Once approved, the self-serve data platform should make it easy for the consumer to access the dataset, without needing to physically copy the dataset.

Let's now take a deeper dive into some of the different types of data consumers that we can find in today's organizations. We will also look at how data engineers can help enable each of these data consumers.

Meeting the needs of business users with data visualization

Some roles within an organization, such as data analysts, have always had easy access to data. For a long time, these roles were effectively gatekeepers of the data, and any "ordinary" business users that had custom data requirements would need to go through the data gatekeepers.

However, over the past decade or so, the growth of big data has expanded the thirst and need for custom data among a growing number of **business users**. Business users are no longer willing to tolerate having to go through long, formal processes to access the data they need to make decisions. Instead, users have come to demand easier, and more immediate, access to wider sets of data.

To remain competitive, organizations need to ensure that they enable all the decision-makers in their business to have easy and direct access to the right data. At the same time, organizations need to ensure that good data governance is in place and that data consumers only have access to the data they need (as we discussed in *Chapter 4, Data Governance, Security, and Cataloging*). Data engineers are key to enabling this.

AWS tools for business users

Business users have mixed skill sets, ranging from those that are Excel power users and are comfortable with concepts such as pivot tables, to executives who want easy access to dashboards that provide visualizations that summarize complex data.

As a data engineer, you need to be able to provide solutions that meet the needs of these diverse business users. Within AWS, the primary tool that's used by business users is **Amazon QuickSight**, a cloud-based **Business Intelligence** (**BI**) application. QuickSight enables the creation of easy-to-access visualizations and reports but also provides functionality for advanced users to dig deeper into the data while providing strong security and governance controls. Amazon QuickSight is cloud-based and can easily be provisioned for hundreds, or even thousands, of users in an organization.

A quick overview of Amazon QuickSight

We will do a deep dive into **Amazon QuickSight** in *Chapter 12, Visualizing Data with Amazon QuickSight*, but in this section, we will have a brief look at some of the primary ways that business users can use this tool.

Amazon QuickSight provides interactive access to data for business users, with many different types and styles of charts supported. A dashboard can display data from multiple different data sources, and users can filter data, sort data, and even drill down into specific aspects of a dataset. In addition to dashboards, QuickSight can also be used to generate multi-page reports.

Business users can elect to receive **dashboards** via regular emails or can access and interact with dashboards on-demand via the QuickSight portal or the QuickSight mobile app. Dashboards can also be embedded into existing web portals and apps, making these rich data visualizations accessible via existing tools that business users have access to.

With a feature called **Amazon QuickSight Q**, business users can ask questions in natural language and receive answers, along with visualizations. This feature uses the power of **Natural Language Processing (NLP)** based machine learning models to understand the intent of a query and to then automatically identify appropriate data sources and create relevant visuals. For example, a sales manager could type in a query such as *"show me sales this month by segment,"* and QuickSight will create a chart showing the relevant information.

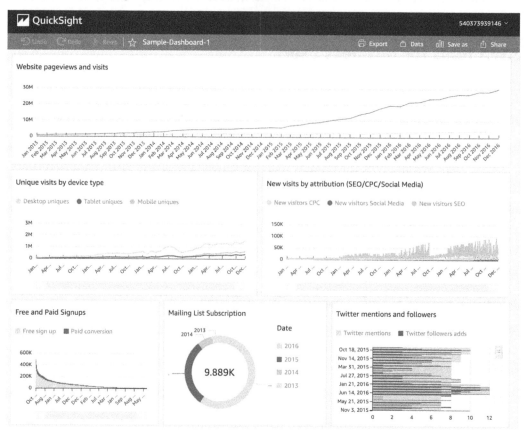

Figure 8.1: A sample QuickSight dashboard

While some users may have previously used spreadsheets to explore datasets using custom-built charts and pivot tables, QuickSight can provide the same functionality but in a much easier-to-use way. QuickSight also provides security, governance, and auditability, which is not possible when users share ad hoc spreadsheets.

QuickSight can use data from many different sources, including directly from an S3-based data lake, databases (such as Redshift, MySQL, and Oracle), SaaS applications (including Salesforce, ServiceNow, Jira, and others), as well as numerous other sources.

As a data engineer, you may be involved in helping set up QuickSight and may need to configure access to the various data sources. QuickSight users with relevant access can combine different data sources directly, thereby enabling them to build the visualizations the business requires without going through traditional data gatekeepers. However, there may also be times when you are asked to create new datasets in a data lake or data warehouse (such as Redshift or Snowflake) so that QuickSight users can access the required data without needing to combine and transform datasets themselves.

We are now going to move on and explore a different type of data consumer – the data analyst. But for a deeper dive into QuickSight, including a hands-on exercise on creating a QuickSight visual, refer to *Chapter 12, Visualizing Data with Amazon QuickSight.*

Meeting the needs of data analysts with structured reporting

While business users make use of data to make decisions related to their job in an organization, a data analyst's full-time job is all about the data – analyzing datasets and drawing out insights for the business.

If you look at various job descriptions for **data analysts**, you may see a fair amount of variety, but some elements will be common across most descriptions. These include the following:

- Cleansing data and ensuring data quality when working with ad hoc data sources.
- Developing a good understanding of their specific part of the business (sometimes referred to as becoming a domain specialist for their part of the organization). This involves understanding what data matters to their part of the organization, which metrics are important, and so on.

- Interpreting data to draw out insights for the organization (this may include identifying trends, highlighting areas of concern, and performing statistical analysis on data). The data analyst also needs to present the information they've gathered, as well as their conclusions, to business leaders.

- Creating visualizations using powerful BI software (such as Amazon QuickSight) that other business users can then interact with.

- Doing an ad hoc analysis of data using structured query languages such as SQL.

A data analyst is often tasked with doing complex data analysis to answer specific business questions. Examples, as described earlier in this book, include identifying which products are the most popular by different age or socio-economic demographics. Another example is what percentage of customers have browsed the company's e-commerce store more than 5 times, for more than 10 minutes at a time, in the last 2 weeks, but have not purchased anything.

At times, a data analyst may make use of data in the data lake that has already been through formal data engineering pipelines, which means it has been cleaned and checked for quality. At other times, a data analyst may need to ingest new raw data, and in these cases, they may be responsible for data cleansing and performing quality checks on the data.

Some of the work a data analyst does may be to use ad hoc SQL queries to answer very specific queries for a certain project, while at other times they may create reports, or visualizations, that run on a scheduled basis to provide information to business users.

AWS tools for data analysts

Data analysts may use a variety of tools as they work with diverse datasets. This includes using query languages, such as SQL, to explore data in a data warehouse such as Redshift or data in a traditional database. A data analyst may also use advanced toolsets such as **Python** or **R** to perform data manipulation and exploration. Visual transformation tools may also be used by the data analyst to cleanse and prepare data when working with ad hoc data sources that have not been through formal data engineering pipelines.

Data analysts also use BI tools, such as **Amazon QuickSight**, to create advanced visualizations or multi-page reports for business users. We covered Amazon QuickSight previously, so let's explore some of the other tools in AWS that can be used by data analysts.

Amazon Athena

Amazon Athena is a service that enables users to run complex SQL queries against a variety of data sources. This can be used to perform ad hoc exploration of data, enabling the data analyst to learn more about the data and test out different queries. Users also have the ability to use an integrated notebook environment to run Spark code for complex queries.

Using Athena, a data analyst can run queries that join data from across tables in different data sources. For example, using Athena, you can run a single query that brings data in from S3 and joins that with data from Redshift.

In *Chapter 11, Ad Hoc Queries with Amazon Athena*, we will do a deeper dive into the Athena service.

AWS Glue DataBrew

Data analysts often need to use new sources of data to answer new questions and may need to perform some data transformation on these datasets. While creating these new insights, the data analyst may work closely with business users to develop the reports, visualizations, metrics, or other data as needed. Part of this iterative process may involve creating ad hoc transformation pipelines to ingest, cleanse, join, and transform data.

Once the deliverable has been finalized (data sources identified, transformations determined, and so on), the data analyst may work with their data engineering team to formalize the pipeline. This is a recommended best practice to ensure that all pipelines are contained in a source control system, are part of formal deployment processes, and so on. As such, data engineers should work closely with data analysts, and always be ready to help formalize the ad hoc pipelines that a data analyst may create and that the business has come to depend on.

One of the AWS tools that is very popular with data analysts is the **AWS Glue DataBrew** service. Using DataBrew, data analysts can easily cleanse new data sources and transform and join data from different tables to create new datasets.

This can all be done with the Glue DataBrew **visual interface**, without the data analyst needing to write any code.

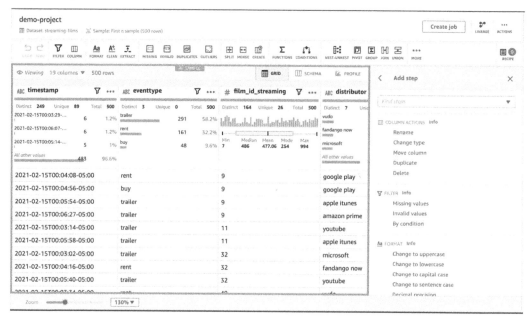

Figure 8.2: The AWS Glue DataBrew visual transform designer

Glue DataBrew can connect to many different data sources, including Redshift and Snowflake, JDBC databases, S3, Glue/Lake Formation tables, as well as other Amazon services such as AWS Data Exchange and Amazon AppFlow. DataBrew also includes over 250 **built-in transforms** that can be used by data analysts to easily perform common data cleansing tasks and transformations. In the hands-on section of this chapter, you will get to use some of these built-in transforms.

Running Python or R in AWS

Some data analysts have advanced coding skills that they put to use to explore and visualize data using popular programming languages such as Python and R. These languages include many functions for statistically analyzing datasets and creating advanced visualizations.

Python code can be run using multiple services in AWS, including the following:

1. **AWS Lambda:** Can run Python code in a serverless environment, for up to a maximum of 15 minutes of runtime

2. **AWS Glue Python shell**: Can run Python code in a serverless environment, with no limit on how long it runs

3. **Amazon EC2**: A compute service where you can install Python and run Python code

In addition, if working with large datasets where a single compute node does not provide the needed processing power, *AWS Glue for Ray* is an engine option on AWS Glue that enables processing large datasets with Python and popular Python libraries. AWS Glue for Ray supports the popular `ray.io` open-source compute framework that enables running Python code over multi-node clusters.

RStudio, a popular IDE that can be used for creating data analytic projects based on the R programming language, can also be run using multiple services in AWS:

1. **RStudio** can be run on Amazon EC2 compute instances, enabling data analysts to create R-based projects for data analysis. See the AWS blog titled *Running R on AWS* (`https://aws.amazon.com/blogs/big-data/running-r-on-aws/`) for more information on how to set this up.

2. If you're working with very large datasets, RStudio can also be run on Amazon EMR, which uses multiple compute nodes to process large datasets. See the AWS blog titled *Statistical Analysis with Open-Source R and RStudio on Amazon EMR* (`https://aws.amazon.com/blogs/big-data/statistical-analysis-with-open-source-r-and-rstudio-on-amazon-emr/`) for more information on how to use R with Amazon EMR.

Data engineers can help enable data analysts who have strong Python or R skills by helping them configure these coding environments in AWS. Data engineers can also help formalize data transformation pipelines in those cases where a data analyst has created an ad hoc pipeline for processing that the business has subsequently come to use on an ongoing basis.

While data analysts are primarily responsible for deriving insights out of data that reflect current trends, as well as the current state of the business, data scientists generally use data to predict future trends and requirements. In the next section, we will dive deeper into the role of the data scientist.

Meeting the needs of data scientists and ML models

Over the past decade, the field of **ML** has significantly expanded, and the majority of larger organizations now have **data science** teams that use ML techniques to help drive the objectives of the organization.

Data scientists use advanced mathematical concepts to develop ML models that can be used in various ways, including the following:

1. Identifying non-obvious patterns in data (based on the results of a blood test, what is the likelihood that this patient has a specific type of cancer?)

2. Predicting future outcomes based on historical data (is this consumer, with these specific attributes, likely to default on their debt?)

3. Extracting metadata from unstructured data (in this image of a person, are they smiling? Are they wearing sunglasses? Do they have a beard?)

Many types of ML approaches require large amounts of raw data to train the **machine learning model** (teaching the model about patterns in data). As such, data scientists can be significant consumers of data in modern organizations.

AWS tools used by data scientists to work with data

Data scientists use a wide variety of tools for many different purposes, such as tools for developing ML models, tools for fine-tuning those models, and tools for preparing data to train ML models.

Amazon SageMaker is a suite of tools that helps data scientists and developers with the many different steps required to build, train, and deploy ML models. In this section, we will only focus on the tools that are used in data preparation, but in *Chapter 13, Enabling Artificial Intelligence and Machine Learning*, we will do a deeper dive into some of the other AWS tools related to ML and AI.

SageMaker Ground Truth

Most ML models today rely on training the model using labeled data. That is, a dataset that includes the attribute that we are trying to predict is available to help train our model.

Let's use an example of a data scientist named Luna who is looking to create an ML model to identify if an image is of a dog or a cat. To train the model, Luna would need loads of pictures of dogs and cats and would need each image to be labeled to indicate whether it is a picture of a dog or a cat. Once Luna has this labeled dataset, she could train her ML model to recognize both dogs and cats.

For our example, let's imagine that Luna was able to acquire a set of 10,000 images of dogs and cats, but the images are unlabeled, which means they cannot be used to train the model. And it would take weeks for Luna to go through the 10,000 images on her own to label each one correctly.

Luckily, Luna has heard about **SageMaker Ground Truth**, a fully managed service for labeling datasets. Ground Truth uses its own ML model to automatically label datasets, and when it comes across data that it cannot confidently label, it can route that data to a team of human data labelers to be manually labeled. You can route data to either your pre-selected team of data labelers, or make use of the over 500,000 independent contractors that are part of the **Amazon Mechanical Turk** program and have them label the data according to your instructions.

Using Amazon SageMaker Ground Truth, Luna can quickly and accurately get her 10,000 images of dogs and cats labeled, ready to help train her ML model.

SageMaker Data Wrangler

It has been estimated that data scientists can spend up to 70% of their time cleaning and preparing raw data to be used to train ML models. To simplify and speed up this process, **Amazon SageMaker Data Wrangler** can be used to aggregate and prepare data for machine learning purposes.

In most organizations, there will be formal datasets that data engineering teams have prepared for consumption by the organization. However, the specific data that a data scientist needs for training a specific model may not be available in this repository, may not be in the required format, or may not contain the granular level of data that is needed. To best enable data scientists to be self-sufficient without needing to depend on other teams, many organizations enable their data science teams to directly ingest and process raw data.

Data Wrangler supports directly ingesting data from sources, including Amazon S3, Athena, Redshift, as well as the Snowflake data warehouse. Once imported, a data scientist can use the SageMaker Studio interface to transform the data, selecting from a library of over 300 built-in data transformations. Data Wrangler also supports writing custom transformations using PySpark and popular Python libraries such as pandas.

Once a Data Wrangler flow has been created in the **SageMaker Studio visual interface**, a user can export the Data Wrangler flow into a **Jupyter notebook** and run it as a Data Wrangler job, or even export the code as Python code and run it elsewhere.

SageMaker Clarify

SageMaker Clarify is a tool for examining raw data to identify potential bias in data that is going to be used to train ML models. For example, let's say that you were developing a new ML model to detect credit risk for new customers. If your proposed training dataset contains data mostly on middle-aged people, then the resulting ML model may be less accurate when making predictions for younger or older people.

SageMaker Clarify has been integrated with **SageMaker Data Wrangler**, enabling users to evaluate their datasets for potential bias as part of the data preparation process. Users can specify the attributes that they want to evaluate for bias (such as gender or age) and SageMaker Clarify will use several built-in algorithms to detect potential bias. SageMaker Clarify also provides a visual report with details on the measurements and potential bias identified.

So far, we have had a look at several types of data consumers that are common in organizations, as well as the types of tools that these data consumers may use. Now, we will move on to this chapter's hands-on exercise – creating a simple data transformation using AWS Glue DataBrew.

Hands-on – creating data transformations with AWS Glue DataBrew

In *Chapter 7, Transforming Data to Optimize for Analytics*, we used AWS Glue Studio to create a data transformation job that took in multiple sources to create a new table. In this chapter, we discussed how **AWS Glue DataBrew** is a popular service for data analysts, so we'll now make use of Glue DataBrew to transform a dataset.

> **Differences between AWS Glue Studio and AWS Glue DataBrew**
>
> Both AWS Glue Studio and AWS Glue DataBrew provide a visual interface for designing transformations, and in many use cases, either tool could be used to achieve the same outcome. However, Glue Studio generates Spark code that can be further refined in a code editor and can be run in any compatible environment. Glue DataBrew does not generate code that can be further refined, although Glue DataBrew recipes can also be run from a Glue Studio job. Glue Studio has fewer built-in transforms, and the transforms it does include are generally aimed at data engineers. Glue DataBrew has over 250 built-in transforms, and these are generally aimed at data analysts. For more information on running Glue DataBrew recipes from within Glue Studio, see the following blog post: https://aws.amazon.com/blogs/big-data/use-aws-glue-databrew-recipes-in-your-aws-glue-studio-visual-etl-jobs/.

In this hands-on task, we will be playing the role of a data analyst who has been tasked with creating a mailing list that can be used to send marketing material to the customers of our now-closed video store, to make them aware that our catalog of movies is now available for streaming.

Configuring new datasets for AWS Glue DataBrew

To start with, we're going to access the Glue DataBrew console and connect to two existing S3-based data sources (the *customer* and *address* tables that we ingested from our MySQL database in *Chapter 6, Ingesting Batch and Streaming Data*):

1. Log in to the **AWS Management Console** and access the **Glue DataBrew** service at `https://console.aws.amazon.com/databrew`.

2. From the left-hand side menu, click on **Datasets**.

3. Click on **Connect new dataset**.

4. Provide a **Dataset name** for the customer table (such as `customer-dataset`).

5. In the **Connect to new dataset** section of the window, click on **Data Catalog S3 tables** on the left-hand side. Then, click on **sakila** from the list of Glue databases.

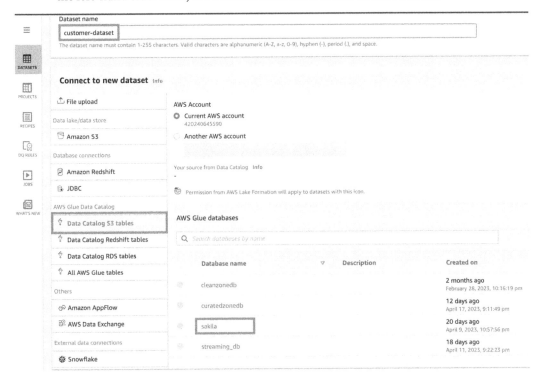

Figure 8.3: Glue DataBrew – Dataset console

6. From the list of tables, click the selector for the `customer` table, and then click **Create dataset** at the bottom right.

7. Repeat *Steps 1–6*, but this time, name the dataset address-dataset, select **Data Catalog S3 tables** and **sakila** again, but select the address table, and then **Create dataset**.

Now that we have configured the two datasets we plan to use, we will start creating the transform steps in a new DataBrew project.

Creating a new Glue DataBrew project

Now, let's create a new Glue DataBrew project where we can join our customer and address tables, and then clean the dataset:

1. In the AWS Glue DataBrew console, click on **PROJECTS** from the left-hand side menu. Then, click **Create project**.

2. For **Project name**, provide a name (such as customer-mailing-list).

3. Under **Recipe details**, leave the default of **Create new recipe** as is.

4. Under **Select a dataset**, select **customer-dataset**:

Figure 8.4: Creating a new Glue DataBrew project (1)

5. Under **Permissions**, from the drop-down list, select **Create new IAM role**.

6. For **New IAM role suffix**, provide a suitable suffix, such as dataengbook.

7. At the bottom right, click on **Create project**:

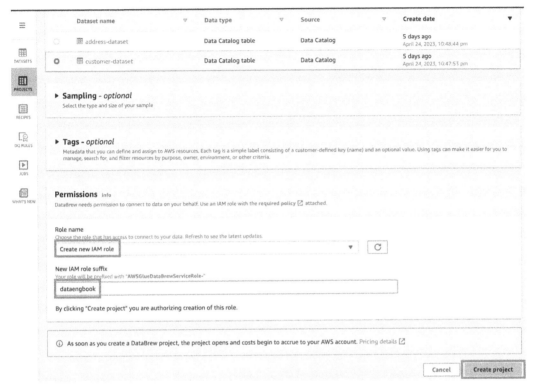

Figure 8.5: Creating a new Glue DataBrew project (2)

Note that there are session costs associated with Glue DataBrew projects ($1.00 per 30-minute session). However, at the time of writing, AWS is offering the first 40 sessions at no charge to new Glue DataBrew customers. For the current pricing, see https://aws.amazon.com/glue/pricing/.

Building your Glue DataBrew recipe

We can now use the interactive Glue DataBrew project session to build out a recipe for our transformation (a recipe is the steps that are taken to transform our data). Note that it may take a few minutes before the session is provisioned and ready.

In the interactive project session window, as shown in the following screenshot, we can see a sample of our customer table data and a panel to the right that allows us to build our recipe:

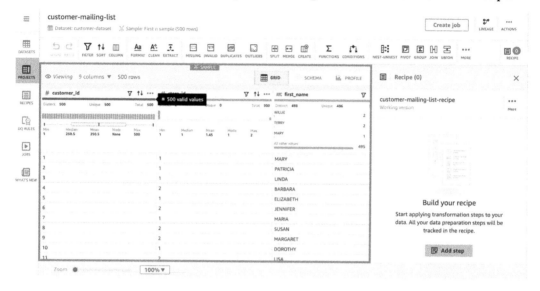

Figure 8.6: AWS Glue DataBrew interactive project session

For our recipe, we want to join this data with our address table, and then make the following changes to the dataset to create a mailing list for our marketing team:

- Change the first_name and last_name columns to capital case.
- Change the email addresses so that they're all in lowercase.

Follow these steps to create the recipe. The first steps will join our data with the address table:

1. Click on **Add step** in the recipe panel on the right-hand side of the console.
2. Scroll down through the list of transformations and select **Join multiple datasets**.
3. From the **Select dataset** dropdown, select **address-dataset**. Dataset metadata, as well as a sample of the dataset, will be displayed. Click on **Next** at the bottom right.
4. For **Select join type**, select **Left join**. This takes all the rows in our left-hand table (the customer table) and joins each row with the matching row in the address table, based on the join keys we specify.
5. For **Join keys**, for **Table A**, select address_id. For **Table B**, also select address_id.

6. Under **Column list**, deselect all the columns, and then select only the following columns (these will be the only columns that our marketing team needs for the mailing list):

   - **Table A**, customer_id
   - **Table A**, first_name
   - **Table A**, last_name
   - **Table A**, email
   - **Table B**, address
   - **Table B**, district
   - **Table B**, postal_code

7. Click **Finish**.

We will now see a preview of our new table, with the customer and address tables joined, and only the columns selected previously showing.

You may notice that our customer list includes addresses from many different countries (look at some of the entries under the district column), and yet we don't have a column for the country. This is because our original data source (a MySQL database) was highly normalized. The address table has a city_id field, and we could have included that and then joined our new dataset with the city table to include the city name and country_id fields. However, we would need to have joined that dataset with the country table (joining on the country_id column) to get the country name. We will not be covering those steps here, but feel free to give that a try on your own.

All the first names and last names were captured in all uppercase in the original data source (MySQL), so let's transform these into capital case, and transform the email address into all lowercase.

1. In the **Recipe** panel, click on **Add step icon** next to **Applied steps**.
2. From the list of transforms, scroll down and select the **FORMAT / Change to capital case** transform.
3. For **Source column**, select the first_name column. Ensure that **Format column to** has **Capital case** selected and then click **Apply**.
4. Repeat *Steps 1–3*, but this time select the last_name column as **Source column**.
5. Repeat *Steps 1–3*, but this time select the **FORMAT / Change to lowercase** transform and select the email column as the **Source** column, and then click **Apply**.

Your Glue DataBrew recipe should look as follows:

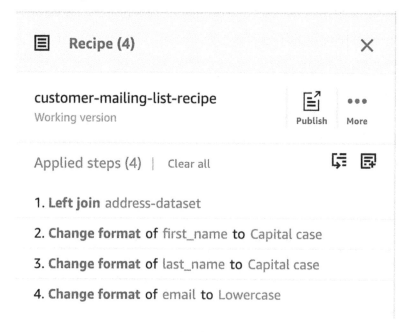

≡ **Recipe (4)**   ✕

customer-mailing-list-recipe   ↗
Working version   **Publish**   **More**

Applied steps (4) | Clear all

1. **Left join** address-dataset

2. **Change format** of first_name **to** Capital case

3. **Change format** of last_name **to** Capital case

4. **Change format** of email **to** Lowercase

Figure 8.7: Completed Glue DataBrew recipe

With that, we have created our recipe and have been able to preview the results of our transform. Our final step will be to run our recipe in a Glue DataBrew job and write out the results to Amazon S3 so that we can provide the mailing list file to our marketing team.

Creating a Glue DataBrew job

In this final section of our hands-on activity, we will run our recipe in a job and write the results of our transform to a file in Amazon S3:

1. In the AWS Glue DataBrew console, click on **Jobs** from the left-hand side menu. Then, click **Create job**.

2. For **Job name**, provide a name for your job (such as mailing-list-job).

3. For **Job input**, select **Project**, and then select your customer-mailing-list project.

4. For **Job output settings**, leave the default settings as is (output to Amazon S3, with CSV set as the file type, the delimiter as a comma, and no compression).

5. For **S3 location**, select a location (such as s3://dataeng-clean-zone-<initial>/ mailing-list but changing the initials to match your unique bucket name).

6. For **Permissions**, select **Create new IAM role** and provide a suffix (such as `mailing-list-job`). By having Glue DataBrew create a new role for this job, DataBrew will automatically provide write access to the location you specified for S3 output.

7. Click **Create and run job**.

    When the job finishes running, the **Job run history** screen will be displayed, showing the status of the job:

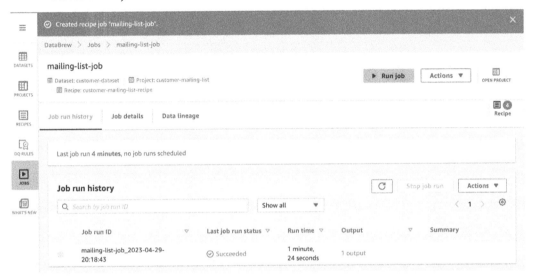

Figure 8.8: Job run history screen showing the job's status

8. Click on **1 output** in the **Output** column to view the S3 destination that you selected for this job. Click on **S3 destination path** to open a new browser tab showing the output's location in the S3 console. Download the CSV file and open it with a text editor or spreadsheet application to verify the results.

In this hands-on exercise, you created a new Glue DataBrew job that joined two tables (customer and address). You then ran various transforms on the dataset to format the columns as needed by the marketing team and created a new CSV output file in Amazon S3.

Summary

In this chapter, we explored a variety of data consumers that you are likely to find in most organizations, including business users, data analysts, and data scientists. We briefly examined their roles and then looked at the types of AWS services that each of them is likely to use to work with data.

In the hands-on section of this chapter, we took on the role of a data analyst, tasked with creating a mailing list for the marketing department. We used data that had been imported from a MySQL database into S3 in a previous chapter, joined two of the tables from that database, and transformed the data in some of the columns. Then, we wrote the newly transformed dataset out to Amazon S3 as a CSV file.

In the next chapter, *Loading Data into a Data Mart*, we will look at how data from a data lake can be loaded into a data warehouse, such as Amazon Redshift.

Learn more on Discord

To join the Discord community for this book – where you can share feedback, ask questions to the author, and learn about new releases – follow the QR code below:

```
https://discord.gg/9s5mHNyECd
```

9

A Deeper Dive into Data Marts and Amazon Redshift

While a **data lake** enables a significant amount of analytics to happen inside it, there are several use cases where a data engineer may need to load data into an external **data warehouse**, or **data mart**, to enable a set of data consumers.

As we reviewed in *Chapter 2, Data Management Architectures for Analytics*, a data lake is a single source of truth across multiple lines of business, while a data mart generally contains a subset of data of interest to a particular group of users. A data mart could be a relational database, a data warehouse, or a different kind of datastore.

Data marts serve two primary purposes. First, they provide a database with a subset of the data in the data lake, optimized for specific types of queries (such as for a specific business function). In addition, they also provide a higher-performing, lower-latency query engine, which is often required for specific analytic use cases (such as for powering **Business Intelligence (BI)** applications).

In this chapter, we will focus on data warehouses and data marts and cover the following topics:

- Extending analytics with data warehouses/data marts
- What not to do – anti-patterns for a data warehouse
- Redshift architecture review and storage deep dive
- Designing a high-performance data warehouse
- Moving data between a data lake and Redshift
- Exploring advanced Redshift features
- Hands-on – deploying a Redshift Serverless cluster and running Redshift Spectrum queries

Technical requirements

For the hands-on exercises in this chapter, you will need permission to create a new IAM role, as well as permission to create a **Redshift** cluster.

You can find the code files of this chapter in the GitHub repository using the following link: `https://github.com/PacktPublishing/Data-Engineering-with-AWS-2nd-edition/tree/main/Chapter09`

Extending analytics with data warehouses/data marts

Tools such as **Amazon Athena** (which we will do a deeper dive into in *Chapter 11, Ad Hoc Queries with Amazon Athena*) allow us to run SQL queries directly on data in the data lake. While this enables us to query very large datasets that exist in an **Amazon S3** data lake, the performance of these queries is generally lower than the performance you get when running queries against data on a high-performance disk that is local to the compute engine.

However, not all queries require this kind of high performance, and we can categorize our queries and data into cold, warm, and hot tiers. Before diving into the topic of data marts and data warehouses, let's first take a look at the different tiers of queries/data storage that are common in data lake projects.

Cold and warm data

We've grouped the cold and warm data tiers into one section, as when building in AWS, both of these tiers generally use Amazon S3 storage. As we have discussed elsewhere in this book, Amazon S3 is low-cost object storage that provides very high durability and an SLA of 99.9% availability, while also being massively scalable.

AWS offers different storage classes for the objects you store in Amazon S3, and some classes are better suited to cold data, while other classes are well suited to warm data. Let's first take a look at the difference between cold and warm data, and then we can do a deeper dive into the different storage classes.

Cold data

This is data that is not frequently accessed but it is mandatory to store for long periods for compliance and governance reasons, or historical data that is stored to enable future research and development (such as for training **Machine Learning (ML)** models).

An example of this is the access logs from a banking website. Unless there is a court-issued legal request to query the logs for some specific data, the chances are that after a few months, we will not need to access this data again. However, due to compliance reasons, we may need to store this data for a number of years.

Another example is detailed data from a range of sensors in a factory. This data may not be queried actively after 30 days, but we want to keep this data available in case there is a future ML project where it would be useful to train the ML model with rich, historical data.

Warm data

Warm data is data that is accessed relatively often but does not require extremely low latency for retrieval. This is data that needs to be queried on demand, such as data that is used in daily ETL jobs, or data used for ad hoc querying and data discovery.

An example of this kind of data is data that is ingested in our **raw** data lake zone daily, such as data from a transactional database system. This data will be processed by our ETL jobs daily, and data will be written out to the **transformed** zone.

Generally, data in the transformed zone will still be batch-processed for further business transforms, before being moved to the curated zone. All of these zones would likely fall into the category of warm data.

Amazon S3 storage classes

Broadly speaking, you can think of Amazon S3 storage classes as being part of one of three different groupings.

General purpose

The **Amazon S3 Standard storage class** is a general-purpose storage class that provides immediate (millisecond) access to data. This storage class is designed for data that is frequently accessed.

The Amazon S3 Standard storage class has a per-GB cost for data stored, and no per-GB cost to read or access the data. As such, it is ideal for storing current data lake data, such as newly ingested data, or data from the past month (or few months) that is queried regularly.

Infrequent Access

There are two different storage classes that are categorized as Infrequent Access – **S3 Standard-Infrequent Access** and **S3 One Zone-Infrequent Access**. Both of these storage classes provide immediate (millisecond) access to data, but the pricing model is different from the Standard storage class.

With the Infrequent Access storage classes, you pay a lower per-GB cost than S3 Standard for storing data, but there is a per-GB charge for reading/accessing the data. Therefore, this storage class is ideal for data that you need to store for longer periods of time and access infrequently. For example, you may store the most recent 3 months of data in the Standard storage class, but store the data for the 24 months prior to that in Infrequent Access, as that data may be queried once a month for month-end reporting.

The difference between Standard-Infrequent Access and One Zone-Infrequent Access is that the One Zone data is only stored in a single availability zone. This reduces the durability of data stored in this storage class, while slightly reducing the data storage costs, and is only intended for data that can be easily recreated.

Note that data stored in the Infrequent Access storage classes is always charged for a minimum of 30 days, therefore it is not suited to data that will be deleted in less than 30 days. Infrequent Access is intended for longer-term data storage.

Archive storage

Amazon S3 has a number of **Glacier storage classes** that are intended for different types of archiving requirements.

The **Glacier Instant Retrieval storage class** offers archival storage for data that is not accessed regularly (for example, once per quarter) but you want to be able to access the data immediately. Objects in the Glacier Instant Retrieval storage class do not need to be restored before you access them, and therefore they can be queried by Athena. The Glacier Instant Retrieval storage class has a lower cost per GB of data stored than the Standard and Infrequent Access classes, but a higher cost to retrieve/access data than the other classes.

The Amazon S3 **Glacier Flexible Retrieval storage class** is intended for long-term storage where access to the data may be required a few times a year, and immediate access is not required. Data can be retrieved from S3 Glacier in minutes to hours (with different price points for the retrieval, based on how quickly the data is required). Data in S3 Glacier cannot be directly queried with Amazon Athena or Glue jobs – it must be retrieved and stored in a regular storage class before it can be queried.

The Amazon S3 **Glacier Deep Archive storage class** is the lowest-cost storage for long-term data retention and is intended for data that may be retrieved at most once or twice a year. Data in this storage class can be retrieved within 12 hours.

Storage charges for objects in S3 Glacier storage classes are for a minimum of 90 days for Instant Retrieval and Flexible Retrieval and 180 days for Deep Archive, so they are not intended for data that is short-lived.

Data that you store in the Glacier Instant Retrieval storage class can still be a part of your data lake, as you are able to immediately access the data and query it with tools such as Amazon Athena. However, because of the data access charges, you need to ensure that data in this class is not queried on a regular basis as this can get very expensive. If data is stored in the Glacier Flexible Retrieval or Deep Archive storage classes, this data cannot be considered active data in the data lake, as the data cannot be queried without first restoring it from the archive.

Using Amazon S3 Lifecycle rules to automatically move data between storage classes

Amazon S3 enables you to configure **Amazon S3 Lifecycle rules** that are used to automatically move your data between the different storage classes. For example, you know that once your granular sales data per store is 3 months old, it is not queried often, so you could configure a lifecycle rule to automatically move data in the sales prefix of the bucket to either Infrequent Access or Glacier Instant Retrieval storage classes.

When creating a lifecycle rule, you can specify multiple transitions that apply at different ages (days after creation) of an object. You can also specify configuration options, including the following:

- You can either limit the scope of the rule to a full bucket or create a rule for a specific prefix in a bucket.
- You can select to exclude files under a specific size or over a specific size.
- You can move objects between storage classes or select to delete an object.

For example, you can create a configuration rule that will move objects to Standard-Infrequent Access after 30 days, and then to Glacier Instant Retrieval 90 days after the object was created. It will then move the object to Glacier Deep Archive 365 days after it was created and, finally, will permanently delete the object 1,095 days (3 years) after creation.

Enabling Amazon S3 to automatically optimize your storage costs

You can also use a special storage class called **Amazon S3 Intelligent Tiering** to automatically move data to the most cost-effective access tier, based on changing access patterns. When you place objects in the S3 Intelligent Tiering storage class, the object is moved between tiers based on when it was last accessed (which is different from how lifecycle rules work, as those are based on the number of days since the object was created).

The default tier is the Frequent Access tier, but if an object in this tier is not accessed for 30 days, it is automatically moved to the Infrequent Access tier. If an object is not accessed for 90 consecutive days, it is automatically moved to the Archive Instant Access tier (which, much like Glacier Instant Retrieval, makes the object available in milliseconds).

You can optionally also enable having the object moved to the Archive Access tier, after anywhere between 90 and 730 days without it being accessed. Once data is moved to the Archive Access tier, it must be retrieved before it can be accessed, and retrieval ranges from minutes to 5 hours, although you can request expedited retrieval (at an additional charge), which restores objects in 1–5 minutes.

An additional option is to activate the Deep Archive Access tier for data that has not been accessed for between 180 and 730 days (configurable). The Deep Archive Access tier is similar to the Glacier Deep Archive storage class in terms of time to retrieve objects (9–12 hours).

When an object that has been moved into an Infrequent Access or Archive tier is accessed, it is moved back into the Frequent Access tier.

There are trade-offs between storage costs, data retrieval costs, and the amount of time required to access data that has been archived (for certain storage classes/tiers), and therefore you need to consider these before enabling either lifecycle rules or the optional archive components of the Intelligent Tiering storage class.

However, in most cases, it is highly recommended that you consider using the S3 Intelligent Tiering storage class (without optional archiving) as your default storage class for data in your data lake, as this can lead to significant cost optimization with very little effort or management overhead.

Each of these storage classes has different pricing plans. S3 Standard's cost is based on storage and API calls (put, copy, get, and more), while S3 Standard-Infrequent Access and Glacier Archive classes also have a cost per GB of data retrieved. S3 Intelligent Tiering does not have a cost per GB for data retrieved, but it does have a small monitoring and automation cost per object. For more details on pricing, see `https://aws.amazon.com/s3/pricing/`.

Hot data

Hot data is data that is highly critical for day-to-day analytics enablement in an organization. This is data that is likely accessed multiple times per day, and low-latency, high-performance access to the data is critical.

An example of this kind of data would be data used by a BI application (such as **Amazon Quick-Sight** or **Tableau**). This could be data that is used to show manufacturing and sales of products at different sites, for example. This is often the kind of data that is used by end user data consumers in the organization, as well as by business analysts who need to run complex data queries. This data may also be used in constantly refreshing dashboards that provide critical business metrics and KPIs used by senior executives in the organization.

In AWS, several services can be used to provide high-performance, low-latency access to data. These include the **RDS database** engines, the **NoSQL DynamoDB** database, as well as **OpenSearch** (for searching full-text data). However, from an analytic perspective, the most common targets for hot data are **Amazon Redshift** or **Amazon QuickSight SPICE** (which stands for **Super-fast, Parallel, In-memory Calculation Engine**):

- **Amazon Redshift** is a super-fast cloud-native data warehousing solution that provides high-performance, low-latency access to data stored in the data warehouse.
- **Amazon QuickSight** is a BI tool from Amazon for creating dashboards. With Amazon QuickSight, you have the option of reading data from sources, such as Amazon Redshift, or loading data directly into the QuickSight in-memory database engine (SPICE) for optimal high-performance, low-latency access.

As we mentioned previously, AWS offers purpose-built storage engines for different data types/temperatures. The decision of which engine to use is generally based on a cost versus performance trade-off.

In many cases, data is time-sensitive. There may be a business application that needs to report on historical statistics, current trends, and a zoomed-in view of the previous few months of data. Some of this data may also need to be refreshed frequently. This requires a data engineer to process the data, clean and transform it, and then load a subset of the data to a high-performing engine, such as Amazon Redshift.

In this chapter, we are going to focus on using Amazon Redshift as a high-performance data mart for hot data access. Data lakes are a great option from a cost and scalability perspective for storing large amounts of data and being the ultimate source of truth.

However, data warehouses provide an application-specific approach to querying large-scale structured and semi-structured data with the best performance and lowest latency.

What not to do — anti-patterns for a data warehouse

While there are many good ways to use a data warehouse for analytics, there are some approaches that at first may seem to be a good fit for a data warehouse but are generally not recommended.

Let's take a look at some of the ways of using a data warehouse that should be avoided.

Using a data warehouse as a transactional datastore

Data warehouses are designed to be optimized for **Online Analytical Processing (OLAP)** queries, so they should not be used for **Online Transaction Processing (OLTP)** queries and use cases.

While there are mechanisms to update or delete data from a data warehouse (such as the merge statement in Redshift), a data warehouse is primarily designed for mostly append-only, or insert, queries. There are also other features of transactional databases (such as **MySQL** or **PostgreSQL**) that are available in Redshift – such as the concept of primary and foreign keys – but these are used for performance optimization and query planning and are **not enforced** by Redshift.

Using a data warehouse as a data lake

Data warehouses offer increased performance by having high-performance storage directly attached to the compute engine. A data warehouse is also able to scale to store vast amounts of data, and while primarily designed to support structured data, they are also able to offer some support for semi-structured data.

However, data warehouses, by design, require upfront thought about schema and table structure. They are also not designed to store unstructured data (such as images and audio), and they generally use SQL as the primary method for data querying and transformation. As data warehouses include a compute engine, their cost is also higher than storing data in low-cost object storage.

In contrast, with data lakes, you can store all the data in low-cost object storage and can ingest data without needing to design an appropriate schema structure first. You can also analyze the dataset directly (using tools such as Amazon Athena) and transform the data with a wide range of tools (**SQL** and **Spark**, for example), and then bring just the required data into the data warehouse.

While it is possible to load raw data in a data warehouse and then transform the data in the warehouse, that is the **Extract, Load, Transform (ELT)** process, this often ends up costing significantly more than storing the raw data in an object store such as S3, transforming the data directly in the data lake, and then loading a subset of data into a data warehouse.

The goal is to avoid storing unnecessary data in a data warehouse. Data warehouses are supposed to store curated datasets with well-defined schemas and should only store hot data that is needed for high-performance, low-latency queries.

Storing unstructured data

While some data warehouses (such as Amazon Redshift and Snowflake) can store semi-structured data (such as JSON data), data warehouses generally cannot be used to store unstructured data such as images, videos, and other media content.

You should always consider which data engine may be best for a specific data type before just defaulting to storing the data in a data warehouse. For example, Health Care FHIR data has a heavily nested JSON structure. While it is possible to store and query this in Amazon Redshift, or another data warehouse solution, you may want to consider using a solution designed for that specific data type, such as **Amazon HealthLake**.

Now that we have reviewed some of the ways that a data warehouse should not be used, let's dig deeper into the Redshift architecture.

Redshift architecture review and storage deep dive

In this section, we will take a deeper dive into the architecture of Redshift clusters, as well as into how data in tables is stored across Redshift nodes. This in-depth look will help you understand and fine-tune Redshift's performance, though we will also cover how many of the design decisions affecting table layout can be automated by Redshift.

In *Chapter 2, Data Management Architectures for Analytics*, we briefly discussed how the Redshift architecture uses leader and compute nodes. Each compute node contains a certain amount of compute power (CPUs and memory), as well as a certain amount of local storage. When configuring your Redshift cluster, you can add multiple compute nodes, depending on your compute and storage requirements. Note that to provide fault tolerance and improved durability, the compute nodes have 2.5–3x the stated node storage capacity (for example, if the addressable storage capacity is listed as 2.56 TB, the actual underlying storage may be closer to 7.5 TB).

Every compute node is split into either 2, 4, or 16 slices, depending on the cluster type and size. Each slice is allocated a portion of the node's memory and storage and works as an independent worker, but in parallel with the other slices.

The slices store different columns of data for large tables, as distributed by the leader node. The data for each column is persisted as 1 MB immutable blocks, and each column can grow independently.

When a user runs a query against Redshift, the leader node creates a query plan and allocates work for each slice, and then the slices execute the work in parallel. When each slice completes its work, it passes the results back to the leader node for final aggregation or sorting and merging. However, this means that a query is only as good as its slowest partition (or slice).

Data distribution across slices

Let's have a look at how data is distributed across slices in Redshift:

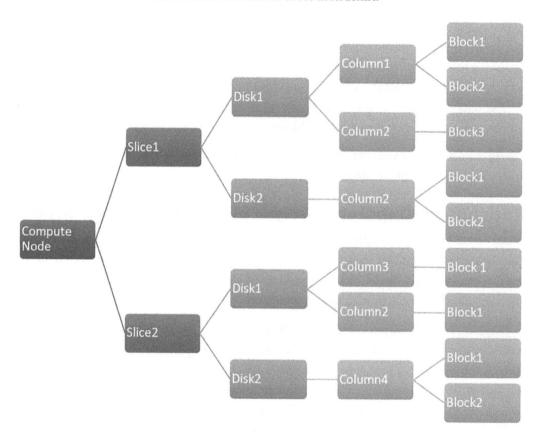

Figure 9.1: Data distribution across slices on a compute node

In the preceding diagram, we can see that Column2 is distributed across Slice1-Disk1, Slice1-Disk2, and Slice2-Disk1. To increase data throughput and query performance, data should be spread evenly across slices to avoid I/O bottlenecks. If most of the data for a specific table were on one node, that node would end up doing all the heavy lifting and diminish the point of parallelism. Redshift supports multiple distribution styles, including EVEN, KEY, and ALL (and can automatically select the best distribution style, as we will discuss later in this chapter).

The distribution style that's selected for a specific table determines which slice a row in a column will be stored on.

One of the most common operations when performing analytics is the JOIN operation. Let's look at an example where we have two tables, one of which is a small dimension table (2–3 million rows) and the other is a very large fact table (potentially with hundreds of millions of rows). For a reminder about data warehouse schema design with fact and dimension tables, refer back to the section *Dimensional modeling in data warehouses* in *Chapter 2, Data Management Architectures for Analytics*.

The small dimension table can easily fit into the storage of a single node, while the large fact table needs to be spread across multiple nodes. One of the biggest impacts on performance regarding a JOIN query is when data needs to be shuffled (copied) between nodes. To avoid this, and to optimize JOIN performance, the smaller dimension table can be stored on all the slices of the cluster by specifying an **ALL distribution style**. For the larger table, data can be equally distributed across all the slices in a round-robin fashion by specifying an **EVEN distribution style**. By doing this, every slice will have a full copy of the small dimension table and it can directly join that with the subset of data it holds for the large fact table, without needing to shuffle the dimension data from other slices.

While this can be ideal for query performance, the ALL distribution style does have some overhead with regard to the amount of storage space used by the cluster, as well as a negative performance impact for data loads.

An alternative approach that can be used to optimize joins, especially if both tables being joined are large, is to ensure that the same slice stores the rows for both tables that will need to be joined. A way to achieve this is by using the KEY distribution style, where a hash value of one of the columns will determine which row of each table will be stored on which slice.

For example, let's say that we have a table that stores details about all of the products we sell, and that this table contains a product_id column. Let's also say we have a different table that contains details of all sales, and that it also contains a column called product_id.

In our queries, we often need to join these tables on the product_id column. By distributing the data for both tables based on the value of the product_id column, we can help ensure that all the rows that need to be joined are on the same slice. Redshift would determine the hash value of, for example, product_id "DLX5992445" and, based on that hash value, determine which slice the data should be stored on. With this approach, all the rows from both tables that contain that product_id would be stored on the same slice.

For grouping and aggregation queries, you also want to reduce data shuffling (copying data from one node to another to run a specific query) to save network I/O. This can also be achieved by using the KEY distribution style to keep records with the same key on the same slice. In this scenario, you would specify the column used in the GROUP BY clause as the key to distribute the data on.

However, if we queried one of these tables with a WHERE filter on the product_id column, then this distribution would create a bottleneck, as all the data that needed to be returned from the query would be on one slice. As such, you should avoid specifying a KEY distribution on a column that is commonly used in a WHERE clause. Finally, the column that's used for KEY distribution should always be one with high cardinality and normal distribution of data to avoid hot partitions and data skew.

While this can be very complex, Redshift can automatically optimize configuration items such as distribution styles, as we will discuss later in this chapter in the *Designing a high-performance data warehouse* section.

Redshift Zone Maps and sorting data

The time it takes a query to return results is also impacted by hardware factors – specifically, the amount of disk seek and disk access time:

- **Disk seek** is the time it takes a hard drive to move the read head from one block to another (as such, it does not apply to nodes that use SSD drives).
- **Disk access** is the latency in reading and writing stored data on disk blocks and transferring the requested data back to the client.

To reduce data access latency, Redshift stores in-memory metadata about each disk block on the leader node in what is called **Zone Maps**. For example, Zone Maps store the minimum and maximum values for the data of each column that is stored within a specific 1 MB data block. Based on these Zone Maps, Redshift knows which blocks contain data relevant to a query, so it can skip reading blocks that do not contain data needed for the query. This helps optimize query performance by magnitudes by reducing the number of reads.

Zone Maps are most effective when the data on blocks is sorted. When defining a table, you can optionally define one or more sort keys, which determines how data is sorted within a block. When choosing multiple sort keys, you can either have a priority order of keys using a **compound sort key** or give equal priority to each sort key using an **interleaved sort key**. The default sort key type is a compound sort key, and this is recommended for most scenarios.

Sort keys should be on columns that are frequently used with range filters or columns where you regularly compute aggregations. While sort keys can help significantly increase query performance by improving the effectiveness of Zone Maps, they can harm the performance of ingest tasks. In the next section, we will look at how Redshift simplifies some of these difficult design decisions by being able to automatically optimize a table's sort key. In most cases, it makes sense to have Redshift automatically optimize the sort key, at least initially, and then over time, investigate manually setting the sort key if you feel further optimization is required.

Designing a high-performance data warehouse

When you're looking to design a high-performing data warehouse, multiple factors need to be considered. These include items such as cluster type and sizing, compression types, distribution keys, sort keys, data types, and table constraints.

As part of the design process, you will need to consider several trade-offs, such as cost versus performance. Business requirements and the available budget will often drive these decisions.

Beyond decisions about infrastructure and storage, the logical schema design also plays a big part in optimizing the performance of the data warehouse. Often, this will be an iterative process, where you start with an initial schema design that you refine over time to optimize for increased performance.

Provisioned versus Redshift Serverless clusters

When creating an Amazon Redshift cluster, you can select to either use a serverless Redshift configuration or provision specific resources. With **Redshift Serverless** clusters, you only pay for compute costs while the cluster is active, and the cluster automatically shuts down during periods of inactivity. With a provisioned cluster, you pay for the compute resources for as long as the cluster is up (although you can manually choose or schedule times to pause and resume the cluster, and when paused, you only pay for storage).

Both provisioned and serverless clusters support the same features, and both can handle complex workloads and advanced queries. With provisioned clusters, you need to determine how many nodes to configure in the cluster, as well as what types of nodes, in order to get the performance you require. With Redshift Serverless, you only need to specify a base number for **Redshift Processing Units** (**RPUs**), and Redshift Serverless will automatically scale in order to handle the load placed on the cluster. As a result, Redshift Serverless is able to more dynamically respond to changes in processing load.

Redshift Serverless clusters also do not require you to specify maintenance windows or to plan for software upgrades. As a serverless service, updated software versions are automatically applied and there is no interruption to existing connections or queries when Redshift changes the underlying software version.

Overall, Redshift Serverless is simpler to deploy and manage than working with a provisioned cluster; however, the costs for Redshift Serverless are harder to predict and manage. To help manage costs, you can set limits on the maximum RPUs consumed over a period of time (daily, weekly, or monthly), and when the limit is reached, either generate a notification or prevent any further queries from being run.

If you have unpredictable workloads, or your cluster is only used at certain times (such as a development or test cluster), then there are many advantages to using Redshift Serverless. However, if you have well-defined and relatively constant workloads, then using a provisioned cluster can provide lower costs (especially when you commit to usage by purchasing a 1-year or 3-year Reserved Instance for Redshift).

Selecting the optimal Redshift node type for provisioned clusters

With provisioned clusters, there are different types of nodes available, each with different combinations of CPU, memory, storage capacity, and storage type. The following are the three families of node types:

1. **RA3 nodes**: These nodes use managed storage, which decouples compute and storage since you pay a per-hour compute fee, and a separate fee based on how much managed storage you use over the month. Storage is a combination of local SSD storage and data stored in S3 and is fully managed by Redshift.

2. **DC2 nodes**: These are designed for compute-intensive workloads and feature a fixed amount of local SSD storage per node. With DC2 nodes, compute and storage are coupled (meaning that to increase either compute or storage, you need to add a new node containing both compute and storage).

3. **DS2 nodes (legacy)**: These are legacy nodes that offer compute with attached large hard disk drives. With DS2 nodes, compute and storage are also coupled.

AWS recommends that for small provisioned clusters (under 1 TB compressed in size), you use DC2 nodes, while larger data warehouses make use of the RA3 nodes with managed storage.

Note that many advanced features of Redshift, such as data sharing, are only available with RA3 nodes. The DS2 node type is a legacy node type that is not generally recommended for use when creating a new Redshift cluster.

When creating a new provisioned Redshift cluster in the console, you have the option of entering information about your data's size, type of data, and data retention, and Redshift will provide a recommended node type and the number of nodes for your workload.

Selecting the optimal table distribution style and sort key

In the early days of Redshift, users had to specifically select the distribution style and sort key that they wanted to use for each table. When a Redshift cluster was not performing as well as expected, it would often turn out that the underlying issue was having a non-optimal distribution style and/or sort key.

As a result, Amazon introduced new functionality that enabled Redshift to use advanced Artificial Intelligence methods to monitor queries being run on the cluster, and to automatically apply the optimal distribution style and/or sort key. Optimizations can be applied to tables within a few hours of a minimum number of queries being run.

If you create a new table and do not specify a specific distribution style or sort key, Redshift sets both of those settings to AUTO. Smaller tables will initially be set to have an ALL distribution style, while larger tables will have an EVEN distribution style.

If a table starts small but grows over time, Redshift automatically adjusts the distribution style to EVEN. Over time, as Redshift analyzes the queries being run on the cluster, it may further adjust the table distribution style to be KEY-based.

Similarly, Redshift analyzes queries being run to determine the optimal sort key for a table. The goal of this optimization is to optimize the data blocks that are read from the disk during a table scan.

It is strongly recommended that you allow Redshift to manage distribution and sort key optimizations for your table automatically, but you do have the power to manually configure these settings if you have a unique use case, or if you find that you need further performance improvements beyond what is achieved with automatic selection.

Selecting the right data type for columns

Every column in a Redshift table is associated with a specific data type, and this data type ensures that the column will comply with specific constraints. This helps enforce the types of operations that can be performed on the values in the column.

For example, an arithmetic operation such as sum can only be performed on **numeric** data types. If you needed to perform a sum operation on a column type that was defined as a **character** or **string** type, you would need to cast it to a numeric type first. This can have an impact on query performance, so it needs to be taken into consideration.

There are broadly six data types that Amazon Redshift currently supports. Let's do a deeper dive into each of these data types.

Character types

Character data types are equivalent to string data types in programming languages and relational databases, and are used to store text.

There are two primary character types:

1. CHAR(n), CHARACTER(n), and NCHAR(n): These are fixed-length character strings that support single-byte characters only. Data is stored with trailing white spaces at the end to convert the string into a fixed length. If you defined a column as CHAR(8), for example, data in this column would be stored as follows:

    ```
    CHAR(8)
    "ABC     "
    "DEF     "
    ```

    However, the trailing white space is ignored during queries. For example, if you were querying the length of one of the aforementioned records, it would return a result of 3, not 8. Also, if you were querying the table for records matching "ABC", the trailing space would again be ignored and the record would be returned.

2. VARCHAR(n) and NVARCHAR(n): These are variable-length character strings that support multi-byte characters. When creating this data type, to determine the correct length to specify, you should multiply the number of bytes per character by the maximum number of characters you need to store.

A column with VARCHAR(8), for example, can store up to eight single-byte characters, four 2-byte characters, or two 4-byte characters. To calculate the value of n for VARCHAR, multiply the number of bytes per character by the number of characters. As this data type is for variable-length strings, the data is not padded with trailing white space.

When deciding on the character type, if you need to store multi-byte characters, then you should always use the VARCHAR data type. For example, the Euro symbol (€) is represented by a 3-byte character, so this should not be stored in a CHAR column.

However, if your data can always be encoded with single-byte characters and is always a fixed length, then use the fixed-width CHAR data type. An example of this is columns that store phone numbers or IP addresses.

AWS recommends that you always use the smallest possible column size rather than providing a very large value, for convenience, as using an unnecessarily large length can have a performance impact for complex queries. However, there is a trade-off because if the value is too small, you will find that queries may fail if the data you attempt to insert is larger than the length specified. Therefore, consider what may be the largest potential value you need to store for a column and use that when defining the column.

Numeric types

Number data types in Redshift include integers, decimals, and floating-point numbers. Let's look at the primary numeric types.

Integer types

Integer types are used to store whole numbers, and there are a few options based on the size of the integer you need to store:

1. SMALLINT/INT2: These integers have a range of -32,768 to +32,767.
2. INTEGER/INT/INT4: These integers have a range of -2,147,483,648 to +2,147,483,647.
3. BIGINT/INT8: These integers have a range of -9,223,372,036,854,775,808 to +9,223,372,036,854,775,807.

You should always use the smallest possible integer type that will be able to store all expected values. For example, if you're storing the age of a person, you should use SMALLINT, while if you're storing a count of product inventory where you expect to have hundreds of thousands of units to potentially a few million units on hand, you should use the INTEGER type.

Decimal type

The DECIMAL type allows you to specify the precision and scale you need to store. The precision indicates the total number of digits on both sides of the decimal point, while the scale indicates the number of digits on the right-hand side of the decimal point. You define the column by specifying DECIMAL(precision, scale).

Creating a column and specifying a type as DECIMAL(7,3) would enable values in the range of -9,999.999 to +9,999.999.

The DECIMAL type is useful for storing the results of complex calculations where you want full control over the accuracy of the results.

Floating-point types

These numeric types are used to store values with variable precision. The floating-point types are known as inexact types, which means you may notice a slight discrepancy when storing and reading back a specific value, as some values are stored as approximations. If you need to ensure exact calculations, you should use the DECIMAL type instead.

The two floating-point types that are supported in Redshift are as follows:

1. REAL/FLOAT4: These support values of up to 6 digits of precision.
2. DOUBLE PRECISION/FLOAT8/FLOAT: These support values of up to 15 digits of precision.

This data type is used to avoid overflow errors for values that are mathematically within range, but the string length exceeds the range limit. When you insert values that exceed the precision for that type, the values are truncated. For a column of the REAL type (which supports up to 6 digits of precision), if you insert 7876.7876, it would be stored as 7876.78. Or, if you attempted to insert a value of 787678.7876, it would be stored as 787678.

Datetime types

These types are equivalent to simple date, time, or timestamp columns in programming languages. The following date/time types are supported in Redshift:

1. DATE: This column type supports storing a date without any associated time. Data should always be enclosed in double quotation marks.
2. TIME/TIMEZ: This column type supports storing a time of day without any associated date. TIMEZ is used to specify the time of day with the time zone, with the default time zone being **Coordinated Universal Time (UTC)**. TIME is stored with up to 6-digit precision for fractional seconds.

3. `TIMESTAMP`/`TIMESTAMPZ`: This column type is a combination of `DATE` followed by `TIME`/`TIMEZ`. If you insert a date without a time value, or only a partial time value, into this column type, any missing values will be stored as `00`. For example, a `TIMESTAMP` of `2021-05-23` will be stored as `20121-05-23 00:00:00`.

Boolean type

The **Boolean** type is used to store single-byte literals with a `True` or `False` state or `UNKNOWN`. When inserting data into a Boolean type field, the valid set of specifiers for `True` is `{TRUE, 't', 'true', 'y', 'yes', '1'}`. The valid set of specifiers for `False` is `{FALSE 'f' 'false' 'n' 'no' '0'}`. And if a column has a `NULL` value, it is considered `UNKNOWN`.

Regardless of what literal string was used to insert a column of the Boolean type, the data is always stored and displayed as t for true and f for false.

HLLSKETCH type

The `HLLSKETCH` type is a complex data type that stores the results of what is known as the **Hyper-LogLog algorithm**. This algorithm can be used to estimate the cardinality (number of unique values) in a large multiset very efficiently. Estimating the number of unique values is a useful analytic function that can be used to map trends over time.

For example, if you run a large social media website with hundreds of millions of people visiting every day, to track trends, you may want to calculate how many unique visitors you have each day, each week, or each month. Using traditional SQL to perform this calculation would be impractical as the query would take too long and would require an extremely large amount of memory.

This is where algorithms such as the HyperLogLog algorithm come in. Again, there is a trade-off, as you do give up some level of accuracy in exchange for a much more efficient way of getting a good estimate of cardinality (generally, the error range is expected to be between 0.01 and 0.6%). Using this algorithm means you can now work with extremely large datasets and calculate the estimated unique values with minimal memory usage and within a reasonable time.

Redshift stores the result of the HyperLogLog algorithm in a data type called `HLLSKETCH`. You could have a daily query that runs to calculate the approximate unique visitors to your website each day and store that in an `HLLSKETCH` data type. Then, each week, you could use Redshift's built-in aggregate and scalar functions on the `HLLSKETCH` values to combine multiple `HLLSKETCH` values to calculate weekly totals.

SUPER type

To support semi-structured data (such as arrays and JSON data) more efficiently in Redshift, Amazon provides the SUPER data type. You can load up to 1 MB of data into a column that is of the SUPER type, and then easily query the data without needing to impose a schema first.

For example, if you're loading JSON data into a SUPER data type column, you don't need to specify the data types of the attributes in the JSON document. When you query the data, dynamic typing is used to determine the data type for values in the JSON document.

The SUPER data type offers significantly increased performance for querying semi-structured data versus unnesting the full JSON document and storing it in columns. If the JSON document contains hundreds of attributes, the increase in performance can be significant.

Amazon did announce support for up to 16 MB of data in the SUPER type; however, at the time of writing, this functionality is still in preview. Also, this functionality currently has a number of known limitations, such as not supporting data sharing, elastic resize, or query federation if a table has a SUPER type that holds objects larger than 1 MB.

Selecting the optimal table type

Redshift supports several different types of tables. Making use of a variety of table types for different purposes can help significantly increase query performance. Here, we will look at the different types of tables and discuss how each type can affect performance.

Local Redshift tables

The most common and default table type in Redshift is a table that is permanently stored on Redshift-managed storage. For RA3 node types, this includes local SSD drives as well as Amazon S3, while with DC2 node types, this would be local SSD storage.

One of the biggest advantages of a lake house architecture is the performance enhancement of placing hot data on high-performance local drives, along with high-network bandwidth and a large high-speed cache, as available in Redshift. With RA3 nodes, Redshift uses Amazon S3-based storage, while automatically loading frequently queried data to local storage, in order to optimize performance (as we cover in more detail later in this section).

Redshift stores data in a columnar data format, which is optimized for analytics and uses compression algorithms to reduce disk lookup time when a query is run. By using ML-based automatic optimizations related to table maintenance tasks such as vacuum, table sort, selection of distribution, and sort keys, as well as workload management, Redshift can turbo-charge query performance.

While the best performance is gained by coupling compute and storage, it can result in an unnecessary increase in cost when you need to scale out either just compute or storage. To solve this, Amazon introduced RA3 nodes with **Redshift Managed Storage (RMS)**, which provides the best of both worlds. RA3 nodes offer tightly coupled compute with high-performance SSD storage, as well as additional S3-based storage that can be scaled separately. No changes need to be made to workflows to use these nodes, as Redshift automatically manages the movement of data between the local storage and S3-managed storage based on data access patterns.

With RMS, data is initially stored on the local SSD drives, but if data on a node exceeds the space available on the SSD storage, Redshift automatically moves colder data to Amazon S3. Redshift uses an advanced algorithm to determine what data should be stored on the local SSD drives and what data is moved to Amazon S3, and automatically moves data between the two storage tiers as required. Some of the factors that the algorithm takes into account include data block temperature, data block age, and workload patterns.

External tables for querying data in Amazon S3 with Redshift Spectrum

To take advantage of our data lake (which we consider to be our single source of truth), Redshift supports the concept of external tables. These tables are effectively schema objects in Redshift that point to database objects in the **AWS Glue Data Catalog** (or optionally an **Amazon EMR Hive metastore**).

Once we have created the external schema in Redshift that points to a specific database in the Glue Data Catalog, we can then query any of the tables that belong to that database, and **Redshift Spectrum** will access the data from the underlying Amazon S3 files. Note that while Redshift Spectrum does offer impressive performance for reading large datasets from Amazon S3, it will generally not be quite as fast as reading that same dataset if it were stored within RMS.

By accessing the data directly from our S3 data lake, we avoid replicating multiple copies of the data across our data warehouse clusters. However, we still get to take advantage of the **Massively Parallel Processing (MPP)** query engine in Redshift to query the data. With Redshift Spectrum, we can still get impressive performance while directly accessing our single-source-of-truth data lake data, without needing to constantly load and refresh data lake datasets into Redshift.

When running queries in Redshift, we are free to run complex joins on data between local and external tables. We can also query data (or a subset of data) from an external S3 table, and then write that data out to a local Redshift table when we want to make a specific dataset, or portion of a dataset, available locally in Redshift for optimal query performance.

A common use case for Redshift Spectrum is where a company knows that 80% of their queries access data generated in the past 12 months, but that 20% of their queries also rely on accessing historical data from the past 5 years. In this scenario, the past 12 months of data can be loaded into Redshift on a rolling basis and queried with optimal performance. However, the smaller portion of queries that need historical data can read that data from the data lake using Redshift Spectrum, with the understanding that reading historical data may not be quite as fast as reading data from the past 12 months.

Redshift Spectrum also supports reading data in Amazon S3 that uses **Open Table Formats**, such as Delta Lake and Apache Hudi. Support for reading Apache Iceberg data with Redshift Spectrum is available in preview at the time of writing (and we will cover Open Table Formats in more detail in *Chapter 14, Building Transactional Data Lakes*).

Another common use case for external tables is to enable Redshift to read data from file formats that are not natively supported in Redshift, such as **Amazon Ion, Grok, RCFile**, and **Sequence** files.

An important point to keep in mind when planning your use of external tables is that the cost of Redshift Spectrum, when run from provisioned clusters, is based on the amount of data that's scanned by a Spectrum query, in addition to the fixed costs of the cluster. With Redshift Serverless, cluster cost is based on the RPUs consumed by queries you run on the cluster, whether the queries are on local tables, or whether they use Redshift Spectrum to query data in the data lake.

Also, while query performance with Redshift Spectrum is often impressive, it still may not match the performance when querying data stored locally in RMS. Therefore, you should consider loading frequently queried data directly into RMS, rather than only relying on external tables. This is especially true for datasets that are used for tasks such as constantly refreshing dashboards, datasets that are frequently queried by a large group of users, or where you need to do a large number of joins across tables.

In the hands-on section of this chapter, we will configure a Redshift Spectrum external table and query data from that table using both Redshift and Athena.

Temporary staging tables for loading data into Redshift

Redshift, like many other data warehousing systems, supports the concept of a **temporary table**. Temporary tables are session-specific, meaning that they are automatically dropped at the end of a session and are unrecoverable.

However, temporary tables can significantly improve the performance of some operations as temporary tables are not replicated in the same way permanent tables are, and inserting data into temporary tables does not trigger automatic cluster incremental backup operations. One of the common uses of temporary tables (also sometimes referred to as staging tables) is for updating and inserting data into existing tables.

Traditional transactional databases support an operation called an UPSERT, which is useful for **Change Data Capture (CDC)**. An UPSERT transaction reads new data and checks if there is an existing matching record based on the primary key. If there is an existing record, the record is updated with the new data, and if there is no existing record, a new record is created.

While Redshift does support the concept of primary keys, this is for informational purposes and is only used by the query optimizer. Redshift does not enforce unique primary keys or foreign key constraints. As a result, the UPSERT SQL clause is not supported natively in Redshift.

However, in April 2023, Amazon Redshift announced support for the MERGE command, which enables applying source data changes into a Redshift table using a simple SQL statement. A common approach is to load the latest snapshot of data from a source system into a temporary table in Redshift, and then use the MERGE command to merge changes in the dataset into a target table.

Data caching using Redshift materialized views

Data warehouses are often used as the backend query engine for BI solutions. A visualization tool such as Amazon QuickSight (which we will discuss in more detail in *Chapter 12, Visualizing Data with Amazon QuickSight*) can be used to build dashboards based on data stored in Amazon Redshift (and other data sources).

The dashboards are accessed by different business users to visualize, filter, and drill down into different datasets. Often, the queries that are needed to create a specific visualization will need to reference and join data from multiple Redshift tables, and potentially perform aggregations and other calculations on the data.

Instead of having to rerun the same query over and over as different users access the dashboards, you can effectively cache the query results by creating what is called a **materialized view**.

Materialized views increase query performance by orders of magnitude by precomputing expensive operations such as join results, arithmetic calculations, and aggregations, and then storing the results of the query in a view. The BI tool can then be configured to query the view, rather than querying the tables directly. From the perspective of the BI tool, accessing the materialized view is the same as accessing a table.

You can choose to either manually refresh a materialized view using the REFRESH MATERIALIZED VIEW statement, or you can configure a materialized view to be automatically refreshed when the underlying base table data changes. Note, however, that Redshift prioritizes other running workloads over auto-refresh, and therefore might not immediately refresh a materialized view if the system is under load.

A common use case for materialized views would be to store the results of the advanced queries and calculations needed to aggregate sales by store daily. Each night, the day's sales can be loaded into Redshift from the data lake, and on completion of the data ingest, a materialized view can be created or refreshed. In this way, the complex calculations and joins required to determine sales by store are run just once, and when users query the data via their BI tool, they access the results of the query through the materialized view.

Now that we've looked at the types of tables that are supported in Redshift, let's look at the best practices involved in ingesting data into Redshift.

Moving data between a data lake and Redshift

Moving data between a data lake and a data warehouse, such as Amazon Redshift, is a common requirement for many use cases. Data may be cleansed and processed with Glue ETL jobs in the data lake, for example, and then hot data can be loaded into Redshift so that it can be queried via BI tools with optimal performance.

In the same way, there are certain use cases where data may be further processed in the data warehouse, and this newly processed data then needs to be exported back to the data lake so that other users and processes can consume this data.

In this section, we will examine some best practices and recommendations for both ingesting data from the data lake and exporting data back to the data lake.

Optimizing data ingestion in Redshift

While there are various ways that you can insert data into Redshift, the recommended way is to bulk ingest data using the Redshift COPY command. The COPY command enables optimized data to be ingested from the following sources:

- **Amazon S3**
- **Amazon DynamoDB**
- **Amazon Elastic MapReduce (EMR)**
- **Remote SSH hosts**

When running the COPY command, you need to specify an IAM role, or the access key and secret access key of an IAM user, that has relevant permissions to read the source (such as Amazon S3), as well as the required Redshift permissions. AWS recommends creating and using an IAM role with the COPY command.

When reading data from Amazon S3, Amazon EMR, or from a remote host via SSH, the COPY command supports various formats, including CSV, Parquet, Avro, JSON, ORC, and many others.

To take advantage of the multiple compute nodes in a cluster when ingesting files into a Redshift-provisioned cluster, you should aim to match the number of ingest files with the number of slices in the cluster. Each slice of the cluster can ingest data in parallel with all the other slices in the cluster, so matching the number of files to the number of slices results in the maximum performance for the ingest operation, as shown in the following diagram:

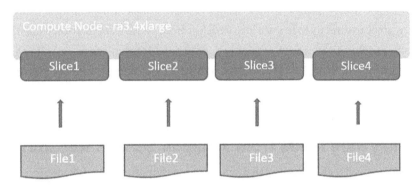

Figure 9.2: Slices in a Redshift compute node

If you have one large ingest file, it should be split into multiple files, with each file having a size between 1 MB and 1 GB (after compression). To determine how many slices you have in your cluster, refer to the AWS documentation on Redshift cluster configuration.

For example, if you had a cluster with 4 x ra3.4xlarge nodes, you would have 16 slices (there are four slices per ra3.4xlarge node). If your ingest file were 64 GB in size, you would split the file into 64 x 1 GB files, and each of the slices in the cluster would then ingest a total of four files.

Note that when using the COPY command to ingest data, the COPY operation is treated as a single transaction across all files. If one of our 64 files failed to be copied, the entire copy would be aborted and the transaction would be rolled back.

While it is possible to use INSERT statements to add rows to a table, adding single rows, or just a few rows, using INSERT statements is not recommended. Adding data to a table using INSERT statements is significantly slower than using the COPY command to ingest data. If you do need to add data using INSERT statements, you can insert multiple rows with a single statement using multi-row insert, by specifying multiple comma-separated rows. You should add as many rows as possible with a single INSERT statement to improve performance and maximize how data blocks are stored.

When loading data from an Amazon EMR cluster, you can use the COPY command in Redshift and specify the EMR cluster ID and the HDFS path that the data should be loaded from. However, before doing this, you need to configure the nodes in the EMR cluster to accept SSH requests from your Redshift cluster, and you need to ensure the appropriate security groups have been configured to allow connections between Redshift and the EMR nodes.

Alternatively, you can directly load data into Redshift from a Spark application using the AWS-optimized Spark-Redshift JDBC driver, available in EMR 6.9, EMR Serverless, and Glue 4.0 and later. In the background, the Spark DataFrame you are loading is written to a temporary S3 bucket, and then a COPY command is executed to load the data into Redshift. You can also read data from Redshift into a Spark DataFrame by using the Spark-Redshift JDBC driver.

Automating data loads from Amazon S3 into Redshift

In November 2022, AWS announced the preview of new functionality in Redshift to perform an auto-copy of data from an S3 bucket into an Amazon Redshift cluster. Using this functionality, you can specify that a COPY command should be created as a job that will monitor an S3 location for new files, and as new files become available, these will automatically be loaded into the Redshift table that you specify.

As of the time of writing, this functionality is still in preview and has some limitations, such as not supporting the loading of Parquet and ORC files. Please refer to the latest Amazon Redshift documentation for the latest supported features for COPY jobs.

Exporting data from Redshift to the data lake

Similar to how the COPY command can be used to ingest data to Redshift, you can use the UNLOAD command to copy data from a Redshift cluster to Amazon S3.

To maximize the performance of UNLOAD, Redshift uses multiple slices in the cluster to write out data to multiple files simultaneously. Each file that is written can be a maximum size of 6.2 GB, although there is an option to specify a smaller maximum file size (and this also gives some control over the number of files that are written out). Depending on the size of the dataset you are unloading, it would generally be recommended to specify a MAXFILESIZE option of 1 GB.

When running the UNLOAD command, you specify a SELECT query to determine what data will be unloaded. To unload a full single table, you would specify SELECT * from TABLENAME in your UNLOAD statement. However, you could use more advanced queries in the UNLOAD statement, such as a query that joins multiple tables, or a query that uses a WHERE clause to unload only a subset of the data in a table. It is recommended that you specify an ORDER BY clause in the query, especially if you plan to load the data back into Redshift.

By default, data is unloaded in a pipe-delimited text format, but unloading data in Parquet format is also supported. For most use cases where you're exporting data to a data lake, it is recommended to specify the Parquet format for the unloaded data. The Parquet format is optimized for analytics, is compressed (so it uses less storage space in S3), and the UNLOAD performance can be up to twice as fast when unloading in Parquet format versus unloading in text format.

If you're performing an UNLOAD on a specific dataset regularly, you can use the ALLOWOVERWRITE option to allow Redshift to overwrite any existing files in the specified path. Alternatively, you can use the CLEANPATH option to remove any existing files in the specified path before writing data out.

Another best practice recommendation for unloading large datasets to a data lake is to specify the PARTITION option and to provide one or more columns that the data should be partitioned by. When writing out partitioned data, Redshift will use the standard Hive partitioning format. For example, if you partition your data by the year and month columns, the data will be written out as follows:

```
s3://unload_bucket_name/prefix/year=2021/month=July/000.parquet
```

When using the PARTITION option with the CLEANPATH option, Redshift will only delete files for the specific partitions that it writes out to.

Let's now look at some of the other advanced features available in Redshift, before moving on to the hands-on part of this chapter.

Exploring advanced Redshift features

While Redshift was first launched a long while back (2013), AWS is continually adding new functionality and features to Redshift. In this section, we are going to look at some of the advanced capabilities launched in the past few years that can help you get the most from your Redshift cluster. You should also regularly review the AWS *What's New* page for Redshift (https://aws.amazon.com/redshift/whats-new/), as well as AWS blog posts tagged with Redshift (https://aws.amazon.com/blogs/big-data/tag/amazon-redshift/), to ensure you keep up to date with new features.

Data sharing between Redshift clusters

There are a number of use cases where you may want to share data from one Redshift cluster with data in another (or multiple other) Redshift cluster. For example, if you implement a data mesh architecture, you may want to make data available from one part of the business easily accessible for other parts of the business without needing to create a duplicate copy of the data. For this use case, a data producer in one part of the business can share data from their Redshift RA3 cluster with the Redshift cluster of data consumers in another part of the business that have been authorized to access the data.

Another example of a use case for sharing data between clusters is where you may want to have the compute resources of a Redshift cluster focused just on data ingestion, transforming data, creating materialized views, etc. without having an impact on consumers who want to query the same data. In this case, you can have a dedicated ELT cluster that does the ingestion and transformation, and then launch a separate cluster that your data consumers will use to query the data. With this scenario, you can share the data from the *ELT cluster* with the *consumer cluster*, enabling each use case to have its own dedicated Redshift compute resources. If you ingest and transform data only once a day, you can even pause the *ELT cluster* once the ingestion and transformation are complete, and the *consumer cluster* will still be able to read the data from the paused *ELT cluster*.

In a similar way, you may have multiple different teams wanting to run queries on the same dataset. Traditionally these teams would end up competing for cluster resources, and it would not be easy to proportionally allocate costs to the different teams based on their usage of the cluster. However, with Redshift data sharing, each team can have its own Redshift cluster, with dedicated resources, and yet they can all access the same dataset. This also means that it is much simpler to allocate data warehousing costs for each team, as they each have their own cluster.

With Amazon Redshift data sharing, you can share live data from a source RA3 Redshift cluster with a target RA3 Redshift cluster in the same, or different, AWS account, as well as across regions (for example, a Redshift cluster in the N. Virginia us-east-1 Region can share data with a Redshift cluster in the Ohio us-east-2 Region). As of the time of writing, data that is shared with another cluster is available in the target cluster as read-only data (i.e., the cluster accessing shared data cannot write or update any of the shared tables). Data that is shared is shared "live," meaning that the target cluster sees the data in its current, most updated form, as it is updated in the source cluster.

You can select to either manage data sharing in Redshift directly, or you can use the AWS Lake Formation service to define and enforce Redshift data shares. This includes the ability to define column and row-level access permissions for shared tables. You can learn more about managing Redshift data shares with Lake Formation in the AWS documentation at `https://docs.aws.amazon.com/redshift/latest/dg/lake-formation-datashare.html`.

Machine learning capabilities in Amazon Redshift

Amazon Redshift includes functionality to integrate with the **Amazon SageMaker** ML service. This functionality, called Redshift ML, enables you to create and train new ML models on data in Redshift, and to perform inference (getting a prediction from the model) as part of a Redshift SQL query.

When you use the Redshift ML functionality to create a new model based on data in Redshift, the data will be automatically exported to Amazon S3, and SageMaker AutoML will then be used to train a new model and make that available in Redshift. Note that using this functionality incurs S3 storage costs for the data exported, as well as Amazon SageMaker costs for the model training.

An example of how you can use this functionality is to use a table in Redshift that contains customer information such as their ZIP/postal code, how long they have had an account with your company, the total revenue you have billed them for, as well as the number of customer service calls they have made. In addition, to train the new model, your dataset should include a field that indicates whether they are still an active customer or not. Based on this data, you can create a model that will predict whether a customer (or group of customers) is likely to cancel their service (often referred to as customer churn).

With the above dataset, you can use the Redshift `CREATE MODEL` statement in a SQL query, and Redshift will export the dataset to S3, and then use the Amazon SageMaker Autopilot feature to train the model. Once trained and validated, Amazon SageMaker will deploy the model and prediction function to Amazon Redshift.

Once complete, you can use SQL statements to provide similar information used to train the model (ZIP code, account length, spend, and customer service calls) to receive a prediction on whether a customer (or group of customers) is likely to cancel their service.

For more information on Redshift ML, see the Amazon Redshift documentation at `https://docs.aws.amazon.com/redshift/latest/dg/machine_learning.html`.

Running Redshift clusters across multiple Availability Zones

For some users, the risk of a Redshift cluster being unavailable for a period of time in the event of an issue with an AWS Availability Zone (AZ) is not a significant risk. In many cases, data warehouse-based queries and reports are not considered critical dependencies for the business, and a business may be willing to take the risk of a certain period of downtime of their Redshift cluster.

With Redshift Serverless, you always configure the serverless cluster with subnets in 3 different availability zones, and this helps ensure the continued availability of the serverless endpoint in the event of an issue impacting an availability zone.

With RA3-provisioned nodes, a feature called cluster relocation is enabled by default, and this allows Redshift to automatically relocate a cluster to a different availability zone in the event of issues impacting cluster operations in the current availability zone. While this can take place automatically, there is a period of downtime while the cluster is relocated. Note however that after relocation, the cluster can still be accessed using the same endpoint (therefore applications do not need to be reconfigured to point to a new endpoint after relocation).

However, there may be other use cases where a business depends heavily on the availability of its data warehouse for running queries and reports and is willing to accept increased costs in exchange for increased availability.

In November 2022, AWS announced the preview availability of a new feature that enables Redshift RA3 clusters to be deployed across multiple AZs. When configuring an RA3 Redshift cluster in multi-AZ mode, you specify the number of nodes you want in a single AZ, and Redshift will deploy those number of nodes in each of the two AZs. All nodes across the AZs can perform read and write workload processing during normal operation.

With multi-AZ, data is stored in RMS, which uses Amazon S3 and makes the data available simultaneously in both AZs where the compute nodes are running. If multiple queries are running against the multi-AZ Redshift cluster, the queries will run on compute nodes in both AZs; however, each individual query will use compute resources in a single AZ only.

Therefore, you need to ensure that you have enough compute nodes in each AZ to be able to handle your most complex queries.

Learn more about running Redshift across multi-AZs by reading the documentation at `https://docs.aws.amazon.com/redshift/latest/mgmt/managing-cluster-multi-az.html`.

Redshift Dynamic Data Masking

In addition to Redshift data access controls that enable row-level security and column-level security, you can also define **Dynamic Data Masking** (DDM) policies to further protect sensitive data stored in Redshift. Using this functionality, you can define policies that mask data values at the time that data is returned to a user. This enables you to protect sensitive data returned in queries, without needing to transform and store the data in Redshift in a protected format.

For example, if you store confidential PII data (such as a national identity number or social security number), you can store the full data in Redshift but can ensure that when users query the data, they are not able to access the PII data directly. The policies you define can completely or partially redact the data, or can apply a hashing function to return a hash instead of the actual data. For example, using this functionality, you could configure a policy that returns just the last 4 digits of a social security number in a query, instead of displaying the full social security number. And you can apply the policy to different user roles, so that some users may be able to access the full number, while other users only see the last 4 digits.

Read more about DDM in the Redshift documentation at `https://docs.aws.amazon.com/redshift/latest/dg/t_ddm.html`.

Zero-ETL between Amazon Aurora and Amazon Redshift

In November 2022, AWS announced the preview support of **zero-ETL** integration between Amazon Aurora and Amazon Redshift. With this functionality, data written to Amazon Aurora can be made available in Amazon Redshift within seconds.

This functionality enables you to analyze data from multiple Amazon Aurora database clusters in an Amazon Redshift cluster, in near real time. Previously, this would have required more complex solutions using ETL pipelines and services such as AWS **Database Migration Service** (DMS) to move data from an Aurora database into Redshift. Using this functionality, you can use Amazon Redshift's advanced analytics and ML capabilities to gain new insights from transactional data.

In the preview announcement, AWS announced zero-ETL support for Amazon Aurora MySQL 3 (with MySQL 8.0 compatibility). At the time of writing, support for Amazon Aurora with PostgreSQL compatibility was not available.

Resizing a Redshift cluster

There may be times when you need to resize your Redshift cluster, either permanently (due to sustained increased load on the cluster) or temporarily (to handle month-end data processing, for example). Redshift enables this through a process known as **elastic resize.**

With elastic resize, you can add or remove nodes from a cluster, or change the node type (for example, from DC2 nodes to RA3 nodes). Elastic resize usually completes within around 10–15 minutes, and while the resize operation takes place, the cluster is in read-only mode. During the process, queries may be temporarily paused, and it is possible that some queries may be dropped. Also, if the cluster has been configured to share data with other clusters, those other clusters may not be able to connect and access data during a portion of the resize.

Elastic resize is recommended when you need to resize a cluster, but there are times when an elastic resize may not be supported for a specific cluster configuration. In those cases, you can perform a classic resize. This process takes longer, but it does support scenarios where elastic resize does not work, such as where you have a cluster that does not use KMS encryption, and you want to now encrypt your cluster.

Now that you have a good understanding of the Redshift architecture, important considerations for optimizing the performance of your cluster, and an understanding of some of the advanced features in Redshift, it is time to get hands-on with deploying a Redshift cluster.

Hands-on – deploying a Redshift Serverless cluster and running Redshift Spectrum queries

In our Redshift hands-on exercise, we're going to create a new **Redshift Serverless** cluster and configure **Redshift Spectrum** so that we can query data in external tables on Amazon S3. We'll then use both Redshift Spectrum and Amazon Athena to query data in S3.

Uploading our sample data to Amazon S3

For this exercise, we are going to use some data generated with a service called Mockaroo (`https://www.mockaroo.com/`). This service enables us to generate fake data with a wide variety of field types and is useful for demos and testing.

We will upload this dataset, containing a list of users, to Amazon S3 and then query it using Redshift Spectrum. Note that all data in this file is fake data, generated with the tool mentioned above. Therefore, the names, email addresses, street addresses, phone numbers, etc. in this dataset are not real.

Let's get started:

1. Download the fake list of users from the GitHub site for this book using the following link: https://github.com/PacktPublishing/Data-Engineering-with-AWS-2nd-edition/blob/main/Chapter09/user_details.csv.

2. Log in to the **AWS Console** and access the **Amazon S3** service. Navigate to your landing zone bucket (for example, dataeng-landing-zone-initials) and create a new prefix called users.

3. Upload the user_details.csv file into the data lake's landing zone bucket (which you created in *Chapter 3, The AWS Data Engineers Toolkit*) under the users prefix. For example:

```
s3://dataeng-landing-zone-gse23/users/user_details.csv
```

4. To verify that the files have been uploaded correctly, we can use **S3 Select** to directly query uploaded files. In the **Amazon S3 console**, navigate to the users prefix in the landing zone bucket, and select the user_details.csv file. From the **Actions** menu, click on **Query with S3 Select**. Leave all the options as their defaults and click **Run SQL query**. This will display a few records from the CSV file.

Having uploaded our users file to the data lake, we now need to create the IAM roles that our Redshift cluster will use, and then create the cluster.

IAM roles for Redshift

Amazon Redshift Spectrum enables our cluster to read data that is in our Amazon S3-based data lake directly, without needing to load the data into the cluster. Redshift Spectrum uses the AWS Glue Data Catalog, so it requires AWS Glue permissions in addition to Amazon S3 permissions. If you are operating in an AWS Region where AWS Glue is not supported, then Redshift Spectrum uses the Amazon Athena catalog, so you would require Amazon Athena permissions.

To create the IAM role that grants the required Redshift Spectrum permissions, follow these steps:

1. Navigate to the **AWS IAM Management console**, click on **Roles** on the left-hand side, and click on **Create role**.

2. Ensure that **AWS service** is selected for **Select type of trusted entity**, and then search for **Redshift** in the drop-down list. For **Use cases for other AWS services**, select **Redshift – Customizable**. Click on **Next**.

3. Attach the following four policies to the role:

    *   `AmazonS3FullAccess`
    *   `AWSGlueConsoleFullAccess`
    *   `AmazonAthenaFullAccess`
    *   `AmazonRedshiftAllCommandsFullAccess`

IMPORTANT NOTE ABOUT PERMISSIONS

The preceding policies provide broad access to various AWS services, including full access to all S3 files in your account. If you are using an account created specifically for the hands-on exercises in this book, or you are using a limited sandbox account provided by your organization, then these permissions may be safe. However, in an AWS account that is shared with others, such as a corporate production account, you should not use these policies. Instead, you should create new policies that, for example, limit access to only the S3 buckets that are used in the hands-on exercises. *Using full access policies, as we have here, is not a good security practice for shared or production accounts.*

4. Then, click on **Next** and provide a **Role name**, such as `AmazonRedshiftSpectrumRole`. Make sure that the three policies listed in *Step 3* are included and that **Trusted entities** includes `redshift.amazonaws.com`. Once confirmed, click **Create role**.

5. Search for the role you just created and click on the role's name. On the **Summary** screen, take note of **Role ARN** as this will be needed later.

Now that we have created an IAM role that provides the permissions needed for Redshift Spectrum to access the required resources, we can move on to creating our cluster.

Creating a Redshift cluster

We are now ready to create our **Redshift Serverless** cluster and attach the IAM policy for Redshift Spectrum to the cluster. Let's get started:

IMPORTANT NOTE ABOUT REDSHIFT COSTS

At the time of writing, AWS offers a free trial for new Redshift Serverless customers, enabling you to create and test out a new Redshift Serverless cluster with $300 of credit that can be used over 90 days. However, this is only available if your organization has not previously created a Redshift Serverless cluster. If you've previously created an Amazon Redshift Serverless cluster, you are not eligible for the free trial and your usage of Redshift Serverless will be billed for. If you are eligible for the free trial but you leave your Redshift cluster running beyond the free trial time limit, you will be charged for usage of the cluster. For more information, see `https://aws.amazon.com/redshift/free-trial/`.

1. Navigate to the **Amazon Redshift** console at `https://console.aws.amazon.com/redshiftv2/`. If you have not created a cluster before, there should be a button marked **Try Redshift Serverless free trial** that you can click in order to quickly configure a new serverless cluster. The option for **Use default settings** should already be checked, which enables us to create a cluster with default settings, so leave this option selected. If **Try Redshift Serverless free trial** is not displayed, then click on **Create workgroup** and provide a workgroup and namespace name, and set the base capacity to 8 RPUs.

2. Scroll down to **Associated IAM roles** and click on **Associate IAM role**. Search for the role you created previously (such as `AmazonRedshiftSpectrumRole`) and select the role, then click **Associate IAM roles**.

3. Select the role you just associated, and then click **Set default** and **Make default**. Click on **Confirm** when prompted.

4. Scroll down to the bottom of the page and click on **Save configuration**.

5. This will now create your Amazon Redshift Serverless cluster and should complete in under 5 minutes. Once complete, click on **Continue**.

You should be redirected to the **Amazon Redshift Serverless** dashboard, which includes information on the default namespace and workgroup you just created (both called **default**), and also includes information on how much of the $300 in credits is still available, if you qualify for the free trial.

Querying data in the sample database

When a new Redshift Serverless cluster is created, it includes easy access to sample datasets that you can query as you explore the Redshift query editor and interface. The following steps show you how to access the sample database:

1. On the **Redshift Serverless dashboard**, click on the **Query data** button to launch the query editor.

2. The query editor will launch in a new window, and a list of workgroups will be displayed on the left. The **Serverless: default** workgroup should be listed. Click to expand the workgroup name, which will display a popup for you to select an authentication method (since this is the first time you are connecting to the workgroup). Select the **Federated user** option, which uses your IAM credentials to generate temporary credentials for accessing the database. There is a default dev database that is created for new clusters, so leave dev set as the database to connect to, and click on **Create connection**.

3. Expand the sample_data_dev schema, and then click on the folder icon next to the tickit table. This loads the sample data into Redshift, but you need a database to store this data. Therefore, when you click on the folder icon (**Open sample notebooks**), you are prompted to allow Redshift to create a sample database. Click on **Create**. It may take a few minutes for the sample data to be loaded.

    The Redshift query editor includes notebook functionality, where you can write up a number of SQL statements, as well as blocks, where you can include comments using Markdown syntax. You can either click on **Run all** to run all the statements in the notebook, or you can click on **Run** in an individual block to run just a single statement.

4. Click on **Run all** to run all the statements in this notebook.

5. In the first block (**Sales per event**), there are two SQL statements, and as a result, there are two **Result** tabs below. The first statement just set the path to use the **tickit** schema, and therefore there is not a lot to show in the result box. Click on **Result 2** to view the results of the second statement, which queries the sales table and shows the total_price for each event in the database.

Up to this point we have loaded and queried some sample data using a query editor notebook, but let's now move on to defining an external schema where we can point to the data we uploaded at the start of the hands-on section. We can then query that data using **Redshift Spectrum**.

Using Redshift Spectrum to directly query data in the data lake

To query data in Amazon S3 using Redshift Spectrum, we need to define a database, schema, and table.

Note that Amazon Redshift and AWS Glue use the term *database* differently. In Amazon Redshift, a database is a top-level container that contains one or more schemas, and each schema can contain one or more tables. When you use the Redshift query editor, you specify the name of the database that you want to connect to, and any objects you create are created in that database. When you query a table, you specify the schema name along with the table name.

However, in AWS Glue, there is no concept of a schema, just a database, and tables are created in the database.

With the command shown in the following steps, we can create a new Redshift schema, defined as an external schema (meaning objects created in the schema will be defined in the AWS Glue Data catalog), and we specify that we want to create a new database in the Glue Data catalog called users. For Redshift to be able to write to the Glue Data Catalog and access objects in S3, we need to specify the ARN for the Redshift Spectrum role that we previously created, as this has access to all data in S3:

1. In the Redshift query editor v2 interface, click on the **PLUS (+)** sign, and then click on **Editor** to create a new tab that provides a simple query interface.

2. In the **database** dropdown, change the database from sample_data_dev to dev, so that our new schema is created in the database called dev. Then run the following command in the new tab to create a new external schema called spectrum_schema, and to also create a new database in the Glue Data catalog called users. Make sure to replace the iam_role ARN with the ARN you recorded previously when you created an IAM role for Redshift Spectrum:

    ```
    create external schema spectrum_schema
    from data catalog
    database 'users'
    iam_role 'arn:aws:iam::1234567890:role/AmazonRedshiftSpectrumRole'
    create external database if not exists;
    ```

Figure 9.3: Creating a Redshift external schema

3.   We can now define an **external table** that will be registered in the Glue Data Catalog under
      our users database in Glue and in the `spectrum_schema` in Redshift. When defining the
      table, we specify the columns that exist, the format of the files (text or comma delimit-
      ed), and the location in S3 where the text files were uploaded. We also include a `table`
      `properties` attribute that indicates that the sample data has a header row, which we
      want to ignore. Replace the previous SQL statement with the following statement, and
      make sure to replace the bucket name of the S3 location with the name of your data lake
      landing zone bucket:

```
CREATE EXTERNAL TABLE spectrum_schema.user_details(
    id INTEGER,
    first_name VARCHAR(40),
    last_name VARCHAR(40),
    email VARCHAR(60),
    gender VARCHAR(15),
    address_1 VARCHAR(80),
    address_2 VARCHAR(80),
    city VARCHAR(40),
    state VARCHAR(25),
    zip VARCHAR(5),
    phone VARCHAR(12)
)
row format delimited
fields terminated by ','
stored as textfile
location 's3://dataeng-landing-zone-initials/users/'
table properties ('skip.header.line.count'='1');
```

4.   We can now run a query against the table to ensure that it was created successfully. In the left-hand navigation pane of the **Redshift query editor v2**, click on the **REFRESH** icon to update the interface to show the newly created objects. Under dev / spectrum_schema / tables, you should see the user_details table. Clicking on this table will show the table schema as we defined it. We can also query a sample of the data from the newly defined table by running the following query in the query editor (making sure that we have the dev database selected in the **database** dropdown of the query editor):

```
select * from spectrum_schema.user_details limit 10;
```

5.   We can also confirm that the new external table was created successfully by checking the Glue Data Catalog. Search for and open the **Glue** service in the AWS Console.

6.   Click on **Databases**, and then click on the **users** database. In the list of tables, click on the **user_details** table.

7.   To view a sample of the data in the table, click on **Actions**, and then click **View data**. If you receive a popup indicating that you will be using the Athena service to query the data and that there may be separate charges, click on **Proceed**. When the Athena console opens (in a new browser tab), you should see 10 records from our user_details table.

With the above tasks, we queried data in our S3 data lake using both Amazon Athena and Amazon Redshift (using the Redshift Spectrum functionality).

DELETE THE SERVERLESS CLUSTER

If you do not plan to explore additional Redshift functionality, you should delete the Redshift Serverless workgroup first, and then the namespace, in order to prevent unnecessary charges from being incurred over time.

Summary

In this chapter, we learned how a cloud data warehouse can be used to store hot data to optimize performance and manage costs (such as for dashboarding or other BI use cases). We reviewed some common "anti-patterns" for data warehouse usage before diving deep into the Redshift architecture to learn more about how Redshift optimizes data storage across nodes.

We then reviewed some of the important design decisions that need to be made when creating a Redshift cluster optimized for performance, before reviewing how to ingest data into Redshift and unload data from Redshift.

Finally, we reviewed some of the advanced features of Redshift (such as data sharing, DDM, and cluster resizing) before moving on to doing some hands-on exercises.

In the hands-on exercise portion of this chapter, we created a new Redshift Serverless cluster, explored some sample data, and configured Redshift Spectrum to query data from Amazon S3.

In the next chapter, we will discuss how to orchestrate various components of our data engineering pipelines.

Learn more on Discord

To join the Discord community for this book – where you can share feedback, ask questions to the author, and learn about new releases – follow the QR code below:

`https://discord.gg/9s5mHNyECd`

10

Orchestrating the Data Pipeline

Throughout this book, we have discussed various services that can be used by data engineers to ingest and transform data, as well as make it available for consumers. We looked at how we could ingest data via **Amazon Kinesis Data Firehose** and **AWS Database Migration Service (DMS)**, and how we could run **AWS Lambda** and **AWS Glue** functions to transform our data. We also discussed the importance of updating a data catalog as new datasets are added to a data lake, and how we can load subsets of data into a data mart or data warehouse for specific use cases.

For the hands-on exercises, we made use of various services, but for the most part, we triggered these services manually. However, in a real production environment, it would not be acceptable to have to manually trigger these tasks, so we need a way to automate various data engineering tasks. This is where data pipeline orchestration tools come in.

Modern-day ETL applications are designed with a modular architecture to facilitate the use of the best purpose-built tool to complete a specific task. A data engineering pipeline (also sometimes referred to as a workflow) stitches all of these components together to create an ordered execution of related tasks, which can then be triggered to automatically run on a given schedule, or in response to another event occurring.

To build our pipeline, we need an orchestration engine to define and manage the sequence of tasks, as well as the dependencies between tasks. The orchestration engine also needs to be intelligent enough to perform different actions based on the failure or success of a task, and should be able to define and execute tasks that run in parallel, as well as tasks that run sequentially.

In this chapter, we will look at how to manage data pipelines with different orchestration engines. First, we will examine some of the core concepts of pipeline orchestration, and then review several different options within AWS for orchestrating data pipelines.

In the hands-on activity for this chapter, we will orchestrate a data pipeline using the AWS Step Functions service.

In this chapter, we will cover the following topics:

- Understanding the core concepts for pipeline orchestration
- Examining the options for orchestrating pipelines in AWS
- Hands-on – orchestrating a data pipeline using AWS Step Functions

Technical requirements

To complete the hands-on exercises in this chapter, you will need an AWS account where you have access to a user with administrator privileges (as covered in *Chapter 1, An Introduction to Data Engineering*). We will make use of various AWS services, including **AWS Lambda**, **AWS Step Functions**, and **Amazon Simple Notification Service (SNS)**.

You can find the code files of this chapter in the GitHub repository using the following link: `https://github.com/PacktPublishing/Data-Engineering-with-AWS-2nd-edition/tree/main/Chapter10`

Understanding the core concepts for pipeline orchestration

In *Chapter 5, Architecting Data Engineering Pipelines*, we architected a high-level overview of a data pipeline. We examined potential data sources, discussed the types of data transformations that may be required, and looked at how we could make transformed data available to our data consumers.

Then, we examined the topics of data ingestion, transformation, and how to load transformed data into data marts in more detail in the subsequent chapters. As we discussed previously, these steps are often referred to as an **Extract, Transform, Load (ETL)** process.

We have now come to the part where we need to combine the individual steps involved in our ETL processes to operationalize and automate how we process data. But before we look deeper at the AWS services to enable this, let's examine some of the key concepts around pipeline orchestration.

What is a data pipeline, and how do you orchestrate it?

A simple definition is that a **data pipeline** is a collection of data processing tasks that need to be run in a specific order. Some tasks may need to run sequentially, while other tasks may be able to run in parallel. You could also refer to the sequencing of these tasks as a **workflow**.

Data pipeline orchestration refers to automating the execution of tasks involved in a data pipeline workflow, managing dependencies between the different tasks, and ensuring that the pipeline runs when it is meant to.

Think of the data pipeline as the smallest entity for performing a specific task against a dataset. For example, if you receive data from a partner regularly, your first data pipeline may involve validating that the data that's received is valid, and then converting the data file into an optimized format, such as **Parquet**. If you have hundreds of partners sending you data files, then this same pipeline may run for each of those partners.

You may also have a second data pipeline that runs at a specific time of day that validates that the data from all your partners has been received, and then runs a Spark job to join the datasets and enrich the data with additional proprietary data.

Once that data pipeline finishes running, you may have a third pipeline that loads the newly enriched data into a data warehouse.

While you could place all of these steps in a single data pipeline, it is a recommended best practice to split pipelines into the smallest logical grouping of steps. In the preceding example of processing files we receive from our partners throughout the day, our first step is getting newly received files converted into Parquet format, but we only want to do that if we can confirm that the file we received is valid. As such, we group those two tasks (confirming that the file is valid, and then converting into Parquet format) into our first pipeline. The goal of our second pipeline is to join the files we received from our partners throughout the day and enrich the new file with additional data. However, our second pipeline should also include a step to validate and report on whether all the expected partner files were received.

Let's explore some of the common concepts that are regularly used when developing data pipelines.

What is a directed acyclic graph?

When talking about data pipelines, you may hear the term **directed acyclic graph**, commonly referred to as **DAG**. If you Google this term, you may find a lot of complex mathematical explanations of what a DAG is. This is because this term not only applies to data pipelines, but is used to define many different types of ordered processes. For example, DAGs are also used to design compilers.

A simple explanation of a DAG is that it represents connections between nodes, with the flow between nodes always occurring in only one direction and never looping back to an earlier node (acyclic means not a cycle).

The following diagram shows a simple DAG:

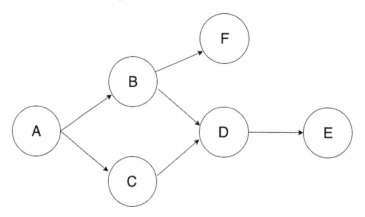

Figure 10.1: A simple example of a directed acyclic graph

If this DAG represented a data pipeline, then the following would take place:

- When event A completes, it triggers event B and event C.
- When event B completes, it triggers event F.
- When events B and C are complete, they trigger event D.
- When event D completes, it triggers event E.

In the preceding example, event F could never loop back to event A, B, or C, as that would break the acyclic part of the DAG definition.

No rule says that data pipelines have to be defined as DAGs, although certain orchestration tools do require this. For example, **Apache Airflow** (which we will discuss in more detail later in this chapter) requires pipelines to be defined as a DAG, and if there is a cycle in a pipeline definition where a node loops back to a previous node, this would not run.

However, **AWS Step Functions** does allow for loop cycles in the definition of a state machine, so Step Functions-based pipelines do not enforce that the pipeline should be a DAG.

How do you trigger a data pipeline to run?

There are two primary types of triggers for a pipeline – **schedule-based pipelines** and **event-based pipelines**.

Traditionally, pipelines were all triggered on a schedule. This could be once a day, every hour, or perhaps even every 15 minutes. This is still a common approach, especially for batch-orientated pipelines. In our prior pipeline example, the second pipeline could be an example of a scheduled pipeline that runs once per day to join and enrich partner files that are received throughout the day.

Today, however, a lot of pipelines are created to be **event-driven**. In other words, the pipeline is triggered in response to some specific event being completed. Event-based workflows are useful for reducing the latency between data becoming available and the pipeline processing that data. For example, if you expect that you will have received the data files you need at some point between 4 A.M. and 6 A.M., you could schedule the pipeline to run at 6 A.M. However, if all the data is available by 5 A.M. on some days, using an event-based trigger can get your pipeline running earlier.

In our earlier example of a pipeline, the first pipeline (to validate files and convert to Parquet format) would be an event-driven pipeline that runs in response to a partner having uploaded a new file. Within AWS, there is strong support for creating event-driven activities, such as triggering an event (which could be a pipeline) based on a file being written to a specific Amazon S3 bucket (and we will get hands-on with an event-driven pipeline in the hands-on section of this chapter).

Using manifest files as pipeline triggers

A **manifest** is often used to refer to a list of cargo carried by a ship, or other transport vehicles. The manifest document may be reviewed by agents at a border crossing or port to validate what is being transported.

In the world of data pipelines, a common concept is to create a **manifest file** that contains information about other files that form part of a batch of files.

In our data pipeline example of receiving files from our partners, we may find that the partner sends hundreds of small CSV files in a batch every hour. We may decide that we do not want to run our pipeline on each file that we receive, but instead to process all the small CSV files in a batch together and convert them into a single Parquet file.

In this case, we could instruct our partners to send a manifest file at the end of each batch of files that they send to us. This manifest file would list the name of each file that's transferred, as well as potentially some validation data, such as file size, or a calculated SHA-256 hash of the file.

We could then configure our S3 event notification to only trigger when a file that begins with the name manifest is written to our bucket. When this happens, we will trigger our pipeline to run, and perhaps the first step in our pipeline would be to read the manifest file, and then for each file listed in the manifest, verify that it exists. We could also calculate the SHA-256 hash of the file, and verify that it matches what is listed in the manifest. Once the files have been verified, we could run our ETL job to read in all the files and write the files out in Parquet format.

This process would still be considered an event-driven pipeline, even though we are not responding to every file upload event, just the completion of a batch of uploads, as represented in the manifest file.

There will, of course, be times when a job will fail, and we need to make sure that we build error handling into our pipelines, as discussed next.

How do you handle the failures of a step in your pipeline?

As part of the orchestration process to automate the processing of steps in a pipeline, we need to ensure that failures are handled correctly. Therefore, it is also important that log files related to each step of the pipeline are easily accessible. In this section, we will look at some important concepts involved in failure handling and logging.

Common reasons for failure in data pipelines

There are many reasons why a specific step in a data pipeline may fail. Some common reasons for errors include the following:

- **Data quality issues:** If one of the steps in your pipeline expects to receive CSV files to process, but instead receives a file in JSON format that it does not know how to process, this would lead to a hard failure (that is, a failure that your job cannot recover from until the data quality issue is resolved).

- **Code errors:** When you update a job, it is possible to introduce a syntax, or logic, error into the code. Testing your code before deploying it into production is very important, but there may be times when your testing does not catch a specific error. This would also be a hard failure, requiring you to redeploy fixed code.

- **Endpoint errors:** One of the steps in your pipeline may involve the need to either read or write data to or from a specific endpoint (such as reading a file in S3 or writing data into a data warehouse). At times, your processing job may not be able to connect to the endpoint, and there may be a number of reasons for this type of error. For example, there could be a temporary network error preventing the connection from being successful, or it could be because of insufficient permissions to access a target database. If it were a temporary network error, this could be considered a soft failure (that is, one that may be overcome by retrying the step). But if it is due to insufficient permissions, the error would be considered a hard failure, and there is no point immediately retrying the step, as you will need the permissions issue to be resolved first.

- **Dependency errors:** Data pipelines generally consist of multiple steps with complex dependencies. This includes dependencies within the pipeline, as well as dependencies between different pipelines. If your job is dependent on a previous step, then the job it is dependent on is referred to as an upstream job. If your job fails, any jobs that depend on it are considered downstream jobs. Dependency errors can be hard failures (such as an upstream job or pipeline having a hard failure) or soft failures (e.g., the upstream job is taking longer than expected to complete, but if you retry your step, it may complete later).

Hard failures generally interrupt processing (and are also likely to cause failures in downstream jobs) until someone takes a specific action to resolve the error. When a hard failure occurs, a data engineer, or operations person, will need to examine the log files to identify the error message, and then take corrective action (such as getting access configured if the error indicated a permissions failure).

Soft failures (such as intermittent networking issues), however, can benefit from having a good retry strategy, as we will discuss next.

Pipeline failure retry strategies

When you're designing your pipeline, you should consider implementing a retry strategy for failed steps. Many orchestration tools (such as Apache Airflow and AWS Step Functions) will allow you to specify the number of retries, the interval between retry attempts, as well as a backoff rate.

The **retry backoff rate** (also known as **exponential backoff**) causes the time between retry attempts to be increased on each retry. With AWS Step Functions, for example, you can specify a BackOffRate value that will multiply the delay between retries by that value. For example, if you specify a retry interval of 10 seconds and a backoff rate of 1.5, Step Functions will wait 15 seconds (10 seconds x 1.5) for the second retry, 22.5 seconds (15 seconds x 1.5) for the third retry, and so on.

Having reviewed some of the core concepts of data pipelines and orchestration, we can now examine the tools that are available in AWS for creating and orchestrating pipelines.

Examining the options for orchestrating pipelines in AWS

As you will have noticed throughout this book, AWS offers many different building blocks for architecting solutions. When it comes to pipeline orchestration, AWS provides native serverless orchestration engines with **AWS Data Pipeline** and **AWS Step Functions**, a managed open-source project with **Amazon Managed Workflows for Apache Airflow (MWAA)**, and service-specific orchestration with **AWS Glue workflows**.

There are pros and cons to using each of these solutions, depending on your use case. When making a decision on this, there are multiple factors to consider, such as the level of management effort, the ease of integration with your target ETL engine, logging, error-handling mechanisms, cost, and platform independence.

In this section, we'll examine each of the four pipeline orchestration options.

AWS Data Pipeline (now in maintenance mode)

AWS Data Pipeline is one of the oldest services that AWS has for creating and orchestrating data pipelines, having been originally released in 2012. However, this service is now in maintenance mode and it is not recommended to build new ETL pipelines using this service.

In December 2022, AWS updated the Data Pipeline documentation to encourage customers to migrate to alternative data integration services, such as AWS Glue, AWS Step Functions, or Amazon MWAA. If you have existing pipelines that use this service, refer to the AWS documentation for a guide on how to migrate to a more modern service at `https://docs.aws.amazon.com/datapipeline/latest/DeveloperGuide/migration.html`.

Let's now take a look at the first of those services that are recommended as an alternative to AWS Data Pipeline, the AWS Glue service.

AWS Glue workflows to orchestrate Glue resources

In *Chapter 3, The AWS Data Engineer's Toolkit*, we introduced **AWS Glue workflows** as a feature of the AWS Glue service. As a reminder, AWS Glue enables you to easily build and run Spark-and Python-based ETL jobs, and the Glue workflows feature can be used to build a pipeline to orchestrate the running of Glue components (Glue Crawlers and Glue ETL jobs).

For use cases where you create a data pipeline that only uses AWS Glue components, the use of Glue workflows can be a good fit. For example, you could create the following pipeline using Glue workflows:

- Run a Glue Crawler to add CSV files that have been ingested into a new partition to the Glue Data Catalog.
- Run a Glue Spark job to read the new data using the catalog, and then transform the CSV files into Parquet files.
- Run another Glue Crawler to add the newly transformed Parquet files to the Glue Data Catalog.
- Run two Glue jobs in parallel. One Glue job aggregates data and writes the results into a DynamoDB table. The other Glue job creates a newly enriched dataset that joins the new data to an existing reference set of data.
- Run another Glue Crawler to add the newly enriched dataset to the Glue Data Catalog.
- Run a Glue Python Shell job to send a notification about the success or failure of the job.

While a fairly complex data pipeline can be created using Glue workflows (as demonstrated above), many use cases require the use of other AWS services, such as EMR for running Hive jobs, or writing files to an SQS queue. While Glue workflows do not support integration with non-Glue services directly, it is possible to run a Glue Python Shell job that uses the Boto3 library to interact with other AWS services. However, this is not as feature-rich or as obvious to monitor as interacting with those services directly.

Glue workflows are a good fit for those pipelines that only use AWS Glue, but other options should be considered if you want to orchestrate additional services outside of the Glue family of services. If your use case only uses AWS Glue services, then the following section will be helpful to understand some best practices for using AWS Glue workflows.

Monitoring and error handling

Glue workflows includes a graphical UI that can be used to monitor job progress. With the UI, you can see whether any step in the pipeline has failed, and you can also resume the workflow from a specific step once you have resolved the issue that caused the error. While the Glue workflows feature does not include a retry mechanism as part of the workflow definition, you can specify the number of retries in the properties of individual Glue jobs.

CloudWatch Events provides a real-time stream of change events that can be generated by some AWS services, including AWS Glue. While Glue does not generate any events related to Glue workflows directly, events are generated from individual Glue jobs. For example, there is a *Glue Job State Change* event that is generated for Glue jobs that reflects one of the following states: SUCCEEDED, FAILED, TIMEOUT, or STOPPED.

Using Amazon EventBridge, you can automate actions to take place when a new event and status you are interested in is generated. For example, you can create an EventBridge rule that picks up Glue job FAILED events, and then triggers a Lambda function to run, which sends an email notification with details of the failure.

Triggering Glue workflows

When you create a Glue workflow, you can select the mechanism that will cause the workflow to run. There are three ways that a Glue workflow run can be started.

If set to **on-demand**, the workflow will only run when it's started manually from the console, or when it's started using the Glue API or CLI.

If set to **scheduled**, you can specify a frequency for running the job, such as hourly, daily, monthly, or for specific days of the week (such as Mondays to Fridays). Alternatively, you can set a custom schedule using a cron expression, which uses a string to set a frequency to run. For example, if you set the cron expression to */30 8-16 * * 2-6, the workflow will run *every 30 minutes between 8 A.M and 4:59 P.M., Mondays to Fridays.*

Glue workflows also support an **event-driven approach**, where the workflow is triggered in response to an EventBridge event. With this approach, you can configure an Amazon EventBridge rule to send events to a Glue workflows as the target, such as an S3 PutObject event for a specific S3 bucket and prefix.

When configuring your workflow, you can also specify triggering criteria, where you specify that you only want the workflow to run after a certain number of events are received, optionally specifying a maximum amount of time to wait for those events.

For example, if you have a business partner that sends many small .csv files throughout the day, you may not want to process each file individually, but rather process a batch of files. For this use case, you can configure the workflow to trigger once 100 events have been received and specify a time delay of 3,600 seconds (1 hour).

This time delay starts when the first unprocessed event is received. If the specified number of events is not received within the time delay you entered, the workflow will start anyway and process the events that have been received.

If you receive 100 events between 8 A.M. and 8:40 A.M., the first run of the workflow will be triggered at 8:40 A.M. If you receive only 75 events between 8:41 A.M. and 9:41 A.M., the workflow will run a second time at 9:41 A.M. anyway and process the 75 received events, since the time delay of 1 hour has been reached.

While Glue workflows can be an ideal service for pipelines that only use Glue services, if you are looking for a more comprehensive solution that can also orchestrate other AWS services and on-premises tools, then you should consider AWS Step Functions or Apache Airflow, which we will discuss next.

Apache Airflow as an open-source orchestration solution

Apache Airflow is open-sourced orchestration software, originally developed at Airbnb, that provides functionality for authoring, monitoring, and scheduling workflows. Some of the features available in Airflow include stateful scheduling, a rich user interface, core functionality for logging, monitoring, and alerting, and a code-based approach to authoring pipelines.

Within AWS, a managed version of Airflow is available as a service called **Amazon Managed workflows for Apache Airflow (MWAA)**. This service simplifies the process of getting started with Airflow, as well as the ongoing maintenance of Airflow infrastructure, since the underlying infrastructure is managed by AWS. Like other AWS managed services, AWS ensures the scalability, availability, and security of the Airflow software and infrastructure. Please refer to the overview of Amazon MWAA in *Chapter 3, The Data Engineer's Toolkit,* for more information on the architecture of this managed service.

When deploying the managed MWAA service in AWS, you can choose from multiple supported versions of Apache Airflow. At the time of writing, Airflow v1.10.12 and Airflow v2.6.3 are supported in the managed service.

Core concepts for creating Apache Airflow pipelines

Apache Airflow uses a code-based (Python) approach to authoring pipelines. This means that to work with Airflow, you do need some Python programming skills. However, having pipelines as code is a natural fit for saving pipeline resources in a source control system, and it also helps with creating automated tests for pipelines.

The following are some of the core concepts that are used to create Airflow pipelines.

Directed acyclic graphs (DAGs)

We introduced the concept of a **directed acyclic graph (DAG)** earlier in this chapter. In the context of Airflow, a data pipeline is created as a DAG (using Python to define the DAG), and the DAG defines the tasks in the pipeline, and the dependencies between the tasks.

In the Airflow user interface, you can also view a graphical representation of the DAG – the pipeline tasks and their dependencies, with tasks represented as nodes and arrows showing the dependencies between tasks.

Airflow Tasks

Airflow Tasks define the basic unit of work that a DAG performs. Each task is defined in a DAG with upstream and downstream dependencies, which defines the order in which the tasks should run. When a DAG runs, the tasks in the DAG move through various states, from None to Scheduled, to Queued, to Running, and then to Success or Failed.

Airflow Hooks

Airflow Hooks define how to connect to remote source and target systems, such as a database, or a system such as Zendesk. These Hooks contain the code that controls the connection to the remote system, and while Airflow includes several built-in hooks, it also lets you define custom hooks. With Amazon MWAA, default hooks are provided for many different AWS services (such as Amazon S3, AWS Glue, AWS Lambda, and more). There are also hooks available for various databases (such as Oracle, MySQL, and Postgres) and systems such as Slack.

Hooks contain the code to connect to remote systems, keeping that code separate from pipeline definitions.

Airflow Operators

Airflow Operators are predefined task templates that provide a pre-built interface for performing a specific task. Airflow includes several built-in core operators (such as BashOperator and PythonOperator, which execute a bash command or Python function).

There is also an extensive collection of additional operators that are released separately from Airflow Core. For example, the LambdaInvokeFunctionOperator, provided by AWS, can be used to invoke an AWS Lambda function.

Airflow Sensors

Airflow Sensors provides a special type of Airflow operator that is designed to wait until a specific action takes place. These Sensors regularly check whether the activity they are waiting on has been completed, and can be configured to time out after a certain period.

Using Airflow Sensors enables you to create event-driven pipelines. For example, you could use S3KeySensor, which waits for a specific key to be present on an S3 path and, once present, triggers a specific DAG to run.

Airflow Connections

Airflow Connections define the configuration information needed to connect to a remote system. For example, a connection may define the URL/hostname, port, username, and password that is used to make a connection to a database. Airflow Connections can be used by hooks, operators and sensors to define authentication credentials for connecting to external systems (such as a database, Amazon S3, or an AWS Lambda function).

Apache Airflow is a popular choice for creating and managing complex data pipelines, and has strong built-in support for AWS and third-party services. However, there is a fixed infrastructure cost for the service, as this is a managed service. Let's now look at AWS Step Functions, a serverless pipeline orchestration solution.

AWS Step Functions for a serverless orchestration solution

AWS Step Functions is a comprehensive serverless orchestration service that uses a low-code approach to develop data pipelines and serverless applications. Step Functions provides a powerful visual design tool that allows you to create pipelines with a simple drag and drop approach. Or, if you prefer, you can define your pipeline using **Amazon States Language** (**ASL**) directly using JSON.

AWS has built optimized, easy-to-use integrations between many different AWS services and Step Functions. For example, in the Step Functions interface you can easily add a step that runs a Lambda function, and select the name of the Lambda function to run from a drop-down list.

Step Functions also makes it easy to specify how to handle the failure of a state with custom retry policies, lets you specify catch blocks to catch specific errors, and takes custom actions based on the error. However, Step Functions does not currently support the ability to restart a state machine from a specific step.

For services where AWS has not built an optimized integration, you can still run the service by using the AWS SDK integration built into Step Functions. For example, there is no direct Step Functions integration for running Glue Crawlers, but you can add a state that calls the Glue StartCrawler API and specify the parameters that are needed by that API call.

In this next section, we review an example of a Step Functions state machine.

A sample Step Functions state machine

With Step Functions, you create a **state machine** that defines the various tasks that make up your data pipeline. Each task is considered a state within the state machine, and you can also have states that control the flow of your pipeline, such as a **choice state** that executes a branch of the pipeline, or a **wait state** to pause the pipeline for a certain period.

When you're executing a Step Functions state machine, you can pass in a payload that can be accessed by each state. Each state can also add additional data to the payload, such as a status code indicating whether a task succeeded or failed.

The following diagram shows a sample state machine in Step Functions:

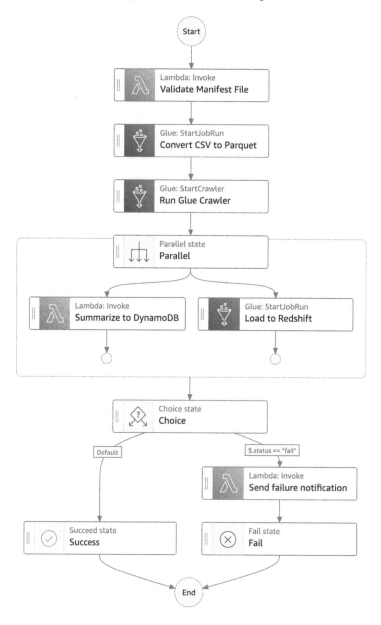

Figure 10.2: Sample Step Functions state machine

In this state machine definition, we can see the following states:

1. We start with a **Task state** that executes a Lambda function that validates a manifest file that has been received (ensuring that all the files listed in the manifest exist, for example).

2. We then have another **Task state**, this time to execute a Glue Job that will convert the files we received from CSV format into Parquet format.

3. Our next step is another **Task state**. This time, the task executes a Glue Crawler to update our data catalog with the new Parquet dataset we have generated.

4. We then enter a **Parallel state**, which is used to create parallel branches of execution in our state machine. In this case, we execute a Lambda function to summarize data from the Parquet file, and store the results in a DynamoDB table. At the same time, we trigger a Glue job to load the new data into our Redshift data warehouse.

5. We then enter a **Choice state**. The choice state specifies rules that get evaluated to determine what to do next. In this case, if our Lambda and Glue jobs succeeded, we end the state machine with a **Success state**. If either of them failed, we run a Lambda function to send a failure notification, and we end the state machine with a **Fail state**.

The visual editor that can be used in the console to create a state machine ultimately ends up generating an **Amazon States Language (ASL)** JSON file that contains the definition of the pipeline. You can store the JSON definition file for your data pipeline in a source control system, and then use the JSON file in a CI/CD pipeline to deploy your Step Functions state machine. You can edit your pipeline using the GUI interface in the console, or by directly editing the JSON file. Any edits you make directly to the JSON file can be imported into the console, and visualized. This enables you to use a combination of both the visual editor and direct edits of the JSON file in order to manage your pipeline.

In the hands-on exercises for this chapter, you will get the opportunity to build out a data pipeline using AWS Step Functions. However, before we do that, let's summarize your choices for data pipeline orchestration within AWS.

Deciding on which data pipeline orchestration tool to use

As we have discussed in this chapter, there are multiple options for creating and orchestrating data pipelines within AWS. And while we have looked at the four different options offered by AWS directly, there are many other options from AWS partners that could also be considered.

As covered previously, AWS Data Pipeline is now in maintenance mode and so it cannot be used for any new projects. If your project only uses AWS Glue jobs and the Glue Crawler, then AWS Glue workflows may be a good option. However, for larger and more complex pipelines, it is worth examining both Amazon MWAA and AWS Step Functions.

The following tables show a comparison of Step Functions and Amazon MWAA based on several different key attributes:

Criteria	AWS Step Functions	Amazon Managed Workflows for Apache Airflow (MWAA)
Short description	Serverless AWS native orchestration service	Managed AWS service for open source Apache Airflow
Graphical pipeline development	Yes	No
Graphical run visualization	Yes	Yes
Error and retry single step	Yes	Yes
Re-run from failed step	Custom workaround	Yes
Open source community support	No	Yes
Cost	Usage-based cost that depends on the complexity of the workflow	Constant base infrastructure cost, plus worker costs that can scale up and down
Scalability	Highly scalable, fully automatic	Highly scalable, managed by user or autoscaling groups, and can be configured
Infrastructure management	No infrastructure management or provisioning as everything handled by AWS	Requires making choices about infrastructure, but AWS manages the infrastructure and software
Language for pipeline development	JSON (or use of visual designer)	Python
Serverless/managed	Serverless	Managed
Integration	Seamlessly integrates with AWS services and manual integration with non-AWS services	Strong integration support for many AWS services, as well as extensive third-party services

Figure 10.3: Comparison of AWS Step Functions and Amazon MWAA

We do not have space to cover getting hands-on with both Amazon MWAA and AWS Step Functions, but since Step Functions is serverless and provides an easy-to-use visual designer, we will look at how to build an AWS Step Functions state machine in the next section.

Hands-on — orchestrating a data pipeline using AWS Step Functions

In this section, we will get hands-on with the AWS Step Functions service, which can be used to orchestrate data pipelines. The pipeline we're going to orchestrate is relatively simple, but Step Functions can also be used to orchestrate far more complex pipelines with many steps. To keep things simple, we will only use Lambda functions to process our data, but you could replace Lambda functions with Glue jobs in production pipelines that need to process large amounts of data.

For our Step Functions state machine, let's start by running a Lambda function that checks the extension of an incoming file to determine the type of file. Once determined, we'll pass that information on to the next state, which is a CHOICE state. If it is a file type we support, we'll call a Lambda function to process the file, but if it's not, we'll send out a notification, indicating that we cannot process the file.

If the Lambda function fails, we'll send a notification to report on the failure; otherwise, we will end the state machine with a SUCCESS status. Once we've created our state machine, we will configure EventBridge to automatically trigger the state machine when a file is uploaded to a specific Amazon S3 path.

Let's get building!

Creating new Lambda functions

Before we can create our state machine, we need to create the Lambda functions that we will orchestrate. We will create three separate Lambda functions in this section.

Using a Lambda function to determine the file extension

Our first Lambda function will check the extension of the file that's uploaded to our Amazon S3 bucket. Once we have the extension, we will return that in a JSON payload. Let's get started:

1. Log in to **AWS Management Console** and navigate to the **AWS Lambda** service at https://console.aws.amazon.com/lambda/home. Make sure that you are in the Region that you used for all the exercises in this book.

2. Click on **Create function**.

3. Select **Author from scratch**. Then, for **Function name**, enter `dataeng-check-file-ext`.

4. For **Runtime**, select **Python 3.10**. Leave the defaults for **Architecture** and **Permissions** as-is and click **Create function**.

5. In the **Code source** block, replace any existing code with the following code. This code receives an EventBridge event when a new S3 file is uploaded and uses the metadata included within the event to determine the extension of the file:

```python
import urllib.parse
import json
import os
print('Loading function')
def lambda_handler(event, context):
    print("Received event: " + json.dumps(event, indent=2))
    # Get the object from the event and show its content type
    bucket = event['detail']['bucket']['name']
    key = urllib.parse.unquote_plus(event['detail']['object']
['key'], encoding='utf-8')
    filename, file_extension = os.path.splitext(key)
    print(f'File extension is: {file_extension}')
    payload = {
        "file_extension": file_extension,
        "bucket": bucket,
        "key": key
        }
    return payload
```

6. Click the **Deploy** button above the code block section to save and deploy your Lambda function.

Now, we can create a second Lambda function that will process the file we received. However, for this exercise, the code in this Lambda function will randomly generate failures.

Using Lambda to randomly generate failures

For this Lambda function, we will use a random number generator to determine whether to cause an error in the Lambda function or allow it to succeed. We will do this by generating a random number that will be either 0, 1, or 2 and then dividing our random number by 10. When the random number is 0, we will get a "divide by zero" error from our function. We do this so that we can explore how Step Functions is able to handle failures in a function.

Let's get started:

1. Repeat *steps 1* to *5* of the previous section to create the first Lambda function, but this time, for **Function name**, enter `dataeng-random-failure-generator`.

2. In the **Code source** block, replace any existing code with the following code:

```python
from random import randint
def lambda_handler(event, context):
    print('Processing')
    #Our ETL code to process the file would go here.
    #However for this exercise we will instead randomly
    #cause the function to succeed or fail
    value = randint(0, 2)
    # We now divide 10 by our random number.
    # If the random number is 0, our function will fail
    newval = 10 / value
    print(f'New Value is: {newval}')
    return(newval)
```

3. Click the **Deploy** button above the code block section.

We now have two Lambda functions that we can orchestrate in our Step Functions state machine. But before we create the state machine, we have a few additional resources to create.

Creating an SNS topic and subscribing to an email address

If there is a failure in our state machine, we want to be able to send an email notification about the failure. We can use the SNS service to send an email. To do this, we need to create an SNS topic that we will send the notification to. Then, we can subscribe one or more email addresses to that topic. Let's get started:

1. Navigate to the **Amazon SNS** service at `https://console.aws.amazon.com/sns`. Ensure that you are in the Region that you have used for all the exercises in this book.

2. In the menu on the left-hand side, click on **Topics**, and then **Create topic**.

3. For **Type**, select **Standard**.

4. For **Name**, enter `dataeng-failure-notification`.

5. Leave all the other items as-is and click on **Create topic**.

6. In the **Subscriptions** section, click **Create subscription**.

7. For **Protocol**, select **Email**.

8. For **Endpoint**, enter your email address. Then, click on **Create subscription**.

9. Access your email and look for an email from *no-reply@sns.amazonaws.com* (this may take a minute or two to arrive). Click the **Confirm subscription** link in that email. You need to do this to receive future email notifications from Amazon SNS.

We now have an SNS topic with a confirmed email subscription that can receive SNS notifications. Next, we will create our new Step Functions state machine.

Creating a new Step Functions state machine

Now, we can orchestrate the various components that we have created so far (our two Lambda functions and the SNS topic we will use for sending emails) using AWS Step Functions:

1. Navigate to the **AWS Step Functions** service at `https://console.aws.amazon.com/states/home`. Ensure that you are in the Region that you have used for all the exercises in this book.

2. In the left-hand menu, click on **State machines**, and then click on **Create state machine**.

3. Select **Blank** for the template.

4. This will show a visual editor with a **Start** block and an **End** block in the **Design** tab. On the left-hand side, we have the components that we can use to design our state machine. Drag the **AWS Lambda Invoke** block into the visual designer, between the **Start** and **End** blocks.

5. On the right-hand side of the screen, set **State name** to `Check File Extension`.

6. Under **API Parameters**, use the drop-down list to set the **Function name** to be the name of the Lambda function that extracts the file extension (such as `dataeng-check-file-ext:$LATEST`).

7. On the right-hand side, click on the **Output** tab, and make sure the selector for **Filter output with OutputPath** is selected, and that the value is set to `$.Payload`. This option configures our **Check File Extension** state to have an output of whatever was returned by our Lambda function (in our case, we have configured our Lambda function to return a JSON payload that contains the S3 bucket, object, and file extension of the file to process).

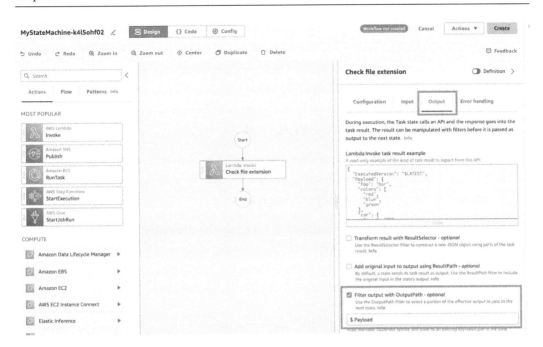

Figure 10.4: Building out a Step Functions state machine

8. On the left-hand side, click on the **Flow** tab. Then, drag the **Choice** state between the **Lambda Invoke** function and the **End** state. We use the **Choice** state to branch out our pipeline to run different processes, based on the output of a previous state. In this case, our pipeline will do different things depending on the extension of the file we are processing.

9. On the right-hand side, under **Configuration** for our new choice state, click the **Pencil Edit** icon next to **Rule #1** and then click **Add conditions**.

10. On the pop-up screen, under **Variable**, enter $.file_extension (our Lambda function returns some JSON, including a JSON path of file_extension that contains a string with the extension of the file we are processing). Set **Operator** to **matches string** and for **value**, enter .csv. Then, click **Save conditions**.

11. On the left-hand side, switch back to the **Actions** tab and drag the **AWS Lambda Invoke** state to the **left-hand side of the two choice boxes**.

12. For our new **Lambda Invoke** state, set **State name** to **Process CSV** (since our **Choice** function is going to invoke this Lambda for any file that has an extension of .csv, as we set in *step 10*).

13. Under **API Parameters**, use the dropdown to set **Function name** to our second Lambda function (`dataeng-random-failure-generator:$LATEST`). In a real pipeline, we would have a Lambda function (or Glue job) that would read the CSV file that was provided as input and process the file. In a real pipeline, we may have also added additional rules to our **Cshoice** state for other file types (such as XLS or JPG) and had different Lambda functions or Glue jobs invoked to handle each file type.

    However, in this exercise, we are only focusing on how to orchestrate pipelines, so our Lambda function code is designed to simply divide 10 by a random number, resulting in random failures when the random number is 0.

14. On the left-hand side, switch back to the **Flow** tab and drag the **Pass** state to the **Default** rule box leading from our **Choice** state. The default rule is used if the output of our Lambda function does not match any of the other rules. In this case, our only other rule is for handling files with a `.csv` extension, so if a file has any other extension besides `.csv`, the default rule will be used.

15. On the right-hand side, for the **Pass** state configuration, change **State name** to `Pass - Invalid File Ext`. Then, click on the **Output** tab and paste the following into the **Result** textbox:

    ```
    {
        "Error": "InvalidFileFormat"
    }
    ```

16. The **Pass** state is used in a state machine to modify the data that is passed to the next state. In this case, we want to pass a JSON-formatted error message about the file format being invalid to the next state in our pipeline.

17. Click the selector for **Add original input to output using ResultPath** so that that option is selected, and ensure that the dropdown is set to **Combine original input with result**. In the textbox, enter `$.Payload`.

18. If we receive an `InvalidFileFormat` error, we want to send a notification using the Amazon SNS service. To do so, on the left-hand side, under the **Actions** tab, drag the **Amazon SNS Publish** state to below our **Pass - Invalid File Ext** state.

19. On the right-hand side, on the **Configuration** tab for the **SNS Publish** state, under **API Parameters**, set **Topic** to our previously created SNS topic (`dataeng-failure-notification`). Your state machine should now look as follows:

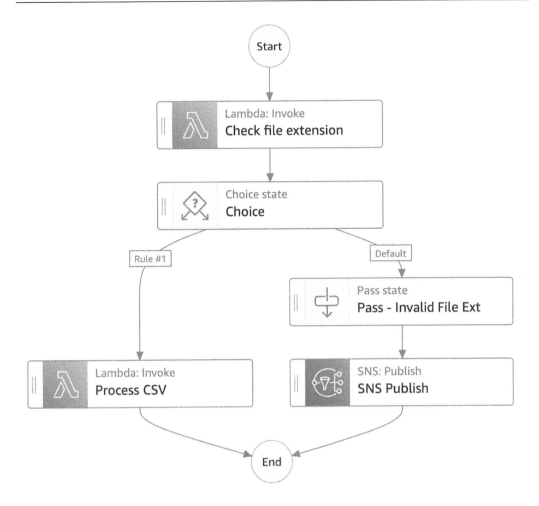

Figure 10.5: The current status of our Step Functions state machine

20. We can now add error handling for our **Process CSV** state. Click on the **Process CSV** state and, on the right-hand side, click on the **Error handling** tab. Under **Catch errors**, click on the **+ Add new catcher** button. For **Errors**, select **States.ALL**, for **Fallback state**, select our **SNS Publish** state, and for **result path**, enter $.Payload. This configuration means that if our Lambda function fails for any reason (States.ALL), we will add the error message to our JSON under a **Payload** key and pass this to our SNS notification state.

21. On the left-hand side, click on the **Flow** tab and drag **Success state** under the **Process CSV** state. Then, drag **Fail state** under the **SNS Publish** state. We do this as we want our Step Functions to show as having failed if, for any reason, something failed and we ended up sending a failure notification using SNS.

Your finalized state should look as follows:

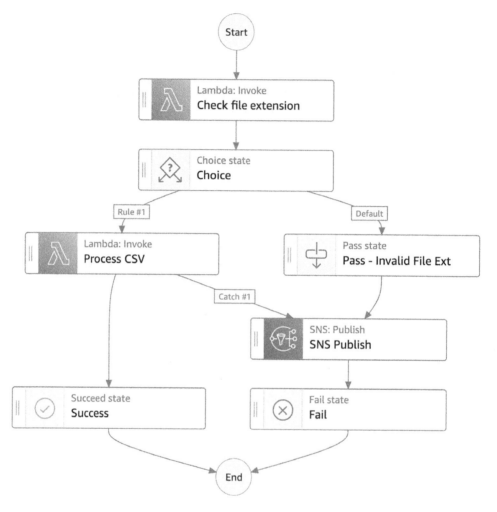

Figure 10.6: The final status of our Step Functions state machine

22. At the top of the screen, click on the **Config** tab.

23. For **State machine name**, enter `ProcessFilesStateMachine`. Leave all the other settings as-is and click **Create** in the top right.

24. On the next screen, click on **Confirm**.

With that, we have created our pipeline orchestration using Step Functions. Now, we want to create an event-driven workflow for triggering our Step Functions state machine. In the next section, we will create a new EventBridge rule that will trigger our state machine whenever a new file is uploaded to a specific S3 bucket.

The **Amazon EventBridge** service is a serverless event bus that can be used to build event-driven workflows. EventBridge can detect events from various AWS services (such as a new file being uploaded to S3) and can be configured to trigger a variety of different targets in response to an event. In our case, we will configure our Step Functions state machine as a target.

Configuring our S3 bucket to send events to EventBridge

In this section, we will configure Amazon EventBridge notifications for our data lake *Clean Zone* bucket. Once this is configured, whenever new files are created in our *Clean Zone* bucket, Event-Bridge will process the event and trigger our Step Functions state machine.

The following steps will take you through the process of configuring the *Clean Zone* bucket:

1. Navigate to the **Amazon S3 service** at https://s3.console.aws.amazon.com/s3/home. Ensure that you are in the Region that you have used for all the exercises in this book.

2. Review the list of buckets, and click on your *Clean Zone* bucket (for example, dataeng-clean-zone-gse23).

3. Click on the **Properties** tab for the bucket, scroll down to the **Event Notifications** section, and click on **Edit** next to the **Amazon EventBridge** sub-section.

4. Click the selector for **On**, in order to ensure that notifications are sent to Amazon Event-Bridge for all events in the bucket. Then, click **Save changes**.

With the above steps, we have configured our *Clean Zone* bucket to send an event containing details about any actions in our S3 bucket (such as new objects created, objects that get read, etc) to EventBridge. In the next section, we will create an EventBridge rule to filter the events, and to send events we are interested in (the creation of new files) to our AWS Step Functions state machine.

Creating an EventBridge rule for triggering our Step Functions state machine

Our final task, before testing our pipeline, is to configure the EventBridge rule that will trigger our Step Functions state machine. Let's get started:

1. Navigate to the **Amazon EventBridge** service at https://console.aws.amazon.com/events/home. Ensure that you are in the Region that you have used for all the exercises in this book.

2. From the left-hand panel, click on **Rules**, ensure that the default **Event bus** is selected, and then click on **Create rule**.

3. For the rule's name, enter dataeng-s3-trigger-rule.

4. For **Rule type**, select **Rule with an event pattern**. Then, click **Next**.

5. For **Event source**, ensure that **AWS events or EventBridge partner events** is selected.

6. Under **Sample event**, for type, ensure that **AWS events** is selected.

7. Under **Sample events**, search for S3, and under **Simple Storage Service (S3)**, select **Object created**. This will display an example **S3 Object Created** notification.

8. Under **Creation method**, select **Use pattern form**.

9. Under **Event pattern**, ensure that **AWS services** is selected for **Event source**, and for **AWS service**, search for and select **Simple Storage Service (S3)**. For **Event type**, select **Amazon S3 Event Notification**.

10. Change the selector from **Any event** to **Specific event(s)**. And then from the dropdown, select **Object created**.

11. Change the selector from **Any bucket** to **Specific bucket(s) by name**.

12. In the text box, enter the name of your data lake *Clean Zone* bucket (for example, `dataeng-clean-zone-gse23`). Then click **Next**.

13. Under **Select target(s)**, for **Target 1**, ensure that **AWS service** is selected, and for **Select a target**, search for and choose **Step Functions state machine**.

14. Under **State machine**, select the state machine we created previously (such as `ProcessFileStateMachine`) from the dropdown.

15. Optionally add tags, and then click **Next**.

16. Review the configuration details, and then click **Create rule**.

With the above steps we have created a new **EventBridge** rule that is triggered whenever a new object is created in the S3 bucket we specified. However, we may only want this rule to run when new objects (files) are created in a specific S3 bucket, rather than fsor every new object in the bucket as a whole. We can do this by editing the rule, as follows:

1. Under **Rules**, click on the name of the rule (such as `dataeng-s3-trigger-rule`).

2. Next to **Event pattern**, click on **Edit**.

3. Under the **Event pattern** JSON, click on **Edit pattern**.

4. Modify the JSON to be as follows, but be sure to keep the bucket name that you created (i.e., change `dataeng-clean-zone-initials` to whatever your *Clean Zone* bucket name is):

```
{
    "source": ["aws.s3"],
    "detail-type": ["Object Created"],
```

```
        "detail": {
          "bucket": {
            "name": ["dataeng-clean-zone-initials"]
          },
          "object": {
            "key": [{
              "prefix": "chapter10"
            }]
          }
        }
      }
```

5. Click on **Next**, and then click on **Next** twice more to continue through the screens and accepting the defaults. Then, click on **Update rule**.

Your completed EventBridge rule should look as follows:

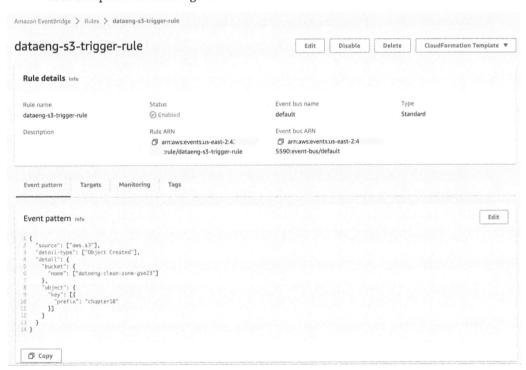

Figure 10.7: Our completed EventBridge rule

With that, we have put together an event-driven workflow to orchestrate a data pipeline using Amazon Step Functions. Our last task is to test our pipeline.

Testing our event-driven data orchestration pipeline

To test our pipeline, we need to upload a file to our *Clean Zone* S3 bucket, into a prefix named chapter10. Once the file has been uploaded, the rule we created in Amazon EventBridge will cause our Step Functions state machine to be triggered:

1. Navigate to the Amazon S3 service at https://s3.console.aws.amazon.com/s3.

2. From the list of buckets, click on the **dataeng-clean-zone-<initials>** bucket.

3. Click on **Create folder** to create a new folder. For **Folder name**, specify chapter10. Then, click **Create folder**.

4. Click on the new folder (chapter10) to move into that folder.

5. Click on **Upload**, and then **Add files**. Browse your computer for a file with a CSV extension (if you cannot find one, create a new, empty file and make sure to save it with an extension of .csv).

6. Leave the other settings as-is and click **Upload**.

7. Navigate to the **AWS Step Functions** service at https://console.aws.amazon.com/states.

8. Click on the state machine we created earlier (ProcessFilesStateMachine). From the list of **Executions**, see whether the state machine **Succeeded** or **Failed**. Click on the **Name** property of the execution for more details.

   Note that you may see two executions, with the first execution failing and the second one succeeding (depending on the random number generator result). The first execution is triggered by the creation of the new folder/prefix (chapter10), and this fails with an invalid file extension failure, as the prefix obviously does not have a .csv extension. The second execution (where you uploaded the file with a .CSV extension) will either succeed or fail, depending on what random number was generated by our second Lambda function.

9. Reupload the same .csv file multiple times and notice how some executions succeed and some fail. The random number generator has a 66% chance of generating the number 1 or 2 and a 33% chance of generating the number 0. When the number 0 is generated, the function will fail, so throughout many executions, approximately one-third should fail.

   The following diagram shows an example of what our state machine looks like after an execution where 0 was generated as a random number, causing the Lambda function to fail:

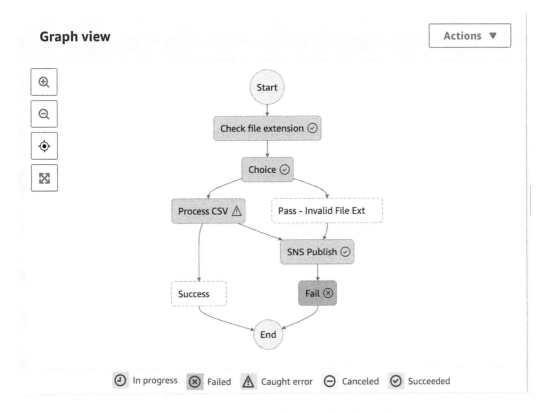

Figure 10.8: An example of a state machine run when the random number generator generated a 0, resulting in a failed state machine

10. After a failed execution, check the email address that you specified when you configured the Amazon SNS notification service. If you previously confirmed your SNS subscription, you should receive an email each time the state machine fails with details on the error (such as "Error":"ZeroDivisionError").

11. Now, upload another file to the same Amazon S3 bucket, but ensure that this file has an extension other than .csv (for example, .pdf). When you're viewing the execution details for your state machine, you should see that the choice state proceeded to the **Pass – Invalid File Ext** state and then also published an SNS notification to your email. The error listed in the email should be "Error":"InvalidFileFormat".

In the hands-on activity for this chapter, we created a serverless pipeline that we orchestrated using the AWS Step Functions service. Our pipeline was configured to be event-driven via the Amazon EventBridge service, which let us trigger the pipeline in response to a new file being uploaded to a specific prefix in our Amazon S3 *Clean Zone* bucket.

You could easily modify this state machine to handle different types of files, in different ways. For example, you could create a Lambda function that converts a CSV file to Parquet format, but that passes an image file (those with JPEG or PNG extensions) to a different Lambda function that creates a thumbnail of the image.

This was a fairly simple example of a data pipeline. However, AWS Step Functions can be used to orchestrate far more complex data pipelines, with advanced error handling and retries. For more information on advanced error handling, see the AWS blog titled *Handling Errors, Retries, and Adding Alerting to Step Functions State Machine Executions* (https://aws.amazon.com/blogs/developer/handling-errors-retries-and-adding-alerting-to-step-function-state-machine-executions/).

Summary

In this chapter, we looked at a critical part of a data engineer's job–designing and orchestrating data pipelines. First, we examined some of the core concepts around data pipelines, such as scheduled and event-based pipelines, and how to handle failures and retries.

We then looked at four different AWS services that can be used for creating and orchestrating data pipelines. This included AWS Data Pipeline (now in maintenance mode), AWS Glue workflows, Amazon MWAA, and AWS Step Functions.

Then, in the hands-on section of this chapter, we built an event-driven pipeline. We used two AWS Lambda functions for processing, and an Amazon SNS topic for sending out notifications about failures. Then, we put these pieces of our data pipeline together into a state machine orchestrated by AWS Step Functions. We also looked at how to handle errors.

So far, we have looked at how to design the high-level architecture for a data pipeline and examined services for ingesting, transforming, and consuming data. In this chapter, we put some of these concepts together in the form of an orchestrated data pipeline.

In the remaining chapters of this book, we will take a deeper dive into some of the services for data consumption, including services for ad hoc SQL queries, services for data visualization, as well as an overview of machine learning and Artificial Intelligence services for drawing additional insights from our data.

In the next chapter, we will do a deeper dive into the Amazon Athena service, which is used for ad hoc data exploration, using the power of SQL.

Learn more on Discord

To join the Discord community for this book – where you can share feedback, ask questions to the author, and learn about new releases – follow the QR code below:

`https://discord.gg/9s5mHNyECd`

Section 3

The Bigger Picture: Data Analytics, Data Visualization, and Machine Learning

In the third section of this book, we examine the bigger picture of data analytics within modern organizations. We learn about the tools that data consumers commonly use to work with data transformed by data engineers, and briefly look into how **Artificial Intelligence (AI)** and **Machine Learning (ML)** can draw rich insights out of data. We also get hands-on with tools for running ad hoc SQL queries on data in the data lake (Amazon Athena), for creating data visualizations (Amazon QuickSight), and for using AI to derive insights from data (Amazon Comprehend).

This section comprises the following chapters:

- *Chapter 11, Ad Hoc Queries with Amazon Athena*
- *Chapter 12, Visualizing Data with Amazon QuickSight*
- *Chapter 13, Enabling Artificial Intelligence and Machine Learning*

11
Ad Hoc Queries with Amazon Athena

In *Chapter 8, Identifying and Enabling Varied Data Consumers*, we explored a variety of data consumers. Now in this chapter, we will start examining the AWS services that some of these different data consumers may want to use, starting with those that need to use SQL to run ad hoc queries on data in the **data lake**.

SQL syntax is widely used for querying data in a variety of databases, and there is a large number of people that know SQL, making it a skill that is fairly easy to find. As a result, there is significant demand from various data consumers for the ability to query data that is in the data lake using SQL, without having to first move the data into a dedicated traditional database.

Amazon Athena is a serverless, fully managed service that lets you use SQL and Spark to directly query data in the data lake, as well as query various other database sources. It requires no set-up, and there are options to either pay for the service based only on the amount of data that is scanned by your SQL queries, or to reserve a specific amount of capacity and pay for that capacity reservation (referred to as provisioned capacity).

In this chapter we will examine Athena features and functionality, such as how Athena can be used to query data directly in the data lake, how you can use Athena to query data from other data sources with Query Federation, and how Athena provides functionality for governance and cost management, with workgroups. We also provide some recommended best practices to help you optimize your Athena SQL queries for both cost and performance.

This chapter covers the following topics:

- An introduction to Amazon Athena
- Tips and tricks to optimize Amazon Athena SQL queries
- Exploring advanced Athena functionality
- Managing groups of users with Amazon Athena workgroups
- Hands-on – creating an Amazon Athena workgroup and configuring Athena settings
- Hands-on – switching workgroups and running queries

Technical requirements

In the hands-on sections of this chapter, you will perform administrative tasks related to Amazon Athena (such as creating a new Athena workgroup) and run Athena queries. As mentioned at the start of this book, we strongly recommend that, for the exercises in this book, you use a sandbox account where you have full administrative permissions.

For this chapter, at a minimum, you will need permissions to manage Athena workgroups, permissions to run Athena queries, access to the **AWS Glue Data Catalog** for databases and tables to be queried, and read access to the relevant underlying S3 storage.

A user that has the **AmazonAthenaFullAccess** and **AmazonS3ReadOnlyAccess** policies attached should have sufficient permissions for the exercises in this chapter. However, note that a user with these roles will have access to all S3 objects in the account, all Glue resources, all Athena permissions, as well as various other permissions, so this should only be granted to users in a sandbox account. Such broad privileges should be avoided for users in production accounts.

You can find the code files of this chapter in the GitHub repository using the following link: https://github.com/PacktPublishing/Data-Engineering-with-AWS-2nd-edition/tree/main/Chapter11.

An introduction to Amazon Athena

Amazon Athena was originally launched as a service that simply provided a way to run **SQL** queries against data in an S3-based data lake. However, over the years, AWS had added a lot of additional functionality to Athena, enabling features like running queries against other databases (not just S3-based data), and supporting the use of Spark based Notebooks for querying data (in addition to SQL queries).

Structured Query Language (SQL) was invented at **IBM** in the 1970s but has remained an extremely popular language for querying data throughout the decades. Every day, millions of people across the world use SQL directly to explore data in a variety of databases, and many more use applications (whether business applications, mobile applications, or others) that, under the covers, use SQL to query a database.

Facebook, the social media network, has very large datasets and complex data analysis requirements and found that existing tools in the Hadoop ecosystem were not able to meet their needs. As a result, Facebook created an internal solution for being able to run SQL queries on their very large datasets, using standard SQL semantics, and in 2013, Facebook released this as an open-source solution called **Presto**.

In late 2016, AWS announced the launch of Amazon Athena, a new service that would enable customers to directly query structured and semi-structured data that exists in Amazon S3. In the launch announcement, Amazon indicated that Athena was a managed version of Presto, with standard SQL support. This provided the power of the **Presto SQL analytics engine** as a serverless service to AWS customers.

SQL is broadly broken into two parts:

- **Data Definition Language (DDL)**, which is used to create and modify database objects.
- **Data Manipulation Language (DML)**, which is used to query and manipulate data.

In 2021, AWS upgraded the Amazon Athena engine to v2, which included support for features such as federated queries, new geospatial functions, and schema evolution support for Parquet files. This was followed by the launch of Athena engine v3 in October 2022, which included reliability improvements, performance improvements, and updates incorporated from the Trino open-source project (https://trino.io/). While both engine versions are available for use at the time of writing, Athena engine v2 will be deprecated at some point, and therefore if starting a new project it is always recommended to configure the project to use the latest Athena engine version.

Amazon Athena requires a Hive-compatible data catalog that provides the metadata for the data being queried. The catalog provides a logical view (databases that contain tables, which consist of rows, along with columns of a specific data type), and this maps to physical files stored in Amazon S3. Athena originally had its own data catalog, but today, it requires the use of the AWS Glue Data Catalog as its Hive compatible data store.

Amazon Athena makes it easy to quickly start querying data in an Amazon S3-based data lake, but there are some important things to keep in mind to optimize SQL queries with Amazon Athena, as we will discuss in the next section.

Tips and tricks to optimize Amazon Athena queries

When **raw data** is ingested into the data lake, we can immediately create a table for that data in the AWS Glue Data Catalog (either using a **Glue crawler** or by running DDL statements with Athena to define the table). Once the table has been created, we can start exploring the table by using Amazon Athena to run SQL queries against the data.

However, raw data is often ingested in plaintext formats such as CSV or JSON. And while we can query the data in this format for ad hoc data exploration, if we need to run complex queries against large datasets, these raw formats are not efficient to query. There are also ways that we can optimize the SQL queries that we write to make the best use of the underlying Athena query engine, which we will review in this chapter.

By default, Amazon Athena's cost is based on the amount of compressed data that is scanned to resolve your SQL query, so anything that can be done to reduce the amount of data scanned improves query performance and reduces query cost. And if using Athena Provisioned Capacity, while you don't pay based on the amount of data scanned, optimized file formats and queries use provisioned resources more efficiently, and queries are also more performant.

In this section, we will review several ways that we can optimize our analytics for increased performance and better cost efficiency.

Common file format and layout optimizations

The most impactful and easiest transformations that a data engineer can apply to raw files are those that transform the raw files into an optimized file format, and that structure the layout of files in an optimized way.

Transforming raw source files to optimized file formats

As we discussed in *Chapter 7, Transforming Data to Optimize for Analytics*, file formats such as **Apache Parquet** are designed for analytics and perform much better than raw data formats such as CSV or JSON. So, transforming your raw source files into a format such as Parquet is one of the most important things a data engineer can do to improve the performance of Athena queries. Review the *Optimizing the file format* section of *Chapter 7, Transforming Data to Optimize for Analytics*, for a more comprehensive look at the benefits of Apache Parquet files.

In *Chapter 7* we also reviewed how the AWS Glue service can be used to transform your files into optimized formats. However, Amazon Athena can also transform files using a concept called **Create Table As Select** (**CTAS**). With this approach, you run a CTAS statement using Athena, and this instructs Athena to create a new table based on a SQL select statement against a different table.

In the following example, customers_csv is the table that was created on the data we imported from a database to our data lake, and the data is in CSV format. If we want to create a Parquet version of this table so that we can query it efficiently, we could run the following SQL statement using Athena:

```
CREATE TABLE customers_parquet
WITH (
      format = 'Parquet',
      parquet_compression = 'SNAPPY')
AS SELECT *
FROM customers_csv;
```

The preceding statement will create a new table called customers_parquet. The underlying files for this table will be in Parquet format and compressed using the Snappy compression algorithm. The contents of the new table will be the same as the customers_csv table since our query specified SELECT *, meaning select all data.

If you are bringing in specific datasets regularly (such as every night), then in most scenarios, it would make sense to configure and schedule an AWS Glue job to perform the conversion to Parquet format. But if you're doing ad hoc exploratory work on various datasets, or a one-time data load from a system, then you may want to consider using Amazon Athena to perform the transformation. Note that there are some limitations in using Amazon Athena to perform these types of transforms, so refer to the *Considerations and Limitations for CTAS Queries* (https://docs. aws.amazon.com/athena/latest/ug/considerations-ctas.html) page in the Amazon Athena documentation for more details.

Partitioning the dataset

This is also a concept that we covered in more detail in *Chapter 7, Transforming Data to Optimize for Analytics*, but we will discuss it again now briefly as, after using an optimized file format such as Parquet, this is the next most impactful thing you can do to increase the performance of your analytic queries. Review the *Optimizing with Data Partitioning* section of *Chapter 7, Transforming Data to Optimize for Analytics*, for more details on partitioning.

A common data partitioning strategy is to partition files by columns related to date. For example, in our sales table, we could have a YEAR column, a MONTH column, and a DAY column that reflect the year, month, and day of a specific sales transaction, respectively. When the data is written to S3, all sales data related to a specific day will be written out to the same S3 prefix path.

Our partitioned dataset may look as follows:

```
/datalake/transform_zone/sales/YEAR=2023/MONTH=9/DAY=29/sales1.parquet
/datalake/transform_zone/sales/YEAR=2023/MONTH=9/DAY=30/sales1.parquet
/datalake/transform_zone/sales/YEAR=2023/MONTH=10/DAY=1/sales1.parquet
/datalake/transform_zone/sales/YEAR=2023/MONTH=10/DAY=2/sales1.parquet
```

NOTE

The preceding partition structure is a simple example because generally, with large datasets, you would expect to have multiple Parquet files in each partition, and not just a single file.

Partitioning provides a significant performance benefit when you filter the results of your query based on one or more partitioned columns using the WHERE clause. For example, if a data analyst needs to query the total sales for the last day of September 2023, they could run the following query:

```
select sum(SALE_AMOUNT) from SALES where YEAR = '2023' and MONTH = '9' and
DAY = '30'
```

Based on our partitioning strategy, the preceding query would only need to read the file (or files) in the single S3 prefix of /datalake/transform_zone/sales/YEAR=2023/MONTH=9/DAY=30.

Even if we want to query the data for a full month or year, we still significantly reduce the number of files that need to be scanned, compared to having to scan all the files for all the years if we did not partition our data.

As covered in *Chapter 7, Transforming Data to Optimize for Analytics*, you can specify one or more columns to partition by when writing out data using **Apache Spark**. Alternatively, you can use Amazon Athena CTAS statements to create a partitioned dataset. However, note that a single CTAS statement in Athena can only create a maximum of 100 partitions.

Other file-based optimizations

Using an optimized file format (such as Apache Parquet) and partitioning your data are generally the two strategies that will have the biggest positive impact on analytic performance. However, several other strategies can fine-tune performance, which we will cover here briefly.

Optimizing file size: It is important to avoid having a large number of small files if you want to optimize your analytic queries. For each file in S3, the analytic engine (in this case, Amazon Athena) needs to do the following:

- Open the file.
- Read the Parquet metadata to determine whether the query needs to scan the contents of the file.
- Scan the contents of the file if the file contains data needed for the query.
- Close the file.

There can be significant **Input/Output (I/O)** overhead in listing out very large numbers of files and then processing each file. **Airbnb** has an interesting blog post on *Medium* (https://medium.com/airbnb-engineering/on-spark-hive-and-small-files-an-in-depth-look-at-spark-partitioning-strategies-a9a364f908) that explains an issue they had where one of their data pipeline jobs ended up creating millions of files, and how this caused significant outages for them.

While there are no hard rules regarding file size, it is generally recommended that to optimize for analytics you should aim for file sizes of at least 128 MB for objects in your S3-based data lake. When using file formats such as Parquet that are splitable (meaning the query engine can split the file and process different parts of the file in parallel), the maximum file size is not as much of an issue. But if processing files that are not splitable, such as Gzipped CSV files, it is important to have multiple files that the query engine can read in parallel, rather than a single large file.

Bucketing: Bucketing is a concept that is related to partitioning. However, with bucketing, you group rows of data together in a specified number of buckets, based on the hash value of a column (or columns) that you specify. Athena engine v2 is not compatible with the bucketing implementation that's used in Spark, but Athena engine v3 supports both Hive bucketing and the Spark bucketing algorithm.

For example, if you have data on all airline flights that you often query based on the airport code of where the flight departed from, you could bucket your data on the origin airport code. That way, all records for flights that originated from a specific airport may be in a single file in each partition, and Athena would only need to scan that file when a query was based on the origin airport and limited to a single partition.

Refer to the Amazon Athena documentation on *Partitioning and bucketing in Athena* for more information (`https://docs.aws.amazon.com/athena/latest/ug/ctas-partitioning-and-bucketing.html`).

Partition Projection: In scenarios where you have a very large number of partitions, there can be a significant overhead for Athena to read all the information about partitions from the Glue catalog. To improve performance, you can configure partition projection, where you provide a configuration pattern to reflect your partitions. Athena can then use this configuration information to determine possible partition values, without needing to read the partition information from the catalog.

For example, if you have a column called YEARMONTH that you partition on, and you have data going back to 2013, you could configure the partition projection range as 201301,NOW and the partition projection format as yyyyMM. Athena would then be able to determine all possible valid partitions for that period without needing to read the partition information from the Glue catalog. For more information on partition projection, see the AWS documentation titled *Partition Projection with Amazon Athena* (`https://docs.aws.amazon.com/athena/latest/ug/partition-projection.html`).

In addition to the file and layout optimizations, there are also ways to write SQL queries so that the queries are optimized for the Athena analytic engine. We will cover some of these optimizations in the next section.

Writing optimized SQL queries

The way that SQL queries are written can also have a significant impact on the performance of the query.

In this section, we will review some best practices that will help provide optimal performance of queries. It's recommended that, as a data engineer, you share these best practices with data analysts and others using Athena to run queries.

That said, there are other ways, beyond the three best practices we will outline here, to go deep into query optimization. For example, you (or your end user data analysts) can use the EXPLAIN statement as part of an Athena query to view the logical execution plan of a specific SQL statement. You can then make modifications to your SQL statement and review the EXPLAIN query plan to understand how that changes the underlying execution plan. For more information, see the AWS Athena documentation titled *Using EXPLAIN and EXPLAIN ANALYSE in Athena*: `https://docs.aws.amazon.com/athena/latest/ug/athena-explain-statement.html`.

Let's look now at three important ways that you can optimize your queries.

Selecting only the specific columns that you need

When exploring data, it is common to run queries that select all columns by specifying the start of the query as select *. However, remember that the Parquet format that we recommend for analytics is a columnar-based file format, meaning that data stored on disk is grouped by columns rather than rows. When you specify a specific column to query, the analytic engine (such as Athena) can read the data for that column only.

If you have a table with a lot of columns (and it is not uncommon for tables to have over a hundred columns), specifying just the columns that are important to your query can significantly increase the performance of your query.

Take a scenario where you have a table with 150 columns, but your specific query only needs data from 15 of the columns. If using a columnar data format such as Parquet, then Athena would only need to scan approximately 10% of the dataset, compared to a query that uses a select * to query all columns.

Using approximate aggregate functions

The Presto and Trino database engines (and therefore Athena) supports a wide variety of functions and operators that can be used in queries. These include functions that can be used in calculations against large datasets in a data lake. They are used for tasks such as the following:

- Working out the sum of all sales for this month compared to last month
- Calculating the average number of orders per store
- Determining the total number of unique users that accessed our e-commerce store yesterday
- Other advanced statistical calculations

For some calculations, you may need to get a fully accurate calculation, such as when determining sales figures for formal financial reporting. At other times, you may just need an approximate calculation, such as for getting an estimate on how many unique visitors came to our website yesterday.

For those scenarios, where you can tolerate some deviation in the result, Presto and Trino provide approximate aggregate functions, and these offer significant performance improvements compared to the equivalent fully accurate version of the function.

For example, if we needed to calculate the approximate number of unique users that browsed our e-commerce store in the past 7 days, and we could tolerate a standard deviation of 2.3% in the result, we could use the `approx._distinct` function, as follows:

```
SELECT
    approx_distinct(userid)
FROM
    estore_log
WHERE
    visit_time > to_iso8601(current_timestamp - interval '7' day)
```

For more information on supported functions in Athena, including approximate functions, refer to the Athena documentation titled *Functions in Amazon Athena*: `https://docs.aws.amazon.com/athena/latest/ug/functions.html`.

Athena also includes some options that you can enable to further improve query performance, such as the ability to reuse query results, as we discuss next.

Reusing Athena query results

One of the options introduced with Athena engine v3, is the ability to specify that you want to reuse query results from previous queries, for a specific time period. When running a query you can opt-in to reusing previous query results, and can specify a maximum age for reusing results (with a default of 60 minutes, but the ability to reuse results for up to 7 days).

When you enable this option for a query, Athena will look for a previous execution of the exact same query within the specified time period, and within the current workgroup. If Athena finds the results of the same query, it does not rerun the query, but rather points to the previous result location or fetches the data from it. This can lead to significant performance improvements and reduced cost.

Note that Athena does not check for changes in the source data, so it is possible that using this feature will result in stale data being returned. Query reuse is based purely on finding an exact match for the query being run, within the same workgroup, and confirming that the result was generated within the time period specified (or 60 minutes if no maximum age is specified).

We don't have space to cover all query optimization techniques in this chapter. However, the AWS documentation provides a deeper dive into these optimizations, so for more information, refer to the AWS Athena documentation titled *Performance Tuning in Athena* at `https://docs.aws.amazon.com/athena/latest/ug/performance-tuning.html`.

Now that you have a good idea of the core functionality provided in Athena, and understand how to optimize your queries, let's move on to how to get even more out of Athena. In the next section we look at advanced functionality, such as how Athena can be used to query other data sources beyond the data files stored in Amazon S3, and how you can also query your data using Spark code through Athena.

Exploring advanced Athena functionality

As we've discussed several times in this book, Athena lets you query data that has been loaded into the data lake using standard SQL semantics. But since the launch of Athena, AWS has added additional functionality to enhance Athena to make it an even more powerful query engine.

One of those major enhancements, which became available in 2021 with Athena query engine v2, was the ability to run federated queries, which we will look at next.

Querying external data sources using Athena Federated Query

Query federation, also sometimes referred to as data virtualization, is the process of querying multiple external data sources, in different database engines or other systems, through a single SQL query statement.

Data lakes are designed to collect data from multiple systems in an organization and bring it into centralized storage, where the data can be combined in ways that unlock value for the business. However, it is not practical to bring every single dataset that an organization has created into the centralized storage of the data lake. For some datasets, the organization either does not need to keep all historical data for a dataset, or the data is currently in a system that already stores historical data. In these scenarios, it may make more sense to query the source dataset directly and combine data from the source with data in the data lake on the fly.

If a dataset needs to be queried by multiple teams, is queried often, and queries need to return very large amounts of data, then it is generally best to load that dataset directly into the data lake. Also, if you need to repeatedly query a system that is already under a relatively heavy load, you can reduce that load by loading data from the system to the data lake in off-peak hours, rather than running federated queries during peak times.

But if you're performing ad hoc queries, or if the data only needs to be queried by a small number of teams with a relatively low frequency of querying, then using the *Athena Federated Query* functionality to access the data makes sense. Several people have run performance testing with Athena Federated Query and have proven the ability to query many tens of thousands of records per second.

Let's look at an example of how this functionality could be used. Athena Federated Query could enable a data analyst to run a single SQL query that combines data from the following datasets:

- Master customer data in Amazon S3
- Current order information in Amazon Aurora
- Shipment tracking data in Amazon DynamoDB
- Product catalog data in Amazon Redshift

An illustration of how this query would work with Athena federation, which uses AWS Lambda based connectors, is shown in the following figure:

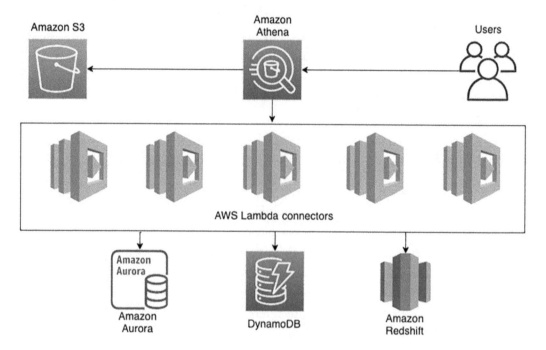

Figure 11.1: Amazon Athena query federation

Another use case would be if you do a nightly load of data from an external system into your data lake, but a few of your queries need to be able to reference some real-time data. For example, if supplier order information was loaded into the data lake each night, but you had a query that needed to calculate the total number of orders for a specific supplier for the year up to the present time, your query could do the following:

- Read supplier order information from the S3 data lake for all orders from the beginning of the year up until yesterday.

- Read any orders from today from your SAP HANA system.

There are many other potential use cases where data processing can be simplified by having the ability to use SQL to read and manipulate data from multiple systems. Rather than having to read independently from multiple systems, and then programmatically process the data, data processing is simplified by processing the data with a single SQL query.

In April 2023, Athena added support for creating views on external data sources. **Views** are a common SQL construct that are used to mask complex queries on data, by effectively creating a virtual table, that when queried, constructs the results by running the underlying query specified in the view definition.

For example, you can create a view based on a select statement that queries only certain columns in an underlying table. This effectively creates a virtual table, and when a user queries this view (or virtual table) with a select * statement, Athena runs the underlying query that only selected specific columns, and only returns those columns. This can be used for use cases such as limiting access to sensitive data (a table may have a column that contains a phone number, but you create the view to select all other columns except the phone number, and when the view is queried the results will not include the phone number column). You could also create a view that queries a number of systems using federated queries, but enables users to query the view without needing to know anything about the external databases.

Athena includes a number of pre-built connectors for querying various data sources, but also enables you to create custom connectors, as we discuss next.

Pre-built connectors and custom connectors

Athena Federated Query uses code running in **AWS Lambda** to connect to and query data, as well as metadata, from external systems. When a query runs that uses a connected data source, Athena invokes the relevant Lambda function/s to read metadata, identifies parts of the tables that need to be read, and launches multiple Lambda functions to read the data in parallel.

AWS has connectors that enable federated queries against over 30 popular data sources, including the following:

- A **JDBC connector** for connecting to sources such as MySQL, Postgres, and Redshift.
- A **DynamoDB connector** for reading from the Amazon-managed NoSQL database.
- A **Redis connector** for reading data from Redis instances.
- A **CloudWatch logs and CloudWatch metrics connector**, enabling you to query your application log files and metrics using SQL.

- An **AWS CMDB connector** that integrates with several AWS services to enable SQL queries against your AWS resources. Integrated services include EC2, RDS, EMR, and S3.
- A **Google BigQuery** connector that enables queries across clouds for data in Google BigQuery tables.
- An **Apache Kafka** connector that enables querying real-time data in Apache Kafka (and Amazon MSK) topics. With this connector you can join data in a Kafka topic with data in other topics, or with data in your Amazon S3 based data lake.

The full list of connectors can be found in the *Using Amazon Athena Federated Query* section of the documentation at `https://docs.aws.amazon.com/athena/latest/ug/connect-to-a-data-source.html`.

In addition to the connectors made available by AWS, anyone can create custom connectors to connect to external systems. If you can make a network connection from AWS Lambda to the target system, whether on-premises or in the cloud, you could potentially create an Athena Federated Query connector for that system.

Third-party companies are also able to create connectors for Athena Federated Query. For example, a company called **Trianz** has created connectors for **GreenPlum** and **GoogleSheets**.

To learn more about building custom connectors, see the Athena documentation titled *Developing a data source connector using the Athena Query Federation SDK*, at `https://docs.aws.amazon.com/athena/latest/ug/connect-data-source-federation-sdk.html`.

Another relatively new feature in Athena (announced at re:Invent 2022) is the ability to use Athena to run Spark based processing of data via Notebooks. We look into this feature in the next section.

Using Apache Spark in Amazon Athena

In November 2022, Amazon announced new functionality for Athena that enables users to interactively explore their data lake data using the power of **Apache Spark**. This functionality includes a simplified notebook experience (compatible with Jupyter notebooks) where users can write and run code in blocks, and immediately see the results of the code execution.

To use this functionality, you need to create a new Athena workgroup (which we cover in more detail later in this chapter) and configure the workgroup engine to be Spark. You can then create a new Notebook associated with the Spark workgroup, and specify options such as the idle timeout, the driver node size, executor size, as well as the maximum concurrent executors. You can then immediately start using Spark code to interactively query your data lake data.

Using Athena notebooks you can also plot your data, creating visualizations based on your data. For example, you can load data into a Spark data frame based on a SQL query, covert the data frame into a Python Pandas data frame, and then use various libraries to plot the data. For an example walk-through of how to do this, refer to the AWS blog *Explore your data lake using Amazon Athena for Apache Spark* at `https://aws.amazon.com/blogs/big-data/explore-your-data-lake-using-amazon-athena-for-apache-spark/`.

Amazon Athena for Apache Spark is useful for data engineers that are familiar with coding with Spark and Python, and want to interactively explore their data using code. Spark compute resources are deployed rapidly and Athena auto-scales compute resources based on the requirements of the queries that are run (up to the maximum concurrency that you specify when creating the Notebook).

Amazon Athena also includes support for a number of open table formats, which we look at in the next section.

Working with open table formats in Amazon Athena

Amazon Athena includes support for working with a number of popular **open table formats**, including **Apache Iceberg, Apache Hudi,** and the **Linux Foundation Delta Lake** table format. These table formats, which we cover in more detail in *Chapter 14, Building Transactional Data Lakes*, enable data lakes to provide data integrity. **ACID transactions** provided by these formats (referring to the properties of **atomicity, consistency, isolation** and **durability**), enable data lakes to perform updates to data and provide a consistent view of data, in a way that is similar to what was previously only available in databases and data warehouses.

However, the Athena support for each table format differs. At the time of writing, Apache Iceberg has the most support, enabling you to both query Iceberg data and perform updates and deletes to data in Iceberg. For Delta Lake format tables, Athena supports read-only queries (statements such as UPDATE, INSERT and DELETE are not currently supported). For the Hudi table format, Athena can read those tables, but does not support writing to those tables.

For the latest support information on these open table formats, see the Athena documentation titled *Using Athena ACID transactions* at `https://docs.aws.amazon.com/athena/latest/ug/acid-transactions.html`.

Let's now look at how you can provision dedicated Athena capacity, instead of using the default on-demand capacity.

Provisioning capacity for queries

By default, Athena usage is priced by the amount of data that a query scans. However, Athena also includes the option to provision a specific amount of capacity to use for queries. When using provisioned capacity, you are charged based on the compute resources you provision, and there is not a per query charge based on data scanned.

When you provision capacity for Athena, you get dedicated processing capacity for your queries. To use this functionality, you specify the number of **Data Processing Units (DPUs)** that you need for your queries, and you assign one or more Workgroups to use that capacity (we discuss Workgroups in more detail in the next section of this chapter).

DPUs are an indication of the compute resources assigned for your provisioned capacity reservation. One DPU provides for 4 CPUs, and 16 GB of memory. The more DPUs assigned, the more concurrent queries you can run. Amazon provides the following guidance for the number of DPUs needed for a specific number of concurrent queries:

- For 10 concurrent queries, Amazon recommends 40 DPUs
- For 20 concurrent queries, Amazon recommends 96 DPUs
- For 30 or more concurrent queries, Amazon recommends 240 DPUs

The above provides general guidance on number of DPUs needed, but the actual number needed is based on your requirements and analysis patterns. If you do not have enough capacity to run all your queries at peak times, Athena will queue you query and run it when capacity becomes available.

At the time of writing, Athena provisioned capacity is billed at $0.30 per DPU hour billed. While billing is per minute, there is a minimum billing period of 8 hours for any capacity that you provision. There is also a requirement to provision a minimum of 24 DPUs in a reservation, and you can increase DPU capacity in 4 DPU increments at any time. Capacity can be held for as long as needed, and can also be cancelled at any time (however you are always billed for a minimum of 8 hours for each capacity reservation).

If you have a few data analysts or data engineers that use Athena on an ad hoc basis to better understand the data in your data lake, then using Athena on-demand makes sense. However, if you have a large number of data consumers that are doing constant queries of your data, or you use Athena for performing data transformation tasks on a regular basis, then Athena provisioned capacity may help you to reduce costs.

When you create an Athena Provisioned Capacity reservation, you need to assign one or more workgroups to that reservation. In the next section we do a deeper dive into Athena workgroups.

Managing groups of users with Amazon Athena workgroups

Athena workgroups are a powerful mechanism for separating different groups and types of user queries (such as SQL based queries, and Spark Notebook queries), for applying cost controls, assigning provisioned capacity, and for implementing strong governance on Athena usage.

All queries within Athena are run in a specific workgroup, and you can apply a number of configuration settings to each workgroup to control costs and governance for the users in that workgroup. The following list shows the configuration items that can be controlled at the workgroup level:

- The analytic engine that users in this workgroup use (either Athena SQL or Apache Spark)
- Whether the Athena engine version used for this workgroup is selected and upgraded automatically, or whether you manually specify the engine version to use
- The S3 location where the results of queries are written to, and whether these files are encrypted or not
- Various general settings, such as the option to publish query metrics to Amazon CloudWatch, and an option to prevent users overriding the workgroup settings
- Limits for each query (the amount of data a single query is allowed to scan)
- Query limits for SQL engine workgroups (how much data can the workgroup as a whole scan within a specified time period)

These options enable administrators to manage governance concerns (where results are written to, and encryption settings), as well as cost controls (how much data can be scanned for SQL queries, at either the user or workgroup level).

Athena workgroups enable administrators to separate groups of users and automated ETL processes into separate workgroups, each with their own settings. By using IAM policy settings, users (or processes) can be restricted to only be able to run their queries within specified workgroups.

Let's start by looking at the cost controls enabled by workgroups.

Managing Athena costs with Athena workgroups

By default, Athena SQL query costs are based on the amount of data that is scanned by a query, and in the first section of this chapter, we looked at some of the ways that data can be optimized so that queries would scan less data, and therefore reduce costs.

However, some of those optimizations are based on writing efficient SQL queries, and it's not unusual for organizations to be concerned that users are going to accidentally run SQL queries that are not optimized and end up scanning massive amounts of data. As such, organizations want a way to control the amount of data that's scanned by different users or teams when they are not using provisioned capacity.

By using Athena workgroups, an administrator can either assign the workgroup to use provisioned capacity (in which case there is no per query cost), or they can place cost controls on the workgroup.

Per query data usage control

You can configure the maximum amount of data that can be scanned by a single SQL query using per query data usage controls. If a user runs a query and Athena ends up trying to scan more data than allowed by the control, the query is cancelled. However, note that the AWS account is still billed for the amount of data that was scanned up until the query was cancelled.

As a practical example, you may have a group of users that are relatively inexperienced with SQL and want to have a sandbox environment where they can run ad hoc queries safely. In this scenario, you could create an Athena workgroup called *sandbox* and configure these users to have access to the sandbox workgroup. You could configure the workgroup to have a per-query limit of 100 GB, for example, which would ensure that no individual query would cost more than $0.50.

Per query data limits are useful for scenarios where you want to have hard control over the amount of data that's scanned by each query. However, this control is restrictive in that it automatically cancels any query that exceeds the specified amount of data that's scanned. An alternative option for controlling costs is to configure workgroup data usage controls.

Athena workgroup data usage controls

With workgroup data usage controls, you have the flexibility to configure the maximum amount of data that's scanned by the entire workgroup, within a specified time period. When the limit for the workgroup is reached, queries are not automatically cancelled, but an **Amazon Simple Notification Service (SNS)** message is triggered, or a Lambda function is run to take some programmatic action.

For each workgroup, you can configure multiple alerts. For example, you can configure an initial workgroup data usage control for a maximum data scan of 3 TB per day, and have that trigger an SNS message to an SNS topic that sends an email to an administrator when the limit is reached.

You can also configure a second alert, that when data scanned reaches 5 TB for the workgroup in a day, another SNS message is sent to a topic, where the SNS topic triggers a Lambda function that programmatically updates the workgroup to have a `STATE` of `DISABLED` (preventing any additional queries from being run within that workgroup).

You also have the option of adding tags to a Workgroup. If that tag is configured as a cost allocation tag in the *Billing and Cost Management* console, the costs associated with running queries in that Workgroup appear in your *Cost and Usage Reports* with that cost allocation tag. This helps you understand and monitor Athena costs by Workgroup. To learn more about monitoring costs with *cost allocation tags*, see the following AWS documentation: `https://docs.aws.amazon.com/awsaccountbilling/latest/aboutv2/cost-alloc-tags.html`.

Having reviewed how to place limits on costs related to Athena SQL queries, let's now look at how to implement additional workgroup settings for implementing strong governance controls.

Implementing governance controls with Athena workgroups

As discussed previously, Athena workgroups enable the separation of query execution between different users, teams, or systems. Every Athena query runs within a workgroup, and you can use IAM policies to limit which workgroups a specific user, or process, has access to.

Most organizations have concerns around governance and security, and workgroups include functionality that can address some of these concerns. Common concerns include the following:

- Athena saves the results of all queries, as well as associated metadata, on S3. These results could contain confidential information, so organizations want to ensure this data is protected.
- Multiple teams in an organization may use Athena in the same AWS account, and organizations want items such as query history to be stored separately for each team.

In the Athena console, users can save queries that they frequently run, and a list of historical queries that they have run are also available. However, these lists only show queries for the workgroup where the query is run, so splitting up teams or projects into different workgroups ensures that query history and saved queries are visible only to the specific team associated with the workgroup. These could be separate workgroups for each team, separate workgroups for different applications, or separate workgroups for different types of users.

By default, each user can control several settings, but workgroups enable an administrator to override the users' settings, forcing them to use the workgroup settings.

The following are some of the configuration items that an administrator can enforce for members of a workgroup:

- **Query Result Location:** This is the S3 path where the results of Athena queries will be written. Users can set a query result location, but if this is set for the workgroup and **Override client-side settings** is set on the workgroup, then this location will be used for all the queries that are run in this workgroup.

  This enables an organization to control where query result files are stored in S3, and the organization can set strict access control options on this location to prevent unauthorized users from gaining access to query results.

  For example, each team can be assigned a different workgroup, and their IAM access policy can be configured to only allow read access to their query results.

- **Encrypt Query Results:** This option can be used to enforce that query results are encrypted, helping organizations keep in line with their corporate security requirements.

- **Metrics:** You can choose to send metrics to CloudWatch logs, which will reflect items such as the number of successful queries, the query runtime, and the amount of data that's been scanned for all the queries that are run within this workgroup.

- **Override client-side settings:** If this item is not enabled, then users can configure their user settings for things such as query result location, and whether query results are encrypted. Therefore, it is important to enable this setting to ensure that query results are protected and corporate governance standards are met.

- **Requester pays S3 buckets:** When creating a bucket in Amazon S3, one of the options that's available is to configure the bucket so that the user that queries the bucket pays for the API access costs. By default, Athena will not allow queries against buckets that have been configured for requester pays, but you can allow this by enabling this item.

- **Tags:** You can provide as many key:value tags as needed to help with items such as cost allocation, or for controlling access to a workgroup. For example, you may have two Workgroups that have different settings for the query output location, based on different projects or use cases. You could provide a tag with the name of the team and then, through IAM policies, provide team members access to all Workgroups that are tagged with their team name.

For examples of how to manage access to workgroups using tags or workgroup names, see the Amazon Athena documentation titled *Tag-Based IAM Access Control Policies* (https://docs.aws. amazon.com/athena/latest/ug/taqgs-access-control.html).

So far in this chapter we have learned more about the features and functionality available in Athena, such as how you can use connectors to query data in a variety of systems (such as Google BigQuery, or a PostgreSQL database) using Athena, and how Workgroups can be used to manage cost and enforce strong governance. We also reviewed some best practices for optimizing your Athena SQL queries from both a cost and performance perspective. Now, let's get hands-on with some of these concepts by creating and configuring a new Athena workgroup, and then running some SQL queries on our data lake data.

Hands-on – creating an Amazon Athena workgroup and configuring Athena settings

In this section, we're going to create and configure a new Athena workgroup, and set a per query data limit:

1. Log into **AWS Management Console** and access the Athena service using this link: https://console.aws.amazon.com/athena.

2. Expand the left-hand menu and click on **Workgroups** to access the workgroup management page.

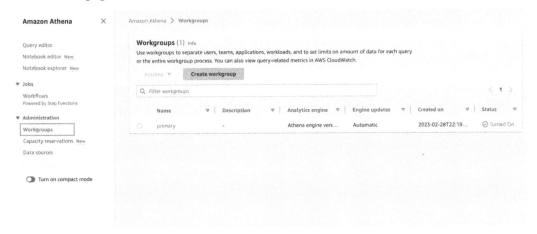

Figure 11.2: Athena Console showing Workgroups

3. On the **workgroup management** page, click on **Create workgroup** and enter the following values for our new workgroup. For the items not listed here, leave the defaults as-is:

    •   **Workgroup name:** Provide a descriptive name for the workgroup, such as datalake-user-sandbox.

- **Description**: Optionally, provide a description for this workgroup, such as `Sandbox workgroup for new datalake-users`.

- **Query result location** (in the **Query result configuration** section): In the hands-on exercises in *Chapter 4, Data Cataloging, Security, and Governance*, we created a bucket to store our Athena query results in (named `aws-athena-query-results-dataengbook-<initials>`). Click the **Browse S3 button** next to **Query result location**, and select the previously created query result bucket selector, and then click **Choose**. To make the location of our query results unique for this workgroup, add the workgroup name to the end of the path. For example, the full path should be something like `s3://aws-athena-query-results-dataengbook-gse23/datalake-user-sandbox/`. Make sure that you include the trailing slash at the end of the path.

- **Encrypt Query Results**: Tick this box to ensure that our query results are encrypted. When you select this, you will see several options for controlling the type of encryption. For our purposes, select **SSE_S3** for **Encryption type** (this specifies that we want to use S3 Server-Side Encryption rather than our own unique KMS encryption key).

- **Override client-side settings** (under the **Settings** section): If we want to prevent our users from changing items such as the query result's location or encryption settings, we need to ensure that we select this option.

4. In the **Per query data usage control** section, we can specify a **Data limit** to limit the scan size for individual queries run in this workgroup. If a query scans more than this amount of data, the query will be canceled. Set the **Data limit** size to `10 GB`.

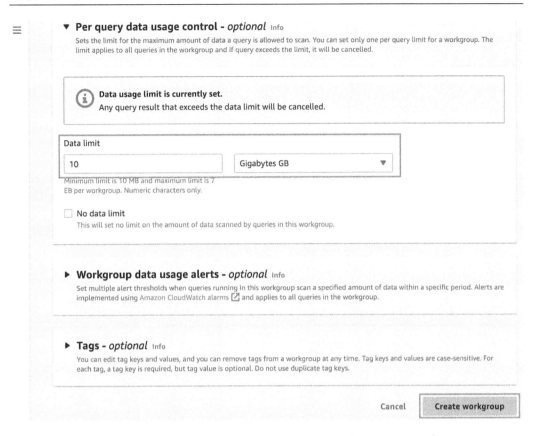

▼ **Per query data usage control -** *optional* Info

Sets the limit for the maximum amount of data a query is allowed to scan. You can set only one per query limit for a workgroup. The limit applies to all queries in the workgroup and if query exceeds the limit, it will be cancelled.

ⓘ **Data usage limit is currently set.**
Any query result that exceeds the data limit will be cancelled.

Data limit

| 10 | Gigabytes GB ▼ |

Minimum limit is 10 MB and maximum limit is 7 EB per workgroup. Numeric characters only.

☐ No data limit
This will set no limit on the amount of data scanned by queries in this workgroup.

▶ **Workgroup data usage alerts -** *optional* Info

Set multiple alert thresholds when queries running in this workgroup scan a specified amount of data within a specific period. Alerts are implemented using Amazon CloudWatch alarms 🗗 and applies to all queries in the workgroup.

▶ **Tags -** *optional* Info

You can edit tag keys and values, and you can remove tags from a workgroup at any time. Tag keys and values are case-sensitive. For each tag, a tag key is required, but tag value is optional. Do not use duplicate tag keys.

Cancel   **Create workgroup**

Figure 11.3: Athena workgroup – Per query data usage control

5. Optionally add any **Tags** you want to specify, and then click on **Create workgroup**.

We can also set a **workgroup data usage control** to manage the total amount of data that is scanned by all users of the workgroup over a specific period. We are not going to cover this now, but if you would like to explore setting this up, refer to the AWS documentation titled *Setting Data Usage Controls Limits*: https://docs.aws.amazon.com/athena/latest/ug/workgroups-setting-control-limits-cloudwatch.html.

Let's now get hands-on with how to switch into our new workgroup, and how to run some queries using Athena.

Hands-on — switching workgroups and running queries

By default, all users operate in the **primary** workgroup, but users can switch between any work-group that they have access to. You can control workgroup access via IAM policies, as detailed in the AWS documentation titled *IAM Policies for Accessing Workgroups* : `https://docs.aws.amazon.com/athena/latest/ug/workgroups-iam-policy.html`

In the previous section, we created and configured a new workgroup, so we can now run some SQL queries and explore Athena's functionality further:

1. In the left-hand menu, click on **Query editor**. Once in the Query editor, use the **Workgroup** drop-down list selector to change to your newly created sandbox workgroup.

Figure 11.4: Switching Workgroups in the Athena Console

2. A pop-up dialog may appear for you to acknowledge that all the queries that are run in this workgroup will use the settings we configured previously. This is because we chose to **Overwrite client-side settings** when creating the workgroup. Click **Acknowledge** to confirm this.

3. In the Query editor, let's run our first query to determine which category of films is most popular with our streaming viewers. We're going to query the streaming_films table, which was the denormalized table we created in *Chapter 7, Transforming Data to Optimize for Analytics*. On the left-hand side of the Athena query editor, select the curatedzonedb from the **Database** dropdown, and then run the following query in the query editor:

```
SELECT category_name,
        count(category_name) streams
FROM streaming_films
GROUP BY category_name
ORDER BY streams DESC
```

This query performs the following tasks:

- It selects the category name and a count of the total number of entries of that category in the table, and then it renames the count of queries column to create a new column heading of streams.

- It selects this data from the streaming_films table. Since we selected the curatedzonedb from the dropdown on the left-hand side, Athena automatically assumes that the table we are querying is in that selected database, so we don't need to specifically reference curatedzonedb in our query, although we could.

- Then, it groups the results by category_name, meaning that one record will be returned per category.

- Finally, it sorts the results by the streaming column, in descending order, so that the first result is the category with the highest number of streams. In the following screenshot, we can see that Sports was the most popular category from our streaming catalog:

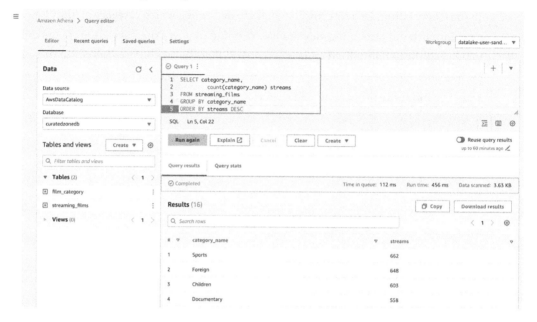

Figure 11.5: Athena query for the top streaming categories

 Note that the data in the streaming_films table was randomly generated by the Kinesis Data Generator utility in *Chapter 6, Ingesting Streaming and Batch Data*, so your results regarding the top category may be different.

4. Notice how under the query results on the right, there is an option for **Reuse query results**, which will re-use the previous result for an identical query run in the last 60 minutes, without rerunning the query (as we covered earlier in this chapter). Optionally run the query again a few times with this option not enabled and note the **run time** for each query. Then enable the **Reuse query results** option, and run the query a few more times, and compare the runtimes. The query we have is a very simple query, but for complex queries, or for cases where you have a BI or dashboarding tool using Athena, this option can make a significant performance difference.

5. If we have a query that we think we may want to run regularly (such as seeing the top category each day), we can **save** the query so that we don't need to retype it each time we want to run it. To do so, click the three dots at the top of the query window, and click on **Save as**, as shown in the following screenshot.

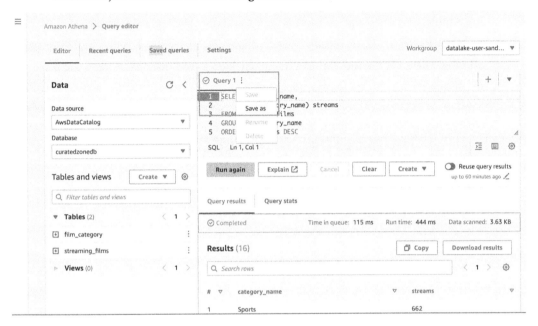

Figure 11.6: Save an Athena Query

6. Provide a name for the query (such as Overall-Top-Streaming-Categories) and a description (such as Returns a list of all categories, sorted by highest number of views). Then, click **Save query**.

7. Now, let's modify our query slightly to find out which State streamed the most movies out of our streaming catalog. Click on the plus (+) sign at the top right of the query window to open a new query window and enter the following query, and then click **Run**:

```
SELECT state,
        count(state) count
FROM streaming_films
GROUP BY state
ORDER BY count desc
```

Running this query using the data I generated indicates that **Alaska** was the most popular state for streaming movies from our catalog. Again, though, your results may be different due to the random data we generated using the **Kinesis Data Generator**:

1. Click on the three dots and then **Save as** and provide a name (such as **Overall-Top-Streaming-States**) and a description for this query, and then click on **Save query**.

2. Click on the down arrow on the top right-hand side of the query editor and click **Close all tabs**. Then, via the top sAthena menu, click on **Saved queries**. Here, we can see the list of queries that we have previously saved, and we can easily select a query from the list if we want to run that query again. Note that saved queries are saved as part of the workgroup, so any of our team members that have access to this workgroup will also be able to access any queries that we have saved. If you click on one of the saved queries, it will open the query in a **New query** tab.

3. At the top of the Athena menu, click on **Recent queries**. Here, we can see a list of all the recent queries that have been run in this workgroup:

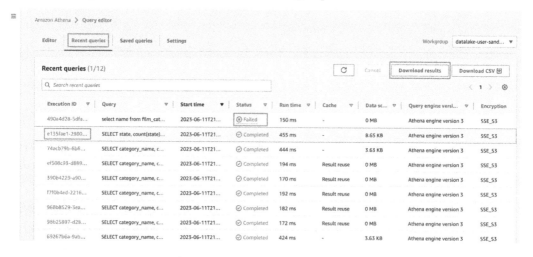

Figure 11.7: Amazon Athena recent queries tab

From here, we can take several actions, as follows:

1. If we want to rerun a query, we can click on the **Execution ID** of the query and it will open the query in a new query window.

2. To download the results that the query generated as a CSV file, click the selector for a query and then click on **Download Results**. Remember that query results are also always stored on S3 in the location set for **Query Result Location**. Note that the **Download CSV** button can be used to download the list of queries, along with the query details, in a CSV file.

3. To see the details of why a query failed, click on **Failed** under the Status column. A pop-up box will provide details of the error message that caused the failure.

4. Other information that we can see in the **Recent queries** tab is the Athena **engine version** that was used, whether the query result was returned from the query **cache** (which happens when we use the **Reuse query** option), as well as the **Run time** for the query.

Note that the **Recent queries** tab keeps a record of all the queries that have been run in the past 45 days.

In these hands-on exercises, you configured an Athena workgroup and made use of that workgroup to run several queries against data that you previously loaded and transformed in the data lake. You also learned how to save queries and view query history.

Summary

In this chapter, we learned more about the Amazon Athena service, an AWS-managed service that builds on the Apache Presto and Trino solutions to enable you to run SQL or Spark based queries against your data. We also looked at how to optimize our data and SQL queries to increase query performance and reduce costs.

Then, we explored advanced Athena functionality, including how Athena can be used as a SQL query engine not only for data in an Amazon S3 data lake, but also for external data sources such as other database systems, data warehouses, and even CloudWatch logs, using Athena Query Federation.

We wrapped up the theory part of this chapter by looking at Athena workgroups, which let us manage governance and costs, and they can be used to enforce specific settings for different teams or projects, and can also be used to limit the amount of data that is scanned by queries. In the last section of this chapter, we got hands-on with Athena, first creating a new workgroup, and then using that workgroup to run a number of SQL queries.

In the next chapter, we will explore another Amazon tool for data consumers as we look at how we can create rich visualizations and dashboards using **Amazon QuickSight**.

Learn more on Discord

To join the Discord community for this book – where you can share feedback, ask questions to the author, and learn about new releases – follow the QR code below:

```
https://discord.gg/9s5mHNyECd
```

12

Visualizing Data with Amazon QuickSight

In *Chapter 11, Ad Hoc Queries with Amazon Athena*, we looked at how **Amazon Athena** enables data analysts to run ad hoc queries against data in the data lake using the power of SQL and Spark. And while this is an extremely powerful tool for querying large datasets, often, the quickest way to understand a summary of a dataset is to visualize the data in graphs and dashboards.

In this chapter, we will do a deeper dive into **Amazon QuickSight**, a **Business Intelligence (BI)** tool that enables the creation of rich visualizations that summarize data, with the ability to filter and drill down into datasets in numerous ways. In addition, QuickSight also enables the creation of formatted, multi-page reports, and brings advanced functionality, such as the ability to ask questions of data in natural language.

In smaller organizations, a data engineer may be tasked with setting up and configuring a BI tool that data consumers can use. Things may be different in larger organizations, where there may be a dedicated team to manage the BI system. However, it is still important for a data engineer to understand how these systems work, as these systems will consume data that the data engineer will have played a part in creating.

The purpose of BI tools is to enable users to quickly understand complex datasets by enabling the exploration of data *visually*. And while we will focus on Amazon QuickSight in this chapter, many of the concepts in this chapter can be applied to other popular BI applications, such as Tableau, Microsoft Power BI, and Qlik.

Amazon QuickSight is a serverless BI solution and is fully managed by AWS. Organizations don't need to pay for any infrastructure or licensing costs, but rather pay a fixed amount per QuickSight user on a subscription basis based on which features are enabled.

In this chapter, we will cover the following topics:

- Representing data visually for maximum impact
- Understanding Amazon QuickSight's core concepts
- Ingesting and preparing data from a variety of sources
- Creating and sharing visuals with QuickSight analyses and dashboards
- Exploring QuickSight's advanced features
- Hands-on – creating a simple QuickSight visualization

Technical requirements

At the end of this chapter, you will get hands-on by creating a QuickSight visual from scratch. To complete the steps in the hands-on section, you will need the appropriate user permissions to sign up for a QuickSight subscription.

If you have administrator permissions for your AWS account, these permissions should be sufficient to sign up for a QuickSight subscription. If not, you will need to work with your IAM security team to create a custom policy. See the AWS documentation titled *IAM Policy Examples for Amazon QuickSight* and refer to the *All Access for Standard Edition* example policy as a reference.

At the time of writing, Amazon QuickSight includes a free trial subscription for 30 days for new QuickSight subscriptions. If you do not intend to use QuickSight past these 30 days, ensure that your user is also granted the `quicksight:Unsubscribe` permission so that you can unsubscribe from QuickSight after completing the hands-on section.

 Note that the *All Access for Standard Edition* example policy has a specific deny for the unsubscribe permission, so this may need to be modified based on your requirements. Work with your security team to implement a custom IAM policy.

You can find the code files of this chapter in the GitHub repository using the following link: https://github.com/PacktPublishing/Data-Engineering-with-AWS-2nd-edition/tree/main/Chapter12

Representing data visually for maximum impact

Data lakes are designed to capture large amounts of raw data and enable the processing of that data to draw out new insights that provide business value. The insights that are gained from a data lake can be represented in many ways, such as reports that summarize sales data and top sales items, **machine learning** (**ML**) models that can predict future trends, and visualizations and dashboards that effectively summarize data. Each of these ways of representing data offers different benefits, depending on the business purpose:

- If you're a data analyst who needs to report sales figures, profit margins, inventory levels, and other data for each category of product a company produces, you would probably want access to detailed tabular data. You would want the power of SQL to run powerful queries against the data to draw varied insights so that you can provide this data to different departments within the organization.

- If you're a logistics manager and are responsible for supplying all your retail stores with the correct amount of inventory, you would want your data science team to develop an ML model that can predict inventory requirements for each store. The model could take in raw data from the data lake and predict how much inventory each store may require.

- If you're a sales manager for a specific product category, you need to have an updated view of sales for the products in your category at all times. You need to be able to determine which products are selling well, and which marketing campaigns are most effective. Seeing a visual representation of relevant data provides you with the most effective way to quickly understand the product and campaign's performance at a high level.

Having raw, granular data available to an organization is important, but when you need to make decisions quickly based on that data, having a visual representation of the data is critical.

It is not practical to identify trends or outliers in a dataset by examining a spreadsheet containing 10,000 rows. However, if you aggregate and summarize the data into a well-designed visual representation of the data, it becomes very easy to identify those trends and outliers.

Of course, you do need to be cautious when creating visualizations to ensure that you do not select a subset of data that is not representative of the full dataset. As Mark Twain (supposedly) said: *"There are three kinds of lies: lies, damned lies, and statistics"*. It is important when designing a visual representation of data that you are careful not to misrepresent the data, and if you are viewing a visualization of data, that you are sure you can trust the author of that visualization.

Benefits of data visualization

A well-designed visual representation of data can reflect multiple different datasets in a single picture. It can do so in a way that enables the consumer of the visual to immediately gain insights that would take significant time and effort to gather from raw data.

There is a common fact often mentioned in articles on the internet that people can process images 60,000 times faster than they can process text. As it turns out, this is just an often-repeated claim with no evidence to back it up. However, while the number may be exaggerated, the basic claim that the human brain can process images quicker than text is without a doubt true.

And you don't need to look too far to validate this claim. For example, look at the rise of visual-based social media sites such as Instagram and Pinterest, or how people use emojis and animated GIFs to quickly and effectively communicate how they feel about something.

In the same way, we can use the power of visuals (images, graphs, word clouds, and many other types) to effectively communicate data from our data lake in a way that makes it easy for the consumer of the visual to quickly draw insights from the data.

Let's examine some common uses of visualizations that enable a user to quickly understand complex information.

Popular uses of data visualizations

Visualizations can be used to draw insights from many different types of data, in various ways. In this section, we will look at a few examples of some common types of visualizations to demonstrate the impact of a well-designed visual.

Trends over time

A common usage of analytic tools is to crunch through raw data to help surface trends, or changes in the data, over time. For example, we may want to understand how our spending on the AWS platform changes over time, as this can help identify areas where we need to focus on cost optimizations. A line graph can be a useful way to illustrate changes in data over a certain period.

The following diagram was created using a popular spreadsheet application and provides a visual of raw Amazon S3 spend per month, over 9 months, for a fictional company:

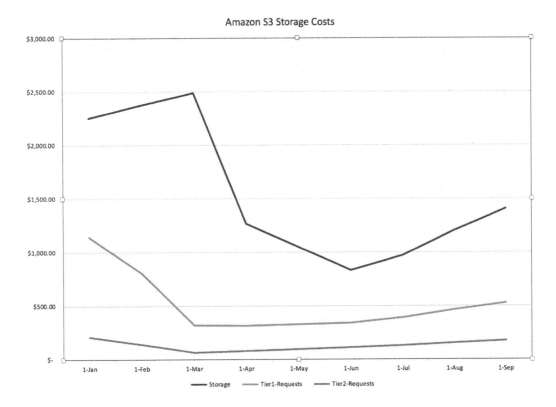

Figure 12.1: Line chart showing data over a certain period

In this visualization, we can see that our Tier1-Requests cost (middle line) significantly decreased from January to March. These costs are for API calls for operations such as PUT, COPY, POST, and LIST. Before February, we used to ingest a large number of small files, resulting in millions of PUT requests when writing these files to Amazon S3. After changing our transformation pipeline to write out fewer, larger files, this visualization clearly shows how those costs decreased.

In the visualization, we can also see that in March, our storage consumption (top line) significantly decreased. This makes sense as, during March, our fictional company had a project to implement Amazon S3 life cycle rules that deleted older versions of data from S3.

Showing summarized data over a certain period in a visual format makes it much easier to track and understand trends in our data, as well as to spot anomalies.

Data over a geographic area

In our first example, we looked at how we could graph trends over time, but another really useful visualization is to look at trends over a geographic area. There are many uses for this type of visualization, such the following:

- Understanding the popularity of a certain product in different geographic regions
- Quickly visualizing hotspots for the spread of an infectious disease (such as flu outbreaks) in different geographic regions
- Visualizing the population sizes of different cities in different regions
- Showing differences in temperature in different geographic areas

These types of charts are often known as **geospatial charts,** although they go by many different names. The chart may also come in different formats, but a common format is to use circles of different sizes on the map, with the size of each circle representing the value of one of the columns in the dataset (the larger the value, the bigger the circle). Circles may also be different colors to represent different rows in the dataset.

For example, the following chart (created with Amazon QuickSight) uses city population data from https://simplemaps.com/data/world-cities. In this chart, we have filtered the data to show all cities with a population above 5 million people, and the size of each circle represents the relative population size. In the hands-on section of this chapter, you will use Amazon QuickSight to recreate this chart so that you can interact with the chart (filter for different values and so on):

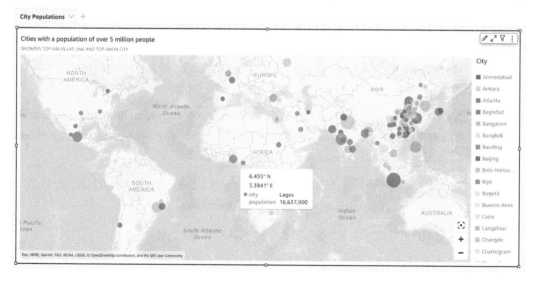

Figure 12.2: Map chart showing data by geographic region

The preceding map chart enables us to quickly understand which parts of the world have the most populated cities, and which parts are less populated. The same type of chart could be used to show the spread of disease, vaccination rates, poverty levels, water quality, or just about any other data that is associated with a specific location.

Heat maps to represent the intersection of data

Another common use of visualization tools is to understand the relationship between different sets of data. Often, we may have a gut feeling that there could be a correlation between two different datasets, but it is only when we explore the data more fully that we can understand those relationships.

As a very simple example, we would probably suspect that sales of ice cream, water, and other cold goods would be more popular in the summer months, and that the sales of coffee, hot chocolate, and soup would be more popular in the winter months:

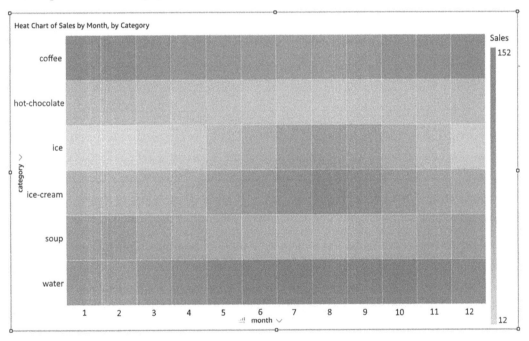

Figure 12.3: Heat map showing product sales by category and month

The preceding diagram shows a heat map that plots the relationship between sales in different categories, by month. The darker squares illustrate a higher sales value, while the lighter squares represent lower sales values.

As you can see, the sales of both coffee and water are strong throughout the year, but we can see that water has higher sales in the Northern Hemisphere summer (months 6 - 9), while coffee has higher sales in winter (months 11 - 2). Another insight we can gain quickly is that sales of ice are very low in the winter months and only have strong sales for a few summer months of the year (months 6 - 10). What other insights can you gain about sales of hot chocolate, ice cream, and soup by examining the heat map?

While this example may have been a fairly simple one, there are many other relationships between datasets that are not always as obvious, and heat maps can be useful to highlight these relationships visually.

We do not have sufficient space in this chapter to cover all the many varied types of charts that can be used to visually represent data, but as we continue on to the other sections of this chapter, we will explore some other common chart types along the way. In the next section, we are going to dive deeper into Amazon QuickSight's core concepts.

Understanding Amazon QuickSight's core concepts

At its core, QuickSight lets us ingest data from a wide variety of sources, perform some filtering or other transformation tasks on the data, and then create dashboards with multiple types of visuals that can be easily shared with others, or highly formatted multi-page PDF reports.

The QuickSight service is fully managed by AWS, and there are no upfront costs for using the service. Instead, the service uses a pricing model of a monthly cost per user and offers both Standard and Enterprise editions. To include specific functionality, such as QuickSight Q (for making natural language queries of data), a higher price per user is charged. There is also an option for capacity pricing, where you pay for the number of sessions per month, or per year, instead of per user.

QuickSight also includes a powerful in-memory storage and computation engine to enable the best performance for working with a variety of data sources. In this section, we'll examine the differences between the Standard and Enterprise editions of QuickSight, and also do a deeper dive into SPICE, the in-memory storage and computation engine.

Standard versus Enterprise edition

The **Standard edition** of QuickSight is useful for those who are just starting to explore the power of a BI tool and enables users to create visualizations from a variety of sources. However, for larger organizations, the **Enterprise edition** of QuickSight provides several additional features that most large organizations would want to make use of.

The following is a subset of some of the additional functionality available in the Enterprise edition, but refer to the Amazon QuickSight pricing page for full details on the differences between the versions. If just getting started with exploring the functionality of a BI application, then it makes sense to start with the Standard edition, as you can upgrade to the Enterprise edition at any time.

However, the following features are only available in the Enterprise edition:

- Integration with **Active Directory (AD)** and the ability to use AD groups for the management of QuickSight resources
- The ability to embed dashboards into custom applications
- The ability to email reports to QuickSight users on a schedule
- Fine-grained access control over AWS data sources (such as S3 and Athena)
- Automatic insight generation using ML Insights
- Encryption of data at rest

Note that if you select to use the Enterprise edition, it is not possible to downgrade to the Standard edition. Therefore, when starting out with QuickSight it's recommended to start with the Standard edition, and then upgrade to the Enterprise edition as you have more users start using QuickSight, and if there are specific features from the Enterprise edition that you require.

While the cost per author for the Enterprise edition is more expensive, if you have a very large number of users that just need to access QuickSight as readers (i.e., do not create visualizations, but only view visualizations created by others), then you can take advantage of the **reader** pricing that is available in the Enterprise edition to reduce your costs overall.

With the Enterprise edition, there is a fixed monthly cost for users that have the author role, while users with the reader role are charged per session. Each session provides access to QuickSight dashboards for a user for up to 30 minutes after they have logged in. During this time, readers can fully interact with the dashboards (filtering data, doing drill-downs into data, and so on).

At the time of writing, a session costs $0.30, and there is a maximum monthly cost of $5 per reader (increased to $10 per reader, if QuickSight Q is enabled), no matter how many sessions are used. In comparison, the Standard edition has a fixed cost (at the time of writing) of $12 per user (if paying month-to-month) and all users have full read and author capabilities.

For example, if you have 50 users that need to access QuickSight, the Standard edition would cost $600/month. However, with the Enterprise edition, if you had 5 authors and 45 readers, the cost would be $345/month.

Refer to the QuickSight pricing page (https://aws.amazon.com/quicksight/pricing/) for the current pricing for your Region, as pricing may change occasionally. Let's now look at the in-memory storage and computation functionality available in QuickSight.

SPICE — the in-memory storage and computation engine for QuickSight

Like many other BI tools, Amazon QuickSight provides a storage engine for storing imported data and performing rapid calculations on that data. In QuickSight, **SPICE** is the acronym that's used to refer to this engine, and it stands for **Super-fast, Parallel, In-memory, Calculation Engine**. When you're creating a new dataset in QuickSight, you can select whether to perform direct queries of the dataset at the source, or whether you want to import data into SPICE.

If you choose to query the dataset directly from the source, then each time the visualization is accessed, QuickSight will make a connection to the data source (such as an Amazon RDS MySQL database) and query the data. This ensures that the dashboard always reflects the latest data. However, there is some latency in making the connection to the data source and retrieving data.

Alternatively, you can choose to import data into the SPICE engine. That way, when the visualization is accessed, QuickSight can read the data directly from SPICE, and this can significantly improve performance. For data that does not change constantly, it makes sense to import data into SPICE and query the data from there.

For example, if you have a dataset covering daily store sales, and the store sales are only updated at the close of business each evening (meaning the data is only updated daily), then it makes sense to import that into SPICE once a day. If you have 5,000 stores, and therefore 5,000 store managers that want to query the previous day's data for their store, having the data in SPICE reduces the number of direct queries of the database, and significantly improves query performance.

However, if creating a dashboard that reflects online sales, and sales are immediately updated in a centralized database, you may want to directly query that database. For example, you may create a dashboard for your marketing team that shows the top 10 products by sales over the past hour, and you may want to enable your marketing team to refresh the dashboard to get the latest data at any moment in time. In this case, you would want to use a direct query of the data source. This is because you always want the most up-to-date data, and the marketing team is relatively small, so there is not a massive load on the source database from direct queries.

You also have the option of scheduling a refresh of the data in SPICE so that QuickSight will regularly connect to the data source and retrieve the latest data to store in SPICE. With both the Standard and Enterprise editions of QuickSight, you can schedule the refresh to be done daily, weekly, or monthly. With the Enterprise edition of QuickSight, however, you gain the additional option of performing incremental refreshes, and the ability to do an incremental refresh as often as every 15 minutes (or a full refresh every hour). You can also use an API call to trigger the refresh of SPICE data, enabling you to build an event-driven strategy for refreshing SPICE data. For more information, see the AWS blog post titled *Event-driven refresh of SPICE datasets in Amazon QuickSight* at https://aws.amazon.com/blogs/big-data/event-driven-refresh-of-spice-datasets-in-amazon-quicksight/.

> **NOTE**
>
> There is a 2-minute timeout for generating visuals in QuickSight. Therefore, if your direct query takes 2 minutes or longer to perform the query and generate the visualization, a timeout will occur. In these cases, you either need to improve the performance of the query (filtering data, only selecting specific columns, and so on) or you should import the data into SPICE. For more information on data source quotas and limitations, refer to the AWS documentation at: https://docs.aws.amazon.com/quicksight/latest/user/data-source-limits.html.

If you're using a data source that charges for each query (such as Amazon Athena in on-demand mode, or Amazon Redshift Spectrum), importing the data into SPICE can help reduce costs. Storing the data in SPICE means you only pay for the query when the data is initially loaded, as well as for when the data is refreshed. With a direct query, you would pay for the query each time the visualization is accessed.

Managing SPICE capacity

Your account is granted 10 GB of SPICE storage for every paid user that has the author role (this would be every user in the Standard Edition, and users with the Author role in the Enterprise edition). SPICE storage is shared by all QuickSight users in an account and is on a per-region basis.

For example, if you have QuickSight Enterprise edition and you have 10 users with the Author role and 100 users with the Reader role, all in the Northern Virginia (us-east-1) Region, then your QuickSight account in us-east-1 would have 100 GB of SPICE storage available.

If additional SPICE storage is needed, you can purchase additional SPICE capacity. For example, if you needed 130 GB of total SPICE storage for the datasets you wanted to import, you could purchase an additional 30 GB of capacity each month. At the time of writing, additional SPICE capacity for the Enterprise edition is charged at $0.38 per GB.

There are also limits on the size of a single dataset in SPICE. At the time of writing, datasets are limited to a maximum of 1 billion rows, or 1 TB, for QuickSight Enterprise edition. For the Standard edition, the limit is 25 million rows, or 25 GB of data. There are also other limits for each dataset (such as the number of columns and the length of column names), so ensure you refer to the latest QuickSight documentation for updated information on these limits (see `https://docs.aws.amazon.com/quicksight/latest/user/data-source-limits.html`).

Now that we have reviewed the core Amazon QuickSight concepts, let's move on and review QuickSight's functionality for importing and preparing data.

Ingesting and preparing data from a variety of sources

Amazon QuickSight can use other AWS services as a source, as well as on-premises databases, imported files, and even some **Software as a Service (SaaS)** applications.

For example, you can easily connect to Oracle, Microsoft SQL Server, Postgres, and MySQL databases, either running as part of the Amazon RDS managed database service, or as instances running on Amazon EC2 or in your own data centers. You can also connect to data warehouse systems such as Amazon Redshift, Snowflake, and Teradata. Other AWS services are also supported as data sources, including Amazon S3, Amazon Athena, Amazon OpenSearch Service, Amazon Aurora, and AWS IoT Analytics.

In addition to these traditional data sources, QuickSight can also connect to various SaaS offerings, including ServiceNow, Jira, Adobe Analytics, Salesforce, GitHub, and Twitter.

Data stored in files, such as a Microsoft Excel Spreadsheet (XLSX files), JSON documents, and CSV files, can also be imported into QuickSight. These files can be directly uploaded through the QuickSight console, or they can be imported from Amazon S3.

The rich variety of potential data sources for QuickSight is shown in the following screenshot:

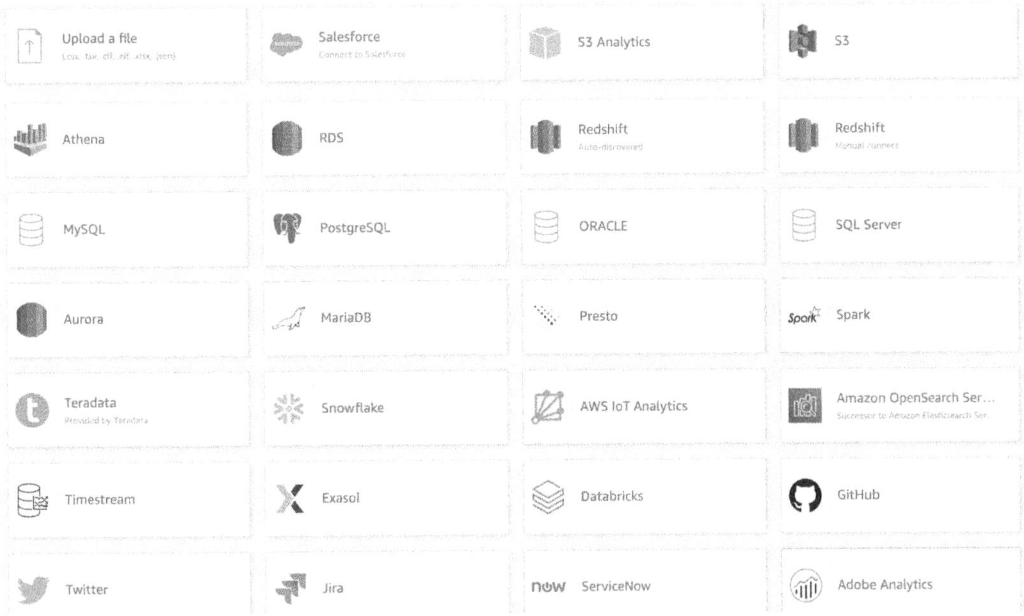

Figure 12.4: Data sources that can be imported into Amazon QuickSight

For the latest list of supported data sources, and to confirm information about supported versions, see the AWS QuickSight documentation topic *Supported Data Sources* at https://docs.aws.amazon.com/quicksight/latest/user/supported-data-sources.html.

For data sources not directly supported, you can use other ingestion methods (such as those discussed in *Chapter 6, Ingesting Batch and Streaming Data*) to ingest data into your S3-based data lake. You can then create visualizations of that data by using the Amazon Athena data source integration to enable QuickSight to query the data directly in Amazon S3.

To learn more about managing your SPICE memory capacity, refer to the AWS documentation at: https://docs.aws.amazon.com/quicksight/latest/user/managing-spice-capacity.html.

Once your data has been imported, you can use QuickSight to do some level of ETL on the datasets, which we will look at in the next section.

Preparing datasets in QuickSight versus performing ETL outside of QuickSight

QuickSight includes functionality for performing data transformations on imported data. For example, you can do the following:

- Join two different datasets
- Exclude specific fields
- Filter data
- Change the data type or name of a field
- Create a new calculated field

All of these data preparation tasks can be done using a simple visual interface.

If you select to join two different datasets, then you need to import the data into SPICE. However, if you're just working with a single data source, the transformations you specify will be applied when the data is read from the data source.

Ultimately, you need to decide whether you should perform data transformations and joins in QuickSight, or whether you should perform those transformations outside of QuickSight. For example, you could join two datasets, drop unneeded columns, change the data types and column names, and create new calculated fields using tools such as AWS Glue DataBrew or AWS Glue Studio.

There are several factors to consider when making this decision, including the following:

- If this dataset may be used outside of QuickSight, such as for queries using Amazon Athena, then it makes sense to perform the ETL with other tools before using the dataset in QuickSight.
- If the required transformations are relatively simple and the resulting dataset will only be used in QuickSight, then you may choose to perform the transformation using QuickSight. This could include transforms such as adding additional calculated fields, changing the names or data types of a few columns, dropping a few columns, and so on.

The decision about where to perform data transformations can be complex, and it may not be an easy decision. However, an important factor to take into account is the controls that may be in place for formal data pipelines, versus those for more informal transformations (such as those performed by data analysts using tools such as Amazon QuickSight).

If you have strong governance controls around your formal data engineering pipelines (such as code reviews and change control), then you may choose to ensure that all the transformations are done within formal processes. However, you need to balance this against ensuring that you don't tie up your end user teams in formal processes that slow the business down.

Often, you need to balance the two sides – ensuring that your business teams have the flexibility to perform minor transformations using tools such as QuickSight, while also ensuring that new datasets or visualizations that business users may use to make important business decisions have the correct governance controls around them.

It is not always easy to find this balance, and there are no specific rules that apply universally when making this decision. Therefore, much thought needs to be given to this decision to find the right balance between enabling the business to make decisions quickly, without being constrained by overly formal processes for even minor data transformations.

The business ultimately needs to take the time required to put in place governance and controls that communicate the types of ad hoc data transformations that data analysts and others can perform. These policies should also make it clear as to when transformations need to be performed by data engineering teams using formal processes.

For more information on the types of transforms you can do in QuickSight, see the QuickSight documentation titled *Preparing data in Amazon QuickSight* at `https://docs.aws.amazon.com/quicksight/latest/user/preparing-data.html`.

Once you have your data ready in QuickSight (whether you did the transforms inside or outside of QuickSight), you are ready to start building your dashboards and reports, as covered in the next section.

Creating and sharing visuals with QuickSight analyses and dashboards

Once a dataset has been imported (and optionally transformed), you can create visualizations of this data using **QuickSight analyses**. This is the tool that is used by QuickSight authors to create new dashboards, with these dashboards containing one or more visualizations that can be shared with others in the business.

When you create a new analysis/dashboard, you choose one or more datasets to include in the analysis (up to a maximum of 50 datasets per dashboard). Each analysis consists of one or more sheets (or tabs, much like browser tabs) that display a group of visualizations. You can have up to 20 sheets (tabs) per dashboard, and each sheet can have up to 30 visualizations.

Once you have created an analysis (consisting of multiple visuals, optionally across multiple sheets), you can choose to publish the analysis as a dashboard. When you're publishing a dashboard, you can select various parameters related to how readers can interact with the dashboard, including the following:

- If they can apply their own ad-hoc filters to the data in the dashboard
- If they can download data in the dashboard as a CSV file
- If they can perform drill-down and drill-up actions (when supported in a dashboard)
- If they can sort the data

Once the dashboard has been published, you can select who to share the dashboard with. You can either share the dashboard with everyone in the account (providing them with read access to the dashboard) or you can select specific users and groups to share with.

By default, when you create a new analysis, the analysis contains a single sheet, with a single empty visualization that is set to a type of **AutoGraph**, as seen in the following screenshot.

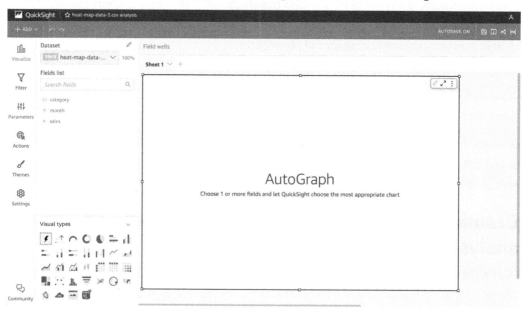

Figure 12.5: New analysis screen in Amazon QuickSight

QuickSight supports many different types of visualizations (as can be seen in the **Visual types** section of the preceding screenshot). Let's dive deeper into some of these visual types.

Visual types in Amazon QuickSight

In this section, we will discuss several **data visualization types** supported by Amazon QuickSight. There are many different types of visualizations that are supported, and in this section, we will cover some of the most popular ones, but you can review the full list of visualizations in the *Amazon QuickSight documentation* (`https://docs.aws.amazon.com/quicksight/latest/user/working-with-visual-types.html`).

AutoGraph for automatic graphing

While this is not an actual type of visual, you can select AutoGraph as a visual type to let QuickSight automatically choose the visual type for you. Based on the number of fields you select, and the data type of each field that is selected, QuickSight automatically uses the most appropriate visual type for your data. This is often a good way to start exploring your data if you're unsure of the specific type of graph you want to use.

Line, geospatial, and heat maps

Earlier in this chapter. we discussed three common types of visualizations:

- **Line charts**: Displays data as a series of data points and is often used to plot data over a certain period
- **Geospatial charts**: Displays data points overlayed on a map, combining geospatial data with other data
- **Heat maps**: Displays data in a chart with values represented by darker or lighter colors

All three of these types of charts (and variations of these charts) are supported by Amazon QuickSight, and can be used to create rich visualizations from many different data sources.

Bar charts

Bar charts are a common visualization type, and QuickSight supports multiple types of bar charts. For example, you can have a simple bar chart showing a single value for a dimension (such as *sales per region*) or a multi-measure bar chart that shows multiple measures for a dimension (such as *sales goal* and *achieved sales per region*).

There are also additional bar chart types that are supported, such as stacked bar charts and clustered bar charts. Bar charts can be displayed horizontally or vertically.

Key performance indicators

A **Key performance indicator** (**KPI**) is often used to show progress against a specific goal. For example, you may have a goal of achieving a specific amount of revenue in a quarter.

A KPI visual could display the current revenue as a percentage of the target revenue in a visual. A dashboard showing this KPI (or multiple KPIs) can help management keep track of how the business is performing based on several key metrics.

In QuickSight, a KPI displays a comparison of two values and includes a progress bar indicating the percentage difference between the values:

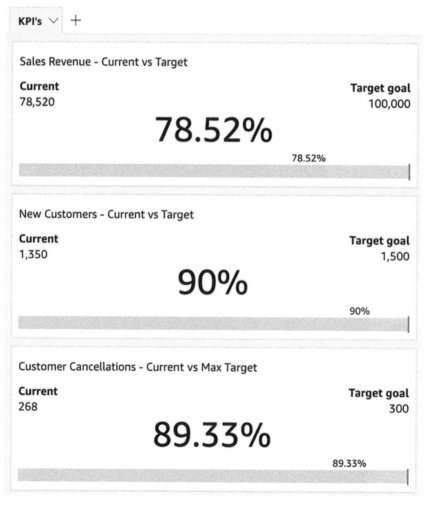

Figure 12.6: Dashboard with KPI visuals

In the preceding screenshot, a sales manager can quickly view how their organization is performing against several key metrics. This chart shows that revenue is nearly at 80% of the target, new customers are at 90% of the target, and that the team is within 11% of the target maximum customer cancellations for that period.

Tables as visuals

There may be use cases where you want to display the raw data of a table on a dashboard, without converting the data into a specific visual.

QuickSight supports displaying tables directly within an analysis/dashboard and supports up to 200 columns in the visual. However, directly displaying raw table data should ideally only be done with small tables, where you display just a limited amount of raw data.

Custom visual types

QuickSight lets you include several **custom visuals** within a dashboard, including the following:

- Custom images (such as a company or product logo)
- Custom videos
- An online form
- An embedded web page

These visual types help you customize and personalize your dashboards. For example, you may want to embed your company logo on a visual, or include a video that provides a guide for working with a specific dashboard.

Note that when you embed custom content in an analysis/dashboard, you need to specify the HTTP URL of the resource. Also, while QuickSight does include functionality for emailing dashboards to users, embedded custom visual types (pictures, videos, forms, and web pages) will not be displayed in the email copy of a dashboard.

There are also other limitations to using embedded content. For example, the web content needs to support opening the content in an iframe; otherwise, the content may not appear in QuickSight. When you're looking to embed content into a QuickSight analysis/dashboard, you should look for content that has an embeddable URL (which is often available when you choose to share content).

Other visual types

There are many other types of charts that are supported in QuickSight, and new types are added over time. These include the following common chart types:

- Pie charts
- Box plots
- Donut charts
- Gauge charts
- Histograms
- Pivot tables
- Sankey diagrams
- Tree maps
- Waterfall charts
- Word clouds

As we have discussed in this section, QuickSight lets us create many different types of visuals, then publish and share those visuals as dashboards. However, QuickSight also includes advanced functionality that can automatically reveal new insights in your data and lets you embed dashboards into custom applications, as we will see in the next section.

Understanding QuickSight's advanced features

The **Enterprise edition** of Amazon QuickSight includes advanced features that can help you draw out additional insights from your data, ask questions of your data using natural language, and enable you to widely share your data by embedding dashboards into applications. We will review some of these features next.

Amazon QuickSight ML Insights

QuickSight ML Insights uses the power of ML algorithms to automatically uncover insights and trends, forecast future data points, and identify anomalies in your data.

All of these ML Insights functionalities can easily be added to an analysis/dashboard without the author needing to have any ML experience or any real understanding of the underlying ML algorithms. However, for those who are interested in the underlying ML algorithms used by QuickSight, Amazon provides comprehensive documentation on this topic.

Review the Amazon QuickSight documentation titled *Understanding the ML algorithim used by Amazon QuickSight* for more information: `https://docs.aws.amazon.com/quicksight/latest/user/concept-of-ml-algorithms.html`.

However, to make use of ML Insights, there are specific requirements for your data, such as having at least one metric and one category dimension. For ML forecasting, the more historical data you have, the better. For example, if you want to forecast based on daily data, you need at least 38 daily data points, or to forecast on quarters, you need at least 35 quarterly data points. The full details on the data requirements are documented in the Amazon QuickSight documentation titled *Dataset requirements for using ML Insights with Amazon QuickSight*: `https://docs.aws.amazon.com/quicksight/latest/user/ml-data-set-requirements.html`.

Let's examine some of the different types of ML Insights in more detail.

Amazon QuickSight autonarratives

Autonarratives provide natural language insights into your data, providing you with an easy-to-read summary of what is displayed in a visual. Effectively, autonarratives enable you to provide a plainly stated summary of your data, as the following autonarrative examples show:

- Year-to-date revenue *decreased* by *4.6%* from $906,123 to $864,441 compared to the same period last year. We are at *89.3%* achievement for the YTD goal and *77.9%* achievement for the annual goal.
- Daily revenue for *Accessories / Cell Phone Covers* on September 3, 2021 was higher than expected at $3,461.21.

You can add a variety of autonarratives to an analysis, such as bottom-ranked items, growth rate, anomaly detection, top movers, and many others. For the full list of available autonarratives, see the Amazon QuickSight documentation titled *Insights that include autonarratives*: `https://docs.aws.amazon.com/quicksight/latest/user/auto-narratives.html`.

ML-powered anomaly detection

Amazon QuickSight can perform **anomaly detection** (also sometimes referred to as outlier detection) across millions of metrics contained in your data, identify non-obvious trends, and highlight outliers in the data. These types of insights are difficult to draw out of data without using the power of modern ML algorithms.

You can add an autonarrative widget to an analysis and specify the type as being anomalous. Then, you can configure several settings related to how QuickSight detects outliers in the data and can set a schedule for when outliers are calculated (ranging from once an hour to once a month). You can also configure QuickSight to analyze the top items that contributed to the anomaly.

Once an anomaly has been detected, you can choose to **explore the anomalies** on the insight. This opens a screen where you can change various settings related to anomaly detection, enabling you to explore different types of anomalies in the dataset.

ML-powered forecasting

Amazon QuickSight can use the power of ML algorithms to provide reliable forecasts against your data. When you create a visual that uses a date field and contains up to three metrics, you can select an option in the widget to add a forecast of future values.

QuickSight will automatically analyze historical data using an ML model and graph out future predicted values for each metric. You can also configure the forecast properties by setting items such as forecast length (how many future periods to forecast and how much historical data to analyze).

The ML model that's used by QuickSight for forecasting automatically excludes data that it identifies as outliers and automatically fills in any missing values. For example, if you had a short spike in sales due to a promotion, QuickSight could exclude that spike when calculating the forecast. Or, if there were a few days where historical data was missing, QuickSight could automatically determine likely values for the missing period.

It is important to remember that the QuickSight ML Insight features (including autonarratives, anomaly detection, and forecasting) are available in the Enterprise edition of QuickSight only, and will not be available if you only have a Standard edition subscription.

In this section, we looked at how QuickSight enables you to draw out powerful new insights from your data using ML. In the next section, we will look at another advanced feature available in QuickSight, and that is the ability to ask questions of your data using natural language.

Amazon QuickSight Q for natural language queries

ML approaches have enabled new abilities in many products, and one of those is the ability to query data with free-form text that uses everyday language. A number of popular BI products offer functionality for **natural language queries** (**NLQ**), and this includes Amazon QuickSight.

With the Amazon QuickSight Q feature, a user could type in a query such as *"Show me the top 3 product categories by revenue for 2023"*, and QuickSight would create a graph displaying that information. However, a QuickSight author does first need to do some work to set up topics for QuickSight Q in order to enable the functionality.

QuickSight Q is a feature that is only available with the QuickSight Enterprise edition, and there is an additional cost to enable this functionality. At the time of writing, there is a $250 charge per month for each account that has QuickSight Q enabled, and authors enabled to use Q have an extra charge of $10/month, and the reader maximum cost increases from $5 to $10 for readers with Q.

Generative BI dashboarding authoring capabilities

In September 2023, AWS announced the preview of new generative BI authoring capabilities as part of Amazon QuickSight Q. The three new capabilities in preview that were part of the announcement provide new functionality for the following:

- Building visualizations by specifying what you want to see using natural language
- Creating complex calculations rapidly, by specifying the expected outcome of the calculation using natural language
- Refining and tweaking visualizations using natural language prompts

These new capabilities are powered by **Amazon Bedrock**, a service that offers a variety of **Large Language Models (LLMs)**, suited for different tasks. For more information on this new functionality, see the QuickSight documentation at `https://docs.aws.amazon.com/quicksight/latest/user/generative-bi-author-experience.html`.

Let's now take a deeper look at **QuickSight Q Topics**, the key concept employed to use QuickSight Q against a dataset.

QuickSight Q Topics

Q Topics are a collection of one (or more) datasets that are used to represent a business subject area that users can ask questions about. Q Topics need to be created by a QuickSight author, and the author then needs to configure the topic to best enable natural language queries.

The easiest way to create and configure a topic, is to create a topic based on an existing analysis/dashboard. When you create a topic using this method, **QuickSight's Automated Data Preparation** automatically configures the topic using the power of ML, including automation of the following:

- **Selection of fields:** With Automated Data Preparation, QuickSight examines the existing analysis to understand which fields are most commonly used in your dashboard, and includes those fields in the topic, and excludes fields that are not commonly used. In addition, it also automatically includes any calculated fields that you created in the analysis.

- **Naming of fields:** It is common to use acronyms and shortened versions of field names in a database or data warehouse, such as naming a column *DOB* for *Date Of Birth*. With Automated Data Preparation, QuickSight can attempt to automatically rename fields to a more natural name that someone is likely to use in a query. In addition, it can automatically add additional synonyms for each field, such as *Birth Date* for the *Date of Birth* field, or *salesperson* and *account representative* for the *SALES_REP* field.

- **Field formatting:** With Automated Data Preparation, QuickSight can automatically determine an appropriate format for a field when using that field in an answer. For example, with a field that shows *sales revenue* value, QuickSight can automatically assign a currency format to that field so that results using this field display the value with a dollar prefix, for example.

When using Automated Data Preparation, authors are strongly encouraged to review the automated configuration that QuickSight applies and edit it further as needed. For example, based on the knowledge that an author has of the business, they may choose to add additional synonyms for certain fields.

If an author creates a new topic directly (i.e., by not creating a topic based on an existing dashboard), then the author needs to perform the above tasks manually to select fields, rename fields, add synonyms, and apply a format to relevant fields.

Once a topic has been created, and your users start querying using natural language prompts, it is important to review how the topic is performing, so that adjustments can be made as needed. Let's take a closer look at how to fine-tune your topics.

Fine-tuning your QuickSight Q Topics

QuickSight Q includes functionality that lets you review the performance of the topics you have created, so that you can fine-tune the topic to further improve performance.

Once your topic has been available to your users for a while, you can review the topic to see information such as the queries that your users have run, whether QuickSight Q was able to provide a result, where users needed to provide more information, etc. This enables you to fine-tune the field names, synonyms, and field formats, in order to improve the results that QuickSight Q provides.

For example, you may find that users typed in a query and no result was available, but you may find that they used a specific term (such as *rep* for *sales representative*) that had not been configured as a synonym, and you can then add a new synonym so that future similar queries will return an appropriate result.

It is important that you regularly review your topics, to understand how users are interacting with the topic, so that you can refine the topic settings to improve results. When a user provides feedback on how well Q responded to a question, this is recorded and available on the topic's **Summary** and **User Activity** tabs.

In the **Summary** tab, you can view metrics such as the number of questions asked over time, as well as a distribution of questions that received positive, negative, or no feedback. In the **User activity** tab, you can see a list of questions that were asked, as well as positive or negative feedback and comments. For more details on monitoring topic feedback, see the Amazon QuickSight documentation at `https://docs.aws.amazon.com/quicksight/latest/user/quicksight-q-topics-performance.html`.

In the next section, we will look at another popular feature of the Enterprise edition of QuickSight, a feature that enables you to easily distribute your published dashboards more widely.

Amazon QuickSight embedded dashboards

For use cases where you don't want your users to have to log in to QuickSight via the AWS Management Console or QuickSight portal, you can embed QuickSight directly into your applications or website.

You can embed either the full console experience (including authoring tools for creating new analyses and managing datasets) or embed published dashboards only. Embedded dashboards have the full interactive capabilities that they do in the console, which means that users can filter and sort data, and even drill down into data (so long as the author enabled those levels of interactivity when they published the dashboard).

Embedding for registered QuickSight users

QuickSight supports several authentication methods, including AD SAML 2.0, as well as SSO using AWS Identity Center (or other identity providers such as Okta, Auth0, and PingOne).

As such, your users can authenticate with your existing website or HTML-based application using one of the supported authentication methods and, using that identity, map to an existing QuickSight user. If that user has not accessed QuickSight before, a new QuickSight user will be created for the user.

You can elect to either embed the full console experience or only embed dashboards. Users will be able to open any dashboards that their QuickSight user has been given access to.

With the QuickSight embedding experience, you can optionally customize the display theme using your branding. This enables the embedded QuickSight objects to appear as a direct part of your application, rather than looking like an embedded external application. However, even when you have a customized theme, the embedded QuickSight application does display a **Powered by QuickSight** label.

Embedding for unauthenticated users

For use cases where your users do not authenticate with your website or application, you still have the option of embedding QuickSight dashboards for anonymous user access.

To enable anonymous access, you need to purchase reader session capacity pricing. This offers a set number of QuickSight sessions per month, or per year (depending on your plan), and these sessions can be consumed by anonymous users. The bonus of purchasing an annual plan for QuickSight sessions is that the **Powered by QuickSight** label can be removed from embedded resources.

An example use case for this functionality is for a local government health department that wants to share the latest information on a virus outbreak with their community. The health department could embed an Amazon QuickSight dashboard into its website that is linked to the latest data on the spread of the virus.

Users accessing the website could interact with the dashboard, filtering data for their specific location, sorting data, or even downloading a CSV version of the data for their additional analysis. These users would not need to log into the health department website to access the dashboard, and the health department could use an annual plan for reader session capacity. For more information on pricing for reader session plans, see the Amazon QuickSight pricing page: `https://aws.amazon.com/quicksight/pricing/`.

When embedding dashboards for unauthenticated users, you need to be *very* aware of what data you make available, and that you do not accidently expose company confidential data via an authenticated embedding.

Let's now look at another advanced feature in Amazon QuickSight: the ability to generate multi-page formatted reports.

Generating multi-page formatted reports

The Amazon QuickSight Paginated Reports functionality (launched in November 2022) enables authors to create highly formatted, multi-page PDF reports. This extends Amazon QuickSight functionality beyond just creating rich visualizations in dashboards, to enabling report generation as well.

With this functionality, QuickSight authors are able to create reports where they specify attributes such as page size, length, orientation (portrait or landscape), as well as the arrangement of images, charts, and tables. These reports can easily be printed, or distributed via email as PDF attachments. A report created with this functionality can generate up to 1,000 pages in a PDF, and reports can be scheduled to run using QuickSight's scheduling mechanism.

Note that there is an extra cost to enable paginated reports in QuickSight. At the time of writing, the cost for 500 reports units a month (with a report unit being 100 pages long, or 100 MB in size) was $500 per month. To learn more about paginated reports, see the QuickSight documentation titled *Working with paginated reports in Amazon QuickSight* at `https://docs.aws.amazon.com/quicksight/latest/user/working-with-reports.html`.

Having learned more about QuickSight's advanced functionality, let's get hands-on by creating a QuickSight visualization.

Hands-on — creating a simple QuickSight visualization

Earlier in this chapter, we discussed how data can be represented over a geographic area. We used the example of data containing information on the population of world cities, and how we could use that to easily visualize how large cities are geographically distributed. The example visual in *Figure 12.2* showed cities with a population of over 5 million people, displayed on top of a map of the world.

For the hands-on section of this chapter, we are going to recreate that visual using Amazon QuickSight.

Setting up a new QuickSight account and loading a dataset

Before we start creating a new dashboard, we need to download a sample dataset of world city populations. We will use the basic dataset available from `https://simplemaps.com/`, which is freely distributed under the *Creative Commons Attribution 4.0* license (`https://creativecommons.org/licenses/by/4.0/`):

1. Use the following link to download the **basic** dataset from simplemaps.com: `https://simplemaps.com/data/world-cities`. If the file downloaded is a ZIP file, make sure to extract the actual city data CSV file.

2. Log into the **AWS Management Console** and use the top search bar to search for, and open, the **QuickSight** service.

3. If you have not used QuickSight before in this account, you will be prompted with a **Sign up for QuickSight** button. Click the button to start the signup process.

4. The default page opens to the QuickSight Enterprise edition. For this exercise, only the Standard edition is needed, so click on the **Sign up for Standard Edition here** link at the very bottom of the page, as per the screenshot in *Figure 12.7*

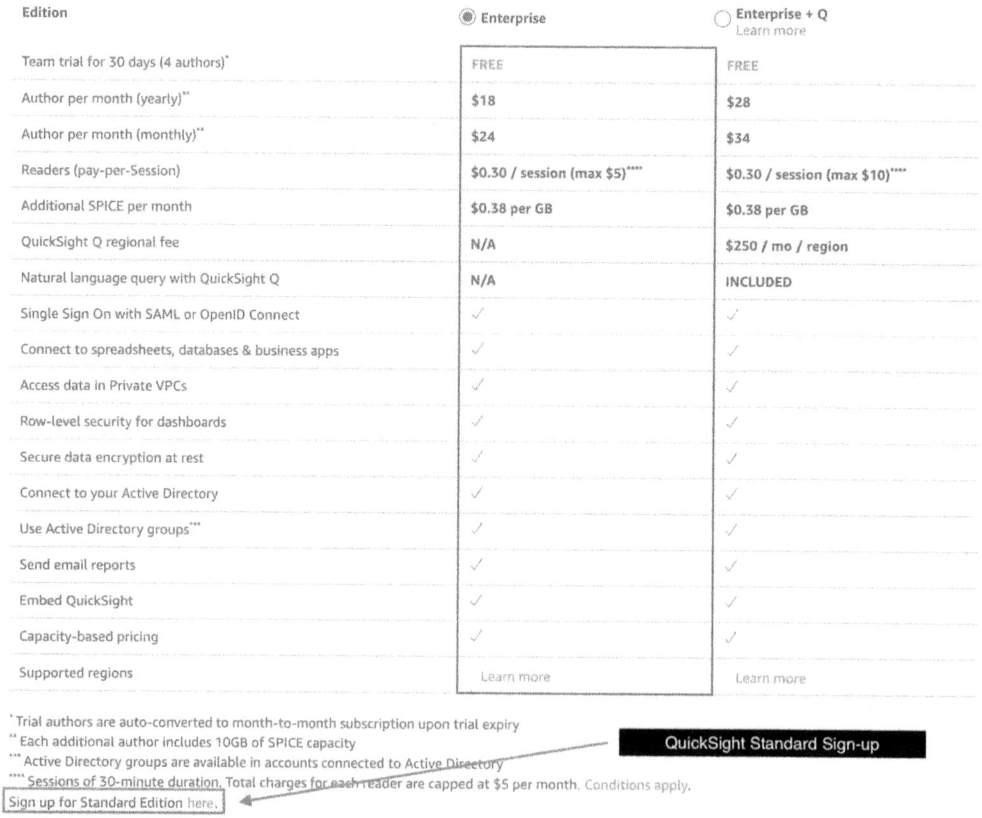

Edition	⦿ Enterprise	◯ Enterprise + Q Learn more
Team trial for 30 days (4 authors)*	FREE	FREE
Author per month (yearly)**	$18	$28
Author per month (monthly)**	$24	$34
Readers (pay-per-Session)	$0.30 / session (max $5)****	$0.30 / session (max $10)****
Additional SPICE per month	$0.38 per GB	$0.38 per GB
QuickSight Q regional fee	N/A	$250 / mo / region
Natural language query with QuickSight Q	N/A	INCLUDED
Single Sign On with SAML or OpenID Connect	✓	✓
Connect to spreadsheets, databases & business apps	✓	✓
Access data in Private VPCs	✓	✓
Row-level security for dashboards	✓	✓
Secure data encryption at rest	✓	✓
Connect to your Active Directory	✓	✓
Use Active Directory groups***	✓	✓
Send email reports	✓	✓
Embed QuickSight	✓	✓
Capacity-based pricing	✓	✓
Supported regions	Learn more	Learn more

* Trial authors are auto-converted to month-to-month subscription upon trial expiry
** Each additional author includes 10GB of SPICE capacity
*** Active Directory groups are available in accounts connected to Active Directory
**** Sessions of 30-minute duration. Total charges for each reader are capped at $5 per month. Conditions apply.

QuickSight Standard Sign-up

Sign up for Standard Edition here.

Figure 12.7: Setting up a new QuickSight account

5. For **Authentication method**, select **Use IAM federated identities only**, and then select your preferred **AWS Region**. Under **Account info**, provide a unique name for your **Quick-Sight account** (such as data-engineering-<initials>) along with a **Notification email address** that can be used to send QuickSight notifications to you. Leave all other settings as-is and click **Finish**:

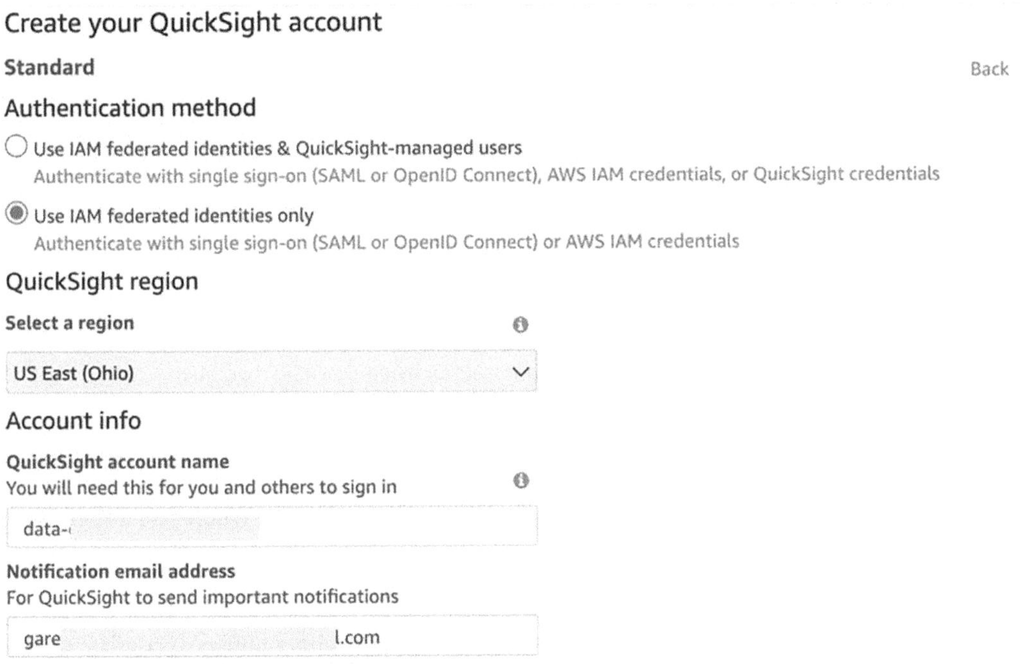

Create your QuickSight account

Standard   Back

Authentication method

○ Use IAM federated identities & QuickSight-managed users
   Authenticate with single sign-on (SAML or OpenID Connect), AWS IAM credentials, or QuickSight credentials

◉ Use IAM federated identities only
   Authenticate with single sign-on (SAML or OpenID Connect) or AWS IAM credentials

QuickSight region

Select a region   ❶

US East (Ohio)   ⌄

Account info

QuickSight account name
You will need this for you and others to sign in   ❶

   data-(

Notification email address
For QuickSight to send important notifications

   gare   l.com

Figure 12.8: Configuring a new QuickSight account

6. After a while, you should receive a pop-up message confirming that you have signed up for Amazon QuickSight. Click on the **Go to Amazon QuickSight link**, and then click through the welcome screens, which provide an overview of Amazon QuickSight's functionality.

7. From the left-hand side menu, click on **Datasets** to go to the dataset management screen. On this screen, you will see several pre-loaded sample datasets:

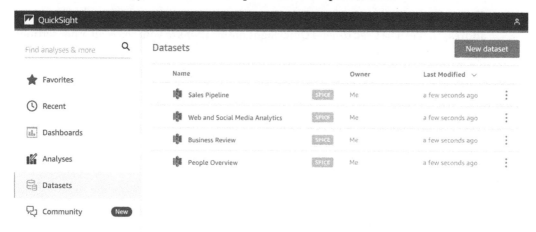

Figure 12.9: Pre-loaded datasets for a new QuickSight account

8. Click on **New dataset** to create a new dataset. On the new dataset screen, click on **Upload a file**.

9. When you're prompted to provide the file to upload, navigate to where you downloaded the World Cities data from *simplymaps.com* (in Step 1 of this exercise) and upload the worldcities.csv file.

10. Once the file has been uploaded, you will be presented with a popup to confirm the file upload settings. Click on **Next**.

11. On the next screen, click on **Visualize**. This will open a new analyses screen where you can create your analysis/dashboard based on the World Cities dataset.

Now that we have subscribed to QuickSight, downloaded our World Cities dataset, and uploaded the dataset to QuickSight, we are ready to create our first visual.

Creating a new analysis

We are now on the analysis authoring page for QuickSight. Using this interface, we can build out new analyses consisting of multiple visualizations and, optionally, containing multiple sheets (tabs). Then, we can publish our analysis as a dashboard that can be consumed by QuickSight readers.

Initially, we will receive a pop-up dialog that enables us to select a layout (with a default of **Tiled**), and to select a resolution to optimize the display. Leave the defaults and click on **Create**.

The following screenshot shows the analysis workspace after importing our worldcities.csv dataset and accepting the defaults:

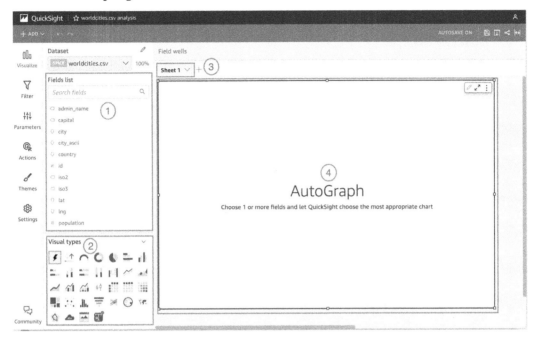

Figure 12.10: The different parts of a new QuickSight analysis

In this screenshot, we can see the following components of the analysis workspace. Note that the numbers in the following list correspond to the component numbers shown in the preceding screenshot:

- A list of fields in our selected dataset (worldcities.csv).
- A list of different types of charts that we can use in our visuals (bar, pie, heat map, and so on).
- The sheet bar, which shows us our current sheet (**Sheet 1**). Clicking the + sign would enable us to create additional sheets (much like tabs in a browser). We can also rename sheets.
- The visual display area. Once we select a chart type and add some fields to the visual, the chart will be displayed here. Notice that the size of the visual area can be dragged to be larger or smaller, and we can click on **+ Add** in the top menu bar if we want to add additional visuals to this sheet.

To create our map of the world showing cities with populations greater than 3 million people, perform the following steps:

1. Click on the **AutoGraph** box, and then in the **Visual types** box, find and select the **Points on map** visual type.

2. From **Fields list**, drag **lat** into the **Geospatial** field well (at the top of the visual-designer workspace), and then drag **lng** into the same **Geospatial** field well. Make sure that you drag **lng** either above or below **lat**; otherwise, you will end up replacing the existing **lat** field.

3. Drag **population** into the **Size** field well and drag **city** into the **Color** field well.

    Your visual designer should look as follows at this point:

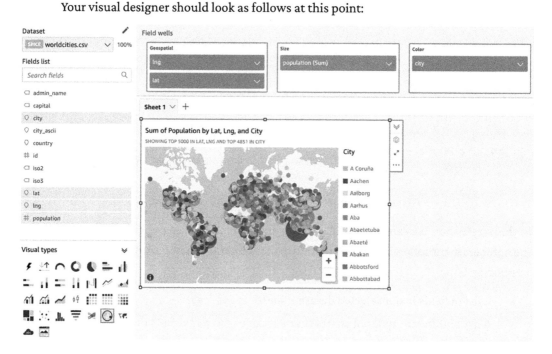

Figure 12.11: Creating a new Points on Map visual

At this point, our visual is displaying population data for all 41,000 cities in the dataset. However, for our use case, we only want to display data for cities that have a population of above 3 million people. Perform the following steps to filter the data to just cities with a population above a certain size.

4. From the left-hand side QuickSight menu, click on **Filter**, and then click **Add Filter** (as shown in the following screenshot):

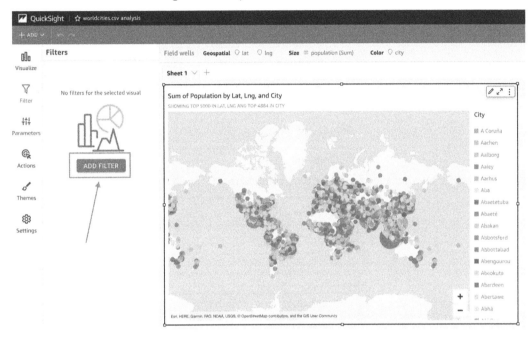

Figure 12.12: Configuring a filter for a visual

5. In the pop-up that shows the list of fields, click on the **population** field. This displays a filters list with **population** showing as the only filter.

6. From the filters list, click on **population**. Change the **Equals** dropdown to **Greater than or equal to** and enter a value of 3000000 (3 million), as shown in the following screenshot. Then, click on **APPLY**:

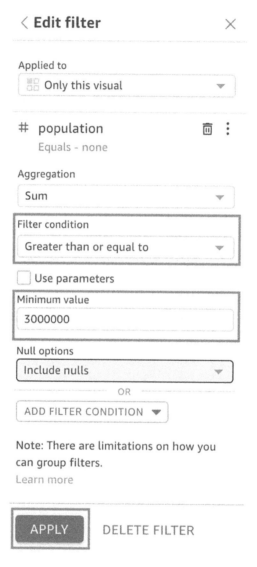

Figure 12.13: Editing the filter for a visual

Our visual now displays only those cities that have a population of 3 million people or more. Note how you can position the mouse over a city to get a popup of the city's name, along with its latitude, longitude, and population details.

You can also modify the following aspects of the visual:

- Drag the corners of the visual to increase the size of the visual.

- Experiment with the visual by changing the filter on population size (for example, change the filter to 5 million people).

- Zoom in and out on the map to size it to display just the parts of the map you want to show.

7. Double-click on the title of the visual to change the title (to something such as Cities with a population of over 5 million people).

8. Click on the **Pencil Icon** (at the top right of the visual) and change the **Base map** to **Streets**.

9. Click the **down arrow** next to the title of the sheet (by default, Sheet 1) and rename the sheet (for example, changing the name to City Populations).

The completed visual now looks as follows:

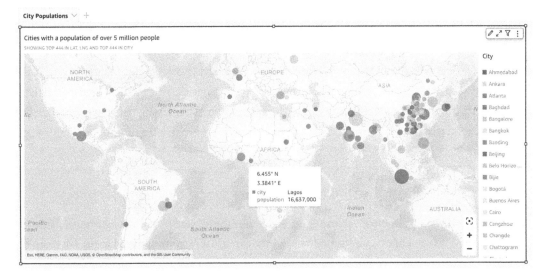

Figure 12.14: A completed visual showing cities with a population of over 5 million people

Let's now look at how to publish our new visual.

Publishing our visual as a dashboard

We can now publish our dashboard to make it available to QuickSight readers.

To publish our analysis, click on the **SHARE** icon in the top menu bar, and then select **Publish dashboard**.

Figure 12.15: The share icon on a QuickSight analysis

On the **Publish a dashboard** pop-up, enter a dashboard name into the **Publish new dashboard as** field, such as World Cities by Population, then click **Publish dashboard**.

Once we have published our analysis, other users in our QuickSight account can access the visual through the QuickSight dashboards tab.

In the hands-on section of this chapter, you signed up for a new QuickSight account and imported a new file-based dataset that contained information on world cities. This included geospatial data (latitude and longitude), as well as the size of the population of the city. Then, you created a new visual based on this data, filtering the data to only show cities with a population of 5 million or more people.

IMPORTANT – AVOIDING FUTURE QUICKSIGHT SUBSCRIPTION COSTS

If you do not intend to use QuickSight after the initial 30-day subscription, ensure that you unsubscribe from QuickSight to avoid future subscription charges. For more information, see the AWS documentation titled *Deleting your Amazon QuickSight subscription and closing the account* (https://docs.aws.amazon.com/quicksight/latest/user/closing-account.html).

Summary

In this chapter, you learned more about the Amazon QuickSight service, a **BI** tool that is used to create and share rich visualizations of data.

We discussed the power of visually representing data, and then explored core Amazon Quick-Sight concepts. We looked at how various data sources can be used with QuickSight, how data can optionally be imported into the SPICE storage engine, and how you can perform some data preparation tasks using QuickSight.

We then did a deeper dive into the concepts of analyses (where new visuals are authored) and dashboards (published analyses that can be shared with data consumers). As part of this, we also examined some of the common types of visualizations available in QuickSight.

We then looked at some of the advanced features available in QuickSight. This included ML Insights (which uses ML to detect outliers in data and forecast future data trends), QuickSight Q (which enables the use of natural language queries to create visualizations), as well as embedded dashboards (which enable you to embed either the full QuickSight console, or specific dashboards, directly into your websites and applications) and paginated reports.

We wrapped up this chapter with a hands-on section that took you through the steps of config-uring QuickSight within your AWS account and creating and customizing a new visualization.

In the next chapter, we will do a deeper dive into some of the many AWS ML and Artificial Intel-ligence services that are available. We will also review how these services can be used to draw new insights and context out of existing structured and unstructured datasets.

Learn more on Discord

To join the Discord community for this book – where you can share feedback, ask questions to the author, and learn about new releases – follow the QR code below:

```
https://discord.gg/9s5mHNyECd
```

13

Enabling Artificial Intelligence and Machine Learning

For a long time, organizations could only dream of the competitive advantage they would get if they could accurately forecast demand for their products, personalize recommendations for their customers, and automate complex tasks. And yet, advancements in **Artificial Intelligence** (**AI**) over the past decade or so have made many of these things, and much more, a reality.

AI describes the process of training computers in a way that mimics how humans learn to perform tasks. And **Machine Learning** (**ML**), which is a subset of AI uses a variety of advanced algorithms and, in most cases, large amounts of data to develop and train an ML model. This model can then be used to examine new data and automatically draw insights from that data.

The difference between AI and ML is not always clear, and people tend to use the terms somewhat interchangeably. AI focuses on creating machines to perform tasks that typically require human intelligence, such as problem-solving, decision-making, and understanding language. ML, more specifically, focuses on developing algorithms and statistical models to enable a model to recognize patterns in data and then make predictions based on those patterns. For example, training an ML model on a dataset that has customer data and an indication of which customers defaulted on their debt, and enabling that model to predict whether other customers may default on their debt.

AI and ML offers a wide range of interesting use cases that are expected to have a growing impact on many different aspects of life. For example, doctors are using ML to analyze a patient's retina scans to identify early signs of Alzheimer's disease. And it is the power of AI, and specifically computer vision, that is enabling advances in self-driving vehicles so that a car can navigate itself along a highway or even navigate complicated city streets unaided.

A self-driving car, as an AI system, makes use of underlying ML models for image classification, object tracking, and route planning.

Large Language Models (LLMs), such as ChatGPT or Bard, are AI systems that enable users to ask queries using natural language on a wide variety of topics, and get comprehensive responses, as well as generate new content (such as stories, poems, or songs).

AWS offers several services to help developers build their own custom advanced ML models, as well as a variety of pretrained models that can be used for specific purposes. In this chapter, we'll examine why AI and ML matter to organizations, and we'll review a number of the AWS AI and ML services, as well as how these services use different types of data.

In this chapter, we will cover the following topics:

- Understanding the value of ML and AI for organizations
- Exploring AWS services for ML
- Exploring AWS services for AI
- Building generative AI solutions on AWS
- Hands-on – reviewing the reviews with Amazon Comprehend

Before we get started, review the following *Technical requirements* section, which lists the prerequisites for performing the hands-on activity at the end of this chapter.

Technical requirements

In the last section of this chapter, we will go through a hands-on exercise that uses **Amazon SQS** and **AWS Lambda**, to send some text to the **Amazon Comprehend** service so that we can extract insights from it.

As with the other hands-on activities in this book, if you have access to an administrator user in your AWS account, you should have the permissions needed to complete these activities. If not, you will need to ensure that your user is granted access to create Amazon SQS and AWS Lambda resources, as well as at least read-only permissions for Amazon Comprehend APIs.

You can find the code files of this chapter in the GitHub repository using the following link: `https://github.com/PacktPublishing/Data-Engineering-with-AWS-2nd-edition/tree/main/Chapter13`

Understanding the value of AI and ML for organizations

More and more companies, of all sizes, are in various stages in the journey of discovering how AI and ML can positively impact their business. While initially, only the largest of organizations had the money and expertise to invest in AI projects, over time, the required technology has become more affordable and more accessible to non-specialist developers.

Cloud providers, such as AWS, have played a big part in making AI and ML technology more accessible to a wider group of users. Today, a developer with no previous ML education or experience can use a pretrained AI service such as **Amazon Lex** to create a customer service **chatbot**. This chatbot will allow customers to ask questions using natural language, rather than having to select from a menu of preset choices. Not all that long ago, anyone wanting to create a chatbot like this would have needed a Ph.D. in ML!

Many large organizations still look to build up data science teams with specialized AI and ML education and experience, and these developers are often involved in cutting-edge research and development. However, organizations of just about any size can use non-specialist developers to harness the power of AI to improve customer experience, financial forecasting, and other aspects of their business.

Let's have a look at some of the ways that ML is having an impact on different types of organizations.

Specialized AI projects

Large organizations in specialized industries make use of advanced AI technologies to develop cutting-edge ML advances. In this section, we'll have a look at a few examples of these technologies.

Medical clinical decision support platform

Cerner, a health information technology services company, has built an AI/ML-powered clinical decision support system to help hospitals streamline their workflows. This solution, built on AWS, uses AI models to predict how busy an emergency room may get on any given day, or time. This helps ensure that the right patients are prioritized for care, that patients are discharged at the right time, and that real-time data is used to create a **Centralized Operations Center** dashboard. This dashboard provides critical, near-real-time information on important metrics for managing hospital workflows, as well as predictions for what these metrics may look like over time.

Cerner has built its *Cerner Machine Learning Ecosystem* platform using **Amazon SageMaker**, as well as other AWS services. As with just about all AI projects, getting the right data to train the underlying ML model is critical, and data engineers play an important role in this. In addition, data engineers are needed to build pipelines that enable near-real-time data to be ingested from multiple sources and fed into the platform. If the pipeline fails to ingest the right data at the right frequency, then the ML models cannot make the predictions that an organization may have come to depend on.

To learn more about the *Cerner clinical decision support system*, you can watch a pre-recorded webinar, available at `https://www.youtube.com/watch?v=TZB8W7BL0eo`.

Early detection of diseases

One of the areas of AI and ML that has massive potential for impacting a significant number of people is the early detection of serious diseases.

A January 2023 article in *MIT News* overviews an AI system developed by researchers at MIT that can detect future lung cancer risk (see `https://news.mit.edu/2023/ai-model-can-detect-future-lung-cancer-0120`). In this article the researches explain how they were surprised that there were lung scans where humans couldn't quite see where the cancer was, and yet the machine learning model they built was able to do better at predicting which lung may eventually develop cancer.

With many terminal diseases, early detection can make a significant difference in the outcome for the patient. For example, early detection, combined with appropriate medical interventions, can significantly increase the chance of survival beyond 5 years for certain cancer patients.

Making sports safer

Another area that AI is having an impact on is improving the safety of athletes for competitive sports. For example, the **National Football League** (**NFL**) in the United States is using Amazon AI and ML services to derive new insights into player injuries, rehabilitation, and recovery.

The NFL has started a project that uses **Amazon SageMaker** to develop a deep learning model to track players on a field, and then detect and classify significant injury events and collisions. There is an expectation that these advanced ML models, along with vast quantities of relevant data (including video data), can be used to significantly improve player safety over time.

To learn more about how the NFL is using AI to improve player safety, you can watch a short video on YouTube from the AWS re:Invent 2020 conference titled *AWS re:Invent 2020 – Jennifer Langton of the NFL on using AWS to transform player safety* (`https://www.youtube.com/watch?v=hXxfCn4tGp4`).

Having had a look at a few specialized use cases, let's look at how everyday businesses are using AI and ML to impact their organizations and customers.

Everyday use cases for AI and ML

Just about every business, ranging from those with tens of employees to those with thousands of employees, is finding ways to improve through the use of AI and ML technologies.

One of the big reasons for this is that AI and ML have become more democratized over the past few years. Whereas AI and ML were once solely the domains of experts with years of experience in the field, today, a developer without specialized ML model-building experience can harness the power of these technologies in impactful ways. And with LLMs like ChatGPT and Amazon Titan, just about every organization can find a use for **generative AI** to improve the productivity of workers.

Let's have a look at a few examples of how AI and ML are widely used across different business sectors.

Forecasting

Just about every organization needs to do forecasting to anticipate a variety of factors that influence their business. This includes financial forecasting (such as sales and profit margin), people forecasting (such as employee turnover, and how many staff are needed for a particular shift), and inventory forecasting (such as how many units we are likely to sell, how many units we need to manufacture next month, and so on).

Forecasting uses historical data over a period (often referred to as time series data) and attempts to predict likely future values over time. Forecasting has been around since long before ML, but traditional forecasts often lacked accuracy due to things such as irregular trends in historical data. Traditional forecasting also often failed to take into account variable factors, such as weather, promotions, and more.

ML has introduced new approaches, techniques and algorithms to forecasting that offer increased accuracy and the ability to take several variable factors into account. AWS offers several services that help bring the power of ML to forecasting problems, as we will discuss later in this chapter.

Personalization

Personalization is all about tailoring communication and content for a specific customer or subscriber. A good example of personalization is the effort Netflix has invested in to provide personalized recommendations about other shows a specific subscriber may be interested in watching, based on the shows they have watched in the past (or shows they have been shown, that they have shown no interest in).

Other examples of where AI is used to power personalized recommendations are the recommended products on the *Amazon.com* storefront, as well as the recommended travel destinations on *booking.com*.

Natural language processing

Natural language processing (NLP) is a branch of AI/ML that is used to analyze human language and draw automated insights and context from the text.

A great example of NLP is the Alexa virtual assistant from Amazon. Users can speak to Alexa using natural language, and Alexa uses NLP algorithms to "understand" (in a sense) what the user is asking. While voice recognition systems have been around for a long time, these generally required users to say very specific phrases for the system to interpret what was wanted. With modern NLP approaches, 10 different users could ask the same question in 10 slightly different ways, and the system would be able to interpret what is being asked.

Traditional NLP technology is different to the new LLMs that have become popular since ChatGPT was launched. While LLMs are very good at responding to a very wide variety of prompts (based on their training on very large amounts of data, and their use of new transformer models), they sometimes may hallucinate (making up answers). Traditional NLP models are less likely to make up answers, but they are also more limited in the scope of prompts they can respond to.

Image recognition

Another area where AI and ML is having an impact on many businesses is through the use of image recognition ML models. With these models, images can be analyzed by the model to recognize objects within them. This can be used for many different types of tasks, such as ensuring employees are wearing appropriate safety gear, or as part of the process of validating the identity of a customer. These models are also able to automatically label images based on what is in the image, such as the breed of dog in a collection of dog photos.

Now that we have reviewed some examples of the typical use cases for AI and ML, we can do a deeper dive into some of the AWS services that enable these use cases.

Exploring AWS services for ML

AWS has three broad categories of AI and ML services, as illustrated in the following diagram (note that only a small sample of AI and ML services are included in this diagram, due to space constraints):

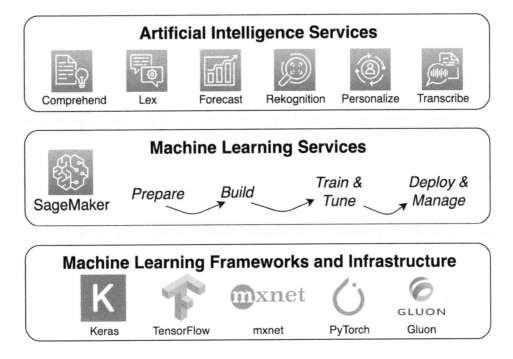

Figure 13.1: Amazon AI/ML stack

In the preceding diagram, we can see a subset of the services that AWS offers in each category – **Pretrained Artificial Intelligence Services**, **Machine Learning Services**, and **Machine Learning Frameworks and Infrastructure**.

At the ML framework and infrastructure level, AWS provides **Amazon Machine Images** (**AMIs**) and prebuilt **Docker containers** that have popular **deep learning ML frameworks** pre-installed and optimized for the AWS environment. While these are useful for advanced use cases that require custom ML environments, these use cases are beyond the scope of this book, and require advanced ML expertise.

> For more information on these ML frameworks, refer to the AWS documentation on AWS Deep Learning AMIs (https://aws.amazon.com/machine-learning/amis/) and *AWS Deep Learning Containers* (https://aws.amazon.com/machine-learning/containers/).

In the remainder of this chapter, we will explore some of the services in the AWS ML services and AWS AI services categories.

AWS ML services

While working in the **Machine Learning Frameworks and Infrastructure** requires advanced ML expertise and experience, AWS makes developing ML models more accessible in the **Machine Learning Services** layer.

In this layer, **Amazon SageMaker** enables users to prepare, build, train, tune, deploy, and manage ML models, without needing to manage the underlying infrastructure. SageMaker is designed to simplify each step of building and deploying an ML model for both data scientists and everyday developers.

SageMaker includes several underlying tools to help with each of the stages of building an ML model.

SageMaker in the ML preparation phase

 Several capabilities within SageMaker simplify and speed up the tasks involved in preparing to build an ML model. We covered these services in *Chapter 8, Identifying and Enabling Data Consumers*, so review that chapter for more information, but here is a quick reminder of these services.

Amazon SageMaker Ground Truth

 The majority of ML models *learn* by being trained on labeled data. That is, the model is effectively given data that includes the attribute the model is designed to predict. Once trained, the model can then predict data where the attribute to be predicted is missing. For example, to train a model that can identify different breeds of dogs in a photo, you would train the model using photos of dogs that are labeled with the breed of dog. Once trained, you could provide a picture of a dog and the model could predict the breed.

SageMaker Ground Truth is a service that uses both ML and/or human curators to label data; for example, labelling the breed of a dog in a photo. This significantly speeds up the process of preparing data to use to train new ML models.

Amazon SageMaker Data Wrangler

The **SageMaker Data Wrangler** service is a visual data preparation tool that data scientists can use to prepare raw data for ML use. The service enables data scientists to select relevant datasets, explore the data, and then select from over 300 built-in transformations that they can easily apply to the dataset, without writing any code.

SageMaker Data Wrangler also includes visualization templates that enable you to preview the results of transformations in **SageMaker Studio**, a full-fledged **integrated development environment (IDE)** for ML.

Amazon SageMaker Clarify

When training an ML model with a training dataset, the dataset may be biased through either a concentration of specific data or because it is missing specific data.

For example, if a dataset is intended to be used to predict responses from people with a wide age range, but the training dataset primarily contains data from people aged 35 – 55, then predictions may be inaccurate for both younger people (under 35) and/or older people (over 55).

The same could be applied to datasets that tend to concentrate on a specific gender, sexual orientation, married versus unmarried, or just about any other attribute. To help avoid this type of potential bias in a dataset, **SageMaker Clarify** can examine some specified attributes in a dataset and use advanced algorithms to highlight the existence of potential bias.

SageMaker in the ML build phase

Once data has been labeled and prepared, a data scientist can move on to building ML models. The following capabilities in SageMaker are used to build new ML models.

SageMaker Studio notebooks

Data scientists typically use notebooks to develop the code for their ML models. A notebook is an interactive web-based environment where developers can run their code and immediately see the results of the running code. An interactive notebook is backed by a compute engine that runs a kernel where notebook code is executed.

With **SageMaker Studio Notebooks**, you can quickly launch a new notebook, backed by an EC2 instance type of your choosing. The notebook environment uses **Amazon Elastic File System (EFS)**, which is network-based storage that persists beyond the life of the instance running the notebook. This enables you to easily start and stop different notebook instances, and have your notebook project files available in each notebook instance.

SageMaker Studio Notebooks also enables users to easily share notebooks, enabling collaborative work between data scientists on a team. In addition, SageMaker Studio Notebooks provides sample projects that can be used as a starting point for developing a new model.

SageMaker Autopilot

For developers that do not have extensive ML experience, **SageMaker Autopilot** can be used to automatically build, train, and tune several different ML models, based on your data.

The developer needs to provide a tabular dataset (rows and columns) and then indicate which column value they want to predict. This could be predicting a number (such as expected spend), a binary category (fraud or not fraud), or a multi-label category (such as favorite fruit, which could be banana, peach, pear, and so on).

SageMaker Autopilot will then build, train, and tune several ML models and provide a model leaderboard to show the results of each model. Users can view each of the models that were generated and explore the results that were generated by each model. From here, a user can select the model that best meets their requirements and deploy it.

SageMaker JumpStart

SageMaker JumpStart provides several preselected end-to-end solutions, ML models, and other resources to help developers and data scientists get their ML projects up and running quickly.

By using these prebuilt resources, developers can easily deploy solutions and models with all the infrastructure components managed for them. Once deployed, the model can be opened with SageMaker Studio Notebooks, and the model can be tested through a notebook environment.

Prebuilt solutions include sample datasets that can be used to test the model, and you can also provide your own dataset to further train and tune the model. Some examples of prebuilt solutions available in JumpStart include the following:

- Foundation models (used to build generative AI solutions)
- Churn prediction
- Credit risk prediction
- Computer vision
- Predictive maintenance

For an example of how to use SageMaker JumpStart to build a custom generative AI solution, see the AWS blog post titled *Fine-tune text-to-image Stable Diffusion models with Amazon SageMaker JumpStart* at https://aws.amazon.com/blogs/machine-learning/fine-tune-text-to-image-stable-diffusion-models-with-amazon-sagemaker-jumpstart/. In this blog post, you learn how to use SageMaker JumpStart to fine-tune the Stable Diffusion model by uploading pictures of a dog, and then having the Stable Diffusion model generate new images of the dog in differing situations (such as the dog on a beach, a pencil sketch of the dog, etc).

SageMaker in the ML training and tuning phase

Once you have built an ML model, you need to train the model on a sample dataset, and then further tune and refine the model until you get the results that meet your requirements.

Training a model is core functionality that's built into SageMaker. You point SageMaker to the location of your training data in Amazon S3, and then specify the type and quantity of SageMaker ML instances you want to use for the training job. SageMaker will provision a distributed compute cluster and perform the training, outputting the results to Amazon S3. The training cluster will then automatically be removed.

SageMaker can also automatically tune your ML model by testing the model with thousands of different combinations of algorithm parameters to determine which combination of parameters provides the most accurate results. This process is referred to as **hyperparameter tuning**, and with SageMaker, you can specify the range of hyperparameters that you want to test.

To keep track of the results of different training jobs, SageMaker also includes something called SageMaker Experiments.

SageMaker Experiments

This process of tracking different ML experiments can be made significantly easier using **SageMaker Experiments**. This feature of SageMaker automatically tracks items such as inputs, parameters, and configurations, and stores the result of each experiment. This helps reduce the overhead and time needed to identify the best performing combinations for your ML model.

When running a training job on SageMaker, you can pass in an extra parameter, defining the name of the experiment. By doing this, all the inputs and outputs of the job will automatically be logged.

This data can then be loaded into a pandas DataFrame (a popular Python data structure for working with data), and you can use the built-in analytics features of pandas to analyze your results. Amazon SageMaker Studio also includes integration with SageMaker Experiments, enabling you to run queries on experiment data, and view leaderboards and metrics.

SageMaker in the ML deployment and management phase

Once you have prepared your data, developed your model, and then trained and tuned the model, you are finally ready to deploy the model. There are several different ways that you can select to deploy the model using SageMaker.

For example, if you want to get predictions on a large dataset, you can use SageMaker's batch transform process. Using this, you point SageMaker to the dataset on S3, select the type of compute instance you want to use to power the transform, and then run the transform job, which will make a prediction for each record in the dataset and write out the transformed dataset to S3.

Alternatively, you can deploy an endpoint for your model that can be used by your applications to pass data to the model to get an ML-powered prediction in real time. For example, you can pass information to the endpoint of a specific credit card transaction (date, time, location, vendor, amount, and so on), and the ML model can predict whether this is a fraudulent or genuine transaction.

ML models can become less accurate over time due to changing trends in your customer base, for example, or because of data quality issues in upstream systems. To help monitor and manage this, you can use SageMaker Model Monitor.

SageMaker Model Monitor

SageMaker Model Monitor can be configured to continuously monitor the quality of your ML models and can send notifications when there are deviations in the model's quality. Model Monitor can detect issues with items such as data quality, model quality, and bias drift.

To resolve issues with model quality, a user may take steps such as retraining the model using updated data or investigating potential quality issues with upstream data preparation systems.

Having briefly covered some of the extensive functionality available for creating custom models using Amazon SageMaker, let's look at some of the AWS AI services that provide prebuilt ML models as a service.

Exploring AWS services for AI

While Amazon SageMaker simplifies building custom ML models, there are many use cases where a custom model is not required, and a generalized ML model that has been pretrained will meet requirements.

For example, if you need to translate from one language into another, that will most likely not require a customized ML model. Existing, generalized models, trained for the languages you are translating between, would work.

You could use SageMaker to develop a French to English translation model, train the model, and then host the model on a SageMaker inference endpoint. But that would take time and would have compute costs associated with each phase of development (data preparation, notebooks, training, and inference).

Instead, it would be massively simpler, quicker, and cheaper to use a pretrained AI service such as **Amazon Translate**, which already incorporates language models trained for this task. This service provides a simple API that can be used to pass in text in one language and receive a translation in a target language. And there would be no ongoing compute costs or commitments – just a small per-character cost for the translation (currently $ 0.000015 per character).

Also, AWS is constantly working to improve the underlying ML algorithms in these pretrained AI services, monitoring data quality, and maintaining the availability of the API endpoints, at no additional cost to you. And if you do need to customize the model (for example, based on specific industry terminology, or a preferred style or tone for the translation), you can provide additional training data for customized translations, although this comes at a slightly higher cost (currently $0.00006 per character).

These types of pretrained AI services have gained in popularity over the past few years, and all of the major cloud providers now offer a range of pretrained ML models that are delivered as an AI service. We don't have space in this chapter to cover all of the AWS AI services, but we'll look at a few of the most popular services in this section.

We started with Amazon Translate as an example of an AWS AI service, so now, let's explore some of the other AI offerings from AWS.

AI for unstructured speech and text

One of the primary benefits of a data lake is the ability to store all types of data, including **unstructured data** such as PDF documents, as well as audio and video files, in the data lake. And while this type of data can be easily ingested and stored in the data lake, the challenge for the data engineer is in how to process and make use of this data.

For example, a large enterprise company may have hundreds of thousands of invoices from a variety of vendors, and they may want to perform analysis or fraud detection on those. Or a busy call center may want to automatically transcribe recorded customer calls to perform sentiment analysis and identify unhappy customers.

For these use cases, AWS offers several AI services designed to extract metadata from text or speech sources to make this data available for additional analysis.

Amazon Transcribe for converting speech into text

Amazon Transcribe is an AWS AI service that can produce text transcription from audio and video files. This can be used to generate subtitles for a video file, to provide a transcription of a recording of a meeting or speech, or to get a transcript of a customer service call.

Transcribe uses **automatic speech recognition (ASR)**, a deep learning process, to enable highly accurate transcriptions from audio files, including the ability to identify different speakers in the transcript and to automatically identify the language of a recording. Transcribe can also detect and remove sensitive personal information (such as credit card numbers or email addresses) from transcripts, as well as words that you don't want to be included in a transcription (such as curses or swear words). Transcribe can also generate a new audio file that replaces these unwanted words with silence.

A data engineer can build a pipeline that processes audio or video files with Transcribe, ensuring that text transcripts from audio sources are generated shortly after new audio sources are ingested into the data lake. Other ML models or AWS AI services can also be built into the pipeline to further analyze the transcript to generate additional metadata.

Amazon Transcribe can work in both batch and streaming mode (although not all features or regions are supported in streaming mode). With batch mode, you point Amazon Transcribe at an audio recording in Amazon S3, while in streaming mode, you send through 'chunks' of the audio that then gets transcribed immediately. Streaming mode can be used for use-cases such as live captioning of meetings or a news broadcast.

Amazon Transcribe also includes functionality targeted at specific types of audio. For example, **Amazon Transcribe Medical** uses an ML model specifically trained to identify medical terminologies such as medicine names, diseases, and conditions. And **Amazon Transcribe Call Analytics** has been specifically designed to understand customer service and sales calls, as well as to identify attributes such as agent and customer sentiment, interruptions, and talk speed.

Amazon Textract for extracting text from documents

Amazon Textract is an AI service that can be used to automatically extract text from unstructured documents, such as PDF or image files. Whether the source document is a scan of printed text or a form that includes printed text and handwriting, Textract can be used to create a semi-structured document for further analysis.

A data engineer may be tasked, for example, with building a pipeline that automatically analyzes uploaded expense receipts to extract relevant information. This may include storing that information in semi-structured files in the data lake, or a different target such as DynamoDB, a relational database, or the Amazon OpenSearch Service.

For example, the following screenshot shows a portion of a hotel receipt bill contained in a PDF file:

DATE	REF NO	DESCRIPTION	CHARGES
4/15/2019	2559498	GUEST ROOM	$179.00
4/15/2019	2559498	STATE TAX	$10.74
4/15/2019	2559498	CITY TAX	$16.11
4/16/2019	2559777	C3 FOOD DRINK	$7.00
4/16/2019	2559811	VS	($212.85)
		BALANCE	$0.00

Hilton Honors(R) stays are posted within 72 hours of checkout. To check your earnings or book your next stay at more than 4,000 hotels and resorts in 100 countries, please visit Honors.com

Thank you for choosing Doubletree! Come back soon to enjoy our warm chocolate chip cookies and relaxed hospitality. For your next trip visit us at doubletree.com for our best available rates!

Figure 13.2: Extract from a PDF document of a hotel invoice

Most traditional analytics tools would not be able to process the data contained within a PDF file, but when this file is sent to the Amazon Textract service, a semi-structured file can be created containing relevant data. For example, the ML model powering Textract can extract information from the preceding table as a CSV file that can be further analyzed in a data engineering pipeline.

The following table shows the CSV file when opened in a spreadsheet application:

DATE	REF NO	DESCRIPTION	CHARGES
4/15/2019	2559498	GUEST ROOM	$179.00
4/15/2019	2559498	STATE TAX	$10.74
4/15/2019	2559498	CITY TAX	$16.11
4/16/2019	2559777	C3 FOOD DRINK	$7.00
4/16/2019	2559811	VS	($212.85)

Figure 13.3: CSV formatted data extracted from a PDF invoice

Textract has been designed to work well with various types of documents, including documents that contain handwritten notes. For example, a medical intake form at a doctor's office, where patients fill out the form by hand, can be sent to Textract to extract data from the form for further processing.

Textract also has advanced functionality for handling specific types of documents, such as the **Textract Analyze Lending** feature that can automate the extraction of information from loan packages, automatically splitting the document package by document type. Textract can also automatically detect signatures, extract data from forms and tables, and process identity documents (such as U.S. passports and drivers licenses). And with a feature called **Textract Queries**, you can enable natural language queries about data extracted from documents. For example, you can enable a user to ask questions such as *"What is the customer name"*, and have Textract automatically provide the relevant answer based on the processing of the document.

Amazon Comprehend for extracting insights from text

We have looked at how Amazon Transcribe can create electronic text from speech, as well as how Amazon Textract can create semi-structured documents from scanned documents and images. Now, let's look at how to extract additional insights from text.

Amazon Comprehend is an AI service that uses advanced ML models to generate additional insights from text documents, such as sentiment, topics, place names, PII information, key phrases, dominant language detection, and more. With Comprehend, you can build a near-real-time pipeline that passes in 1 to 25 documents in a single API call for analysis, or build a batch pipeline that configures Comprehend to analyze all documents in an S3 bucket.

When you call the API or run an asynchronous batch job, you specify the type of comprehension that you want in the results. For example, you can have Comprehend analyze text to detect the dominant language, entities, key phrases, PII data, sentiment, or topics (each type of comprehension has a different API call).

Comprehend can be used for several use cases, such as identifying important entities in lengthy legal contracts (such as location, people, and companies), or understanding customer sentiment when customers interact with your call center. As a data engineer, you may be tasked with building a pipeline that uses Amazon Transcribe to convert the audio of recorded customer service calls into text, and then run that text through Comprehend to capture insight into customer sentiment for each call.

Another use case could be to analyze social media posts to identify which organizations were being referenced in a post, and what the sentiment of the review was. For example, we could analyze the following fictional post made to a social media platform:

"I went to Jack's Cafe last Monday, and the pancakes were amazing! You should try this place, it's new in downtown Westwood. Our server, Regina, was amazing."

When Amazon Comprehend analyzes this text, it returns the following insights:

1. **Entities detected:**

    *   Jack's café, Organization, 93% confidence

    *   Westwood, Location, 71% confidence

    *   Regina, Person, 99% confidence

    *   last Monday, Date, 94% confidence

2. **Sentiment:**

- Positive, 99% confidence

As we can see from the previous results, Comprehend can accurately detect entities and sentiment. At the end of this chapter, we will go through an exercise with Amazon Comprehend to determine customer sentiment from online reviews, which will allow you to get hands-on with how Amazon Comprehend works.

Note that there is also a specialty version of Comprehend, called **Amazon Comprehend Medical**, that has been designed to extract medical information from electronic text, such as medical conditions, medications, treatments, and protected health information. You can also train a **Comprehend custom entity detection** model using your data to recognize specialized entities (such as a model trained to recognize different makes and models of cars and motorbikes).

AI for extracting metadata from images and video

In the previous section, we reviewed AI services for processing text – including audio transcribed into text (Amazon Transcribe), images and scanned documents converted into text (Amazon Textract), and insights drawn out of electronic text (Amazon Comprehend).

In this section, we will change focus and look at how we can extract insights out of videos and images using the power of AI.

Amazon Rekognition

Amazon Rekognition uses the power of pretrained ML models to extract metadata from images and videos, enabling users to get rich insights from this unstructured content.

With traditional data warehouses and databases, the ability to store unstructured data, such as images and videos, was very limited. In addition, until recently, it was difficult to extract rich metadata from these unstructured sources, without having humans manually label data. And, as you can imagine, this was a very time-consuming and error-prone process.

For organizations that stored a lot of images or videos, they needed to manually build catalogs to tag the media appropriately. For example, these organizations would need someone to manually identify celebrities in photos or add labels to an image to tag what was shown in the image.

As ML technologies advanced, these organizations could build and train ML models to automatically tag images (or stills from a video), but this still required deep expertise and an extensive labeled catalog for training the ML model.

With new pretrained AI services, such as **Amazon Rekognition**, vendors do the hard work of building and training the ML models, and users can then use a simple API to automatically extract metadata from images. And, with **Amazon Rekognition Video**, users can also gain these insights from video files. When passed a video file for analysis, the results that are returned include a timestamp of where the object was detected, enabling an index of identified objects to be created.

For example, the following photo could be sent to the Amazon Rekognition service to automatically identify elements in the photo:

Figure 13.4: Photo of a dog and a Jeep in the snow

When passed to Amazon Rekognition, the service can automatically identify objects in the photo. The following is a partial list of the identified objects (with the confidence level of the ML model shown in brackets):

- Outdoors (99.8%)
- Dog (98.3%)
- Winter (96.8%)
- Car (96.6%)
- Snow (90.7%)
- Wheel (87.8%)

A data engineer could use this type of service to build a data pipeline that ingests images and/or video, and then calls the Amazon Rekognition service for each file, building an index of objects in each file, and storing that in DynamoDB, for example.

Some of the features included in Amazon Rekognition include label detection (such as objects, activities and landmarks), dominant color detection, facial recognition (including facial comparison and search), celebrity detection, unsafe images (used for content moderation), text in images, and more.

The AI services we have discussed so far are used to extract data from unstructured files such as PDF scans and image and video files. Now, let's take a look at AWS AI services that can be used to make predictions based on semi-structured data.

AI for ML-powered forecasts

A common business need is to forecast future values, whether these be the number of staff an entertainment venue is likely to need next month, or how much revenue an organization is likely to receive on a specific product line over the next 12 months.

For many years, organizations would use formulas to forecast future values, based on historical data that they had built up. However, these formulas often did not take into account seasonal trends and other third-party factors that could significantly influence the actual values that are realized.

Modern forecasting tools, such as Amazon Forecast, can provide significantly more accurate forecasts by using the power of ML.

Amazon Forecast

Amazon Forecast is a powerful pretrained AI service for predicting future time series data, based on complex relationships between multiple datasets. Using Forecast, a developer can train and build a customized forecast ML model, without needing ML expertise.

To train the custom model, a user would provide historical data for the attribute that they want to predict (for example, daily sales at each store over the past 12 months). In addition, they can include related datasets, such as a dataset listing the total number of daily visitors to each store.

If the primary dataset also includes geolocation data (identifying, for example, the location of the store) and timezone data, Amazon Forecast can automatically use weather information to help further improve prediction accuracy.

For example, the model can take into account how the weather has affected sales in the past, and use the latest 14-day weather forecast to optimize predictions for the upcoming period based on the weather forecast.

A data engineer may be involved in building a pipeline that uses Amazon Forecast. The following could be some of the steps in a pipeline that the data engineer architects and implements:

1. Use an **AWS Glue** job to create an hourly aggregation of sales for each store, storing the results in Amazon S3.

2. Use **AWS Step Functions** to call Lambda functions that clean up previous predictions, and generate new predictions based on the latest data. Use a Lambda function to create an export job to export the newly generated predictions to Amazon S3.

3. Use **a Redshift COPY** job to load the newly generated predictions from Amazon S3 to Amazon Redshift for further analysis.

> Refer to the AWS blog post titled *Automating your Amazon Forecast workflow with Lambda, Step Functions, and CloudWatch Events rule* (`https://aws.amazon.com/blogs/machine-learning/automating-your-amazon-forecast-workflow-with-lambda-step-functions-and-cloudwatch-events-rule/`) for more details on building a pipeline that incorporates Amazon Forecast.

AI for fraud detection and personalization

The AI services we discussed previously are often incorporated into data engineering pipelines as these services are useful for advanced analytics (such as extracting metadata from images, text transcripts from audio files, or making forecasts). However, other AI services are often used as a part of transactional systems, rather than data engineering pipelines, which we will briefly look at in this section.

Amazon Fraud Detector

Amazon Fraud Detector is an AI service that helps organizations detect potentially fraudulent transactions and fake account registrations.

Fraud Detector enables an organization to upload its historical data regarding fraudulent transactions. It then adds this to a model trained with fraud data from Amazon and AWS to optimize fraud detection.

Using Fraud Detector, an organization can build fraud prediction into their checkout process, getting a prediction within milliseconds as part of the checkout process.

Amazon Personalize

Amazon Personalize is an AI service that helps organizations provide personalized recommendations to their customers. Using Personalize, developers can easily integrate personalized product recommendations, marketing initiatives, and other ML-powered personal recommendations into existing customer-facing systems.

With Personalize, developers can design systems that capture live events from users (such as data extracted from a website click-stream) and combine this with historical user profile information to recommend the most relevant items for a user. This can be used to recommend other products a customer may be interested in, or the next movie or TV show a customer may like to watch.

Before we get to the hands-on section of this lab, let's have a look at how you can build generative AI solutions (such as those made popular with ChatGPT and Bard) on AWS.

Building generative AI solutions on AWS

In November 2022, a company called OpenAI launched ChatGPT, a chatbot built on a new type of ML technology. This very quickly went viral and became a world-wide sensation, as people were amazed at the ability of this new chatbot to have conversations on just about any topic. OpenAI explained the abilities of this new chatbot as follows:

> *We've trained a model called ChapGPT which interacts in a conversational way. The dialogue format makes it possible for ChaptGPT to answer follow-up questions, admit its mistakes, challenge incorrect premises, and reject inappropriate requests.*

Using AWS services, it is possible for anyone to create new solutions or services that take advantage of the same type of technology that powers ChatGPT. But before we get into the AWS services that can be used for generative AI, let's have a brief look at the details of the technology behind these new machine learning services.

Understanding the foundations of generative AI technology

The technology behind ChatGPT is a model known as **Generative Pretrained Transformer** (**GPT**), which is based on the **Transformer architecture**, a type of neural network designed for processing sequential data, such as text. This technology is an example of a LLM, which is designed to both interpret, and generate, conversational text in natural language.

A **foundational model** (**FM**) is a model, such as ChatGPT, that can be used as a foundation for building more specialized models and applications. Beyond ChatGPT, there are many other companies and organizations that have created FM (such as Jurassic-2 from AI21labs, Claude from Anthopic, and Bard from Google) that can be used to build advanced AI applications. These models have been trained on a massive quantity of data (with many being trained on all publicly available internet sites), enabling them to respond to a wide range of queries and to handle many different tasks. Some models, such as ChatGPT, are primarily used for text based interactions, while others, such as DALL-E and Stable Diffusion, are orientated for visual based tasks (such as generating new images).

Text-based models can be used for use-cases such as effectively summarizing a large amount of text, answering questions on just about any topic, translating between languages, or generating content (such as marketing copy, stories, or even poems and songs). Image-based models can be used for generating images (creating realistic images based on whatever prompt is provided), detecting objects within an image, or modifying an existing image (such as changing the style of an image, or changing the background).

Both text-based and image-based solutions that use this new ML technology can be built on AWS, as we look at in the following sections.

Building on foundational models using Amazon SageMaker JumpStart

Amazon SageMaker JumpStart (which we covered earlier in this chapter) includes options that can accelerate the process of building new solutions that harness the power of LLMs, as well as large-scale image models. Using JumpStart, you can use either publicly available models, or proprietary FMs, to build new solutions.

When building a custom solution using SageMaker and FM, any data you use to train the model, as well as prompts you provide when using the model, are kept private. This ensures that any data that may be confidential to your organization is not exposed to a service provider, where they may potentially be able to incorporate the data you provided in the training of future versions of their model.

SageMaker JumpStart enables users to easily build solutions using state-of-the-art foundation models for a variety of use cases, such as code generation, summarization, content writing, image generation, and much more. With SageMaker JumpStart, AWS provides and maintains foundation models that can be integrated into your machine learning lifecycle using popular publicly available models (such as HuggingFace, Stable Diffusion, and more) as well as proprietary models that you can subscribe to (such as models from AI21 Labs, Cohere, and LightOn).

For more information on selecting an appropriate model for your use case, see the AWS documentation titled *Choose a foundation model* at `https://docs.aws.amazon.com/sagemaker/latest/dg/jumpstart-foundation-models-choose.html`.

However, if your use case would benefit from a pre-built solution that is accessible via API, instead of building with SageMaker JumpStart, then keep reading as we explore the Amazon Bedrock service.

Building on foundational models using Amazon Bedrock

In September 2023, AWS launched a new service for building generative AI on AWS called **Amazon Bedrock**. This service makes FMs from multiple sources available via an API, providing an easy way for customers to build and scale generative AI-based applications. Bedrock includes FMs from leading AI companies like AI21 Labs, Anthropic, Cohere, Meta, Stability AI, and Amazon.

Amazon Bedrock provides a serverless environment, meaning that users do not need to manage any infrastructure. With Bedrock, customers can privately customize (or fine-tune) popular FMs with their own data, and then easily integrate and deploy these models into their existing applications.

Along with the announcement of Amazon Bedrock, Amazon also announced the launch of Amazon Titan Embeddings, an LLM that translates text into a numerical representation, which can be used in ML applications for personalization and search. In addition, Amazon announced the preview of LLMs for text use cases, including Amazon Titan Text Express (offering a balance of price and performance), and Amazon Titan Text Lite (offering an affordable and compact model, ideal for basic tasks and fine-tuning).

Common use cases for LLMs

LLMs by design are very versatile, meaning that this technology can be applied to many different potential use cases. For example, you could create a chatbot application that makes use of LLM technology and acts like an unhappy customer. You could then use this as part of the training for your call center staff, to train them on dealing with unhappy customers and evaluate how well they handle the "customer."

You could also build a Q&A chatbot that is connected to some of your internal datasets (such as FAQ documents), enabling users to ask questions using natural language and to get answers that come from your official corporate documents.

There are many other common use cases, as well as many use cases that are yet to be discovered. To review some of the common use cases and understand how you can use Amazon Bedrock for these use cases, see the Amazon Bedrock workshop at `https://github.com/aws-samples/amazon-bedrock-workshop`.

Having learned more about AWS services for AI and ML, let's now get hands-on with one of the pretrained AI services we discussed earlier in this chapter, Amazon Comprehend.

Hands-on – reviewing reviews with Amazon Comprehend

Imagine that you work for a large hotel chain and have been tasked with developing a process for identifying negative reviews that have been posted on your website. This will help the customer service teams follow up with the customer.

If your company was getting hundreds of reviews every day, it would be time-consuming to have someone read the entire review every time a new review was posted. Luckily, you have recently heard about Amazon Comprehend, so you decide to develop a small **Proof of Concept (PoC)** test to see whether Amazon Comprehend can help.

If your PoC is successful, you will want to have a decoupled process that receives reviews once they have been posted, calls Amazon Comprehend to determine the sentiment of the review, and then takes a follow-up action if the review is negative or mixed. Therefore, you decide to build your PoC in the same way, using Amazon **Simple Queue Service** (**SQS**) to receive reviews and have this trigger a Lambda function to perform analysis with Comprehend.

Setting up a new Amazon SQS message queue

Create a new Amazon SQS message queue for receiving reviews by following these steps:

1. Log in to **AWS Management Console** and navigate to the **Amazon SQS** service at `https://console.aws.amazon.com/sqs/v2/`. Make sure you are in the same region you have been using for the other hands-on activities in this book.

2. Click on **Create queue**.

3. Leave the defaults for the **Standard** queue as-is and fill in the **Name** field for your queue (such as `website-reviews-queue`):

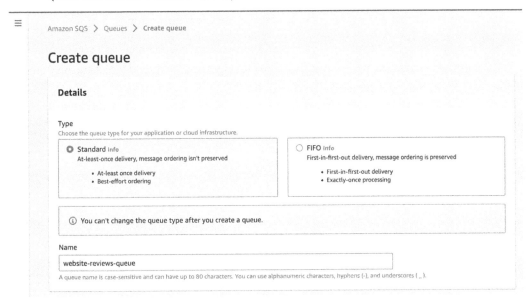

Figure 13.5: Creating a new Amazon SQS message queue

4. Leave all other options as their default values and click on **Create queue** at the bottom of the page.

Now that our queue has been created, we want to create a Lambda function that will read items from the queue and submit the website review text to Amazon Comprehend for analysis.

Creating a Lambda function for calling Amazon Comprehend

The following steps will create a new Lambda function to call Amazon Comprehend to analyze the text that's passed in from the SQS queue:

1. In the Amazon Management Console, navigate to the **AWS Lambda** service at `http://console.aws.amazon.com/lambda/home`.

2. Click on **Create function**.

3. Select the option to **Author from scratch**.

4. Provide a **Function name** value (such as `website-reviews-analysis-function`) and select the most recent version of **Python** for **Runtime**.

5. Expand the **Change default execution role** section, and for **Execution role**, select **Create a new role from AWS policy templates**.

6. Provide a **Role name value** (such as `website-reviews-analysis-role`).

7. For **Policy templates,** search for SQS and add **Amazon SQS poller permissions**.

8. Leave everything else as the defaults and click on **Create function**.

    Having created our function, we can add our custom code, which will receive the SQS message, extract the review text from the message, and then send it to Amazon Comprehend for sentiment and entity analysis.

9. Scroll down a little, and replace the `lambda_function` code, in the **Code source** section, with the following block of code:

```python
import boto3
import json
comprehend = boto3.client(service_name='comprehend',
                region_name='us-east-2')


def lambda_handler(event, context):
    for record in event['Records']:
        payload = record["body"]
        print(str(payload))
```

10. In this preceding block of code, we imported the required libraries (boto3, and json) and initialized the Comprehend API, which is part of boto3. Make sure that you modify the preceding Comprehend API initialization code to reflect the region you are using for these exercises (in the example above, we use us-east-2, which is the Ohio region). Then, we defined our Lambda function and read in the records that we received from Amazon SQS. Finally, we loaded body of rescord into a variable called payload.

    Continue your Lambda function with the following block of code:

```python
        print('Calling DetectSentiment')
        response = comprehend.detect_sentiment(Text=payload,
                    LanguageCode='en')
        sentiment = response['Sentiment']
        sentiment_score = response['SentimentScore']
        print(f'SENTIMENT: {sentiment}')
        print(f'SENTIMENT SCORE: {sentiment_score}')
```

In this preceding block of code, we called the Comprehend API for sentiment detection, passed in the review text (payload), and specified that the text is in English. In the response we receive from Comprehend, we extracted the sentiment property (positive, mixed, or negative), as well as the SentimentScore property.

11. Now, let's look at our last block of code:

```
print('Calling DetectEntities')
response = comprehend.detect_entities(Text=payload,
            LanguageCode='en')
#print(response['Entities'])
for entity in response['Entities']:
    entity_text = entity['Text']
    entity_type = entity['Type']
```

And finally, to correctly print over two lines, we need the following code:

```
print(
    f'ENTITY: {entity_text}, '
    f'ENTITY TYPE: {entity_type}'
    )
return
```

In this final part of our code, we called the Comprehend API for entity detection, again passing in the same review text (payload). Multiple entities may be detected in the text, so we looped through the response and printed out some information about each entity.

12. Then, we returned without any error, which indicates success, which means the message will be deleted from the SQS message queue. Note that for a production implementation of this code, you would want to add error-catching code to raise an exception if there were any issues when calling the Comprehend API.

13. Click **Deploy** in the **Lambda** console to deploy your code.

Now, we just need to add permissions to our Lambda function to access the Comprehend API and add our function as a trigger for our SQS queue. Then, we can test it out.

Adding Comprehend permissions for our IAM role

When we created our Lambda function, we were able to select from a preset list of common permissions to add permission for our Lambda function to poll an SQS message queue. However, our function also needs to call the Comprehend API, so let's add permission for that as well:

1. In the **AWS Lambda console**, with your website reviews analysis function open, click on the **Configuration** tab along the top, and then the **Permissions** tab on the left.

2. The name of the role you specified when creating the Lambda function will be shown as a link. Click on **Role name** (such as **website-reviews-analysis-role**) to open the **IAM** console so that we can edit the permissions, as shown below.

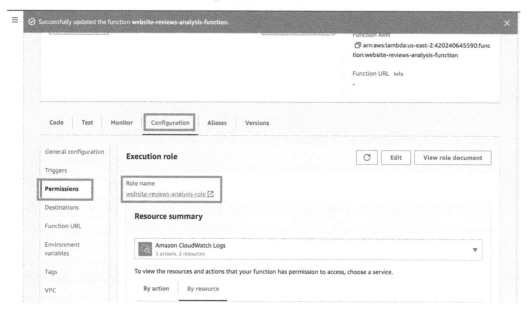

Figure 13.6: Lambda Permissions > Configuration tab > Execution role

3. In the **IAM** console, click on the **Add permissions** drop-down, and then click **Attach policies**.

4. Search for a policy called **ComprehendReadOnly**, which has sufficient permissions to enable us to call the Comprehend API from our Lambda function.

5. Select the checkbox for **ComprehendReadOnly**, and then click on **Add permissions**.

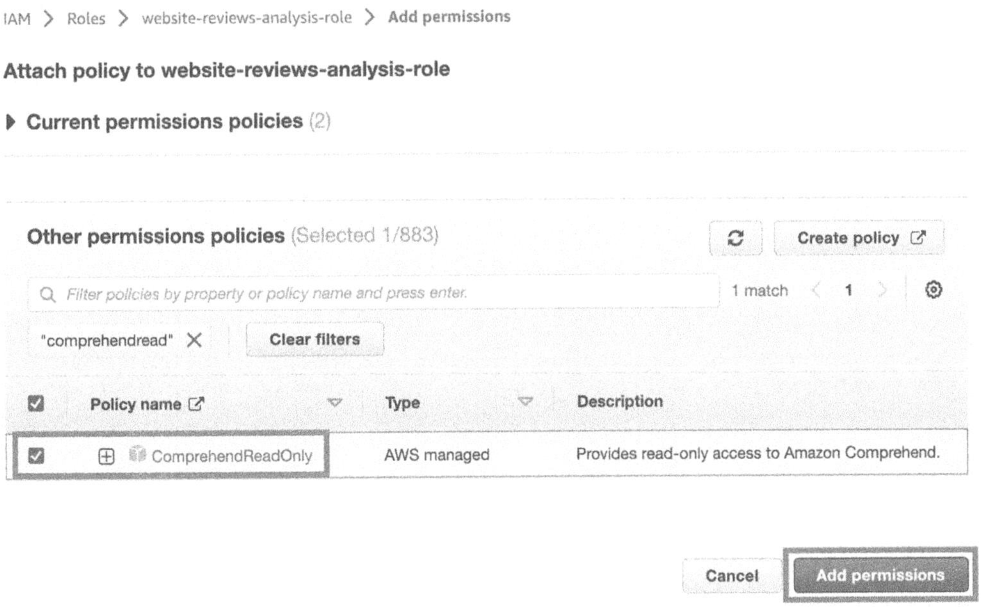

IAM > Roles > website-reviews-analysis-role > **Add permissions**

Attach policy to website-reviews-analysis-role

▶ **Current permissions policies** (2)

Other permissions policies (Selected 1/883)   ⟳   Create policy ⧉

Q *Filter policies by property or policy name and press enter.*   1 match < 1 > ⚙

"comprehendread" ✕   **Clear filters**

☑	Policy name ⧉	▽	Type	▽	Description
☑	⊕ ▦ ComprehendReadOnly		AWS managed		Provides read-only access to Amazon Comprehend.

                                                    Cancel   **Add permissions**

Figure 13.7: Finding and selecting the required Comprehend permissions in IAM

We are just about ready to test our function. Our last step is to link our SQS queue and our Lambda function.

Adding a Lambda function as a trigger for our SQS message queue

With the following steps, we'll configure our Lambda function to be able to pick up new messages that are added to our SQS message queue for processing:

1. Navigate back to the **Amazon SQS** message queue console at `https://console.aws.amazon.com/sqs/v2/`.

2. Click on the name of the SQS queue you previously created (such as **website-reviews-queue**).

3. Click on the **Lambda triggers** tab, and then click **Configure Lambda function trigger**.

4. Make sure that **Region** is set to the region you have been using for the exercises in this chapter, and then select your Lambda function from the drop-down list (such as `website-reviews-analysis-function`).

5. Click **Save** to link your SQS queue and Lambda function.

And with that, we are now ready to test out our solution and see how Amazon Comprehend performs.

Testing the solution with Amazon Comprehend

Using the following steps, test the solution and get Amazon Comprehend to analyze the text you have provided for both sentiment and entity detection:

1. Ensure that you are still on the **Amazon SQS** console and that your SQS queue is open.

2. At the top right, click on **Send and receive messages**:

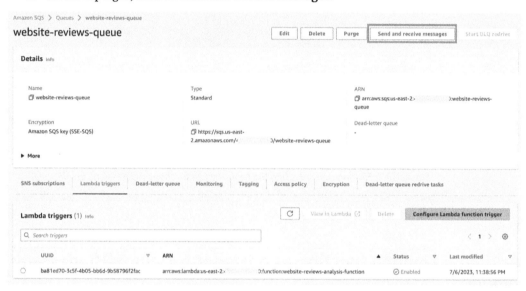

Figure 13.8: Amazon SQS queue detail view

We can now send a message directly to our SQS queue, which will trigger our Lambda function to process the message and send it to Amazon Comprehend. When moved to production, we would build integration into our website to automatically send all new reviews to our Amazon SQS message queue as the reviews are posted.

3. Paste the following text (or your own, similar text) into the **Message Body** section of **Send and receive messages**:

    "I recently stayed at the Kensington Hotel in downtown Cape Town and was very impressed. The hotel is beautiful, the service from the staff is amazing, and the sea views cannot be beaten. If you have the time, stop by Elizabeth's Kitchen, a coffee shop not far from the hotel, to get a coffee and try some of their delicious cakes and baked goods."

4. Then, click on the **Send message** option at the top right.

5. To view the results of the Comprehend analysis, we can review the output of our Lambda function in CloudWatch Logs. If it's not already open in a separate browser tab, open a new browser tab and navigate back to your **Lambda function**. Click on the **Monitor** tab, and then click **View CloudWatch logs**. This will open the **CloudWatch** console in a new browser tab.

6. The **CloudWatch** console should have opened at the log group for your Lambda function (for example, the log group named /aws/lambda/website-reviews-analysis-functions). Click on the latest log stream to open the log, which should look similar to the following screenshot.

Figure 13.9: Amazon CloudWatch logs for our Lambda function

In the CloudWatch logs, you can see the output of our Lambda function. This includes the text that was analyzed, the sentiment (**POSITIVE**), the sentiment score, as well as the three entities Comprehend detected in our text (the hotel and coffee shop names, and the city location).

7.   Go back to your browser tab for the **Amazon SQS console** and click **Clear content** and then provide a negative review for the message body. You can either write your own fictional negative review or copy and paste a negative review that you find via Google. Send the message via SQS and review the analysis results in CloudWatch to see how Comprehend detects the negative sentiment, and see which other entities Comprehend can detect.

After testing and validating that Amazon Comprehend can reliably detect sentiment from published reviews, you may decide to move forward with implementing this solution in production. If you do decide to do this, you could use Amazon Step Functions to build a workflow that runs a Lambda function to do the sentiment analysis. Then, depending on the results (positive, negative, neutral, or mixed), the Step Function state machine could run different Lambda functions based on the next steps (such as sending a negative review to customer service to follow up with the customer or sending a mixed review to a manager to decide on the next steps).

With this hands-on exercise, you got to experiment with how Amazon Comprehend can detect both sentiment and entitles in written text. If you have time, you can explore the functionality of other Amazon AI services directly in the console. This includes Amazon Rekognition, Amazon Transcribe, Amazon Textract, and Amazon Translate.

Summary

In this chapter, you learned more about the broad range of AWS ML and AI services that AWS provides, and had the opportunity to get hands-on with Amazon Comprehend, an AI service for extracting insights from written text.

We discussed how ML and AI services can apply to a broad range of use cases, both specialized (such as detecting cancer early) and general (business forecasting or personalization).

We examined different AWS services related to ML and AI. We looked at how different Amazon SageMaker capabilities can be used to prepare data for ML, build models, train and fine-tune models, and deploy and manage models. SageMaker makes building custom ML models much more accessible to developers without existing expertise in ML.

We then looked at a range of AWS AI services that provide prebuilt and trained models for common use cases. We looked at services for transcribing text from audio files (Amazon Transcribe), for extracting text from forms and handwritten documents (Amazon Textract), for recognizing images (Amazon Rekognition), and for extracting insights from text (Amazon Comprehend). We also briefly discussed other business-focused AI services, such as Amazon Forecast and Amazon Personalize.

Finally, we had a brief look at how you can build generative AI solutions based on Foundation Models, using either Amazon SageMaker JumpStart, or the Amazon Bedrock service (a new service that AWS has announced, but not yet released as of the time of writing).

We're near the end of a journey that has had us look, at a high level, at several tasks, activities, and services that are part of the life of a data engineer. In the final part of this book, we will bring a lot of the previous concepts together and look at how you can build a modern data platform on AWS.

Learn more on Discord

To join the Discord community for this book – where you can share feedback, ask questions to the author, and learn about new releases – follow the QR code below:

`https://discord.gg/9s5mHNyECd`

Section 4

Modern Strategies: Open Table Formats, Data Mesh, DataOps, and Preparing for the Real World

In the final section of this book, we take a look at some of the most recent changes and trends in the data engineering space. We review the emergence of new open table formats, such as Apache Iceberg, that bring traditional data warehouse type functionality to data lakes. We explore the move from traditional data lake implementations to a data mesh approach, and take an overall look at how to use AWS to build a modern data platform with a DataOps approach. Finally, we end the book by reviewing how data engineering works in the real world, with all of the added complexities and considerations that brings.

This section comprises the following chapters:

- *Chapter 14, Building Transactional Data Lakes*
- *Chapter 15, Implementing a Data Mesh Strategy*
- *Chapter 16, Building a Modern Data Platform on AWS*
- *Chapter 17, Wrapping Up the First Part of Your Learning Journey*

14

Building Transactional Data Lakes

In the last few years, new technologies have emerged that have significantly enhanced the capabilities of traditional data lakes, enabling them to operate similarly to a data warehouse. These new technologies provide all the benefits of data lakes (such as low-cost object storage, and the ability to use serverless data processing services) while also making it much easier to update data in the data lake (amongst other benefits).

Traditional data lakes were built on the Apache Hive technology stack, which enables you to store data in various file formats (such as CSV, JSON, Parquet, and Avro). Hive enabled many tens of thousands of data lakes to be built on object storage, but over the years the limitations of Hive became more clear, as we will discuss in this chapter.

To overcome these limitations, a number of new table formats have been created by a number of different companies and open-source organizations. Keep reading to learn more about how these new table formats enable you to build a transactional data lake. The topics that we will cover in this chapter include:

- What does it mean for a data lake to be transactional?
- Deep dive into Delta Lake, Apache Hudi, and Apache Iceberg
- AWS service integrations for building transactional data lakes
- Hands-on – Working with Apache Iceberg tables in AWS

Before we get started, review the following *Technical requirements* section, which lists the prerequisites for performing the hands-on activity at the end of this chapter.

Technical requirements

In the last section of this chapter, we will go through a hands-on exercise that uses Amazon Glue to read data, and write the data out using the Apache Iceberg table format.

As with the other hands-on activities in this book, if you have access to an administrator user in your AWS account, you should have the permissions needed to complete these activities. If not, you will need to ensure that your user is granted access to create and run AWS Glue jobs, and to read and write data from Amazon S3.

You can find the SQL statements that we run in the hands-on activity section of this chapter in the GitHub repository for this book, using the following link: `https://github.com/PacktPublishing/Data-Engineering-with-AWS-2nd-edition/tree/main/Chapter14`.

What does it mean for a data lake to be transactional?

Transactional data lakes is a common way to refer to the abilities enabled by these new table formats, but what does that mean?

Let's start by looking at the definition of a database transaction in general, from Wikipedia (`https://en.wikipedia.org/wiki/Database_transaction`):

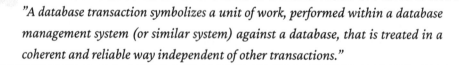

> *"A database transaction symbolizes a unit of work, performed within a database management system (or similar system) against a database, that is treated in a coherent and reliable way independent of other transactions."*

What this means is that you have the ability to update a database in a way that may potentially make multiple updates as part of the transaction, and you have the guarantee that all the individual updates will work and be applied consistently, or the whole transaction will fail. That means that if there are five updates as part of the transaction, and the third update fails, then the two previous updates that had been applied will be rolled back, and the last two updates will not be applied. Either everything in the transaction succeeds, or the database is returned to the state that it was in prior to the transaction being attempted.

This has been standard functionality in traditional databases and data warehouses pretty much since they were invented, but it was not easy to implement that same functionality when working with Hive-based data lakes (although Spark did have some functionality that attempted to emulate this). But there were also other limitations in Hive that were challenges for anyone building a data lake.

Limitations of Hive-based data lakes

Being unable to easily apply multiple updates in a transaction consistently was just one of the limitations of **Hive** that made data processing more complex, with another big limitation being the inability to update rows in a table without having to rewrite the entire table (or at least a partition of the table). Most data lakes are built on object storage, where data in the file (object) cannot be modified. If you needed to update a row (such as deleting a record), you would read the table, or at least the relevant partition of the table, then remove the row, and rewrite the table or partition.

Let's say you have a data lake that contains a customer table, partitioned by state, so that your files in the storage layer are laid out as follows:

```
/datalake/customer/state=new_york/parquetfile.1
/datalake/customer/state=new_york/parquetfile.2
/datalake/customer/state=new_york/parquetfile.3
/datalake/customer/state=new_jersey/parquetfile.1
/datalake/customer/state=new_jersey/parquetfile.2
/datalake/customer/state=new_jersey/parquetfile.3
```

If you have a customer from New York that requests that you delete all records that contain their information, and you want to honor that request, you would effectively need to do the following in your Spark code:

1. Read the records from the customer table for all customers in New York (such as select
   * from customers where state = "new_york") into a temporary Spark dataframe

2. Create a new dataframe that excludes the customer information of the customer that you want to remove from your data lake

3. Write this new dataframe (that now excludes the specific customer) back to the *new_york* partition, overwriting all the existing files in that partition

However, for a large organization, it is possible that they may have many millions of customers in New York State (so they may have 300 Parquet files in the New York partition, and not just the 3 files shown in the above example). And with Hive, there is no built-in mechanism to find out which physical file in the data lake contains the record for a specific customer. As a result, you end up using a significant amount of compute power, and time, in order to just delete a single record from the data lake, as you need to replace all the files in the relevant partition.

In addition, if the update job is running, at some point it will delete the existing files from the partition, and then start writing out the new 300 files. If during this process, someone queries the data lake to list customers in New York, they will get inaccurate results, as only a subset of the 300 files may exist at the time they do the query. Even worse, if two jobs both attempt to update the table at the same time, there is a chance that both jobs fail at some point, and the underlying table, or partition, is left in an inconsistent state.

For a long time, customers that have built data lakes using Hive have struggled with these issues and had to invent complicated processes to try and ensure that their data stays consistent, and to ensure adequate performance. Three companies that built solutions to overcome some of these challenges ended up making their solutions available to the wider community.

Uber created a table format called Hudi, which was adopted as a top level project by Apache in 2020 and became Apache Hudi.

Netflix created a table format called Iceberg, and this was later donated to the Apache foundation and became a top-level Apache project in 2021.

Databricks (a company created by the original developers of Spark) created a table format called Delta Lake. They released an open-source version as a sub-project of the Linux Foundation, but also have a commercial version that is part of their Databricks Lakehouse Platform.

Each of these new table formats provide similar, although not identical, functionality, and we will examine each of these table formats in more detail in later sections of this chapter. First, we take a look at some of the specific benefits provided by these new table formats.

High-level benefits of open table formats

Each of the **open table formats** we will be examining provide the following functionality, although the way they implement this functionality may be different.

ACID transactions

The common properties that are enabled in transactions are often referred to by the acronym **ACID (Atomicity, Consistency, Isolation, Durability)**:

- **Atomicity** refers to the fact that every update contained in a transaction is treated as a single unit. If any one of the updates fail, then the transaction as a whole fails, and any updates that had been applied are rolled back.

- **Consistency** refers to ensuring that reads and writes are always consistent. For example, if a transaction is running and performing a number of updates, someone querying the data must get a consistent result (i.e., not get a result that contains part of the updates only). This means any queries running against a table where updates are happening at the same time must either get results as the table was before the update started, or must get the results of the table as the table is after the update has been successfully completed and committed.

- **Isolation** refers to ensuring that transactions are isolated from each other. This means that if two updates are run at the same time, they must not interfere with each other. One of the transactions must first complete before the second transaction is run.

- **Durability** refers to ensuring that once an update has been applied, that it is permanent (well, at least until another update is applied to change that data). Once a transaction has been committed, all future reads must reflect the new state of the data.

Record level updates

Each of these new open table formats make it much easier and more performant to do updates (inserts, deletes, or changes) to a single row of a table. These open table formats handle the underlying complexities of working at the record level with very large datasets in a data lake. With some of the table formats, you are able to configure whether you want write or read performance to be optimized.

Schema evolution

Schema evolution refers to the ability to change the schema of the table without breaking the ability to query the table. This includes the ability to make changes such as adding columns, deleting columns, changing the column name, changing the order of columns, and even changing the type of a column (for example, changing an *integer* to a *long* data type).

Time travel

Time travel queries provide the ability to query a table as it was at some point in the past. Whenever an update is made to a table, the open table format effectively creates a new version of the table. This enables you to run a query and specify a timestamp, and the query result will be as the data was at the timestamp specified. Alternatively, you can choose to roll back a table to the state that it was in at a prior point in time.

An example of how this can be used is to recover from an incorrect change to a table. For example, if you have a new data pipeline job that performs some transformation, but you discover after it runs that there was some logic error with the job, you can return the table to the version that it was at prior to the job running. Ideally, though, you should have strong change control and testing processes, so this should never happen in a production environment. However, you can use this feature to roll back a table to a previous version in your development or testing environment if you discover a code error during development or testing.

While this is very useful, it does mean that the physical files stored in the data lake end up being larger than the actual dataset (since you have all versions of the data). It also means that if you delete data for governance reasons (such as deleting a customer record because they requested that you remove all their information), it may be possible to still access the data through time travel.

Therefore, each of the table formats provides a method to delete older versions, or snapshots, of a table.

And even though they are implemented differently, at a high level each of these table formats provides the above functionality by managing metadata related to the table, and by managing the layout of files in the object storage. Let's take a high-level look at how this works.

Overview of how open table formats work

For a long time, modern file formats (such as Parquet) have worked by collecting and storing metadata related to the data that they store. For example, with Parquet, different types of metadata is stored in the file, along with the actual data. This includes metadata about the file (such as number of columns and rows in the file) and column metadata (such as the data type stored in the column, as well as statistics such as the min and max values for that column).

Storing this type of metadata in the file enables a process that is reading data from the Parquet file to optimize query performance. For example, let's say we have a table that contains transaction information, and our table has around 20 million rows. The data is stored in Parquet format in a data lake, and is spread over 200 Parquet files. When a query runs and wants to report on transactions that were over 1,000 in value (stored in a column called *amount*), the query engine is able to use the metadata to avoid having to scan the data in every file. It does this by reading the metadata in each file, through which it can immediately identify if this specific file has data that needs to be read. If, for example, the metadata indicates that the minimum value for the *amount* column is 2.20 and the maximum value is 780.56, then the data in this file does not need to be scanned (as we are only querying for transactions with a value over 1,000). This can significantly improve query performance.

In a similar way, the new table formats we are looking at store metadata about the table, and the files that make up the table. Using this information enables them to further optimize performance and also overcome some of the limitations of the Hive format, which we discussed previously.

The exact metadata captured and tracked differs between the table formats, but each format has a way to track the current state of a table, as well as a history of how the table has evolved. Some of the formats also track key statistics for each file that makes up the table. For example, with **Apache Iceberg**, there are Manifest files that store metadata for each file that makes up a table, including column-level metrics and stats that can be used to optimize the query.

In this way, the table metadata will store some of the same data that is stored in a Parquet file, such as the min and max values for a column, the number of `null` values, etc. These details are stored for each file that makes up the table, enabling a query planner (an analytic engine that is querying the data) to identify the exact path of each file that has data relevant to a specific query, without even having to open the file to read the metadata.

With Hive, the analytic engine would have needed to list all files in an S3 partition, and then open each file to read the Parquet metadata, for example. A partition may have had hundreds, or even thousands, of files, and listing every file and then opening every file to read the file metadata could significantly slow down a query. By maintaining metadata on every file that makes up a table, the query engine just needs to read the table format metadata files, and from there it can determine exactly which files contain data that it needs to scan to fulfil the query. Reading the metadata file to determine which files to query can significantly increase performance over having to list all files in a partition, and then individually read the metadata from every file.

Another item that is common between the table formats is the approaches used to enable updates to a file. Again, these may be implemented slightly differently, but at a high level, there are two common approaches for updating tables, as we will see in this next section.

Approaches used by table formats for updating tables

There are two common approaches that are currently used by the different open table formats for applying updates to a table. All three formats support both the **copy-on-write (COW)** and the **merge-on-read (MOR)** approaches.

Let's start with a detailed look at the COW approach.

COW approach to table updates

With the COW approach to updates and deletes, whenever a record is updated or deleted, a new copy of the underlying files that contain that record are created, with the updated data. At the same time, the metadata files are updated to reflect that there is a new version, or snapshot, of the data. These files contain metadata that points to the updated files so that when a query is run, the latest metadata files point to the latest data files. However, the metadata files for earlier versions/snapshots of the table still contain the pointers to the original file, with the older data. It is this mechanism that enables time travel.

Using COW does have a performance impact on updating records in a table (or deleting records from a table) because each of the underlying affected files need to be recreated with the new data. However, it does provide better *read* performance than the MOR approach (which we will discuss shortly).

Imagine that you have a user that purchases from your online eCommerce store every month for a full year, and that you have transaction data partitioned by month. Every month, you end up with approximately 300 Parquet files in that month's partition, and a subset of those files contain transactions for the specific user we mentioned earlier. If at some point you need to delete all records related to that user, with the COW approach, there will be a subset of files in every partition that will need to be rewritten. Even if just one of the 300 Parquet files in each partition needed to be updated, if the average file size was 1 GB, that would still require 12 GB of new data files to be written (since COW creates a new version of a file, rather than replacing the existing file).

COW is ideal for use cases where updates/deletes of records in a table are infrequent, and for where you want to optimize write performance, over read performance.

MOR approach to table updates

With the MOR approach to handling record updates and deletes, affected files are not rewritten when data inside those files is updated. Instead, if a record is either deleted or updated, a delete tracking metadata file is created to record the information about the deleted/updated record. For updated records, the newly updated record is also written to a new file. When a user queries the table, the query engine will know to ignore the records listed in the delete file, and will merge the original data with the file containing the updated data.

With this approach, writes are much faster (since a new version of the underlying Parquet files with changes do not need to be written when data is updated); however, reads are slower since the query engine needs to merge information from the deleted files and the files containing updated records with the original data whenever that table is queried.

Each of the table formats supports a process that you can run that will merge the updates and deletes into new copies of the Parquet files. Therefore with this approach, if you have a write-heavy workload you can use MOR tables to enable fast writes, and then in off-peak times you can run a process to create newly updated Parquet files to improve read performance.

Apache Hudi has supported the MOR approach since 2018, while Apache Iceberg introduced comprehensive MOR support with v2 of the Iceberg table format. Delta Lake traditionally only supported COW, but in a July 2023 blog post on the *delta.io* website, they announced a new feature called *Deletion Vectors* that provides a MOR approach for Delta Lake tables.

Let's now do a deeper dive into each of the open table formats that we are looking at in this chapter, starting with Delta Lake.

Choosing between COW and MOR

As discussed above, there are pros and cons of each approach to updating tables. The following table summarizes the differences between the two approaches.

	Copy-On-Write (COW)	Merge-On-Read (MOR)
Action on record update/delete	New version of affected file is created containing newly updated records, or skipping deleted records	Deleted and updated rows are written to a deletion tracking file, and updated records are written to a new file
Action when table is read	The metadata for the table tracks the files that have the latest data, and only those files are read	The metadata for the table tracks the original file, the file tracking deleted records, and files containing new/updated data. The query engine needs to merge each of these files to query the data.
Optimized for reads or writes?	Optimized for table reads	Optimized for table writes

Figure 14.1: Comparison of COW and MOR

Let's now examine each of the open table formats that we are looking at in this chapter, starting with Delta Lake.

An overview of Delta Lake, Apache Hudi, and Apache Iceberg

The three table formats that we are reviewing in this book all provide similar functionality, as outlined above, but they also all have their own unique features and slightly different implementations. In this section, we are going to do a deep dive into each of the three open table formats.

Deep dive into Delta Lake

Let's start by looking at **Delta Lake**; however, we will not be covering the enhanced capabilities available as part of the paid Databricks offering. For example, Delta Live Tables provides ETL pipeline functionality, but is not open-sourced, so is not covered here.

Delta Lake has become a very popular table format, in large part as a result of Databricks having a very popular Lakehouse offering that incorporates Delta Lake. Databricks has made all Delta Lake API's open-source, including a number of performance optimization features that they initially built for their paying customers. Delta Lake also includes advanced features, such as Delta Sharing, an open protocol for secure data sharing across different organizations. There are also stand-alone readers and writers for Delta Lake, which enables clients written in popular languages such as Python, Ruby, and Rust to write data directly to Delta Lake tables without requiring a big data engine such as Apache Spark. However, while some of the other table formats support multiple file formats, Delta Lake only supports the Apache Parquet file format.

Delta Lake is built on an open-source standard called Delta Lake transaction log protocol. This standard specifies how data transactions should be recorded, and all implementations of Delta Lake must follow the Delta Lake transaction log protocol strictly. This is what enables one implementation of Delta Lake to be able to read and update files that were created by a different implementation.

There are various implementations of Delta Lake by open-source providers and commercial companies. For example, there is the delta-io implementation (`https://github.com/delta-io/delta/`), which is open-source, and there is an implementation by Microsoft called the Microsoft Fabric Lakehouse, as well as an implementation by Databricks called *Databricks Delta Lake*. Each of these implementations has its own additional functionality, but they should all be interoperable.

Advanced features available in Delta Lake

Let's take a look at some of the advanced features that are available in Delta Lake.

Delta Lake shallow clones

Some of the advanced functionality included in Delta Lake includes the ability to create a *shallow clone* of an existing table. You can create a shallow clone of any available version of a table, and when you make changes to the shallow clone version of the table, the original table is not impacted. Shallow clones reference the underlying files of the source table, but track any changes (updates, deletes, and inserts) separately. This means that you can test changes to a table using a shallow clone without impacting the original source table.

Use cases for shallow clones include making a clone of a production table, and then doing testing on the cloned table (such as changing the schema, or other major changes). Another use case is for machine learning state capture, where you create a copy of a table as it was at a specific point in time, using a shallow clone. You can then retest or retrain a model using a static version of the table. The changes to the shallow clone will have no impact on the original table, and changes to the original table do not reflect in the shallow clone.

Delta Lake Z Ordering

While we won't go into the details of how **Delta Lake Z Ordering** works under the hood, let's examine the basic principles of Z Ordering and how this helps improve query speed.

With Delta Lake, you can run a command to reorganize how the data is stored in files, and you can specify that you want to use Z Ordering to sort the data. While standard sorting of files allows you to optimize data sorting by one column, Z Ordering enables you to optimize data by multiple columns.

This is useful if you regularly run queries where you filter the data by a number of different columns. When you run the command to sort the data using Z Ordering, you can specify one or more columns to sort the data on. The Z Ordering algorithm will store the data in files in such a way as to optimize any queries that use those columns for filtering. Note, however, that the more columns you specify, the less effective the sorting is overall.

Therefore, if you mainly run queries where you filter by one specific column, there may not be much benefit gained from Z Ordering. However, if you regularly query your data and filter by two or three columns, then Z Ordering can be beneficial.

When you run a command to reorganize your data using Z Ordering, all the underlying Parquet files are rewritten with the objective of clustering data for the columns you specify in as few files as possible. So if you have 50 files, for example, and you regularly query the data on column1 and column2, if you organize by those columns then queries will need to read fewer files in order to scan the needed data.

For a deeper dive into how Z Ordering works, see the following article from delta.io: `https://delta.io/blog/2023-06-03-delta-lake-z-order/`.

Delta Lake Change Data Feed (CDF)

With **Delta Lake Change Data Feed**, all the inserts, updates, and deletions to a table can be captured in an audit log. This is functionality that can be enabled at a table level, so you are able to decide on which tables you may want to enable this functionality.

There are two primary use cases for enabling Change Data Feed on a table. The first one is purely for a governance and audit perspective, where you want to be able to query all the changes that have been made to a table over time. Note, however, that the transaction log generated by this functionality does not include information on *who* made the change, but rather just records the changes made to a table.

The second use case enables you to optimize operations for performing updates on incremental downstream tables (such as an aggregation table). For more information on Change Data Feed functionality and an example of how this can be used to update downstream tables, see the delta.io blog post at `https://delta.io/blog/2023-07-14-delta-lake-change-data-feed-cdf/`

Let's now move on to our next table format, Apache Hudi, and do a deep dive into this table format.

Deep dive into Apache Hudi

Apache Hudi, originally developed at Uber for their massive data lake, has become a popular choice for building transactional data lakes and has broad support in modern analytic tools. Hudi is probably the oldest of the open table formats; it was developed at Uber in 2016, and its name is as an acronym for *Hadoop Updates, Deletes, and Incrementals.*

Let's look at some of the key concepts that make Hudi different to the other open table formats, and that will help you better understand how Hudi works under the hood.

Hudi Primary Keys

Hudi has a concept of a **primary key**, which is made up of a record key and the partition path that the record belongs to. Using this key enables Hudi to ensure that there are no duplicate records in the data lake (or at least that records are unique within a partition).

Hudi is highly customizable, and this includes the ability to choose from a number of different key generators. Here are a few of the built-in key generators:

- **SimpleKeyGenerator** is used to create a primary key where the record key consists of a single field (column) and the partition path is also based on a single field. For example, we may specify that the record key is based on the *customer_id* column, and the partition path is based on the *state* column.

- **ComplexKeyGenerator** is used to create a primary key where the record key and the partition path consist of one or more fields.

- **NonpartitionedKeyGenerator** is used for use cases when you do not need to partition your dataset. This effectively is used to set the partition path to be empty.

In addition to the standard key generators, you also have the ability to write your own key generator and use that.

File groups

The file layout in object storage for Hudi tables is based on a **partition path**, and within each partition, files are organized into **file groups**. Each file group contains several **file slices**, with each slice consisting of one or more base data files, which are produced at a certain commit/compaction event, along with a set of delta log files that record all the inserts/updates/deletes to the base file since the file was initially created.

Note that the delta log files are used for tables that are configured as MOR. When a table is configured as COW, updates are made directly to the base file at the time of writing.

Compaction

When working with Hudi MOR table types, you need to regularly run a **compaction** process that will update the base Parquet file with all the updates contained in the delta logs, in order to optimize read performance. With MOR tables, any updates to a table are contained in an Avro formatted delta log file (with Avro providing the best performance for writing out rows of data). When you read a table, the base Parquet file is merged with the delta log files in order to return the latest state of the table. However, merging the delta log Avro file with the Parquet file does add overhead to the query.

When you run the compaction process, all updates from the delta logs are merged into the Parquet file so that reads made directly after the compaction process completes only need to query the Parquet file. Of course, as new updates are made to the table, new delta logs are created, and therefore you need to run the compaction process on a regular basis.

Record level index

While each of the open table formats captures metadata about the files and the data they contain (such as column min and max values), Hudi is currently the only one that stores record-level metadata in an index file. With the record-level index, Hudi is able to immediately identify exactly which files contain data for a specific record, and therefore knows exactly which files need to be scanned to resolve a query, or which need to be rewritten when a specific record is updated or deleted (or which transaction log files needs to be updated in the case of MOR tables).

The index does this by recording the details of each record key, along with the relevant group/file ID that contains the data for that record. Again, with Hudi being very configurable, you can select from multiple different types of indexes, or even write your own custom index mechanism. For a more in-depth understanding of how Hudi indexes work, refer to the following Hudi documentation: `https://hudi.apache.org/docs/indexing`.

Let's now move on to a deep dive into the Apache Iceberg format, after which we'll have a look at the current state of support in AWS services for each of these formats.

Deep dive into Apache Iceberg

Apache Iceberg is the table format that appears to be getting the broadest support across vendors, and some industry experts feel it may end up becoming the most popular table format (although all three table formats have their benefits and supporters).

Much like the other two formats, Iceberg has its own metadata format to track the data files that make up a table and, more specifically, to track table snapshots (the state of a table at a specific point in time).

In the directory for an Iceberg table in S3 (for example, `dataeng-curated-zone-gse23/iceberg/streaming_films`) there are two directories. One is the **metadata** directory, and the other is the **data** directory. All the metadata is, as expected, stored in the **metadata** directory. Let's do a deep dive into the Apache Iceberg metadata files.

Iceberg Metadata file

The top level metadata file in the **metadata** directory is a file that begins with a sequence number (for example, the first file starts with 00000) followed by a **Universally Unique Identifier** (UUID), and that ends with metadata.json. Whenever there is a new commit to the Iceberg table (a commit being an operation that ran against the table and changed it in some way), a new metadata.json file will be created, with an incrementing sequence number. So after the first update to a table, there will be a new file that starts with 00001, followed by a unique UUID, and ending again with metadata.json.

We won't do a deep dive into everything that is tracked in this file, but the following are some of the metadata items stored in this file:

- The table format version (the current Iceberg version is V2)
- The location of the table as stored in Amazon S3
- The date and time of when the table was last updated (in Unix epoch format)
- The table schema (a list of all columns, with column name, type, and an ID number for the column)
- Details about how the table has been partitioned (such as which column the table is partitioned on)
- The properties of the table (such as that the files are stored in Parquet format and the S3 storage path for data)
- The UUID of the current snapshot (every time the table is updated, a new snapshot is created)

Statistics for each of the existing snapshots (such as the append or delete operation that was applied to the table, the snapshot timestamp, and the total size of the table and number of records contained in this snapshot)

For each snapshot, the metadata.json file also has a reference to the relevant metadata list file for that snapshot

When a query is run against the table, the query engine first queries the catalog (such as the AWS Glue catalog) to find out what the current metadata.json file is. It then reads the current metadata.json file and can then determine which manifest list file to query in order to read the relevant data. Let's now look at what is stored in the manifest list file.

The manifest list file

The manifest list file is another metadata file created and managed by Iceberg. Whenever an update is made to a table, a new snapshot is created, and a new manifest list file is created that contains a list of the manifest files that are relevant to this snapshot. Manifest list files are stored in Avro format, and the filenames start with a prefix of *snap*.

When the table is queried, the query engine can read the relevant **manifest list file** for the snapshot that needs to be queried, and from the manifest list it can read a list of the **manifest files** that are needed to query the data in this snapshot.

By using a manifest list file that is associated with a specific snapshot, Iceberg is able to read only relevant manifest files, and doesn't need to open and read all manifest files.

Let's take a look at the last of the metadata files, the manifest files.

The manifest file

The manifest file tracks detailed metadata about a subset of the data files that make up a table. For larger tables, there will be multiple manifest files, which enables the query engine to read multiple files simultaneously through parallelism.

The manifest file contains valuable metadata about the data contained in a data file that the query engine can use in query planning to improve efficiency and performance. For example, for each data file, the manifest file contains information about which partition the data file stores data for, the number of records, the lower and upper bounds of columns, etc.

Putting it together

Apache Iceberg is able to read the metadata files (the metadata,json file, the metadata list file for a snapshot, and then the manifest files for that snapshot) and use this to determine exactly which data files need to be read in order to return results for a specific query. For large tables, this can significantly speed up query performance by minimizing the number of data files that need to be read for a specific query. The following figure illustrates the different metadata and data files:

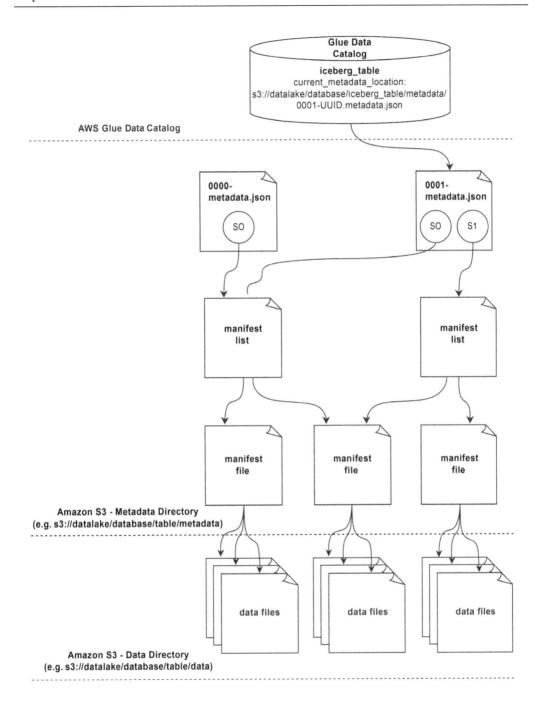

Figure 14.2: Apache Iceberg File Structure

In *Figure 14.2*, we see the following different levels of metadata and data for an Apache Iceberg table.

At the top of the diagram we have the **AWS Glue Data Catalog**, which stores the location of the latest metadata.json file for a table. When a query engine needs to query a table, it starts by querying the Glue Data Catalog for the location of the current metadata.json file.

In the next level down, we see two metadata.json files, which are written to the S3 **metadata** directory for the table. Every time there is a commit to a table, a new metadata.json file is generated containing details about the manifest list files for each snapshot. In the example illustrated in *Figure 14.2*, we can see that the latest snapshot (S1) points to a specific metadata list file. Note that the metadata.json and metadata list files are stored in the Amazon S3 metadata prefix for the table (such as s3://datalake/database_name/table_name/metadata).

We then see that the metadata.list file for a specific snapshot points to one or more manifest files. Multiple snapshot versions may point to the same manifest files.

Finally, we see the actual data files (multiple formats are supported, but most commonly these files are in Parquet format). The data files are stored in the Amazon S3 data prefix for the table (such as s3://datalake/database_name/table_name/data).

By capturing metadata for each snapshot, Iceberg enables time travel – the ability to query data as it was at a specific point in time by determining which snapshot was current at that point in time and then reading the relevant metadata and data files for that snapshot.

In the hands-on section of this chapter, we will get hands-on with creating an Apache Iceberg formatted table and have a closer look at the metadata files and how they change as we perform different operations on the table.

Because Iceberg works on the basis of snapshots, with every commit to the table creating a new snapshot, you can end up with a lot of metadata files, as well as delete files that are used to track data that has been deleted. Keeping this data is useful for time travel queries (where you query the table as it was as a previous point in time), but you generally do not want, or need, to keep all data from the point that the table was created. In order to remove some of the old data and metadata files that are not needed to query recent data, there are various maintenance tasks that can be applied to your Iceberg tables, as we discuss in the next section.

Maintenance tasks for Iceberg tables

There are two primary operations that can be used to clean up your Iceberg tables: optimizing the files that make up the table to improve read performance or deleting old data and metadata files that you may no longer need.

Let's take a look at how Amazon Athena implements Iceberg table maintenance.

Amazon Athena provides the OPTIMIZE statement, which can be used to compact the underlying data files that make up an Iceberg table. When you run the OPTIMIZE statement against an Iceberg table, Athena rewrites the underlying data files into a more optimized layout (this is also sometimes referred to as a **compaction** process).

One of the ways it does this is by rewriting underlying data files to exclude any records that were included in a delete file so that future reads do not need to merge the base data file and the delete file to return relevant results. Instead, the query engine can can just read the base file without having to merge any records from delete files.

The other optimization applied by the OPTIMIZE process is to rewrite files into an optimal size. Over time, as some smaller commits are applied against a table, you may end up with a significant number of small files, which are not efficient to read. By running the OPTIMIZE process, small files can be merged into bigger files to increase performance.

Vacuuming a table

The other table maintenance task supported by Amazon Athena is the VACUUM statement. When you run a VACUUM statement against an Iceberg table, Athena removes data and metadata files related to old snapshots that are no longer needed. There are various table properties that you can set to control how many snapshots to keep, such as vacuum_max_snapshot_age_seconds, and vacuum_min_snapshots_to_keep.

Keeping more snapshots enables you to perform time travel to older points in time, but it does mean that you use more storage space to store those additional snapshots (and this additional space may be a significant amount of space). Therefore, you need to balance how far in the past you need to be able to run time-travel queries against how much storage space the old snapshots consume, and what the cost implications are. You should also consider any data governance requirements when deciding on how much old data to keep versus when data should be deleted.

At the time of writing, the default value for vacuum_max_snapshot_age_seconds was set to be 5 days, meaning that any snapshots older than 5 days would be deleted. This means that after running the VACUUM command using the default table setting, you would not be able to do time travel queries on data older than 5 days.

If you had a use case that required you to be able to query data for the last month, then you could update the value of this setting to be 31 days, and this would ensure that you could always query the status of the table as it was at any point in the last 31 days. If you had a table that was updated 3 times every day, this would mean that 93 snapshots would be kept.

For the `vacuum_min_snapshots_to_keep` setting, the default at the time of writing was 1, meaning that at least one snapshot would be kept, irrespective of the snapshot age setting. If you set this value to 100, and your table had 3 snapshots per day, then even if you had max snapshot age set to 31 days (covering 93 snapshots), additional snapshots would still be kept beyond the 31 days (at least 33 day's worth of snapshots would be kept). Effectively, the `vacuum_max_snapshot_age_seconds` property is ignored if it would result in keeping fewer snapshots than are set in the `vacuum_min_snapshots_to_keep` setting.

The previous two tasks are based on the way Amazon Athena implements the clean-up of Apache Iceberg tables. However, other tools that support the Apache Iceberg table format may implement these maintenance tasks differently. For details of the underlying specification for table maintenance operations, see the Apache Iceberg specification at `https://iceberg.apache.org/docs/1.2.0/maintenance/`.

When it comes to selecting which table format to use out of the three, it seems that Apache Iceberg currently has the most momentum, and is gaining broad support across many different analytic vendors. However, all three table formats have their own pros and cons, and AWS has a great blog post that compares the three different table formats in detail to help you make a decision about which table format may be right for your use case. See the blog post titled *Choosing an open table format for your transactional data lake on AWS* at `https://aws.amazon.com/blogs/big-data/choosing-an-open-table-format-for-your-transactional-data-lake-on-aws/`.

Now that we have a better understanding about the three table formats, let's take a look at the current state of support for these new transactional open table formats in different AWS services.

AWS service integrations for building transactional data lakes

AWS services constantly evolve as new services are introduced and existing services have new functionality added. This applies to the AWS analytic services as well, with many of these services introducing support for these new transactional open table formats over the last few years. In this section, we will look at the support for open table formats in various services, as at the time of publishing.

However, make sure to review the latest AWS documentation to understand the latest status of support across the services.

Open table format support in AWS Glue

AWS Glue has broad support for open table formats across the different components of the Glue service. In this section, we examine open table support in two of the key Glue components.

AWS Glue crawler support

As covered earlier in this book, the **AWS Glue crawler** is a component of the Glue service that can scan a data source (such as Amazon S3) and automatically register table information in the Glue Data Catalog. A common use case is when you have data in an Amazon S3 data lake and you want to automatically populate the catalog.

The AWS Glue crawler supports crawling data sources that are in Amazon S3 in Delta Lake, Apache Hudi, and Apache Iceberg format. When the crawler examines the objects in S3 that belong to these table formats, it is able to recognize the different metadata schemas, and successfully register the tables in the Glue Data Catalog, and correctly identify the open table format type.

For more information about current support for open table formats with the AWS Glue Crawler, see the AWS documentation at `https://docs.aws.amazon.com/glue/latest/dg/crawler-data-stores.html`.

AWS Glue ETL engine support

In November 2022, AWS announced support for the popular open table formats – Delta Lake, Apache Hudi, and Apache Iceberg—in AWS Glue for Apache Spark. With this announcement, AWS Glue for Apache Spark introduced native integration with these formats, meaning that users do not need to install a separate connector in order to work with these tables.

For more information on how to use AWS Glue for Apache Spark with these three table formats, see the AWS blog post titled *Introducing native support for Apache Hudi, Delta Lake, and Apache Iceberg on AWS Glue for Apache Spark* at `https://aws.amazon.com/blogs/big-data/part-1-getting-started-introducing-native-support-for-apache-hudi-delta-lake-and-apache-iceberg-on-aws-glue-for-apache-spark/`.

Open table support in AWS Lake Formation

AWS Lake Formation, which we discussed previously in this book, is a service that enables you to configure fine-grained permissions on data in an Amazon S3 data lake at the database and table level (and even down to the row, column, and cell level).

AWS Lake Formation also enables you to configure sharing of both S3-based tables and Redshift tables across AWS accounts.

The support for Lake Formation fine-grained access controls across different AWS services is complex, with different AWS services supporting different levels of integration with Lake Formation permissions. For example, Amazon EMR 6.9.0 and later supports Lake Formation column-level permissions on Apache Hudi tables, but at the time of writing does not support Lake Formation permissions on Apache Iceberg or Delta Lake tables. And while AWS Glue can read and write Iceberg tables that are controlled using IAM permissions, it does not support Iceberg (or the other table formats) when they are managed using Lake Formation permissions.

At the time of writing, the best Lake Formation support for open table formats can be found in the Amazon Athena and Amazon Redshift Spectrum services. With both of these services you can read data from tables that are controlled by Lake Formation permissions for Delta Lake, Apache Hudi, and Apache Iceberg formats.

For more information on the current state of Lake Formation permissions support for open table formats across various AWS services, see the AWS Lake Formation documentation titled *Working with other AWS services* at `https://docs.aws.amazon.com/lake-formation/latest/dg/working-with-services.html`. Underneath this section of the documentation there is detailed information for each of the compatible AWS services, including a discussion about the support for transactional table formats for each service.

Open table support in Amazon EMR

As of **Amazon EMR** release 6.9.0, all three of the open table formats that we have been discussing are now supported in EMR, without having to manually install additional libraries to the cluster.

However, depending on which packages you are using (such as Spark, Presto, Trino, or Flink) some additional configuration may be required, and there may be certain limitations. For details on how to configure EMR for each of the table formats, see the following documentation:

- Using Amazon EMR with Delta Lake: `https://docs.aws.amazon.com/emr/latest/ReleaseGuide/emr-delta.html`

- Using Amazon EMR with Apache Hive: `https://docs.aws.amazon.com/emr/latest/ReleaseGuide/emr-hudi.html`

- Using Amazon EMR with Apache Iceberg: `https://docs.aws.amazon.com/emr/latest/ReleaseGuide/emr-iceberg.html`

Note that the support in **Amazon EMR Serverless** is slightly different, and requires a different configuration in certain cases. However, all three table formats can be used with Amazon EMR Serverless. See the *Tutorials* section of the EMR Serverless documentation for information on the required configuration: `https://docs.aws.amazon.com/emr/latest/EMR-Serverless-UserGuide/tutorials.html`.

For a comprehensive guide to using Amazon Iceberg on Amazon EMR, see the AWS blog post titled *Build a high-performance, ACID compliant, evolving data lake using Apache Iceberg on Amazon EMR* at `https://aws.amazon.com/blogs/big-data/build-a-high-performance-acid-compliant-evolving-data-lake-using-apache-iceberg-on-amazon-emr/`.

Open table support in Amazon Redshift

Amazon Redshift Spectrum enables you to run queries against data in Amazon S3 and, optionally, also join that data with other data that has been loaded into your Redshift cluster. We discussed this earlier in the book, when we used an example of loading the most recent 12 months of frequently queried data into the Redshift cluster for optimal performance, and then being able to join that with 5 years of historical data that is in Amazon S3. Most queries would be querying recent data, so for the smaller percentage of queries that need to query the historical data, you can tolerate the slightly slower query performance of Redshift Spectrum.

In September 2020, AWS announced support for reading both Apache Hudi and Delta Lake formatted tables in an S3 data lake using Amazon Redshift Spectrum. However, for Apache Hudi, at the time of writing, only COW-formatted Hudi tables were supported (Hudi MOR tables are not supported).

In July 2023, AWS announced preview support for querying Apache Iceberg formatted tables via Redshift Spectrum.

Note that Redshift Spectrum only supports limited write operations, such as insert into, and therefore you cannot update tables in any of the open table formats using Redshift Spectrum.

Open table support in Amazon Athena

Amazon Athena provides a serverless way to query data in a data lake without needing to provision or manage any infrastructure (as we have discussed previously in this book). Once a table has been added to the AWS Glue Data Catalog, Amazon Athena can query and update the data using standard SQL statements.

Amazon Athena provides strong support for open table formats, especially for the Apache Iceberg format. At the time of writing, Athena can be used to read data in all three of the table formats we have been discussing, and also supports insert, update, delete and maintenance operations for Apache Iceberg tables. In the hands-on section of this chapter, we will use Amazon Athena to create a new Iceberg table, and then perform various operations on the table using SQL commands.

When looking to implement an open table format in AWS, you have a wide variety of different AWS services that can be used, and of course you can use multiple different AWS services to work on the same table in a transactionally consistent way. For example, you can create an Iceberg table using Amazon Athena and have an ETL job that runs in AWS Glue to regularly load and update data in the table. You may then have a different team that uses an EMR cluster for their ETL, and they may read some of the data in your Iceberg table. Finally, a different team may have a visualization tool (such as Amazon QuickSight or Power BI) that connects to Redshift and uses Redshift Spectrum to visualize data contained in the Iceberg table.

As we discussed in this section, support for different features of the open table formats differs across services, so make sure to read the latest AWS documentation to understand any considerations or limitations when architecting solutions that will make use of one of the open table formats.

Let's now get hands-on to apply some of what we have learned about open table formats and how they work in AWS. In the next section, we will use Amazon Athena to create and work with an Apache Iceberg table.

Hands-on – Working with Apache Iceberg tables in AWS

As discussed in the previous section, Amazon Athena has strong support for the Apache Iceberg format, and as a serverless service, it is the quickest and simplest way to work with Apache Iceberg tables.

For the hands-on section of this chapter, we are going to use the Amazon Athena service to create an Apache Iceberg table, and then explore some of the features of Iceberg as we query and modify the table. To do this, we will create an Iceberg version of one of the tables we created earlier in this book.

Creating an Apache Iceberg table using Amazon Athena

To create our Apache Iceberg table, we will access the Athena console and then run DDL statements to specify the details of the table we want to create. At the time of writing, Amazon Athena supports the creation of Iceberg v2 tables. Remember to refer to the GitHub site for this book for a copy of the SQL statements used in this section (as mentioned at the start of this chapter):

1. Log into the **AWS Management Console** and use the top search bar to search for, and open, the **Athena** service.

2. Open a new **Query** tab and run the following statement to create a new database to hold our Iceberg tables:

    ```
    create database curatedzonedb_iceberg;
    ```

3. Create a new version of our existing `streaming_films` table in Apache Iceberg format using the following statement. Make sure to change the S3 location specified in this statement to reflect the name of your S3 curated zone bucket:

    ```
    CREATE TABLE curatedzonedb_iceberg.streaming_films_ib(
        timestamp string,
        eventtype string,
        film_id_streaming int,
        distributor string,
        platform string,
        state string,
        ingest_year string,
        ingest_month string,
        category_id bigint,
        category_name string,
        film_id bigint,
        title string,
        description string,
        release_year bigint,
        language_id bigint,
        original_language_id double,
        length bigint,
        rating string,
        special_features string
    )
    ```

```
PARTITIONED BY (category_name)
LOCATION 's3://dataeng-curated-zone-gse23/iceberg/streaming_films/'
TBLPROPERTIES ('table_type' = 'ICEBERG', 'format' = 'parquet')
```

4. Open a new tab in your browser and navigate to the Amazon S3 console at `https://s3.console.aws.amazon.com/s3`, and then navigate to the location that you specified for your new Iceberg table (for example, `dataeng-curated-zone-gse23/iceberg/streaming_films/`).

You will notice that there is a metadata folder here, and in the folder there should be a single file ending in `metadata.json`. Download this file, open it with a text editor, and review the metadata that has been captured.

Having created our new Iceberg table, let's now populate the table with the data from the original table.

Adding data to our Iceberg table and running queries

In *Chapter 7, Transforming Data to Optimize for Analytics*, we created the `streaming_films` table by joining two other tables. We will now take the data from that table and write it into our Iceberg version of the table, before querying both the data and the metadata:

1. Go back to your browser tab where you had the **Athena console** open, open a new **Query** tab, and run the following to insert data from our `streaming_films` table into our new Iceberg formatted table:

    ```
    insert into curatedzonedb_iceberg.streaming_films_ib
    select *
    from curatedzonedb.streaming_films
    ```

2. Go to your browser window where you had opened the **Amazon S3 console** and review the files in the `metadata` directory (note that you may need to click to refresh the list of files). Notice that we now have additional metadata files – the new `metadata.json` files as well as other files (for example, `.stats` files and `.avro` files). These files all contain different metadata that is used by Iceberg to track statistics, snapshots, and data files that make up the table, as we discussed in the *Deep dive into Apache Iceberg* section of this chapter.

3. In a new browser window, open up the **AWS Glue console** (`https://console.aws.amazon.com/glue`), navigate to the Glue **Data Catalog**, and open up the list of Glue databases. Select the `curatedzonedb_iceberg` database and then click on the `streaming_files_ib` table. Click on the **Advanced properties** tab to view some Iceberg-specific table properties.

AWS Glue > Tables > streaming_films_ib

streaming_films_ib

Last updated (UTC)
July 23, 2023 at 18:33:55 | Version 1 (Current version) ▼ | Actions ▼

Table overview | Data quality New

Table details | **Advanced properties**

Serde parameters (0)

Key	Value
	No parameters
	No parameters to display.

Table properties (3)

Key	Value
metadata_location	s3://dataeng-curated-zone-gse23/iceberg/streaming_films/metadata/00001-ec5cdb77-7b7b-4277-abae-
previous_metadata_location	s3://dataeng-curated-zone-gse23/iceberg/streaming_films/metadata/00000-b118a8c2-eeea-485f-8f79-5
table_type	ICEBERG

Figure 14.3: Glue advanced properties for the streaming_films_ib table

Note that the Glue Data Catalog is used to keep track of the location of the current (most recent) metadata file for a table, as well as the location of the previous version of the metadata file. Download the most recent version of the metadata file from Amazon S3 and compare it to the previous version.

4. Let's now query our new table using Athena. Go back to your browser tab where you have the Athena console open and run the following query:

```
select * from curatedzonedb_iceberg.streaming_films_ib limit 50;
```

5. We can also query the Iceberg metadata to view information on the manifests and data files that Iceberg uses to manage the table. Run the following queries (one at a time) and view the metadata results:

```
select * from "curatedzonedb_iceberg"."streaming_films_ib$manifests"
select * from "curatedzonedb_iceberg"."streaming_films_ib$files"
select * from "curatedzonedb_iceberg"."streaming_films_
ib$partitions"
```

In the results of the manifests query, you can see information such as how many data files make up the current snapshot (in my case, it's 127) and the number of records (for my dataset, it is 8,550 records).

In the results of the files query, you can see details about each file that makes up the current snapshot, including items such as record_count and the file size. Note that there may be many small files that make up this dataset.

In the results of the partitions query, you can see details of how many partitions there are. We partitioned our table by film category, and in my dataset I have 16 different categories of films, so 16 partitions.

When we added data to the table, Iceberg registered a snapshot, which can be used to query the state of a table at a point in time. In the next section, we will modify the data in our table so that we can see how new snapshots are created, and how they can be queried.

Modifying data in our Iceberg table and running queries

So far, we have created a new Iceberg table and then added some data to the table, resulting in the creation of our first snapshot. Let's now delete one category of records from our table, and this change should result in the creation of a new snapshot:

1. Go back to your browser tab where you had the Athena console open and open a new **Query** tab and run the following to delete data that is in the *Documentary* category:

    ```
    delete from curatedzonedb_iceberg.streaming_films_ib where category_
    name='Documentary'
    ```

2. Find your browser window with the S3 console and refresh the listing of files in the metadata directory. Your listing of metadata files should look similar to the following:

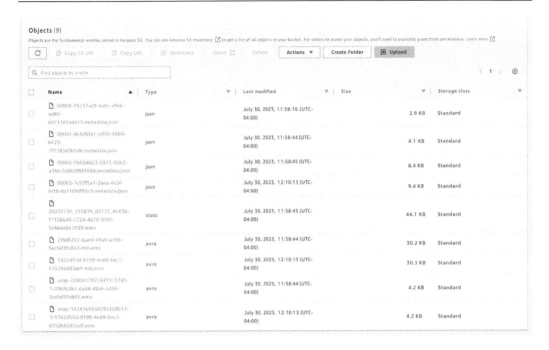

Figure 14.4: Listing of Iceberg metadata files

We now have four versions of the master metadata.json file. If you were to look at the table in the Glue Data Catalog, and examine **Advanced properties**, you will see that the metadata_location attribute now points to the file starting with 00003, and the previous_metadata_location attribute points to the file starting with 00002.

3. We now have two snapshots, and for each snapshot there is a manifest list file (Avro files starting with a UUID) and a manifest file (the Avro files starting with snap). And if you open the most recent metadata.json file, you will find that it lists the current snapshot ID (in the field current-snapshot-id) but has metadata for the current and previous snapshot/s. If you compare the **summary** section for the snapshots, you will see that it identifies the operation that created the new snapshot (append for the first snapshot and delete for the most current snapshot). It also lists the number of records and files that were added or deleted, partitions changed, total data files, total records, etc.

Below is a screenshot of a portion of the most recent metadata.json file:

```
d6ec39.metadata.json        {} 00002-1d77459b-273a-4e6d-adf6-f3c62379a6f9.metadata.json  ×

{} 00002-1d77459b-273a-4e6d-adf6-f3c62379a6f9.metadata.json > {} refs > {} main > abc type
130        "current-snapshot-id" : 1954287477388955304,
131        "refs" : {
132          "main" : {
133            "snapshot-id" : 1954287477388955304,
134            "type" : "branch"
135          }
136        },
137        "snapshots" : [ {
138          "sequence-number" : 1,
139          "snapshot-id" : 8054068847429778299,
140          "timestamp-ms" : 1690137234995,
141          "summary" : {
142            "operation" : "append",
143            "trino_query_id" : "20230723_183350_00145_y5gpr",
144            "added-data-files" : "127",
145            "added-records" : "8550",
146            "added-files-size" : "665754",
147            "changed-partition-count" : "16",
148            "total-records" : "8550",
149            "total-files-size" : "665754",
150            "total-data-files" : "127",
151            "total-delete-files" : "0",
152            "total-position-deletes" : "0",
153            "total-equality-deletes" : "0"
154          },
155          "manifest-list" : "s3://dataeng-curated-zone-gse23/iceberg/streaming_films/m
156          "schema-id" : 0
157        }, {
158          "sequence-number" : 2,
159          "snapshot-id" : 1954287477388955304,
160          "parent-snapshot-id" : 8054068847429778299,
161          "timestamp-ms" : 1690143975094,
162          "summary" : {
163            "operation" : "delete",
164            "trino_query_id" : "20230723_202612_00037_gpms6",
165            "deleted-data-files" : "11",
166            "deleted-records" : "558",
167            "removed-files-size" : "54404",
168            "changed-partition-count" : "1",
169            "total-records" : "7992",
170            "total-files-size" : "611350",
171            "total-data-files" : "116",

                          Ln 134, Col 24   Spaces: 2   UTF-8   LF   {} JSON
```

Figure 14.5: Most recent metadata.json file

The metadata file allows a query engine to identify which snapshot contains the latest state of data and to find the relevant manifest list files needed to query the latest state of data.

4. If you query the Iceberg metadata, such as by querying the partitions, you will see that there are now 15 partitions, where previously you had 16 partitions. Run the following query to list the Iceberg metadata for partitions, and note how the *Documentary* partition is no longer listed:

```
select * from "curatedzonedb_iceberg"."streaming_films_
ib$partitions"
```

If we now query the manifest files, we will see that just the most recent manifest file is listed, and this contains data about the current snapshot:

```
select * from "curatedzonedb_iceberg"."streaming_films_ib$manifests"
```

5. Examine the results and notice that there are columns that provide information about the snapshot, such as the number of files, number of records, number of deleted files (which track data that has been deleted), number of deleted rows, etc.

6. Another special Iceberg query that we can run in Athena is a query that shows us all our **snapshots**. Use the following query statement to display a history of snapshots:

```
select * from "curatedzonedb_iceberg"."streaming_films_ib$history"
```

We should have two snapshots listed here. The first one is the original snapshot from when we added data to our table. The second snapshot (the one that shows a snapshot parent_id) is from when we deleted the Documentary category from our data.

7. Remember that with Iceberg, data is not physically deleted from files until you run table maintenance operations (as we discussed earlier in this chapter). This enables us to run a query that references a previous snapshot. Run the following **time travel** query, but **make sure to change the timestamp to a time prior to when you deleted the data** for the Documentary category. Note that the timestamp used in this query is specified in the UTC timezone, so make sure to specify a time **in the UTC timezone** for before you deleted the Documentary category. You can use the output of the previous command (the history query) to see the UTC timestamp for when the second snapshot was created, and then modify the query below to specify a timestamp between the first and second snapshots:

```
SELECT * FROM "curatedzonedb_iceberg"."streaming_films_ib" FOR
TIMESTAMP AS OF TIMESTAMP '2023-07-23 19:00:00 UTC' where category_
name = 'Documentary'
```

If you selected an appropriate time, you should find that you received results that showed all the movies in the Documentary category.

We can now move on to looking at the maintenance activities for Iceberg tables.

Iceberg table maintenance tasks

Over time, your Iceberg tables can end up using significantly more storage than the actual size of the current data. That is because with the snapshot approach, all data is kept forever ... or at least until you run table maintenance tasks.

In the hands-on section of this chapter, we created a new table, inserted data into the table, and then deleted the data for a specific category. However, as we saw with the last query, we can specify a timestamp and query the table as it was prior to the deletion, demonstrating that all the data still exists.

In this section, we are going to run two table maintenance tasks. First, we will **optimize** the data layout by creating a new snapshot with the files reorganized in an optimized format. After that, we will run a **vacuum** command to delete older snapshots.

Before we do this, let's check on the size of our table in S3 as it currently is:

1. Open your browser window where you have the **Amazon S3** console.

2. Navigate to your `curated-zone` bucket, then to the folder for your `iceberg` database. For example, `dataeng-curated-zone-gse23/iceberg`.

3. Select the `streaming_films` prefix and then click on **Actions / Calculate total size**. Make a note of the number of files and size of data. For my dataset, I have 136 objects with a total size of 789 KB.

Optimizing the table layout

We firstly use the `OPTIMIZE` command to create a new snapshot of our data, but this time we ensure that the physical files in S3 are optimized. This covers items such as merging smaller files into larger files and merging delete files (which contain information on data that has been deleted) into the underlying base files:

1. Open your browser window where you have the **Amazon Athena** console.

2. Before we run the optimization process against our Iceberg table, let's first look at the file metadata for our table to understand how our data is distributed across files. Execute the following statement in a query window. This lists the files that make up our current snapshot:

```
select * from "curatedzonedb_iceberg"."streaming_films_ib$files"
```

For my dataset, I have 116 files listed. Some of these files only have a single record, while others may have 100's of records.

3. In this step, we are going to optimize our table (sometimes also referred to as a compaction process) which involves merging small files into bigger files, and merging delete data into the underlying base files. Refer to the section earlier in this chapter titled *Maintenance tasks for Iceberg tables* for more details on how the OPTIMIZE statement works:

```
OPTIMIZE curatedzonedb_iceberg.streaming_films_ib REWRITE DATA USING
BIN_PACK
```

Note that Athena is not always consistent with where it allows database or table names to be quoted. For example, when querying metadata, such as by adding $files to the table name as we did in *Step 2*, you must have the table name in quotes. However, with the OPTIMIZE statement, if you put the database and table names in quotes, the query may not run and you will receive a confusing error indicating that OPTIMIZE is not a valid command.

Let's run the query to list file metadata for the current snapshot to determine whether our files are now more optimized:

```
select * from "curatedzonedb_iceberg"."streaming_films_ib$files"
```

For my dataset, I now have 15 files listed, one for each category of data. Recall that I started with 16 categories, but deleted the Documentary category, so I now have 15 categories, with all data for a category in a single file. This is a significant optimization from the 116 files that contained the data prior to this step. Each file is of course larger, with a higher record count (no more files with just 1 or 2 records in it), and this is optimized for querying.

We have now optimized the table so that when queries run against the most recent snapshot, the queries will be optimized for performance. However, all the data files for the previous snapshots are still there, as is the data for the deleted category. Go back to the S3 console and calculate total size for your streaming_films prefix. For my dataset, I now have 155 objects (compared to 136 prior to running the optimize) and total size is now 1 MB.

Reducing disk space by deleting snapshots

If we want to actually delete the data from storage (thereby reducing the size of data in S3), we can run a VACUUM operation, as we discussed earlier in this chapter. Let's take a look at how to run a VACUUM on our table in order to remove deleted data, and older snapshots:

1. Open your browser window where you have the **Amazon Athena** console.

2.   Re-run the query to list the snapshot history for your table:

```
select * from "curatedzonedb_iceberg"."streaming_films_ib$history"
```

We should now have three snapshots listed. One from when we inserted data into the table, a second one from when we deleted the Documentary category data, and a third snapshot resulting from running the OPTIMIZE command.

3.   When we run the VACUUM command, we clean up old snapshots based on the value set in two table properties, as we discussed in the *Maintenance tasks for Iceberg tables* section earlier in this chapter. The defaults are to keep at least 1 snapshot and to keep at most 5 days worth of snapshots. If we want to delete the original snapshot that included the data on the Documentary category (which will reduce the size of data in S3) we should set the vacuum_max_snapshot_age_seconds property to have a much shorter duration. In the statement below, we change this value to be just 60 seconds, but because we have the default value of vacuum_min_snapshots_to_keep set to 1, this will result in the oldest snapshots being deleted but will ensure that just the latest is kept.

4.   Execute the following statement to modify the relevant table property:

```
ALTER TABLE curatedzonedb_iceberg.streaming_films_ib SET
TBLPROPERTIES (
  'vacuum_max_snapshot_age_seconds'='60'
)
```

5.   To confirm that this setting was successfully applied, run the following command to show the table properties:

```
SHOW TBLPROPERTIES curatedzonedb_iceberg.streaming_films_ib
```

Note that Athena is not always consistent with where it allows database or table names to be quoted. For example, when querying metadata, such as by adding $history to the table name as we did in *Step 2*, you must have the table name in quotes. However, with the SHOW TBLPROPERTIES statement, if you put the database and table names in quotes, the query may not run and you will receive an error indicating the command is invalid.

Let's now run the VACUUM command, which will result in only our most recent, optimized snapshot being kept:

```
VACUUM curatedzonedb_iceberg.streaming_films_ib
```

After running this command, we should only have one snapshot remaining (which you can confirm by running the $history query), and any files that were used only by the original snapshot (such as files containing data on the Documentary category) will have been deleted.

If we now re-run **Calculate total size** on the streaming_files prefix in Amazon S3, we should see fewer files, and a smaller total size. For my dataset, after running the VACUUM statement the number of files in the streaming_films prefix went down to 27 objects, and the total size down to 273 KB.

In the hands-on activity for this chapter, we used Amazon Athena to work with Apache Iceberg tables. We created a new table, inserted data, updated the table by deleting some data, and then optimized and vacuumed the table. As we went through that process, we examined how this changed the underlying metadata that Apache Iceberg uses to track the table state.

Summary

In this chapter, we looked at how new open table formats are helping to solve some of the challenges experienced with traditional data lakes. This includes challenges around updating data at the record level, ensuring that users can consistently query a table even while it is being updated, managing changes to the underlying table schema, and more.

We did a deep dive into how three popular new table formats – Delta Lake, Apache Hive, and Apache Iceberg – use metadata to manage tables consistently and to provide advanced features such as the ability to query a table as it was at a point in the past (commonly referred to as time travel queries). We then examined how different AWS analytical services support different table formats, and even different features of those table formats.

Finally, we used the Amazon Athena service to get hands-on with working with Apache Iceberg, one of the most popular of the new table formats. After creating a new Apache Iceberg formatted table we did a number of operations on the table (such as inserting and deleting data), and also looked at how to perform table maintenance activities.

The new table formats we discussed in this chapter are having a big impact on the ability to treat a data lake more like a traditional data warehouse, and it is becoming increasingly popular to use these table formats when building new data lakes. However, there are other trends we have seen over the last few years that are having an impact on how organizations work across the multiple data lakes that may end up being created. And these trends are also leading to a new strategy where different teams in an organization own their own data lakes, rather than attempting to centralize all data. This new approach is often referred to as a data mesh approach, and we will do a deep dive into what a data mesh is in the next chapter.

Learn more on Discord

To join the Discord community for this book – where you can share feedback, ask questions to the author, and learn about new releases – follow the QR code below:

`https://discord.gg/9s5mHNyECd`

15

Implementing a Data Mesh Strategy

The original definition of a data lake, which first appeared in a blog post by James Dixon in 2010 (see `https://jamesdixon.wordpress.com/2010/10/14/pentaho-hadoop-and-data-lakes/`), was as follows:

> *If you think of a datamart as a store of bottled water – cleansed and packaged and structured for easy consumption – the data lake is a large body of water in a more natural state. The contents of the data lake stream in from a source to fill the lake, and various users of the lake can come to examine, dive in, or take samples.*

In his vision of what a data lake would be, Dixon imagined that a data lake would be fed by a single source of data, containing the raw data from a system (so not pre-aggregated like you would have with a traditional data warehouse). He imagined that you may then have multiple data lakes for different source systems, but that these would be somewhat isolated.

Of course, new terms and ideas often seem to take on a life of their own and regularly don't end up looking like the original vision of the creator. And that is true of data lakes, as what happened in the decade between 2010 – 2020 was that many organizations attempted to build centralized data lakes that would contain data from across the organization.

There were of course different implementations and approaches to data lakes, but it was common for an organization to set up a central data engineering team that would become responsible for collecting and processing data into a data lake. Raw data would be collected from across the organization, and a central data engineering team would be responsible for running transformations on the data to further enrich it and to join data across diverse systems. Different lines of business would then make requests to the central data engineering team for new types of transforms or new data sources they wanted to be ingested into the lake.

This approach was common for a long time, but had some significant limitations, as we will discuss in this chapter. In this chapter, we will also introduce a new approach to data lakes that has become popular over the past few years, with a concept known as a data mesh. Specifically, we cover the following topics in this chapter:

- What is a data mesh?
- Challenges that a data mesh approach attempts to resolve
- The organizational and technical challenges of building a data mesh
- AWS services that help enable a data mesh approach
- A sample architecture for a data mesh on AWS
- Hands-on – Implementing a data mesh approach on AWS

Before we get started, review the following *Technical requirements* section, which lists the prerequisites for performing the hands-on activity at the end of this chapter.

Technical requirements

In the last section of this chapter, we will go through a hands-on exercise that uses Amazon DataZone to implement a basic data mesh approach.

As with the other hands-on activities in this book, if you have access to an administrator user in your AWS account, you should have the permissions needed to complete these activities.

You can access more information about running the exercises in this chapter using the following link: `https://github.com/PacktPublishing/Data-Engineering-with-AWS-2nd-edition/tree/main/Chapter15`

What is a data mesh?

The concept of a **data mesh** was introduced around 2019 by Zhamak Dehghani, who at the time was a consultant for a company called ThoughtWorks. The data mesh architecture was built around four principles:

- Domain-oriented, decentralized data ownership
- Data as a product
- Self-service data infrastructure as a platform
- Federated computational governance

Over time, as with data lakes, the term began to mean different things to different people. Some organizations would claim they had implemented a data mesh because they had enabled data sharing between multiple data lakes, while others would go all in with organizational change, in addition to building technology stacks to support a data mesh.

I believe that it is okay for a term to evolve and change, but that does mean that when someone uses a term such as data mesh, you need to ask them exactly what that means to them. If someone defines a data mesh as the ability to share data between multiple data lakes or analytical systems, then that is fine, as long as you understand their limited definition. Other people you speak to may define their data mesh as an organization-wide program that is intended to modify their approach to how data is produced, transformed, and consumed, in a way that involves both organizational (people, process, culture) changes and technology changes. The second definition is closer to what Dehghani envisioned for a data mesh.

In this chapter, we will dig deeper into the original intention for the data mesh, mostly following the concept as defined by Dehghani. In the original blog posts about the data mesh concept (`https://martinfowler.com/articles/data-monolith-to-mesh.html`), Dehghani made it clear that she was not proposing a data mesh as a technical solution. Rather, she defined the data mesh as an approach for how to organize responsibilities around analytical data, and the fundamental requirements that needed to be in place to gain maximum value for analytical data across an organization. So, as we start to look at the four principles that Dehghani defined for building a data mesh, remember that these are approaches, and not technical solutions or designs. Later in this chapter, we will review potential architectures for building a data mesh on AWS.

Let's dive into the four principles for a data mesh, starting with domain-oriented, decentralized ownership.

Domain-oriented, decentralized data ownership

This first principle is around organization structure and who is responsible for creating the analytics data that is developed out of the transactional data that runs the business. A core idea with a data mesh, in the way that Dehghani laid it out, is that you no longer attempt to have a central team that collects and processes all the analytical data for an organization. It is important that transactional and analytical data responsibilities and ownership instead be defined in terms of business domains.

If we use an example of a company that streams music (such as Spotify, Amazon Music, or Apple Music), then there may be a business domain responsible for managing users/customers, and a separate domain for managing the music catalog (in addition to many other domains for items like partners, playlists, etc.). Based on the modern microservices approach to application development, each of these teams is likely to be responsible for creating APIs for managing their domain (such as creating a new user, or adding a new song to the catalog), and will also own the transactional data that they generate (the user database, or the song catalog database).

With a traditional approach, a centralized data engineering team may have worked with these teams to ingest their data into a central data lake, and the centralized team would also be responsible for performing various ETL-related tasks (cleaning data, ensuring data quality, reacting to schema changes, joining across different datasets, etc.).

However, with a data mesh approach, one of the core principles is that analytical data is now also domain-oriented and decentralized. There is no longer a central team that collects data from across domains in order to process the data for analytics, but rather each domain becomes responsible for not only their transactional data and related APIs, but also for creating an analytical set of data for their domain. For example, the music catalog team creates an analytical dataset that groups all artists in the catalog by the country where their music is published, and the user team creates a cleaned, master list of all users, as well as a dataset showing the number of users per country.

Each team supporting a specific business domain works independently (in other words, analytical data is decentralized), but, as we discuss later, there is a central governance team that helps to ensure standards and controls for data that is part of the data mesh.

Let's now look at the second principle for developing a data mesh, and that is around treating analytics datasets produced by a domain team as a *data product*.

Data as a product

Along with this new approach of having decentralized, domain-oriented teams creating analytical data, there comes a concept of treating the data that is created as a product. Much as a team may create a software product, in the data mesh world, the team will create a **data product**.

When you create a software product, you are responsible for knowing who your customers are and what they want, and for delivering a high-quality product that is well documented, easily accessible, reliable, regularly updated, etc. You need to apply the same type of thinking to building a data product.

For example, the team that owns the music catalog may also have data related to streams of each song in the catalog. They also know that identifying the top 20 streamed songs for each day, month, and year is useful to other teams in the organization (such as the marketing team). As a result, the music catalog team creates three new tables in the data lake – top daily songs, top monthly songs, and top songs of the year so far.

Other parts of the business rely on having access to this aggregated data on top streaming songs, and it is the responsibility of the music catalog team to ensure that they deliver this data on time. Dehghani outlined some of the attributes, or properties, that a data product should have, including:

- **Discoverability and accessibility** (ability for other teams in the business to discover that the dataset exists and learn how to access it, or request access to the data)
- **Security** (the data should only be accessible to people who have a right to access it, and ideally there should be fine-grained access controls in place so that some people may be able to see all columns, while others will have a limited view)
- **Understandability** (data consumers should be able to understand the data, such as what data is stored in each column and how that data is defined for the business. Additional documentation may also provide examples of how to use the data, etc.)

Other aspects of data product thinking include agreeing on an **SLA (Service Level Agreement)** for your data product, which sets expectations between the data producer and data consumer around both the quality of the data and the timeliness of the data being updated. You should also have a cross-domain governance team that defines some standards for data products, such as agreement on a date format used in all analytical products, or data types for specific fields.

One of the recommendations for implementing this approach for the creation of data products is to create a new role in each domain team for a **data product manager**/owner. Much as each software product has one or more people that are product managers, responsible for understanding customer requirements, setting the roadmap, and delivering a high-quality product, the same can be applied to the data product. Specifically tasking someone with the responsibility of developing and maintaining a data product for the domain is one of the organizational changes that should be implemented when developing a data mesh.

Let's now move on to some of the technical aspects of building a data mesh, as we look at the next principle, which is having *self-service data infrastructure as a platform*.

Self-service data infrastructure as a platform

One of the concerns about having domain-oriented, decentralized teams is that there could be duplication of effort and expense if each team is responsible for setting up their own data infrastructure. Therefore, a recommendation for organizations that are looking to implement a data mesh is that you create a central team that is responsible for data infrastructure, but not responsible for implementing business logic in data pipelines.

That distinction between the data pipeline infrastructure and the actual data pipelines that implement business logic is important. The central data mesh team is responsible for building out infrastructure and systems that make it easy for data engineers working in a data domain to easily build ETL pipelines that apply business logic to create data products.

Some of the components that the central data mesh team may provide include:

- Scalable storage buckets (such as Amazon S3) for storing data
- Ingestion tooling (such as Amazon DMS, Glue, or third-party tools such as Upsolver)
- Data quality tools (such as Glue DataBrew, Glue Studio Data Quality, or third-party tools such as Deequ)
- Data transformation tools (such as Glue Studio, or third-party solutions such as Databricks)
- A central data catalog for making data products discoverable (such as Amazon DataZone, or third-party tools such as Collibra)
- Automation for routing data access requests to a data owner, and automated sharing of data once a request is approved (such as with Amazon DataZone, or can be built on top of a third-party tool such as Collibra)
- Data warehouse solution for low-latency data access (such as Amazon Redshift, or third-party solutions such as Snowflake)

- Data access control solutions (such as AWS Lake Formation, or third-party tools such as Privacera)

- Data orchestration tools (such as Amazon MWAA, AWS Step Functions, or third-party tools such as Apache Airflow)

- **Continuous Integration (CI)/Continuous Delivery (CD)** infrastructure for deploying pipelines (such as AWS CodePipeline, or third-party tools such as GitHub Actions)

The central data mesh engineering team should provide the infrastructure, as well as documentation and support for using that infrastructure. The purpose of this team is to enable the domain specific data engineers to easily build high-quality data products, make them discoverable through a central catalog, and ensure they are easily accessible with data sharing (i.e., make sure that other teams can access the data in place, without needing to make a copy of the data they want to access).

Let's now look at the last principle suggested by Dehghani, *federated computational governance*, which addresses the interoperability and governance of data products.

Federated computational governance

Federated computational governance is a complex phrase, but effectively means that all data product owners and the data platform owner are represented in a central group that agrees on governance policies for data in the data mesh, and that governance is enforced/monitored through automation.

Previously, you may have had a central governance team that wrote up standards and governance policies that a central data engineering team would then work to implement; however, this changes with the decentralized data mesh approach. You still need certain standards and governance agreements in order to ensure a good level of interoperability between different data products, and to ensure that corporate governance requirements are met. However, these are now decided by a governance group that is made up of representatives that include data owners and the data platform owner.

The goal is to provide as much independence and flexibility as possible to the individual domain teams, while also ensuring good interoperability between data products. To do this, the data governance team can define certain standards, such as the date format that should be used, and how columns should be named for something like customer ID (for example, ensuring all columns with the customer ID are named `customer_id`, instead of having different data products use variations such as `cust-id`, `customer_identifier`, `customer_key`, etc.).

Other examples of items that the data governance team may create standards for include items around data quality metrics that must be reported for each data product, and a minimum set of metadata that must be captured for each data product registered in the data mesh catalog. The goals of these standards are to ensure that high-quality, trustworthy data products are easily discoverable in the data mesh, and that the data products can easily be joined through common field names and items like date formats. However, as far as possible, each data domain team should have as much freedom as possible to create data products, with only minimal and necessary standardization and governance policies being applied from the federated governance team.

Finally, as far as possible, the data platform team should create automation to monitor compliance with the standardization and governance rules that the governance teams put in place. This should include the automated monitoring of published data products to verify compliance, along with alerting to notify relevant data product owners and the governance team of data products that are out of compliance.

For example, there should be an automated process that runs data quality checks against published data products, ensuring that data quality requirements are being met. For data products that are not meant to contain any PII (such as those where the PII is obfuscated in some way), there can be an automated process that scans data products, looking for PII, and notifying relevant stakeholders if PII is detected.

In addition to the four principles that we have outlined above, there is another important concept to understand when talking about a data mesh, and that is the concept of data producers and data consumers, which we discuss next.

Data producers and consumers

When people talk about a data mesh approach, you will often hear them talk about data producers and data consumers. These are used to identify two distinct personas that work within a data mesh, and how each of them interacts differently with the data mesh.

Data producers are teams that publish new data products within the data mesh. Teams within a domain will create analytical data products, from their transactional data, and publish the resulting dataset on the data mesh.

Data consumers are other teams within an organization that will search the data catalog for data that they need, and then subscribe to a dataset published by another team. For example, the marketing team may discover a dataset in the data catalog that contains the top 1000 songs that are streamed from the music catalog of a streaming service. They subscribe to the dataset to use this top 1000 songs data in their marketing campaigns.

However, data consumers may also be data producers. For example, if there is a dataset listing the top 1000 songs streamed from the music catalog, the marketing team may join that dataset with a dataset that contains details about artists and create a new dataset that lists the top 10 artists with the most popular songs on the streaming service. For example, in a specific week, Taylor Swift may not have the top-streamed song, but she may have 10 different songs that are in the top 1000 list. As a result, she may be the most popular artist in the list of the top 1000 songs. The marketing team may choose to publish this list of the most popular artists in the top 1000 streaming songs as a new and separate dataset, and publish this to the data mesh, making them both a data consumer and data producer.

Having a better understanding of what is meant by a data mesh, let's now look at some of the items that a data mesh approach helps to fix.

Challenges that a data mesh approach attempts to resolve

Traditional data lakes and approaches served many organizations well for a long time, but as with everything, there are always new developments and approaches that help drive improvements.

In the previous chapter, we looked at how new table formats (such as Apache Iceberg) introduced new functionality that improved querying and processing data in data lakes. In a similar way, the concepts and approaches introduced by a data mesh help solve some different challenges of traditional data lakes and how data teams are structured.

Let's look at a few of the traditional challenges that a data mesh helps solve.

Bottlenecks with a centralized data team

While not the case for every data lake, it was common for large enterprises to create a centralized team that would ingest data from transactional systems across the organization and then perform ETL tasks on that data (cleaning the data, joining data from across different sources, etc.). This team would respond to requests from different parts of the business when they needed new data sources ingested or new reports created.

However, this was not always the most efficient way to get the analytics insights that each team needed. Often the central team would be overloaded with new ingestion or transformation requests, and this central team would also often need time to learn about and understand the new data they were ingesting. This was because the central team was taking data from across the organization and could not be expected to be experts about the data and business logic of every part of the organization.

The central team would also end up having to try and prioritize the different requests coming from across the business, without necessarily having visibility into which request would have the biggest business impact.

One of the big benefits of a decentralized data mesh approach is that data stays within a domain and therefore close to domain experts. If each domain team hires data engineers to create analytical products of their data, those data engineers can become experts in the data for that specific domain. These domain experts will have a good idea of what good data quality looks like, and will more easily identify data quality problems. They will also get to know that part of the business well, and be in the best position to respond to the reporting and visualization requirements for that specific business domain (as well as know which data sources they need and how best to apply business logic transforms to create the required reports).

Finally, with the self-service approach that is core to a data mesh, each business domain can easily discover data that has been generated by other business domains and can directly request access to that data without needing to go through a central team to coordinate everything.

The "Analytics is not my problem" problem

When you create a central team that is responsible for doing all the data engineering tasks and creating the datasets and reporting that the business requires, there can be friction between this team and the data source owners.

Traditionally, there was strong separation of duties between the engineers responsible for building and running transactional systems and the engineers responsible for creating analytic reporting for the business. And when data engineers need data from a source system, the owners of the source system may get nervous about how that data is going to be extracted from the source database.

This would sometimes cause the owners of the source system to complain that analytics was not their problem (meaning not their responsibility). And strictly, they were correct – their primary responsibility to the organization is to keep the transactional systems up and running and performing well. Anything that potentially could jeopardize that (such as a data engineering system trying to read the full database) is considered a risk, and a source system owner may fight against accepting that risk. This of course can lead to delays in data engineers being able to build the reports that another part of the business may be requesting.

Therefore, when implementing a data mesh and, as part of that, changing the organizational culture regarding how data is comprehensively viewed and who is responsible for creating it (both transactional and analytical data), much of that friction can be removed.

For this to be successful does require organizational and cultural change (which can be difficult). But the end goal is to have business domains take responsibility for both the transactional data and analytical data for their domain. And if a team building a new transactional data source is aware that their wider team will also be responsible for making the analytics data available, and they involve data engineers from the design phase of the new system, this can significantly smooth the process of ensuring that required data can be efficiently extracted from the transactional system.

No organization-wide visibility into datasets that are available

When we discussed data products in the previous section, we spoke about how there are various attributes of data products that are core to the data mesh approach, and this included discoverability and accessibility.

With a centralized approach to data lakes, there ends up being a core data engineering team that collects all the data and then reactively responds to requests from across the organization to build new reports or to make specific data available. Often business requests go to that team from business users that don't know what data or existing reports the central team has. The data engineering team may find that they already have the required data, but at times they will need to go to a different part of the business to find the source data and arrange to ingest it (as discussed in the **"Analytics is not my problem"** problem section above).

With traditional data lakes, a lot of activity was reactive. But with a data mesh approach, it is far more of a proactive, self-service approach. Each domain is responsible for creating analytical products for the data that they own, and the data platform team creates automation to enable new data products to be added to a central data catalog. All users across the organization can search the catalog to discover datasets, and from the catalog should have the ability to request access to a specific dataset. Once that is approved by the data owner, there should be automatic data sharing that makes the data available to the data consumer that requested it.

The above are just a few of the challenges that a data mesh approach helps to overcome. Let's now do a deeper dive into the other side of the coin – the organizational and technical challenges of building a data mesh.

The organizational and technical challenges of building a data mesh

As we discussed at the start of this chapter, a data mesh may mean different things to different people. Some people approach a data mesh implementation as though it were just a technical challenge about improving the sharing and creation of analytical data. But as we have seen, the way that Dehghani proposed a data mesh approach is not about technical solutions to data sharing, but much more about the overall way that an organization approaches analytical data.

In this section, we look at some of the challenges (both organizational and technical) of implementing a data mesh.

Changing the way that an organization approaches analytical data

While there are technical challenges to building a data mesh, the more difficult part is changing the way that an organization views analytical data, and changing who is responsible for creating analytical data.

While there is no "traditional" way to creating analytical data, it has been very common for this to be the job of a central analytics team. Many companies, even today, still have a data & analytics team that is responsible for ingesting transactional data into a central data store (such as a data warehouse or data lake). Once ingested, this central team is also responsible for cleansing the data (ensuring data quality) and for building ETL pipelines to transform the transactional data into analytics data. A data mesh approach changes this completely.

Let's take a look at how a data mesh changes things for the centralized data & analytics team.

Changes for the centralized data & analytics team

With a data mesh approach, the centralized data mesh team now has a different responsibility – they need to build and run a data platform that domain teams throughout the organization can use for building analytical data products. Where as their customers used to be business users that wanted specific data or reports for analyses, their new customers are now data engineers in different business teams that want a platform that enables them to easily build data products.

Where as previously they were responsible for implementing and running technology that they then used to build ETL pipelines, they are now focused on building a data platform that others can use to build ETL pipelines. They effectively are now responsible for building and running an internal **Software-as-a-Service (SaaS)** data platform for internal data engineers.

This is a change in their focus, but they are using existing skills they already had for deploying data-related infrastructure.

As part of the changing role of the data platform team, a new data platform owner role should be created. This role should work with the data domain teams in the different lines of business to learn about their requirements and expectations from the data platform, and in turn develop a data platform development roadmap that is regularly updated. The data platform owner takes on the responsibility of ensuring that the data platform features and functionality meet both the central governance team requirements and the requirements of the individual domains.

The change within the lines of business is more fundamental, as it introduces brand-new responsibilities and skills requirements, as we will discuss next.

Changes for line of business teams

The more challenging organizational change is making lines of business responsible for generating not just transactional data, but also relevant analytical data products. This means that a line of business now needs to upskill for various roles, as we outline here.

Data product owners

Each line of business needs to appoint data product owners/managers that will be responsible for the development of analytical data products. The data product owners need a strong understanding of their specific line of business and must also understand the bigger picture of how other lines of business may want to use their data.

The data product owner is ultimately responsible for the creation of data products, as well as for the quality of those products. They need to work with the owners of transactional data systems to facilitate the ingestion of data from those systems, work with data architects or engineers to confirm ingestion methods and required transformations, and ensure that the finished data product is added to the central data catalog.

They are also ultimately responsible for ensuring the usability of the data that is generated, communicating any schema changes to downstream customers, and taking feedback from other parts of the business on any new requirements. The data product owner also needs to determine how the data should be delivered (such as batch updates to the data lake, making the data available via a streaming source such as Kafka or Kinesis, or loading the data into a data warehouse for access via JDBC).

Data architects/engineers

Each line of business also needs to hire data engineers (or repurpose existing data engineers) that are capable of developing ETL pipelines that can use the central data platform to ingest data from line of business transactional systems and transform that data into analytical data products that can be shared with the rest of the organization.

Depending on the size of the line of business, they may choose to separate the role of data architect and data engineer. If separated, the data architect would work with the data product owner to design end-to-end pipelines from data ingestion to making the data available to consumers, and then work with data engineers to communicate the requirements for the pipeline.

The data engineers will either work closely with the data architect or directly with the data product owner to understand business requirements, enable ingestion of data from transactional systems, implement business logic in ETL pipelines for transforming data, and load the data product into a final destination where it can be consumed (data lake, data warehouse, streaming target, etc.). They will also play a key role in ensuring data quality.

Some teams may already have data architects/engineers; however, for other organizations, this may be a new role for a line of business. In some cases, the line of business may be able to move existing data architects/engineers from the centralized data engineering team into the line of business, reallocating existing resources as part of the organizational restructuring to implement the data mesh. Otherwise, the line of business may need to create new roles to fill the data architect/engineer positions.

Data stewards

The other role that is key in a data mesh is that of the **data steward**, a role that is responsible for ensuring that the data products created by a data producer meet the requirements of the central governance team policies. In addition to meeting the central governance policies, the data steward may also create governance policies that are specific to their line of business.

As discussed previously, the central governance team is responsible for implementing the minimum required policies to meet corporate governance standards, and governance standards that all domain producers agree should be common for the data mesh. However, a specific line of business, such as the HR team, may have additional governance requirements for their data products. The data steward helps define, and enforce, these policies.

Some of the functions that the data steward may be responsible for include ensuring that all published data products for their line of business have required metadata, and that any PII privacy requirements are enforced. The data steward may also take on the responsibility of ensuring that data quality is maintained for all published data products.

Data stewards will work with data product owners, as well as the data architects and engineers, in ensuring that governance and related requirements are met.

Data stewards may also be nominated to join the federated governance team that works with other data stewards across the organization to set minimum data governance requirements.

For any organization that is looking to adopt a data mesh approach to their data, it is critical that they first address the organizational changes that we have discussed here before they look into implementing any type of *technical* solution.

For this to be successful, it is critical that there is executive buy-in to implementing a data mesh approach. Without executive-level sponsorship of the data mesh, it will not be possible to implement the organizational changes that are required. The executive that sponsors the project needs to be able to work with teams across the organization in order to educate them on the business value of moving to a data mesh approach, and to then secure the required buy-in from business leaders.

Once support has been secured, a comprehensive education program can be put in place to educate people from all parts of the organization on what a data mesh is, how it will be implemented, and what changes can be expected.

The organizational changes required for implementing a data mesh are often the biggest challenge, but there are also significant technical challenges, which we look at in the next section.

Technical challenges for building a data mesh

While many vendors advertise that they have the technical solution for building a data mesh, the reality is that there are no single solutions that out of the box enable everything that is needed for data mesh implementation at enterprise scale. In large enterprises, there is likely to already be a wide variety of technologies in use, and many different tools will need to be integrated into the new data mesh approach. For smaller organizations though, out-of-the-box solutions may be suitable.

Integrating existing analytical tools

If you are building a brand-new platform (such as for a new company, or in the event you're looking to modernize legacy on-prem solutions as you move to the cloud), then this is not a significant challenge. You can select a single vendor that supports a data mesh approach and use their suite of products. For example, you could build a data mesh using AWS-native services, or select a vendor such as Databricks or Snowflake, and use their data mesh solutions.

However, large organizations often already have a wide range of established analytical tools in use across the organization. And different parts of the organization may have different toolsets. For example, it's not uncommon to have an organization where one team has built a data lake in AWS, and another team has built a data lake in Azure or **Google Cloud Platform (GCP)**. Even if all data is in AWS, for example, you may find that different teams use different tools – such as one team using AWS-native services, while another team uses Databricks, and another team uses Snowflake. Integrating those different tools into a data mesh is certainly possible, but it generally takes a lot of custom development to build the required integrations. We look at one aspect of that integration in the next section, where we discuss the centralized data catalog.

Centralizing dataset metadata in a single catalog and building automation

A key part of a data mesh is having a centralized catalog where metadata for all data products is published. This enables all data consumers within the organization to go to a central catalog to search for and discover published data products, learn more about the data product (through comprehensive metadata that should be published with the data product), and request access to the data.

For large enterprises, there may already be one or more data catalogs in existence. Your challenge in this environment is to select a single data catalog solution that provides the needed functionality for your data mesh, and then get agreement from all lines of business to use this new catalog for all new data products.

However, you will not want to just "lift and shift" existing catalogs into the new catalog, because the data mesh has specific requirements around governance, required metadata, data quality, etc. Therefore, a line of business may end up continuing to use their existing data catalog for "legacy" datasets, while needing to publish all new data mesh data products into the new catalog. Therefore, this is both a technical and organizational/process change and challenge.

A big focus of the data mesh approach is about creating a self-serve environment for data producers and consumers. This means building in as much automation of processes as possible. One common place for this automation is in requesting, approving, and provisioning access to data products.

In an ideal world, a data consumer should be able to log in to the central data catalog using their corporate credentials, and from there they should be able to search for relevant data for their use case. The search terms that they provide should be matched against attributes of the data products, such as column names, table descriptions, and additional metadata associated with the data product.

Once a data consumer finds a data product in the catalog, they should be able to learn more about the data product by reviewing the provided metadata, and ideally also viewing the lineage of the data product (which sources were used in the creation of the product, and what transforms and joins were applied). They may also be able to view a sample of the dataset.

If the data consumer decides that a specific data product is well suited to their use case, they should be able to request a subscription to the data product from within the catalog. Some data products may be marked as being available to all users in the organization without additional approval being required, in which case the data consumer should immediately receive access to the data. Access to the data product may be via a JDBC connection, or it could be provided via the data being shared with the consumer (such as the dataset being shared from a source Redshift or Snowflake data warehouse, with a target Redshift or Snowflake data warehouse that the data consumer has access to).

Other datasets may require the data owner or data steward from the publishing domain to approve the request for access. In this case, the data consumer should be able to provide a justification for why they want access, and the request should be routed to the data producer. Once the data producer approves the request for access, the data should be automatically made available to the data consumer.

If an enterprise has a wide variety of analytic tools, then this will generally require custom development to enable this level of automation. Alternatively, if an organization is using analytical tools from one primary vendor, the integration will be much simpler.

Compromising on integrations

Because of the complexities of integrating different analytical tools, across different vendors and perhaps even different clouds and on-prem data sources, an organization may compromise on their vision of what a data mesh is. The data mesh is a good approach to making analytical data available across an organization, but it is not always practical to enable every integration to reach the full vision of what a data mesh should be, as defined by Dehghani.

As a result, organizations may implement limited aspects of the data mesh approach, or they may build a new data mesh that operates alongside existing analytical systems. This approach may be viewed by some as failing to really implement a data mesh, but my view is that if you gain at least some of the benefits of the data mesh approach, and you are able to do this in a reasonable time frame and cost, and in a way that brings concrete business benefits, then you should go with that. Ideally, over time, you will mature your data mesh to be more in line with the vision created by Dehghani. This is why at the start of this chapter we discussed how the term data mesh means different things to different people.

AWS services that help enable a data mesh approach

Most analytics vendors have been adding functionality to their solutions to support a data mesh approach over the past few years. And while there is currently no single solution that enables a data mesh across a complex selection of analytical tools and hybrid environments, many companies have made good progress in supporting the data mesh approach, at least within their own "ecosystem" of tools.

AWS has supported sharing both S3-and Redshift-based datasets across AWS accounts for a while. And while easy sharing of data across different AWS accounts (and different teams within an organization generally have their own AWS accounts) is a key component of a data mesh architecture, it is only a piece of building a data mesh. Another key component is the ability to centrally catalog data and add rich business metadata for each dataset, which can be done with the **Amazon DataZone** service. In this section, we explore the AWS services that can help build an AWS-based data mesh in more detail.

Querying data across AWS accounts

In AWS, two of the primary query engines that are used for data consumption are Amazon Athena (for ad-hoc queries of data in an S3 data lake, and federated queries to other data sources) and Amazon Redshift (for low-latency use cases, such as for powering dashboards or visualizations in BI tools). Both tools can access data that has been shared across accounts using AWS Lake Formation.

Sharing data with AWS Lake Formation

We previously discussed the AWS Lake Formation service (in *Chapter 4, Data Governance, Security, and Cataloging*) and how it provides the ability to enforce granular data access controls. Using AWS Lake Formation, in conjunction with the Glue Data Catalog, you can control access to data in your S3-based data lake by granting or revoking permissions for users through the Lake Formation console (or API). This includes the ability to control access at the column or row level.

With Lake Formation, you can also enable the sharing of data between different AWS accounts. As a reminder, in the Glue Data Catalog you have databases, which contain tables, and each table has one or more columns. When you share a database or table from a source AWS account to a target AWS account using Lake Formation, the database tables become visible in the target account's catalog. Once a user in the target account is granted access to the shared database/table, they can query the table using Amazon Athena as though it were locally in the account, even though the data files are still in the source AWS account's S3 bucket. With Lake Formation data sharing, the data is *not copied* to a target account, but rather *made accessible* in the target account.

In a similar way, you can use Lake Formation to manage Redshift data shares. This enables you to configure the sharing of a Redshift table from a data producer's Redshift cluster directly to a data consumer's Redshift cluster. Using Lake Formation, you can share both S3 and Redshift data between separate AWS accounts, as well as share data between different AWS Regions within the same account.

From a data mesh perspective, this enables data producers in one domain to grant access to their data products to data consumers in a different domain. A common pattern would be to have a business data catalog where data consumers can find datasets that they wish to subscribe to. Within the data catalog, the consumer should be able to request access to a dataset, and once approved by the data producer, access should be granted to the dataset. For data products that are S3-or Redshift-based, you can build an automation that uses Lake Formation to share the relevant table/s from the data producer account to the data consumer account.

Once S3-based data has been shared to a data consumer's account, a data consumer can query the data using Amazon Athena, Amazon Redshift Spectrum, or Amazon QuickSight, as though the table were in the account locally. And in a similar way, if a Redshift table has been shared across accounts using Lake Formation, a data consumer can view the table in Redshift as though it were a local table in their cluster, and immediately start querying it.

In October 2023, AWS launched a new service that provides business data catalog functionality integrated with Lake Formation data sharing, called Amazon DataZone. Let's explore how this service can significantly simplify the process of building a data mesh on AWS for environments that use AWS analytic services.

Amazon DataZone, a business data catalog with data mesh functionality

Amazon DataZone is a service from AWS that provides built-in data governance features, helping to unlock the power of data across an organization.

While AWS does not specifically market Amazon DataZone as a data mesh solution, the service does include functionality that simplifies building out a data mesh, via integration with AWS Lake Formation. Let's review some of the core concepts and components found in DataZone.

DataZone concepts

The following are some of the core DataZone concepts that you need to understand before we move on to examine the various components that make up DataZone.

Domains

The first concept to understand is that of **domains**, which are a way of organizing data assets, projects, associated AWS accounts, and data sources.

Most commonly, a domain will align with a specific organizational boundary, such as a business unit or specific function. As such, you may have domains for finance, HR, manufacturing, sales, marketing, etc.

Data sources

DataZone supports publishing data to the business data catalog from the Glue Data Catalog and Amazon Redshift. While traditionally the Glue Data Catalog is used to catalog Amazon S3-based data lake resources, it can also be used to capture database and table information from other sources, such as relational databases or a Snowflake data warehouse. All sources that are supported by AWS Glue crawlers can also be imported as a DataZone data source.

Business glossaries

A business glossary is effectively a dictionary used to define business-related metadata, and to ensure the consistent use of business terms. For example, an organization may have datasets related to their business in different countries around the world. If you allow the free-form capture of metadata associated with a dataset, different people may label countries differently, making it difficult to consistently search the data catalog based on the country that the data applies to. For example, you could have the following metadata applied to different datasets:

- Country: United States
- Country: USA
- Region: U.S.
- Geography: united_states

If the data catalog had the metadata shown above, it would be difficult to search the catalog to find all datasets with data from the United States. Therefore, you can instead create a business glossary called *Country*, and then create a list of all countries that your organization operates in, as shown below:

- Country

    - United States

    - South Africa

    - New Zealand

    - India

    - United Kingdom

When adding metadata to a dataset, a data producer or data steward can select to apply metadata from the *Country* glossary and select the specific country the dataset applies to. This ensures consistency in metadata, making it easier to find related datasets.

Metadata forms

Metadata forms can be used to ensure that datasets for a specific domain contain a consistent set of metadata. A domain data steward creates metadata forms, where they specify metadata that should be captured for datasets. Multiple metadata forms can be created, and then a data steward can select forms to be applied to all datasets in the domain. Optionally, a data publisher can also elect to attach additional metadata forms to datasets that they publish.

A metadata form lists field names for each metadata item, and then a field type. The field type could be a string (allowing for free-form entry), Boolean value, date, integer, or decimal. Alternatively, the field type could be tied to a specific business glossary term. The following is a simple example of items that could be included in a metadata form.

Field Name	Field Type	Description
Sales Region	*Country* Business Glossary	The sales region for this dataset
Sales Quarter	*Quarter* Business Glossary	The calendar quarter that this dataset covers
Dataset Support	String	Provide the email address to use for queries about this dataset
Last Audit Date	Date	Provide the date that this dataset was last audited

Figure 15.1: Sample items for a metadata form in Amazon DataZone

Metadata forms are critical to ensuring that all data in the business data catalog has good metadata that can be used to help discover datasets, and to better understand the dataset.

Associated AWS accounts

A DataZone domain is deployed to a specific AWS account, and you can then associate additional AWS accounts with the domain.

This enables teams that have their own AWS accounts where they produce or consume data to continue to use those accounts. They can publish data from their account into the DataZone business data catalog, and when they subscribe to a data product from another project in a different account, they can have the data shared into their account for local consumption.

Having reviewed some of the core DataZone concepts, let's now look at the key components of the DataZone service.

DataZone components

DataZone has a number of components that are used to provide an environment where users can search for and discover data, subscribe to a data product, and publish a data product. In this section, we will review two key DataZone components.

Data portal

When you configure Amazon DataZone, a data portal UI is created that is accessible from outside of the AWS console via a unique URL generated for your DataZone domain. The data portal provides the ability to manage your data products and is also a full business data catalog that enables data consumers to easily search for and discover data products.

As part of your data mesh, it is important that all potential data consumers across the domain can easily access the data catalog. By creating the data portal UI outside of the AWS console, it means that you do not need to grant AWS console access to all data producers and consumers in your domain. Instead, you can integrate the data portal UI with your **Single Sign-On** (**SSO**) provider, enabling users to easily log in to the data portal using their corporate credentials.

While DataZone administrators may still need AWS console access for some aspects of managing DataZone, most regular users will only work in the data portal UI. Within the data portal, data producers can do tasks such as add business metadata to their data products, view and approve (or reject) subscription requests from data consumers, etc. And for data consumers, the data portal allows them to search for and discover data products, as well as to request access to a data product directly from the portal.

Projects and environments

Projects provide a way to group different resources together, including people, data assets, and analytical tools. When you create a project in the DataZone data portal UI, you are enabling a collaborative environment where a group of users can discover, subscribe to, and consume data registered in the business data catalog, as well as create new data products and publish them as part of a project.

Within a DataZone project, you can create environments, which are collections of configured resources (such as Amazon S3 buckets, AWS Glue databases, or Amazon Athena workgroups). Each environment also has a set of IAM principals that are granted access to use those resources. **DataZone environment profiles** are pre-configured sets of resources and blueprints that are a template for creating a new environment.

Instead of access to data products being granted to individuals, with DataZone, access is granted to a project. As a project administrator, you can then add people to the project, and they can use the access granted to the project to access the data.

Having a better understanding of the Amazon DataZone service, let's look at what an architecture for a data mesh on AWS looks like. In the following section, we will illustrate how DataZone can be a technical enabler of a data mesh approach to managing data.

A sample architecture for a data mesh on AWS

We have looked at what a data mesh is, some of the organizational and technical challenges of building a data mesh, and finally some of the AWS services that can be used to build a data mesh. Now, in this section, let's bring it all together with a sample architecture for a data mesh on AWS.

Architecture for a data mesh using AWS-native services

Earlier in this chapter, we discussed how a data mesh is easier to build if starting new, or if just using AWS-native services. In this section, we will look at a sample architecture for when you only use AWS-native services, and in the section after this, we will review an architecture for environments that use analytic tools from other vendors.

The following architecture diagram shows a data mesh that is built using Amazon DataZone, with data in an Amazon S3-based data lake (a similar architecture would support data in Amazon Redshift) and using AWS Lake Formation for data sharing.

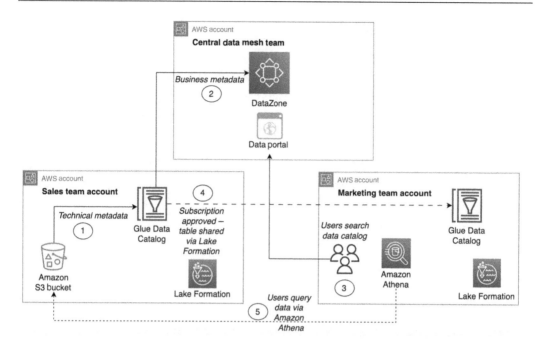

Figure 15.2: Sample data mesh architecture when using AWS analytic services

In the preceding diagram, we see how there is an account for the *central data mesh team*, and this is the account where we have created our DataZone domain (and therefore is also the account that hosts the DataZone data portal). This account doesn't host data producers or data consumers but is owned and managed by the central data mesh team. Here they create the DataZone domain and also manage the high-level administrative tasks for DataZone. The central data mesh team will also associate AWS accounts from data producers and consumers with the DataZone domain.

In addition to the central data mesh account that deploys the domain for Amazon DataZone, we also see two other accounts. On the left, we see a data producer account. This account is owned by the *sales* team, and in this account the data engineers on the sales team create data products to be part of the DataZone *sales* project. On the right, we see the account for the *marketing* team, who in this case are consumers of a sales data product.

While this diagram may look somewhat complicated, the architecture is relatively simple. Let's go through each of the numbers in the preceding diagram to explain the process:

1.   A data product is created and stored in an Amazon S3-based data lake. A Glue crawler (or other method) is used to register the technical metadata for the data product in the AWS Glue Data Catalog of the sales team's AWS account.

2. A member of the sales team that has been added to a DataZone project adds the data product to the DataZone catalog. They do this by creating a new DataZone data source that points to the database in the AWS Glue Data Catalog. This effectively imports the table metadata from the Glue Data Catalog, and they can then add relevant business metadata via a metadata form and the business glossary.

3. A user in the marketing team (who has been added to a relevant DataZone project for the marketing domain) searches the catalog and discovers the dataset from the sales team. They choose to subscribe to the data product, and a data steward or the data publisher in the sales team approves the subscription.

4. Once the subscription is approved, DataZone automatically uses AWS Lake Formation to share the dataset from the sales account Glue Data Catalog to the marketing team's Glue Data Catalog.

5. The marketing team users can now use the deep-links in the DataZone data portal UI to access Amazon Athena and query the sales team data. When they run a SQL query, Athena accesses the data in the S3 bucket of the sales team, using Lake Formation-provisioned permissions.

This architecture is a good solution for where you are primarily using AWS-native services. In the preceding diagram, we showed an architecture that uses data in Amazon S3, but this architecture would also support Amazon Redshift tables in a similar way.

Let's now review an architecture for an environment where there is a broad range of analytic services, from multiple vendors.

Architecture for a data mesh using non-AWS analytic services

As we have discussed in this chapter, Amazon DataZone (at the time of writing) supports the automated sharing of data in an Amazon S3-based data lake and data in Amazon Redshift. However, if you have data in other systems (such as Snowflake, or Databricks data cataloged in the Databricks Unity catalog), as well as perhaps on-premises data in other data warehouses (such as Teradata), then a data mesh architecture is more complex.

While most of these data sources could be cataloged in the Glue Data Catalog and then imported to Amazon DataZone from there, DataZone would not support enabling the automated sharing of those data sources across different domains.

Also, if you have more advanced catalog and data governance requirements (such as data lineage, which is not currently supported in Amazon DataZone), then you may want to consider a different business data catalog solution, such as Collibra, Atlan, or Alation.

There are many different ways that you could build out a data mesh architecture in this environment, so the following example is just one potential pattern that you could use, although this is a pattern that is relatively common. In this example, we use just a single analytic service (Snowflake), but later on we will discuss approaches for when you have multiple analytic solutions from various vendors.

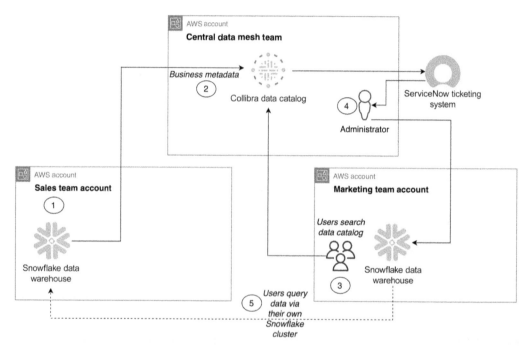

Figure 15.3: Sample data mesh architecture when not using AWS analytic services

The preceding diagram shows a simplified architecture where just Snowflake is used as an analytic service, but the same architecture could be expanded to include additional analytic services such as Databricks, an on-premises Teradata data warehouse, Oracle, and others. We will talk about that in a moment, but let's first work through the steps shown in *Figure 15.3*:

1. A data product is created and stored in the Snowflake data warehouse.

2. Using the Collibra JDBC driver for Snowflake, the data producer registers the data product in Collibra and adds the relevant business metadata. Note that we are using Collibra as an example, but this could be replaced with Atlan, Alation, or any other business data catalog of your choosing.

3. A user in the marketing team searches the Collibra data catalog and discovers the dataset from the sales team. They choose to subscribe to the data product, and a data steward or the data publisher in the sales team approves the subscription.

4. Once the subscription is approved, Collibra automatically creates a ticket in ServiceNow (this could be using a custom-built integration, or an integration downloaded from the Collibra marketplace). An administrator is notified of the approved data share via ServiceNow, and they then log in to Snowflake and share the specified dataset from the sales Snowflake cluster to the marketing team's Snowflake cluster.

5. The marketing team users can now use their Snowflake cluster to query the data from the sales team.

Of course, there are multiple variations and different ways that this integration could have been built. Let's discuss a few different options that we could use to modify the above architecture.

Automating the sharing of data in Snowflake

If Snowflake were the only analytic tool that we were using, then it would make sense to simplify things and remove the step of having an administrator manually do the datashare from the source Snowflake cluster to the target Snowflake cluster.

In the Collibra marketplace, there is an integration that enables Collibra to automatically share the relevant dataset between Snowflake clusters. See `https://marketplace.collibra.com/listings/snowflake-data-share-to-collibra-integration/`

In the architecture shown in *Figure 15.3*, we used the ServiceNow integration, as a typical environment may have many different analytic tools, and there may not be a Collibra integration for each of those tools. Therefore, in a more complex environment, the simplest solution may be to just have Collibra raise a ServiceNow ticket, and then have an administrator do the share manually, as each analytic tool would have a different process for sharing data.

Using query federation instead of data sharing

In the architecture shown in *Figure 15.3*, we used the built-in functionality of Snowflake to make data in the producer Snowflake cluster (the sales team) available in the consumer Snowflake cluster (the marketing team). To the marketing team, the sales data would appear as though it were a local table, and they could easily use the Snowflake query tool on their cluster to join the sales data with their marketing data.

However, not every analytic tool may support this type of data sharing. For example, if you have on-premises legacy data warehouses, it is unlikely that they would support data sharing to a different cluster. Therefore, an alternate approach is to use query federation to enable users in one team (such as marketing) to be able to easily access and query data from another team (such as sales), without needing to copy the data.

In *Chapter 11, Ad-Hoc Queries with Amazon Athena*, we discussed Athena query federation. As a reminder, this functionality enables you to create connectors to other database systems, and then run queries that can join data in the S3-based data lake with data from other database systems. To configure this in Amazon Athena, you need to install and configure the appropriate connector, which does require some relatively advanced technical skills.

As an alternative, there are commercial solutions from vendors that enable the same type of functionality but with an easy-to-use tool. One of the popular products in this space is Starburst. With Starburst, you can easily configure integrations with many popular database and analytical solutions. Starburst then sits between SQL clients and the target database. Users connect their SQL client to Starburst, and Starburst has connectors to various database systems. A data consumer can then query any of the database systems that they have been granted access to via Starburst.

If we were to incorporate Starburst into the architecture shown in *Figure 15.3*, when a subscription is approved for a data product, an administrator would grant access to the data product in the sales team Snowflake cluster to the marketing team consumers via Starburst. The marketing team could then connect to Starburst to query the sales data.

The benefit of query federation is that it allows a data consumer to subscribe to multiple datasets, all in different analytic tools, and access them all via Starburst. However, it does mean that the data platform team has to license and manage additional infrastructure (such as the Starburst server), and in certain cases there may be increased query latency when querying via query federation.

Having looked at sample architectures, let's now get hands-on with setting up a simple data mesh environment in the AWS console using Amazon DataZone.

Hands-on – Setting up Amazon DataZone

In the hands-on section of this chapter, we are going to set up and configure the Amazon DataZone service. We will then create a DataZone project, import a data source, add business metadata, and publish a data product. Finally, we will access the DataZone data portal as a data consumer, to search for and subscribe to a data product.

At the time of publication of this book, the Amazon DataZone service has just recently been released. There are sometimes a number of changes made to a service shortly after it becomes Generally Available (GA), so make sure to reference the GitHub page for this chapter to check for any updates related to these hands-on exercises. The GitHub page is available at https://github.com/PacktPublishing/Data-Engineering-with-AWS-2nd-edition/tree/main/Chapter15

Let's get started.

Setting up AWS Identity Center

To log in to the **Amazon DataZone data portal**, you can either use your AWS IAM credentials, or you can log in using an identity configured in **AWS Identity Center**. With AWS Identity Center, you can create local users, or you can perform identity federation using SSO by configuring Identity Center to work with your identity provider (such as Azure Active Directory, Okta, Ping Identity, etc.). For this hands-on exercise, we are going to set up AWS Identity Center with local users.

Note that Identity Center is an AWS Organizations-wide service, meaning that to configure Identity Center, you must log in with the credentials of your AWS Organizations management account. If you created a new account for performing the activities in this book, then the instructions provided here will help you get Identity Center configured. However, if you are using a sandbox or other work account that is part of AWS Organizations, then you will either need to work with your cloud management team to configure Identity Center, or you can use local IAM accounts instead of Identity Center:

1. Log in to the **AWS Management Console** and use the top search bar to search for, and open, the **IAM Identity Center** service.

2. Ensure that you are in the Region that you have been using for the exercises in the previous chapters of this book.

3. Within the Identity Center console, click the **Enable** button in the **Enable IAM Identity Center** box. If your account is not currently configured to be part of an AWS organization, you will be prompted to allow Identity Center to create an organization for you. Click on **Create AWS Organization**. Note that you will receive an email verification request, and you must verify your email address within 24 hours.

4. By default, the **Identity Source** is configured to be the **Identity Center directory,** which is what we will use to create local users in this exercise. Therefore, you do not need to edit the Identity Source, but if you wanted to link Identity Center to your SSO provider, this could be done at this point.

5. Using the left-hand menu, navigate to the **Groups** page, and click on **Create group**.

6. Provide a **Name** for the group, such as **DataZone Users**.

7. Optionally provide a **Description** for this group, and then click on **Create group**.

8. Using the left-hand menu, navigate to the **Users** page, and click on **Add user**.

9. We want to create a user that will be used to manage our DataZone domain. So, for **User-name**, set this to film-catalog-team-admin. In a production environment, we would use the username of an actual person, but to make it easier to track the different roles that we will log in to DataZone with, we are setting the name to be more descriptive of the role.

10. Provide an email address to be associated with this user. As we have done elsewhere in this book, we can create a unique email address that will go to our primary email by specifying our email address with a PLUS sign and a unique identifier after the name portion of the email. Gmail and Outlook both support this mechanism, but not all email providers may support this, in which case you should first create a new email address with a provider to use for this step. If your provider supports this, and your email was, for example, gareth-eagar@ example.com, then you could use gareth-eagar+film-catalog-team-admin@example.

11. Fill in **First Name** and **Last Name**, and then click on **Next**.

12. On the **Add user to groups** screen, select the **DataZone Users** group and then click **Next**.

13. Review the details, and then click **Add user**.

14. Check your email for a message titled **Invitation to join AWS IAM Identity Center**. Click **Accept Invitation** in that message. In the page that opens, provide a password for your new account. **NOTE:** Identity Center requires passwords to be a minimum of 8 characters, and must contain lowercase, uppercase, numbers, and a special character.

15. **Repeat steps 8 – 14** to add a second user. Set the **Username** for this user to be marketing-team-admin.

In the above steps, we enabled AWS Identity Center, created a new user and group, and set the password for our new user. Let's now configure our DataZone domain.

Enabling and configuring Amazon DataZone

Amazon DataZone domains are used to organize your data assets, users, and associated projects. In this section, we will set up Amazon DataZone by configuring a domain:

1. Log in to the **AWS Management Console** and use the top search bar to search for, and open, the **DataZone** service.

2. Click on **Create domain**.

3. Under **Domain details**, provide a name for the domain. We will be creating a domain that manages data related to our movie streaming business, so let's call our domain streaming.

4. Optionally provide a description, and then under **Quick setup** click the checkbox for **Set-up this account for data consumption and publishing**.

   By selecting Quick setup, DataZone will enable default blueprints for working with Data Lake and Data Warehouse data. This will also automate the configuration of required permissions and resources, and create a default DataZone project and environment profiles.

5. Leave all other defaults, scroll to the bottom of the page, and click on **Create domain**.

6. It may take a few minutes for your domain to be created. Once it is created, the **Welcome to your DataZone Domain** screen is displayed. Scroll down this screen, and in the **Summary** section, click on **Update domain to enable IAM Identity Center** (or alternatively, display your list of domains, click on the **streaming** domain, and then click **Edit**).

7. In the **User management** screen, click the **checkbox** for **Enable users in IAM Identity Center**. Leave the default option of **Do not require assignments**, which will allow any Identity Center user to access the DataZone portal. In a production environment, you may want to require assignments, so that only approved users can access the DataZone portal.

8. Scroll down and click on **Update domain**.

9. In the **Data Domain** console, scroll down to the **Summary** section again, and click the **Copy** icon to the left of the **Data portal URL**.

Figure 15.4: DataZone console showing Data Portal URL

10. Open a **new private/Incognito browser** window, and paste the **Data Portal URL** in that window. Note that if you do this in your current browser, you will be automatically logged in as your IAM user, but we want to log in as the **movie-catalog-team-admin** user. Therefore, use a private/Incognito window.

11. Log in to the data portal using the username (film-catalog-team-admin) and password you configured in AWS Identity Center.

12. In the **Welcome to Amazon DataZone** popup, click on **Create New Project**.

13. In the **Create project** popup, enter `Film Catalog Project` for **Name**. Optionally provide a description, and then click **Create**.

14. On the **Your project is ready to use** popup, click on **Create environment**.

15. For the environment **Name**, enter `Film Datasets S3` as this is the project where we will produce datasets related to our catalog of films, using data in Amazon S3.

16. For **Environment profile**, select **DataLakeProfile**. This creates an environment that can be used to work with data in an Amazon S3-based data lake.

17. You can optionally customize the environment to specify the name to use for a Glue database that is used for data that you publish, as well as the name of a Glue database that is used to contain tables that you subscribe to from other environments. You can also optionally specify the name of the Athena workgroup that you want to use. These are optional, so you can skip these and just click **Create environment**. DataZone will now create Glue objects (producer and consumer database), an S3 bucket, and other resources, as well as configure default Lake Formation permissions for the objects. This may take a few minutes to complete.

With the above steps, we have configured our DataZone domain and created a new project and environment that we will use to produce datasets related to our catalog of films. We can now move on to adding a data source to our project.

Adding a data source to our DataZone project

We are now ready to add one of our existing Glue datasets to DataZone. To do this, we need to configure a data source:

1. In the **DataZone data portal**, make sure you are in the **Film Catalog Project** and on the **Overview** tab.

2. In the **Working with Projects** section, click on **Create data source**.

3. For **Name**, enter `films-CuratedZoneDB`, optionally provide a description, and then for **Data source type**, select **AWS Glue**.

4. For **Select an environment**, chose the **Film Datasets S3** environment from the dropdown.

5. In the **Data Selection** section, enter `curatedzonedb` for **Database name**. This is the name of the AWS Glue database that we have been using throughout this book in order to store our curated datasets.

6. For **Table selection criteria**, leave the default of the wildcard asterisk, which will add all of the tables in our **curatedzonedb** to DataZone. Then click **Next**.

7. For **Publishing settings**, leave the default of **No** for **Publish assets to the catalog**. This will add the tables to the project inventory, and later, after reviewing and adding additional metadata, we can choose to publish the tables to the data catalog.

8. Leave the default setting of having **Automated business name generation** enabled.

9. Click on **Next**.

10. For **Run preference**, select **Run on demand** and then click **Next**.

11. Review the summary of settings, and then click **Create.**

12. On the `films-CuratedZoneDB` summary page, click on **Run** to run the data import process.

13. When the import completes, the three tables in the **curatedzonedb** in our Glue Data Catalog should now be listed, as shown in the following screenshot. Even though we have multiple tables, for this exercise we will focus on the `film_category` table.

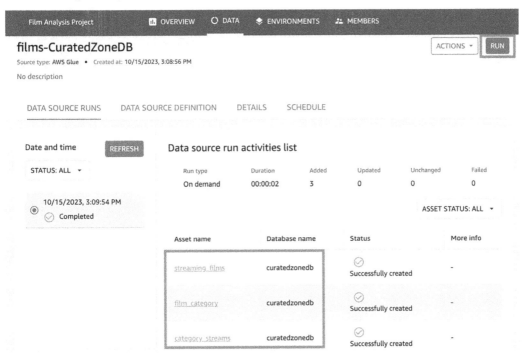

Figure 15.5: DataZone import from the Glue Data Catalog

Now that we have imported data into DataZone, we can add additional business metadata and then publish to the data catalog.

Adding business metadata

We can now review the current metadata for one of the tables we imported and add additional business metadata:

1. In the DataZone data portal, click on the **Data** tab along the top. This provides an overview of data for this project.

2. On the left-hand side menu, click on **Inventory data**, and then click on the `film_category` table. Inventory data contains tables that we have imported into DataZone but that have not yet been published into the DataZone business data catalog.

3. Click on **Schema** to view the schema of this table. For each column, a green icon indicates where automated metadata has been generated. For example, the first column in this table is `category_id`, and DataZone has automatically provided a label of **Category ID** for this column. You could approve each automatic metadata item individually, but in this exercise, we will accept all the changes by clicking the **ACCEPT ALL** button at the top of the screen, as shown in the following screenshot.

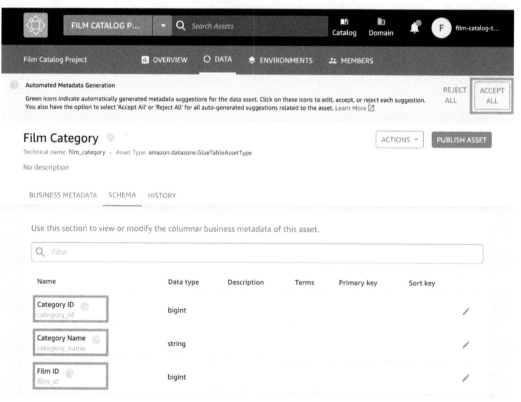

Figure 15.6: Automated metadata for the Film Category table

4. Let's make this dataset easier to discover for our business users by adding additional business metadata. At the top right, click on **Actions**, and then select **Edit** from the dropdown.

5. In the **Edit Asset** popup, change the name to Movie listings with category. For **description**, provide the following: *This table contains a complete listing of all films in our streaming movie catalog, including category/genre information for each film, as well as a list of special features.*

6. Click on **Update Asset**.

7. Click on the **Schema** tab, then click the **Pencil** icon next to the **Category Name** field. For description, add the following: *This field contains the movie category/genre. Sample categories include Animation, Comedy, Sports, Children, Drama, Action, and more.*

8. Click **Save**.

9. We could add additional metadata for each of the columns, but to save time we are going to publish the data asset to the category as it is now. Click on **Publish asset**, and then in the confirmation popup, click **Publish asset** again.

This table is now added to the business data catalog, and is discoverable by other users of the catalog.

Creating a project for data analysis

We can now create a new project that will be used by our marketing team to do data analysis:

1. Log out of the DataZone data portal by clicking on your username in the top right and clicking **Log out**.

2. Sign back in to the DataZone data portal with SSO, but sign in as the marketing-team-admin user. Note that you may be signed back in as the film-catalog-team-admin automatically, but if you are logged out again and you attempt to log in a second time, you should be prompted for your username.

3. Once logged in, click on **Create Project**.

4. For the project name, enter marketing-team-analysis. Optionally provide a description, and then click **Create**.

5. In the popup confirming that the project has been created, click on **Create environment**.

6. For the environment **Name**, enter marketing-team-datalake, and optionally provide a description.

7. Under **Environment profile**, select **DataLakeProfile** from the dropdown.

8. Leave all other defaults, and then click **Create environment**.

Now that our analysis project is ready, we can search for and subscribe to data.

Search the data catalog and subscribe to data

In this section, our marketing team searches the business data catalog and subscribes to a dataset:

1. The marketing team wants to analyze the movie catalog in order to identify the most popular genres of films. Use the search bar along the top of the DataZone data portal console and search for movie genre.

2. In the results, you should see the Movie listings with category table. Note how even though the original table in the Glue Data Catalog was called films_category, we were able to find the table based on the business metadata we had added in DataZone. **Click on the table name** to select it.

3. We can now review details of the table, including schema information for the table. We decide that this table will be good for our analysis, so click on **Subscribe**.

Note the warning message on this page, indicating that this dataset is an **unmanaged asset**. With DataZone, if an S3-based table uses Lake Formation for permissions management, or you have a Redshift table, these are considered **managed assets** and DataZone can enable the automatic sharing of these resources between different projects/teams.

Because our film_category table has not been configured to use Lake Formation permissions, it is listed as unmanaged. This means we can still request a subscription to the dataset, and the data owner will receive a notification to approve access. However, once they approve the subscription, they will need a process outside of DataZone to grant permissions to the team that requested the data. This could be, for example, working to add IAM-based permissions for the Glue database, table, and S3 data location for the film_category table to the marketing team IAM role.

In addition to modifying the table to use Lake Formation permissions, to configure the table for automatic sharing managed by DataZone, a DataZone administrator would also need to grant a set of permissions to a specific IAM role that is auto created by DataZone to be used by our marketing-team-analysis project. This is beyond the scope of this book, but refer to the following documentation for more information on this topic: https://docs.aws.amazon.com/datazone/latest/userguide/lake-formation-permissions-for-datazone.html

4. In the **Subscribe popup**, select the **marketing-team-analysis** project from the drop-down, and then provide a **Reason for request**. For example, this could be *Need access to the movie listings with category table for a new marketing project we are running.*

5. Click on **Subscribe**.

Approving the subscription request

We now log in to the DataZone portal as the film-domain-admin (the owner and publisher of the film_category table) so we can approve the request:

1. Log out of the DataZone data portal by clicking on your username in the top right and clicking **Log out**.

2. Sign back in to the DataZone data portal with SSO, but sign in as the **film-catalog-team-admin** user.

3. Click on the **Notifications icon** at the top right (just to the left of your username). You should see a list of alerts, with the most recent alert being **Subscription request created**. Click on the notification.

4. Review the **Subscription request** popup, which provides details about the requestor (marketing-team-admin) and the subscriber (the marketing-team-analysis project). This page also lists the **Reason for access** that the subscriber provided. Leave a short comment on your decision in the **Decision comment** box, and then click on **Approve** to approve the request.

As mentioned previously, since this dataset is not managed using AWS Lake Formation permissions, the dataset will not have been automatically shared with the marketing team. Therefore, a process would need to be in place to now grant the marketing team access, such as by updating the marketing team IAM policies to grant access. In order to get the full benefits of DataZone automated data sharing between projects and accounts, it would be recommended to ensure that all your S3 data is managed by Lake Formation.

Summary

In this chapter, we looked at the concept of a data mesh, a relatively new approach to data management. And while this concept has only been around since 2019, it has been rapidly adopted in many organizations.

The data mesh approach moves away from centralizing data analytics within a single team, and instead uses a decentralized approach, moving the responsibility for creating analytic data products closer to the teams that produce, or own, the operational data. In this chapter, we examined several different aspects of a data mesh, including the people, process, and organizational changes required to implement a data mesh, as well as some of the architecture approaches to implementing the technology required to enable a data mesh.

We also explored the core concepts and components of the Amazon DataZone service, which provides data governance functionality, including a business data catalog. After looking at potential data mesh architectures within AWS, we then got hands-on with the Amazon DataZone service. In the hands-on exercise, we set up DataZone, imported a dataset from the AWS Glue Data Catalog, and added business metadata to the dataset. We then had a look at how to search the DataZone business data catalog and how to subscribe to a data product.

As we near the end of this book, we will look at some of the key concepts required to build a modern data platform on AWS, which we will cover next.

Learn more on Discord

To join the Discord community for this book – where you can share feedback, ask questions to the author, and learn about new releases – follow the QR code below:

`https://discord.gg/9s5mHNyECd`

16

Building a Modern Data Platform on AWS

As we near the end of this book, we will review high-level concepts around building a modern data platform on AWS. We could easily devote another whole book to this topic alone, but in this chapter, we will provide at least an overview to give you a strong foundation on how to approach the build-out of a modern data platform.

There are many different pieces to the puzzle of building a modern data platform, and this chapter will build on many of the other topics we have covered in this book (such as data meshes and modern table formats) alongside introducing topics we have not yet covered (such as Agile development and CI/CD pipelines).

The goal of this chapter is to help you think through how to bring together many of the different concepts you have learned in this book to create a data platform that supports both the data producers and data consumers in your organization. This chapter is not a complete guide to building a data platform, but rather introduces important concepts and tools to enable you to start planning the building of your own modern data platform on AWS.

In this chapter, we will cover the following topics:

- Goals of a modern data platform
- Deciding whether to build or buy your data platform
- DataOps as an approach to building data platforms
- Hands-on – automated deployment of data platform components, and data transformation code

Before we get started, review the following *Technical requirements* section. This lists the prerequisites for performing the hands-on activity at the end of this chapter.

Technical requirements

In the last section of this chapter, we will go through a hands-on exercise that automates the deployment of components that could be used in a data platform, as well as the code for a data engineering pipeline. This will require permission for services such as AWS CloudFormation, AWS CodeCommit, AWS CodeDeploy, as well as AWS Glue and various other services. As with the other hands-on activities in this book, having access to an administrator user in your AWS account should give you the permissions needed to complete these activities.

You can access more information about running the exercises in this chapter using the following link: `https://github.com/PacktPublishing/Data-Engineering-with-AWS-2nd-edition/tree/main/Chapter16`

Goals of a modern data platform

In *Chapter 15, Implementing a Data Mesh Strategy*, we discussed how a central data platform team is responsible for building a platform that makes it easy for both data producers and data consumers to work with organizational data.

A data platform is intended to provide a system where multiple teams from across an organization can easily ingest data (including both structured and semi-structured, via batch and streaming), process the ingested data, and create new data products by joining datasets. It should also provide data governance controls, a catalog for making data discoverable across the organization, and the ability to easily share datasets across different teams/data domains.

Let's review some of the top goals for a modern data platform, after which we will explore approaches to building these data platforms.

A flexible and agile platform

As we all know, the only constant is change. We have seen this throughout this book as we spoke about new table formats, including Apache Iceberg, and new data architecture approaches such as the data mesh approach. AWS services also constantly evolve, and new services are introduced (both by AWS and other vendors). In this second edition of the book, there are three new chapters (including this one), as well as countless updates related to new AWS services and features (such as EMR Serverless, Bedrock, Redshift support for Iceberg, Glue support for Ray.io, DataZone, and more).

As a result, it is critical when building a data platform to ensure that the platform is flexible enough to incorporate new technologies and approaches. And not only should the platform be adaptable, but also agile enough to adapt and incorporate changes quickly. This requires an agile approach to the development of the platform, as we discuss later in this chapter.

A scalable platform

When building a new platform, you want to be able to start with a minimally viable product (MVP), or minimally loveable product (MLP), as some people prefer to call it. This means that you build a working platform with a minimal set of critical features, and then over time you add additional features. It also means that you do a staged roll-out of the platform, starting with perhaps a single domain, and then onboarding additional domains over time.

This means that right from the start, you need to build a platform that is scalable. On day one of the platform being live, you may have just one or two datasets of a few hundred GBs. But as you onboard additional domains/lines of business, the data volumes may grow to tens, and then hundreds, of TBs.

One of the big advantages of building a modern data platform on the cloud is the built-in scalability. For example, an Amazon S3 bucket can be used to store hundreds of GBs of data to start with, and yet without any additional configuration, the bucket can scale to store hundreds of TBs of data. The same goes for most other AWS services, specifically those that are serverless. For example, Amazon Kinesis in on-demand mode is able to automatically scale in response to changing data traffic.

As a result, one of the key enablers of a data platform that can easily scale is the use of AWS serverless services.

A well-governed platform

Another key attribute for a modern data platform is that it must support good governance of all data that is stored and processed on the platform.

In *Chapter 15, Implementing a Data Mesh Strategy*, we discussed how one of the key principals of a data mesh is *federated computational governance*. In summary, a central governance team, made up of representatives from each of the domains, works together to decide on the minimal required governance standards for the platform (such as compliance with data governance regulations, etc.). Each domain must then comply with those governance standards, but they may also implement their own additional governance requirements for their specific domain.

The central data platform needs to be able to support both the central common data governance requirements, and the governance requirements for each individual domain. This means that strong data governance functionality needs to be a core part of the platform from the start. Good data governance controls must be considered part of the minimally viable/lovable product that we spoke about earlier.

A secure platform

Another obvious but key requirement is that the data platform must be secure. This is an aspect of data governance generally, but since it is so critical, we call it out separately here.

Security on the platform needs to cover things such as ensuring that all data both at rest and in transit is encrypted. In addition, security also involves access control, making sure that only authorized users have access to data on the data platform, and then only the level of access to the data they need as opposed to system-wide data access. Another aspect of security is ensuring that data access is logged, so that access attempts can be audited by the security team.

In an overlap with data governance, security may also include using a service such as **Amazon Macie** to identify whether any PII information is contained in data files so that it can be secured if so.

An easy-to-use, self-serve platform

Even if you get all the previous goals correct – you have an agile, scalable, well-governed, and secure platform – but that platform is difficult to use, then its success will always be limited and it is likely to fail.

It is critical that different domains/lines of business are able to easily onboard onto the platform, and that users can quickly become productive with producing and/or consuming data. This requires both organizational effort (ensuring that you have a team that helps domains onboard to the platform), and making sure that use of the platform is well documented and the platform is easy to use from a technical standpoint. The platform should also support self-service – that is, once onboarded, teams should be able to add new data products, subscribe to data products from other teams, and perform most functions without needing to depend on a central data platform team to perform certain tasks.

The goal is to have the tools available that make it easy to ingest data into the platform, transform that data, apply required governance controls, register the data in a central catalog, and then enable data consumers to search for, subscribe to, and consume data products from across the organization. All of this should be doable without needing to raise tickets or request help from the central data platform team.

Having reviewed some of the key goals for central data platforms, let's now look at a critical decision point – whether to build a data platform or buy one.

Deciding whether to build or buy a data platform

The question of whether to build or buy applies to many different purchasing decisions that an organization needs to make. Some of these decisions are pretty obvious – for example, not many organizations will choose to build their own power plant and generate their own power, rather than just purchasing power from their local utility company.

Within the IT realm, there is likely to be a mix of building and buying, depending on the size of the organization. For example, most organizations that need systems for HR, Customer Relationship Management (CRM), or Enterprise Resource Planning (ERP) will purchase these from one of the many vendors that have built these products for many years. However, many organizations will choose to build and manage their own website and mobile app, including the microservices that power those systems.

Organizations also have a choice when it comes to their approach to implementing a modern data platform. However, there are a number of factors that you need to take into consideration when deciding whether to build or buy a data platform. Let's start by looking at what may be involved when you choose to buy a platform.

Choosing to buy a data platform

One option is to purchase a unified data platform that provides the processing and query engine and most of the components an organization needs, and then integrate other components as required (such as BI tools or database ingestion tools). Many vendors provide data platform products, however, in this section, we will primarily reference two of the most common data platforms – Databricks and Snowflake.

Databricks offers the **Databricks Lakehouse Platform**, designed to *"provide all the components needed to unify data, analytics, and AI."* **Snowflake** offers the **Snowflake Platform**, designed to *"connect businesses globally, across any type of scale of data and many different workloads."*

Depending on the vendor and platform you select, most data platforms that you purchase include the following components:

- **Data storage:** When you ingest data into most vendor-provided data platforms, the data is converted into an optimized format. This may be in a proprietary format, such as the compressed, columnar format that Snowflake stores data in, or an open format, such as the Delta Lake format that Databricks uses to store and manage data tables. Modern data platforms mostly make use of object storage such as Amazon S3 to physically store files.

- **Data transformation engine:** A core part of these platforms is an engine that enables you to create ETL/ELT jobs to transform your data, applying business logic across multiple datasets. The most popular languages for performing data transformation are SQL and Python (including PySpark, a Python API for Apache Spark). Databricks provides the ability to transform data using either Apache Spark or SQL, while Snowflake primarily provides a SQL-based interface.

- **Data query editor:** Another key component of data platforms is a query editor that enables data producers and consumers to interact with the data on the platform. This may be a SQL-based editor for running SQL queries against data, or something different, such as a notebook interface that enables users to work with platform data using code. Both Databricks and Snowflake provide a rich SQL query editor that also enables the ability to visualize query results (i.e., viewing the results as a bar chart, line chart, heat grid, etc.).

- **Data services:** Each platform will provide a number of services that you can use to manage and monitor your data platform, implement data governance, etc. This may include a data catalog for managing metadata related to your datasets (such as the Databricks Unity Catalog), as well as services that enable data sharing within the data platform and across different teams (such as Snowflake Secure Data Sharing, or Databricks Delta Share). Advanced services may also be included, such as the ability to securely combine data with a partner's dataset in a way that protects data privacy and limits access to the underlying granular data (such as with the clean room solutions offered by both Databricks and Snowflake).

Note that even when you purchase a platform from a vendor, you are still likely to need to integrate other third-party services and applications with your data platform. For example, you may have an application that streams data via Kinesis Data Streams or Amazon MSK (a managed streaming Kafka service), and you need to integrate that into your data platform. You may also want to use a commercial tool that enables easy data ingestion from many different data sources (such as Upsolver, Striim, Matillion, Fivetran, and others).

On the data consumption side, you are also likely to need to integrate a BI visualization tool such as QuickSight or Tableau.

When to buy a data platform

The primary benefit of purchasing a data platform from a vendor is that they provide and integrate all the common components that are needed for a modern data platform. This makes the implementation of the platform much simpler and reduces the skillsets required by the organization to implement and manage the platform. For organizations without existing engineering skills, this is a significant benefit.

However, when you purchase a data platform from a vendor, you are limited to the functionality that the vendor provides. As a result, it is important to fully evaluate different vendor offerings to ensure that the platform meets your needs and is likely to continue to do so as your requirements change over time. Once an investment has been made in a specific vendor's data platform, it can be very difficult to change to a different platform, and therefore it is critical that you evaluate your vendor's ability to support your organization over a 5-10 year timeframe.

Purchasing a platform is also often more expensive than using equivalent cloud-native services. The data platform vendors provide the integration between components managing the infrastructure and software for you and provide support when you run into issues. However, this often comes at a premium cost. Therefore it is important that you understand all the factors that can influence the cost of the vendor solution (for example, some vendors charge an additional premium for more advanced features) and project what your costs are likely to be over a longer time period, based on your expected data volume growth and additional features you may need over time.

Another benefit of purchasing a data platform is that, often, these platforms are supported across multiple clouds. For many organizations, it is simpler to standardize, and build on, a single cloud, but for large organizations, different teams may have elected over time to use different cloud providers. If your organization already has teams building in different clouds, then the ability to have a single data platform (such as Databricks or Snowflake) that can be run in AWS, Azure, and GCP may be a significant benefit.

Let's now look at some of the reasons that it may make sense to build a platform using cloud-native services and third-party tools, instead of purchasing a platform from a vendor.

Choosing to build a data platform

An alternative to buying a data platform from a vendor is to build your own platform using cloud-native services. Throughout this book, we have discussed a number of AWS services that can be integrated together to build a data platform:

- **Data storage:** Most modern data platforms are built using cloud object stores, and within AWS you can build your data platform with Amazon S3 as the physical storage layer. As we discussed in *Chapter 14, Building Transactional Data Lakes*, you can also use one of the modern open-table formats to store your data in an optimized format, such as Apache Iceberg. For smaller projects and environments where the primary skillset is SQL, you may decide to store your data in Amazon Redshift (although with Redshift RA3 nodes, the persistence layer does use Amazon S3 under the hood).

- **Data transformation engine:** We have discussed a number of AWS services that can be used to transform data as part of an ETL or ELT solution. For example, you can transform data using Apache Spark with the AWS Glue or Amazon EMR services, or use Python and pandas for light data transformation tasks using AWS Lambda. Alternatively, you can use SQL to transform your data using Amazon Athena or Amazon Redshift.

- **Data query editor:** If you primary storage platform is Redshift, you can use Redshift Query Editor for working with your data. Alternatively, if using Amazon S3 to store your data, you can use Amazon Athena as your query editor.

- **Data services:** AWS has a wide range of analytic services that can be integrated as part of your data platform. For example, AWS Lake Formation and Amazon DataZone can be used as a technical and business catalog respectively, and Lake Formation can also be used to manage access control and for sharing data across accounts. The AWS Clean Rooms service can be used to share data in S3 with partners in a secure, privacy-protecting way, and AWS Data Exchange can be used to directly access data from third-party data suppliers.

While building a data platform using cloud-native components is not the appropriate choice for all organizations, it does carry a number of advantages over buying one, as we discuss next.

When to build a data platform

One of the primary advantages of building a data platform is that you have a lot of flexibility in which components you use, and cloud-native services are often available at a lower cost than buying a data platform solution from a vendor.

When you build a data platform, you get to customize the platform based on your specific business requirements and have a wider variety of tools that you can integrate with the platform to meet the requirements of different teams within your organization. You can also more easily swap out different components of the platform over time than if you had purchased a full data platform solution from a single vendor.

In most cases, you will need some level of data engineering skills regardless of whether you use a vendor-provided data platform or a platform that you build yourself. These data engineers need to apply business logic to datasets in order to build analytical data products, which can be done through SQL or code-based transforms. Your data engineers also need to integrate the platform with other components, such as data ingestion services and BI visualization tools. However, when building a platform, your engineering team will also be responsible for creating integrations between the various AWS components that make up the core data platform (such as AWS Glue, Lambda, Lake Formation, DataZone, etc.).

Companies that have generalist developers and DevOps skills are well suited to building their own data platform. This is true for both small start-up type companies and large enterprises. In small start-ups, where budgets are tight, engineers can build their own data platform and start small with very low costs, and then scale up over time as the business grows. For large enterprises, there is often already a mix of different analytic tools used by different lines of business, and it may be easier to integrate these different technologies into a custom-built modern data platform than it would be to force all lines of business to standardize and migrate to a solution from a single vendor.

However, for mid-size companies that do not have developers and DevOps-type resources, it may make more sense for them to purchase a data platform solution from a vendor, and have the vendor (or a partner recommended by the vendor) implement and integrate the solution for them.

A third way — implementing an open-source data platform

As somewhat of a compromise between buying a vendor-provided data platform and building one from scratch, another option is to implement an open-source data platform. This is closer to building a data platform, as implementing most open-source data platforms requires downloading the source code from a repository such as GitHub, and then having engineering teams implement and customize the solution. Your engineering teams will also need to integrate your different data sources with the platform, as most open-source data platforms do not have connectors for all common sources.

However, it does give the engineering team a headstart and provides a mature platform with many features. In addition, it allows the engineering team to customize the platform based on the requirements of the business.

In the following section, we provide a brief overview of a data platform created and open-sourced by AWS Professional Services.

The Serverless Data Lake Framework (SDLF)

The **Serverless Data Lake Framework (SDLF)** is an open-source project that provides a data platform that accelerates the delivery of enterprise data lakes on AWS. This includes a number of production-ready best-practice templates that speed up the process of implementing data pipelines on AWS. This framework has been implemented at a number of large organizations, including Formula 1 motorsports racing, Amazon retail in Ireland, and Naranja Finance in Argentina (amongst many other companies).

Some of the best practices that are implemented via the SDLF include:

- **Infrastructure-as-Code and version control:** The base SDLF implementation, along with customizations and data transformation tasks, are all managed through a CI/CD pipeline and a code repository. The SDLF avoids the need to do any manual implementation via the AWS console, instead deploying infrastructure and code via DevOps pipelines. This also means that any changes to the data platform or data transformation pipelines are managed via a code repository, providing version control.

- **Scalability using serverless technologies:** The SDLF makes extensive use of serverless technologies for the core of the data platform. Serverless services can easily scale from low data volumes to handling much larger data volumes, and are often the most cost-effective approach as you only pay for resources when tasks are running (you never pay for idle time).

- **Built-in monitoring and alerting:** The SDLF data platform includes built-in monitoring (using the ELK stack) and alerting (via CloudWatch alarms). This ensures that issues can be detected quickly and that logs are easily accessible for troubleshooting issues.

Deploying and managing the SDLF does require DevOps skills, so is not intended for environments that do not have relevant engineering skills. Deploying the SDLF should not be viewed as an alternative to purchasing a data platform from a vendor like Databricks or Snowflake; however, if you are considering building a data platform, then the SDLF can help accelerate the data platform build while ensuring many best practices are applied.

In this next section, we will look at some of the key components of the SDLF.

Core SDLF concepts

There are various layers that make up the SDLF, starting from the foundational layer that provides the core data platform functionality. Once the **foundations** have been deployed, **teams** are able to build **pipelines** (which control the **transformation** processes that are applied to a **dataset**). Let's look into each of these terms in more detail.

Foundations

When you deploy the SDLF foundation layer, you are deploying components to be used by all teams and all pipelines. This includes components such as Amazon S3 buckets for storage, DynamoDB tables (for configuration and the metadata catalog that tracks pipeline executions), and the ELK stack for monitoring.

Teams

The team layer deploys resources for a specific team (that is, a group of people that work together, such as a specific line of business, or a smaller team within a line of business). A team develops and deploys datasets, transformations, pipelines, and code repositories that are unique to that specific team.

Datasets

With the SDLF, a dataset is a logical grouping of data – this could be a single table, or an entire database consisting of multiple tables. For example, a dataset could constitute the tables imported from a relational database, or a group of files coming from a streaming data source (such as IoT data from a factory system).

Pipelines

A pipeline is a logical view of an ETL process, laying out the steps that data goes through as it is transformed. Teams create pipelines, and may create multiple pipelines for different datasets.

With the SDLF, each pipeline is split into multiple stages, most commonly Stage A (which is intended for doing an initial light transform on a single file), and Stage B (which is intended for heavier transforms, such as joining datasets or applying business logic).

The orchestration of these pipelines is done using AWS Step Functions. Each stage has a Step Functions workflow that defines the transformation steps that will be completed as part of the pipeline.

Transformations

Transformations perform the data transformation tasks – converting files to Parquet format, joining datasets, aggregating columns, etc. These transformations are run by the different stages of the pipeline. For example, a pipeline may consist of a Step Functions workflow that runs a Glue job to apply business logic to data, and then runs a Glue crawler to crawl the new data and add it to the Glue Data Catalog. The transformation would be the Spark code that the Glue job runs.

To learn more about the **Serverless Data Lake Framework (SDLF)**, use the following links:

- **SDLF GitHub page**: `https://github.com/awslabs/aws-serverless-data-lake-framework`
- **SDLF documentation**: `https://sdlf.readthedocs.io/en/latest/index.html`

Having looked at options for buying, building, or implementing an open-source solution for a data platform, let's now review how you can use a DataOps approach to building and maintaining your data platform and transformation code.

DataOps as an approach to building data platforms

DataOps is a term that has been around since at least 2015 and refers to an agile approach to building data platforms and data products that borrows from some of the concepts of DevOps. Where DevOps transformed the approach to how software is engineered, DataOps transforms the approach by which data products are built.

Much like it is difficult to give an exact definition or outline an exact approach for other concepts we have discussed (such as data lakes and data meshes), it is similarly difficult to tie down one clear-cut definition for what is meant by DataOps. The original author of the term may have had a clear definition of what they meant, but over time, the term may come to mean different things to different people, and the meaning of the term as a whole may evolve.

In this section, we will attempt to focus on some of the core concepts of DataOps, and specifically, how they apply to building a data platform and data products. There is more to DataOps than we can cover in a single chapter, so in this section, we will focus on two of the key aspects – automation and observability.

Automation and observability as a key for DataOps

While there may be different definitions of what DataOps is, at its core it is about automation and observability. This includes automating the deployment of the data platform (and updates to the platform), as well as deployment and updates to the transform code that produces data products.

A key part of this automation is managing infrastructure for the data platform and logic for data transformations as version-managed code.

In addition, there should be automation for monitoring and alerting for the data platform and data transformations. If the platform is designed to trigger an AWS Lambda job to run in response to a specific event (such as a new data file being received) and the Lambda function fails to execute, a data platform engineer should receive an alert. In the same way, if the code within a Lambda function causes an error and the function fails, a data engineer should be alerted.

There should also be observability dashboards that enable data platform owners and data engineers to view key metrics related to their area of responsibility. A platform engineer should easily be able to view the throughput of Kinesis Data Streams or the number of executions of a Lambda function, and a data engineer should be able to easily view the status of a specific pipeline they have engineered. When there is a failure, engineers should be able to easily access relevant log files in order to troubleshoot and identify the root cause of the issue.

Another key success factor for DataOps is ensuring that teams work with an **Agile approach**, working in short sprints in order to constantly evolve and enhance the data platform and products, rather than planning months-long release cycles. To learn more about the Agile approach to software development, see `https://www.atlassian.com/agile`.

Let's take a closer look at the topic of automating infrastructure and code deployment.

Automating infrastructure and code deployment

When you deploy data platform infrastructure (such as a Snowflake or Redshift cluster, a Databricks cluster or an AWS Glue job, or a Kinesis Data Stream) the deployment should **not** be done manually using the console or by typing commands on the command line, but should be automated using a provisioning tool. Two common tools for this purpose are **Terraform** (by HashiCorp) and **CloudFormation** (an AWS service).

In the same way, when deploying data transformation code (such as the code for a Glue job or Databricks job, or a SQL transform in Snowflake or Redshift), this code should be managed and deployed from a version-controlled code repository. Common tools for this include **GitHub**, **GitLab**, **AWS CodeCommit**, **Bitbucket**, and **Azure DevOps**.

When developing code, developers should build unit tests (among other types of tests), and as part of the automation of code deployment, the pipeline should use these tests to validate the code. It is also recommended to perform security scans of code as part of the pipeline and to implement other software development best practices.

While it may be argued that managing the code for these deployments via these tools may add additional overhead to the deployment process, it significantly increases the reliability and security of the deployment and improves the reliability of making updates to either infrastructure or data transformation code. If an update does fail, then having all infrastructure, pipeline, and transformation code managed in a version control system means that rolling back to the previous version of the code can be done quickly.

For example, let's say someone deploys some data transformation code in a Glue job by directly writing the code for the Glue job in the AWS console. When that code needs to be updated, another engineer may use the AWS Management Console to modify the code. With this approach, no history of the code changes will be stored and an engineer can change the code without anyone else needing to approve those changes.

In comparison, if the code for the Glue job is managed via a code management solution (such as AWS CodeCommit or GitHub), then each version of the code is stored and available to review. When code is updated, you can build in approval requirements which require the code to be reviewed by other members of the team, and perhaps a security engineer, before the code is deployed via an automated pipeline. In addition, code can be developed and tested in a development environment and then promoted to be deployed in the QA or production environment via a pipeline.

Let's now look at the importance of observability for data platforms and data engineering pipelines.

Automating observability

The other key part of building data platforms and products is to ensure that there is clear observability – this means that teams can monitor the current status of operations, identify trends that indicate when things are starting to go wrong, and deep-dive to find the root cause of issues when things do go wrong.

There are three primary tools that enable this:

- **Dashboards:** Having dashboards that are constantly updated enables a team to get an accurate view of current operations. By looking at various dashboards, teams can view Key Performance Indicators (KPIs) that show the health of a system. For example, a platform engineer can view a **CloudWatch dashboard** for **Simple Queue Service (SQS)** to determine whether the queue size is growing, indicating an issue with processing the queue. In a similar way, a data engineer can view a list of all DAGs in **Apache Airflow** and easily see when a specific DAG last ran, the recent tasks for a DAG, the number of runs, etc.

- **Alerts:** The platform should have a way of sending automated alerts when things are not operating normally or if failures are detected. For example, **CloudWatch alarms** can be configured to send an email or text alert if a queue grows beyond a certain threshold, and **Airflow Service Level Agreements (SLAs)** can be used to generate an email if the expected time it takes for a specific task to complete exceeds an agreed length of time.

- **Logs:** The other tool that teams need is an effective log collection system that includes functionality for doing advanced searches against logs. When things do go wrong (as they will!), teams need an effective way to search through logs to help troubleshoot the issue. For example, **CloudWatch Logs** or **Amazon OpenSearch** can be used to store logs from the various systems across a data platform and engineers can easily search through the logs to troubleshoot failures.

To learn more about DataOps, you can access a free, on-demand DataOps certification course titled *The Fundamentals of DataOps*. This course, along with a certification assessment, is offered by *DataKitchen*, a commercial provider of DataOps solutions. Access the course at `https://info. datakitchen.io/training-certification-dataops-fundamentals`.

Having briefly discussed a DataOps approach to developing data platforms and data products, let's now look at some of the core AWS services that can be used to implement a DataOps approach.

AWS services for implementing a DataOps approach

In this section, we'll explore a quick overview of some of the core AWS services that can help you implement a DataOps approach to building your data platform and data products. Then, in the hands-on section of this chapter, you can follow along to get some practical experience by putting some of these services into action.

AWS services for infrastructure deployment

There are two primary tools within AWS that enable you to manage and deploy your **Infrastructure as Code (IaC)**, instead of manually deploying resources via the AWS console or the command line.

AWS CloudFormation

AWS CloudFormation enables you to define your AWS resources within a template (in either YAML or JSON format), and then automatically deploy those resources into your AWS account. When you need to modify some aspect of the infrastructure, you can modify and redeploy the template and CloudFormation will intelligently update the resources.

For example, you can define a simple AWS Glue job using the following YAML template:

```
AWSTemplateFormatVersion: '2010-09-09'
# Sample template to define an AWS Glue job (in YAML format)
Resources:
# The script file already exists in S3 and is called by this job
  GlueSampleJob:
    Type: AWS::Glue::Job
    Properties:
      Role: DataEngGlueCWS3CuratedZoneRole
      Description: Glue job to denormalize film and category tables
      Command:
        Name: glueetl
        ScriptLocation: "s3://aws-glue-assets-1234567890-us-east-2/
scripts/Film Category Denormalization.py"
      WorkerType: G.1X
      NumberOfWorkers: 2
      GlueVersion: "3.0"
      Name: Film Category Denormalization via CFN
```

The above template deploys a Glue job to run the Film Category Denormalization job (which we created in an earlier chapter using the Glue Studio console).

CloudFormation also supports the ability to use parameters in templates, and at deployment time the parameter values can be passed to CloudFormation. This enables you to use the same template to deploy resources into different environments, such as your dev, test, and production environments. For example, the ScriptLocation could be referenced as a parameter, and then at the time of deployment the correct S3 bucket name for the specific environment could be passed in. Or the WorkerType and NumberOfWorkers could be parameters, so that you deploy smaller resources in the dev and test environments, and more powerful resources for the production job deployment.

If you are building a data platform using all AWS services, then **CloudFormation** is a good option for automating your infrastructure deployments and updates. However, if you have a multi-cloud approach, or you also want to automate the deployment of other non-AWS services (such as Snowflake or Databricks), then **Terraform** (a product from HashiCorp) provides similar functionality for both AWS and non-AWS resources. For more information on Terraform, see https://www.terraform.io/.

Let's now look at another related service that enables us to create CloudFormation templates with recommended best practices via code.

AWS Cloud Development Kit (CDK)

The AWS CDK enables you to define resources using popular programming languages including TypeScript, JavaScript, Python, Java, C#/.Net, and Go. You define the resources in your code and the CDK then creates a CloudFormation template that incorporates best practices for the specific type of resource that you are creating.

Some of the benefits of using the AWS CDK to define your AWS resources as code are as follows:

- **It allows you to specify high-level constructs in your code, and have CDK automatically create CloudFormation templates that provide best practice and contain secure defaults:**

  This enables you to define resources that follow best practices, with less code. For example, the AWS documentation demonstrates how just 13 lines of Python code that provides high-level constructs can be used to create a CloudFormation template of over 500 lines. See: https://docs.aws.amazon.com/cdk/v2/guide/home.html.

- **It allows you to use common programming approaches to model the design of your system:**

  For example, you can use the AWS CDK to write Python code that defines AWS resources that make up your data platform, and make use of programming constructs such as parameters, if … then … else conditions, loops, and more.

- **It enables the import of existing CloudFormation templates for use in your AWS CDK code:**

  With this approach, you can migrate any existing CloudFormation template to the AWS CDK one piece at a time. See the AWS documentation on this at https://docs.aws.amazon.com/cdk/v2/guide/use_cfn_template.html.

- **It enables you to centralize the code that defines your data platform resources alongside the code for data transformation jobs, CI/CD pipelines, etc.:**

  Source Control Management (SCM) systems such as Git (which we will cover in more detail in the next section) enable you to securely manage your code in a centralized location and include features that simplify collaboration and help manage conflicts. By defining your resources using the AWS CDK, you can manage all your code in central repositories.

AWS has a blog post that demonstrates how to use the AWS CDK to create a continuous integration and continuous deployment (CI/CD) pipeline to define, test, provision, and manage changes to an AWS Glue-based pipeline. We will not cover the AWS CDK in any more detail here, but refer to the following AWS blog post to learn more about how the CDK can be used with data pipelines: https://aws.amazon.com/blogs/big-data/build-test-and-deploy-etl-solutions-using-aws-glue-and-aws-cdk-based-ci-cd-pipelines/.

Let's now look at AWS services for managing and deploying code.

AWS code management and deployment services

Source Control Management (SCM) systems enable you to store code (along with documentation and other files) in a way that each version of a file is stored and tracked. It also helps manage potential conflicts when you have multiple engineers working to update the same set of files. This has many benefits, including:

- The ability to easily revert to a previous version of code
- Being able to check which person on the team made a change to a specific part of the code
- The ability for multiple people to work on different parts of the same file (such as different functions in code), easily merge their changes to the file, and resolve any potential conflicts
- Ensuring that there is a central copy of all code, enabling administrators to handle code backups centrally

The most popular code management toolkit is Git, an open-source solution that is freely available. Many vendors, however, have created commercial SCM solutions that use the underlying Git toolset. This means that once you have a good understanding of how Git works, there are multiple different solutions that you can use with ease that add additional functionality and a user interface to the underlying Git toolset.

Let's look at the AWS service for hosting Git repositories, as well as related services that can be used to create CI/CD pipelines.

AWS CodeCommit

AWS CodeCommit is a cloud-based service that provides a managed source control system to host Git repositories. CodeCommit stores code, binaries, and metadata in a way that provides resilience, redundancy, and high availability. CodeCommit encrypts all files that it stores, and through integration with AWS Identity and Access Management (IAM), you can assign specific permissions to different users for different code repositories.

With CodeCommit you can create a code repository to store code related to the data platform and separate code repositories for each of your data domains (where data producers can store code for their data engineering transforms and pipelines). You can also integrate popular development tools with AWS CodeCommit, such as **AWS Cloud9**, **Visual Studio**, and **Eclipse**. Certain AWS services also offer direct integration with CodeCommit, such as support in **AWS Glue** for managing code for your Glue jobs in CodeCommit (and AWS Glue also supports another popular code management solution, GitHub).

CodeCommit currently offers 5 active users per month at no cost as part of the AWS Free Tier. If you need more than 5 active users, the cost is $1 per additional user per month. This comes with a set limit of storage and Git requests per user per month, and if these limits are exceeded there is an additional charge. See the CodeCommit pricing page at `https://aws.amazon.com/codecommit/pricing/`.

We will use CodeCommit in the hands-on section of this chapter, but first let's have an overview of a related service, AWS CodeBuild.

AWS CodeBuild

AWS CodeBuild is a managed service that can be used to compile source code, run unit tests, and produce software packages ready for deployment.

For example, you can use CodeBuild to deploy an environment where you can use an AWS Glue public Amazon ECR image (Docker container) to run unit tests against your code. Once the tests have run, assuming they complete successfully, you can use CodeBuild to write the updated code to an Amazon S3 bucket.

AWS CodePipeline

AWS CodePipeline is a managed service providing **continuous delivery**, enabling you to automate the steps to deploy and update code and infrastructure for your data platform and products.

For example, you can create a pipeline in CodePipeline that instructs CloudFormation to perform an update on resources, based on an updated CloudFormation template. You can then configure that pipeline to be automatically triggered when a new commit is made to the associated CodeCommit repository and branch combination. By doing this, every time you update the CloudFormation template in CodeCommit, the pipeline will be triggered and will use CloudFormation to deploy the update to the existing resources.

Another example is data producers using CodePipeline to manage updates to their data engineering transform and pipeline code. When a data engineer updates the code for a Glue job and commits that to CodeCommit, this can trigger a pipeline that calls CodeBuild to run unit tests against the Python code, and then writes the updated file to Amazon S3. When Glue jobs run, they read the code file from Amazon S3, so the next time the Glue job is triggered it will use the latest version of the code file placed there by CodeBuild. For an example of this implementation, see the following AWS blog post: https://aws.amazon.com/blogs/devops/how-to-unit-test-and-deploy-aws-glue-jobs-using-aws-codepipeline/.

Having reviewed a number of AWS services that help implement a DataOps approach to building a data platform, let's now get hands-on with some of these services.

Hands-on — automated deployment of data platform components and data transformation code

While we do not have space to cover all aspects of building a modern data platform, in this section we will cover how to use various AWS services to deploy some components of a data platform. We start by setting up an AWS CodeCommit repository that will contain all the resources for our data repository (such as Glue ETL scripts and CloudFormation templates). We then use AWS CodePipeline to configure pipeline jobs that push any code or infrastructure changes into our target account.

Setting up a Cloud9 IDE environment

Our first step is to create a **Cloud9** IDE environment, which we can use for writing our code and committing code to a CodeCommit repository. Cloud9 is an AWS service that can be used to provision a managed EC2 instance to provide us with a browser-based **Integrated Development Environment** (**IDE**) that we can use to write, run, and debug code from within our web browser. Cloud9 environments come preinstalled with various tools that are useful for developing in an AWS environment, such as the **AWS Command Line Interface** (**CLI**) and a **Git** client.

Let's get started:

1. Log in to the **AWS Management Console** and use the top search bar to search for and open the **Cloud9** service.

2. On the **Cloud9** dashboard page, click on **Create environment** at the top right.

3. For **Name**, provide a name for your environment, such as dataeng-ide, and optionally provide a description that explains what you are using the environment for (this will be visible to other AWS users in this account).

4. For **Environment type**, ensure that **New EC2 instance** is selected, and for **Instance type**, select **t2.micro**. If there are no **t2.micro** instances available when you launch your Cloud9 IDE, either wait a while and try again, or use a different instance size (just be aware of the pricing differences for the different instance types).

5. Leave all other settings at their defaults, and click **Create**.

6. On the list of your Cloud9 environments, click on the link to **open** your Cloud9 IDE. Note that it takes a few minutes for your environment to be created.

7. Once the environment has been created, use the terminal at the bottom of the Cloud9 environment to run the following command: git --version. This should return the version of Git that is preinstalled in the Cloud9 environment.

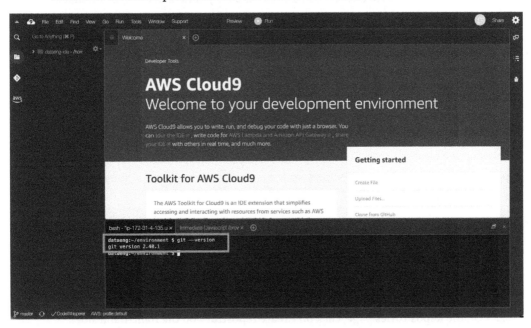

Figure 16.1: AWS Cloud9 console

8. You can now configure a username and email that will be associated with your Git commits by running the following commands in the Cloud9 terminal. Modify the following commands to use a username of your choice and specify your email address:

```
git config --global user.name "Gareth Eagar"
git config --global user.email gareth.eagar@example.com
```

9. We can now configure the AWS CLI credential helper, which will automate the provisioning of credentials needed to authenticate to CodeCommit. Run the following two commands to configure the credential helper:

```
git config --global credential.helper '!aws codecommit credential-
helper $@'
git config --global credential.UseHttpPath true
```

10. For the last step in this part of the hands-on exercise, let's create a new directory in our Cloud9 environment to contain our Git repositories. By default, you should be in the /home/ec2-user/environment directory in the terminal window, and you can run the following commands to create a new git subdirectory, and then change into that directory:

```
mkdir git
cd git
```

Now that we have configured our IDE environment, let's move on to creating our **CodeCommit** repositories.

Setting up our AWS CodeCommit repository

In this step, we create an AWS CodeCommit repository to store a CloudFormation template that deploys a Glue job, and to store PySpark code for the Glue job. We then clone the repository in our Cloud9 environment.

Let's get started:

1. We will be going back to our Cloud9 IDE environment shortly, so use a new browser tab to open the **AWS Management Console** and use the top search bar to search for, and open, the **CodeCommit** service.

2. On the **Repositories** page, click on **Create repository** on the right-hand side.

3. For **Repository name,** set the name to data-product-film, and optionally provide a **Description**. Then, click **Create**.

4. In the left-hand side menu, make sure **Repositories** is selected, and then click on the **Clone HTTPS** link under the **Clone URL** column for your data-product-film repository. This will copy the HTTPS URL for the repository to our clipboard, which we will need in the next step.

5. Go back to your browser tab with the **Cloud9** IDE environment, and in the terminal/console window, run pwd to make sure you are in the home/ec2-user/environment/git directory.

6. In the **terminal/console** window, run git clone <https-repo-link>, replacing <https-repo-link> with the link you copied in *step 5*. For example:

```
git clone https://git-codecommit.us-east-2.amazonaws.com/v1/repos/
data-product-film
```

7. In the **terminal/console** window, change into the data-product-film directory and create new subfolders – one for our Glue PySpark code, and one for CloudFormation templates:

```
cd data-product-film
mkdir glueETL_code
mkdir cfn_templates
```

8. We also want to create a new S3 bucket to store resources related to our data product. In the **terminal/console** window, run the following command to create a new bucket, but make sure to replace initials with your own initials or unique identifier:

```
aws s3 mb s3://data-product-film-initials
```

So far, we have created a repository in AWS CodeCommit, cloned the repository into a Cloud9 IDE environment, and created an Amazon S3 bucket and directories to store our files. We can now move on to our next exercise, where we will add a Glue ETL script and a CloudFormation template into our repository.

Adding a Glue ETL script and CloudFormation template into our repository

In this section, we will create a new CloudFormation template file that defines an AWS Glue job, and will also create a file that contains the code for the Glue job:

1. Log in to the **AWS Management Console** and use the top search bar to search for, and open, the **Cloud9** service.

2. In the list of your environments, click on the dataeng-ide environment (which we created earlier), and then click on **Open in Cloud9**. Note that if your Cloud9 environment has been idle for more than 30 minutes, it will have automatically shut down and you will need to wait a few minutes while the environment restarts.

3.   Once your Cloud9 environment is ready, click on **File | New File**. Paste the following code into the editor. Note that you can also copy and paste this code from the GitHub site for this chapter of the book:

IMPORTANT: Make sure you change the S3 path to reference the name of the curated zone bucket.

```python
import sys
from awsglue.transforms import *
from awsglue.utils import getResolvedOptions
from pyspark.context import SparkContext
from awsglue.context import GlueContext
from awsglue.job import Job
from awsglue.dynamicframe import DynamicFrame


args = getResolvedOptions(sys.argv, ["JOB_NAME"])
sc = SparkContext()
glueContext = GlueContext(sc)
spark = glueContext.spark_session
job = Job(glueContext)
job.init(args["JOB_NAME"], args)


# Load the streaming_films table into a Glue DynamicFrame from the
Glue catalog
StreamingFilms = glueContext.create_dynamic_frame.from_catalog(
    database="curatedzonedb",
    table_name="streaming_films",
    transformation_ctx="StreamingFilms",
)


# Convert the DynamicFrame to a Spark DataFrame
spark_dataframe = StreamingFilms.toDF()


# Create a SparkSQL table based on the steaming_films table
spark_dataframe.createOrReplaceTempView("streaming_films")


# Create a new DataFrame that records number of streams for each
# category of film
```

```
CategoryStreamsDF = glueContext.sql("""
SELECT category_name,
         count(category_name) streams
FROM streaming_films
GROUP BY category_name
""")


# Convert the DataFrame back to a Glue DynamicFrame
CategoryStreamsDyf = DynamicFrame.fromDF(CategoryStreamsDF,
glueContext, "CategoryStreamsDyf")


# Prepare to write the dataframe to Amazon S3
############# NOTE #############
#### Change the path below to
#### reference your bucket name
###############################
s3output = glueContext.getSink(
  path="s3://dataeng-curated-zone-gse23/streaming/top_categories",
  connection_type="s3",
  updateBehavior="UPDATE_IN_DATABASE",
  partitionKeys=[],
  compression="snappy",
  enableUpdateCatalog=True,
  transformation_ctx="s3output",
)
# Set the database and table name for where you want this table
# to be registered in the Glue catalog
s3output.setCatalogInfo(
  catalogDatabase="curatedzonedb", catalogTableName="category_
streams"
)
# Set the output format to Glue Parquet
s3output.setFormat("glueparquet")
# Write the output to S3 and update the Glue catalog
s3output.writeFrame(CategoryStreamsDyf)
job.commit()
```

4. Ensure that in the previous step, you modified the name of the S3 bucket on line 47 to match the name of your curated zone bucket, and then click **File | Save As**. Make sure to select the glueETL_code directory, give the file a name of Glue-streaming_views_by_category. py, and then click **Save:**

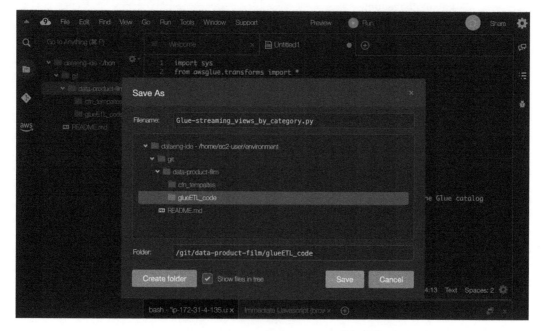

Figure 16.2: Cloud9 – saving the Glue ETL code

5. Now we can create our CloudFormation template, which will be used to deploy a new Glue job. Click on **File | New File**. Paste the following code for our CloudFormation template into the text editor for the new file. Note that you can also copy and paste this code from the GitHub site for this chapter of the book:

    IMPORTANT: Make sure you change the S3 script location parameter to reference the name of the bucket that you created earlier in this chapter.

```
AWSTemplateFormatVersion: '2010-09-09'
# CloudFormation template to deploy the streaming view by category
# Glue job.
# In the Parameters section we define parameters that can be passed
to
# CloudFormation at deployment time. If no parameters are passed in,
then the
# specified default is used.
```

```
Parameters:
# JobName: The name of the job to be created
  JobName:
    Type: String
    Default: streaming_views_by_category
# The name of the IAM role that the job assumes. It must have access
to data,
# script, and temporary directory. We created this IAM role via the
AWS
# console in Chapter 7.
  IAMRoleName:
    Type: String
    Default: DataEngGlueCWS3CuratedZoneRole
# The S3 path where the script for this job is located. Modify the
default
# below to reference the specific path for your S3 bucket
  ScriptLocation:
    Type: String
    Default: "s3://data-product-film-initials/glueETL_code/Glue-
streaming_views_by_category.py"
# In the Resources section, we define the AWS resources we want to
deploy
# with this CloudFormation template. In our case, it is just a
single Glue
# job, but a single template can deploy multiple different AWS
resources
Resources:
# Below we define our Glue job, and we substitute parameters in from
the
# above section.
  GlueJob:
    Type: AWS::Glue::Job
    Properties:
      Role: !Ref IAMRoleName
      Description: Glue job to calculate number of streams by
category
      Command:
        Name: glueetl
```

```
     ScriptLocation: !Ref ScriptLocation
     WorkerType: G.1X
     NumberOfWorkers: 2
     GlueVersion: "3.0"
     Name: Streaming Views by Category
```

6.   Ensure that in the previous step, you modified the name of the S3 bucket on line 22 to
     match the name of your data product film bucket, and then click **File | Save As**. Make sure
     to select the cfn_templates directory, give the file a name of CFN-glue_job-streams_by_
     category.cfn, and then click **Save.**

7.   Let's now commit the two new files we created to our data-product-film repository. To
     do this, use the **terminal/console** window in Cloud9. Make sure you are in the /home/ec2-
     user/environment/git/data-product-film directory and run the following commands
     to commit the file to the repository:

```
git add .
git commit -m "Initial commit of CloudFormation template and Glue
code for our streaming views by category data product"
git push
```

 Note that you can type out the above commands or copy and paste them
from the GitHub repo for this book, but be careful about copying and pasting
from the eBook or PDF versions, as it may use quote characters that will not
work correctly when you paste the code into Cloud9.

The above git add command stages all files in the current directory and its subdirec-
tories to be added to Git. The git commit command prepares the file to be written to
our CodeCommit Git repository, along with a message explaining the purpose of this
specific commit. The git push command takes the prepared files and copies them into
the CodeCommit repository.

8.   Now, access the **AWS Console** and navigate to the **CodeCommit** service. If you review
     the data-platform-film repository in CodeCommit, you should see the files that we just
     created in the repository.

We have now created a CloudFormation template and Glue ETL code and committed the files to
our CodeCommit repository. Next, we create pipelines to automate the deployment of the Glue
job and code.

Automating deployment of our Glue code

When a Glue job runs, it reads the code for the job from Amazon S3. In this section, we will set up a pipeline using AWS CodePipeline that will copy the contents of our data product film repository to Amazon S3 whenever a change is made to any of the files:

1. Log in to the **AWS Management Console** and use the top search bar to search for and open the **CodePipeline** service.

2. On the page listing pipelines, click on **Create pipeline** on the top right-hand side.

3. For **Pipeline name**, enter `data-product-film-resources`, and for **Role name**, accept the default. Leave **Advanced settings** as the default, and then click on **Next**.

4. For **Source provider**, select **AWS CodeCommit** from the drop-down list.

5. For **Repository name**, select **data-product-film**.

6. For **Branch name**, select the default (usually the default branch is called **master**, but it may also be called **main**, depending on the tool that was used to commit the first file to the repository).

7. For **Change detection options**, select **Amazon CloudWatch Events**.

8. Leave other settings as default, and click **Next**.

9. For **Build – optional**, click **Skip build stage**. Then click **Skip** to confirm.

10. For **Deploy provider**, select **Amazon S3** from the drop-down list.

11. For **Bucket**, select the bucket we created earlier for our data product (such as **data-product-film-initials**).

12. Select the **Extract file before deploy** option, leave **Deployment path – optional** blank, then click **Next**.

13. Review the settings, then click **Create pipeline**.

14. Open the **Amazon S3** console and confirm that the files from your repo have now been copied into your `data-product-film-initials` bucket.

Our Glue code is now deployed, so let's now set up a pipeline that will deploy our Glue job using CloudFormation.

Automating the deployment of our Glue job

Let's create a new pipeline that will be triggered whenever the CloudFormation template for our Glue job is updated. In order to do this, we first need to update one of our IAM roles.

When we deploy a CloudFormation template via the console, by default it will use the credentials of the user that we are logged in as to create the required resources (such as a Glue job). However, when doing an automated deployment via CodePipeline, we need to specify an IAM role that has the necessary permissions to deploy the resources instead.

For our use case, we can use the `DataEngGlueCWS3CuratedZoneRole` role, which we created in *Chapter 7* to run our Glue job. However, we need to modify the role so that CloudFormation is able to assume it when deploying resources, which we do by adding a trust relationship for CloudFormation to the role. We also want to add permissions to allow this role (which is also used to run our Glue job) to access the new bucket we created that contains the Glue ETL code:

1. Log in to the **AWS Management Console** and use the top search bar to search for, and open, the **IAM** service.

2. In the left-hand menu, click on **Roles**, and then search for `DataEngGlueCWS3CuratedZoneRole`, and then click on the role name so we can edit it.

3. Select the **Trust relationships** tab, and then click **Edit trust policy.**

4. Modify the **Service** portion of the policy to also include the **CloudFormation** service, as follows:

```json
{
    "Version": "2012-10-17",
    "Statement": [
        {
            "Effect": "Allow",
            "Principal": {
                "Service": [
                    "cloudformation.amazonaws.com",
                    "glue.amazonaws.com"
                ]
            },
            "Action": "sts:AssumeRole"
        }
    ]
}
```

5. Once the policy JSON is updated, click on **Update policy**.

6. Click on the **Permissions** tab, expand the `DataEngGlueCWS3CuratedZoneWrite` policy, and click **Edit**.

7. Add your `data-product-film-initials` bucket in the list of resources that provide `s3:GetObject` permissions as follows (making sure to modify the bucket name initials to reflect your bucket name):

```
"Resource": [
    "arn:aws:s3:::dataeng-landing-zone-initials/*",
        "arn:aws:s3:::dataeng-clean-zone-initials/*",
        "arn:aws:s3:::data-product-film-initials/*"
    ]
```

Now that we have permissions configured as needed, let's create the pipeline:

1. Log in to the **AWS Management Console** and use the top search bar to search for, and open, the **CodePipeline** service.

2. On the page listing pipelines, click on **Create pipeline** at the top right-hand side.

3. For **Pipeline name**, enter `data-product-film-glue-streaming-views-by-category-job`, and for **Role name**, accept the default. Leave **Advanced settings** as default, and then click on **Next**.

4. For **Source provider**, select **AWS CodeCommit** from the drop-down list.

5. For **Repository name**, select `data-product-film`.

6. For **Branch name**, select the default (usually the default branch is called **master**, but it may also be called **main**, depending on the tool that was used to commit the first file to the repository).

7. For **Change detection options**, select **Amazon CloudWatch Events.**

8. Leave other settings as default, and click **Next**.

9. For **Build – optional**, click **Skip build stage**. Then click **Skip** to confirm.

10. For **Deploy provider**, select **AWS CloudFormation** from the dropdown.

11. For **Action mode**, select **Create or update a stack.**

12. For **Stack name**, enter `glue-job-streaming-views-by-category-job`.

13. For **Template**, select **SourceArtifact** for **Artifact name.**

14. For **File name**, enter the name of our CloudFormation template: `cfn_templates/CFN-glue_job-streams_by_category.cfn`.

15. For **Role name**, select **DataEngGlueCWS3CuratedZoneRole** from the dropdown.

16. Leave all other settings blank and then click **Next**.

17. Review the settings, then click **Create pipeline**.

18. The pipeline should run, deploying the Glue job to your account. In the **AWS Management Console**, go to the **CloudFormation** service to confirm that the template was deployed, and then go to the **AWS Glue** console to confirm that the job has been created. You can also optionally run the Glue job in order to create the new top_categories table.

Testing our CodePipeline

We created our CodePipeline so that when a change to our CloudFormation template (which deploys our Glue job) is committed to CodeCommit, the change will automatically be deployed by CodePipeline.

Let's test it out:

1. Log in to the **AWS Management Console** and use the top search bar to search for, and open, the **CodeCommit** service.

2. Click on the **data-product-film** repository, then click on the **cfn_templates** folder, and then click on the name of our CloudFormation template (CFN-glue_job-streams_by_category).

3. Click on the **Edit** button at the top right.

4. Let's increase the number of workers for our Glue job from 2 to 3. Look for the NumberOfWorkers attribute (around line 38) and change the number from 2 to 3.

5. At the bottom of the page, complete the form for **Commit changes to master** by providing details for **Author name, Email address**, and **Commit message**.

6. Click on **Commit changes**.

7. Now navigate back to the **CodePipeline** service in the AWS console. When you review the list of pipelines, you should see that your **cloudformation-glue-job-deployment** pipeline is listed as **In progress** (although it may take a few moments before the status updates).

8. Navigate to the CloudFormation service, click on your stack name, then view the **Events** tab and confirm that your Glue job is being updated. You can also optionally go to the AWS Glue console and confirm in the **Job details** tab that the number of workers is now set to **3**.

We've now created a CloudFormation template to deploy a Glue job, and linked that with a CodePipeline pipeline to automatically deploy updates to the job whenever we commit a new version of the CloudFormation template to our CodeCommit repository. With this, we are now managing our code through an SCM system (Git with CodeCommit, in this case), and we can automate the deployment of our pipeline whenever a change is made to our transformation code or the configuration of our AWS Glue Job CloudFormation template.

Summary

In this chapter, we introduced a number of approaches to implementing a modern data platform. We looked at the high-level goals of a data platform (flexibility, scalability, good governance, secure, and self-serve enabled), and then discussed the pros and cons of building versus buying a data platform.

We then discussed how a DataOps approach brings automation to the process of developing data products. We looked at how the deployment and management of infrastructure (such as Glue jobs) can be automated, as well as how code for transforms can be managed with an SCM system.

We then got hands-on with some of the AWS services that can be used to automate data platforms, including CloudFormation, CodeCommit, and CodePipeline. We created a Git repository in CodeCommit and used it to store both the PySpark code for our Glue ETL job and a CloudFormation template to deploy the Glue job. We then looked at how we could create a pipeline that would automatically deploy our Glue job (as well as any updates to the Glue job configuration). Any updates to our ETL code are also automatically pushed to the Amazon S3 location where the Glue job reads the ETL code, ensuring that updates to the code would be run with any future executions of the Glue job.

A modern data platform should be managed by a central team, and should enable data producers to easily build data products and catalog those in a way that data consumers can find and access the data products. The platform should also make it easy to use modern table formats (such as Apache Iceberg), and data producers should be able to use automation to deploy and manage their transformation code.

There is a lot more to building a modern data platform than we could cover in this chapter, and you are encouraged to read further on this topic. But we'll now move on to the last chapter of this book, where we will wrap up by looking at the bigger picture of analytics, real-world data pipelines, and potential future developments and trends in this space.

Learn more on Discord

To join the Discord community for this book – where you can share feedback, ask questions to the author, and learn about new releases – follow the QR code below:

`https://discord.gg/9s5mHNyECd`

17

Wrapping Up the First Part of Your Learning Journey

In this book, we have explored many different aspects of the data engineering role by learning more about common architecture patterns, understanding how to approach designing a data engineering pipeline, and getting hands-on with many different AWS services commonly used by data engineers (for data ingestion, data transformation, orchestrating pipelines, and consuming data).

We examined some of the important issues surrounding data security and governance and discussed the importance of a data catalog to avoid a data lake turning into a data swamp. We also reviewed data marts and data warehouses and introduced the concept of a data lake house.

We learned about data consumers – the end users of the product that's produced by data engineering pipelines – and looked into some of the tools that they use to consume data (including Amazon Athena for ad hoc SQL queries and Amazon QuickSight for data visualization). Then, we briefly explored the topics of **machine learning (ML)** and **Artificial Intelligence (AI)** and learned about some of the AWS services that are used in these fields.

We also looked at some recent developments, such as the **data mesh** approach, which moves away from a centralized data engineering team and has teams that produce the data and also own the process of creating analytical versions of that data. We also discussed open table formats, such as **Apache Iceberg**, which overcome some of the technical challenges of traditional data lakes, such as doing record-level updates. Finally, we introduced some important concepts for building a modern data platform, including the pros and cons of building versus buying, and how a **DataOps** approach can help bring automation and observability to a modern data platform.

In this chapter, we're going to review the complexities of real-world data engineering environments (including some examples of real-world data pipelines) and discuss some emerging trends in the field. We'll then look at how to clean up your AWS account in the hands-on portion of this chapter.

In this chapter, we will cover the following topics:

- Understanding the complexities of real-world data environments
- Examining examples of real-world data pipelines
- Imagining the future – a look at emerging trends
- Hands-on – cleaning up your AWS account

Technical requirements

There are no specific technical requirements for the hands-on section of this chapter as we will just be cleaning up resources that we have created throughout this book. Optionally, however, there will be a section that covers deleting your AWS account. If you choose to do this, you will need access to the account's root user to log in with the email address that was used to create the account.

You can find the code files of this chapter in the GitHub repository using the following link: `https://github.com/PacktPublishing/Data-Engineering-with-AWS-2nd-edition/tree/main/Chapter17`

Understanding the complexities of real-world data environments

This book was never intended as a deep dive into one specific area of data engineering, although there are many other great books and resources out there that do focus on a single area (such as books that focus on Apache Spark programming, or on just how to use Kafka to ingest streaming data). Rather, we took a broad look at the many different areas that are covered by data engineering.

Because of this broad topic coverage, you have probably already begun to form a good idea of the different aspects of the bigger picture of data analytics. While it is quite common for data engineering roles to focus on just writing data transform jobs, or just managing the infrastructure to ingest and process streaming data, it is helpful to understand how this integrates with data warehouses/data marts, how different data consumers use data, and how ML and AI fit into the bigger data picture, as we have reviewed in this book. Having this broader understanding of the big data landscape makes you a better data engineer, no matter what your specific focus is.

We have also been focusing on the tasks from the perspective of a single data engineer, but in reality, most data engineers will work as part of a larger team. There may be different teams, or team members, focused on different aspects of the data engineering pipeline, but all team members need to work together. This is why DataOps processes are so important, as they help teams work together effectively in the process of building data products.

In most organizations, there are also likely to be **multiple environments**, such as a development environment, a test/**quality assurance (QA)** environment, and a production environment. The data infrastructure and pipelines must be deployed and tested in the **development environment** first, and then any updates should be pushed to a **test/QA environment** for automated testing, before finally being approved for deployment in the **production environment**.

In the following diagram, we can see that there are multiple teams responsible for different aspects of data engineering resources. We can also see that the data engineering resources are duplicated across multiple different environments, such as the development environment, test/ QA environment, and production environment (and these would generally be separate AWS accounts). Each organization may structure its teams and environments a little differently, but this is an example of the complexity of data engineering in real life:

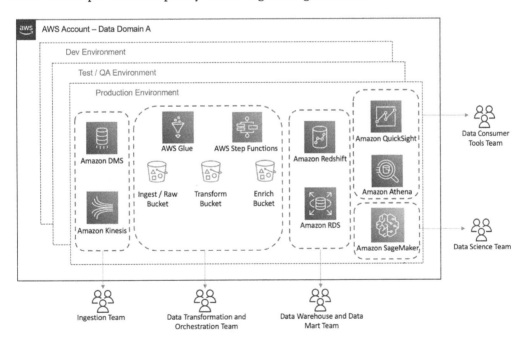

Figure 17.1: Data engineering teams and environments

If using a data mesh approach to organize your data teams, then each data domain would have multiple environments and teams, as shown in *Figure 17.1*. However, for smaller data domains, there may be a single team with a variety of skills that manages all of the aspects shown in the diagram. There is no best way to structure teams within a domain, as it mostly depends on the scale of the data (including the number and complexity of data sources), and the range and complexity of required data transforms. For a small domain with just a few data sources that are creating just one or two data products, it is possible that all the functions shown in *Figure 17.1* will be managed by a single data engineer, building on automation and functionality provided by the central data mesh team (which we discussed in *Chapter 15, Implementing a Data Mesh Strategy*).

Let's now look at what this may look like for an organization with multiple data domains, and how the different domains come together with a central data mesh platform, as shown in *Figure 17.2*.

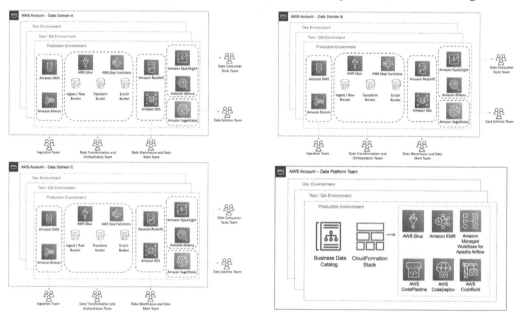

Figure 17.2: Data engineering environments in a data mesh

In *Figure 17.2*, we see three data domains, and at the bottom right, a central data platform. Note how the central data platform team is responsible for a business data catalog, which each data domain uses to publish metadata for their data products. The central data platform team may also create and manage **CloudFormation** stacks, which are used to automate the deployment of resources such as AWS Glue, Amazon EMR, and Amazon **Managed Workflows for Apache Airflow** (**MWAA**). The data platform team may also deploy AWS CodeBuild, CodeDeploy, and CodePipeline, which each domain uses to implement DevOps processes.

In this way, the data platform team helps simplify the process of implementing data engineering pipelines for each data domain, by providing automation for resource and code deployment.

Having discussed some of the complexities of real-world data environments, let's now look at some examples of real-world data pipelines.

Examining examples of real-world data pipelines

The data pipeline examples that we have used in this book have been based on common types of transformations and pipelines, but they have been relatively simple examples. As you can imagine, in large organizations, the types of data pipelines that are built can be a lot more complex and may end up processing extremely large sets of data.

In this section, we will examine two examples of more complex data engineering pipelines from two very well-known organizations – **Spotify** and **Netflix**. Both of these companies have public blogs that cover software and data engineering, and the details provided about their pipelines in this section have been taken from the public information that's been made available in a variety of blog posts and articles.

By learning more about these real-world big data pipelines, you can be better prepared for what to expect when you start working with very large datasets. Also, these examples teach valuable lessons from cutting-edge companies about how they approach complex big data processing tasks, and you can apply these types of approaches and lessons learned to your own complex engineering challenges in the future.

A decade of data wrapped up for Spotify users

Each year, the music streaming service *Spotify* uses the extensive data they have on their users' listening history to generate interesting stats for each user. This information is made available to each user at the end of the year and includes information such as how many minutes of Spotify audio they streamed that year, as well as their top artist, top track, and top genre for the year.

In 2022, Spotify added a new feature – an overview of a user's "listening personality" that displayed a four-letter code that was a combination of four binary attributes that each try to measure and describe one aspect of *how* a user listens to music, independent of *what* music they like. For example, it analyzed how much a user listened to their favorite artists versus how much they explored new artists, and how much they listened to newly released songs versus listening to older songs.

To generate these statistics and metrics related to each user of the platform, the data engineering team at Spotify has to gather and analyze detailed information about every user's listening history, such as:

- Which songs they played
- Which artists they listened to
- The top genres they listen to
- Whether the user listens to the same artist all the time, or often listens to different artists
- The age of each song they listened to, in order to determine whether they listened to more new songs or preferred older songs

A summary of the information is then generated for users, and users can review this in a feature called **Spotify Wrapped**. Putting this all together is a massive undertaking for multiple teams at Spotify, including marketing, frontend app engineering, and, of course, data engineering.

While Spotify has been presenting the Spotify Wrapped feature for several years, in 2019, they decided to add a new feature that reports a user's listening trends for each year of the past decade (2010 – 2019). In an official Spotify blog post, *Spotify Unwrapped: How we bought you a decade of data* (`https://engineering.atspotify.com/2020/02/18/spotify-unwrapped-how-we-brought-you-a-decade-of-data/`), the Spotify data engineering team revealed some of the behind-the-scenes work they did to aggregate user data by year, over 10 years.

In this blog post, the data engineering team talks about some challenges they faced with the Wrapped project in 2018, and how they had to work closely with Google (their cloud provider) to be able to achieve the required processing scale. For 2019, they were planning to do something similar to 2018, but they had more users (totaling 248 million monthly active users at the time) and were planning to do this for 10 years of listening history. As a result, they used the lessons they had learned from their 2018 experience to modify their approach for 2019.

Spotify considers each statistic they want to report for an individual user (such as top artist or top track) as a separate data story. So, to meet the scale requirements for a decade of data, they decided to persist intermediate data and final data for Spotify Wrapped 2019 in **Google BigTable** (a NoSQL database that is somewhat similar to Amazon DynamoDB). For every Spotify user, they had a row in BigTable with a column for each data story, for each year of the decade. This was a significant change from how they had processed and collected different data stories for each user in previous years, but this led to a significantly improved process as data was now pre-grouped and collated per user in BigTable.

They could then write separate jobs for most data stories (decoupling the data stories from each other) and run these individually, but could also run multiple different data story jobs in parallel. The output of each of these data story jobs would then be saved in BigTable, with a row for each Spotify user. End-of-decade top statistics could then be aggregated directly from the data in BigTable.

The key takeaways that we can learn from this example are as follows:

- It is good to iterate on data engineering pipelines and continually reevaluate the architecture and approach you use to identify better ways to do things.

- Breaking down large jobs into smaller, decoupled jobs can lead to improved efficiencies. Keep a modular design for your jobs and avoid the temptation to create a single job that does everything.

- Be versatile and flexible in the tools you use. While we did not have space to cover NoSQL databases in any significant way in this book, a NoSQL database may be an ideal target for storing some of the output from your big data processing jobs. For example, **DynamoDB** was designed to handle billions of rows of data in a table, as well as enable extremely fast access to individual rows from that large dataset.

Data engineers are often challenged to come up with innovative new ways to draw insights out of extremely large datasets, as demonstrated in this real-world example from Spotify. Now, let's look at another real-life data processing example, this time from Netflix.

Ingesting and processing streaming files at Netflix scale

Netflix, the world's leading streaming video platform, with over 230 million subscribers worldwide, predominantly uses AWS for its compute infrastructure. As you can imagine, it takes a lot of compute power, and many different microservices and applications, to support a user base of that size.

Monitoring and understanding how network traffic flows between all the different Netflix microservices, across many separate AWS accounts, is key for the following:

- Maintaining a resilient service
- Understanding dependencies between services
- Troubleshooting when things do go wrong
- Identifying ways to improve the user experience

One of the features of the Amazon **Virtual Private Cloud** (**VPC**) service (a private cloud-based network environment in an AWS account) is the ability to generate **VPC Flow Logs**, which capture details on network traffic between all network interfaces in a VPC.

However, most AWS services make use of dynamic IP addresses, meaning that the IP address that's used by a system can frequently change. So, while VPC Flow Logs provide rich information on network communications between IP addresses, if you don't know which applications or services had the IP addresses being reported on at that time, the Flow Logs are largely meaningless.

Enriching VPC Flow Logs with application information

To have data that was meaningful, Netflix determined that they needed to enrich VPC Flow Logs with information about which application was using a specific IP address at the point in time recorded in the VPC Flow Log. To capture this information, Netflix created an internal system called Sonar that uses CloudWatch Events, Netflix Events, API calls, and various other methods to capture a stream of IP change events.

At the 2017 AWS Summit in Chicago, Netflix presented a breakout session about this solution (available on YouTube at https://www.youtube.com/watch?v=8tsIqfvizpU). In the video, Netflix explains how they used a large **Kinesis Data Streams cluster** (with hundreds of shards) to process incoming VPC Flow Logs. An internal Netflix application known as **Dredge** was created to read incoming data from the Kinesis data stream, as well as enrich the VPC Flow Log data with application metadata from the Sonar stream of IP change events, identifying the applications or microservices involved with each VPC Flow Log record. This enriched data was then loaded into an open-source, high-performance, real-time analytics database called **Druid**, where users could efficiently analyze network data for troubleshooting and to gain improved insights into network performance (to learn more about Apache Druid, see https://druid.apache.org/).

Amazon VPC enhancements and changing the architecture

In the cloud, things change frequently, and AWS is constantly enhancing its services and adding additional services in response to customer feedback. In August 2018, AWS enhanced the VPC Flow Logs service so that logs could be delivered directly to Amazon S3, without needing to be processed via Kinesis first.

In May 2020, Netflix posted a public blog post titled *How Netflix is able to enrich VPC Flow Logs at Hyper Scale to provide Network Insight* (https://netflixtechblog.com/hyper-scale-vpc-flow-logs-enrichment-to-provide-network-insight-e5f1db02910d). This blog post shows how Netflix has changed its architecture to make the best use of the updated functionality in the VPC Flow Logs service.

In this blog post, Netflix talks about a common pattern that they have for processing newly uploaded S3 files. When a new file is uploaded to S3, it is possible to configure an action to take place in response to the newly uploaded file (as we did in *Chapter 3, The AWS Data Engineer's Toolkit*, where we triggered a Lambda function to transform a CSV file into Parquet format whenever a new CSV file was uploaded to a specific S3 bucket prefix).

Netflix commonly uses this pattern to write details of newly uploaded files to an Amazon SQS queue, and they can then read events from the queue to process the newly arrived files. This enables them to decouple the S3 event from the action that they wish to perform in response to this event.

In this case, Netflix intended to read through the entries on the SQS queue and use the file size information included in the event notification to determine the number of newly ingested VPC Flow Log files to process in a batch (which they refer to as a *mouthful* of files). They intended to use an Apache Spark job that would enrich the VPC Flow Log with application metadata based on the IP addresses recorded in each record. They would tune the Apache Spark job to optimally process a certain amount of data, which is why they would read the file size information contained in the SQS messages to create an optimally sized *mouthful* (batch) of files to send to the Spark job.

With the Amazon SQS service, messages are read from the queue and processed. If the processing is successful, the processed messages are deleted from the queue. During the time that a batch of messages is being processed, the messages are considered to be *in flight* and will be hidden from the queue so that no other application attempts to process the same files. If something goes wrong and the files are not successfully processed and deleted from the queue, the messages will become visible again after a certain amount of time (known as the *visibility timeout period*) so that they can be picked up by an application again for processing.

In the case of Netflix, they would send a mouthful of files to an Apache Spark job, and once the Spark job successfully processed the messages, the messages would be deleted from the queue.

However, the Amazon SQS service has a limit on the number of files that can be considered to be in flight at any point (the default quota limit is 120,000 messages). Netflix found that because the Spark jobs would take a little while to process the files, they were regularly ending up with 120,000 or more messages in flight, causing issues. As a result, they came up with an innovative way to work around this by using two different SQS queues.

Working around Amazon SQS quota limits

The re-architected Netflix solution reads the SQS queue containing the S3 events and runs a process to create a mouthful of files (evaluating each file's size to create a batch that is the optimal size for their Spark jobs).

This process can complete very quickly as it does not need to read or process the files, just read the metadata contained in the SQS messages to group a mouthful of files to be processed by a Spark job.

The output of the first job writes a message to a second SQS queue, and each message contains the list of files in a single mouthful. While the blog does not provide any indication of how many files may usually be contained in a mouthful of files, if we assumed it was, on average, around 10 files, it would reduce the number of messages on the second SQS queue by 90%. If a mouthful of files was, on average, 100 files, then the number of messages written to the secondary SQS queue would be reduced by 99%.

The Netflix blog does not provide enough details to be able to describe the exact architecture of the solution, but the following diagram shows an example of a potential architecture we could design for this solution (however, this may be very different from the architecture that Netflix implemented):

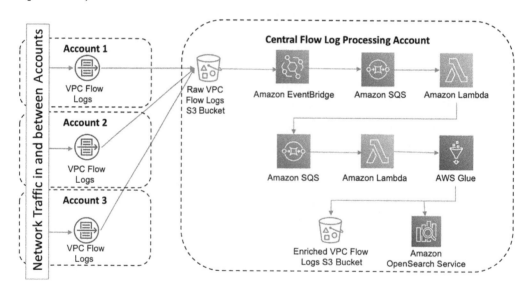

Figure 17.3: A potential architecture for VPC Flow Logs processing and enrichment

In the preceding diagram, we have VPC Flow Logs configured to write to an Amazon S3 bucket in a central flow log processing account. As each new Flow Log is written into this central bucket, it triggers an **EventBridge** rule with details about the newly written file, including the size of the file.

The EventBridge rule has an Amazon SQS queue configured as a target, so as each new file is written to the Amazon S3 bucket, EventBridge forwards the event information to an Amazon SQS queue.

A Lambda function has been configured to read messages from the Amazon SQS queue and uses the file size metadata contained in the message to create a batch of files of an optimal size. The list of files in the batch is written to a separate SQS queue as a single message. At this point, our first Lambda function can complete, and remove messages from the first SQS queue very quickly, since it is only processing metadata in the SQS message, not reading/writing S3 files, and running a Spark job to enrich the files.

A separate Lambda function processes the much smaller number of messages in the secondary SQS queue by reading the list of files (the mouthful of files) in each message. The list of files is passed to a Spark job (in our example architecture, we are using AWS Glue to run the job), and this job enriches the VPC Flow Log files in this mouthful with data from other sources. Enriched files are written to another Amazon S3 bucket, and/or a system designed for storing and searching through log-style data, such as **Amazon OpenSearch Service**.

The key takeaways that we can learn from this example are as follows:

- It is important to know what the AWS quotas/limits are for the services that you use. Some limits can be raised by contacting AWS support, but some limits are hard limits that cannot be increased.

- It is important to stay up to date with *what's new* announcements from AWS. AWS regularly launches new services, as well as major new features, for existing services. Bookmark the following web page, which lists all new AWS features and services: https://aws.amazon. com/new.

As shown in this blog post, new features launched by AWS may help you significantly simplify existing architectures and reduce costs (based on this blog post, it would seem that Netflix may no longer need their Kinesis Data Streams cluster, configured with hundreds of shards, in order to process VPC Flow Logs).

In the next section, we will look at upcoming trends and what the future may hold for data engineers.

Imagining the future — a look at emerging trends

Technology seems to progress at an increasing velocity. For decades, relational databases from vendors such as Oracle were the primary technology for managing all data. Today, there is a wide range of different database types that can be used, depending on the use case (such as graph databases for highly connected datasets, NoSQL databases for low-latency reading and writing of very large tables, and vector databases, which have become popular for ML applications such as generative AI).

It was also not all that long ago that **Hadoop MapReduce** was the state-of-the-art technology for processing very large datasets, but today, most new projects would choose **Apache Spark** over a MapReduce implementation. Apache Spark itself continues to progress from its initial release, with Spark 3.4 having been released in April 2023. We have also seen the introduction of **Spark Streaming**, **Spark ML**, and **Spark GraphX** for different use cases.

No one can tell for certain what the next big thing will be, but in this section, we will look at a few emerging concepts and technologies, as well as expected trends, that are likely to be of relevance to data engineers.

Increased adoption of a data mesh approach

In the past few years, we have seen a rapid increase in the number of companies that are looking to implement a data mesh-type approach to how they organize and structure data responsibilities. This will continue to lead to a move away from centralized data engineering teams to data engineers being assigned to specific data domains.

This will also lead to an increase in dedicated *data platform engineer* roles, with the platform engineers being responsible for the central data platform and catalog, and not responsible for developing ETL pipelines that perform data transformation. Instead, data engineers responsible for developing data transformation pipelines will be embedded in data domains, and make use of infrastructure templates managed by the central data platform team.

There will also be an increase in roles that are responsible for data governance, ensuring that data quality is high and that data lineage and protection of PII data are prioritized.

As discussed in *Chapter 15, Implementing a Data Mesh Strategy*, the term data mesh means different things to different people and was never intended as a technical solution but more of a theoretical approach. Therefore, not every data mesh implementation will be the same, and we will not always see a role for people who are focused on architecting the data mesh implementation for a company.

Requirement to work in a multi-cloud environment

While this book focuses on data engineering using AWS services, it is not uncommon for many larger companies to have a **multi-cloud strategy**, where they use more than one cloud provider for services.

Having a multi-cloud strategy can introduce numerous challenges across **information technology (IT)** teams, including challenges for data engineering teams that need to work with data stored with different cloud providers.

Another challenge for IT teams and data engineers is the need to learn the different service implementations for each cloud provider (for example, AWS, Azure, and Google Cloud each offer a managed Apache Spark environment, but the implementation details are different for each provider).

From a data analytics perspective, each of the cloud providers is starting to do more to support querying analytics data across clouds. For example, Amazon Athena and AWS Glue both have connectors that you can deploy to enable those services to read data from sources such as Google BigQuery and Azure Data Lake Storage.

Perhaps a bigger challenge is to have a unified data catalog that can efficiently span across multiple clouds, in order to create a centralized repository of business data, no matter which cloud the data is stored in.

There are many different reasons for organizations wanting to adopt a multi-cloud strategy, but the pros and cons need to be carefully thought through. However, in many cases, data engineers will have no option but to take up the challenge of becoming comfortable with working in, and across, multiple different cloud provider environments.

Migration to open table formats

As we discussed in *Chapter 14, Building Transactional Data Lakes*, the last few years have seen the development of a number of **open table formats**, which provide a modern approach to developing data lakes that are able to be easily updated in a consistent manner (in addition to other features).

While difficult to predict which of the table formats will become dominant, it appears that **Apache Iceberg** has the most momentum currently. But whichever format (or formats) ends up becoming the most popular, you can expect that many organizations will be working on migrating to one of the open table formats over the next few years.

This will involve migrating existing Hive-based data lake tables to one of the new open table formats, and modifying existing ETL jobs to make use of the new features provided. Considering that most large organizations likely have thousands of datasets and transformation jobs, this will be a significant undertaking. However, there are significant benefits provided by these table formats, so it will be a worthwhile project for these organizations. These migration projects are likely to be long-term projects, and it may take a number of years to migrate all existing data lake tables and transformation jobs to a new open table format.

Managing costs with FinOps

In recent years, there has been increasing focus on monitoring and managing cloud-related spend, and this of course also applies to data-related spend.

This trend is likely to continue, and as a result, organizations are increasingly developing a **FinOps** function. The purpose of FinOps is to create a cross-functional team that helps monitor IT-related spend and bring engineering, finance, technology, and business teams together to work on making data-driven spending decisions.

It is important for data teams to have a program in place that helps educate the data engineering team, the central data platform team, and all other associated teams about best practices for cloud cost management. This team should be part of, or be represented within, the FinOps function.

While the cloud offers incredible scale, flexibility, and agility, it can be more challenging to predict future costs. It is great to provide a data engineering team access to a development environment where they can create and run AWS Glue Spark-based jobs on demand, and then deploy those to production. But a data engineer's primary role is to transform the data, and the cost of that transformation is often not a priority for the data engineer.

By default, a Glue job is assigned 10 DPUs, but many smaller jobs may not require that many DPUs. Also, auto-scaling is an option in Glue jobs (where Glue automatically uses only the needed DPUs, up to a maximum number of DPUs), but this needs to be enabled for each job. If only using the default Glue settings, a job may cost more than required. But with just a little bit of education, each team can learn how to easily cost-optimize their Glue jobs.

To be a successful data engineer, it is increasingly important that you learn how to manage and optimize costs for your data engineering pipelines and data platform. And ensuring that your organization has a cross-functional FinOps team is, or will become, critical to the success of your cloud projects.

The merging of data warehouses and data lakes

Another trend that we have seen over the past few years is the merging of data warehouses and data lakes.

Snowflake architecture resembles that of a data warehouse, and the **Databricks** platform architecture provides more of a data lake approach. However, in their marketing, one of the Snowflake messaging campaigns is about *"Snowflake for Data Lakes."* The Databricks documentation talks about their Databricks Lakehouse platform providing a *"complete end-to-end data warehousing solution."*

For a while, many companies used variations of the term "Data Lake House" to describe a combination of a data lake and a data warehouse. These terms were used by different marketing teams to mean slightly different things, but ultimately it was used to describe how data lake and data warehouse technologies were becoming more interoperable.

For example, within AWS, Redshift Spectrum can be used to query data in an Amazon S3-based data lake, Amazon Athena can be used to query and join data in multiple sources (including an Amazon S3-based data lake, and an Amazon Redshift data warehouse), and AWS Glue works with open table formats to enable more data-warehouse-type functionality.

This trend continues, even if the terms somewhat change. Over the next few years, we are likely to continue to see the lines blur between data lakes and data warehouses, with traditional solutions for each encompassing more of the features and functionality of the other. The advent of open table formats (previously discussed) is enabling and accelerating this trend.

Data warehouses are increasingly able to query open table formats that exist on object storage (such as Amazon S3), and data lake technologies are increasingly including functionality that enables them to act more like a data warehouse (also enabled by open table formats). Ultimately, as we see the increase in the adoption of open table formats, it will become more difficult to separate the functions of a data lake and a data warehouse.

The application of generative AI to business intelligence and analytics

With the growing popularity of **generative AI** solutions (such as **ChatGPT**) in recent times, there is increasing interest in being able to query data in a data store (such as a data lake) using natural language. The ultimate goal would be to enable an executive to type something like *"On which day of the week do we see the highest sales of our chocolate flavored ice cream?"*. And in response, the generative AI-powered assistant may ask some necessary clarifying questions, but will ultimately return an accurate result, or perhaps even a visualization showing the requested data.

Today, there are some experimental approaches that attempt to use **generative AI/LLMs** to generate the SQL required to query a data store, in response to a prompt (for an example, see the following AWS blog post – https://aws.amazon.com/blogs/machine-learning/reinventing-the-data-experience-use-generative-ai-and-modern-data-architecture-to-unlock-insights/). However, these are not yet at a point where they are can be counted on to provide guaranteed accurate and high-quality results to all potential queries.

Over the next few years, we can expect to see improvements in applying generative AI/LLMs to data analytics. For example, in July 2023, AWS announced new generative **business intelligence** (**BI**) features were coming to Amazon QuickSight. This functionality builds on the existing functionality of QuickSight Q (which we covered in *Chapter 12, Visualizing Data with Amazon QuickSight*).

In the announcement, AWS explained that the new generative BI capabilities would include functionality for:

- Rapidly creating visuals using a new QuickSight Q-powered visual authoring experience
- Fine-tuning and formatting visuals using natural language
- Creating calculations using natural language without needing to know specific syntax
- Enabling business users to create generative BI-powered *stories*, which automates much of the process of generating narrative and visual presentations around a data topic by simply entering a description of the story they want to tell

For example, with *stories*, a business user can type something such as *"Build a story about how we can increase the conversion of free trial customers into paying accounts so we can boost sales."* QuickSight will put together a document that includes visuals, along with narrative text, that explores the topic. To learn more about this, see the AWS blog post at `https://aws.amazon.com/blogs/business-intelligence/announcing-generative-bi-capabilities-in-amazon-quicksight/`.

The application of generative AI to building transformations

In addition to generative AI being used to simplify BI and analytic tasks, we can expect to see increasing usage of these new LLMs for building ETL-type transformations.

For example, AWS Glue already supports **Amazon CodeWhisperer**, an AI coding companion that can help developers as they write ETL transformation code, such as PySpark code. CodeWhisperer has been built into AWS Glue Studio notebooks, enabling a developer to enter a comment in their code describing what they are trying to do and have CodeWhisperer generate suggested code to achieve that function.

For example, if a developer has a Spark DataFrame that includes a column named `quantity` and another named `price`, they can write the following comment in their Glue Studio notebook:

```
# Add a column to calculate the total price
```

CodeWhisperer will then generate some suggested code, and the developer can use the up and down arrows to look through different code suggestions and then hit **TAB** to accept the suggestion. For example, CodeWhisperer may suggest the following code, which the developer can accept by hitting **TAB**:

```
df = df.withColumn('total_price', df.quantity * df.price)
```

For more details on using Amazon CodeWhisperer with AWS Glue, see the following blog post: https://aws.amazon.com/blogs/big-data/build-data-integration-jobs-with-ai-companion-on-aws-glue-studio-notebook-powered-by-amazon-codewhisperer/. For general information on CodeWhisperer and integrations with various IDEs, such as Visual Studio Code, see the following documentation: https://docs.aws.amazon.com/codewhisperer/latest/userguide/setting-up.html.

Over the next few years, we can expect that these AI coding assistants will significantly improve, perhaps to the point where an analyst can describe the transformation they want to apply to a dataset in natural language, and the AI assistant will generate all the code required and then show a sample of the result for the analyst to approve. Once approved, the AI assistant can then automatically commit the code to a code repository. The analyst can then describe, in natural language, a pipeline that runs multiple transformations, and the AI assistant will generate an Apache Airflow DAG for the pipeline, commit the DAG to a code repository, and then deploy the pipeline.

It is not possible to know exactly how generative AI and LLMs will impact the future of data engineering, but it will be an interesting topic to watch and keep up with.

Having looked at some practical implementations of real-world data engineering, examples of real-world data pipelines, and emerging trends and concepts, we will now move on to our final hands-on section of this book.

Hands-on — cleaning up your AWS account

In the hands-on section of *Chapter 1, An Introduction to Data Engineering*, we went through how to create a new AWS account. If you created a new account at that point, and have used that account to work through the exercises in this book, you may want to delete that account now that you have reached the final chapter of this book. We'll include instructions on how to do that here.

However, if this was your first AWS account, you may decide that you want to keep the account open so that you can continue to explore and learn more about AWS using other resources. If that is the case, we'll include some instructions on how to check your account billing to detect which resources you are still being charged for.

Reviewing AWS Billing to identify the resources being charged for

While many of the services that we have used in this book are included in the AWS Free Tier (where you are not charged for certain limited usage of specific services), other services will have had a cost associated with their use.

In this section, we will go through how to review the AWS Billing console to determine which resources you are being charged for:

1. Log in to the **AWS Billing** console using the following link: `https://console.aws.amazon.com/billing/home`.

2. On the **Billing Dashboard**, we can immediately see a forecast of what the current month's spend will be, as well as the actual month-to-date cost, and a comparison of the current month's spend compared to the previous month at the same point:

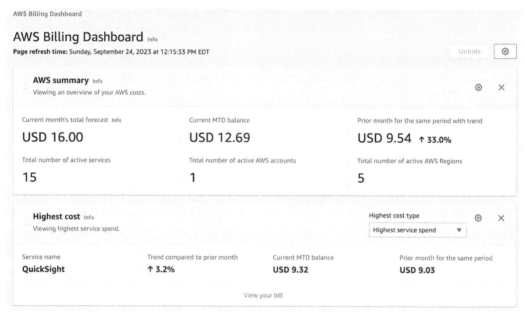

Figure 17.4: AWS Billing Dashboard

In the preceding screenshot, you can see that I have spent **$12.69** so far this month, and that the forecast for the full month is a total of **$16.00**.

3. Scroll further down the Billing Dashboard and review the section titled **Cost trend by top five services**.

Figure 17.5: AWS Billing Dashboard – Cost trend by top five services

I did not cancel my **QuickSight** subscription after completing the exercises in *Chapter 12, Visualizing Data with Amazon QuickSight*, and my free 30-day trial ended. If I wanted to cancel my QuickSight subscription now to avoid any future charges after this month, I could follow the instructions in *Deleting your Amazon QuickSight subscription and closing the account* (`https://docs.aws.amazon.com/quicksight/latest/user/closing-account.html`).

4. I can also see charges for **Relational Database Service** and **Redshift**. I am not sure what these charges relate to, so to investigate this further, I can click on **Bills** in the left-hand menu. Once on the **Bills** page, I can scroll down and review the section titled **Amazon Web Services, Inc. charges by service**.

On this page, I can expand the **Redshift** item to examine those costs.

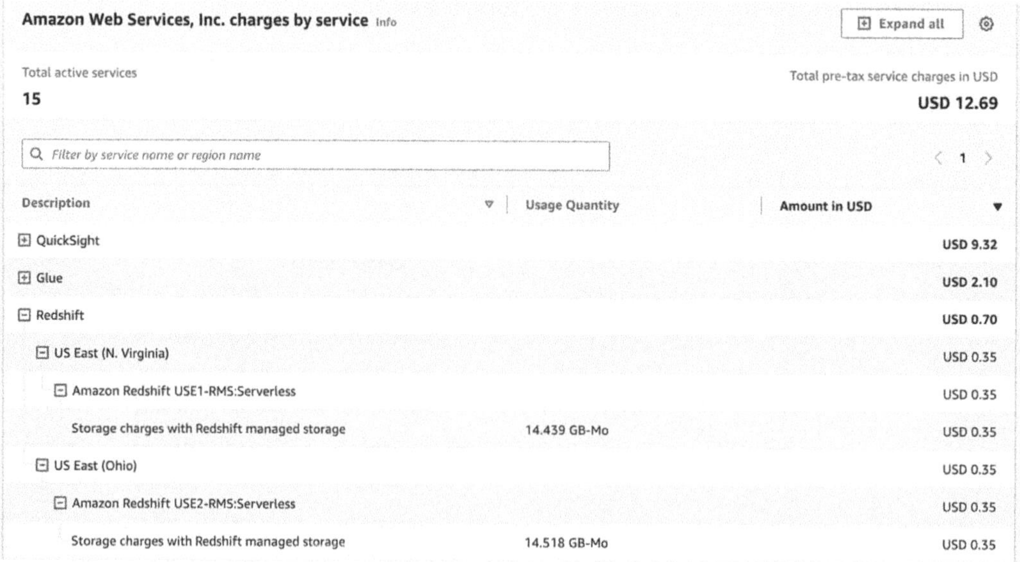

Description	Usage Quantity	Amount in USD
Amazon Web Services, Inc. charges by service Info		Expand all
Total active services		Total pre-tax service charges in USD
15		USD 12.69
Filter by service name or region name		< 1 >
⊞ QuickSight		USD 9.32
⊞ Glue		USD 2.10
⊟ Redshift		USD 0.70
⊟ US East (N. Virginia)		USD 0.35
⊟ Amazon Redshift USE1-RMS:Serverless		USD 0.35
Storage charges with Redshift managed storage	14.439 GB-Mo	USD 0.35
⊟ US East (Ohio)		USD 0.35
⊟ Amazon Redshift USE2-RMS:Serverless		USD 0.35
Storage charges with Redshift managed storage	14.518 GB-Mo	USD 0.35

Figure 17.6: AWS bill details view

Here, I can see that the Redshift charges are related to two Amazon Redshift Serverless clusters that I had previously created – one in the US East (N. Virginia) Region and one in the US East (Ohio) Region. I have not performed any queries with the cluster recently, but I am being billed for the amount of storage I am using, from when I previously loaded data into the serverless cluster. If I no longer needed the cluster and data, then to avoid being charged in the future, I could go to the Redshift console, view the configured **namespace**, then delete any associated **workgroups** within that namespace, and then delete the namespace. I would of course need to do this for each Region where I had Redshift Serverless configured.

In a similar way, I could expand the lines for **Glue** and **Relational Database Service** (**RDS**), and identify what items I am being charged for. In my case, the Glue charges were related to a Glue job that I had run, so as long as I am not running any future jobs, I will not have any future Glue charges. For RDS, the charges were for backups that I had taken of database instances, so I could delete those snapshots if no longer needed, and that way I would not have any future RDS charges.

If I canceled my QuickSight subscription, deleted my Redshift workgroups and namespaces, and deleted my RDS snapshots, I could continue using my AWS account without incurring additional charges for those items. However, it is strongly recommended that you regularly check the Billing console and set billing alarms to alert you of spending above the limit you've set.

For more information, see `https://docs.aws.amazon.com/AmazonCloudWatch/latest/ monitoring/monitor_estimated_charges_with_cloudwatch.html`.

If you want to keep your AWS account so you can continue to explore and experiment with AWS services, then going through the Billing console to identify what AWS services you are paying for and deleting those resources you don't need is all you need to do for now. However, in the next section, we'll cover what to do if you want to fully delete your account.

Closing your AWS account

If you decide that you want to close your AWS account, you can do so with the following steps.

Before proceeding, make sure that you have read the *Considerations before you close your AWS account* section of the AWS documentation at `https://docs.aws.amazon.com/awsaccountbilling/ latest/aboutv2/close-account.html`. If you want to close your account, use the following steps:

1. Log in to your AWS account as the root user of the account (that is, using the email address and password you registered when you opened the account). Use the following link to log in: `https://console.aws.amazon.com`.

    If you're prompted for an IAM username and password, click on the link for **Sign in using root user email**.

2. Enter your root user email address and password when prompted.

3. Open the Billing console with the following link: `https://console.aws.amazon.com/ billing/home#/`.

4. In the top-right corner, select the dropdown next to your account number (or account alias, if set). From this dropdown, select **Account**:

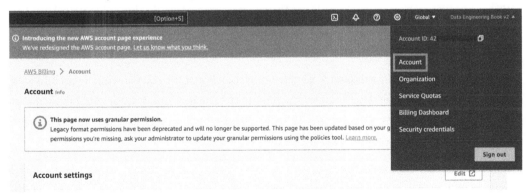

Figure 17.7: Accessing the Account screen in the AWS Management Console

5. Scroll to the bottom of the **Account** page. Read and ensure you understand the account closure guidance. If you still want to close your account, click **Close account:**

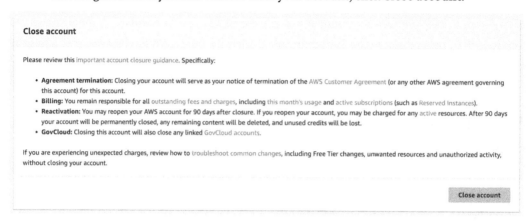

Figure 17.8: Closing your AWS account

6. In the pop-up box, click **Close account** to confirm that you want to close your account.

Subsequently, if you change your mind about closing your account, it may still be possible to reopen your account within 90 days of choosing to close it. To do so, contact AWS support.

Summary

Data engineering is an exciting role to be in and is one that offers interesting challenges, constant learning opportunities, and increasing importance in helping organizations draw out the maximum value that they can from their data assets. And the cloud is an exciting place to build data engineering platforms and pipelines.

AWS has a proven track record of listening to their customers and continuing to innovate based on their customers' requirements, so you can expect new features and services at a virtually constant pace. Things move quickly with AWS services, so hold on tight for the ride.

If you're new to data engineering on AWS, then this book is just the start of what could be a long and interesting journey for you. There is much more to be learned than what could ever be captured in a single book, or even a volume of books. Much of what you will learn will be through practical experience and things you learn on the job, as well as from other data engineers.

But this book, and other books like it, as well as resources such as podcasts, YouTube videos, and blogs, are all useful vehicles along your journey. Let the end of this book be just the end of the first chapter of your learning journey about data engineering with AWS.

Learn more on Discord

To join the Discord community for this book – where you can share feedback, ask questions to the author, and learn about new releases – follow the QR code below:

`https://discord.gg/9s5mHNyECd`

packt.com

Subscribe to our online digital library for full access to over 7,000 books and videos, as well as industry leading tools to help you plan your personal development and advance your career. For more information, please visit our website.

Why subscribe?

- Spend less time learning and more time coding with practical eBooks and Videos from over 4,000 industry professionals
- Improve your learning with Skill Plans built especially for you
- Get a free eBook or video every month
- Fully searchable for easy access to vital information
- Copy and paste, print, and bookmark content

At www.packt.com, you can also read a collection of free technical articles, sign up for a range of free newsletters, and receive exclusive discounts and offers on Packt books and eBooks.

Other Books You May Enjoy

If you enjoyed this book, you may be interested in these other books by Packt:

Data Engineering with dbt

Roberto Zagni

ISBN: 9781803246284

- Create a dbt Cloud account and understand the ELT workflow
- Combine Snowflake and dbt for building modern data engineering pipelines
- Use SQL to transform raw data into usable data, and test its accuracy
- Write dbt macros and use Jinja to apply software engineering principles
- Test data and transformations to ensure reliability and data quality
- Build a lightweight pragmatic data platform using proven patterns
- Write easy-to-maintain idempotent code using dbt materialization

Data Engineering with Python

Paul Crickard

ISBN: 9781839214189

- Understand how data engineering supports data science workflows
- Discover how to extract data from files and databases and then clean, transform, and enrich it
- Configure processors for handling different file formats as well as both relational and NoSQL databases
- Find out how to implement a data pipeline and dashboard to visualize results
- Use staging and validation to check data before landing in the warehouse
- Build real-time pipelines with staging areas that perform validation and handle failures
- Get to grips with deploying pipelines in the production environment

Packt is searching for authors like you

If you're interested in becoming an author for Packt, please visit authors.packtpub.com and apply today. We have worked with thousands of developers and tech professionals, just like you, to help them share their insight with the global tech community. You can make a general application, apply for a specific hot topic that we are recruiting an author for, or submit your own idea.

Share your thoughts

Now you've finished *Data Engineering with AWS, Second Edition*, we'd love to hear your thoughts! Scan the QR code below to go straight to the Amazon review page for this book and share your feedback or leave a review on the site that you purchased it from.

https://packt.link/r/1804614424

Your review is important to us and the tech community and will help us make sure we're delivering excellent quality content.

Index

Download a free PDF copy of this book

Thanks for purchasing this book!

Do you like to read on the go but are unable to carry your print books everywhere? Is your eBook purchase not compatible with the device of your choice?

Don't worry, now with every Packt book you get a DRM-free PDF version of that book at no cost.

Read anywhere, any place, on any device. Search, copy, and paste code from your favorite technical books directly into your application.

The perks don't stop there, you can get exclusive access to discounts, newsletters, and great free content in your inbox daily

Follow these simple steps to get the benefits:

1. Scan the QR code or visit the link below

https://packt.link/free-ebook/9781804614426

2. Submit your proof of purchase
3. That's it! We'll send your free PDF and other benefits to your email directly

Milton Keynes UK
Ingram Content Group UK Ltd.
UKHW032145070124
435550UK00008B/537